Modern Library Technologies for Data Storage, Retrieval, and Use

Chia-Hung Wei
Chien Hsin University of Science and Technology, Taiwan

Chih-Ying Gwo
Chien Hsin University of Science and Technology, Taiwan

Managing Director: Lindsay Johnston
Editorial Director: Joel Gamon
Book Production Manager: Jennifer Yoder
Publishing Systems Analyst: Adrienne Freeland
Assistant Acquisitions Editor: Kayla Wolfe
Typesetter: Christy Fic
Cover Design: Jason Mull

Published in the United States of America by
Information Science Reference (an imprint of IGI Global)
701 E. Chocolate Avenue
Hershey PA 17033
Tel: 717-533-8845
Fax: 717-533-8661
E-mail: cust@igi-global.com
Web site: http://www.igi-global.com

Library of Congress Cataloging-in-Publication Data

Modern Library Technologies for Data Storage, Retrieval, and Use / Chia-Hung Wei and Chih-Ying Gwo, Editors.
   pages cm
 Includes bibliographical references and index.
 Summary: "This book highlights new features of digital library technology in order to educate the database community in the efforts to understand the applications of data acquisition, retrieval and storage"-- Provided by publisher.
  ISBN 978-1-4666-2928-8 (hardcover) -- ISBN 978-1-4666-2929-5 (ebook) -- ISBN 978-1-4666-2930-1 (print & perpetual access) 1. Digital libraries. 2. Information storage and retrieval systems. 3. Multimedia systems. I. Wei, Chia-Hung, 1973- editor of compilation. II. Gwo, Chih-Ying, editor of compilation.
 ZA4080.M63 2013
 025.042--dc23
                     2012039283

British Cataloguing in Publication Data
A Cataloguing in Publication record for this book is available from the British Library.

Associate Editors

List of Reviewers

Table of Contents

Detailed Table of Contents

Section 1
Retrieval

Chapter 1

Sekhar Mandal, Bengal Engineering & Science University, Shibpur, India

Amit K. Das, Bengal Engineering & Science University, Shibpur, India

Partha Bhowmick, Indian Institute of Technology Kharagpur, India

Bhabatosh Chanda, Indian Statistical Institute, Kolkata, India

This paper presents a unified algorithm for segmentation and identification of various tabular structures from document page images. Such tabular structures include conventional tables and displayed math-zones, as well as Table of Contents (TOC) and Index pages. After analyzing the page composition, the algorithm initially classifies the input set of document pages into tabular and non-tabular pages. A tabular page contains at least one of the tabular structures, whereas a non-tabular page does not contain any. The approach is unified in the sense that it is able to identify all tabular structures from a tabular page, which leads to a considerable simplification of document image segmentation in a novel manner. Such unification also results in speeding up the segmentation process, because the existing methodologies produce time-consuming solutions for treating different tabular structures as separate physical entities. Distinguishing features of different kinds of tabular structures have been used in stages in order to ensure the simplicity and efficiency of the algorithm and demonstrated by exhaustive experimental results.

Chapter 2

Mousumi Dutt, Bengal Engineering & Science University, India

Aisharjya Sarkar, Bengal Engineering & Science University, India

Arindam Biswas, Bengal Engineering & Science University, India

Partha Bhowmick, Indian Institute of Technology, Kharagpur, India

Bhargab B. Bhattacharya, Indian Statistical Institute, India

Analysis of handwritten documents is a challenging task in the modern era of document digitization. It requires efficient preprocessing which includes word segmentation and baseline detection. This paper proposes a novel approach toward word segmentation and baseline detection in a handwritten document. It is based on certain structural properties of isothetic covers tightly enclosing the words in a handwritten document. For an appropriate grid size, the isothetic covers successfully segregate the words so that each cover corresponds to a particular word. The grid size is selected by an adaptive technique that classifies the inter-cover distances into two classes in an unsupervised manner. Finally, by using a geometric heuristic with the horizontal chords of these covers, the corresponding baselines are extracted. Owing to its traversal strategy along the word boundaries in a combinatorial manner and usage of limited operations strictly in the integer domain, the method is found to be quite fast, efficient, and robust, as demonstrated by experimental results with datasets of both Bengali and English handwritings.

Chapter 3

Jinn-Ming Chang, Chi Mei Foundation Hospital, Tainan, Taiwan

Pai-Jung Huang, Tungs' Taichung MetroHarbor Hospital, Chi Mei Foundation Hospital, Taipei Medical University Hospital, & Taipei Medical University, Taiwan

Chih-Ying Gwo, Ching Yun University, Taiwan

Yue Li, Nankai University, China

Chia-Hung Wei, Ching Yun University, Taiwan

In hospitals and medical institutes, a large number of mammograms are produced in ever increasing quantities and used for diagnostics and therapy. The need for effective methods to manage and retrieve those image resources has been actively pursued in the medical community. This paper proposes a hierarchical correlation calculation approach to content-based mammogram retrieval. In this approach, images are represented as a Gaussian pyramid with several reduced-resolution levels. A global search is first conducted to identify the optimal matching position, where the correlation between the query image and the target images in the database is maximal. Local search is performed in the region comprising the four child pixels at a higher resolution level to locate the position with maximal correlation at greater resolution. Finally, this position with the maximal correlation found at the finest resolution level is used as the image similarity measure for retrieving images. Experimental results have shown that this approach achieves 59% in precision and 54% in recall when the threshold of correlation is 0.5.

Chapter 4

Chee-Chiang Chen, Tungs' Taichung MetroHarbor Hospital, Taiwan

Pai-Jung Huang, Tungs' Taichung MetroHarbor Hospital, Chi Mei Foundation Hospital, Taipei Medical University Hospital, & Taipei Medical University, Taiwan

Chih-Ying Gwo, Ching Yun University, Taiwan

Yue Li, Nankai University, China

Chia-Hung Wei, Ching Yun University, Taiwan

Content-based image retrieval (CBIR) has been proposed by the medical community for inclusion in picture archiving and communication systems (PACS). In CBIR, relevance feedback is developed for bridging the semantic gap and improving the effectiveness of image retrieval systems. With relevance feedback, CBIR systems can return refined search results using a learning algorithm and selection strategy. In this study, as the retrieving process proceeds further, the proposed learning algorithm can reduce the influence of the original query point and increase the significance of the centroid of the clusters comprising the features of those relevant images identified in the most recent round of search. The proposed selection strategy is used to find a good starting point and select a set of images at each round to show that search result and ask for the user's feedback. In addition, a benchmark is proposed to measure the learning ability to explain the retrieval performance as relevance feedback is incorporated in CBIR systems. The performance evaluation shows that the average precision rate of the proposed scheme was 0.98 and the learning ability reach to 7.17 through the five rounds of relevance feedback.

Chapter 5

Yue Li, Nankai University, China
Wei Wang, Nankai University, China

Artificial intelligent (AI) driving is an emerging technology, freeing the driver from driving. Some techniques for automatically driving have been developed; however, most can only recognize the traffic signs in particular groups, such as triangle signs for warning, circle signs for prohibition, and so forth, but cannot tell the exact meaning of every sign. In this paper, a framework for a traffic system recognition system is proposed. This system consists of two phases. The segmentation method, fuzzy c-means (FCM), is used to detect the traffic sign, whereas the Content-Based Image Retrieval (CBIR) method is used to match traffic signs to those in a database to find the exact meaning of every detected sign.

Section 2
Storage

Chapter 6

Lung-Chun Chang, Ching Yun University, Taiwan
Yueh-Jyun Lee, Ching Yun University, Taiwan
Hui-Yun Hu, Ching Yun University, Taiwan
Yu-Ching Hsu, Ching Yun University, Taiwan
Yi-Syuan Wu, Ching Yun University, Taiwan

To obtain high resolution images, some low resolution images must be processed and enhanced. In the literature, the mapping from the low resolution image to the high resolution image is a linear system and it is only enlarged by an integer scale. This paper presents a real scaling algorithm for image resolution enhancement. Using a virtual magnifier, an image resolution can be enhanced by a real scale number. Experimental results demonstrate that the proposed algorithm has a high quality for the enlarged image in the human visual system.

Chapter 7

Yue Li, Nankai University, China

Today, many digital forensic techniques for digital images are developed to serve the purpose of the origin identification and integrity verification for security reasons. Generally speaking, these methods can be divided into two classes, the methods based on the extracted features, which are usually the high frequency noise inside the investigating images and the methods based on the contents of the images. Different techniques may be developed specially against different forging attacks, while be vulnerable to other malicious manipulations on the images. This paper reviews the most popular techniques in order to help the user to understand the techniques and find the most proper methods for variety forensic purpose in different situations.

Yue Li, Nankai University, Tianjin, China

Chia-Hung Wei, Ching Yun University, Taiwan

Digital image authentication refers to all the techniques performing anti-falsification, digital image copyright protection, or access control. A large number of DIA techniques have been developed to authenticate digital images, including cryptography-based digital image authentication (CBDIA) techniques and data-hiding-based digital image authentication (DHBDIA) techniques. This paper not only provides some practical applications on image authentication, but also describes general frameworks of image watermarking and the general techniques, including robust watermarking, fragile watermarking, and semi-fragile watermarking. This paper also addresses the potential issues on future research directions, including managing the PRNU database, development of advanced PRNU-based blind authentication techniques, and search for digital fingerprints.

Yue Li, Nankai University, China

Today, the digital forensic techniques for digital images are developed with the origin identification and integrity verification functions for security reasons. Methods based on photo-response-non-uniform (PRNU) are widely studied and proved to be effective to serve the forensic purposes. However, due to the interpolation noise, caused by the colour filtering and interpolation function the accuracy of the PRNU-based forensic method has been degraded. Meanwhile, the tremendous physical storage requirement and computation consumption limit the applications of PRNU-based method. Therefore, an innovative DPRNU-based forensic method has been proposed in order to solve the above problems. In the method, the artificial component and physical component are separated according to the colour filtering array (CFA) and the PRNU are only extracted from the physical component in order to remove the interference caused by the interpolation noise, which increases the accuracy of the camera identification and integrity verification. Meanwhile, due to the separation, the DPRNU are only 1/3 of the size of the traditional PRNU, which saves considerable physical storage in setting up the digital library and fasters the comparison speed between the fingerprints.

Yueh-Jyun Lee, Ching Yun University, Taiwan

Ji-Chyun Liu, Ching Yun University, Taiwan

Shih-Wen Liu, Ching Yun University, Taiwan

Yuh-Fong Lin, Ching Yun University, Taiwan

Lung-Chun Chang, Ching Yun University, Taiwan

In this paper, image reconstruction technique (IRT) is used to reconstruct a 3-D profile of typhoons from MTSAT satellite cloud image data and based on a 1691 MHz receiver and iDAP system. The satellite cloud image data gives a single line profile slicing from a surface cloud image which does match the typhoon distribution. The line profile is presented with the temperature of the cloud top. The 3-D profiles of typhoons are constructed with the surface cloud images and the temperatures. IRT is conducted using the data of the 2010 Megi event. The typhoon feature is studied and the various typhoon eyes in three time intervals are analyzed. An effective early-warning system may become feasible based on this work.

Chapter 11

Menq-Wen Lin, Ching Yun University, Taiwan

Chia-Hung Wei, Ching Yun University, Taiwan

Pei-Cheng Cheng, Ching Yun University, Taiwan

With the growing demand for water, and many challenges related to water availability, food security, pollution, and environmental degradation, it becomes imperative to establish good water policy planning for a sufficient supply of water consumption. This paper presents a general problem-solving framework for modeling multi-issue agent negotiation in water policy planning via fuzzy constraint processing. All participants involved in water policy planning are modeled as agents. Agent negotiation is formulated as a distributed fuzzy constraint satisfaction problem. Fuzzy constraints are used to define each participant's professional views and demands. The agent negotiation simulates the interactive process of all participants' water policy planning. This approach provides a systematic method to reach an agreement that benefits all participants' water policy planning with a high satisfaction degree of fuzzy constraints, and move towards the deal more quickly since their search focuses only on the feasible solution space. An example application to Negotiation for Water Policy Planning is considered to demonstrate the usefulness and effectiveness of the proposed approach.

Chapter 12

Wei Wang, Nankai University, China

Mei Chang, Neusoft Institute of Information, China

Xiaofei Wang, University of Toyama, Japan

Zheng Tang, Toyama University, Japan

This paper proposes an affinity based complex artificial immune system considering the fact that the different eptitopes located on the surface of antigen can be recognized by a set of different paratopes expressed on the surface of immune cells. A neighborhood set consisting of immune cells with different affinities to a certain input antigen is built to simulate the nature immune behavior. Furthermore, the complex numbers are adopted as the data representation, besides the weight between different layers. In the simulations, the recognition on transformation patterns is performed to illustrate that the proposed system is capable of recognizing the transformation patterns and it has obviously higher noise tolerance ability than the previous system models.

Section 3
User Studies

Chapter 13

Edwin I. Achugbue, Delta State University, Nigeria

Sylvester O. Anie, Delta State Polytechnic, Nigeria

The attitude of librarians in Nigerian university libraries has the potential to encourage or discourage digital libraries in e-learning. This paper addresses and discusses the attitudes of librarians towards digital library in e-learning, the imperativeness of training and knowledge for effective functionality of digital libraries in Nigerian universities. The paper uses the descriptive survey method to explore the attitudes of librarians towards digital libraries, advantages of digital libraries, and the types of e-learning that can be supported by digital libraries. It was discovered that training and knowledge are sine qua non of a positive attitude towards digital libraries in e-learning. And there was a high interest in the use of online information by researchers and learners but lack of awareness and how best to integrate e-learning resources into digital libraries pose a great challenge to the librarians in Nigerian universities.

Chapter 14
Owajeme Justice Ofua, Delta State University, Nigeria
Ogochukwu Thaddaeus Emiri, Delta State University, Nigeria

This paper reviews the role of public libraries in bridging the digital divide in Delta State. It calls for the adoption of appropriate infrastructure and other innovative measures like introduction of appropriate computer related programmes in schools, encouraging citizenry to pick up carrier in the area of science and technology, embanking on enlightenment and awareness programmes and setting up regional/local information resource centers by government especially through the use of the internet also, the challenges of digital divide was revealed. The work concludes that unless appropriate measures are taken in Delta State and Nigeria generally they will be relegated to the background in this knowledge age.

Chapter 15
Owajeme Justice Ofua, Delta State University, Nigeria
Ogochukwu Thaddaeus Emiri, Delta State University, Nigeria

This study was conducted in December 2010 to find out students perception and attitude toward vandalism in the library. To gather the required information, a questionnaire was distributed to 1400 randomly selected students of university libraries in the South-South zone of Nigeria out of which 718 responded. Results of their responses revealed that vandalism of library materials in the form of theft, mutilation and hiding of books and journals, is largely regarded as a form of academic survival, this makes student to put up "I Don't care" attitude to library materials. The major causes of vandalism of library materials include limited library collections; restrictions in the use of some materials; number and duration of loans; insufficient number of copies of recommended textbooks; unaffordable cost of personal textbooks; high cost of photocopying as well as peer-influence. Amongst others, researchers recommend the following: training and retraining programme for users, extension of loan period; adequate funding; robust security measures and punishment of offenders.

Chapter 16
Pereware A. Tiemo, Niger Delta University, Nigeria
Nelson Edewor, Delta State Polytechnic, Nigeria

This article surveys the Information Communication Technology (ICT) readiness of higher institution libraries in Delta State, Nigeria. By means of questionnaires and observation techniques, data were collected from the higher institution libraries. Frequency counts and percentages were used to analyze the data generated. Findings revealed the higher institution libraries ICT demographics, available ICT facilities and equipment, critical service areas automated in these libraries, as well as constraints to ICT use to include poor funding, inadequate skilled manpower, non reliability of electricity supply, inadequate technical support, and poor implementation of policies and lack of maintenance. The study concludes that higher institution libraries in Delta State, Nigeria, are yet to fully embrace ICT in library and information service delivery. Some recommendations that can facilitate the use of ICT in these libraries were also set forth.

In traditional SCW environments, related web services are integrated into business processes. Web service still brings less than expected benefits to small corporations and end-users for two reasons: 1) the web service only focuses on data level and is difficult to implement the presentation-centric business contexts. 2) The small corporations and end-users usually do not have enough IT competences to write a client or user interface to interact with web service(s). In order to solve these problems, the author proposes a presentation-preserved compositional approach for service-oriented architecture (PCSOA), which extends the existing data-oriented compositional approaches for web services to provide a more flexible methodology to orchestrate both data level and presentation level services during the workflow integration. A prototype is also built to validate the feasibility of the approach.

Chapter 18

This study examines technostress, its effects, and measures taken to avoid it among librarians at university libraries in Nigeria. The descriptive survey design was adopted and 5 (five) university libraries in Edo and Delta States were used for the study. The sample size for the study was 79, using the purposive sampling technique, a questionnaire was the main instrument used for data collection, and simple percentage and Chi square were used to analyze the data collected. The authors found that technostress could be avoided by librarians, by taking the following measures: purchasing user friendly interface software, regular staff training on ICTs, and developing positive attitude toward technology, and so forth.

Universities are investing heavily in electronic resources. As a way of embracing new developments, the University of Ilorin, Nigeria, has spent millions of dollars building a usable e-library. However, research indicates that potential users may still not use e-libraries. This study examines user acceptance of e-library from the perspective of technology acceptance mode (TAM). E-library system characteristics, organisational context, and individual characteristics are identified as variables that determine acceptance. Data was collected through self-designed questionnaire from 1,500 undergraduate users of the e-library. The findings revealed that the acceptance constructs, ease of use, perceived usefulness, actual use, satisfaction, relevance, awareness, computer/internet self-efficacy, and social influence, significantly correlate with e-library acceptance. The study suggests that all eight factors jointly pulled 69% prediction of the users' acceptance of e-library. The study recommends that e-library users at the university increase their computer and internet self-efficacy, which significantly enhances their use of the e-library system. The university can assist in this matter by organising computer training for the students.

Hsin-Ju Wei, Information Technology Total Services Corp., Taiwan
Chia-Liang Wei, Allis Electric Co. Ltd., Taiwan

Enterprise Resource Planning (ERP) has become the core of successful information management and is also the foundation of corporate information systems for treating with everything related to corporate processes. The ERP implementation has been considered a complicated process because introducing process is involved with different potential conditions and factors so that they may affect the ultimate performance of ERP systems. The aim of this study is to analyze success factors of introducing SAP system for ERP implementation in small and midsized firms. The authors first found out past critical factors affecting the ERP implementation by means of literature review in order to understand results of past studies. Next, the authors widely collected the critical success factors from previous studies and sifted out representative factors to make up a questionnaire. Through the pilot study and questionnaire revision, the authors identified the content of the questionnaire and started interviewing job. When interviewing activities were finished, they began to study and analyze the data. Survey results indicate that three of the most important factors affecting ERP implementation are "top management support and commitment", "project manager's competence" and "communication and coordination effectiveness".

Preface

This book is divided into the retrieval section, the storage section, and the user study section.

RETRIEVAL

Sekhar Mandal *et al.* present a unified algorithm for segmentation and identification of various tabular structures from document page images. Such tabular structures include conventional tables and displayed math-zones, as well as Table of Contents (TOC) and Index pages. After analyzing the page composition, the algorithm initially classifies the input set of document pages into tabular and non-tabular pages. A tabular page contains at least one of the tabular structures, whereas a non-tabular page does not contain any such. The approach is unified in the sense that it is able to identify all tabular structures from a tabular page, which leads to a considerable simplification of document image segmentation in a novel manner. Such unification also results in speeding up the segmentation process, since the existing methodologies produce time-consuming solutions for treating different tabular structures as separate physical entities. Distinguishing features of different kinds of tabular structures have been used in stages in order to ensure the simplicity and efficiency of the algorithm, as explained in this paper and demonstrated by exhaustive experimental results.

Creation of a document image library involves a chain of thorough and intense activities like scanning, per-processing, segmentation, layout analysis, storage and retrieval, etc. Hence, it is still constrained with the requirement of huge manual workloads—particularly for the segmentation and identification of page constituents as a part of the layout analysis. Despite being the most researched field in the domain of Document Image Analysis (DIA), the problems are yet to be solved up to the desired level of accuracy and efficiency. Most of the currently used methods have been designed and tested with some typical applications in mind and have moderate performance apropos the huge variety of document pages in real life. An integrated approach to segmentation and physical analysis of document images is, therefore, imminent for broad classification of the pages utilizing some common criteria. A classification based on the presence of any tabular structure in a page may lead to better segmentation at a lower computing cost. It may be noted that, by the term "tabular structure," which means anything that visually resembles a table. Careful observation would reveal that tabular items are quite common in document pages; for, any table, table of content (TOC), index page, and most of the displayed math-zones exhibit the tabular nature. Moreover, a simple test based on spatial criteria is enough to detect these tabular structures. With this backdrop, here, a novel approach is presented, treating any page as tabular or non-tabular for reaping its benefit in subsequent DIA tasks.

Handwriting bears the touch of personality traits of an individual, and hence has been studied in numerous disciplines including experimental psychology, neuroscience, engineering, anthropology, forensic science, etc. In the realm of computer science, analysis of handwriting has been an important field that strives to interpret, verify, and recognize a particular handwritten document. The segmentation of cursive handwriting is one of the most difficult problems in the area of handwriting recognition. The infinitude of different types of human handwritings amidst the similarities in the shapes of different characters, renders the problem even more difficult. Hence, over the last few years, various works have been presented for specific domains, e.g., Bengali character recognition, text line identification, numeral recognition, address reading, tax reading, office automation, automated postal system, etc.

Handwriting recognition techniques are based on either holistic or analytic strategies. In the holistic method, a top-down approach is employed where the whole word is recognized by comparing its global features against a limited size lexicon. On the other hand, analytic strategies adopt the bottom-up approach starting with characters, strokes etc., eventually producing the meaningful text. Clearly, in connection with handwriting recognition, it is important to extract/segment the words in a cursive writing such that the task of segregating the individual characters and strokes may be taken up. The segmented regions may be found out from the peaks of the projection profile of a gray-level image. It is also important to properly extract the baselines such that the words can be segmented properly. Information about the upper and the lower baselines are necessary to avoid problems arising out of ascending and descending portions of the characters. In general, the baselines are extracted from the projection profile. As per the existence practice, the text line segmentation is usually done by considering a subset of the connected components in a document image. Word segmentation is achieved using the distinction of inter- and intra-word gaps using a combination of two different distance metrics.

To overcome the disadvantage of different distance measures in word segmentation, a gap metric based on the average distance is used for word segmentation. A number of works have been reported in the literature for line and word segmentation in other languages, e.g., Chinese, Arabic, etc. Chinese word segmentation has various applications on Chinese text processing. The algorithm for detection of straight or curved baselines for Arabic handwritten text can be applied on online handwriting or off-line handwritten writing. A method for precise identification of ascending or descending parts of the words has been proposed using lexicon based search.

Mousumi Dutt *et al.* have devised a novel method to segment out the words in a cursive handwriting by using the outer isothetic covers of the words constituting the handwritten document. The method has also the advantage of extracting the upper and the lower baselines by analyzing these covers corresponding to the handwritten words. Owing to the combinatorial nature of its traversal strategy while deriving the minimum-area isothetic covers corresponding to the words, and hence describing the covers as sequences of their vertices (or/and edges), it is endowed with an easy solution to locate the baselines of different words — whatsoever be their patterns and letter-wise constitution — as shown in this chapter. A fast decision policy based on the covers, coupled with usage of operations strictly in the integer domain, make it fast, robust, and efficient, thereby depicting its compliance for real-time applications.

In hospitals and medical institutes, a large number of mammograms are produced in ever increasing quantities and used for diagnostics and therapy. The need for effective methods to manage and retrieve those image resources has been actively pursued in the medical community. The author Jinn-Ming Chang proposes a hierarchical correlation calculation approach to content-based mammogram retrieval. In this approach, images are represented as a Gaussian pyramid with several reduced-resolution levels. A global search is first conducted to identify the optimal matching position, where the correlation between the query image and the target images in the database is maximal. Local search is performed in the region comprising the four child pixels at a higher resolution level in order to locate the position with maximal correlation at greater resolution. Finally, this position with the maximal correlation found at the finest resolution level is used as the image similarity measure for retrieving images. Experimental results have shown that this approach achieves 59% in precision and 54% in recall when the threshold of correlation is 0.5.

Breast cancer is the most common cancer among women. The National Cancer Institute (NCI) recommends that women over the age of 40 and older should have routine screening mammography every one to two years. The U.S. Preventive Services Task Force (USPSTF) recommends biennial screening mammography for women aged 50 to 74 years. An enormous number of digital mammograms have been generated in hospitals and breast screening centers as mammography is an accurate and reliable method for the detection and diagnosis of breast cancers. These valuable mammograms which show various symptoms, allow radiologists to conduct medical studies and assist them in diagnosing new cases. The most important aspect of image database management is how to effectively retrieve the similar images based on the lesion of a given example. This approach of searching images is known as content-based image retrieval (CBIR), which refers to the retrieval of images from a database using information directly derived from the content of the images themselves, rather than from accompanying text or annotation. CBIR can help radiologists to retrieve mammograms with similar contents.

Due to the nature of mammograms, content-based retrieval for similar lesions is faced with some challenges. Low resolution and strong noise are two common characteristics. With these characteristics, Lesions in mammograms cannot be precisely segmented and extracted for the visual content of their features. In addition, mammograms obtained from different scanning devices may display different features, though some approaches to image correction and normalization have been proposed; Mammograms are represented in gray level rather than color. Even with the change of intensity, monochrome may fail to clearly display the actual circumstance of lesion area.

Content-based image retrieval (CBIR) has been proposed by the medical community for inclusion into picture archiving and communication systems (PACS). In CBIR, relevance feedback is developed for bridging the semantic gap and improving the effectiveness of image retrieval systems. With relevance feedback, CBIR systems can return refined search results using a learning algorithm and selection strategy. In the study presented by Chee-Chiang Chen, as the retrieving process proceeds further, the proposed learning algorithm can reduce the influence of the original query point and increase the significance of the centroid of the clusters comprising the features of those relevant images identified in the most recent round of search., The proposed selection strategy is employed to find a good starting point and to select a set of images at each round to show that search result and ask for the user's feedback. In addition, a benchmark is proposed to measure the learning ability to explain the retrieval performance as relevance feedback is incorporated in CBIR systems. The performance evaluation shows that the average precision rate of the proposed scheme was 0.98 and the learning ability reach to 7.17 through the five rounds of relevance feedback.

Nowadays artificial intelligent (AI) driving has become an emerging technology, freeing the driver from the boring travels. More important, the AI system for automatically driving is supposed to be more secure in theory than the human drivers, because the system will never be too exhaustive to response the accident in time. In automatic driving, Geographic Positioning System (GPS) has become an essential component, which aids AI to find the correct route and drive to the destination along the route following the directions predefined on the electronic map. In theory, AI system should be able to drive only depending on GPS, following the directions, such as speed limit, one way only, and etc, on electronic map. However, one inevitable situation may happen where the route may be updated due to the road work, route adjusting and etc, while the corresponding directions on the e-map will be updated periodically in half a year. This asynchronization on directions of e-maps and the actual traffic signs will cause the AI system fail from the real time driving.

Some techniques for automatic driving have been developed in recent years, however, most of these developments can only recognize the traffic signs in particular groups, such as triangle signs for warning, circle signs for prohibition and etc but could not tell the exact meaning of every sign. Without understanding the exact meaning of every sign, the AI system cannot drive automatically but need the driver to determine the route when it encounters any traffic signs. Subsequently, it is an essential work to design a system could recognize the exact meaning of every traffic signs. In this paper, Yue Li and Wei Wang propose a framework on traffic system recognition system, which consists of two phrases that a segmentation method is used to detect the traffic sign while the Content-Based Image Retrieval (CBIR) method is used to match the detect traffic signs and the traffic signs in the database.

STORAGE

For image analysis, to investigate more closely a specific area within the image is desired. For this desire, to enlarge the specific area is engaged. In the video sequence, for a specific area within an image frame, zoom in on it could enlarge it. The enlarged area can be recognized efficiently. Image resolution enhancement refers to image processing algorithm which produces a high quality and high resolution image from a low quality and low resolution image. It includes two procedures. The first is the problem for finding a mapping between high resolution image and low resolution image. The second is the problem for calculating all the pixel values of the high resolution image from its low resolution version. The mapping between them is always chosen by a linear mapping system in the literature proposed by Lung-Chun Chang *et al.* However, for the CCD (charged-coupled devices) camera, the resolution of enlarged images is produced by the lens. The linear mapping system is not suitable. In addition, due to the linear mapping system, the scale of the image to be enlarged is always an integer scale once. Thus, in this paper, they focus on the design of the mapping system and the mapping system can enlarge the image by a real scale. In the second procedure, image interpolation addresses the problem of generating a high resolution image from its low resolution version. Conventional linear interpolation schemes (e.g., bilinear and bicubic) based on space-invariant models fail to capture the fast evolving statistics around edges and annoying artifacts. Linear interpolation is generally preferred not for the performance but for computational simplicity. Many algorithms have been proposed to improve the subjective quality of the interpolated images by imposing more accurate models.

The magnifier is a perfect optics tool. It is easy to enlarge the resolution of images by a real scale. In this paper, a virtual magnifier is constructed and simulated. Using the virtual magnifier, the mapping between high resolution pixels and low resolution pixels is obtained. Further, a traditional interpolation algorithm is applied into the mapping of the high resolution image and low resolution image. With three real images, experimental results demonstrate that the proposed algorithm has a high quality in the human visual system.

Nowadays many digital forensic techniques for digital images are developed to serve the purpose of the origin identification and integrity verification for security reasons. Generally speaking, these methods can be divided into two classes, the methods based on the extracted features, which are usually the high frequency noise inside the investigating images and the methods based on the contents of the images. Different techniques may be developed specially against different forging attacks, while be vulnerable to other malicious manipulations on the images. This chapter presented by Yue Li is to review the most popular techniques in order to help the user to understand the techniques and find the most proper methods for variety forensic purpose in different situations.

The widely applied digital imaging devices bring great convince to the people in daily life. At any time, people can capture scenes around them by the portable cameras or the built-in camera in the mobile; the government can achieve 24-hour surveillance by the widely installed CCTV; the journalists can records the 1/24-second-motions by the professional camera. However, the security of the captured digital images remains unprotected and such problem needs urgently investigation by the research and the engineer. The malicious user can easily forge an image with modified contents or replace the output images of the camera with a fake one. These operations are defined as attacks in the study of security of multimedia and protection of digital libraries while the users who operated these attackers are defined as attackers. Practically, these attacks may be operated for different purposes. For example, the attacker may fake an origin marks in the image to announce an illegal copyright of the digital multimedia products, or the attacker may modify the contents inside an image or a video, which is used as evident in court. It is obvious that these attacks will cause tremendous loss in practical if no proper protections are implied, and therefore, many security techniques have been developed to fight against these attacks.

Digital watermarking is traditionally developed to protect the digital multimedia products. The term of digital watermarking, which is similar to the real watermarking implanting a mark in the secret paper documents or bank notes, refers to an operation embedding an imperceptible mark into the digital multimedia products to authorize the integrity and origin of the images. The user, who needs to authorize the products, extracts and investigates the integrity of the embedded watermark. If the watermark is broken or destroyed, then the product is deemed as forged. Digital watermarking techniques may be developed to achieve advance functions. For example, some techniques can localize which area is modified by the attacker, whereas other techniques can survival after the attack and can be further used to reconstruct the images.

Despite of the advantages in theory and effectiveness in practices, digital watermarking is not widely applied in the implementation due to some disadvantages. Forensic techniques are developed rapidly in recent years and tends to replace digital watermarking as the most effective and applied techniques for digital products and library protection. In this paper, Yue Li reviewed the main classes forensic methods currently used.

Digital image authentication refers to all the techniques performing anti-falsification, digital image copyright protection or access control. A large number of DIA techniques have been developed to authenticate digital images, including cryptography-based digital image authentication (CBDIA) techniques and data-hiding-based digital image authentication (DHBDIA) techniques. This paper presented by Yue Li is not only to provide some practical applications on image authentication, but also describe general framework of image watermarking and the general techniques, including robust watermarking, fragile watermarking and semi-fragile watermarking. Finally, this paper also addresses the potential issues on future research directions, including managing the PRNU database, development of advanced PRNU-based blind authentication techniques, and search for digital fingerprints.

The digital forensic techniques for digital images are developed with the origin identification and integrity verification functions for security reasons. Methods based on photo-response-non-uniform

(PRNU) are widely studied and proved to be effective to serve the forensic purposes. However, due to the interpolation noise, caused by the color filtering and interpolation function the accuracy of the PRNU-based forensic method has been degraded. Meanwhile, the tremendous physical storage requirement and computation consumption limit the applications of PRNU-based method. Therefore, an innovative DPRNU-based forensic method has been proposed in order to solve the above problems. In the method, the artificial component and physical component are separated according to the color filtering array (CFA) and the PRNU are only extracted from the physical component in order to remove the interference caused by the interpolation noise, which increases the accuracy of the camera identification and integrity verification. Meanwhile, due to the separation, the DPRNU are only 1/3 of the size of the traditional PRNU, which saves considerable physical storage in setting up the digital library and fasters the comparison speed between the fingerprints.

The widely applied digital imaging devices bring great convince to the people in daily life. At any time, people can capture scenes around them by the portable cameras or the built-in camera in the mobile; the government can achieve 24-hour surveillance by the widely installed CCTV; the journalists can records the 1/24-second-motions by the professional camera. However, the security of the captured digital images remains unprotected and such problem needs urgently investigation by the research and the engineer. The security problem can be summarized as which person/device produces the image and whether the image is modified. As a result, the digital forensic techniques for digital images are developed with the origin identification and integrity verification functions in order to solve the aforementioned problems.

Generally speaking, the forensic techniques extract a fingerprint, which is a digital feature left by the digital imaging device, and compared it to the reference fingerprints representing a set of imaging devices in the database. Depending on the comparing result, the forensic techniques can identify the origin and verify the integrity of the digital images. Due to the necessity of the reference fingerprint, setting up a digital library, which stores the majority reference fingerprints of the digital devices and connect to internet/intranet, is essential to serve the forensic purposes. With the aids of the digital fingerprint library, the user can identify the source cameras by comparing the fingerprints of the camera under investigation and the fingerprint stored in the library and representing sample cameras. Meanwhile, the user can investigate the integrity of the photo using the fingerprints. Compared to the sample fingerprint in the library, if the investigated fingerprint is partially broken or entirely destroyed, then the corresponding photo can be verified as tampered in the corresponding area or entirely faked due to the destroyed fingerprint. As a result, the digital library of the fingerprint can greatly benefits the user in the forensic application. However, in setting up such digital library, the user may face the serious problem in the physical storage requirement and tremendous time consuming in the computation. The most representative and widely applied forensic method based on PRNU is reviewed and the corresponding limitations in setting up a library on this method in the paper are discussed by the author Yue Li.

The distribution of typhoon and its variation are very important for disaster prevention and worthy of study. The satellite data provides typhoon cloud image for analyzing the cloud structure and wind driven velocity of typhoon. The typhoon cloud images are not clear often, there are many kinds of noise in it, which may affect to accurately segment the helical cloud band or extract some information from the typhoon cloud images. Both noise reduction and contrast enhancement are usually applied in a typhoon cloud image for location, rotation, tracking, and forecast.

Recently, the typhoon eye is the interested behavior for research. Since the portion surrounding the eye will do the most damage, the typhoon center recognition is important for weather forecast and typhoon analysis. When the typhoon reaches to certain strength, there will be an eye appeared at the center. As the strength of the typhoon getting stronger, the eye tends to a circle and also becomes clearer. When the typhoon arrive the land, its strength will decrease and the eye may be non-clear. However, the typhoon cloud images are planar pictures. Recently a 3-D profile reconstruction is an interesting research topic for recognizing the practical typhoon. The segmentation of the satellite cloud image was sliced in horizontal plane to obtain a series of 2D surfaces, and reconstruct the 3D cloud or storm.

Based on the vertical segmentation, IRT is used to reconstruct a 3-D profile of typhoons from MT-SAT satellite cloud image data. The objectives of this paper presented by Yueh-Jyun Lee *et al.* are three folds: first, to slice the line profile from that satellite cloud image data and present the height variations under the conversion of the temperature; second, to construct the mesh-amplitude model in depicting the height distribution of the cloud top from a surface cloud image. The 3-D profiles of typhoons are constructed with the surface cloud images and the temperatures; third, to recognize the eye of the typhoon. IRT is conducted using the data of the 2010 Megi typhoon in three time interval. An effective early-warning system may become feasible based on this work. They present the numerical results with discussion and conclusions finally.

With the boosting demand for water, and many challenges related to water availability, food security, pollution, and environmental degradation, it becomes an imperative and necessity to establish good water policy planning for sufficient supply of water consumption. An agent with autonomy, self-learning, and coordination can serve as an efficient approach for water policy planning in view of its following features. Firstly, an agent can stand for different institutes or groups related to water resource and fulfill autonomously its duty that is assigned to itself. Secondly, an agent can self-learn and anticipate the oncoming water demand and trend in water resource development, in a changeable and unpredictable environment of water resource. Thirdly, an agent can coordinate and solve a problem in water policy planning from perspectives of its self- and overall-interest. In Addition, agent negotiation is an iterative process through which a joint decision is made by two or more agents in order to reach a mutually acceptable agreement. Many approaches to such negotiation have been proposed, including negotiation support systems (NSSs), a game theory-based model, a Bayesian model, evolutionary computation, and distributed artificial intelligence.

NSSs emphasize support, rather than automation. In the game theory-based model, the agent's utility for each possible outcome of an interaction is used to construct into a pay-off matrix. The aim of the game theory-based model is to formalize agent negotiation in a context in which each agent tries to maximize its own utility with respect to other agents. However, the pay-off matrices are generally based on some unrealistic assumption that all agents have common knowledge of the pay-off matrix. Even if the pay-off matrix is known, it may quickly become intractable for large games that involve multiple issues and agents. As a result, the use of negotiation strategies based on game theory should generally be treated with skepticism. In the Bayesian model, a Bayesian network is used to update an agent's knowledge and beliefs about other agents, and Bayesian probabilities are employed to generate offers.

Fuzzy constraints can serve as a natural means of modeling a buyer's requirements over products' single issues and the combination of the products' multiple issues. They are also appropriate for modeling trade-offs between different issues of a product, and capturing the process by which a buyer relaxes his constraints to reach a partially satisfactory deal. Hence, the authors Menq-Wen Lin *et al.* present a general problem-solving framework for modeling multi-issue agent negotiation in e-marketplace via fuzzy constraint processing. In this framework, all participants involved in water policy planning are modeled as agents. Agent negotiation is formulated as a distributed fuzzy constraint satisfaction problem (DFCSP). Fuzzy constraints are used to define each participant's professional views and demands.

The agent negotiation can simulate the interactive process of all participants' water policy planning. A concession strategy, based on fuzzy constraint-based problem-solving, is proposed to relax demands and a trade-off strategy is presented to evaluate existing alternatives. This approach provides a systematic method to reach an agreement that benefits all participants' water policy planning with a high satisfaction degree of fuzzy constraints, and move towards the deal more quickly since their search focuses only on the feasible solution space. An example application for modeling water policy planning via agent negotiation is considered to demonstrate the usefulness and effectiveness of the proposed approach.

Along with the interest in studying the immune system increasing over the last few years, a new field of research called artificial immune systems has arisen. The artificial immune systems, which is inspired by theoretical immunology and observed immune functions, principles and models, has been applied to the various fields of engineering science to solve many complex problems, such as pattern recognition, robotics, anomaly detection, data mining and optimization.

The authors Wei Wang *et al.* propose an affinity based complex artificial immune system model to simulate the actual immune response. In this model, they build a neighborhood set consisting of several immune cells with higher affinities to a certain input antigen than the other immune cells based on the SOM principles. All the weights of cells located in the neighborhood set have their weights updated according to the affinities. The results of simulation on pattern recognition show that the proposed system model can recognize the transformation patterns in high accuracy and it has obvious higher noise tolerance ability than the previous system models.

USER STUDIES

The attitudes of librarians in Nigerian university libraries have the potential to encourage or discourage digital libraries in e-learning. The author Edwin I. Achugbue addressed and discussed the attitudes of librarians towards digital library in e-learning, the imperativeness of training and knowledge for effective functionality of digital libraries in Nigerian universities. The paper uses descriptive survey method to explore the attitudes of librarians towards digital libraries, advantages of digital libraries and the types of e-learning that can be supported by digital libraries. It was undoubtedly discovered that training and knowledge are sine qua non of a positive attitude towards digital libraries in e-learning. And there was a high interest in the use of online information by researchers and learners but lack of awareness and how best to integrate e-learning resources into digital libraries pose a great challenge to the librarians in Nigerian universities. This paper provides a useful insight into the attitudes of librarians towards digital libraries, the role and influence of digital libraries and online resources on e-learning.

To review the role of public libraries in bridging the digital divide in Delta State is conducted by Justice Owajeme Ofua and Ogochukwu Thaddaeus Emiri. It calls for the adoption of appropriate infrastructure and other innovative measures like introduction of appropriate computer related programs in schools, encouraging citizenry to pick up carrier in the area of science and technology, embanking on enlightenment and awareness programs and setting up regional/local information resource centers by government especially through the use of the internet also, the challenges of digital divide was also revealed. The work concludes that unless appropriate measures are taking in Delta State and Nigeria generally they will be relegated to the background in this knowledge age.

Justice Owajeme Ofua and Ogochukwu Thaddaeus Emiri found out students' perception and attitude to vandalism in the library in their study. To gather the required information, a questionnaire was distributed to 1400 randomly selected students of university libraries in the South-South zone of Nigeria out of which 718 responded. Result of their responses revealed that vandalism of library materials in the form of theft, mutilation and hiding of books and journals, is largely regarded as a form of academic survival, this makes student to put up "I don't care" attitude to library materials. The major causes of vandalism of libraries materials include limited library collections; restrictions in the use of some materials; number and duration of loans; insufficient number of copies of recommended textbooks; unaffordable cost of personal textbooks; high cost of photocopying as well as peer-influence. Amongst others, researchers recommend the following: training and retraining program for users, extension of loan period; adequate funding; robust security measures and punishment of offenders.

The article conducted by Pereware A. Tiemo and Nelson Edewor is to survey the Information Communication Technology (ICT) readiness of higher institution libraries in Delta State, Nigeria. By means of questionnaires and observation techniques, data were collected from the higher institution libraries. Frequency counts and percentages were used to analyze the data generated. Findings revealed the higher institution libraries ICT demographics, available ICT facilities and equipment, critical service areas automated in these libraries, as well as constraints to ICT use to include poor funding, inadequate skilled manpower, non reliability of electricity supply, inadequate technical support, poor implementation of policies, and lack of maintenance. The study concludes that higher institution libraries in Delta State, Nigeria, are yet to fully embrace ICT in library and information service delivery. Some recommendations that can facilitate the use of ICT in these libraries were also set forth.

In the traditional SCW environments, related Web services are integrated into business processes. The author Fang-Chuan Ou Yang points out that web service still bring less than expected benefits to small corporations and end-users for two reasons: 1) the web service only focuses on data level and is difficult to implement the presentation-centric business contexts. 2) The small corporations and end-users usually do not have enough IT competences to write a client or user interface to interact with web services. In order to solve these problems, the author propose a presentation-preserved compositional approach for service-oriented architecture (PCSOA), which extends the existing data-oriented compositional approaches for web services to provide a more flexible methodology to orchestrate both data level and presentation level services during the workflow integration. A prototype is also built to validate the feasibility of our approach.

The study proposed by Justice Owajeme Ofua and Tiemo Aghwotu Pereware is to focus on technostress, effects and measures taken to avoid it among librarians in university libraries in Nigeria. The descriptive survey design was adopted and five university libraries in Edo and Delta States were used for the study. The sample size for the study was 79 using the purposive sampling technique, the questionnaire was the main instrument used for data collection, simple percentage and Chi square was used in analyzing the data collected. Among the findings were technostress can be avoided by librarians, by taking the following measures; purchasing user friendly interface software, regular Staff training on ICTs, and develops positive attitude towards technology etc.

Universities around the world are now investing heavily on electronic resources especially academic libraries where users are exposed to various e-resources through the Internet. As a way of embracing the new development in e-library, the University of Ilorin, Nigeria, have spent millions of dollars on building usable e-library. However, previous research has indicates that potential users may still not use them. Not this alone, there have been no single study indicating use and acceptance of this library in the context of this university and Nigeria as a whole.

The study is to examine user acceptance of e-library from the perspective of technology acceptance mode (TAM). E-library system characteristics, organizational context and individual characteristics are identified as variables that determine the acceptance of e-library. Design: A survey design approach was adopted to carry out the study. Data was collected through self-designed questionnaire from 1,500 undergraduate users of e-library. Results/Findings: The findings of the study revealed that the entire acceptance constructs: ease of use, perceived usefulness, actual use, satisfaction, relevance, awareness, computer/internet self-efficacy and social influence significantly correlate with e-library acceptance. Moreover, the study suggests that all eight factors jointly pulled 69% prediction of the users' acceptance of e-library; and that, all the constructs are good predictors of e-library acceptance.

This study recommends among other that users of e-library users in the university should increase their computer and internet self-efficacy as this is expected to further enhance significantly their use of the e-library system. The university was as well call upon to assist in this matter by organizing computer training for the students. If this is done, it assumed that it will help the students to develop internet browsing skills. This study constitutes one of the pioneer studies predicting acceptance of e-library from technology acceptance model point of view. The study extended and modified technology acceptance model thereby contributing to literature in this area.

Enterprise Resource Planning (ERP) has become the core of successful information management and is also the foundation of corporate information systems for treating with everything related to corporate processes. The ERP implementation has been considered a complicated process because introducing process is involved with different potential conditions and factors so that they may affects the ultimate performance of ERP systems. The study presented by Hsin-Ju Wei and Chia-Liang Wei is to analyze success factors of introducing SAP system for ERP implementation in small and midsized firms. To achieve the aim, they firstly found out past critical factors affecting the ERP implementation by means of literature review in order to understand the results of past studies. Next, they widely collected the critical success factors from previous studies and sifted out representative factors to make up the questionnaire in according with the purpose of the research. Through the pilot study and questionnaire revision, they identified the content of the questionnaire and started interviewing job. When interviewing activities were finished, they began to study and analyze these data. Finally, they generated results. Their survey results indicate that three of the most important factors affecting ERP implementation are "top management support and commitment," "project manager's competence" and "communication and coordination effectiveness."

Chia-Hung Wei
Chien Hsin University of Science and Technology, Taiwan

Chih-Ying Gwo
Chien Hsin University of Science and Technology, Taiwan

Section 1
Retrieval

Chapter 1
A Unified Algorithm for Identification of Various Tabular Structures from Document Images

Sekhar Mandal
Bengal Engineering & Science University, Shibpur, India

Amit K. Das
Bengal Engineering & Science University, Shibpur, India

Partha Bhowmick
Indian Institute of Technology Kharagpur, India

Bhabatosh Chanda
Indian Statistical Institute, Kolkata, India

ABSTRACT

This paper presents a unified algorithm for segmentation and identification of various tabular structures from document page images. Such tabular structures include conventional tables and displayed math-zones, as well as Table of Contents (TOC) and Index pages. After analyzing the page composition, the algorithm initially classifies the input set of document pages into tabular and non-tabular pages. A tabular page contains at least one of the tabular structures, whereas a non-tabular page does not contain any. The approach is unified in the sense that it is able to identify all tabular structures from a tabular page, which leads to a considerable simplification of document image segmentation in a novel manner. Such unification also results in speeding up the segmentation process, because the existing methodologies produce time-consuming solutions for treating different tabular structures as separate physical entities. Distinguishing features of different kinds of tabular structures have been used in stages in order to ensure the simplicity and efficiency of the algorithm and demonstrated by exhaustive experimental results.

DOI: 10.4018/978-1-4666-2928-8.ch001

INTRODUCTION

Billions of pages are to be scanned and analyzed to create document image libraries targeted to real-world applications. The task is daunting; however, there is a pressing need for these libraries, as we witness a spurt of activities in recent times in industries as well as in academia. Creation of a document image library involves a chain of thorough and intense activities like scanning, per-processing, segmentation, layout analysis, storage and retrieval, etc. Hence, it is still constrained with the requirement of huge manual workloads—particularly for the segmentation and identification of page constituents as a part of the layout analysis. Despite being the most researched field in the domain of Document Image Analysis (DIA), the problems are yet to be solved up to the desired level of accuracy and efficiency. Most of the currently used methods have been designed and tested with some typical applications in mind and have moderate performance apropos the huge variety of document pages in real life. An integrated approach to segmentation and physical analysis of document images is, therefore, imminent for broad classification of the pages utilizing some common criteria. A classification based on the presence of any tabular structure in a page may lead to better segmentation at a lower computing cost. It may be noted that, by the term "tabular structure", we mean anything that visually resembles a table. Careful observation would reveal that tabular items are quite common in document pages; for, any table, table of content (TOC), index page, and most of the displayed math-zones exhibit the tabular nature. Moreover, a simple test based on spatial criteria is enough to detect these tabular structures. With this backdrop, here, a novel approach is presented, treating any page as *tabular* or *non-tabular* for reaping its benefit in subsequent DIA tasks.

The paper is organized as follows. The next section presents a brief review of the existing works in the related field. The basic stages of our algorithm have been explained in two subsequent sections: In the first one, we show how a document page is classified as a tabular or a non-tabular page using certain characteristic features of tables, index pages, and math-zones. The detailed procedures of finally classifying all sorts of tabular structures are explained with examples in the second one. The next section contains experimental results including performance-wise comparison with some existing methods. Finally, we conclude the paper with the future possibilities that evolve out of our work.

PAST WORK

The approach of treating the text as either tabular or non-tabular is not yet proposed by others. Hence, citation with similar approaches is not possible. However, there are various works available in the literature for detection/ segmentation of tabular components, e.g., table, TOC, displayed math, etc. In this section we present a brief review of the past work under the following categories.

1. **Table:** Table detection and segmentation have been done in several ways (Chandran et al., 1996; Mandal et al., 2006b; Tsuruoka et al., 2001; Watanabe et al., 1995). The algorithms may be classified broadly into two types: one based on the presence of rule lines in the table and the other based on the knowledge of table layout. Watanabe et al. (1995) have proposed a tree for representation of the structure of various kinds of tables. In Chandran et al. (1996), the horizontal and vertical lines of the table are used to recognize the structure of the tabulated data. In Itonori (1993), a similar technique is found, which also uses row-column pairing and the relationship of cells and ruled lines. Zuyev (1997) has defined a table grid, and has described simple and compound cells of any table based on the table grid. Node

property matrix has been used by Tanaka and Tsuruoka (1998) in the processing of irregular rule lines and generation of HTML files. Method of analysis for unknown table structure has been proposed by Belaid, Panchevre, and Belaid (1998). Tersteegen and Wenzel (1998) have proposed a system for extraction of tabular structure (table only) with the help of predefined reference table. Tsuruoka et al. (2001) have presented a segmentation method for complex tables with or without rule lines. A technique has been described by Das and Chanda (1998a) to separate out tables and headings in document images. Ramel et al. (2003) have used a flexible representation scheme based on clear distinction between the physical table and its logical structure.

Only a few approaches for table detection are based on the spatial layout of the document, of which two representative cases are the following. In Kieninger (1998), individual words are clustered and a block segmentation graph is constructed based on the overlaps of the individual items (words) in consecutive lines. It may be noted that in tables, the overlaps are limited to individual columns and the block segmentation graph will be distinctly different from a block of normal text. The authors claim that this approach works well for ASCII files and may be extended for a scanned document. In the second (Hu, Kashi, Lopresti, & Wilfong, 2000), a structured approach based on dynamic programming is taken to find the input line(s) that can be taken as a part of the table. This is done by computing characteristics such as *score*, *merit*, and *line correlations* to ascertain the gain (or loss) if the candidate line is taken (or rejected) as a part of the table. This approach has a strong theoretical foundation and the detection rate is 81% for the scanned image and 83% for ASCII text. Interested readers may see Embley et al. (2006) Lopresti and Nagy (1999) and Zanibbi

et al. (2004) for a comprehensive survey on table recognition schemes.

2. **TOC and Index pages:** Several works are available in the literature for detection and segmentation of TOCs (Belaid, 2001; Le Bourgeois & Bensafi, 2001; He, Ding, & Peng, 2004; Lin, Niwa, & Narita, 1997; Lin & Xiong, 2006; Liu, 2003; Luo, Watanabe, & Nakayama, 1996; O'Gorman, 1992; Satoh, Takasu, & Katsura, 1995; Story, O'Gorman, Fox, Schaper, & Jagadish, 1992; Tsuruoka, Hirano, Yoshikawa, & Shinogi, 2001); however, to the best of our knowledge, there is none for Index pages. O'Gorman (1992) and Story et al. (1992) have proposed methods for TOC structure extraction in their Right Pages Electronic Library Systems utilizing OCR techniques. By *Docstrum analysis*, blocks are first extracted and then the articles are indexed with the help of *a priori* model, fed manually, derived out of the TOCs of different journals. The relationship information is used to help human user to quickly go to the relevant sections (say, from the article title to the exact pages), on mouse clicks.

Satoh et al. (1995), in the CyberMagazine project, have introduced a technique using training data to learn decision trees for different kinds of journals for conversion of TOC pages of the journals to bibliographic database. Lin et al. (1997) have proposed a TOC page analysis and logical structure extraction by layout modeling and headline matching for books in Japanese. He et al. (2004) have combined indentations and typical text sequences identifying chapters and sections to extract hierarchical logical structure in Chinese books. Parts-of-speech tagging, a labeling approach for automatic recognition of TOCs, has been suggested in (Belaid, 2001; Belaid, Pierron, & Valverde, 2000) using *a priori* model of the regularities present in the document. A probability relaxation method is used by Le Bourgeois and Bensafi (2001) to analyze the structure of periodicals through training on layouts of several representative samples to recognize TOCs; recognition rate is reported to exceed 98%.

In a recent work, Lin and Xiong (2006) have reported a TOC detection technique based on content association with the assumption that the contents (title, author name(s), start page number, etc.) of an article will repeat on the title page (i.e., the first page of an article). Though it does not rely on layout information, the technique is applicable only for journals where the underlying assumption is true. Several other contemporary layout-based approaches for TOC and index page detection are reported in Mandal, Chowdhury, Das, and Chanda (2003a, 2006a, 2003b). It may be noted that, all the previous approaches assume that either the TOC pages are located on some fixed pages for certain type of publications or they are manually selected. An exception to this is the work reported by Luo et al. (1996), which has used layout information for automatic identification. However, it depends on the recognition of the connectors (solid or dotted lines used to associate article/section/chapter name and corresponding page numbers) instead of identifying the tabular layout of TOCs.

3. **Math-zone:** Segmenting out the math-zone still remains a challenging problem. Most of the previous works (Anderson, 1977; Ha, Haralick, & Philips, 1995; Okamoto & Miyazawa, 1992) are directed towards recognition of either the math-symbols or the equations, as cited in existing literature. Many researchers in recent years have reported a number of approaches (Anderson, 1977; Belaid & Haton, 1984; Chang, 1970; Fateman, Tokuyasu, Berman, & Mitchell, 1996; Grbavec & Blostein, 1995; Ha et al., 1995; Kacem, Belaid, & Ahmed, 2001; Lee & Lee, 1993; Mandal, Chowdhury, Das, & Chanda, 2003c; Okamoto & Miyazawa, 1992) for mathematical document processing with a focus on recognition and understanding of mathematical expressions. They assume that the math-zones have already been segmented out from the document image manually or through semi-/fully automated segmentation logic. Following is a brief review of the existing approaches for math-segmentation.

Fateman et al. (1996) have proposed a scheme that utilizes character size and font information to identify all the connected components. Two bags, namely text and math, are then defined, which contain all the items. The "text bag" includes all letters and italic numbers, whereas the "math bag" collects punctuation marks, special symbols, Roman digits, italic letters, dots, and lines. The objects in math bag are then grouped together according to their spatial proximity. Grouping of items in text bag is also done, followed by review and correction, to move the isolated items to their proper destinations.

Math segmentation by Toumit, Garcia-Salicetti, and Emptoz (1999) uses physical and logical analysis of spatial characteristics of the math-zone and identification of some math symbols. A survey on the methods of mathematical symbol recognition has been carried out by Chan and Yeung (2000). Methods proposed in (Chou, 1989; Nakayama, 1993; Okamoto & Miao, 1991; Okamoto & Miyazawa, 1992) are based on traditional template matching for recognizing mathematical symbols. Later, template matching based on Hausdorff distance has been proposed by a few researchers (Berman & Fateman, 1994; Fateman & Tokuyasu, 1996; Miller & Viola, 1998). Belaid and Haton (1984) and Chan and Yeung (1999) have used structural approaches for symbol recognition. Statistical approaches for recognition of mathematical symbols have also been suggested by several researchers (Chen & Yin, 1992; Fateman et al., 1996; Lee & Lee, 1993, 1994; Lee & Wang, 1995, 1997). Mathematical symbol recognition using neural network has been suggested by Dimitriadis and Coronado (1995) and by (Ha et al., 1995). Recently, computational geometry has also been used for the identification of mathematical notations from English text (Drake & Baird, 2005).

CLASSIFICATION OF TABULAR AND NON-TABULAR STRUCTURES

The objective of the present work is to detect tabular structures, such as tables, table of contents, index page, and displayed math. It is based on certain simple-yet-effective structural properties without resorting to individual solutions for different entities. This approach was, to the best of our knowledge, first reported by the present authors in (Mandal, Chowdhury, Das, & Chanda, 2004) as a naive attempt to classify page entities on the basis of tabular and non-tabular text. The present work is an all-round improvement of our earlier scheme in several important aspects.

The flow-diagram in Figure 1 shows the stages for detection and identification of various tabular structures in document pages. Our tabular structure detection algorithm assumes a half-tone removed, skew-corrected binary image of the document as input (Das & Chanda, 1998b, 2001). Since processing is done column-wise, a multi-column document is first stripped into separate columns. Detection of tabular structures in a document page is done by analyzing mainly the spatial properties

of these structures. Before explaining the identification steps in detail, it would be meaningful to look at these properties, as presented next.

Observation

Most of the documents, created with standard typesetting rules, are structurally homogeneous. The gap between adjacent fields/columns of a tabular structure is usually more than the interword gap in normal text. This subtle difference is crucial in detection of tabular structure and is reflected in projection profile. The spatial properties of various tabular structures, which form the foundation of their detection, are as follows.

Table: A table contains at least 2 rows and 2 columns, which may be fully or partly embedded in boxes formed by horizontal and vertical rule lines.

TOC: TOC pages are of two types: (1) Some have right-aligned page numbers and (2) others have non-aligned page numbers appearing just after the title field. We call the former type as TOC-I and the latter as TOC-II. Examples of these two types of TOC pages are shown in Figure 2(a, b).

Index Page: Index pages are mostly printed in the multi-column format. Average number of characters (or probability of occurrence of characters) decreases from left to right in each column. An index page is also characterized by the presence of a number of words separated by commas in a majority of text lines. An example is shown in Figure 2(c).

Math-zone: Displayed math-zones are usually centrally aligned. Subscripts and superscripts are frequently used in math expressions. Tall symbols whose heights are significantly greater than the median height of normal text characters may be present in math expressions. The characters and symbols are less dense in comparison with normal text lines. Presence of a horizontal line separating the numerator and the denominator portions is also common. Multiple lines with a nearby tall vertical separator(s) may be present so as to indicate the beginning or end of a matrix, determinant,

Figure 1. A schema of the proposed work for identification of tabular structures

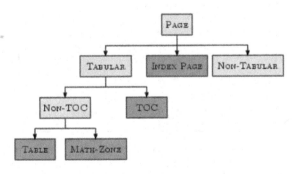

Figure 2. Examples of tabular structures (except tables): (a) TOC-I; (b) TOC-II; (c) Index page; (d) Tabular math-zones

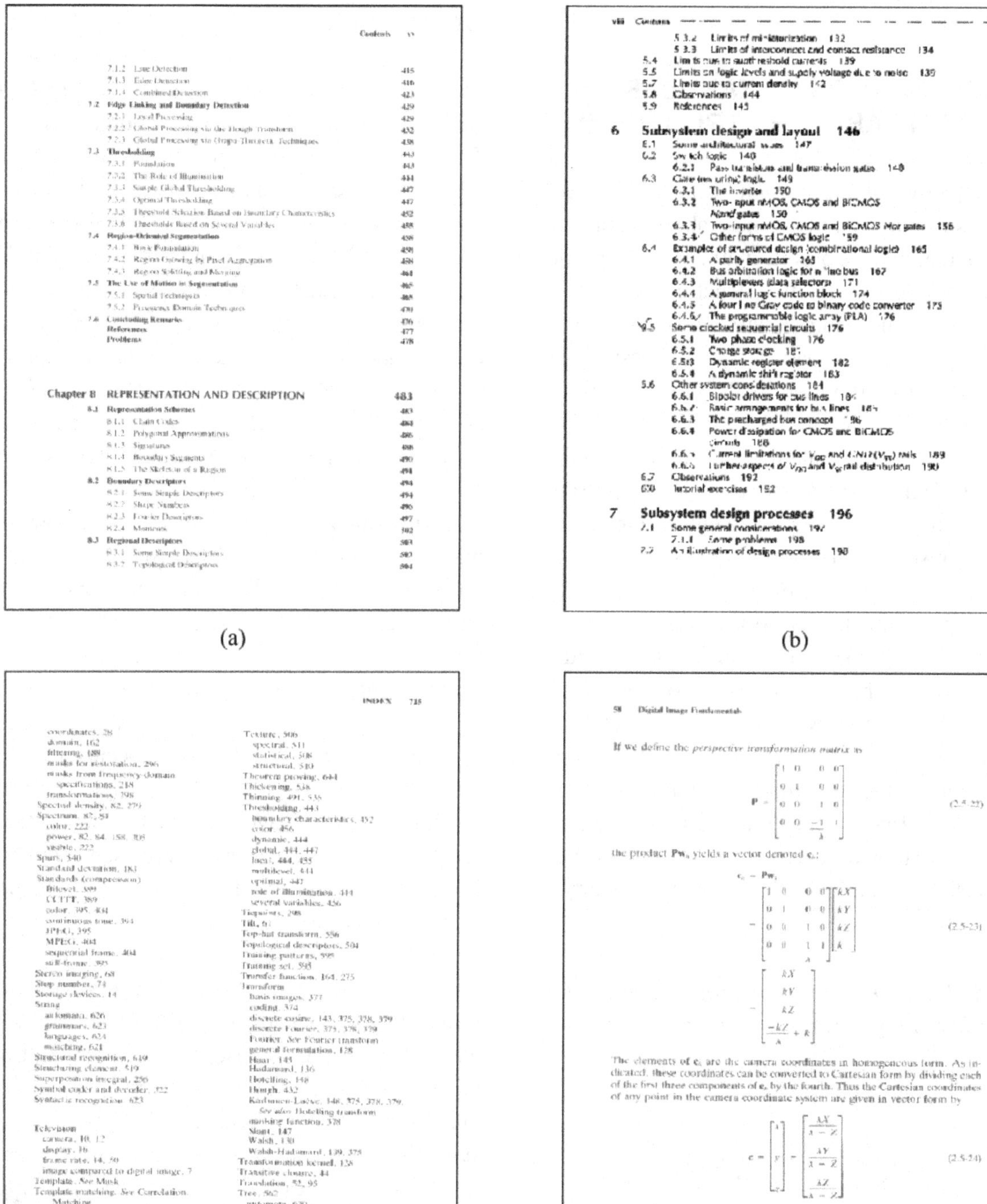

(a)

(b)

(c)

(d)

a group of conditional equations, etc. A set of consecutive text lines with one or more special characters/symbols in each line indicates the presence of an equation array. Such an instance of a page containing displayed math-zones is shown in Figure 2(d).

A careful study of the aforesaid observations reveals that all tabular structures (except index pages) have a common unique spatial property. The property is that, the gap between adjacent fields/columns is significantly larger than the normal word gap in any text line. This feature is primarily utilized in our algorithm to detect tabular structures within a document page.

The Algorithm

The tabular structure detection algorithm primarily depends on the periodic nature of the vertical projection profile. To facilitate the analysis, creation of word blobs in text lines and hence finding the consecutive text lines are performed in succession as a pre-processing step. Word blobs are formed by morphological operations, and in order to determine the size of its structuring element, connected component analysis is done first. Each line is also marked by a unique id according to its order of physical appearance from top to bottom in the concerned document page.

Creation of Word Blobs in Text Lines: This is done by coalescing the words in a line. By this technique, a text line would be normally converted to a single rectangular block, whereas a row of a tabular structure would normally give rise to multiple smaller blocks. Such a word coalescing process depends on the accuracy in detecting the normal word gap and the gap between consecutive connected components (i.e., characters and punctuation marks) in that text line. The mathematical formulation for blob formation is as follows.

Consider a binary image I, which consists of connected components, $\{Ck: k = 1, 2,..., n\}$ (Gonzalez & Wood, 1992). Let $L(Ck)$, $R(Ck)$, $T(Ck)$, and $B(Ck)$ be the respective coordinates

of left column, right column, top row, and bottom row of the kth connected component. Let f be a function that decides whether two connected components, Ca and Cb, lie in the same text line or not. We define f as

$$f(C_a, C_b) = \{ \ 1 \text{ if } T(C_a) \leq B(C_b) \text{ and } T(C_b) \leq B(C_a)$$

0 otherwise.

Now, for grouping the horizontal connected components, we extract the information on interword gap. This is obtained from the histogram $H1$ of the distance d measured between every pair of consecutive connected components, Ca and Cb. The distance function, d, between Ca and Cb is defined as

$$d\,(C_a, C_b) = L(C_b) - R(C_a).$$

The histogram $H1$ registers the gap between two consecutive characters. It may be noted that there may be more than two distinct humps in $H1$; the first one represents the character gaps and the second one represents the word gaps in text lines. An example page and its corresponding histogram are shown respectively in Figure 2a and Figure 3a. To combine the consecutive words into a single blob, the upper limit/bound α of the second hump is taken as the length of the structuring element. Morphological closing operation with a structuring element of size $\alpha \times 1$ forms the blobs comprising the set $\{Vs: s = 1, 2, ..., m\}$, m being the total number of blobs. The blob formation is dictated by the following two conditions:

1. If there are two connected components Ca and Cb ($1 \leq a, b \leq n$), n being the number of connected components, such that $f\,(Ca, Cb) = 1$ and $d(Ca, Cb) \leq \alpha$, then Ca and Cb should belong to the same blob.
2. $V_s \cap V_t = \Phi$ for all (s, t), $s \neq t$.

An example of typical blob formation is shown in Figure 3(b). Each text line consists of a set of blobs such that each blob is not shared by more than one line (see Figure 4a and 4b). A document page is declared to contain the tabular structure if the vertical projection of two or more consecutive lines after closing exhibits a wave-like structure with its number of peaks greater than unity. The number of peaks may be estimated from the number of blobs in a line. Major steps for selection of consecutive text lines are as follows.

1.   After the morphological close operation, all small components such as dots of "i's" are removed from the document on the basis of their small height and width.

2.   Text lines with more than one blob are separated (see Figure 4c).

3.   Next, only the consecutive text lines are selected (see Figure 4d). Headings with higher font size and with multiple blobs are eliminated.

It has already been pointed out earlier that in an index page, the gap between the 'index term' and the 'page number' is not distinguishable from the normal word gap in a text line. As a result, consecutive text lines appear without multiple blobs after morphological close operation. Hence, in order to detect an index page, vertical projection profile (see Figure 5) is derived for each column of the document page. We observe that this projection profile is asymmetric with respect to its

Figure 3. Blob formation based on histogram analysis: (a) Histogram corresponding to the page of Figure 2a. (b) Blob formation based on the histogram

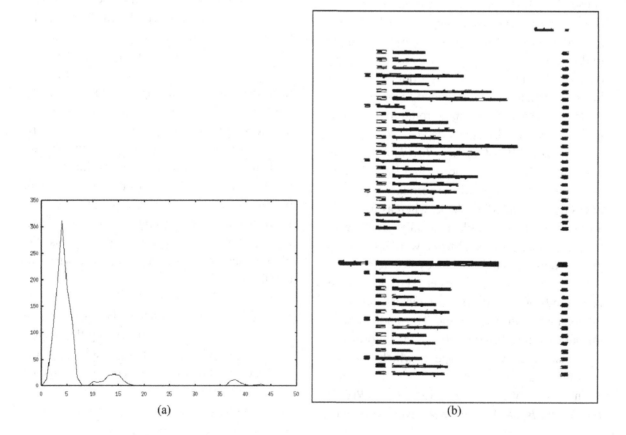

(a)   (b)

orientation and it has a decreasing trend from left to right for any index column. The salient information which should be extracted out of such non-uniform distribution is the primitive relationship characterizing the distribution, i.e., mean (μ) and standard deviation (σ). It is interesting to note that the ratio of these two parameters for an index page differs widely from a conventional text page. The experimental results in Table 1, carried out from 77 randomly chosen index and other document pages, supports this observation. Hence, we resort to this feature for detection of an index page from the document image by an elementary projection operation.

CLASSIFICATION INTO TOCS, INDEX PAGES, MATH-ZONES, AND TABLES

Out of four possible tabular structures, considered in this work, first-level identification of index pages is already done, as explained earlier, while other pages are marked as containing tabular or non-tabular text (i.e., running text). Pages marked as index pages as a whole or containing some tabular structure are now used for further classification.

Identification of TOC Pages

Document pages with tabular structures are first checked to identify TOCs. A TOC in a book, a journal, or a magazine provides information about section/subsection number, title/article, and the corresponding starting page number.

Table 1. Characterization of Index page and running text page

Page type	No. of pages	Ratio μ/σ	
		Minimum	Maximum
Text	40	3.70	4.95
Index	37	1.26	2.49

Observations about the structural information, as pointed out earlier, have led us to the formulation of certain rules for detection of TOCs from other tabular structures. TOCs have many possible structures, yet they can be broadly classified into two categories, namely, TOC-I and TOC-II. In TOC-I, page numbers are printed in a right-aligned fashion, while in TOC-II, they appear without any alignment after the title, as shown in Figure 2(a, b).

Identification of the TOC is based on finding text segments containing page numbers associated with the titles or headings. It is important to note that the page number, considered as a word, will be available as the rightmost word of a text line. However, as an added complexity, the rightmost word of a particular line may not always indicate the page number, as the text associated with a title or heading may continue over a couple of lines. The steps for identification of TOC pages are elaborated in Figure 7.

1. The blob formation with the text lines, as mentioned earlier, converts almost all text lines into three parts. These are section/sub-section number, title of the section/sub-section, and its page number, as shown in Figure 3(b). However, in an exceptional case, a line may not get coalesced into those three parts, e.g., when a section heading has characters with font-size larger than that used for other lines.

2. In case of TOC-I, the rightmost word (i.e., the page number) of a line is right-aligned and a significant gap exists between the page number and the last word of the title. The right-aligned page numbers will have their reflection in the vertical projection profile of the whole image in the form of a narrow hump at the rightmost location, as shown in Figure 7.

3. TOC-II is characterized by the presence of page numbers at the ends of almost all lines, but they are not printed in the right-aligned fashion. As a result, there is no tall hump at

Figure 4. Example of selection of consecutive text lines for a document image: (a) A document page contains tabular structures. (b) Formation of clusters. (c) Lines with multiple blobs. (d) Selected consecutive lines

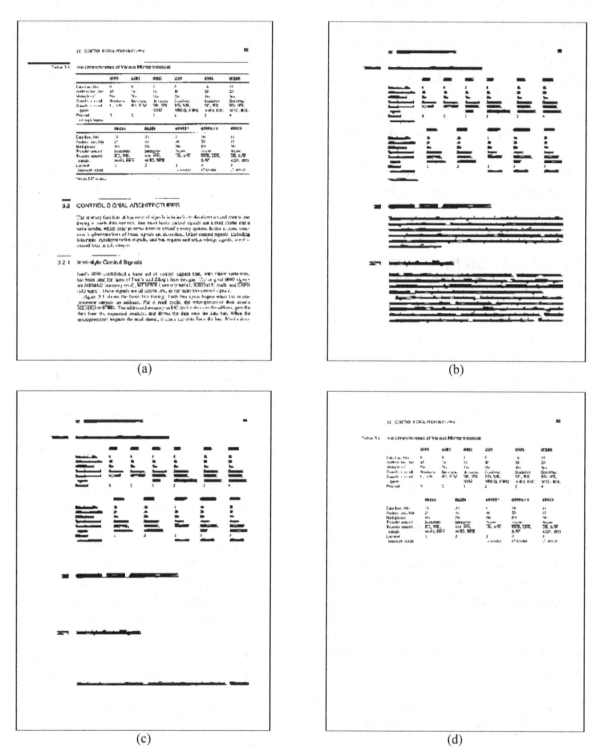

Figure 5. (a) Portion of an index page; (c) Portion of running text page; (b, d): Vertical projection profiles of (a, c).

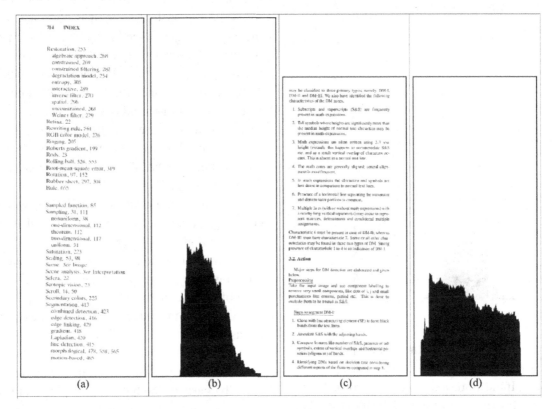

Figure 6. Features of TOC-II corresponding to the image used in Figure 2b: (a) coalesced fields of TOC lines (b) Vertical projection (c) Spatial distribution of the rightmost words and their constituent characters

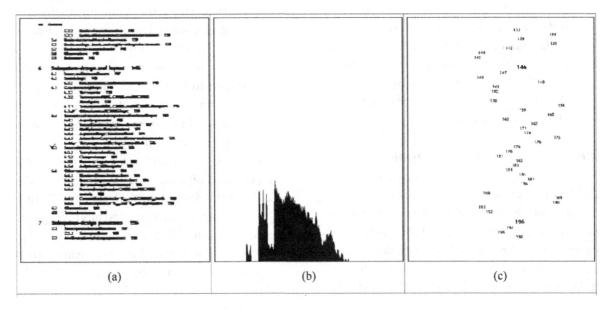

Figure 7. Vertical projection of document image shown in Figure 2a. Rightmost hill corresponds to the right-aligned page number

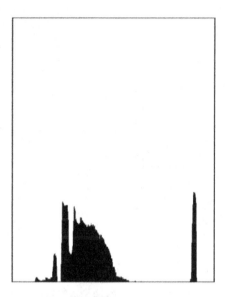

the right hand side of the vertical projection profile for the entire document page (Figure 6b). If the aforesaid projection profile has a short narrow hump at its left side, then the number of characters in rightmost words of all lines as obtained from blob formation (Figure 6a) is counted, and a histogram of number of characters in the rightmost words for the entire page is also computed. The difference between the number of characters in the rightmost word of each line and the median of the said histogram is checked. If the difference is 0 or 1 for most of the lines (Figure 6c), then the document under test is classified as TOC-II page.

Identification of Index Pages

Detection of commas (',') plays a crucial role in the identification of index pages. In order to make the algorithm robust and fully automated irrespective of the font size used for index pages, a sample of 61 index pages with different fonts and styles has been selected from our database. The area histogram of all characters within an index page is computed. Figure 8 shows two such plots for two different font sizes. It is observed from this area histogram (see Figure 8) that, irrespective of font sizes and styles, there is a wide gap between the area of small components (such as comma, dot, etc.) and other characters (indicated by the wide multi-modal hill, as shown in Figure 8). Hence, a local threshold for a particular index page may be chosen on this gap occurring before the said multi-modal hill, on a page-by-page basis, for removing alpha-numerals.

Index pages are identified, in the 2nd level, by counting the number of commas present in the page (see Figure 9). It may be noted that OCR is not used for detection of commas; it is done by utilizing the *a priori* knowledge about the presence of small components along the baseline of any text line. Major steps to identify index pages are as follows.

1. The baseline (median line computer on the basis of the bottommost pixels of each component in a line) of each text line is determined.
2. Alpha-numerals are removed using the threshold determined from the area histogram. Components are morphologically closed using the vertical structuring element (SE) of length equal to the average character height. In order to join the dot of a semicolon with its lower (and larger) comma-shaped part, and to join the dot of an 'i' with its lower (and larger) part, this close operation is deployed. Further, this technique also joins broken characters, if any.
3. Components, which have got protruding portions only below the baseline, are identified by tracking along the baseline. All other components, which have no protruding part below the baseline, are eliminated thereby.
4. Semicolons, where dots are already joined with their lower parts, are taller than the

commas and are removed straightaway on the basis of this argument.

5. A page is declared as an index page if its number of commas counts to at least twice the number of lines obtained for that page.[1]

Identification and Segmentation of Math-Zones

After identification of TOCs and index pages, attention is focused on the other tabular structures, namely, tables and tabular math-zones. However, it is now prudent to mention about the importance of the order in which they should be dealt with. At first, the identification of tabular math-zones (i.e., displayed math in tabular form) is done, since the spatial features of tabular math-zones are very close to those for conventional tables. In either case, there are distinct columns (such as determinants and matrices, conditional identities, etc.). This leads to the formation of multiple blobs in each line after morphological close operation. Hence, identification of tables should follow detection of tabular math-zones; otherwise, tabular math-zones are very likely to be interpreted as tables (see Figure 10).

Algorithm for Identification of Displayed Math-Zone

The algorithm to identify tabular math-zones is described here. Let us take a note of the input to the algorithm first. It is the original binary image I of a page having tabular structures, on which the identification process is applied. The major steps are as follows.

1. Find the connected components in I and create the set $C = \{C_i : i = 1, 2, …, n\}$.
2. For each $C_i \in C$, compute its height h_i and width w_i.
3. Find the median height h_m and the median width w_m of all components in C.

4. Let $T = \{C_t : h_t > \mu h_m \text{ and } w_t < w_m\}$ be the set of all tall components and $W = \{C_u : w_u > \mu w_m \text{ and } h_u < h_m\}$ be the set of all wide components. Let $S = C - (T \cup W)$.
5. Let I_1 be the image containing elements of S. Apply morphological close operation on I_1 with a suitable structuring element for blob formation (as explained earlier). Let the closed image be denoted by I_2.
6. (i) for each pair of tall components (C'_i, C''_i) in $T \times T$
   a. if there exists a vertical overlap between C'_i and C''_i and there exist multiple text lines (each with multiple blobs) between C'_i and C''_i in I_2
   b. then identify the area bounded by C'_i and C''_i as a tabular math-zone, and remove C'_i and C''_i from T.
   (ii) for each C_t in T
   c. if there is a single text line to the left of C_t in I_2 and there are multiple text lines
   d. with multiple blobs to the right of C_t in I_2
   e. then identify the horizontal area in which C_t lies as a tabular math-zone.
7. For each wide component C_w in W merge the components of I_1 that lie immediately above and below C_w, and prepare I_3 containing the components of I_1 after merging (I_3 is prepared to obtain the correct dimension of each text line in I_1)
8. (i) for each centrally aligned line in I_1
   a. apply morphological close operation
   (ii) if there are two or more consecutive centrally aligned text lines in $I1$ with multiple small components in each text line then identify these text lines as tabular math-zones in I

The explanatory notes on the different steps of the above algorithm are given sequentially as follows.

Figure 8. Histograms of area of connected components present in the text portion of the two document images with dierent font sizes. Irrespective of the font size, a significant gap exists between small items (i.e., commas and other punctuation marks) and alphanumerals. 't' denotes the threshold for analysis

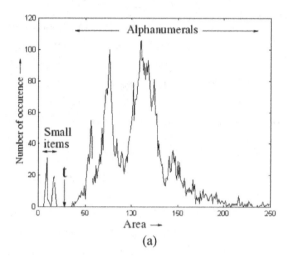
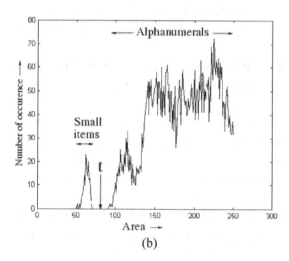

(a) (b)

Figure 9. Identification of index page: (a) Portion of an index page; (b) Result after removal of alphanumerals

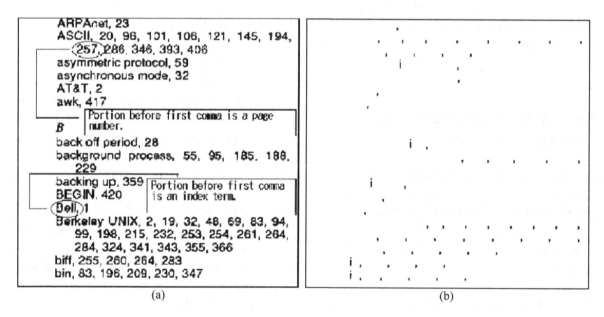

(a) (b)

- In Steps 1 through 4, component analysis is performed, and the median height and the median width of components are computed. Tall and wide components are separated on the basis of these medians.

The multiplying factor μ, used to detect tall and wide components, is set to 3 in our experiments. Sets of tall and of wide components, namely T and W, are also created at this point.

Figure 10. Tabular math-zones in document pages: (a) Matrices; (b) Mathematical expressions; (c) Conditional equations; (d) Fractions

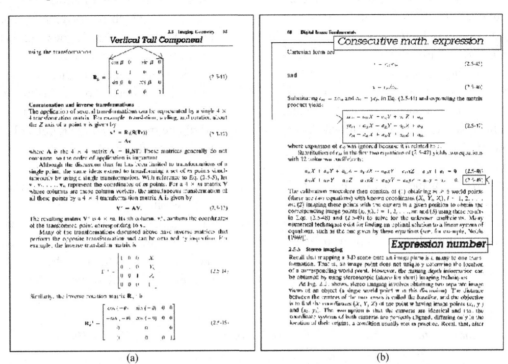

(a)

(b)

(c)

(d)

- In Step 5, the morphological close operation is carried out with a suitable structuring element for blob formation. This process is shown in Figure 11a.

- In Step 6(i), tabular math-zones containing matrices and determinants are identified. Portions of the document bounded by two vertical tall components are the candidates of information for such identification, as shown in Figure 11b. This is followed by identification of conditional identities in Step 6(ii) using the fact that, to the right of a tall component C_t, there exist multiple lines with multiple blobs each, and to its left lies a single line, as shown in Figure 12.

- Operations in Step 7 are carried out to merge the portions of numerator and denominator, which are originally separated by a horizontal line appearing between them. The numerator and the denominator lines are joined to the separator line to combine these three as a single logical entity (Figure 13b). Otherwise, they would be treated as three unrelated entities and it would not be possible to associate them with the intervening math-symbols ('+', '-', '=', etc.) so as to form a single expression.

- In Step 8, the supposedly tabular math equations are identified and separated from the document. The morphological close operation is carried out on the separated

Figure 11. Demonstration of displayed math detection on the page used in Figure 10a: (a) Blob formation; (b) Clusters of adjacent lines with multiple blobs

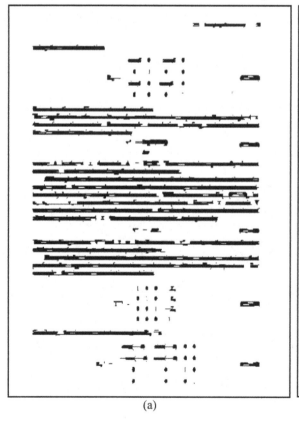
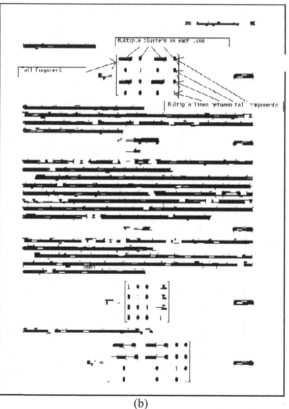

(a)   (b)

Figure 12. Example of identifying conditional equation as displayed math

centrally aligned text lines with a line-like structuring element whose length is half the length of structuring element used in Step 5. The output after this close operation is shown in Figure 14a. After this close operation, the area (number of pixels) of a mathematical symbol is significantly smaller than most of the alpha-numerals. It is also to be noted that the close operation increases the average area of alpha-numerals, as neighboring alpha-numerals coalesce together. Hence, on the basis of the area, alpha-numerals are removed from the output after close operation, leaving behind most of the mathematical symbols (Figure 14b). In any centrally aligned text line, the presence of two or more "small components" (i.e., with their individual areas smaller than the average area of al-

pha-numerals) would indicate that the text line under consideration is a mathematical expression.

Identification and Segmentation of Tables

The last stage in extraction of different tabular structures is the identification and segmentation of conventional tables. After extraction of all other tabular items (i.e., TOCs, index pages, and tabular math-zones) from the identified tabular portion, we are left with pages containing conventional tables, misclassified pages that are actually pages with math- zones, and a few TOC-II pages. Without further processing, all these misclassified pages will be identified as table- containing pages. Hence, exclusion of those pages calls for further processing, though identification of all those misclassified pages may not be possible at this stage. The table detection algorithm is discussed below.

All the lines that have more than one blob, are taken as candidate text lines (see Figure 16). It may be noted that all the words in a text line are coalesced to a single blob, whereas we get multiple blobs for rows of tables. Mathematically,

$$Q(L_a) = \{\ 1 \text{ if } \#(L_a) > 1$$

0 otherwise.

where $a = 1, 2, \ldots, N$ and $\#(\cdot)$ counts the number of blobs in a line. Thus, $Q = 1$ indicates the possibility that the candidate text line may belong to a table. It is to be noted that this first level of selection may not detect all the potential candidate lines; moreover, it may include a couple of unwanted lines (see Figure 16). Hence, to prevent splitting errors, the missing candidate lines are to be included and the unwanted lines are to be excluded.

Imposing candidature on missing lines is based on the test that decides whether their immediate neighbors are candidate lines or not. This

Figure 13. Identification of mathematical expression with fractions: (a) Bounding rectangles; (b) Clustering

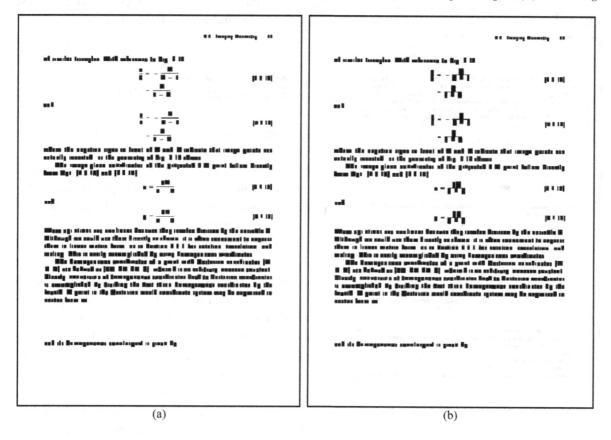

| (a) | (b) |

Figure 14. Identifying centrally aligned math expressions: (a) Blob formation; (b) Isolated math symbols. Page used in this example is shown in Figure 10b

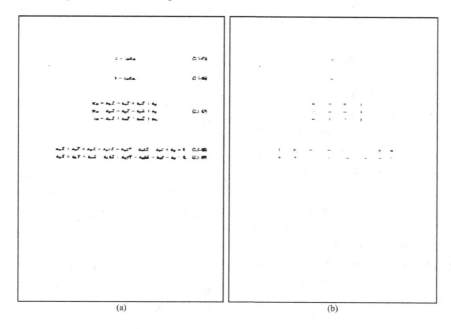

| (a) | (b) |

Figure 15. Example of table detection: (a) A document page image; (b) Corresponding image after blob formation

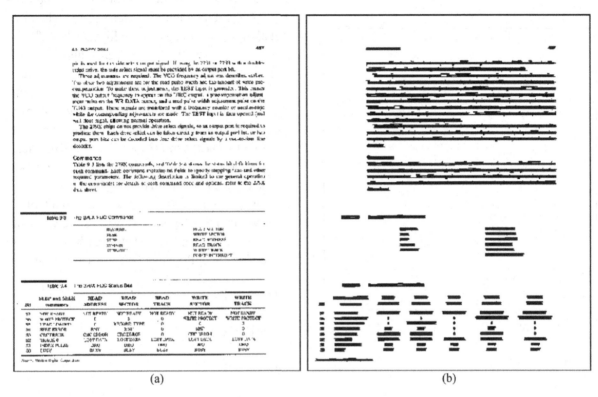

(a)   (b)

Table 2. Overall identification and segmentation performance by our algorithm for various tabular structures (Detailed explanation given in text.)

		Actual					
					General Text Page (GTP)		
		TOC			GTP containing at least one tabular zome (934 pages)		GTP with no tabular zone
		TOC-I	TOC-II	Index page	TABL	MATH	NTABL
	Number of input images	86	121	184	385	1321	1935
Indentified	TOC-I	86			10		
	TOC-II		112				
	Index page			172			
	TABL		9		371	14	17
	MATH					1249	
	NTABLE			12		58	1918

[a] 8 tables (multi-column) detected as 4 tables (*see text*).

Figure 16. Lines containing multiple blobs in the document shown in Figure 15

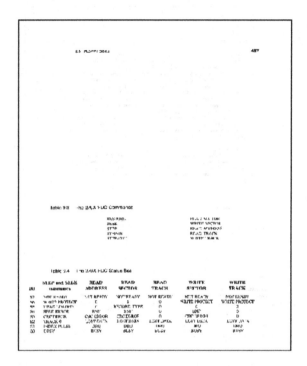

calls for the computation of vertical gap between each pair of consecutive lines, and hence obtain a measure of the maximum gap, gm_{ax}, that exists between two consecutive rows of a table. Now, by considering the possible presence of a horizontal rule line between two consecutive text lines, the gap between La and La_{+1} is computed as

$$g(a) = \{ \ (T(L_{a+1}) - B(L_a))/2 \text{ if a horizontal rule line lies between } L_a \text{ and } L_{a+1}$$

$$(T(L_{a+1}) - B(L_a)) \text{ otherwise.}$$

where $T(La_{+1})$ is the top abscissa line of La_{+1} and $B(La)$ is the bottom abscissa line of La. An example histogram $H2$ of $g(a)$ is shown in Figure 17a. The histogram $H2$ exhibits a line spectrum because the size of sample is small. As a result, we cannot obtain a proper value of $gmax$ from $H2$. To convert the line spectrum into an equivalent band spectrum, we have applied a Gaussian

filter iteratively on $g(a)$ starting with a standard deviation $\sigma = 0.5$. Median mg of $g(a)$ is computed from $H2$ and the iteration is terminated when we get all non-zero values for the line gap $^{between\ 0.5 \times m}g$ $_{and\ 3.0 \times m}g$. It may be noted that most of the gaps between two consecutive text lines will lie on this range. After applying Gaussian filter, the resultant histogram $H3$ is shown in Figure 17b. The threshold value of gm_{ax} is set to the lowest point of the valley between the first two peaks of $H3$ (see Figure 17b). Thus, gm_{ax} is more than the gap between any two rows of the table but less than the gap between (1) two successive tables and (2) a text line and a table.

Based on the gap $g(a)$ as well as the value of gm_{ax}, we infer that the text line La belongs to a table if all the following conditions are satisfied.

$$Q(L_{a-1}) = 1$$

$$g(a_{-}1) \leq g_{max}$$

$$Q(L_{a+1}) = 1$$

$$g(a) \leq g_{max}$$

where $1 < a < N$, N being the number of lines in the document page. Therefore, based on the above criteria, the missing candidate lines are successfully included as parts of a table.

The above conditions may not be enough to include the first and the last lines of a table, as

Table 3. Performance-wise comparison of the proposed method with the existing ones

Problem	% Recognition		
	Existing Methods		Proposed Method
TOC Detection/ segmentation	Lin *et al.* [37]	94.40%	95.65%
Math-zone Detection/seg-mentation	Chaudhuri *et al.* [14]	94.54%	94.62%
Table Detection/ segmentation	Wang *et al.* [60]	93.86%	96.28%

they have not been marked in the first level. For the first (last) line, as there is a preceding (succeeding) line, the conditions need modification. To include the first line, the conditions are as follows.

$$Q(L_{a+1}) = 1$$

$$g(a) \leq g_{max}$$

where a is set to 1.

Similarly, for the last line, the following conditions are checked.

$$Q(L_{a-1}) = 1$$

$$g(a - 1) \leq g_{max} \text{ with the setting } a = N.$$

Now, we are left with the issue of excluding the unwanted lines. It has already been mentioned that during the first-level selection, some extra lines, which are not actually table rows (e.g., paragraph heading), are also marked (see Figure 16). These are easily eliminated as isolated lines (see the first line of Figure 16) on the argument that no table consists of only a single row. Similarly, if a text line is accidentally coalesced into a number of blobs, then also it is eliminated as an isolated text line, since its immediate neighbors in the coalesced text are not candidate text lines.

Finally, a vertical projection of the area that has been detected as a table is taken in order to check multiple humps and troughs. This is done as a measure against getting multiple consecutive text lines as candidate lines with multiple blobs. This can occasionally happen when the inter-word gaps are stretched in a couple of consecutive lines to solve the text alignment problem. An example of the extraction of tables from the candidate lines is given in Figure 18.

EXPERIMENTAL RESULTS

All our experiments have been carried out in DEC ALPHA DS server running UNIX. The algorithms are implemented in C language. Our database used in this investigation contains 3250 document images out of which there are 184 index pages, 207 TOC pages, 1321 displayed math-zones, and 385 tables. These are distributed in 924 pages and 1935 non-tabular pages that contain only text. The database consists of mainly UW English Document Image Databases I & II (University of Washington), some document sets collected by us from Internet, and pages scanned and processed by us from books and journals. The results on these document pages with tabular portions are shown in Table 2. All 86 TOC-I pages in our database are identified correctly; however, there are 10 pages with conventional tables that are misclassified as TOC-I. The reason is the presence of tabular structures, which are spread over the entire width of the page with a narrow rightmost column. Success in identification of TOC-II is not that high due to two reasons: (1) variation in number of components in the page-number field due to broken numerals and (2) small gap (resembling the inter-word gap) between the title field and the page number field. Further, it may be noted that, usually a lot of characters are found broken in case of old documents. Also, sufficient/standard gap between the fields is not always maintained by printers due to lack of standardization. In the first case, our identification fails, as the algorithm is based on minimum variation of the number of components in the page number field, whereas, in the second case, the error creeps in as the page number merges with the title. It may be noted that, our algorithm is not able to detect TOC pages whose page numbers appear on the left-hand-side of the document.

Results of index page detection and identification are quite encouraging. After the first level of screening, 192 pages are marked as index pages, out of which 179 are truly index pages, and 13

Figure 17. (a) Histogram of the text line gap g(a) of the preprocessed document page in Figure 15a. (b) Band spectrum of g(a) after applying Gaussian filter on (a) starting with σ= 0.5

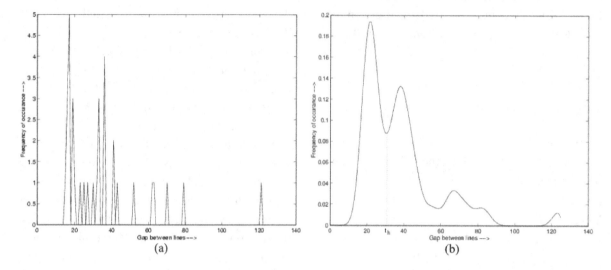

Figure 18. Example of table extraction from candidate lines: (a) Extracted lines for Figure 15a; (b) Table within the preprocessed image.

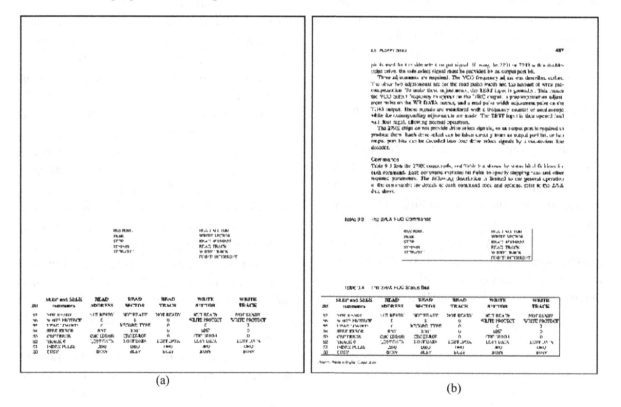

text pages are misclassified as index pages. The 5 index pages, on the other hand, are misclassified as normal text pages. In the 2nd level of identification process, all those 13 text pages are properly identified as non-index pages. However, a couple of pages without the presence of comma (',') separator between the indexed word(s) and the corresponding page numbers are declared as normal text pages for the obvious reason. It may be noted that this type of format is quite unusual for index pages.

Segmentation of matrices and determinants, i.e., objects within thin vertical components resembling ideal tabular components, is almost perfect. Segmentation performance of conditional equalities is also very successful. However, segmentation of equation arrays is not very encouraging due to their close similarities with normal text lines. As a result, some pages containing equation arrays have not been marked as tabular in the higher level identification process. Moreover, a number of pages with left-aligned equation arrays are also wrongly identified, since the "central alignment" nature of equations is used as a discerning criterion. The major sources of false alarms for different types of displayed math are broken tall components, which are not uncommon in matrices/determinants as well as in conditional equalities and math-arrays without central alignment.

Performance for table detection is also quite satisfactory. We could identify 371 tables out of a total of 385, giving a success rate of 96.28%. Ten tables have been misclassified as TOC-I. Multiple tables placed side by side are considered wrongly as a single table by our algorithm and we have 4 such pairs. Thus, 8 tables are detected as 4 tables, reducing the total no of detected tables by 4. A total of 40 pages without any table are misclassified as table-containing pages. There are three sources of error: (1) The math-zones (mostly equation arrays without central alignment) exhibiting table-like property may be misclassified as tables. (2) The remnants of TOC-II are also detected as tables. (3) The plain text pages where the words,

in consecutive lines, are not coalesced properly to a single blob will be treated as tables. So, the total number of tables detected by our algorithm will be higher than the actual number of tables, owing to the problem of misclassification. On the other hand, as mentioned earlier, two similar-sized tables that are placed side by side would also be segmented as a single table, thereby reducing the count.

Performance comparison: The proposed unified treatment of tabular structures is new and not reported by other researchers, and thus, direct comparison is not possible. However, as a datum for a broad-level comparison, the segmentation performances for TOC pages, displayed math-zones, and table by certain well-known existing approaches are presented. It is important to note that those algorithms have been designed specifically for the segmentation of specific tabular items and have not considered a unified treatment. The three references made here have been chosen due to their high performance. The summary of their results along with ours is presented in Table 3. It is reassuring to note that the performance of the proposed method is either comparable to or even better than some of the well-known techniques.

Time requirement: The average time required to classify a page as tabular is 1.17 seconds. In addition to it, pre-processing takes a total of about 0.5 second for half-tone removal, binarization, and skew correction. The next phase, i.e., classifying the tabular structure into table, displayed math-zone, index page, and TOC, takes an average time of 0.23 second. Also the unified treatment of tabular structures has given an improved timing performance. The proposed algorithms have been tested for identifying and segmenting the four different tabular structures in a discrete manner. With same database and pre-processing, excluding the broad identification step, time required by the total process is approximately 2.5 times more than that of the unified approach. This is mainly due to the advantages accrued out of the unified treatment of the tabular structures as well as the reduction in the number of images in the input set by broad identification step.

CONCLUSION

Treating all table-like objects as tabular structures is a new approach in DIA. In this work, efforts have been made to establish that it facilitates a unified and simpler treatment of all tabular structures in their identification phase. Exploitation of a simple-yet-distinctive spatial property of each individual tabular structure is also important as it drastically reduces many heuristics and related thresholds that are commonly used in many DIA tasks. It is an important feature of this work because a truly automatic system demands minimum heuristics and nominal use of threshold values.

The present work may be extended in future in a number of ways out of which the following two are very important. First, documents with non-Manhattan layout should be included in the dataset and the algorithms should be modified to accommodate processing of those documents. Secondly, form documents may be included for processing as they are also tabular in nature.

REFERENCES

Anderson, R. H. (1977). Two-dimensional mathematical notation. In *Proceedings of the Syntactic Pattern Recognition Applications* (pp. 147-177).

Belaid, A. (2001). Recognition of table of contents for electronic library consulting. *International Journal on Document Analysis and Recognition, 4*(1), 35–45. doi:10.1007/PL00013572

Belaid, A., & Haton, J. P. (1984). A syntactic approach for handwritten mathematical formula recognition. *IEEE Transactions on Pattern Analysis and Machine Intelligence, 6*(1), 105–111. doi:10.1109/TPAMI.1984.4767483

Belaid, A., Pierron, L., & Valverde, N. (2000). Part-of-speech tagging for table of contents recognition. In *Proceedings of the 15th International Conference on Pattern Recognition*, Barcelona, Spain (Vol. 4, pp. 451-454).

Belaid, Y., Panchevre, J. L., & Belaid, A. (1998). Form analysis by neural classification of cells. In *Proceedings of the 3rd Workshop on Document Analysis Systems*, Nagano, Japan (pp. 69-78).

Berman, B. P., & Fateman, R. J. (1994). Optical character recognition for typset mathematics. In *Proceedings of the International Symposium on Symbolic and Algebraic Computation*, Oxford, UK (pp. 348-353).

Chan, K. F., & Yeung, D. Y. (1999, July). Recognizing on-line handwritten alphanumeric characters through flexible structural matching. *Pattern Recognition, 32*(7), 1099–1114. doi:10.1016/S0031-3203(98)00155-1

Chan, K. F., & Yeung, D. Y. (2000). Mathematical expression recognition: A survey. *International Journal on Document Analysis and Recognition, 3*(1), 3–15. doi:10.1007/PL00013549

Chandran, S., Balasubramanian, S., Gandhi, T., Prasad, A., Kasturi, R., & Chhabra, A. (1996). Structure recognition and information extraction from tabular documents. *International Journal of Imaging Systems and Technology, 7*(4), 289–303. doi:10.1002/(SICI)1098-1098(199624)7:4<289::AID-IMA4>3.0.CO;2-4

Chang, S. K. (1970). A method for the structural analysis of 2-d mathematical expression. *Information Sciences, 2*(3), 253–272. doi:10.1016/S0020-0255(70)80052-4

Chen, L. H., & Yin, P. Y. (1992). A system for on-line recognition of handwritten mathematical expressions. *Computer Processing of Chinese and Oriental Languages, 6*(1), 19–39.

Chou, P. (1989). Recognition of equations using a two-dimensional stochastic context-free grammar. *Visual Communications and Image Processing,* 852-863.

Das, A. K., & Chanda, B. (1998a, February 18-20). Detection of tables and headings from document image: A morphological approach. In *Proceedings of the International Conference on Computational Linguistics, Speech and Document Processing,* Calcutta, India (pp. 57-64).

Das, A. K., & Chanda, B. (1998b, April 6-8). Extraction of half-tones from document images: A morphological approach. In *Proceedings of the International Conference on Advances in Computing,* Calcutta, India (pp. 15-19).

Das, A. K., & Chanda, B. (2001). A fast algorithm for skew detection of document images using morphology. *International Journal of Document Analysis and Recognition, 4,* 109–114. doi:10.1007/PL00010902

Dimitriadis, Y. A., & Coronado, J. L. (1995). Towards an art based mathematical editor that uses on-line handwritten symbol recognition. *Pattern Recognition, 28*(6), 807–822. doi:10.1016/0031-3203(94)00160-N

Drake, D., & Baird, H. (2005). Distinguishing mathematics notation from English text using computational geometry. In *Proceedings of the 8th International Conference on Document Analysis and Recognition,* Seoul, South Korea (pp. 1270-1274).

Embley, D. W., Hurst, M., Lopresti, D., & Nagy, G. (2006). Table processing paradigms: A research survey. *International Journal on Document Analysis and Recognition, 8,* 66–86. doi:10.1007/s10032-006-0017-x

Fateman, R. J., & Tokuyasu, T. (1996). Progress in recognizing typeset mathematics. *Proceedings of the Society for Photo-Instrumentation Engineers, 2660,* 37–50.

Fateman, R. J., Tokuyasu, T., Berman, B., & Mitchell, N. (1996). Optical character recognition and parsing of typeset mathematics. *Visual Communication and Image Representation, 7*(1).

Gonzalez, R. C., & Wood, R. (1992). *Digital image processing.* Reading, MA: Addison-Wesley.

Grbavec, A., & Blostein, D. (1995). Mathematical expression recognition using graph rewriting. In *Proceedings of the International Conference on Document Analysis and Recognition* (pp. 417-421).

Ha, J., Haralick, R. M., & Philips, I. T. (1995). Understanding mathematical expressions from document images. In *Proceedings of the International Conference on Document Analysis and Recognition* (pp. 956-959).

He, F., Ding, X., & Peng, L. (2004). Hierarchical logical structure extraction of book documents by analyzing table of contents. *Proceedings of the Society for Photo-Instrumentation Engineers, 5296,* 6–13.

Hu, J., Kashi, R., Lopresti, D., & Wilfong, G. (2000). Medium-independent table detection. *Proceedings of the Society for Photo-Instrumentation Engineers, 3967,* 291–302.

Itonori, K. (1993). Table structure recognition based on textblock arrangement and ruled line position. In *Proceedings of the International Conference on Document Analysis and Recognition* (pp. 765-768).

Kacem, A., Belaid, A., & Ahmed, M. B. (2001). Automatic extraction of printed mathematical formulas using fuzzy logic and propagation of context. *International Journal of Document Analysis and Recognition, 4*(2), 97–108. doi:10.1007/s100320100064

Kieninger, T. G. (1998). Table structure recognition based on robust block segmentation. *Proceedings of the Society for Photo-Instrumentation Engineers, 3305,* 22–32.

Le Bourgeois, H. E., & Bensafi, S. S. (2001). Document understanding using probabilistic relaxation: Application on tables of contents of periodicals. In *Proceedings of the 6th International Conference on Document Analysis and Recognition*, Seattle, WA (p. 508-512).

Lee, H. J., & Lee, M. C. (1993). Understanding mathematical expression in a printed document. In *Proceedings of the International Conference on Document Analysis and Recognition* (pp. 502-505).

Lee, H. J., & Lee, M. C. (1994). Understanding mathematical expressions using procedure-oriented transformation. *Pattern Recognition, 27*(3), 447–457. doi:10.1016/0031-3203(94)90121-X

Lee, H. J., & Wang, J. S. (1995). Design of mathematical expression recognition system. In *Proceedings of the International Conference on Document Analysis and Recognition* (pp. 1084-1087).

Lee, H. J., & Wang, J. S. (1997). Design of a mathematical expression understanding system. *Pattern Recognition Letters, 18*, 289–298. doi:10.1016/S0167-8655(97)87048-1

Lin, C., Niwa, Y., & Narita, S. (1997). Logical structure analysis of book document images using contents information. In *Proceedings of the International Conference on Document Analysis and Recognition* (pp. 1048-1054).

Lin, X., & Xiong, Y. (2006). Detection and analysis of table of contents based on content association. *International Journal of Document Analysis and Recognition, 8*(2-3), 132–143. doi:10.1007/s10032-005-0149-4

Liu, X. (2003). Text mining based journal splitting. In *Proceedings of the International Conference on Document Analysis and Recognition*, Edinburgh, UK.

Lopresti, D., & Nagy, G. (1999). Automated table processing: An opinionated survey. In *Proceedings of the 3rd International Workshop on Graphics Recognition*, Jaipur, India (pp. 109-134).

Luo, Q., Watanabe, T., & Nakayama, T. (1996). Identifying contents page of documents. In *Proceedings of the International Conference on Document Analysis and Recognition* (pp. 696-700).

Mandal, S., Chowdhury, S. P., Das, A. K., & Chanda, B. (2003a). Automated detection and segmentation of table of contents page and index pages from document images. In *Proceedings of the 12th International Conference on Image Analysis and Processing* (p. 213-218).

Mandal, S., Chowdhury, S. P., Das, A. K., & Chanda, B. (2003b). Automated detection and segmentation of table of contents page from document images. In *Proceedings of the International Conference on Document Analysis and Recognition* (pp. 398-402).

Mandal, S., Chowdhury, S. P., Das, A. K., & Chanda, B. (2003c). Automated segmentation of math-zones from document images. In *Proceedings of the International Conference on Document Analysis and Recognition* (pp. 755-759).

Mandal, S., Chowdhury, S. P., Das, A. K., & Chanda, B. (2004). A complete system detection and identification of tabular structures from document images. In *Proceedings of the International Conference on Document Analysis and Recognition* (pp. 217-225).

Mandal, S., Chowdhury, S. P., Das, A. K., & Chanda, B. (2006a, April 27-28). Detection and segmentation of table of contents and index pages from document images. In *Proceedings of the 2nd IEEE International Conference on Document Analysis for Libraries*, Lyon, France (pp. 70-81).

Mandal, S., Chowdhury, S. P., Das, A. K., & Chanda, B. (2006b). A simple and effective table detection system from document images. *International Journal on Document Analysis and Recognition, 8*(2-3), 172–182. doi:10.1007/s10032-005-0006-5

Miller, E. G., & Viola, P. A. (1998). Ambiguity and constraint in mathematical expression recognition. In *Proceedings of the 15th National Conference on Artificial Intelligence*, Madison, WI (pp. 784-791).

Nakayama, Y. (1993). A prototype pen-input mathematical formula editor. In *Proceedings of the Ed-Media World Conference on Educational Multimedia and Hypermedia*, Orlando, FL (pp. 400-407).

O'Gorman, L. (1992). Image and document processing techniques for the right pages electronic library system. In *Proceedings of the 11th International Conference on Pattern Recognition* (pp. 260-263).

Okamoto, M., & Miao, B. (1991). Recognition of mathematics by using the layout structures of symbols. In *Proceedings of the International Conference on Document Analysis and Recognition* (pp. 242-250).

Okamoto, M., & Miyazawa, H. (1992). An experimental implementation of a document recognition system for papers containing mathematical expression. *Structured Document Image Analysis, 36-53*.

Ramel, J. Y., Crucianu, M., Vincent, N., & Faure, C. (2003). Detection, extraction and representation of tables. In *Proceedings of the International Conference on Document Analysis and Recognition*, Edinburgh, UK (pp. 374-378).

Satoh, S., Takasu, A., & Katsura, E. (1995). An automated generation of electronic library based on document image understanding. In *Proceedings of the International Conference on Document Analysis and Recognition* (pp. 163-166).

Story, G. A., O'Gorman, L., Fox, D., Schaper, L. L., & Jagadish, H. V. (1992). The right pages image-based electronic library for alerting and browsing. *Computer, 25*(9), 17–26. doi:10.1109/2.156379

Tanaka, T., & Tsuruoka, S. (1998). Table form document understanding using node classification method and HTML document generation. In *Proceedings of the 3rd IAPR Workshop on Document Analysis Systems*, Nagano, Japan. (pp. 157-158).

Tersteegen, W. T., & Wenzel, C. (1998). Scantab: Table recognition by reference tables. In *Proceedings of the 3rd IAPR Workshop on Document Analysis Systems*, Nagano, Japan (pp. 356-365).

Toumit, J. Y., Garcia-Salicetti, S., & Emptoz, H. (1999). A hierarchical and recursive model of mathematical expressions for automatic reading of mathematical documents. In *Proceedings of the International Conference on Document Analysis and Recognition* (pp. 116-122).

Tsuruoka, S., Hirano, C., Yoshikawa, T., & Shinogi, T. (2001). Image-based structure analysis for a table of contents and conversion to a XML documents. In *Proceedings of the Workshop on Document Layout Interpretation and its Application*

Tsuruoka, S., Takao, K., Tanaka, T., Yoshikawa, T., & Shinogi, T. (2001). Region segmentation for table image with unknown complex structure. In *Proceedings of the International Conference on Document Analysis and Recognition* (pp. 709-713).

Watanabe, T., Luo, Q. L., & Sugie, N. (1995). Layout recognition of multi-kinds of table-form documents. *IEEE Transactions on Pattern Analysis and Machine Intelligence, 17*(4), 432–446. doi:10.1109/34.385976

Zanibbi, R., Blostein, D., & Cordy, J. R. (2004). A survey of table recognition: Models, observations, transformations, and inferences. *International Journal on Document Analysis and Recognition*, 7, 1–16.

Zuyev, K. (1997). Table image segmentation. In *Proceedings of the International Conference on Document Analysis and Recognition* (pp. 705-707).

ENDNOTES

[1] An index page usually consists of *two columns*. Each column contains index terms, each of which has one or more page numbers, separated by commas. Hence each line of an index page contains at least *two commas*.

This work was previously published in the International Journal of Digital Library Systems, Volume 2, Issue 2, edited by Chia-Hung Wei, pp. 27-54, copyright 2011 by IGI Publishing (an imprint of IGI Global).

Chapter 2
Efficient Word Segmentation and Baseline Localization in Handwritten Documents Using Isothetic Covers

Mousumi Dutt
Bengal Engineering & Science University, India

Arindam Biswas
Bengal Engineering & Science University, India

Aisharjya Sarkar
Bengal Engineering & Science University, India

Partha Bhowmick
Indian Institute of Technology, Kharagpur, India

Bhargab B. Bhattacharya
Indian Statistical Institute, India

ABSTRACT

Analysis of handwritten documents is a challenging task in the modern era of document digitization. It requires efficient preprocessing which includes word segmentation and baseline detection. This paper proposes a novel approach toward word segmentation and baseline detection in a handwritten document. It is based on certain structural properties of isothetic covers tightly enclosing the words in a handwritten document. For an appropriate grid size, the isothetic covers successfully segregate the words so that each cover corresponds to a particular word. The grid size is selected by an adaptive technique that classifies the inter-cover distances into two classes in an unsupervised manner. Finally, by using a geometric heuristic with the horizontal chords of these covers, the corresponding baselines are extracted. Owing to its traversal strategy along the word boundaries in a combinatorial manner and usage of limited operations strictly in the integer domain, the method is found to be quite fast, efficient, and robust, as demonstrated by experimental results with datasets of both Bengali and English handwritings.

DOI: 10.4018/978-1-4666-2928-8.ch002

INTRODUCTION

A handwriting portrays the characteristics of an individual, and hence has been studied in numerous disciplines including experimental psychology, neuroscience, engineering, anthropology, forensic science, etc. (Plamondon, 1993; Plamondon & Leedham, 1990; Simner et al., 1994, 1996; Galen & Morasso, 1998; Galen & Stelmach, 1993; Wan et al., 1991). The analysis of handwritings has been quite important in recent times with the advancements of document digitization (Hole & Ragha, 2011; Saba, 2011; Terrades, 2010; Zhu et al., 2009), biometric authentication (Henniger & Franke, 2004; Hoque et al., 2008; Low et al., 2009; Makrushin, 2011; Schimke et al., 2005; Vielhauer, 2006; Vielhauer & Scheidat, 2005), forensic science (Franke & Köppen, 2001; Máadeed et al., 2008; Mahmoudi et al., 2009; Pervouchine et al., 2008), etc. The result of analysis strives to interpret, verify, and recognize a particular handwritten document. The most difficult problem in the area of handwriting recognition is segmentation of cursive handwriting. The infinitude of different types of human handwritings amidst the similarities in the shapes of different characters renders the problem even more difficult. Hence, over the last few years, various works have been presented for specific domains, e.g., Bengali character recognition (Majumdar & Chaudhuri, 2007; Parui et al., 2008), text line identification (Chaudhuri & Bera, 2009), numeral recognition (Bhattacharya & Chaudhuri, 2009), check sorting (Gorski et al., 1999), address reading (Srihari & Keubert, 1997), tax reading (Srihari et al., 1996), office automation (Gopisetty, 1996), automated postal system (Vajda et al., 2009), etc.

Handwriting recognition techniques are based on either holistic or analytic strategies. In the holistic method, a top-down approach is employed where the whole word is recognized by comparing its global features against a limited size lexicon (Guillevic & Suen, 1998). On the other hand, analytic strategies adopt the bottom-up approach starting with characters, strokes, etc., eventually producing the meaningful text (Wang & Jean, 1994; Mohamed & Gader, 1996; Mao et al., 1998; Kim & Govindaraju, 1997). Clearly, in connection with handwriting recognition, it is important to extract/segment the words in a cursive writing such that the task of segregating the individual characters and strokes may be taken up. The segmented regions may be found out from the peaks of the projection profile of a gray-level image (Lee et al., 1996). Proper baseline extraction is important to segment out words correctly. To avoid the problems arising out of ascending and descending portions of the characters, information about the upper and the lower baselines are necessary. In general, the baselines are extracted from the projection profile (Guillevic & Suen, 1998).

As per the existence practice, the text line segmentation is usually done by considering a subset of the connected components in a document image (Louloudis et al., 2009). Word segmentation is achieved using the distinction of inter- and intra-word gaps using a combination of two different distance metrics.

To overcome the disadvantage of different distance measures in word segmentation, a gap metric based on the average distance is used for word segmentation (Huang & Srihari, 2008). A number of works have been reported in the literature for line and word segmentation in other languages, e.g., Chinese, Arabic, etc. Chinese word segmentation has various applications on Chinese text processing (Haizhou & Baosheng, 1998). The algorithm for detection of straight or curved baselines for Arabic handwritten text can be applied on online handwriting or off-line handwritten writing (Boubaker et al., 2009). A method for precise identification of ascending or descending parts of the words has been proposed using lexicon based search in Aida-zade & Hasanov (2009).

In our work, we have devised a novel method to segment out the words in a cursive handwriting by using the outer isothetic covers of the words constituting the handwritten document (see Figure 1). The method has also the advantage of extracting the upper and the lower baselines by analyzing these covers corresponding to the handwritten words. Owing to the combinatorial nature of its traversal strategy while deriving the minimum-area isothetic covers corresponding to the words, and hence describing the covers as sequences of theirs vertices (or/and edges), it is endowed with an easy solution to locate the baselines of different words — whatsoever be their patterns and letter-wise constitution — as shown in this paper. A fast decision policy based on the covers, coupled with usage of operations strictly in the integer domain, make it fast, robust, and efficient, thereby depicting its compliance for real-time applications.

Proposed Work

The outer isothetic cover (OIC) of a 2D object of any shape can be obtained using the algorithm TIPS, given in Biswas et al. (2010). It may be noted that, since the algorithm TIPS cannot find out multiple polygons (for multiple objects), it has been modified in the proposed work to obtain the complete set of isothetic polygons for the objects present in the handwritten document. In Figure 1, two handwritten Bengali words chosen from a handwritten text, and their corresponding OICs and baselines detected by our algorithm are shown. The outer isothetic covers (shown in blue) in this example are obtained for grid size g = 3; the upper and the lower baselines (shown in red) are extracted by analyzing these isothetic covers.

Construction of the OIC

In order to segment out the words in a handwritten text, we construct the outer isothetic covers (OIC) of the corresponding handwritten document image after its binarization (Otsu, 1979). To do this, we impose an isothetic set of grid lines having the grid size g on the binarized image. Let Q_1,

Q_2, Q_3, and Q_4 be the four quadrants incident at a grid point $p(i, j)$, as shown in Figure 2. The grid point p is decided to be a vertex depending on how many of the quadrants have object containment. Interestingly, there arise $2^4 = 16$ different arrangements considering object containments of these four quadrants, which can be reduced to five cases. Let C_q ($q = 0, 1, ..., 4$) denote the case of all the arrangements for which q out of 4 squares are occupied by the object. If p belongs to Case C_1, then it is a 90^0 vertex of the isothetic polygon; and if it is a 270^0 vertex, then it belongs to C_3. For Case C_2, if the diagonal quadrants are occupied, then p is considered as a 270^0 vertex; otherwise, p is a non-vertex grid point lying on some edge of the polygon. For case C_0, p is just an ordinary grid point lying outside the polygon, whereas, for case C_4, p is a grid point lying inside the polygon.

Word Segmentation

As mentioned earlier, in order to draw multiple polygons corresponding to multiple words in a handwritten document image, we have modified the algorithm TIPS [24]. With a proper grid size, each polygon corresponds to a single word barring intermingled words, punctuation marks, or dot marks over certain characters of the alphabet.

Figure 1. (a) Two handwritten words; (b) their outer isothetic covers (OIC); (c) corresponding upper and lower baselines

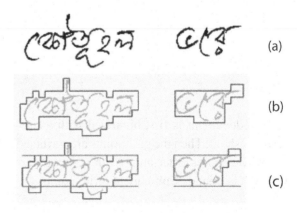

Figure 2. Five combinatorial cases (having 2 =16 possible subcases depending on the arrangement of object-containing and object-free cells). Object boundaries are shown in black, object interiors in gray, and traversed edges by arrowed grid-lines. Note that, the object always lies left while traversing the edges of OIC.

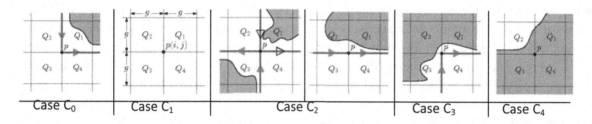

Case C$_0$ | Case C$_1$ | Case C$_2$ | Case C$_3$ | Case C$_4$

Figure 3. Segmentation of words in a handwritten document by the proposed technique. Top: input image; bottom: output word polygons.

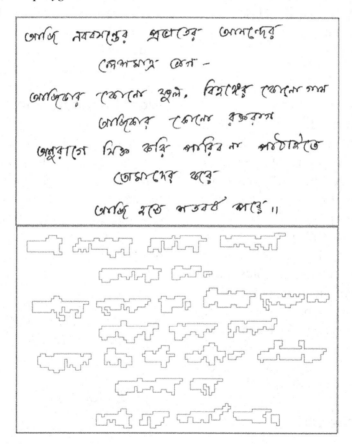

The document is first binarized with a suitable threshold. Then the grid points are traversed in the row-major order until a 90^0 vertex ('start vertex') is found. Subsequent grid points are classified, marked as 'visited', and the direction is determined from each such grid point until the start vertex is reached. This completes the outer isothetic cover corresponding to a word. The procedure is iterated over the remaining set of unvisited grid points until the next 90^0 vertex is found, which will subsequently derive the polygon corresponding to another word. Finally, all the grid points are visited and the algorithm reports the vertex sequences of all the isothetic polygons corresponding to the words in the input document.

The set of extracted polygons may contain some small (in perimeter) polygons, which may be due to the dot over a character of the alphabet or some punctuation mark. These smaller polygons are easily identified by their perimeters. If two or more words are unusually close or unmanageably inter mingled with respect to the grid size, then we get a single polygon for these words. However, the major strength of the algorithm is that words with usual inter-word spacing can be easily segmented from skewed handwriting without resorting to skew correction. Figure 3 shows a handwritten

paragraph and the segmentation result of its constituent words. The polygons (shown in blue) represent the different words. It has also rightly extracted the small perimeter objects like dots and punctuation marks in Bengali, which can be useful for further analysis of the document, if required.

Setting the grid size g: In order that each isothetic polygon corresponds to a word and hence results in a sequence of vertices, specifying an appropriate grid size is necessary to get a correct output of word segmentation and subsequent baseline extraction. Based on the fact that the inter-character gap in a word is smaller than the inter-word gap in a handwritten document, we have designed our algorithm to adaptively change the value of g depending on the font size and word spacing, as follows.

Figure 4. Setting the grid size g in an adaptive way

	'P (g)'	d_{min}	d_{max}
(a) input	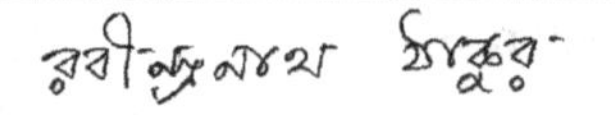 রবি-ন্দ্র নাথ ঠাকুর	–	–
(b) $g = 1$	 রবি-ন্দ্র নাথ ঠাকুর	1	50
(c) $g = 2$	 রবি-ন্দ্র নাথ ঠাকুর	2	48
(d) $g = 3$	 রবি-ন্দ্র নাথ ঠাকুর	3	45
(e) $g = 4$		4	44
(f) $g = 5$		5	45
(g) $g = 6$	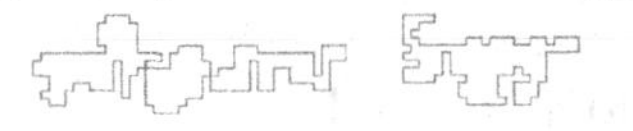	0	42

Results for $g = 1, 2, \ldots, 6$.

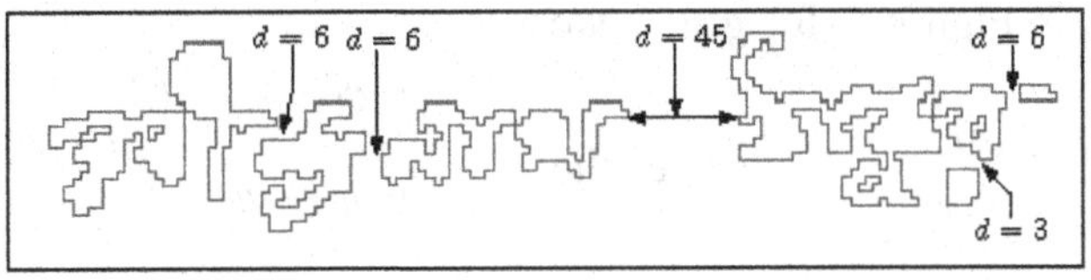

$$g = 3 : d_{min}^{(g)} = 3, d_{max}^{(g)} = 45$$

Let $P_k^{(g)}$ and $P_{k+1}^{(g)}$ be two consecutive polygons in a line corresponding to the grid size g. For each grid point $p_k \in P_k^{(g)}$ (i.e., lying on the boundary of $P_k^{(g)}$, we find the nearest point $p'_{k+1} \in P_{k+1}^{(g)}$ and store the corresponding distance, which is given by

$$d\left(p_k, P_{k+1}^{(g)}\right) = \min_{p'_{k+1} P_{k+1}^{(g)}} d(p_k, p'_{k+1}) \quad \text{where}$$

$$d\left(p_k, p'_{k+1}\right) = \max(\mid x_k - x'_{k+1} \mid, \mid y_k - y'_{k+1} \mid),$$

considering that (x_k, y_k) and (x'_{k+1}, y'_{k+1}) are the respective coordinates of p_k and p'_{k+1}. Then the distance between $P_k^{(g)}$ and $P_{k+1}^{(g)}$ is estimated as $d(P_k^{(g)}, P_{k+1}^{(g)}) = \min_{p_k \in P_k^{(g)}} d(p_k)$.

We consider all inter-polygonal distances and find their minimum and maximum, namely $d_{min}^{(g)}$ and $d_{max}^{(g)}$, respectively (see Figure 4). Interestingly, as the value of g is gradually increased, $d_{min}^{(g)}$ increases and $d_{max}^{(g)}$ decreases. Each distance is classified to the Class $C_{min}^{(g)}$ or Class $C_{max}^{(g)}$, depending on its closeness to $d_{min}^{(g)}$ and $d_{max}^{(g)}$. For example, in Figure 4, for $g = 2$, we have $d_{min}^{(g)} = 2$ and $d_{max}^{(g)} = 46$; hence, the distance $d = 4$ is classified to $C_{min}^{(g)}$. Until the

number of distances in $C_{min}^{(g)}$ falls below that in $C_{max}^{(g)}$, g is made to increase, and the lowest value of g for which $\mid C_{min}^{(g)} \mid < \mid C_{max}^{(g)} \mid$ is considered in our algorithm for word segmentation. For example, in Figure 4, when $g = 6$, we have $\mid C_{min}^{(g)} \mid = 0 < \mid C_{max}^{(g)} \mid = 1$, and so $g = 6$ is chosen (see Table 1).

The algorithm WordSegment takes the input handwritten document as a digital object, A (see Figure 5). Initializations are done in Step 1. The while loop (Step 2) continues as long as the condition ($\mid C_{min}^{(g)} \mid > \mid C_{max}^{(g)} \mid$) is satisfied. The set of isothetic polygons, $P(A)$, is obtained using the

Table 1. Algorithm WordSegment

Steps:

1. $g \leftarrow 1$, $\mid C_{min}^{(g)} \mid \leftarrow 1$, $\mid C_{max}^{(g)} \mid \leftarrow 0$

2. **while** $\mid C_{min}^{(g)} \mid > \mid C_{max}^{(g)} \mid$

3. $P(A) \leftarrow OIC(A, g)$

4. **for** each $(P_k^{(g)}, P_{k+1}^{(g)})$

5. $d(P_k^{(g)}, P_{k+1}^{(g)}) \leftarrow DIST(P_k^{(g)}, P_{k+1}^{(g)})$

6. $(d_{min}, d_{max}) \leftarrow \textsc{FindMaxMin}(d)$

7. **for** each d_i

8. $\textsc{Classify} \leftarrow (d_i, d_{min}, d_{max})$

9. $g \leftarrow g + 1$

Figure 5. Analysis of edge-length array E[j] for a word polygon to detect the baselines

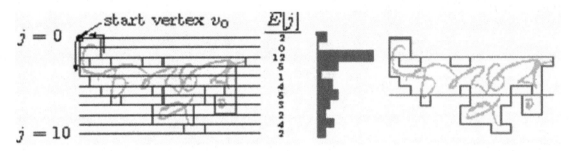

Figure 6. Baselines of the extracted words for g = 3

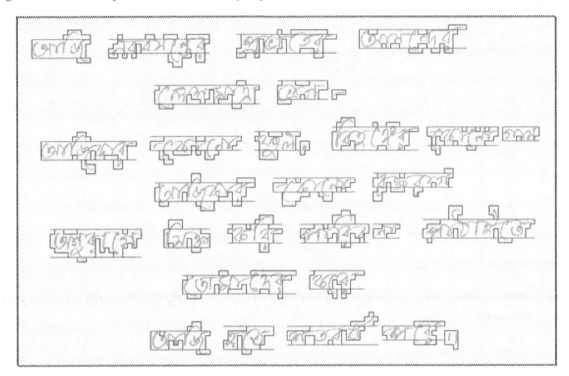

procedure *OIC* (Step 3). The distances between each two consecutive polygons in a line, $P_k^{(g)}$ and $P_{k+1}^{(g)}$, are obtained (Steps 4-5). The procedure *DIST* computes the smallest distance between any two vertices in the two polygons. Once the inter-polygon distances are computed, the minimum and the maximum amongst these dis-

tances are determined by *FindMaxMin* (Step 6). Finally, all the distances (computed in Steps 4-5) are classified using the procedure *Classify*. The procedure *Classify* (Step 8) classifies each distance d_k. If the value of d is closer to d_{min} (checked by calling a procedure *Nearest*, not shown here for its obviousness), then it is in class C_{min} (Steps 2-3), otherwise d_k is closer to d and hence classified to C_{max} (Steps 4-5).

Figure 7. Result of word segmentation (left, in blue) and baseline extraction (right, in red) of handwriting samples of five different persons

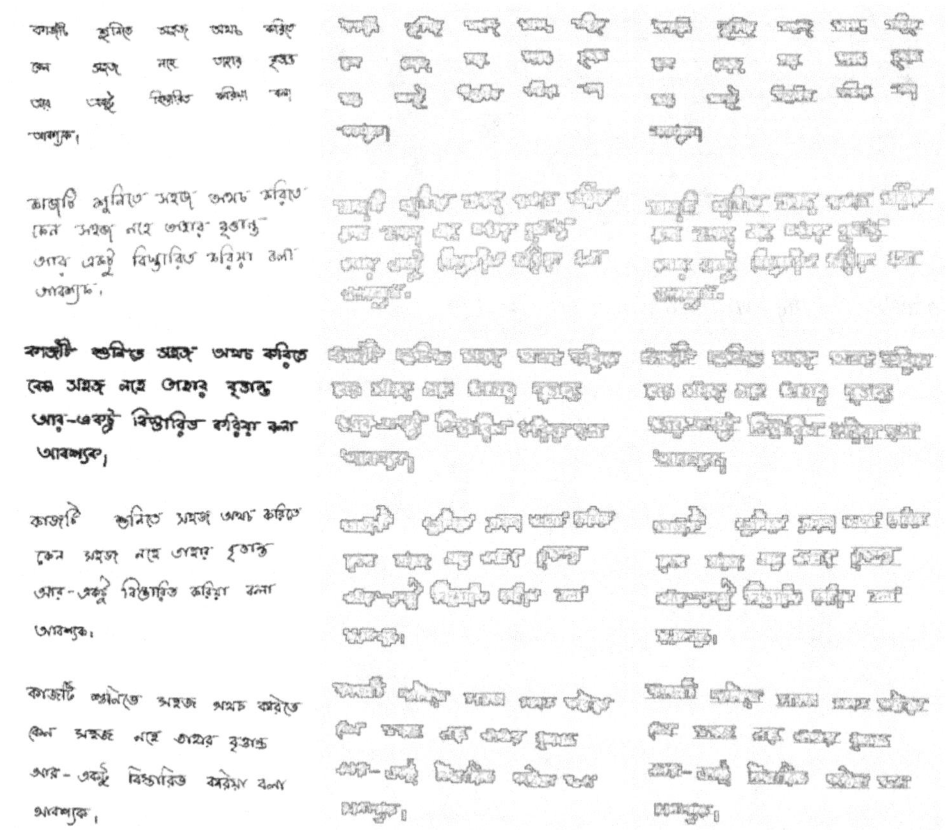

Figure 8. Result of Word Segmentation (left, in blue) and baseline extraction (right, in red) of two English handwritten samples

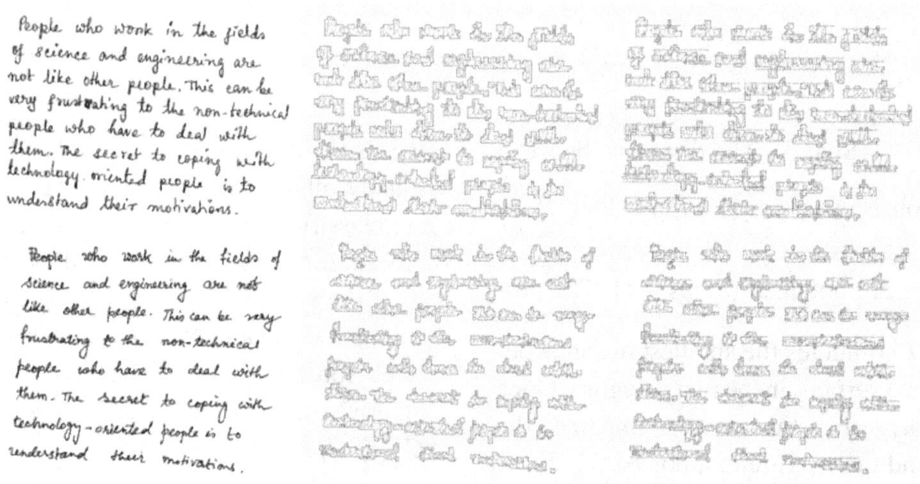

Figure 9. Segmented words (in blue) detected by our algorithm on two handwritten English script

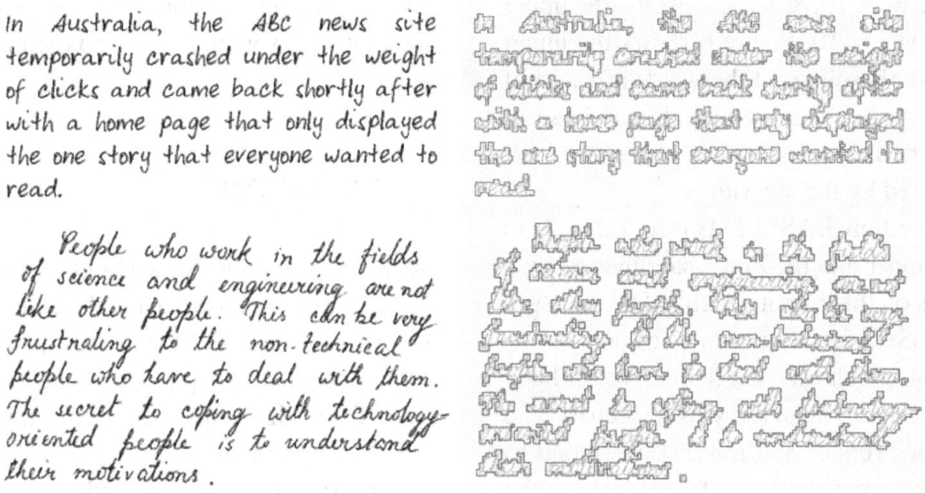

Baseline Extraction

The baselines, upper and lower, are determined after determining the word polygons. It is easy to see that (i) the number of vertices of any isothetic polygon (here, a word polygon) is always even (to be precise, it is a multiple of 4), and (ii) the number of its horizontal edges equals that of its vertical edges. Hence, if there are $n = 2m$ vertices in the word polygon, P_k, corresponding to the kth word, w_k, then P_k contains m horizontal and m vertical edges. As the algorithm starts from the top-left 90^0 vertex of P_k, namely v_0, and traverses along the edges of P_k in a way such that the corresponding word w_k always lies left (see Figure 2), the length of the horizontal edge $e_h^{(2i+1)}$ $(i = 0, 1, ..., m)$ outgoing from the vertex $v_{2i+1} \in P_k$ and ending at the next vertex $v_{2i+2} \in P_k$ is computed.[1] If the respective coordinates of v_{2i+1} and v_{2i+2} be (x) and (x_{2i+1}, y_{2i+1}) and $(x_{2i+2}, y_{2i+2} = y_{2i+1})$, then the value stored at the array $E[y_{2i+1}]$ is increased by the length of $e_h^{(2i+1)}$, i.e., $|x_{i+2} - x_{i+1}|$. Note that E is a 1-D array and $E[j]$ is initialized as 0 for $j = 0, 1, ..., m$ before envisaging each new word, w_k. For each word w_k, we reconsider a local coordinate system with its origin at $v_0 := (0, 0)$. Thus, after traversing m horizontal edges of P_0 outgoing from the vertices v_0, v_2, ..., v_{2m} in succession, the entry $E[j]$ contain the sums of lengths of all the horizontal edges whose ordinates (in the local coordinate system of w_k) are j.

A detailed demonstration on a typical handwritten Bengali word is given in Figure 6. As evident from this figure, after considering the lengths of all horizontal edges in E (blue histogram in Figure 5), we find two local maxima in E. As we traverse along $E[0], E[1], ...$, the first maximum gives the upper baseline and the next maximum gives the

Table 2. Algorithm of baseline detection

Steps:

1. **for** $i = 0...m$

2. **for** edge $v_{2i+1} v_{2i+2} \in w_k$

3. $e_h^{2i+1} \leftarrow |x_{i+2} - x_{i+1}|$

4. $E[y_{2i+1}] \leftarrow E[y_{2i+1}] + e_h^{2i+1}$

5. FINDBASEMAX(E)

lower. For example, Figure 5 shows that $E = \langle 2, 2, 15, 11, 2, 3, 3, 10, 8, 3, 3 \rangle$, whereby the upper baseline is at $j = 10$. Figure 6 shows the upper and the lower baselines of the words of a part of the document shown in Figure 3. It may be seen, almost all the baselines (shown in red) are correctly detected by the algorithm.

The algorithm BASELINE (see Table 2) to detect the upper and the lower baselines of each word works on the output generated by the algorithm WORDSEGMENT. For each word polygon w, the length of each horizontal line, e, is calculated (Step 3) and stored in an array $E[y]$ (Step 4). The two baselines (upper and lower) correspond to the two maximum values (i.e., frequencies) in the array $E[j]$, and are detected by calling the procedure FINDBASEMAX (Step 5).

Experimental Results

The algorithm is implemented in C on an Intel(R) Core(TM)2 Duo CPU E4500 2.20 GHz machine, the OS being Mandriva Linux Release 2008. The algorithm is tested on a different variety of handwritten documents. Results of word segmentation and baseline detection on a Bengali handwriting have been already shown in Figure 7 with necessary explanations. English handwriting is shown in Figure 8. To show the algorithm works on different handwriting traits, the algorithm is tested on various text samples written by five different persons. Figure 9 shows some results produced by our algorithm on the samples collected from these five persons. As evident from these results, the proposed algorithm has significant strength and efficiency in detecting the words and their baselines irrespective of the scripting style.

The algorithm is also tested on English handwritings where it works with quite a high level of accuracy. Results of word segmentation and baseline extraction of two English handwriting samples are shown in Figure 10. It may be noted that in case of very small gaps between adjacent lines of handwritten documents, two words of two adjacent lines may lie "too close", thereby giving rise to a single polygon. Such erroneous results are quite unlikely to occur, and exhibited in Figure 11.

CONCLUSION

A novel technique to segment out words in a handwriting document using the concept of outer isothetic covers (OIC) for an appropriate grid size is presented in this paper. The procedure for selection of grid size, explained in this paper, uses an adaptive technique. The baselines of words can also be successfully extracted by analyzing the OICs of words. The word segmentation technique may be used to design an improved algorithm that will work efficiently even on a skewed document. Apart from the word segmentation, the OICs can be used to develop several other document processing tools, such as writer identification or handwriting analysis, skew detection, etc. As evident from this paper, the combinatorial image analysis, if applied in an appropriate way, is quite useful to solve various real-world problems of image processing and pattern recognition in general, and document image analysis in particular.

ACKNOWLEDGMENT

A preliminary version of this paper appeared in the Proceedings of 12th International Conference on Frontiers in Handwriting Recognition, Kolkata, India, 2010 (Sarkar et al., 2010).

REFERENCES

Aida-zade, K. R., & Hasanov, J. Z. (2009). Word base line detection in handwritten text recognition system. *International Journal of Electrical and Computer Engineering, 4*(5), 310–314.

Bhattacharya, U., & Chaudhuri, B. B. (2009). Handwritten numeral databases of Indian scripts and multistage recognition of mixed numerals. *IEEE Transactions on Pattern Analysis and Machine Intelligence, 31*(3), 444–457. doi:10.1109/TPAMI.2008.88

Biswas, A., Bhowmick, P., & Bhattacharya, B. B. (2010). Construction of isothetic covers of a digital object: A combinatorial approach. *Journal of Visual Communication and Image Representation, 21*(4), 295–310. doi:10.1016/j.jvcir.2010.02.001

Boubaker, H., Kherallah, M., & Alimi, A. M. (2009). New algorithm of straight or curved baseline detection for short Arabic handwritten writing. In *Proceedings of the 10th International Conference on Document Analysis and Recognition* (pp. 778-782).

Chaudhuri, B. B., & Bera, S. (2009). Handwritten text line identification in Indian scripts. In *Proceedings of the 10th International Conference on Document Analysis and Recognition* (pp. 636-640).

Gopisetty, S., Lorie, R., Mao, J., Mohiuddin, M., Sorin, A., & Yair, E. (1996). Automated forms processing software and services. *IBM Journal of Research and Development, 40*(2), 211–230. doi:10.1147/rd.402.0211

Gorski, N., Anisimov, V., Augustin, E., Baret, O., Price, D., & Simon, J. C. (1999). A2iA check reader: A family of bank check recognition systems. In *Proceedings of the 5th International Conference on Document Analysis and Recognition* (pp. 523-526).

Guillevic, D., & Suen, C. Y. (1998). Recognition of legal amounts on bank cheques. *Pattern Analysis & Applications, 1*(1), 28–41. doi:10.1007/BF01238024

Haizhou, L., & Baosheng, Y. (1998). Chinese word segmentation. In *Proceedings of the 12th Pacific Asia Conference on Language, Information, and Computation* (pp. 212-217).

Huang, C., & Srihari, S. (2008). Word segmentation of off-line handwritten documents. In *Proceedings of the IST/SPIE Annual Symposium on Document Recognition and Retrieval*.

Kim, G., & Govindaraju, V. (1997). A lexicon driven approach to handwritten word recognition for real-time applications. *IEEE Transactions on Pattern Analysis and Machine Intelligence, 19*(4), 366–379. doi:10.1109/34.588017

Lee, W., Lee, D. J., & Park, H. S. (1996). A new methodology for gray scale character segmentation and recognition. *IEEE Transactions on Pattern Analysis and Machine Intelligence, 18*(10), 1045–1050. doi:10.1109/34.541415

Louloudis, G., Gatos, B., Pratikakis, I., & Halatsis, C. (2009). Text line and word segmentation of handwritten documents. *Journal of Pattern Recognition, 42*(12), 3169–3183. doi:10.1016/j.patcog.2008.12.016

Majumdar, A., & Chaudhuri, B. B. (2007). Curvelet-based multi-SVM recognizer for offline handwritten Bangla: A major Indian script. In *Proceedings of the 9th International Conference on Document Analysis and Recognition* (pp. 491-495).

Mao, J., Sinha, P., & Mohiuddin, K. (1998). A system for cursive handwritten address recognition. In *Proceedings of the 14th International Conference on Pattern Recognition* (pp. 1285-1287).

Mohamed, M., & Gader, P. (1996). Handwritten word recognition using segmentation free hidden markov modeling and segmentation based dynamic programming techniques. *IEEE Transactions on Pattern Analysis and Machine Intelligence, 18*(5), 548–554. doi:10.1109/34.494644

Otsu, N. (1979). A threshold selection method from graylevel histogram. *IEEE Transactions on Systems, Man, and Cybernetics*, 9(1), 62–66. doi:10.1109/TSMC.1979.4310076

Parui, S. K., Guin, K., Bhattacharya, U., & Chaudhuri, B. B. (2008). Online handwritten Bangla character recognition using HMM. In *Proceedings of the 19th International Conference on Pattern Recognition* (pp. 1-4).

Plamondon, R. (Ed.). (1993). Handwriting processing and recognition. *Pattern Recognition*, 26(3), 379. doi:10.1016/0031-3203(93)90165-S

Plamondon, R., & Leedham, C. G. (Eds.). (1990). *Computer processing of handwriting*. Singapore: World Scientific.

Sarkar, A., Biswas, A., Bhowmick, P., & Bhattacharya, B. B. (2010). Word segmentation and baseline detection in handwritten documents using isothetic covers. In *Proceedings of the 12th International Conference on Frontiers in Handwriting Recognition* (pp. 445-450).

Senior, A. W., & Robinson, A. J. (1998). An off-line cursive handwriting recognition system. *IEEE Transactions on Pattern Recognition and Machine Intelligence*, 20(3), 309–322. doi:10.1109/34.667887

Simner, M., Hulstijn, W., & Giouard, P. (Eds.). (1994). *Forensic, developmental and neuropsychological aspects of handwriting*. Journal of Forensic Document Examination.

Simner, M. L., Leedham, C. G., & Thomassen, A. J. W. M. (Eds.). (1996). *Handwriting and drawing research: Basic and applied issues*. Amsterdam, The Netherlands: IOS Press.

Srihari, S. N., & Keubert, E. J. (1997). Integration of handwritten address interpretation technology into the United States postal service remote computer reader system. In *Proceedings of the 4th International Conference on Document Analysis and Recognition* (pp. 892-896).

Srihari, S. N., Shin, Y. C., Ramanaprasad, V., & Lee, D. S. (1996). A system to read names and addresses on Tax Forms. *Proceedings of the IEEE*, 84(7), 1038–1049. doi:10.1109/5.503302

Vajda, S., Roy, K., Pal, U., Chaudhuri, B. B., & Bela¨ıd, A. (2009). Automation of Indian postal documents written in Bangla and English. *International Journal of Pattern Recognition and Artificial Intelligence*, 23(8), 1599–1632. doi:10.1142/S0218001409007776

Van Galen, G. P., & Morasso, P. (Eds.). (1998). Neuromotor control in handwriting and drawing. *Acta Psychologica*, 100(1-2), 236.

Van Galen, G. P., & Stelmach, G. E. (Eds.). (1993). Handwriting: Issues of psychomotor control and cognitive models. *Acta Psychologica*, 82(1-3).

Wan, J., Wing, A. M., & Sovik, N. (Eds.). (1991). *Development of graphic skills: Research, perspectives and educational implications*. London, UK: Academic Press.

Wang, J., & Jean, J. (1994). Segmentation of merged characters by neural networks and shortest path. *Pattern Recognition*, 27(5), 649–658. doi:10.1016/0031-3203(94)90044-2

ENDNOTES

[1] The first edge $e_0 := <v_0, v_1>$ is always vertical as the algorithm traces a polygon with the object always lying to its left (see Figure 2).

This work was previously published in the International Journal of Digital Library Systems, Volume 2, Issue 3, edited by Chia-Hung Wei, pp. 1-13, copyright 2011 by IGI Publishing (an imprint of IGI Global).

Chapter 3
Hierarchical Correlation of Multi-Scale Spatial Pyramid for Similar Mammogram Retrieval

Jinn-Ming Chang
Chi Mei Foundation Hospital, Tainan, Taiwan

Chih-Ying Gwo
Ching Yun University, Taiwan

Pai-Jung Huang
Tungs' Taichung MetroHarbor Hospital, Chi Mei Foundation Hospital, Taipei Medical University Hospital, & Taipei Medical University, Taiwan

Yue Li
Nankai University, China

Chia-Hung Wei
Ching Yun University, Taiwan

ABSTRACT

In hospitals and medical institutes, a large number of mammograms are produced in ever increasing quantities and used for diagnostics and therapy. The need for effective methods to manage and retrieve those image resources has been actively pursued in the medical community. This paper proposes a hierarchical correlation calculation approach to content-based mammogram retrieval. In this approach, images are represented as a Gaussian pyramid with several reduced-resolution levels. A global search is first conducted to identify the optimal matching position, where the correlation between the query image and the target images in the database is maximal. Local search is performed in the region comprising the four child pixels at a higher resolution level to locate the position with maximal correlation at greater resolution. Finally, this position with the maximal correlation found at the finest resolution level is used as the image similarity measure for retrieving images. Experimental results have shown that this approach achieves 59% in precision and 54% in recall when the threshold of correlation is $\geq$ 0.5.

DOI: 10.4018/978-1-4666-2928-8.ch003

1. INTRODUCTION

Breast cancer is the most common cancer among women (Buciu & Gacsadi, 2011; Eltoukhy, Faye, & Samir, 2010; Meselhy Eltoukhy, Faye, & Belhaouari Samir, 2012). The National Cancer Institute (NCI) recommends that women over the age of 40 and older should have routine screening mammography every one to two years. The U.S. Preventive Services Task Force (USPSTF) recommends biennial screening mammography for women aged 50 to 74 years (DeAngelis & Fontanarosa, 2010). An enormous number of digital mammograms have been generated in hospitals and breast screening centers as mammography is an accurate and reliable method for the detection and diagnosis of breast cancer (Wei & Li, 2006). These valuable mammograms which show various symptoms, allow radiologists to conduct medical studies and assist them in diagnosing new cases. The most important aspect of image database management is how to effectively retrieve the similar images based on the lesion of a given example. This approach of searching images is known as content-based image retrieval (CBIR), which refers to the retrieval of images from a database using information directly derived from the content of the images themselves, rather than from accompanying text or annotation. CBIR can help radiologists to retrieve mammograms with similar contents (El-Naqa, Yang, Galatsanos, Nishikawa, & Wernick, 2004).

Due to the nature of mammograms, content-based retrieval for similar lesions is faced with some challenges. Low resolution and strong noise are two common characteristics (Wei, Li, & Wilson, 2006). With these characteristics, Lesions in mammograms cannot be precisely segmented and extracted for the visual content of their features. In addition, mammograms obtained from different scanning devices may display different features, though some approaches to image correction and normalization have been proposed; Mammograms are represented in gray level rather than color.

Even with the change of intensity, monochrome may fail to clearly display the actual circumstance of lesion area.

The purpose of this paper is to present a multi-resolution correlation calculation approach is presented to mammogram retrieval. The rest of this report is organized as follows: The third section discusses the problems of measuring image similarity by correlation. The fourth section provides a background review of the image pyramid method. The fifth section proposes a novel approach for CBIR. The sixth section describes the experiment and evaluates the effectiveness of the proposed approach for mammogram retrieval. The last section presents the conclusions for this work.

2. LITERATURE REVIEW

An image pyramid is a multi-scale spatial structure, represented at progressively lower resolution at higher levels of the structure. Since the pyramidal structures preserve spatial information and, they have been widely used for content-based image retrieval (Urdiales, Dominguez, de Trazegnies, & Sandoval, 2010). Several studies have applied pyramid-based methods for image retrieval and recognition (Brun & Kropatsch, 2006; Dong & Kim, 2001; El Aroussi, El Hassouni, Ghouzali, Rziza, & Aboutajdine, 2011; Gangolli & Tanimoto, 1983; Kountchev, Rubin, Milanova, & Todorov, 2007; Grauman & Darrell, 2007; Kwon & Yeom, 2004; Liu et al., 2011; Elfiky, Shahbaz Khan, van de Weijer, & Gonzàlez, 2012; Milanova, Kountchev, Rubin, Todorov, & Kountcheva, 2009; Qiao, Lu, Pan, & Sun, 2010; Su, Zhuang, Huang, & Wu, 2005; Urdiales et al., 2010). This study (Milanova et al., 2009) presents an approach to image retrieval using cognitive representation with pyramidal decomposition. This approach is based on object model creation with inverse difference pyramid controlled by neural network. The main advantages of the method are the high flexibility and the ability to create general models for various views and scaling with relatively low computational complexity. The study (Kountchev et al., 2007) decomposes an image from the inverse difference pyramid. The method permits the evaluation of the images similarity to be performed in the consecutive decomposition layers and to compare parts of the images with increasing resolution, which corresponds to different image scaling. The study (Grauman & Darrell, 2007) present a new fast kernel function called the pyramid match that measures partial match similarity in time linear in the number of features. The pyramid match maps unordered feature sets to multi-resolution histograms and computes a weighted histogram intersection in order to find implicit correspondences based on the finest resolution histogram cell where a matched pair first appears.

3. IMAGE SIMILARITY BY CORRELATION

Correlation, in the context of image analysis, refers to the degree of similarity between images. When an image convolves with another image, a two-dimensional correlation can be generated to indicate individual matching degrees at different positions. To obtain such a correlation matrix, it is required to perform a neighborhood operation where each output pixel is the weighted sum of neighboring input pixels. This matrix of weights is also called the correlation kernel. The value of each output pixel indicates the relative matching degree between the two images.

For a query image $f(x, y)$ of size $M \times N$ and a candidate image $w(s, t)$ of the same size, the correlation between the two images $f(x, y)$ and $w(x, y)$ is expressed as follows (Gonzalez, Woods, & Eddins, 2002).

$$c(x, y) = \sum_{s=0}^{M-1} \sum_{t=0}^{N-1} w(s, t) f(x + s, y + t) \quad (1)$$

for $x = 0, 1, 2, \ldots, M - 1$, $y = 0, 1, 2, \ldots, N - 1$. However, the correlation given in Equation (1) is sensitive to changes in the amplitude of w and f. A correlation coefficient is used to overcome this drawback, with the correlation defined as follows (Dong & Kim, 2001):

$$\gamma(x, y) = \frac{\sum_{s,t} [w(s, t) - \overline{w}(s, t)][f(x - u, y - v) - \overline{f}]}{\{\sum_{x,y} [w(x, y) - \overline{w}_{u,v}]^2 \sum_{x,y} [f(x - u, y - v) - \overline{f}]^2\}^{\frac{1}{2}}} \quad (2)$$

where $x = 0, 1, 2, \ldots, M\text{-}1$, $y = 0, 1, 2, \ldots, N\text{-}1$, $\overline{w}$ and $\overline{f}$ are the means of the pixels in w and f. The maximal correlation value $\gamma(x, y)$ is expressed as

$$\gamma(x^*, y^*) = \arg \max_{x,y} \gamma(x, y) \quad (3)$$

The highest correlation coefficient $\gamma(x, y)$ occurs at the position (x^*, y^*), where the best match between w and f is found. However, the correlation is by no mean a time-efficient process. For example, an exhaustive search for the maximal correlation between two images of $M \times N$ pixels requires $M \times N$ correlation coefficients to be calculated before the maximum can be found, and each correlation coefficient requires $M \times N$ multiplications and $M \times N$ additions. This computational cost is far too high for the application of image database retrieval. It is our intention in this work to propose an efficient way for correlation calculation within a multi-resolution framework.

4. A FRAMEWORK OF MULTI-SCALE SPATIAL PYRAMID

An image pyramid represents a digital image in the multi-resolution system. It consists of a sequence of versions of an original image wherein both sample density and resolution are decreased in regular steps. These reduced resolution levels of the pyramid are generated through an iterative procedure. In an image pyramid, the zero level of the pyramid, G_0, is equal to the original images. To generate the next pyramid level G_1, G_0 is low-pass filtered and sub-sampled by a factor of two. Similarly, G_1 is filtered and sub-sampled in the same procedure to generate G_2, and so on. By repeating the filtering/sub-sampling procedure, pyramids like that shown in Figure 1 can be constructed. The sequence of images G_0, G_1, ..., G_n is called the Gaussian pyramid as the low-pass filtering is performed by a process which is equivalent to convolution with Gaussian weighting functions.

The main characteristic of an image pyramid is that the lower levels of the pyramid contain more detailed content whereas the higher levels provide an approximation of the original image. Figure 1 illustrates an image pyramid structure, which is a stack of digital images describing the same content with decreasing resolution. The base of the pyramid is the image at the original resolution. As you move up the pyramid, the size of the image becomes smaller and the resolution becomes lower. The top of the pyramid contains the lowest resolution representation of the image.

Figure 1. An image is represented in the multi-scale spatial system

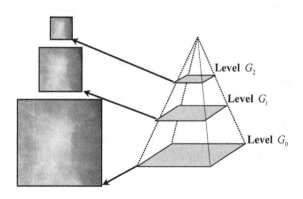

Another important characteristic of the structure of an image pyramid is the parent-child relation between adjacent levels. Each site/pixel, except those at the bottom level, of an image pyramid contains four child sites/pixels at the next level. Therefore, the pixel $P(x,y)$ in level G_n is regarded as the parent of the four child pixels $(2x,2y)$, $(2x-1,2y)$, $(2x,2y-1)$, $(2x-1,2y-1)$ in level G_{n-1}. Such a parent-child relation will provide a basis for the development of the proposed approach, which is described in the following section.

5. HIERARCHICAL CORRELATION

The higher levels of a Gaussian pyramid are an approximation of the original image at the bottom level. Our concept of hierarchical correlation calculation is based on the assumption that the maximal correlation at a finer resolution level is likely to appear within the neighborhood comprising the four child positions of the position in the immediate coarser resolution level where maximal correlation is found. By performing an exhaustive/global search at the nominal top level and confining further search at finer resolution levels to the local neighborhood comprising the four child positions of the optimal position found in the higher level, the computational complexity of an exhaustive search for the maximal correlation can be significantly reduced. However, due to the nature of the low-pass filtering, at higher levels of the pyramid, more details (the high-frequency component) of the image are lost. Therefore, instead of starting from the very top level of the pyramid with only one pixel, which is pointless, the search has to start from a nominal top level where structural details are still preserved. Therefore, for images of $M \times N$ pixels, if we start the search at level n, the number of correlation coefficients E to be calculated is

$$E = \frac{M \times N}{2^{2n}} + 4n \qquad (4)$$

where the first term accounts for the global search at the nominal top level while the second term corresponds to the local search at the n finer resolution levels, including level 0. For example, suppose an image with 200×200 pixels can be reduced down to 25×25 pixels at the nominal top level of a 4 level pyramid (i.e., $n = 3$). A global search is first carried out by computing the correlation and finding its optimal matching position in the smallest-scale image. 625 (25×25) positions were scanned to compute their correlations at this level. A local search within the neighborhood comprising the four child pixels at the new resolution level is then conducted to find the maximal correlation among its corresponding four points in a 50×50 image. A local search is then iteratively performed in the 100×100 and 200×200 images. The correlation of the original image is the maximal value in the local search of the 200×200 image. In the example, the proposed approach only needs to computes 637 ($625 + 4 + 4 + 4 = 637$) correlation coefficients whereas an exhaustive search on the original image would require the calculation of 40,000 (200×200) correlation coefficients. As the size and number of images increases, the efficiency of this approach increases significantly. The computational cost of constructing a Gaussian pyramid is trivial, compared to the cost for an exhaustive search on the original image, but additional storage for the different resolution images is required. Given the fact that the cost of storage is continually decreasing as technology advances, storing the Gaussian pyramid of each image in the database is a worthwhile trade-off for reduced computational cost because the extra storage required for each image is less than a half of the original.

To demonstrate this concept, a 4-level Gaussian pyramid of an original image was constructed, as shown in Figure 2. A new image was then cre-ated by *circularly* shifting the original image in this pyramid by (59, 78) to the upper left corner and a Gaussian pyramid was constructed based on the new image. This is shown in Figure 3. Then, correlation computation was performed by sliding the images in the first pyramid over the images of the same level in the second pyramid to look for optimal positions. The optimal positions for each level of the second Gaussian pyramid are showed in Table 1. It was observed that

Figure 2. A Gaussian pyramid of a mammogram with an architectural distortion at center

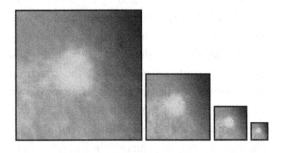

Figure 3. A Gaussian pyramid of a mammogram with an architectural distortion at left top

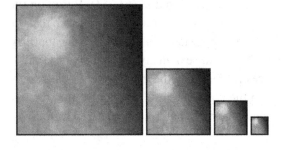

Figure 4. Two original mammograms with an architectural distortion

the optimal position was also moved to the top left of each level of the Gaussian pyramid and these positions reveal the parent-child relation, i.e., the optimal positions at level G_3, G_2, G_1 reflect the optimal positions at the next level G_2, G_1, G_0, respectively. Based on the results of this investigation, it was found that when an optimal position P at G_n is determined, the optimal position at G_{n-1} must be located at one of its four corresponding pixels, which have a parent-child relation with P.

Another investigation was conducted to examine the difference between the optimal position of a Gaussian pyramid found by the hierarchical approach and the optimal position found by an exhaustive/global search directly carried out at the pixel level. Firstly, the hierarchical approach is applied to find the position of the maximal correlation coefficient using the two images shown in Figure 4. The optimal position (61, 33) was found at the bottom level of the pyramid. Secondly, the two original images in Figure 4 were used to conduct the exhaustive/global search for the maximal correlation coefficient at pixel level. This position with the maximal correlation coefficient was also found at (61, 33). Based on the results of this investigation, it can be seen that the proposed approach can find the same optimal position as an exhaustive/global search, but is more efficient than the exhaustive/global search.

In the context of a CBIR application, the retrieval algorithm can be summarized as follows.

- **Step 1:** Construct a Gaussian pyramid, called the query pyramid, based on the query image.
- **Step 2:** For each candidate image in the database,
  - **Step 2.1:** Construct a Gaussian pyramid, called a candidate pyramid, based on the candidate image.
  - **Step 2.2:** Compute the correlation between the top levels of the query pyramid and the candidate pyramid and locate the optimal position where the maximal correlation coefficient occurs.
  - **Step 2.3:** Propagate the optimal position to the next finer resolution level and locate the optimal position from the four child positions of the position where the maximal correlation coefficient occurs.
  - **Step 2.4:** Repeat Step 2.3 until the maximal correlation coefficient C_b at the bottom level is calculated.
- **Step 3:** Retrieve the H images whose C_b is the highest.

6. EXPERIMENTS

A. Mammogram Data Set

Mammograms were obtained from the database of the Mammographic Images Analysis Society

Table 1. The optimal position of different levels using different images

Level of Pyramid	Size of Image	Position
Level G3	25x25	(8, 10)
Level G2	50x50	(15, 20)
Level G1	100x100	(29, 39)
Level G0	200x200	(59, 78)

Table 2. Criteria for measuring performance evaluation

Score	Criteria
1.0	The retrieved image belongs to the class of query image.
0.5	The retrieved image belongs to one of the abnormal classes, but not the class of query image.
0	The retrieved image does not belong to any abnormal class.

(MIAS) (Suckling et al., 1994). The size of each image was 1024×1024 pixels. All of the images have been annotated for class, severity and location of abnormality, character of background tissue, and radius of circle enclosing the abnormality. Sub-images of size 200×200 pixels were cropped as ROIs from each mammogram. 250 sample ROIs were selected deliberately from abnormal tissues. Another 207 ROIs were obtained arbitrarily from normal tissues. These 457 ROIs were used to evaluate the performance of the CBIR system.

B. Retrieval Frameworks

This content-based retrieval framework is divided into off-line preprocessing and on-line image retrieval (Wei, Li, & Wilson, 2005). In the off-line preprocessing part, the mammograms in the database are decomposed into different levels of Gaussian pyramids. The different-level versions of each candidate image constitute a sub-image dataset stored in the database. In the on-line image retrieval part, the user submits a query example to the retrieval system in search of the desired mammograms. The system immediately builds a Gaussian pyramid for this example. The optimal matching position of each of the candidate mammograms is found by the proposed hierarchical

correlation calculation approach. The similarity between the query example and those mammograms in the feature dataset are then computed and ranked. Retrieval is conducted by applying an indexing scheme to provide an efficient way of searching the image database. Finally, the system ranks the search results and then returns the results that are most similar to the query example.

C. Performance Evaluation

Relevance judgment is a vital part of performance evaluation. The relevance criteria described in Table 2 were used in this work. For example, suppose the query image belonged to the circumscribed masses class, the retrieved image would score 0.5 if it belonged to any of the following abnormal classes: ill-defined masses, speculated masses, architectural distortion, and asymmetry.

Precision and recall are basic measures used in evaluating the effectiveness of an information retrieval system (Müller, Müller, Squire, March-and-Maillet, & Pun, 2001). Precision is the ratio of the number of relevant records retrieved to the total number of irrelevant and relevant records retrieved. It indicates the subject score assigned to each of the top images in this experiment. The formula is expressed as follow:

Table 3. Performance evaluation for precision and recall with the correlation value ≥ 0.5

	CIRC	SPIC	MISC	ARCH	ASYM	Mean
Precision	54%	58%	57%	61%	64%	**59%**
Recall	43%	61%	52%	54%	59%	**54%**

(Notes: CIRC = circumscribed masses, SPIC = speculated masses; ARCH = architectural distortion; ASYM = asymmetry; MISC = other or ill-defined masses.)

Table 4. Performance evaluation for precision and recall with the correlation value ≥ 0.75

	CIRC	SPIC	MISC	ARCH	ASYM	Mean
Precision	57%	63%	55%	63%	61%	**60%**
Recall	31%	50%	43%	37%	43%	**41%**

$$p = \frac{\sum_{i=1}^{n} S_i}{H} \qquad (5)$$

where, S_i is the score assigned to the ith hit, H is the number of top hits retrieved.

Recall is the ratio of the number of relevant records retrieved to the total number of relevant records in the database. It is defined as follow:

$$R = \frac{R_n}{T_n} \qquad (6)$$

where R_n is the number of retrieved relevant hits, and T_n is the total number of relevant images in the database.

Table 3 shows the precision and recall rates for CIRC, SPIC, ARCH, ASYM and MISC when the threshold of correlation is ≥ 0.5. The average precision and recall are 59% and 54% in this experiment. When the threshold of correlation ≥ 0.75, it was found that the mean of precision rises slightly to 60% and the mean of recall drops to 41% (see Table 4). We also found that target images were not always returned in the top ten images. As the total number of target images in the database is small and the threshold of correlation is raised, the recall value is likely to drop greatly.

7. CONCLUSION

This work presents a novel approach to content-based mammogram retrieval, which utilizes hierarchical correlation of multi-scale spatial pyramid to efficiently find the optimal position for image similarity. Correlation can be used as an index to describe the similarity between two images. However, looking for an optimal matching position directly at pixel level for two-dimensional images, where the correlation is maximal, is com-putationally expensive as one image has to slide over the other image to measure the correlations at different matching positions. As the size and number of images in a database becomes larger, performing correlation computation becomes a serious burden, especially for CBIR systems that are expected to response rapidly to a user's query. This study also demonstrates that the mean of precision reaches 60% and the mean of recall is 41%, respectively. The results reflect the effectiveness of the proposed approach to similar lesion retrieval. Future work on the development of this approach may include the deletion of noise and detection of regions of interests on mammograms at several distinct scales. We will extract the mammographic features based on ACR BI-RADS standards (Eberl, Fox, Edge, Carter, & Mahoney, 2006).

REFERENCES

Brun, L., & Kropatsch, W. (2006). Contains and inside relationships within combinatorial pyramids. *Pattern Recognition*, *39*(4), 515–526. doi:10.1016/j.patcog.2005.10.015

Buciu, I., & Gacsadi, A. (2011). Directional features for automatic tumor classification of mammogram images. *Biomedical Signal Processing and Control*, *6*(4), 370–378. doi:10.1016/j.bspc.2010.10.003

DeAngelis, C. D., & Fontanarosa, P. B. (2010). US preventive services task force and breast cancer screening. *Journal of the American Medical Association*, *303*(2), 172–173. doi:10.1001/jama.2009.1990

Dong, H., & Kim, H.-J. (2001). A fast content-based indexing and retrieval technique by the shape information in large image database. *Journal of Systems and Software*, *56*(2), 165–182. doi:10.1016/S0164-1212(00)00095-9

Eberl, M. M., Fox, C. H., Edge, S. B., Carter, C. A., & Mahoney, M. C. (2006). BI-RADS classification for management of abnormal mammograms. *Journal of the American Board of Family Medicine, 19*(2), 161–164. doi:10.3122/jabfm.19.2.161

El Aroussi, M., El Hassouni, M., Ghouzali, S., Rziza, M., & Aboutajdine, D. (2011). Local appearance based face recognition method using block based steerable pyramid transform. *Signal Processing, 91*(1), 38–50. doi:10.1016/j.sigpro.2010.06.005

El-Naqa, I., Yang, Y., Galatsanos, N. P., Nishikawa, R. M., & Wernick, M. N. (2004). A similarity learning approach to content-based image retrieval: Application to digital mammography. *IEEE Transactions on Medical Imaging, 23*(10), 1233–1244. doi:10.1109/TMI.2004.834601

Elfiky, N. M., Shahbaz Khan, F., van de Weijer, J., & Gonzàlez, J. (2012). Discriminative compact pyramids for object and scene recognition. *Pattern Recognition, 45*(4), 1627–1636. doi:10.1016/j.patcog.2011.09.020

Eltoukhy, M. M., Faye, I., & Samir, B. B. (2010). Breast cancer diagnosis in digital mammogram using multiscale curvelet transform. *Computerized Medical Imaging and Graphics, 34*(4), 269–276. doi:10.1016/j.compmedimag.2009.11.002

Gangolli, A. R., & Tanimoto, S. L. (1983). Two pyramid machine algorithms for edge detection in noisy binary images. *Information Processing Letters, 17*(4), 197–202. doi:10.1016/0020-0190(83)90040-6

Gonzalez, R. C., Woods, R. E., & Eddins, S. L. (2002). *Digital image processing* (2nd ed.). Knoxville, TN: Gatesmark.

Grauman, K., & Darrell, T. (2007). The pyramid match kernel: Efficient learning with sets of features. *Journal of Machine Learning Research, 8*, 725–760.

Kountchev, R., Rubin, S., Milanova, M., & Todorov, V. (2007, 13-15 Aug. 2007). Image multi-layer search based on spectrum pyramid. In *Proceedings of the IEEE International Conference on Information Reuse and Integration*.

Kwon, J. B., & Yeom, H. Y. (2004). Generalized data retrieval for pyramid-based periodic broadcasting of videos. *Future Generation Computer Systems, 20*(1), 157–170. doi:10.1016/S0167-739X(03)00151-1

Liu, Y.-Y., Chen, M., Ishikawa, H., Wollstein, G., Schuman, J. S., & Rehg, J. M. (2011). Automated macular pathology diagnosis in retinal OCT images using multi-scale spatial pyramid and local binary patterns in texture and shape encoding. *Medical Image Analysis, 15*(5), 748–759. doi:10.1016/j.media.2011.06.005

Meselhy Eltoukhy, M., Faye, I., & Belhaouari Samir, B. (2012). A statistical based feature extraction method for breast cancer diagnosis in digital mammogram using multiresolution representation. *Computers in Biology and Medicine, 42*(1), 123–128. doi:10.1016/j.compbiomed.2011.10.016

Milanova, M., Kountchev, R., Rubin, S., Todorov, V., & Kountcheva, R. (2009). Content based image retrieval using adaptive inverse pyramid representation. In G. Salvendy & M. Smith (Eds.), *Proceedings of the International Symposium on Human Interface and the Management of Information: Information and Interaction* (LNCS 5618, pp. 304-314).

Müller, H., Müller, W., Squire, D. M., Marchand-Maillet, S., & Pun, T. (2001). Performance evaluation in content-based image retrieval: overview and proposals. *Pattern Recognition Letters, 22*(5), 593–601. doi:10.1016/S0167-8655(00)00118-5

Qiao, Y.-L., Lu, Z.-M., Pan, J.-S., & Sun, S.-H. (2010). Fast k-nearest neighbor search algorithm based on pyramid structure of wavelet transform and its application to texture classification. *Digital Signal Processing, 20*(3), 837–845. doi:10.1016/j.dsp.2009.10.011

Su, C., Zhuang, Y., Huang, L., & Wu, F. (2005). Steerable pyramid-based face hallucination. *Pattern Recognition, 38*(6), 813–824. doi:10.1016/j.patcog.2004.11.007

Suckling, J., Parker, J., Dance, D., Astley, S., Hutt, I., Boggis, C., et al. (1994). The mammographic images analysis society digital mammogram database. *Experta Medica International Congress Series, 1069*, 375-378.

Urdiales, C., Dominguez, M., de Trazegnies, C., & Sandoval, F. (2010). A new pyramid-based color image representation for visual localization. *Image and Vision Computing, 28*(1), 78–91. doi:10.1016/j.imavis.2009.04.014

Wei, C.-H., & Li, C.-T. (2006). Calcification descriptor and relevance feedback learning algorithms for content-based mammogram retrieval. In *Proceedings of the 8th International Workshop on Digital Mammography.*

Wei, C.-H., Li, C.-T., & Wilson, R. (2005). A general framework for content-based medical image retrieval with its application to mammogram retrieval. In *Proceedings of the SPIE International Symposium on Medical Imaging.*

Wei, C.-H., Li, C.-T., & Wilson, R. (2006). *A content-based approach to medical image database retrieval.* Hershey, PA: Idea Group.

This work was previously published in the International Journal of Digital Library Systems, Volume 2, Issue 4, edited by Chia-Hung Wei, pp. 13-23, copyright 2011 by IGI Publishing (an imprint of IGI Global).

Chapter 4
Mammogram Retrieval:
Image Selection Strategy of Relevance Feedback for Locating Similar Lesions

Chee-Chiang Chen
Tungs' Taichung MetroHarbor Hospital, Taiwan

Chih-Ying Gwo
Ching Yun University, Taiwan

Pai-Jung Huang
Tungs' Taichung MetroHarbor Hospital, Chi Mei Foundation Hospital, Taipei Medical University Hospital, & Taipei Medical University, Taiwan

Yue Li
Nankai University, China

Chia-Hung Wei
Ching Yun University, Taiwan

ABSTRACT

Content-based image retrieval (CBIR) has been proposed by the medical community for inclusion in picture archiving and communication systems (PACS). In CBIR, relevance feedback is developed for bridging the semantic gap and improving the effectiveness of image retrieval systems. With relevance feedback, CBIR systems can return refined search results using a learning algorithm and selection strategy. In this study, as the retrieving process proceeds further, the proposed learning algorithm can reduce the influence of the original query point and increase the significance of the centroid of the clusters comprising the features of those relevant images identified in the most recent round of search. The proposed selection strategy is used to find a good starting point and select a set of images at each round to show that search result and ask for the user's feedback. In addition, a benchmark is proposed to measure the learning ability to explain the retrieval performance as relevance feedback is incorporated in CBIR systems. The performance evaluation shows that the average precision rate of the proposed scheme was 0.98 and the learning ability reach to 7.17 through the five rounds of relevance feedback.

DOI: 10.4018/978-1-4666-2928-8.ch004

1. INTRODUCTION

Content-based image retrieval (CBIR) refers to the retrieval of images whose contents are similar to a query example, using information derived from the images themselves, rather than relying on accompanying text indices or external annotation (El-Naqa, Yang, Galatsanos, Nishikawa, & Wernick, 2004). One of the key challenges in CBIR is bridging the gap between low-level representations and high-level semantics. The semantic gap exists because low-level features are formulated in the system design process while high-level queries are used at the starting point of the retrieval process (Lew, Sebe, & Eakins, 2002). Relevance feedback is developed for bridging the semantic gap and improving the effectiveness of image retrieval systems (El-Naqa et al., 2004; Wei & Li, 2008). With relevance feedback, CBIR systems can return refined search results using a learning algorithm and selection strategy.

Content-based image retrieval has been proposed by the medical community for inclusion into picture archiving and communication systems (PACS) (Lehmann et al., 2004). The idea of PACS is to integrate imaging modalities and interfaces with hospital and departmental information systems in order to manage the storage and distribution of images to radiologists, physicians, specialists, clinics, and imaging centres (Huang, 2003). A crucial requirement of PACS is to provide an efficient search function for accessing images that are relevant to the query example. The contents of medical images provide useful information, which can be used to search for other images containing similar content.

An enormous number of digital mammograms have been generated in hospitals and breast screening centres in recent years. As hospitals and breast screening centres are connected together through PACS, content-based approaches can be applied to efficiently retrieve mammograms from distributed databases. However, content-based retrieval approaches are usually developed for specific contents of medical images. Given this motivation, the goal of this study is to develop a novel and complete scheme for incorporating the relevance feedback into a content-based mammogram retrieval system.

The rest of the paper is organized as follows. Prior work is reviewed and described in Section 2. An overview of the proposed content-based retrieval framework is described in Section 3. The proposed learning algorithm and selection strategy for relevance feedback is presented in Sections 4 and 5, respectively. Section 6 evaluates the retrieval performance, and Section 7 discusses the results of the experiments. Section 8 makes a conclusion on this study.

2. PRIOR WORK

To incorporate relevance feedback into content-based image retrieval, two main approaches are developed: the *query point movement approach* and *re-weighting approach*. The concept behind the first approach is to modify the query that is originally submitted by the user. It is assumed that there exists at least one image which completely conveys the intentions of the user, and its high-level concept has been modeled in low-level feature space (Kushki, Androutsos, Plataniotis, & Venetsanopoulos, 2004). The query point movement approach is to move the point of the query toward the region of the feature space that contains the ideal image (Zhong, Hongjiang, Li, & Shaoping, 2003). Based on this concept, the classic Rocchio algorithm was originally developed to improve the effectiveness of information retrieval system (Rocchio, 1971). The MARS system has applied the query point movement approach as one of methods for relevance feedback (Rui, Huang, & Mehrotra, 1998). The method used in the MARS system is called $tf \times idf$ (term frequency-inverse document frequency), which generates pseudo-document vectors from image feature vectors and then applies the Rocchio algorithm to find the ideal point.

The concept used in the re-weighting approach is to modify the similarity measure in an attempt to re-index images and re-rank the results. Since each image is represented by an N dimensional feature vector, the feature vector can be regarded as a point in an N dimensional space. The re-weighting approach is to adjust the weights assigned to each feature or modify the similarity measure used (i.e., important features with larger weights, and less important features with smaller weights). Based on the re-weighting concept, the MARS system uses a refined method (standard deviation method) for relevance feedback. If the variance of the positive examples is high along the j-th axis, any point on the j-th axis may be acceptable to the user. The feature presenting j-th axis should be assigned a lower weight w_j. Hence, the inverse of the standard deviation of the j-th feature values in the feature matrix can be used as the weight w_j for the feature j (i.e., $w_j = 1/\sigma_j$). In the MindReader system, the feedback learning is regarded as a minimization problem on parameter estimation which avoids the use of ad-hoc heuristics, such as α, β, and γ in the Rocchio algorithm (Ishikawa, Subramanya, & Faloutsos, 1998). Moreover, the MindReader system, unlike the other systems whose distance function is represented by ellipses aligned with the coordinate axis, applied a distance function which is not necessarily aligned with the coordinate axis, thereby allowing for the assignment of different weights of each feature and correlations between features.

3. OVERVIEW OF CONTENT-BASED IMAGE RETRIEVAL FRAMEWORK

The proposed content-based retrieval framework as shown in Figure 1 can be divided into *off-line feature extraction* and *on-line image retrieval*.

In the component of off-line feature extraction, the contents of the images in the database are extracted and described with a feature vector, also called a descriptor. The feature vectors of the images constitute a feature dataset stored in the database. In the component of on-line image retrieval, the user can submit a query example to the retrieval system to search for desired images. The system represents this example with a feature vector. The similarities between the feature vectors of the query example and those of the media in the feature dataset are then computed and ranked. Retrieval is conducted by applying an indexing scheme to provide an efficient way of searching the image database. Finally, the system ranks the search results and returns the results that are most similar to the query example. If the user is not satisfied with the search results, the user can provide relevance feedback to the retrieval system in order to search further. To supply relevance feedback, the user simply identifies the positive image that is relevant to the query. The system subsequently recalculates the feature of the user's feedback using a learning algorithm and then employs a selection strategy to return refined results. This relevance feedback process can be iterated until the user is satisfied with the results or unwilling to offer any more feedbacks.

4. QUERY POINT MOVEMENT APPROACH

In this study query point movement is adopted to move the point of the refined query toward the region in the feature space that contains the relevant images specified by the user. When the feature point of the original query example $q(1)$ is moved to the refined point $q(2)$ in the feature space, the system comes closer to the center of the region containing more relevant images and less irrelevant ones, wherein the chance of retrieving more relevant images is higher.

Figure 1. The framework of the proposed CBIR framework

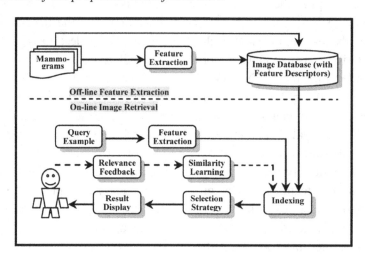

The learning algorithm in Equation (1) is proposed to learn the relevance feedbacks from the user in each round of the search and to determine the new query point for the next retrieval. To provide relevance feedbacks after being presented with the retrieved images of *t*th round of search, the user is allowed to identify an arbitrary number $n(t)$ of images as *relevant*. Let us denote the feature of the *pseudo query* to be used in the *t*th round of search by $q(t)$, $t >= 1$ and the feature of the *k*th image identified as relevant in the *t*th round of search by $f(t, k)$. Therefore, $q(1)$ is the feature of the original query example—a physical image. Apart from $q(1)$, all new query points do not correspond to any physical image in the feature space. This indicates the use of the phrase 'pseudo query'. The proposed learning algorithm for calculating the refined pseudo query point $q(t+1)$ in the feature space is described as follows.

The new query point is calculated as the centroid of the clusters comprising the feature of the original query example and the features of those images identified as relevant in the most recent round.

$$q(t+1) = e^{-\alpha t} \cdot q(1) + (1 - e^{-\alpha t}) \cdot \frac{\sum_{j=1}^{n(t)} f(t,j)}{n(t)} \quad , \quad t \geq 1$$

(1)

By giving variable weights $e^{-\alpha t}$ and $(1 - e^{-\alpha t})$ to the two terms in Equation (1), Equation (1), as the retrieving process proceeds further, reduces the influence of $q(1)$ and increases the significance of the centroid of the clusters comprising the features of those relevant images identified in the *t*th round of search only. Parameter α determines the rate at which the influences of the two terms changes. α is set to 1 in this study.

5. SELECTION STRATEGY

5.1. Proposed Selection Strategy

As conducting relevance feedback in search of desired images generally needs more than one round of user interaction, it is very important to employ a strategy to select the set of images at each round to show that search result and ask for the user's feedback so that the total number of iterations which are required to reach the target image is minimal. The most-positive-images strategy and the most-informative-image strategy are often used to investigate the user's information need. The most-positive-images strategy returns those images that are currently considered by the learning mechanism as the most relevant to the query (Tong & Chang, 2001) while the most-informative-image strategy mainly investigates the user's information needs and learn from the feedback information by returning the most ambiguous images (Cox, Miller, Minka, Papathomas, & Yianilos, 2000).

In this study it is assumed that the user is unwilling to spend too much time conducting relevance feedback. Therefore, a hybrid strategy combining the most-positive-images strategy and the most-positive-images strategy is used to not only provide the most positive images but also display the most informative images at the same time. It is very important to compromise two kinds of different purposes at each search result page of the limited number. The proposed strategy is described as follows:

- The proposed strategy is firstly to select two images in an attempt to find a good starting point at the exploratory stage. The image selection will follow the procedure: The first image A is the one with the certain degree of relevance to the query example Q. Normally, the low degree of relevance is taken in order to explore the other far areas of the feature space. To determine the second image B, the point representing the

query example Q is regarded as the origin of the multidimensional space and then a point in correspondence to the first image A is found in the feature space. As there, in the most circumstances, may be no image found in the exactly corresponding location, the image with the nearest distance to the corresponding point is seen as the second image B. As image A and B are located in corresponding position of the feature space in terms of the query image Q, the contents of the two images are supposed to contain completely different features. These two images shown at the first page of the search result are used to investigate the user's information need.

- If image A is identified as relevant ones at the feedback round (r), a new query point is estimated using Equation (1) described in Section 4 and those with the shortest distance to the new query point in the feature space will be return to the user. Based on the number of relevance feedback of image A, the number of images (I) returned from image A for the next feedback round $(r+1)$ is calculated as follows:

Figure 2. The proposed relevance feedback scheme

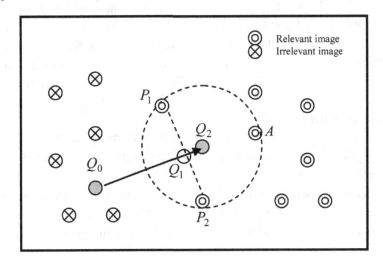

$$I_{r+1} = S \cdot \frac{N}{M} \qquad (2)$$

where S is the number of images shown to the user at the $(r+1)$ round, N represents the number of images which are identified as relevant one and provided from image A, and M represents the number of all images identified as relevant one in this feedback round. The procedure is also applied to calculate the number of images provided based on relevance feedback of image B.

For the estimation of the new query point for the original query point, all relevance feedback, including those from image A and B in the feedback round (r), is taken into account using Equation (1). As the new query point is determined, the number (H) of images provided from the new query point is obtained by Equation (3).

$$H = I_{total} - I_{r+1} \qquad (3)$$

where I_{total} is the total number of images returned to the user.

The proposed learning algorithm and selection strategy is visually illustrated in Figure 2. Q_0 is the original query point and P_1 and P_2 represent those images identified as relevant images. As using only Equation (1) without the selection strategy, the point Q_1 will be the new query point. If the selection strategy is employed, point A would be identified as the relevant one so that point Q_2 will be obtained and comes close to more relevant images.

5.2. Fundamental Requirements

In addition to the proposed scheme, three fundamental requirements have to be made when implementing relevance feedback in the proposed CBIR system. These requirements for images, users, and the system, are specified as follows.

- If candidate images in the database have been displayed to the users for evaluating their relevance to the query example, those images should not be shown in later search results. All images will be eventually displayed once if the search is not terminated.
- Users have to provide relevance feedback by labeling images which are relevant ones to the current query. Since training data is analyzed by finding the correlation among labeled images, the training data should contain more than one image.
- The system has to update the degree of similarity for all candidate images after obtaining the user's relevance feedback. As more images are labeled as relevant and irrelevant, the system has an increasing amount of data available to predict the user's target image or class.

6. EXPERIMENTS

6.1. Mammogram Data Set

The CBIR system using the proposed learning algorithm and selection strategy has been developed to perform the content-based retrieval (see Figure 3). This system allows the user to provide relevance feedbacks by identifying the relevant images to the query example. There are 750 images with the size 200×200 pixels, each image cropped from the Region Of Interest (ROI) of one mammogram. Among the 750 images, 250 images contain calcification phenomenon while other 500 do not.

6.2. Extraction of Calcification Features

Three features extracted to respond the calcification degree for each image are denoted as f_1, f_2 and f_3. (For the method used to extract the three

Figure 3. A search result from the content-based image retrieval system

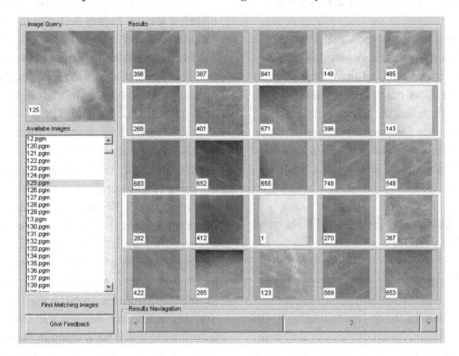

features, please refer to Wei and Li (2006), for detailed descriptions.) The Euclidean distance of the three calcification degrees is then used to compare the similarity of the image content between the query mage and each mammogram in the database.

Figure 4. The comparison of LS and LW in average precision rate (LS = the proposed learning algorithm and selection strategy; LW = the proposed learning algorithm without selection strategy)

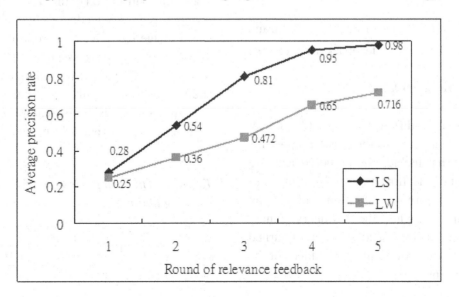

6.3. Process of Relevance Feedback

In the process of relevance feedback, five images with calcification phenomenon were used as query examples to retrieve other similar images. If the returned images have calcification phenomenon, they will be regarded as the relevant images. Five rounds of relevance feedback were conducted for each query example. In each round only relevant images are required to be identified as feedback.

7. PERFORMANCE EVALUATION AND DISCUSSION

7.1. Benchmark

Precision is one of basic measures used in evaluating the effectiveness of a retrieval system. Precision is defined as the ratio of the number of relevant is retrieved to the total number of irrelevant and relevant records retrieved. In addition to the precision rate, a proposed benchmark L for the learning ability to relevance feedback is expressed as follows

$$L = \frac{P_i - P_0}{P_0} \qquad (4)$$

where p_i and p_j are precision rates at the (i) th and (j) th round of relevance feedback, respectively.

7.2. Results and Discussion

In this section two different schemes LS and LW are evaluated for their effectiveness. LS represents the scheme that include the proposed learning algorithm and selection strategy. LW only uses the proposed learning algorithm without any selection strategy, where the new query point is also estimated using Equation (1) and returned images are those with the nearest distance of the new query point.

LS and LW are compared on their precision and learning ability. Figure 4 shows that LS outperforms LW after five rounds of relevance feedback. It was observed that if images provided by selection strategy are identified as relevant ones, the precision rate can bring more relevant images to be shown at the next round. The selection strategy in LS can usher the new query point into the high probability density area while LW has to conduct more rounds only using the learning algorithm.

Table 1 indicates that LS can lead to 1.33, 3.50 5.75, 6.92, and 7.17 times the number of relevant images from the 1st to 5th relevance feedback round as compared with the performance without conducting any relevance feedback. In other words, this CBIR system can only return one relevant image at the initial search (i.e., without conducting any relevance feedback). However, after learning feedback back through five rounds, the same retrieval system can return seven relevant images to the user. Although the learning ability of LW is not as significant as that of LS, LW can also achieve up to 4.97 times retrieval performance at the fifth feedback round.

8. CONCLUSION

The main contribution of this work is to present a complete relevance feedback scheme for content-based image retrieval. The proposed algorithm, as the retrieving process proceeds further, can reduce the influence of the original query point and increases the significance of the centroid of the clusters comprising the features of those relevant images identified in the most recent round of

Table 1. The comparison of LS and LW in learning ability

	1st	2nd	3rd	4th	5th
LS	1.33	3.50	5.75	6.92	7.17
LW	1.08	2.00	2.93	4.42	4.97

search. The proposed selection strategy can assist in finding a good starting point so that the CBIR system can rapidly improve its retrieval ability and reach to the high precision rate through few interactive rounds. In addition, a benchmark is proposed to measure the learning ability to compare the retrieval performance as relevance feedback is incorporated. The performance evaluation shows that the average precision rate of the proposed scheme was 0.98 and the learning ability reach to 7.17 at the fifth rounds of relevance feedback.

REFERENCES

Cox, I. J., Miller, M., Minka, T. P., Papathomas, T., & Yianilos, P. (2000). The Bayesian image retrieval system, PicHunter: Theory, implementation, and psychophysical experiments. *IEEE Transactions on Image Processing*, *9*(1), 20–37. doi:10.1109/83.817596

El-Naqa, I., Yang, Y., Galatsanos, N. P., Nishikawa, R. M., & Wernick, M. N. (2004). A similarity learning approach to content-based image retrieval: Application to digital mammography. *IEEE Transactions on Medical Imaging*, *23*(10), 1233–1244. doi:10.1109/TMI.2004.834601

Huang, H. K. (2003). *PACS, image management, and imaging informatics*. New York, NY: Springer.

Ishikawa, Y., Subramanya, R., & Faloutsos, C. (1998). MindReader: Querying databases through multiple examples. In *Proceedings of the 24th International Conference on Very Large Data Bases*.

Kushki, A., Androutsos, P., Plataniotis, K. N., & Venetsanopoulos, A. N. (2004). Query feedback for interactive image retrieval. *IEEE Transactions on Circuits and Systems for Video Technology*, *14*(5), 644–655. doi:10.1109/TCSVT.2004.826759

Lehmann, T. M., Guld, M. O., Thies, C., Plodowski, B., Keysers, D., Ott, B., et al. (2004). IRMA - content-based image retrieval in medical applications. In *Proceedings of the 14th World Congress on Medical Informatics*

Lew, M. S., Sebe, N., & Eakins, J. P. (2002). Challenges of image and video retrieval. In *Proceedings of the International Conference on Image and Video Retrieval.*

Rocchio, J. J. (1971). Relevance feedback in information retrieval . In Salton, G. (Ed.), *The SMART retrieval system - Experiments in automatic document processing* (pp. 313–323). Upper Saddle River, NJ: Prentice Hall.

Rui, Y., Huang, T. S., & Mehrotra, S. (1998). Human perception subjectivity and relevance feedback in multimedia information retrieval. In *Proceedings of the IS&T/SPIE Storage and Retrieval of Image and Video Database.*

Tong, S., & Chang, E. (2001). Support vector machine active learning for image retrieval. In *Proceedings of the Ninth ACM International Conference on Multimedia.*

Wei, C.-H., & Li, C.-T. (2006). Calcification descriptor and relevance feedback learning algorithms for content-based mammogram retrieval. In *Proceedings of the 8th International Workshop on Digital Mammography.*

Wei, C.-H., & Li, C.-T. (2008). *Content analysis from user's relevance feedback for content-based image retrieval*. Hershey, PA: Idea Group.

Zhong, S., Hongjiang, Z., Li, S., & Shaoping, M. (2003). Relevance feedback in content-based image retrieval: Bayesian framework, feature subspaces, and progressive learning. *IEEE Transactions on Image Processing*, *12*(8), 924–937. doi:10.1109/TIP.2003.815254

This work was previously published in the International Journal of Digital Library Systems, Volume 2, Issue 4, edited by Chia-Hung Wei, pp. 45-53, copyright 2011 by IGI Publishing (an imprint of IGI Global).

Chapter 5
Traffic–Signs Recognition System Based on FCM and Content–Based Image Retrieval

Yue Li
Nankai University, China

Wei Wang
Nankai University, China

ABSTRACT

Artificial intelligent (AI) driving is an emerging technology, freeing the driver from driving. Some techniques for automatically driving have been developed; however, most can only recognize the traffic signs in particular groups, such as triangle signs for warning, circle signs for prohibition, and so forth, but cannot tell the exact meaning of every sign. In this paper, a framework for a traffic system recognition system is proposed. This system consists of two phases. The segmentation method, fuzzy c-means (FCM), is used to detect the traffic sign, whereas the Content-Based Image Retrieval (CBIR) method is used to match traffic signs to those in a database to find the exact meaning of every detected sign.

1. INTRODUCTION

Currently, artificial intelligent (AI) driving has become a emerging technology, freeing the driver from the boring travels. More important, the AI system for automatically driving is supposed to be more secure in theory than the human drivers, because the system will never be too exhaustive to be response the accident in time (Wang, 2006). In automatically driving, Geographic Positioning System has become (GPS) is an essential component, which aids AI to find the correct route and drive to the destination along the route following the directions predefined on the electronic map (Wang, Zeng, & Yang, 2006). In theory, AI system should be able to drive only depending on GPS, following the directions, such as speed limit, one

DOI: 10.4018/978-1-4666-2928-8.ch005

way only, etc., on an electronic map. However, one inevitable situation may happen where the route may be updated due to the engineering request, route adjusting, etc., while the corresponding directions on the e-map will be are updated periodically in half a year. This asynchronization on directions on e-maps and the actual traffic signs fail the AI system from the real time driving unless the system could recognize the traffic signs in the real-time.

Some techniques for automatically driving have been developed in recent years (Blancard, 1992; Kehtarnavaz, Griswold, & Kang, 1993; Kang, Griswold, & Kehtarnavaz, 1994; Kang, 1994; Aoyagi & Asakura, 1996); however, most of these developments can only recognize the traffic signs in particular groups, such as triangle signs for warning, circle signs for prohibition, etc., but could not tell the exact meaning of every sign. Without understanding the exact meaning of every sign, the AI system cannot drive automatically but need the driver to determine the route when it encounters any traffic signs. Subsequently, it is an essential work to design a system could recognize the exact meaning of every traffic sign. In this paper, we propose a framework on traffic system recognition system, which consist of two phrase that a segmentation method is used to detect the traffic sign while the Content-Based Image Retrieval (CBIR) method is used to match the detected traffic signs to the traffic signs in the database in order to find out the exact meaning of every detected sign. The rest of this paper is organized as follows: Section 2 reviews the relevant works on traffic sign recognition, Section 3 presents the proposed method for traffic sign recognition. Section 4 demonstrates the experimental results. Finally, conclusions are made in Section 5.

2. LITERATURE REVIEW

The works on traffic signs recognitions can be traced back to the 1990's. At the very beginning of the studies on traffic signs recognitions, most works were focusing on detecting the traffic signs from a images about real-scene on the street while those method left the contains of the traffic signs not recognized. For example, Blancard (1992) recognized the signs by their color and form. In order to classify the colors, he used a band-pass filter to filter out most color but the chosen red colors attached to a black and white background. Meanwhile, a Sobel filter is applied to the images in order to find the edges inside the images. Associating with the edges, some features, including perimeter, length, gravity center and compactness are calculated and sent to a neural-network to recognitions. The method is fast (about 0.7s ~1s) but quite limited since it can only recognize the red background sign "stop" or similar warning signs while leaving other signs not recognized. Similar method is proposed in (Kehtarnavaz, Griswold, & Kang, 1993; Kang, Griswold, & Kehtarnavaz, 1994; Kang, 1994), where the combination of color and shape processing are used as the feature of the traffic sign. Besides the "stop" sign, Aoyagi and Asakura (1996) present a genetic algorithm to detect speed limit signs. They only work with the bright image due to the limitation of the Hue variations used in their method. After obtaining the Laplacian of the original image, the pixels are thresholded for recognition. However, they method do not take into account different scales for the horizontal and vertical axes; thus they do a matching only with a circular pattern. However, these results still remain on recognize the "stop" or similar red sign only.

As the developing the computer techniques, the AI driving system requests the method to recognize the meaning of variety traffic signs instead of only detecting the sign from the image or only recognizing "stop". Then Kehternavaz and Ahmad (1995) suggest to use the Fourier descriptor as the feature of the traffic sign detected based on the color. The Fourier descriptor is then sent to a neural network for determine the meaning of the signs. However, the time consuming of Kehternavaz and Ahmad's method is 80s, which is far too expensive for a real-time driving system. In de la Escalera and Salichs (1997), in order to obtain a more detailed recognition result, the traffic signs are grouped to triangle, circle and square since these shapes represents warning, prohibition, and instruction respectively. The corners of the edge are extracted as the feature of the signs, then the signs are grouped according to the location of the corners. However, de la Escalera and Salichs (1997) can only recognize the traffic sign accurate to different shapes.

After 2000, more advanced methods are proposed to further assign the traffic signs to more detailed groups of meanings. In methods (de la Escalera & Salichs, 2003; Viola & Jones, 2001; Bahlmann, Zhu, Ramesh, Pellkofer, & Koehler, 2005; Fang, Chen, & Fuh, 2003), a general framework is setup and widely accepted. In the framework, the system is separated to traffic sign segmentation/detection and traffic sign recognition. In de la Escalera and Salichs (2003), a genetic algorithm is applied based on the colors of the pixels to detect the traffic signs in complex situations, and a neural network is used to classify the traffic signs to similar groups sharing similar colors then the detected signs will be assigned to one of the groups by the neural network. In Viola and Jones (2001) and Bahlmann, Zhu, Ramesh, Pellkofer, and Koehler (2005) the AdaBoost method, based on the wavelet features of the Harr transform is applied for traffic signs detection while a Bayesian classifier with temporal hypothesis fusion is used to partition the traffic signs to different groups, and determines which group the detected sign belongs to. In Fang, Chen, and Fuh (2003) the authors compute a feature map of the entire image frame based on color and gradient information, while incorporating a geometry model of signs. Method in Fang, Chen, and Fuh (2003) requires a manual threshold tuning, and the method is reported to be computationally rather expensive. All of the aforementioned approaches (de la Escalera & Salichs, 2003; Viola & Jones, 2001;

Bahlmann, Zhu, Ramesh, Pellkofer, & Koehler, 2005; Fang, Chen, & Fuh, 2003) could not match one detected sign exactly to an exact meaning but a group of similar signs in the database, unless every traffic sign is classified as a solo-group. On the other hand, classifying every traffic sign as a solo-group greatly increases the computation load of the system and causes great time consumption.

Beside the traditional methods that separate the recognition system to two phrase, detection and recognition, Goedeme (2008) use local features Speeded Up Robust Features (SURF) to detect and recognize the traffic signs at the same time. The SURF feature represents the interest points inside the images while these points are extracted and matched with the visual word vocabulary. As a result, the signs consist of the interest points are linked to and explained by the visual word and hence recognized. However, the drawbacks of this method is that without the traffic sign detection phrase, the SURF feature is not robust enough against the noise and distortions and hence the input image must be an captured in an ideal situation.

3. METHOD PRESENTATION

The proposed scheme consists of two essential phrases, traffic sign segmentation and traffic-sign recognition. In the first phrase, the traffic sign must be detected from the real-scenes. Here the real scene refers to the scene captured from the built-in camera in the car. These scenes may include variety background and foreground, be deflected or faked by the lights, or contains incomplete traffic signs cut by the object around the signs. Therefore, detecting the traffic-signs from the real-scene image becomes a tough task. On the other hand, the segmentation algorithm employed in the driving system must be fast enough to satisfy the request on the real-time driving. In order to solve overcome these difficulties, the proposed scheme separates the segmentation phrase and the recognition phrase into two independent sections and the algorithms used in either section can be replaced without the necessarily of adjusting the other sections. This design consequently improved the flexibility of the proposed scheme to advanced algorithms. If advanced algorithms on either segmentation or recognition are developed in recent future, the ones used in the corresponding section in proposed scheme can be easily replaced while the performance of the proposed scheme will be correspondingly improved. Figure 1 demonstrates the framework of the proposed scheme.

In Figure 1, the image is firstly acquired by the built-in camera and then transmitted to the real-time segmentation system, and the output, which is highly possible to be a traffic sign, is further recognized by the recognition system and saved in the memory. In the scheme, fuzzy c-means (FCM) (Bezdek, Ehrlich, & Full, 1984) clustering algorithm is used as the candidate segmentation algorithm. According to the design of the proposed scheme, the segmentation algorithm is independent to the recognition algorithm, and hence, FCM algorithm can be replaced by any other advanced unsupervised segmentation algorithm while the frame of the proposed scheme is maintained. After the segmentation, the possible traffic mark is further send to the recognition system based on

CBIR system (Wei, Li, Chau, & Li, 2009; Wei, 2008), so that the system can identify the traffic signs by querying the system.

3.1. Traffic Sign Segmentation

The segmentation method for detecting the traffic signs from the images are discussed in this section. As discussed in the previous section, any unsupervised segmentation algorithm can be employed under the frame proposed in this paper. Here the algorithm is request to be unsupervised due to the complexity of the contents in the images about the real-scene on the road. The user can hardly obtain enough *prior*-information on how many regions representing different objects exist in the images, and hence, the employed segmentation method is requested to be a unsupervised method which could determine the regions without pre-acquired information. After different regions are classified, the next step in the detection is to judge whether the detected region, called Region of Interest (ROS), contains the traffic signs. The segmentation method and the corresponding ROI identification methods are presented as follows.

Figure 1. Process of image recognition and retrieval using features

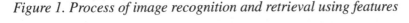
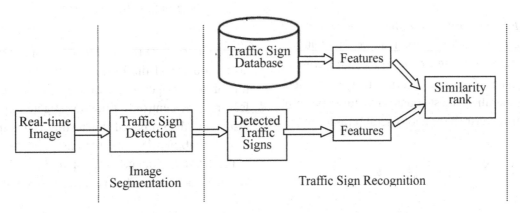

3.1.1. FCM Method for Traffic Sign Segmentation

In the proposed method, fuzzy c-means (FCM) method is used for segmentation (Bezdek, Ehrlich, & Full, 1984). The FCM method is intended to assign a membership of each regions to each pixel and separate all pixels of the image into different groups, where the number of the groups could be predetermined.

Let $X = \{I(x,y)\}$ is the set of the intensity values of the pixels in the images, where the images are transferred from RGB images to gray value images. Then a pixel $I(x_i, y_i)$ belongs to group C^j is represented by a probability p_i^j, where

$$p_i^j = p(I(x_i, y_i) \in C^j) \tag{1}$$

The cluster C^j is grouped by the intensity values, and at the very beginning, we have all p_i^j set randomly, and the centroid c^j of the each group C^j also set randomly. Then FCM algorithm is best description of recasting conditions for grouping the intensity values that C^j satisfies

$$\begin{cases} C^j \neq \phi \\ C^j \cap C^i = \phi \\ \cup C^j = E \end{cases} \tag{2}$$

where E is the entire set of the pixels.

After the random initialization, FCM iteratively improve p_i^j and c^j until they converge to stable values. The iteration is normally controlled by the generalized least-square error function with p_i^j determined in the previous iteration as followed

$$D_m(i,j) = \sum_{i=i}^{N} \sum_{j=1}^{K} \left(p_i^j\right)^m \left\| I(x_i, y_i) - c^j \right\|_2 \tag{3}$$

In Equation (3), D_m is the square distance for a cluster j, m counts the iterations, and K is the number of clusters predetermined by the users. $\|\cdot\|$ calculates the 2-order form of the equations. By adapting p_i^j and c^j in each iteration, D_m achieves the minimal value smaller than the threshold, and then FCM gives the best partition of the input images

3.1.2. Traffic Sign Identified

After the segmentation, the output image may be separated into several connected region. Although the number of the clusters, m, in FCM should be pre-determined, the connected regions inside the images are still not cleared. FCM only partitions the pixels inside the image into groups according to their intensities, where the pixels in the same groups own similar intensities and are marked with the same group number. Whereas these pixels are distributed through the image and consequently, these pixels in the same group may formed variety regions in the image (see Figures 2 and 3 in the Experiment Section). On the other hand, the traffic signs must be one certain connect region containing meaningful contexts or marks. Therefore, the traffic sign region must be further identified from all of the grouped regions. The information about location, shape and color are used to determined whether the region represent traffic signs.

A. Location of the Traffic Signs

In the video, most the traffic signs appear firstly at the top 1/5 of the images, counting from the top of the image. Therefore, according to this features, the centroid of the investigate region is tested and the output of this testing is a generalized probability describe how far the centroid is to the 1/5 of the image from top to down. Let the y_c be y-coordinate of the centroid, calculated as

Figure 2. Segmentation result of the image with different initialization group numbers

(a) Original Image

(b) Segmented Images with initialized group number equal to 2

(c) Segmented Images with initialized group number equal to 4

Figure 3. Traffic region identification result

(a) Image with connect region highlighted

(b) Identified Traffic Region, ranked by likelihood

$$y_c^m = \frac{1}{M} \sum_{y_i \in R_m} y_i \qquad (4)$$

where M is the number of pixels in the region R_m. Please notice that R_m is a connected region containing pixels with similar intensities, and many R_m form a group C_k, with is the output of FCM. Then the generalized probability for the region R_m is calculated as follow,

$$p_l = 1 - \left(\frac{y_c^m - y_{1/5}}{y_{1/5}} \right)^2 \qquad (5)$$

where $y_{1/5}$ is the coordinate of the top 1/5 of the images.

B. Color of the Region

From the normal situations, the most frequently used color in the traffic signs are black, white, blue, red, yellow, since red, yellow and blue has the longest frequency and hence the traffic signs in these color are most attractive to the drivers and black and white provides strongest contract to the formal colors (Kehtarnavaz, Griswold, & Kang, 1993; Kang, Griswold, & Kehtarnavaz, 1994). Therefore, a generalized probability p_c is determined how a regions could be a region for traffic signs from the colors.

Firstly, a color histogram is calculated as H, and the bins representing black, white, blue, red, and yellow are calculated respectively, as h_{bk}, h_w, h_{be}, h_r and h_y. Then the probability p_c is calculated as

$$p_c = \frac{h_{bk} + h_w + h_{be} + h_r + h_y}{M}$$

C. Shape of the Region

It is obvious and understandable that the shape of the region are normally circle, triangle or square (Bahlmann, Zhu, Ramesh, Pellkofer, & Koehler, 2005). Therefore, the region containing traffic signs should be one of the shapes. We use Zernike (Papakostas, Boutalis, Karras, & Mertzios, 2007) as the globe feature for the shape measurement. The Zernike moments derive from a set of complex polynomials orthogonal over the interior of a unit circle and defined in polar coordinates. As Zernike moments are the projection of the image function on orthogonal basis functions, Zernike moments can overcome the drawbacks of information redundancy present in the popular geometric moments.

The Zernike moments derive from a set of complex polynomials orthogonal over the interior of a unit circle $U : x^2 + y^2 \leq 1$ and defined in polar coordinates. The form of a 2-dimensional Zernike polynomial $V_{n,m}$ is expressed as

$$V_{n,m}(\rho,\theta) = R_{n,m}(\rho) \exp(jm\theta), \qquad (6)$$

where n and m are called order and repetition, respectively. The order n is a non-negative integer, and the repetition m is an integer satisfying $n - |m| =$ an even number and $|m| \leq n$. j is an imaginary unit $\sqrt{-1}$. $R_{n,m}(\rho)$ is the 1-dimensional radial polynomial, which is defined as

$$R_{n,m}(\rho) =$$
$$\sum_{s=0}^{\frac{(n-|m|)}{2}} (-1)^s \frac{(n-s)!}{s! \left(\frac{n+|m|}{2} - s \right)! \left(\frac{n-|m|}{2} - s \right)!} \rho^{n-2s}$$
$$\qquad (7)$$

As the Zernike moments are the projection of image $I_i = f(x_i, y_i)$ onto these orthogonal basis functions, image I_0 can be decomposed into a weighted sum of the Zernike polynomials

$$f = \sum_{n=1}^{\infty} \sum_{m=-n}^{n} A_{n,m} V_{n,m} \qquad (8)$$

where $A_{n,m}$ are the Zernike moments, which are the coefficients of the Zernike polynomials. The Zernike moments of image $f(x,y)$ with continuous intensity are calculated according to the following equation

$$A_{n,m} = \frac{n+1}{\pi} \iint_U f(x,y) V_{n,m}(\rho,\theta) dx dy \qquad (9)$$

As discussed before, Zernike moment is an ideal moment to describe the shape of the regions. In the identification for the regions of traffic signs, three standard shapes, as circle, triangle and square, are filled in black and take as the input to Zernike moment calculation, and the corresponding output, R_c, R_t, R_s, are taken as the standard moment. Then the generalized probability of shape descriptor are calculated as

$$p_s = \frac{\|Ri - R_j\|}{\|R_j\|},$$

where

$$j = \arg\min_{j \in \{c,t,s\}} \|R_i - R_j\|$$

With the determined generalized probability p_l, p_c and p_c, the final probability of whether a region being a traffic sign can be easily calculated as

$$p = \frac{1}{3}(p_l + p_c + p_s)$$

If p is higher than the threshold t, then the region is detected as a traffic region, otherwise, it will be identified as an irrelevant region.

3.2. Traffic Sign Identification

After ROI is detected, the next phrase is to identify the contents inside the ROI. In the identification, the CBIR system (Bezdek, Ehrlich, & Full, 1984; Wei, Li, Chau, & Li, 2009) is applied. The standard traffic sign database are setup and saved in the AI system database, meanwhile the features of the traffic signs are also extracted and saved in the database. Then the features describing the ROI is extracted and compared to the features in the database representing different traffic signs, and the ROI is matched to one traffic signs with the highest similarity.

3.2.1. Feature Extraction

The features used to describe the traffic signs can be classified to the globe feature and local features. The global feature vectors capture the gross essence of the shapes while the local feature vectors capture the interior details of the shapes from the image. The globe feature, used in the proposed scheme is the Zernike moment, which has been discussed in Section 3.1. The local features in the scheme includes Fourier Descriptor and the Curvature Scale Space (CSS) descriptor. These features are defined as local feature because these features focus on examining the points on edges of the objects inside the region and owning maximal or minimal curvature.

A. Fourier Descriptor

Suppose that the boundary of the object O is described by n pixels numbered from 0 to $n-1$. Firstly, each point along the boundary is represented by means of chain code (Zhang & Lu, 2002). Then, the position (x_k, y_k) of the k-th pixel along the boundary can be transformed in the complex form, $s(k) = x(k) + jy(k)$, where $k = 0, 1, 2, \cdots, K-1$. Fourier descriptors $a(u)$ can be obtained computing the discrete Fourier transform of $s(k)$ by the following equation,

$$a(u) = \sum_{k=0}^{k-1} s(k)e^{-j2\pi uk/K} \qquad (10)$$

where $k = 0, 1, 2, \cdots, K - 1$. The resulting coefficient vector can be used as a feature vector, representing the shape of the object O. Since Fourier descriptors involve chain code presentation of the contour (Forsyth & Ponce, 2003), they are therefore sensitive to the selection of the starting point for the chain coding and rotation of an image object. In addition, Fourier descriptor is poor in describing disjoint shape, and slight variations of the object boundary can cause significant changes.

B) Curvature Scale Space (CSS) Descriptor

The development of curvature scale space descriptor begins with applying Gaussian smoothing progressively on the boundary of an image object. Then, the inflection points are obtained by finding the curvature zero-crossings of a curve, which are points where the sign of curvature changes. Given a plane curve $y = f(x)$, the curvature k can be expressed as

$$k = \frac{y''}{\left(1 + \left(y'\right)^2\right)^{\frac{3}{2}}} \qquad (11)$$

With different amount of convolutions on the contour, different number of the inflection points can be obtained to represent the shape information of the image object.

3.2.2. Feature Comparison

The most important part of the image retrieval stage is the feature matching. In the proposed algorithm, a multi-level matching strategy was used to enhance the accuracy of the search. There are altogether 3 features in 259 dimensions, including 15 Zernike moments, 4 groups of Fourier Descrip-

tor in 51 dimensions each, and a 36-dimension vector representing the CSS for each image stored in the database. In order to improve the system performance, the features are compared separately in different levels.

The proposed algorithm utilises two levels of feature matching. The first level utilises Zernike moments during the match. Meanwhile, the second level utilises standard deviation of curvature, the mean and standard deviation of centroid distance in order to match the subtle features of the traffic signs. By utilizing the Euclidean distance to compute the similarity between the query image features and the features stored in the database in each level, the similarity between two images can be obtained. In order to discriminate the relevant images from the irrelevant images through the distance computation, the distance difference is normalized into the range [0,1] and a threshold of 0.3 is set up for both levels. In other words, if the distance difference obtained for a candidate image is greater than 0.3 in either one of the levels, a penalty value 1 will be added to its current distance value, whereas a penalty value 2 will be added to its current distance value if the values obtained are greater than 0.3 in both levels. The strategy ensures that the relevance is determined by both the two-level features, and precludes extreme cases. The final value obtained for each image can be used to rank the images in ascending order. The candidate images with a smaller distance are placed on the top while the candidate images with a larger distance are placed at the bottom.

4. EXPERIMENTS AND DISCUSSION

4.1. Traffic Sign Database Setup

In the experiment, we first set up the original traffic sign database. We obtained 30 common traffic-sign images with the size 30 x 30 pixels. As seen in Table 1, these images are in white/ yellow and black background which means no need of image segmentation. They are stored in the database with their features and annotations for later recognition.

4.2. Experiments for Traffic Sign Segmentation

After setting up the database, the next step is to detect the traffic signs in the images with variety objects inside. Figure 2 demonstrates a images captured by the camera, and it is clearly that this image contains many objects on the road, including trees, other vehicles, buildings, etc. We use FCM to segment this image. As presented in Eq 2, all of the pixels are partitioned into number of groups where the number must be predetermined. In the experiments, we choose the group number to be 2 and 4 respectively for testing. In the image demonstrated in Figure 2(b), the pixels are grouped into 2 groups and these pixels are represented as black and with respectively. While in Figure 2(c), the pixels are partitioned into 4 groups, and hence the pixels are marked with four different gray scale values from white to blacks. It is obvious that the grouping the pixels into 2 groups is enough to find two separated connected regions for the traffic signs, whereas grouping the pixels into 4 groups may cause some noise, marked as different gray values, inside the traffic sign region. This noise indicates the inaccuracy and distortion in the segmentation. As a result, this experiment proves

segments the image with input group number as 2 is enough for detection.

This experiment also tests the time complexity of FCM method since FCM is rather a well-known time-consuming method. In the experiment, the input image is in the resolution of 372*500 pixels, and the pixels are partitioned into 2 groups. On a PC with CPU Pentium Core 2, RAM 2 GB, the time consumption is 5.14 second. If the system use image with smaller resolution, the time consuming can be further decreased.

The next step is testing the performance of correctly identify the traffic region from the segmented regions. The system further identifies 13 regions with the size limitation of 290 pixels, which are marked as white in Figure 3(a), with identification described in Section 3.1.2, the three regions with highest likelihood of being traffic region are listed in Figure 3(b) by the rank. In this result, the first two regions are correctly identified while the third region are erroneous identified due to the similar color and shape of this region. The identification operation is finished in less than 1 second.

4.3. Experiments for Traffic Sign Identification

With the three identified traffic regions, the system further recognize the traffic sign by the CBIR system. Table 2 lists the recognition results. In the recognition result, we can see that the first

Table 1. Original traffic-sign images in the database

Index	No.1	No.2	No.3	No.4	No.5	...
Examples						...
Annotation	Prohibition: No pedestrain	Warning: junction of three roads	Prohibition: No bicycle	Warning: junction of four roads	Forbidden: No vechiles	...

and second traffic sign are correctly recognized while the third region is erroneously recognized, because region 3 is not a correct traffic sign.

Since the features of the traffic signs are pre-extracted and saved in the database, the time consumption on the recognition is rather small, which is about 1.1 seconds. However, as the size of the database grows from 30 traffic signs, the time consumption on recognition may be reasonably increased.

4.4. Discussion

Experiment in Sections 4.2 and 4.3 prove the effectiveness of the propose scheme, and the speed of this scheme is acceptable for less than 10 seconds in total. Compared to the method only detect the traffic signs, which cost about 1s or less, the time consumption in the proposed scheme is rather expensive. However, it is noticeable that the proposed scheme is more advanced to recognize the exact meaning of the traffic sign instead of find out the groups that a traffic signs belonging to. Therefore, the time consumption is reasonable for this more advanced performance. Meanwhile, compared to the traditional methods mainly based on the characters and must consider the motion features that strongly related to the speed of the vehicle and the angles of the camera, the proposed

scheme can generally correctly recognized the traffic signs in the traffic sign recognition phrase.

On the other hand, it is obvious that the bottle-neck of the proposed scheme is the segmentation method from two sides. Firstly, the experiment takes about 8~10 second for the entire recognition operations depending on the images, where the most time is spend on segmentation. Subsequently, if other unsupervised method can give out similar result in short time, the total time consumption may be greatly decreased. Secondly, in the previous experiment, a type I error (an error represented by false positive rate) happens due to the erroneously segmentation. With an erroneous input, the CBIR system could impossible to recognize any correct traffic signs. As a result, it is predictable that a more accurate segmentation result can enhance the performance of the system. On the other hand, in the frame of the proposed scheme, the segmentation method and the recognition method are independent to each other. Therefore, if a faster but more accurate unsupervised segmentation method is developed and replace the FCM method used in the current scheme, then the performance of the system can be easily improved.

Table 2. Recognition result

ROI			
Recog-nition Result			

5. CONCLUSION

In this paper, we propose a framework on traffic system recognition system, which consist of two phrase that FCM method is used to detect the traffic sign while the Content-Based Image Retrieval (CBIR) method is used to match the detect traffic signs to the traffic signs in the database in order to find out the exact meaning of every detected sign. Compared to the traditional method, the proposed scheme can extract the exact meaning of the traffic signs in the real-scene image on the road. Experiment proves the effectiveness of the proposed method.

ACKNOWLEDGMENT

This paper is supported by the "Fundamental Research Funds for the Central Universities".

REFERENCES

Aoyagi, Y., & Asakura, T. (1996). A study on traffic sign recognition in scene image using genetic algorithms and neural networks. In *Proceedings of the 22nd International Conference on Industrial Electronics, Control, and Instrumentation.*

Bahlmann, C., Zhu, Y., Ramesh, V., Pellkofer, M., & Koehler, T. (2005). A system for traffic sign detection, tracking, and recognition using color, shape, and motion information. In *Proceedings of the Intelligent Vehicles Symposium* (pp. 255-260).

Bezdek, J. C., Ehrlich, R., & Full, W. (1984). FCM: The fuzzy c-means clustering algorithm. *Computers & Geosciences*, *10*(2-3), 191–203. doi:10.1016/0098-3004(84)90020-7

Blancard, M. (1992). Road sign recognition: A study of vision-based decision making for road environment recognition. In Masaki, I. (Ed.), *Vision based vehicle guidance* (pp. 162–175). Berlin, Germany: Springer-Verlag. doi:10.1007/978-1-4612-2778-6_7

de la Escalera, A., & Salichs, A. M. (1997). Road traffic sign detection and classification. *IEEE Transactions on Industrial Electronics*, *44*(6). doi:10.1109/41.649946

de la Escalera, A., & Salichs, A. M. (2003). Traffic sign recognition and analysis for intelligent vehicles. *Image and Vision Computing*, *21*, 247–258. doi:10.1016/S0262-8856(02)00156-7

Fang, C.-Y., Chen, S.-W., & Fuh, C.-S. (2003). Road-sign detection and tracking. *IEEE Transactions on Vehicular Technology*, *52*(5), 1329–1341. doi:10.1109/TVT.2003.810999

Forsyth, D. A., & Ponce, J. (2003). *Computer vision: A modern approach*. Upper Saddle River, NJ: Prentice Hall.

Goedemé, T. (2008). Traffic sign recognition with constellations of visual words. In *Proceedings of the International Conference on Informatics in Control, Automation and Robotics* (pp. 222-227).

Kang, D. (1994). *Invariant pattern recognition system based on sequential processing and geometrical transformation* (Unpublished doctoral dissertation). Texas A&M University, College Station, TX.

Kang, D., Griswold, N., & Kehtarnavaz, N. (1994). An invariant traffic sign recognition system based on sequential color processing and geometrical transformation. In *Proceedings of the IEEE Southwest Symposium on Image Analysis* (pp. 88-93).

Kehtarnavaz, N., & Ahmad, A. (1995). Traffic sign recognition in noisy outdoor scenes. In *Proceedings of the Intelligent Vehicles Symposium.*

Kehtarnavaz, N., Griswold, N., & Kang, D. (1993). Stop-sign recognition based on color and shape processing. *Machine Vision and Applications, 6,* 206–208. doi:10.1007/BF01212298

Papakostas, G. A., Boutalis, Y. S., Karras, D. A., & Mertzios, B. G. (2007). A new class of Zernike moments for computer vision applications. *Information Sciences, 177*(13), 2802–2819. doi:10.1016/j.ins.2007.01.010

Viola, P., & Jones, M. (2001). *Robust real-time object detection (Tech. Rep. No. CRL 2001/01).* Cambridge, MA: Cambridge Research Laboratory.

Wang, F.-Y. (2006). Driving into the future with ITS. *IEEE Intelligent Systems, 21*(3), 94–95. doi:10.1109/MIS.2006.45

Wang, F.-Y., Zeng, D., & Yang, L. (2006). Smart cars on smart roads: An IEEE intelligent transportation systems society. *IEEE Pervasive Computing / IEEE Computer Society [and] IEEE Communications Society, 5*(4), 68–69. doi:10.1109/MPRV.2006.84

Wei, C.-H. (2008). *Content-based mammogram retrieval* (Unpublished doctoral dissertation). University of Warwick, Coventry, UK.

Wei, C.-H., Li, Y., Chau, W. Y., & Li, C.-T. (2009). Trademark image retrieval: Using synthetic features for describing global shape and interior structure of trademark. *Pattern Recognition, 42*(3), 386–394. doi:10.1016/j.patcog.2008.08.019

Zhang, D., & Lu, G. (2002). A comparative study of curvature scale space and fourier descriptors for shape-based image retrieval. *Journal of Visual Communication and Image Representation, 14*(1), 39–57. doi:10.1016/S1047-3203(03)00003-8

This work was previously published in the International Journal of Digital Library Systems, Volume 2, Issue 4, edited by Chia-Hung Wei, pp. 1-12, copyright 2011 by IGI Publishing (an imprint of IGI Global).

Section 2
Storage

Chapter 6
Virtual Magnifier–Based Image Resolution Enhancement

Lung-Chun Chang
Ching Yun University, Taiwan

Hui-Yun Hu
Ching Yun University, Taiwan

Yueh-Jyun Lee
Ching Yun University, Taiwan

Yu-Ching Hsu
Ching Yun University, Taiwan

Yi-Syuan Wu
Ching Yun University, Taiwan

ABSTRACT

To obtain high resolution images, some low resolution images must be processed and enhanced. In the literature, the mapping from the low resolution image to the high resolution image is a linear system and it is only enlarged by an integer scale. This paper presents a real scaling algorithm for image resolution enhancement. Using a virtual magnifier, an image resolution can be enhanced by a real scale number. Experimental results demonstrate that the proposed algorithm has a high quality for the enlarged image in the human visual system.

INTRODUCTION

For image analysis, we often want to investigate more closely a specific area within the image. To do this we need to enlarge the specific area. In the video sequence, for a specific area within an image frame, we can *zoom* in on it by enlarged it. The enlarged area can be recognized efficiently.

Image resolution enhancement refers to image processing algorithm which produces a high quality and high resolution image from a low quality and low resolution image. It includes two procedures. The first is the problem for finding a mapping between high resolution image and low resolution image. The second is the problem for calculating all the pixel values of the high resolution image from its low resolution version. In the literature, the mapping between them is always chosen by a linear mapping system. However, for the CCD (charged-coupled devices) camera, the resolution of enlarged images is produced by the lens. The linear mapping system is not suitable. In addition, due to the linear mapping system,

DOI: 10.4018/978-1-4666-2928-8.ch006

the scale of the image to be enlarged is always an integer scale once. Thus, in this paper, we will focus on the design of the mapping system and the mapping system can enlarge the image by a real scale. In the second procedure, image interpolation addresses the problem of generating a high resolution image from its low resolution version. Conventional linear interpolation schemes (e.g., bilinear and bicubic) based on space-invariant models fail to capture the fast evolving statistics around edges and annoying artifacts. Linear interpolation is generally preferred not for the performance but for computational simplicity. Many algorithms (Algazi, Ford, & Potharlanka, 1991; Carrato, Ramponi, & Marsi, 1996; Early & Long, 2001; Lee & Paik, 1993; Li & Orchard, 2001; Nguyen, Milanfar, & Golub, 2001) have been proposed to improve the subjective quality of the interpolated images by imposing more accurate models.

The magnifier is a perfect optics tool. It is easy to enlarge the resolution of images by a real scale. In this paper, a virtual magnifier is constructed and simulated. Using the virtual magnifier, the mapping between high resolution pixels and low resolution pixels is obtained. Further, a traditional interpolation algorithm (Gomes, Darsa, Costa, & Velho, 1999) is applied into the mapping of the high resolution image and low resolution image. Under three real images, experimental results demonstrate that the proposed algorithm has a high quality in the human visual system.

The remainder of this paper is organized as follows. In the next section, we describe the imaging model by using a magnifier. The proposed algorithm is then presented, followed by experimental results illustrated to demonstrate the advantages of the proposed algorithm. Finally, some conclusions are addressed.

IMAGING MODEL

In the optics, the trace of a ray of light is a straight line. When the ray passes through a medium, the rule of the refraction is followed by the Snell's Law (Jenkins & White, 1976; Meyer-Arendt, 1989; Pedrotti & Pedrotti, 1987) and the Snell's Law is defined below.

Law of Refraction (Snell's Law) (Pedrotti & Pedrotti, 1987): When a ray of light is refracted at an in θ_1 and θ_2 denote the incident angle and the refraction angle, respectively, n_1 and n_2 denote the two media with refractive indices. Figure 1 shows a ray of light passing from medium n_1 into a optically denser medium n_2, where N is a normal line. According to the Snell's Law, an object M with height h is located at the left side of the lens and passes through the lens, then the imaging object M'' with height h'' is formed on the right side of the lens (see Figure 2). In Figure 2, L_1 and L_2 denote the left spherical surface and the right spherical surface of the lens, respectively.

Image resolution enhancement refers to image processing algorithm which and θ_2 denote the angles of the incidence and refraction, respectively. Angles of the incidence and refraction are positive when the angle from the normal line to the ray must be rotated counterclockwise. φ_1 $(.\varphi_2.)$ denotes the angle of the axis and the inci-

Figure 1. Refraction of light

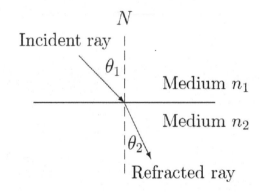

Figure 2. The imaging model

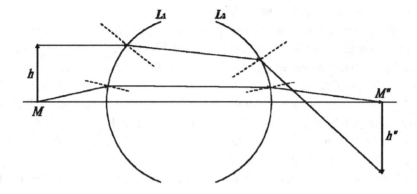

Figure 3. The construction for refraction at a single spgerical surface

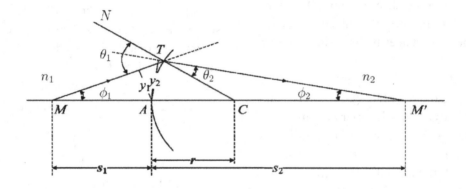

Figure 4. The transition model

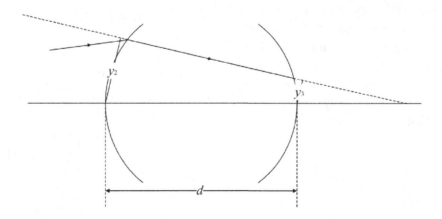

Figure 5. The imaging position

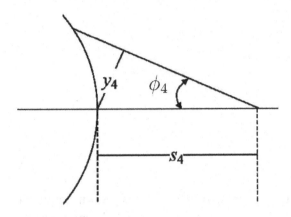

dent ray (refracted ray). φ_1. and φ_2. are positive when the angle from the axis to the ray must be rotated clockwise. s_1 (s_2) denotes the distance between the spherical surface at A and M (M'). r is a radius of the spherical surface.

A line with length y_1 (y_2) passes through A and is a vertical line of the incident ray (refracted ray). Thus,

$$y_1 = s_1 \sin |\varphi_1|.$$

In addition, y_1 can be written by

$$y_1 = r \sin \theta_1 + r \sin \varphi_1$$

$$\Rightarrow \sin \theta_1 = \frac{y_1}{r} - \sin \varphi_1.$$

By using the Snell's Law,

$$\sin \theta_2 = \frac{n_1}{n_2} \sin \theta_1.$$

Then, the angle of θ_2 is obtained by applying the inverse sine function. The angle $\angle ACT$ (as shown in Figure 3) is equal to $\theta_2 + \varphi_2$. And, θ_1 is the sum of $-\varphi_1$ and $\angle ACT$. Thus,

$$\theta_1 = -\varphi_1 + \angle ACT = -\varphi_1 + (\theta_2 + \varphi_2).$$

Then, $\varphi_2 = \theta_1 + \varphi_1 - \theta_2$. After obtaining the values of θ_2 and φ_2, we can calculate $y_2 = r \sin \varphi_2 + r \sin \theta_2$. separating two media of index n_1 and n_2.

In the refraction of the right single spherical surface, the refracted ray of the left single spherical surface is the incident ray of the right single spherical surface. Suppose the distance of the two

Figure 6. The imaging model of a 2-D image

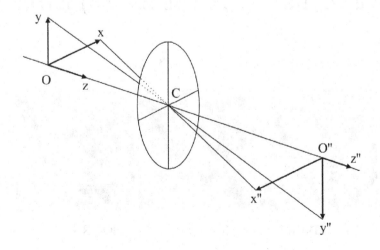

Figure 7. The process of the proposed algorithm

$$I_H \xrightarrow{\text{coordinate mapping}} I_L$$
$$I_H(x_H, y_H) \longmapsto I_L(x_L, y_L)$$

$$\left\downarrow \begin{array}{l}\text{generating the gray level}\\ \text{of the point at } (x_L, y_L)\end{array}\right.$$

$$G_H \xleftarrow{\text{gray level mapping}} G_L$$
$$G_H(x_H, y_H) \longleftarrow G_L(x_L, y_L)$$

single spherical surfaces is d (see Figure 4). The value of y_3 is obtained by

$$y_3 = y_2 - d \sin \varphi_2.$$

Further, the process of refraction of the right single spherical surface is same as that of the left single spherical surface. Note that the radius of the right single spherical surface is negative. Finally, the refracted ray of the right single spherical surface is found, and the value of y_4 and the angle of φ_4 are obtained (see Figure 5). The position of the imaging object is given by

$$s_4 = \frac{y_4}{\sin \varphi_4}.$$

Figure 8. Three real images with size 64×64

(a) Lena.　(b) Pepper.　(c) F16.

Figure 9. Three enlarged Lena images with size 128×128

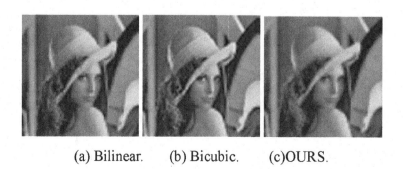

(a) Bilinear.　(b) Bicubic.　(c)OURS.

Figure 10. Three enlarged pepper images with size 128×128

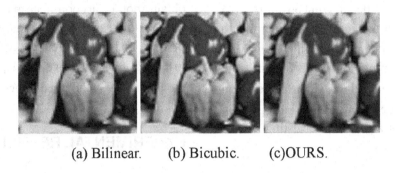

(a) Bilinear.　　(b) Bicubic.　　(c)OURS.

Figure 11. Three enlarged F16 images with size 128×128

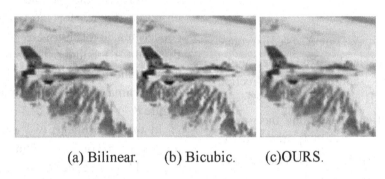

(a) Bilinear.　　(b) Bicubic.　　(c)OURS.

Figure 12. Three enlarged images with size 145×145

(a) Lena.　　(b) Pepper.　　(c) F16.

In this imaging model, the effect of the enlarged scale of object is different when the position of the object is different. So, the value of the enlarged scale is a real value. After presenting the imaging model, an image to be enlarged will be presented in next section.

PROPOSED ALGORITHM

According to the different position of an object, the object is enlarged by different real scale. A 1-D object to be enlarged has been presented by using a lens. In this section, the concept described in Section II is applied to the superresolution of a 2-D image. Figure 6 shows the imaging model of a 2-D image.

Suppose a low resolution image I_L is enlarged by r, we can calculate the imaging position of the enlarged high resolution image I_H. According to the reverse property of a ray of light, we can find the coordinate mapping from I_H to I_L. Thus, the center of I_H is found and we put the center O on the optical axis (see Figure 6). For each pixel in I_H, our proposed algorithm consisting of two steps is shown below.

Step 1: (Mapping the Coordinate from the High Resolution Image to the Low Resolution Image)

For the pixel at (x_H, y_H) in I_H, we first rotate the point to the *y*-axis and keep the rotated angle. Using the imaging system described in Section II, the rotated point is mapped to I_L by passing through the magnifier. Then, using the rotated angle of that pixel at (x_H, y_H) in I_H, the mapping point in I_L is rotated back and then its coordinate in I_L is (x_L, y_L). Here, x_H and y_H are integer values and x_L and y_L are real values.

Step 2: (Generating the Gray Level of the High Resolution Pixel)

After obtaining the point at (x_L, y_L) in I_L, we use some nearest integer points in I_L to generate the gray level of the point. Here, the bilinear interpolation method and the bicubic interpolation method are applied. The bilinear interpolation method determines the gray level from the weighted average of the four closest pixels to the specified point at (x_L, y_L) in I_L, and assigns that value to the point at (x_H, y_H) in I_H. The bicubic interpolation method uses a 4×4 pixel neighborhood to calculate the gray level of the point at (x_L, y_L) in I_L, and assigns that gray level to the point at (x_H, y_H) in I_H.

In summary, Figure 7 shows the process of the proposed superresolution algorithm. Using the magnifier to enlarge an image, in Step 1, we can obtain a nonlinear coordinate mapping. According to the nonlinear coordinate mapping, each point in I_H is mapped to a real coordinate in I_L. Due to the real coordinate of each mapped point in I_L, the feature of an enlarged image is clearer.

EXPERIMENTAL RESULTS

In this section, some experiments are carried out to demonstrate the performance among the bilinear algorithm, the bicubic algorithm, and our proposed (OURS for short) algorithm. All the concerning algorithms are implemented using Borland C++ builder. Three real images, Lena, pepper, and F16, with size 64×64 are used as the benchmarks in the experiment and shown in Figure 8.

In the experiment, two enlarged scales are used, scale = 2 or 2.265. Figure 9, Figure 10, and Figure 11 include the comparison of the portions of the enlarged images with scale by 2. It is observed that our proposed algorithm has a high quality in the human visual system when compared to the previous two algorithms. In addition, our proposed algorithm can enlarge an image by a real scale. Figure 12 shows the images to be enlarged with scale by 2.265. From the experiment results, our proposed algorithm can obtain the enlarged image with a real scale number easily.

CONCLUSION

Based on the magnifier model, this paper has presented an optimal scaling algorithm for image resolution enhancement. Some experimental results have been carried out to confirm the good performance of our proposed method in terms of image quality among our proposed algorithm and the previous algorithms.

REFERENCES

Algazi, V. R., Ford, G. E., & Potharlanka, R. (1991). Directional interpolation of images based on visual properties and rank order filtering. In *Proceedings of the IEEE Int. Conf. Acoustics, Speech. Signal Processing, 4*, 3005–3008.

Carrato, S., Ramponi, G., & Marsi, S. (1996). A simple edge--sensitive image interpolation filter. In *Proceedings of the IEEE Int. Conf. Image Processing* (Vol. 3, pp. 711-714).

Early, D. S., & Long, D. G. (2001). Image reconstruction and enhanced resolution imaging from irregular samples. *IEEE Transactions on Geoscience and Remote Sensing, 39*, 291–302. doi:10.1109/36.905237

Gomes, J., Darsa, L., Costa, B., & Velho, L. (1999). *Warping and morphing of graphical objects*. San Francisco: Morgan Kaufmann.

Jenkins, F. A., & White, H. E. (1976). *Fundamentals of Optics*. New York: McGraw-Hill.

Lee, S. W., & Paik, J. K. (1993). Image interpolation using adaptive fast B--spline filtering. In *Proceedings of the IEEE Int. Conf. Acoustics, Speech. Signal Processing, 5*, 177–180.

Li, X., & Orchard, M. T. (2001). New edge--directed interpolation. *IEEE Transactions on Image Processing, 10*, 1521–1527. doi:10.1109/83.951537

Meyer-Arendt, J. R. (1989). *Introduction to Classical and Modern Optics*. Upper Saddle River, NJ: Prentice-Hall.

Nguyen, N., Milanfar, P., & Golub, G. (2001). Efficient generalized cross--validation with applications to parametric image restoration and resolution enhancement. *IEEE Transactions on Image Processing, 10*, 1299–1308. doi:10.1109/83.941854

Pedrotti, F. L., & Pedrotti, L. S. (1987). *Introduction to Optics*. Upper Saddle River, NJ: Prentice Hall.

This work was previously published in the International Journal of Digital Library Systems, Volume 2, Issue 1, edited by Chia-Hung Wei, pp. 58-66, copyright 2011 by IGI Publishing (an imprint of IGI Global).

Chapter 7
A Survey of Digital Forensic Techniques for Digital Libraries

Yue Li
Nankai University, China

ABSTRACT

Today, many digital forensic techniques for digital images are developed to serve the purpose of the origin identification and integrity verification for security reasons. Generally speaking, these methods can be divided into two classes, the methods based on the extracted features, which are usually the high frequency noise inside the investigating images and the methods based on the contents of the images. Different techniques may be developed specially against different forging attacks, while be vulnerable to other malicious manipulations on the images. This paper reviews the most popular techniques in order to help the user to understand the techniques and find the most proper methods for variety forensic purpose in different situations.

1. INTRODUCTION

Nowadays, the widely applied digital imaging devices bring great convince to the people in daily life. At any time, people can capture scenes around them by the portable cameras or the built-in camera in the mobile; the government can achieve 24-hour surveillance by the widely installed CCTV; the journalists can records the 1/24-second-motions by the professional camera. However, the security of the captured digital images remains unprotected

and such problem needs urgently investigation by the research and the engineer (Chen, Fridrich, Goljan, & Lukas, 2008). The malicious user can easily forge an image with modified contents or replace the output images of the camera with a fake one. These operations are defined as attacks in the study of security of multimedia and protection of digital libraries while the user who operated these attackers are defined as attackers. Practically, these attacks may be operated for different purposes. For example, the attacker may fake an origin marks in the image to announce an illegal copyright of the digital multimedia products, or the attacker may modify the contents inside an image or a video,

DOI: 10.4018/978-1-4666-2928-8.ch007

which is used as evident in court. It is obvious that these attacks will cause tremendous loss in practical if no proper protections are implied, and therefore, many security techniques have been developed to fight against these attacks.

Digital watermarking are traditionally developed to protect the digital multimedia products (Rey & Dugelay, 2006; Liu & Qiu, 2002; Lu & Liao, 2001; Li & Hong, 2008; Wolfgang & Delp, 1997). The term of digital watermarking, which is similar to the real watermarking implanting a mark in the secret paper documents or bank notes, refers to an operation embedding an imperceptible mark into the digital multimedia products to authorise the integrity and origin of the images. The user, who needs to authorise the products, extracts and investigates the integrity of the embedded watermark. If the watermark is broken or destroyed, then the product is deemed as forged. Digital watermarking techniques may be developed to achieve advance functions. For example, some techniques can localise which area is modified by the attacker (Liu & Qiu, 2002; Lu & Liao, 2001; Wolfgang & Delp, 1997) whereas other techniques can survival after the attack and can be further used to reconstruct the images (Rey & Dugelay, 2004; Liu & Qiu, 2002; Lu & Liao, 2001).

Despite of the advantages in theory and effectiveness in practices, digital watermarking are not widely applied in the implementation due to some disadvantages,

1. Firstly, digital watermarking is a class of intrusive security techniques that modify the contents inside the images. Although this modification is imperceptible and the embedded images preserve high visual qualities, the contents inside the embedded images are altered more or less due to the modification (Swaminathan, Wu, & Liu, 2007; Cox, Doerr, & Furon, 2006). Digital watermarking techniques are inappropriate in the applications where identical images are

requested. For example, the images submit to court as evident cannot be watermarked in most situations due to the laws, which request the images must be original without any modification.

2. Multiple watermarking methods cannot be applied on the same multimedia products. According to the research, one watermarking techniques may be only limited attacks (Cox, Miller, Bloom, Fridrich, & Kalker, 2007). For example, the watermarking techniques developed in spatial domain and based on block dependency are always fragile to localise the modified area but cannot survive under the (Rey & Dugelay, 2002; Liu & Qiu, 2002; Lu & Liao, 2001; Li & Hong, 2008; Wolfgang & Delp, 1997; Swaminathan, Wu, & Liu, 2007; Cox, Doerr, & Furon, 2006; Cox, Miller, Bloom, Fridrich, & Kalker, 2007). While the techniques in transform domain are normally robust and able to be clearly identified after the attack but unable to point out the modified regions. In contrast, the attackers normally applies many attacking techniques in one attack. For example, the attacker may modifies the contents of the multimedia products while destroy the origin marks left in the images. If fragile watermarking techniques are applied to localise the tampered area, the origin marks will not be protected. When the robust watermarking is applied to implant the marks into the image and robust the attacks, the robustness make the localisation function fails. Although several works are done (Osborne, Abbott, Sorell, & Rogers, 2004; Li, 2010) aiming to employ different watermarking techniques at the same time, the employed techniques are normally owning similar function, such as robust or fragile, but unable to serve the two purposes at the same time.

3. Due to the aforementioned two disadvantages, in the implementation of digital watermarking, the user must first determine

which attack they may face in protecting the products, and judge which watermarking technique is most appropriate. The receiver has to passively accept the embedder's decision. At the same time, there is no commonly accepted third-party or standard who can authorise which is the best watermarking techniques for each situations. As a result, every media producer and administrator of the digital library practically applies different watermarking methods and it is impossible to transform product between libraries or reuse some products on different player client provided from different producer.

The major reason of the aforementioned disadvantages is that digital watermarking are intrusive techniques which must implant information and modify the content of the image for protection. The intrusion cause inconvenience in some legally situation, but also makes conflictions among different techniques. Because of the intrusion, different techniques need to modify the image in different ways and one modification may inevitably effect others' modification (Cox, Miller, Bloom, Fridrich, & Kalker, 2007). Regarding to the disadvantages of the intrusion of digital watermarking, a class of non-intrusive methods, which are generally named as digital forensic techniques, are subsequently developed to protect the digital multimedia products and the corresponding digital library (Fridrich, 2009; Caldelli, Amerini, Picchioni, De Rosa, & Uccheddu, 2009; Cao & Kot, 2009; Popescu & Farid, 2005; Kirchner & Boehme, 2008). Compared to the intrusive techniques, forensic techniques do not implant any information into the products, but passively extract the high frequency noise as a fingerprint of the image when the images are examined. By investigating the noise, the techniques can further serve the origin identification and integrity verification purposes. Due to the non-intrusive property, the forensic techniques outperform watermarking methods in the three areas,

1. The forensic methods preserve the identical contents of the images. Because of the non-intrusion (Swaminathan, Wu, & Liu, 2007), no information is implanted into the image and therefore, the contents of the image is perfectly preserved.
2. Multiple forensic methods can be applied to the same products for different investigation purpose. Similar to digital watermarking, one forensic method can only be against limited attacks. However, due to the non-intrusion property, there is no conflictions between the different forensic techniques and hence, multiple techniques can be applied to the same products at the same time.
3. No need for the three party in the implementation. Without the confliction between different forensic techniques, the investigator can apply many techniques under the limitation of computation load, Therefore, there is no need to establish a widely accepted third party or standard to judge only one technique with best performance.

Due to the aforementioned advantages, digital forensic techniques are developed rapidly in recent years and tends to replace digital watermarking as the most effective and applied techniques for digital products and library protection, In the following of this paper, we will review the main classes forensic methods currently used.

2. REVIEW OF THE FORENSIC TECHNIQUES

Nowadays, many digital forensic techniques for digital images are developed to serve the origin identification and integrity verification purposes Generally speaking, these techniques can be divided into two classes, the methods based on the extracted features, which are usually the high frequency noise inside the investigating images and the methods based on the contents of the images. The two classes of techniques are reviewed respectively as follows.

2.1. Feature-Based Forensic methods

Generally speaking, most feature-based forensic techniques works in a similar work flow where firstly, they extract a fingerprint, which is a digital feature left by the digital imaging device or the manipulations, and secondly compare it to the reference fingerprints in the database (Fridrich, 2009; Caldelli, Amerini, Picchioni, De Rosa, & Uccheddu, 2009; Cao & Kot, 2009; Popescu & Farid, 2005; Kirchner & Boehme, 2008). Depending on the comparing result, the forensic techniques can identify the origin and verify the integrity of the digital images. In the following description of Figure 1, either the features left by the digital image device or the manipulations, are all expressed as S_I of image I. And the fingerprint saved in the library is named as fingerprint S_D. If a correlation between a reference fingerprint and S_I is maximal among all correlations and greater than a predefined threshold, then the corresponding device is identified as the source device of the image under investigation. To verify content integrity, the fingerprint database consists of fingerprints on different areas of the reference image. If a reference fingerprint on a special area results in a correlation lower than the threshold, then this area is identified as a forged area.

Based on the features used, the feature-base techniques can be separated into two major types, techniques based on the digital imaging device's left-over features and methods based on manipulation left-over features. In practical, forensic techniques based on the digital imaging device's left-over features are preferred to protect and authenticate the digital images captured from an known or suspicious device, while forensic methods based on the manipulation's left-over features are applied to investigate the images after post-processing.

2.1.1. Colour Filter Array

Forensic methods based on Colour Filter Array (CFA) is developed based on the image acquisition process inside a digital camera. A digital camera follows the process demonstrated in Figure 2 to produce a photo (Nakamura, 2006). A colour photo is represented in three components (i.e., Red (R), Green (G), and Blue (B)). During the acquisition process, the lenses capture the light of all the three colour components of the scene, but for every pixel only the light of one colour component is passed through the CFA and subsequently converted into electronic signals by the sensor. This colour filtering is determined by the CFA, which is a 2×2 array, as demonstrated in Figure 2(a). In the array, one element only contains one colour according to the predetermined CFA. The array is repeatedly mapped to the sensor so that for every pixel, only the colour that appears in the element of the array is captured by the sen-

Figure 1. A general framework of forensic techniques

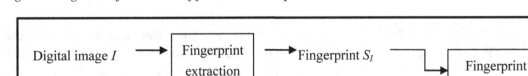

Figure 2. The image acquisition process of a digital camera

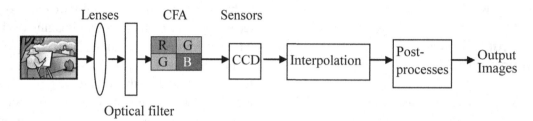

sor and converted into an electronic signal. After the conversion, the interpolation function generates (i.e., interpolates) the other two colour components for every pixel according to the colour intensities of the neighbouring pixels. The signal may then undergo additional operations such as white balancing, gamma correction, and image enhancement. Finally, the signal is stored in the camera's memory in a customised format, primarily the JPEG format.

Figure 3(a) illustrates a typical Bayer CFA (Nakamura, 2006) which is the most widely applied CFA, consisting of two green, one red and one blue component in the 2×2 pixel square. In addition to the CFA, manufacturers also develop and employ different Interpolation Matrixes (IM) for interpolating/demosaicing signals. Figure 3(b) illustrates two commonly used bilinear IM of the size 3×3 and 7×7 pixels.

$$IM_{3\times3} = \begin{bmatrix} 0 & 1 & 0 \\ 1 & 4 & 1 \\ 0 & 1 & 0 \end{bmatrix}$$ (b) Bilinear IM in the size

of 3×3

Figure 3. The Bayer CFA and the bilinear IM (a) A Bayer CFA

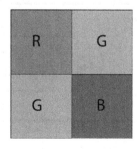

$$IM_{7\times7} = \begin{bmatrix} 0 & 0 & 0 & 1 & 0 & 0 & 0 \\ 0 & 0 & -9 & 0 & -9 & 0 & 0 \\ 0 & -9 & 0 & 81 & 0 & -9 & 0 \\ 1 & 0 & 81 & 256 & 81 & 0 & 1 \\ 0 & -9 & 0 & 81 & 0 & -9 & 0 \\ 0 & 0 & -9 & 0 & -9 & 0 & 0 \\ 0 & 0 & 0 & 1 & 0 & 0 & 0 \end{bmatrix}$$ (c)

Bilinear IM in the size of 7×7

As previously discussed, for each pixel in an interpolated image, only one colour component is converted to the electronic signals by the camera's sensor, while the other two components are interpolated according to their neighbouring pixels and the IM. Let $I_{s,c}$ be the image after the CFA filtering and

$$I_{s,c}(x,y) = \begin{cases} I_c(x,y), & if \quad t(x,y) = c \\ 0, & otherwise \end{cases}$$ (1)

where $t(x,y)$ is the CFA pattern and c is the colour component, which can be R, G or B. $I_c(x,y)$ is the signal of the scene through the optical lenses. Then $I_{s,c}$ is interpolated by the equation in Box 1.

Since different manufacturers use different CFAs and IMs in their products, the CFA and IM together can be utilised as a digital fingerprint for authentication. Bayram et al. (2005) proposed a method for CFA and IM estimation by solving linear equations. Sets of linear equations are es-

Box 1.

$$I'_c(x,y) = \begin{cases} I_{s,c}(x,y), & \text{if } t(x,y) = c \\ \sum_{u,v=-N}^{N} a_{u,v} I_{s,c}(x+u,y+v) & \text{if } t(x,y) \neq c, \ a_{u,v} \in IM \end{cases} \quad (2)$$

where $a_{u,v}$ is the (u,v)th coefficient in the $IM_{N\times N}$, which is of size $N \times N$.

tablished from exhaustive colour configurations of CFA. The solutions to these sets of equations are defined as the candidate IMs. To determine the real IM and CFA adopted in the camera, simulated interpolation images are calculated based on the candidate IMs and the corresponding CFAs. After that, an Expectation Maximisation algorithm is applied to identify the optimal simulated result, which minimises the expected Euclidean distance to the original image. Finally, the IM and CFA, which correspond to the optimal simulated image, are defined as the real IM and CFA adopted by the manufacturer. Swaminathan, Wu, and Liu (2007) and Poilpre, Perrot, and Talbot (2008) applied this CFA and IM estimation algorithm to identify the origin of digital photos. In their approaches, the IM is estimated from the image under investigation and compared the IMs, which are stored in the CFA and IM database as reference fingerprints representing different cameras. The camera model corresponding to the CFA and IM pair that highly correlates with the estimated CFA and IM pair of the image under investigation is taken as the source camera model.

In the applications of CFA on the protection of the image, the device camera identification and integrity verification can be achieved in the following way.

Device Camera Identification

Because every type of camera applies one and only one pattern of CFA and the corresponding IM, the user can identify the origin device by as-

certain the CFA pattern and the IM employed in the device. In a more detailed investigation, since many devices in the same type employs same CFA and IM, the identification is quite limited that can only identify the type of the camera but fails for the individual cameras. OnN the other hand, since Bayer CFA is most commonly employed in different devices (Nakamura, 2006), the user cannot identify the origin devices only according to the CFA if all of them are employing the same Bayer CFA. To solve this problem, the IM must be estimated and compared between each other as the same time. Subsequently, a very accurate IM must be estimated by the advanced statistic tools, which leads to a gap in the research of evaluation of the IM estimation currently.

Integrity Verification

The user can identify the integrity of the image under the assumption that one camera only employ one CFA inside one image. When different CFA pattern and IM are extracted in different area the images, then the image is deemed as a modified image. However, this working process only works in theory because current producer only employ one CFA to each camera but multiple IM corresponding to the CFA. Meanwhile the IM are kept as business secret for keeping high imaging quality. As a result, the user cannot prove the assumption that only one IM is applied.

Vulnerabilities of Forensic Techniques based on CFA

The core idea of CFA-based techniques is to detect the linear relationship, described as the linear equations among pixels inside the images. Therefore, these methods is not robust enough against any attacks that resample the images (Kirchner & Boehme, 2008). For example, if the images are rescaled to double size by a linear interpolation, than the detected IM is not the accuracy corresponds to employed CFA any more, but a combination of the original IM and the matrix for rescaling. On the other hand, IM is calculatcd according to the intestines of the pixels. As a result, any manipulations, which alter the intensities values, may fail the forensic detections. These altering manipulations include nonlinear correction techniques, such as a gamma correction, smoothing and enhancement (Gonzalez & Woods, 2002).

At the same time, setting up a accurate library of IM is also quite impossible because the employed CFA and, more important, the IM as kept as business secret by the manufacturer. An improvement IM can essentially improved the quality of the output image from the device, and hence the manufacturer tends to register the IM as business pattern and keep private from the manual books of the product. As a result, setting up a fingerprint library for CFA detection is not practical due to the business protection.

Due to the vulnerabilities of CFA-based techniques, another forensic techniques based on the unique feature inside the camera is developed.

2.1.2. Photo Response Non-Uniformity

Forensic methods based on Photo Response Non-Uniformity(PRNU) is developed based on the assumption that the digital camera are not perfected produced and the image captured by every camera will contains an identical and recognisable high frequency noise dependent on the imperfection of the camera.

In acquiring an image (see Figure 2 in the section of CFA), the signal will inevitably be distorted when passing through each process and these distortions result in slight differences between the scene and the camera-captured image (Lukas, Fridrich, & Goljan, 2006). Such distortions are called camera noise. With camera noise, even if the camera takes pictures of the same scene, the resulting digital images will still exhibit slight differences (Lukas, Fridrich, & Goljan, 2006). This is partly because of the *shot noise* (also known as photonic noise, Holst, 1998) is a random component being different in every acquisition process, and partly because of *pattern noise*, which is a deterministic component that remains the same in pictures of the same scene taken by the same camera (Lukas, Fridrich, & Goljan, 2006). Due to this property, pattern noise can be utilised as a camera fingerprint for photo authentication.

Figure 4 demonstrates the composition of the camera noise, in which the camera noise is separated into shot noise and pattern noise, and the pattern noise can be further classified into fixed pattern noise (FPN) and photo response pattern noise, known-as photo response non-uniformity (PRNU). Table 1 lists the definition of the three major types of noise and the dominant component of each noise. Fixed pattern noise (FPN) is caused by dark currents, which occurs when the sensor array is not exposed to light (Goesele, Heidrich, & Seidel, 2001). On the other hand, the dominant part of the pattern noise is the PRNU (Lukas, Fridrich, & Goljan, 2006), which is defined as the different sensitivity of pixels to light. This different sensitivity is due to the inhomogenities of silicon wafers and imperfections during the sensor manufacturing process. The imperfections are unique to every sensor therefore can be used as a fingerprint to indentify individual cameras.

In mathematics of PRNU, the distortions can be described as additive noise to the signals, and hence the general expression for captured images is

Figure 4. The composition of the camera noise

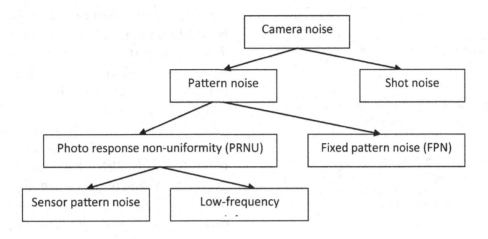

$$I = Y + N \qquad (3)$$

where I is the captured image, Y is the perfect representation of the scene and N is the additive noise representing the distortion.

With regard of the noise classification and the definition (see Table 1), a complete camera output model (Lukas, Fridrich, & Goljan, 2006) can be expressed as

$$I = c^{\gamma}\left[(1+K)Y + \Lambda + \Theta_s + \Theta_r\right]^{\gamma} + \Theta_q \qquad (4)$$

where I is the output image, and Y is the input signal of the scene in the c colour component before demosaicking $(c \in \{R, G, B\})$. K is the zero-mean multiplicative factor responsible for PRNU, and Λ, Θ_s, Θ_q stand for dark current, shot noise, read-out noise and quantisation (lossy compression) noise, respectively. γ is the gamma correction factor. In Equation (4), Θ_s and Θ_r belong to shot noise (random noise) and Λ is the FPN that is tied to every camera and can be removed by subtracting a dark frame from every image taken by the same camera (Goesele, Heidrich, & Seidel, 2001). After applying a Taylor expansion to Equation (4), we obtain

$$I = I^{(0)} + \gamma \cdot I^{(0)} \cdot K + \Theta \qquad (5)$$

where $I^{(0)}$ is the denoised image and Θ is the ensemble of independent noise components, which consist of Λ, Θ_s, Θ_r and Θ_q. The PRNU pattern noise K can then be calculated as follows

$$K = \frac{n - \Theta}{\gamma \cdot I^{(0)}} \qquad (6)$$

where $n = I - I^{(0)}$ is the noise obtained by applying a denoising filter on the images. Although various denoising filters can be used, the wavelet-based denoising process, i.e., a discrete wavelet-transform followed by a Wiener filtering operation, described in Appendix A of Lukas, Fridrich, and Goljan (2006) has been reported as effective in producing good results. Equation (4) demonstrates how to extract the PRNU pattern noise K from the images with the denoising filter.

The basic idea of using the PRNU noise pattern in the image authentication is as follows. Firstly, the PRNU noise patterns of imaging devices, e.g., digital cameras, are extracted from a number (say S) of low-contrast images and then the weighted average of them are calculated to

Table 1. Noise type definitions

Noise type	Definition	Dominant component
Shot noise	Random noise: It differs in every picture, even in the pictures of the same scene taken by the same camera.	Photonic noise [130]
PRNU	Content-dependent noise: It differs in the pictures of the different scenes, but remains the same in the pictures of the same scene taken by the same camera.	Sensor pattern noise [16]
FPN	Content-independent noise: It is fixed to the camera and is constant in every picture taken by the same camera.	Dark current [131]

serve as the reference fingerprints r of the devices according to

$$r = \frac{1}{\gamma} \frac{\sum_{s=1}^{S} n_s I_s}{\sum_{s=1}^{S} (I_s)^2} \qquad (7)$$

as suggested by Chen et al. (2008), where γ is gamma correction factor ($\gamma \approx 0.455$), I_s and n_s are the s th image and the corresponding noise extracted from I_s. Note the multiplication operation in Equation (7) is element-wise. Secondly, the noise n_I of the image, I, under investigation is extracted and compared against the reference fingerprint r_d of each device d available to the investigator in the hope that it will match one of the reference fingerprints, thus identifying the source device that has taken the image under investigation (Chen, Fridrich, Goljan, & Lukas, 2008; Goesele, Heidrich, & Seidel, 2001; Lukas, Fridrich, & Goljan, 2006). The normalised cross-correlation

$$\rho(Ir_d, n_I) = \frac{\left(I \cdot r_d - \overline{I \cdot r_d}\right) \cdot \left(n_I - \overline{n_I}\right)}{\left\|I \cdot r_d - \overline{I \cdot r_d}\right\| \cdot \left\|n_I - \overline{n_I}\right\|} \qquad (8)$$

is used to compare the noise n_I against the reference fingerprint r_d, where $\overline{\bullet}$ is the mean function. Note in Equation (7), instead of using r_d, we used $I \cdot r_d$ as suggested in Goesele, Heidrich, and Seidel (2001). Again the multiplication operation in Equation (8) is element-wise.

Figure 5 demonstrates two enhanced PRNU of different cameras. Figure 5(a) shows the PRNU pattern from the Canon Power Shot A610 camera. In this figure, the PRNU has a circular distribution in the middle of the pattern. Figure 5(b) is the PRNU pattern for the Fuji FinePix F50fd camera, in which the noise has a striped rather than a circular distribution.

Many techniques have been developed to identify source camera device and to verify image integrity by investigating the PRNU in images (Goesele, Heidrich, & Seidel, 2001; Lukas, Fridrich, & Goljan, 2006; Chen, Fridrich, Lukas, & Goljan, 2008; Chen, Fridrich, Goljan, & Lukas, 2007). The methods of two applications are listed as follow:

Device Camera Identification

The PRNU-based device identification is carried out in the following manner. Firstly, the PRNU is obtained from low-contrast images taken by the camera and registered as the reference PRNU for the camera. Secondly, the PRNU is extracted from the image under investigation and then correlations between the reference PRNU of each camera and the extracted PRNU are calculated. The reference PRNU which leads to the highest correlation, if greater than a predetermined threshold, is identified and the corresponding camera is reported as the some camera of the image under investigation (Goesele, Heidrich, & Seidel, 2001; Chen, Fridrich, Goljan, & Lukas, 2007; Li, 2009).

Figure 5. Illustration of the PRNU pattern noise of different cameras

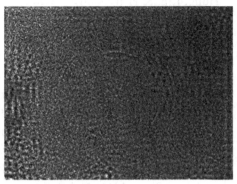 

(a) PRNU of camera Conon Power Shot A610   (b) PRNU of camera Fuji FinePix F50fd

Integrity Verification

To verify content integrity, the PRNU is extracted from the image under investigation. Then a sliding window is moved across the PRNU, and the PRNU block contained by the window is compared to the corresponding the reference PRNU block of the camera which has taken the image under investigation. An authentic PRNU block leads to a higher correlation, while a manipulated block gives rise to a lower correlation than the predetermined threshold (Holst, 1998; Li, 2009).

Vulnerabilities of Forensic Techniques Based on PRNU

According to definition of PRNU, the feature can be destroyed by the wavelet domain manipulations, including JPEG2000 compression (Grgic, Mrak, Grgic, & Zovko-Cihlar, 2003) and some image filtering manipulations. All of these manipulations will alter the coefficients in the wavelet domain and hence break or remove the high frequency noise used for PRNU. As a result, the PRNU based forensic methods must be used on the images without any wavelet domain processing.

Another disadvantage of PRNU based techniques is the heavy burden to the data storage and computation load. In the digital library of PRNU, each PRNU represents a camera and therefore, the number of the fingerprint is determined the number of the camera need to be included in the database. Regarding to the huge amount of portable cameras, built-in cameras in the mobile, CCTV cameras and etc., the library of the PRNU will cost tremendous physical storage, which is a great challenge in setting up a fingerprint library (Li & Li, 2011). On the other hand, identifying PRNU fingerprints from the database need exhaustive comparisons, which consume considerable computation time. As a result, a method can decrease the digital library size and increase the comparison speed is in need to improve the applicability of this kind of forensic method.

Besides these techniques based CFA and PRNU, there are also many techniques on the left features of black and white balance of the camera, the gamma correction employed inside the camera, and etc. Because of the strong restriction in the application, these techniques are not widely applied and hence not reviewed in detail in this paper.

2.1.3. Feature on Quantization Estimation and JPEG Compression

To investigate the features by the manipulations, the most widely applied forensic method examines the quantization step used in the JPEG compression and MPEG video compression. In both of the aforementioned lossy compression, the core idea is to quantize the input signal, discrete transform (DCT) coefficients in JPEG for example, to the integers and transform them same integer at the same time as the compressed information to save the channel capacity.

Let the coefficient be D, then the quantized coefficient is

$$D_q = round\left(\frac{D}{q}\right) * q \qquad (9)$$

Figure 6 demonstrates the histogram of quantized Lena in spatial domain as an visual example for quantization. The frequencies of the occurrence of most intensity values become zero, which represents the disappearance of the intensity values in the quantised images. Therefore, gaps appear in the histogram due to the quantization.

In attacking the multimedia products, the attacker may need to modify the intercepted products and recompressed them before sending it to the legal receiver. As a result, the products will be quantized and compressed twice. As a result, the investigator can identify the double-compressed products as suspicious ones. When the images are quantized twice, the histogram of the numbers will be further modified. Instead of the column and gap, a more complex result with peaks and hills appears in the histogram (Fridich, Lukas, & Soukal, 2003; Hsu, Hung, Lin, & Hsu, 2008). Different distribution will be exhibited in the histogram depending on the relationship between the quantizers in the two quantizations. If the quantizers are relatively dividers, the hills are less obvious; otherwise, the relatively primes results

to a more obvious peaks in the histogram (Hsu, Hung, Lin, & Hsu, 2008).

Origin Identification

The method cannot be used for integrity verification because the quantization is a globe processing that the whole image are quantized at the same time, subsequently, this technique can only be used to detected whether the products are suspiciously double compressed. However, with the knowledge of quantization table (which defines every quantizers used in for different DCT coefficients) planted in the source imaging device and the establishment of the quantization table library, the investigator can identify the quantization table and further ascertain the imaging device or software applying the compression.

Vulnerabilities of Forensic Techniques based on Quantization Estimation

As the name refers to, the investigator needs to estimate the quantizers as the feature of the JPEG images or MEPG videos. This estimation is applied on the histogram of the quantized DCT coefficients. Therefore, any attacks, modify the histogram of the DCT coefficients, can destroy the feature and crack the technique. These attacks including another quantization, filtering in transform domain, and etc.

Form the above analysis, we can know that the forensic method based on the feature in high frequency and left by the device and image processing manipulation can also be destroyed by the similar manipulations, including rescaling, resampling, smoothing, and correction. On the other hand, all of these manipulations are the common processing techniques frequently applied to forge the image. As a result, an alternative method is to investigate the image according to the contents. Whichever technique is applied by the attacker, the purpose of the attacking is to create a forge image with

Figure 6. The histograms of the original Lena and the watermarked Lena

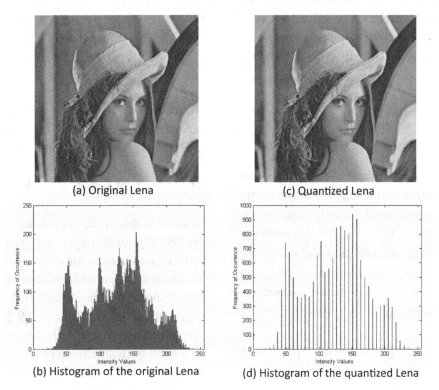

meaningful but fake contents. If the investigator can identify the forge contents directly, then the attack is resisted. Therefore, the techniques based contents of the images are developed and accordingly reviewed as follows.

2.2. Content-Based Forensic Methods

Due to the aforementioned disadvantages, the accuracy of feature-based forensic methods is easily effected by the image processing methods, such as rotation, resizing and etc. Subsequently, methods based on the contents of the images are more widely applied to server forensic purposes. According to the practical, we can find that in most situations, the attack cannot "create" some contents inside the images/videos by freehand but mostly copy some contents from other images/ frames in other videos and replace some contents

inside the original copies (Kutter, Voloshynovskiy, & Herrigel, 2000). After the copy-and-paste manipulation, many image processing techniques may be applied to achieve best visual quality. As a result, the applied image processing techniques may destroy the features left by the imaging devices and make the feature-based forensic method ineffective. Because of this reason, the content-based forensic methods are more widely applied. Since the copied and pasted contents are transplanted from other images/videos, the user can investigate the similarity between different area to detect the copied and pasted area.

2.2.1. Forensic Methods based on Correlation

When being considered as a high dimensional mathematical matrix, the images/videos can be compared by the cross correlations between the matrixes or the auto-correlations insides the images. The term of correlation is derived from the Euclidean distance that the distance between two images I_1 and I_2 (Dietrich, 1991) is

$$
\begin{aligned}
d(u,v) &= \sum_{x,y}\left(I_1(x,y)-I_2(x-u,y-v)\right)^2 \\
&= \sum_{x,y}\left(I_1^2(x,y)+I_2^2(x-u,y-v)-2I_1(x,y)I_2(x-u,y-v)\right)
\end{aligned}
$$

(10)

where *x, y* are the coordinate of the images and *u, v* are the position of the window, which limits the regions being compared. Under the assumption that $I_1^2(x,y)$ and $I_2^2(x-u,y-v)$ are approximately constant in statistic analysis, the major component in Equation (10) is $2I_1(x,y)I_2(x-u,y-v)$, which is used to define the cross correlation as

$$
c(u,v) = \sum_{x,y} I_1(x,y)I_2(x-u,y-v) \qquad (11)
$$

However, using Equation (10) may face several disadvantages (Dietrich, 1991). Firstly, If the energier of the images, which are $I_1^2(x,y)$ and $I_2^2(x-u,y-v)$ varies seriously with position, the correlation may be affected by the contents insides each images rather than exhibit the similarity between images. For example, the correlation between the pasted region and an exactly copied region in the image may be less than the correlation between the pasted region and a bright area. Secondly, the range of $c(u,v)$ depends on the size of the images. Larger size of sliding windows results in a higher correlation than the smaller size of sliding window, even the similarity inside the larger windows is much lower.

The correlation coefficient (Dunn, 2005) is proposed to overcome the difficulties by introducing the mean value and variance of the images. Let $\overline{I_1}$ and $\overline{I_2}$ be the mean values of I_1 and I_2, then the correlation coefficient of I_1 and I_2 is

$$
c(u,v) = \frac{\sum\limits_{x,y}\left(I_1(x,y)-\overline{I_1}\right)\left(I_2(x-u,y-v)-\overline{I_2}\right)}{\sqrt{\sum\limits_{x,y}\left(I_1(x,y)-\overline{I_1}\right)^2\sum\limits_{x,y}\left(I_2(x-u,y-v)-\overline{I_2}\right)^2}}
$$

(12)

The correlation coefficient is robust to the variance of contents and size of the images and hence can be used to detection the copy and paste attack.

Detection of Copy-And-Paste Attack

In order to detect the copied and pasted region, the investigator can apply an exhaustive search between two images (or inside the images if the investigator suspect the regions is copied and pasted inside an image) and find out the most similar regions (Fridich, Lukas, & Soukal, 2003). The exhaustive search method save the investigator's time in manually determine the regions in two regions with alike contents. However, the computation load for the exhaustive searching in correlation is normally unacceptable. For an investigation on two images of $M \times N$ pixels and a sliding window of $W \times H$ pixels, the step count is approximately $(M-W)(N-H)WH$ and the complexity of is $O(MNWD)$. In circumstance, an image of 512×512 and the sliding window is 64×64, then step count in the exhaustive searching is about 822,083,584, which is quite unacceptable for the investigator. In a more practical usage, the investigator needs to ascertain the suspicious areas by visually examination and set the correlation methods to only compute the correlations between the areas (Hsu, Hung, Lin, & Hsu, 2008). If the similarity is higher than the predetermined threshold, then the investigated area is deemed as a pasted region copied from the suspicious area. The threshold is usually determined by assuming that the similarity should follow the Gaussian distribution, in which the parameter is estimated by the statistic method, and the threshold is set up in the multiple standard derivations of Gaussian distribution (Hsu, Hung, Lin, & Hsu, 2008).

Vulnerable Attacks

According to Equation (11) and (12), correlation is a linear computation strictly relates to the coordinate of the pixels inside the images (or frames inside the videos). Subsequently, if the attack modifies the related position in regions, then the investigator cannot identify the similar area however the window is slide. The modification manipulation includes resampling, such as interpolation which inserts pixels between the original ones and make the original pixels furthers. In this way, the copied regions are rescaled to a larger size before pasted to the target image. Correspondingly, the investigator without the pre-knowledge of the rescaling will fails to obtain a correlation higher than the threshold. Another common modification manipulation is rotation. Since the copied area are not in the perfect angle and must be rotated before pasted into the target image. The rotation applied in this situation moves pixels to different locations and sometimes generate new pixel values in the old position. Consequently, the contents in the forged images and original images are different and leading to a correlation lower than the pre-determined threshold, no matter how the window is slide along the suspicious area.

Due to the high complexity, vulnerability to common image processing manipulations, forensic methods based on scale-invariant feature transform are developed to examine the similarity between the images.

2.2.2. Forensic Methods based on Scale-Invariant Feature Transform(SIFT)

Scale-invariance feature transform (SIFT) (Lowe, 1999) is one of the popular methods to detect keypoints of an object so that the same object in another image can be recognized with invariance to scale, rotation, translation and illumination. The basic idea behind the keypoint detection method assumes that most salient points exist in corners of objects and are seen as interest points. It is denoted that though salient points do not only exist in corners, those points in corners are considered more stable and useful than those in edges for object recognition and similarity matching applications.

The first step of the SIFT is to identify stable points from shoeprint pattern which is invariant to scale, rotation and translation. Assume x, y represent the coordinates of a pixel in image I. The scale space $L(x, y, \sigma)$ can be constructed by utilizing Gaussian filter $G(x, y, \sigma)$ to smooth the base image $I(x, y)$ as described in Equation (13).

$$L(x, y, \sigma) = G(x, y, \sigma) * I(x, y) \tag{13}$$

where σ is defined as the width of the filter, and $*$ is the convolution operation. Then, Difference-of-Gaussian (DoG) images of a shoeprint image I, as shown in Equation (13)), can be created by subtracting each Gaussian image from the previous Gaussian image in scale.

$$DoG(x, y, \sigma) = L(x, y, k\sigma) - L(x, y, \sigma) \tag{14}$$

where k is a constant multiplicative factor used for varying the scale. Subsequently, DoG images are used to detect potential keypoints through the findings of local maxima and minima across different scales. To find local maxima and minima, each pixel in the DoG image is compared to eight neighbors in the same scale and nine neighbors in the neighboring scales. The pixel is considered as a candidate keypoint only if it is local maxima or minima. However, some pixels may be mistakenly localized because those with low contrast are sensitive to noise (Lowe, 1999). To rule out those improper keypoints, we have to verify whether each point could reasonably be selected in another image of the same shoeprint pattern. A 3D quadratic function is fitted to the selected points in order to filter the point in low contrast. $D(\overline{x})$, described in Equation (15), is expanded at the select point $\overline{x}$ by Taylor expansion.

$$D(\bar{x}) = D + \frac{\partial D}{\partial \bar{x}} \bar{x} + \frac{1}{2} \bar{x}^T \frac{\partial^2 D}{\partial \bar{x}^2} \bar{x} \qquad (15)$$

where D and its derivatives are evaluated at the selected point and $\bar{x} = (x, y)^T$ is the offset from this point. Taking the derivative of this function with respect to $\bar{x}$ and setting it equal to zero, we can determine the extremum, $\bar{x}$, to be

$$\tilde{x} = -\frac{\partial^2 D^{-1}}{\partial \bar{x}^2} \frac{\partial D}{\partial \bar{x}} \qquad (16)$$

The extremum can help us verify the keypoints in low contrast and reject those points. We substitute Equation (17) into Equation (16) which result in

$$D(\tilde{x}) = D + \frac{1}{2} \frac{\partial D^T}{\partial \tilde{x}} \tilde{x} \qquad (17)$$

A given point is rejected if $|D(\tilde{x})|$ is less than 0.03. To determine if an extrema point is along an edge, using the Hessian matrix

$$H = \begin{bmatrix} D_{xx} & D_{xy} \\ D_{xy} & D_{yy} \end{bmatrix} \qquad (18)$$

where D is the second partial derivative of the DoG image at a scale, The following inequality is used to find edge and corner points. If

$$\frac{trace(H)^2}{\det(H)} = \frac{(\lambda_1 + \lambda_2)^2}{\lambda_1 \lambda_2} < \frac{((r+1)\lambda_2)^2}{r\lambda_2^2} = \frac{(r+1)^2}{r}, \qquad (19)$$

where $\lambda_1 < (1 + r)\lambda_2$ As $r = 10$, the extrema point is considered to be a corner; otherwise, the point is rejected as an edge point. After rejecting points based on contrast, edge value, and stability, the remaining points are assigned to describe the pattern of the given shoeprints.

For each selected keypoint, the dominant orientation of the gradient of the points within a window around the point is determined from the quantized histogram of orientations. The magnitude and orientation of the gradient of each point is found and its orientation is stored within one of 36 bins. For each point within a window of W around thee keypoint, the weighted gradient magnitude is added to the bin corresponding to that point's orientation and the gradient magnitude is weighted by a Gaussian centered at the keypoint with standard deviation. The two feature descriptors magnitude and orientation of keypoints can be extracted from each shoeprint image. For similarity matching cross correlation for each feature is computed so as to determine the similarity between the query shoeprint and the database shoeprint images. Cross correlation c is a measurement of estimating the degree to which two vectors are correlated. A_i and B_i denote the i-th elements in vector A and B, respectively. Finally, the values of c for the two features are summed to represent the final score of the similarity.

SIFT algorithm extracts the features based on the contents of the images and compares these features to examine the similarity between the contents. The comparison results are measured by the number of groups of successfully matched keypoints. In the output, each group of matched keypoint is linked by a line. It is noticed that this matching relationship is not one-to-one but many-to-many according to the SIFT algorithm. Therefore, many lines may start at one points and end at different points or conversely start at many points and end at one point. It is also noticeable that that the number of the matched point is not the only measurement of the similarity, because sometimes they may be errantly matched. We also need to measure the parallel line among the matching. Because in the common manipulations, the contents between the copied and pasted area mostly related by a linear projection and therefore the lines representing the matching should be parallel to each other. As a result, in visual observation, if the lines are mainly cross to each, then the key points are mainly errantly matched.

Detection of Copy-And-Paste Attack

Forensic techniques based on SIFT operate an globe comparison with the aids of the keypoints (Li, 2011; Amerini, Ballan, Caldelli, Del Bimbo, & Serra, 2011). Therefore, the user needs to precisely localise the suspicious region for comparison, although a very precise region results in a higher accuracy with less irrelevant keypoints. Much more, the user can firstly compare the region suspiciously copied from other images to a full size image as the suspicious origin. The SIFT technique can localise the copied region approximately, allowing the investigator to apply a further detailed comparison.

Figure 7 demonstrates a comparison result of the forensic methods based on SIFT. A forged image is created by copying a flower from area A, which is highlight and marked as A in the image,

and paste it to area B. After copying, we rotate the flower slightly, enhance the grayscale value of the area and smooth the edge of the flower by Photoshop in order to achieve the best visual result. Because they are plenty flowers similar to each other, the investigator can hardly identify the copy-and-paste area by visual observation. For comparison, another area C which is highly similar to area A visually.

Figure 8(a) and (b) demonstrates the result, that the area B is highly similar to similar A with more lines linking the keypoints while be less similar to Area C with less lines. Meanwhile, if area B is compared to the full images excluding area B itself, area A is highlighted as a suspicious origin region of area B as in Figure 8(b). Since the SIFT area detect the contents inside the images, the common manipulations such as rotation, smoothing, enhancement cannot degrade the identification rate of the forensic method, as demonstrated in Figure 9(a),(b),(c)

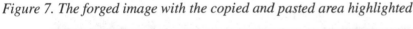

Figure 7. The forged image with the copied and pasted area highlighted

Figure 8. Similarity comparison between different areas. (a) copied and pasted areas; (b) pasted and other areas, (c) pasted area and globe area

(a) (b) (c)

Figure 9. Similarity comparison between different areas. (a) Comparison between copied area and pasted area with noise inserted (b), copied area with pasted area rotated, (c) copied area with pasted area enhanced

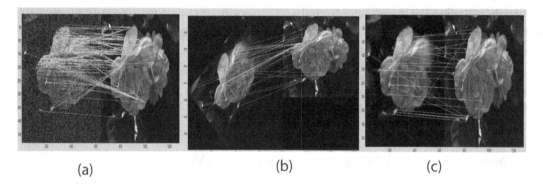

(a) (b) (c)

Disadvantages of SIFT Techniques

Compared to the techniques based on correlation, SIFT save a great amount of time, which is however not enough in managing a digital library of huge amount of the digital products. When the keypoints are extracted, SIFT algorithm need to run an exhaustive comparison between the two classes of features inside the two images. As a result, the computation load is strongly effected by the size of the keypoint class, and more directly, by the size of the images. When the digital library contains image in high resolution, the SIFT technique may not be appropriate for forensic investigation.

3. CONCLUSION

This paper has reviewed many forensic techniques, mainly based on the features inside the images or the contents of the images. The review and analysis demonstrates that currently there is no perfect techniques can serve all forensic techniques at the same time. However, the investigator can applied multiple forensic techniques at the same time to achieve the best performance.

REFERENCES

Amerini, I., Ballan, L., Caldelli, R., Del Bimbo, A., & Serra, G. (2011). A SIFT-based forensic method for copy–move attack detection and transformation recovery. *IEEE Transactions on Information Forensics and Security, 3*(6).

Bayram, S., Sencar, H. T., Memon, N., & Avcibas, I. (2005). Source camera identification based on CFA interpolation. In *Proceedings of the IEEE International Conference on Image Processing* (pp. 69-72).

Caldelli, R., Amerini, I., Picchioni, F., De Rosa, A., & Uccheddu, F. (2009). Multimedia forensic techniques for acquisition device identification and digital image authentication. In Li, C.-T. (Ed.), *Handbook of research on computational forensics, digital crime and investigation: Methods and solutions*. Hershey, PA: Information Science Reference. doi:10.4018/978-1-60566-836-9.ch006

Cao, H., & Kot, A. C. (2009). Accurate detection of demosaicing regularity for digital image forensics. *IEEE Transactions on Information Forensics and Security, 4*(4), 899–910. doi:10.1109/TIFS.2009.2033749

Chen, M., Fridrich, J., Goljan, M., & Lukas, J. (2007). Source digital camcorder identification using sensor photo response non-uniformity. *Proceedings of the Society for Photo-Instrumentation Engineers, 6505*.

Chen, M., Fridrich, J., Goljan, M., & Lukas, J. (2008). Determining image origin and integrity using sensor noise. *IEEE Transactions on Information Security and Forensics, 3*(1), 74–90. doi:10.1109/TIFS.2007.916285

Chen, M., Fridrich, J., Lukas, J., & Goljan, M. (2008). Imaging sensor noise as digital x-ray for revealing forgeries. In *Proceedings of the 9th Information Hiding Workshop* (pp. 342-458).

Cox, I. J., Doerr, G., & Furon, T. (2006). Watermarking is not cryptography. In *Proceedings of the 5th International Workshop on Digital Watermarking* (pp. 1-15).

Cox, I. J., Miller, M., Bloom, J., Fridrich, J., & Kalker, T. (2007). *Digital watermarking and steganography* (2nd ed.). San Francisco, CA: Morgan Kaufmann.

Dietrich, C. F. (1991). *Uncertainty, calibration, and probability: the statistics of scientific and industrial measurement*. Bristol, UK: Institute of Physics.

Dunn, P. F. (2005). *Measurement and data analysis for engineering and science*. New York, NY: McGraw-Hill.

Fridich, J., Lukas, J., & Soukal, D. (2003). Detection of copy-move forgery in digital images. In *Proceedings of the Digital Forensics Research Conference*.

Fridrich, J. (2009). Digital image forensics. *IEEE Signal Processing Magazine, 26*(2), 26–37. doi:10.1109/MSP.2008.931078

Goesele, M., Heidrich, W., & Seidel, H.-P. (2001). Entropy based dark frame subtraction. In *Proceedings of the Image Processing, Image Quality, Image Capture Systems Conference* (pp. 293-298).

Gonzalez, R. C., & Woods, R. E. (2002). *Digital image processing*. Upper Saddle River, NJ: Prentice Hall.

Grgic, S., Mrak, M., Grgic, M., & Zovko-Cihlar, B. (2003). Comparative study of JPEG and JPEG2000 image coders. In *Proceeding of the 17th International Conference on Applied Electromagnetics and Communications* (pp. 109-112).

Holst, G. C. (1998). *CCD arrays, cameras, and displays* (2nd ed.). Winter Park, FL: JCD Publishing & SPIE Press.

Hsu, C. C., Hung, T. Y., Lin, C. W., & Hsu, C. T. (2008). Video forgery detection using correlation of noise residue. In *Proceedings of the IEEE 10th Workshop on Multimedia Signal Processing.*

Kirchner, M., & Boehme, R. (2008). Hiding traces of resampling in digital images. *IEEE Transactions on Information Forensics and Security, 3,* 582–592. doi:10.1109/TIFS.2008.2008214

Kutter, M., Voloshynovskiy, V., & Herrigel, A. (2000). Watermark copy attack. *Proceedings of SPIE Security and Watermarking of Multimedia Contents, II,* 3971.

Li, C. M., & Hong, L. X. (2008). Adaptive fragile watermark for image authentication with tampering localization. In *Proceedings of the Second International Conference on Anti-counterfeiting, Security and Identification* (pp. 22-25).

Li, C.-T. (2009). Source camera linking using enhanced sensor pattern noise extracted from images. In *Proceedings of the 3rd International Conference on Imaging for Crime Detection and Prevention.*

Li, C.-T. (2009). Unsupervised classification of digital images of unknown cameras using filtered sensor pattern noise. In *Proceedings of the International Workshop on Digital Watermarking.*

Li, C.-T. (2010). Medical image protection through steganography and digital watermarking. In Li, C.-T. (Ed.), *Handbook of research on computational forensics, digital crime and investigation: Methods and solutions.* Hershey, PA: IGI Global.

Li, Y. (2011). A robust forensic method based on scale-invariance feature transform. In *Proceeding of the 2nd International Conference on Multimedia Technology.*

Li, Y., & Li, C. T. (2011). Optimized digital library for digital forensic based on decomposed PRNU. In *Proceeding of the 2nd International Conference on Multimedia Technology.*

Liu, T., & Qiu, Z.-D. (2002). A survey of digital watermarking-based image authentication techniques. In *Proceedings of the 6th International Conference on Signal Processing* (pp. 26-30).

Lowe, D. G. (1999). Object recognition from local scale-invariant features. In *Proceedings of the International Conference on Computer Vision.*

Lu, C. S., & Liao, H. Y. M. (2001). Multipurpose watermarking for image authentication and protection. *IEEE Transactions on Image Processing, 10*(10), 1579–1592. doi:10.1109/83.951542

Lukas, J., Fridrich, J., & Goljan, M. (2006). Detecting digital image forgeries using sensor pattern noise. *Proceedings of SPIE Electronic Imaging, 6072,* 362–372.

Lukas, J., Fridrich, J., & Goljan, M. (2006). Digital camera identification from sensor noise. *IEEE Transactions on Information Security and Forensics, 1*(2), 205–214. doi:10.1109/TIFS.2006.873602

Nakamura, K. (2006). *Image sensors and signal processing for digital still cameras.* Boca Raton, FL: Taylor & Francis Group.

Osborne, D., Abbott, D., Sorell, M., & Rogers, D. (2004). Multiple embedding using robust watermarks for wireless medical images. In *Proceedings of the Third International Conference on Mobile and Ubiquitous Multimedia* (pp. 245-250).

Poilpre, M. C., Perrot, P., & Talbot, H. (2008). Image tampering detection using Bayer interpolation and JPEG compression. In *Proceedings of the First International Conference on Forensic Applications and Techniques in Telecommunications, Information and Multimedia.*

Popescu, A. C., & Farid, H. (2005). Exposing digital forgeries in color filter array interpolated images. *IEEE Transactions on Signal Processing*, *53*(10), 3948–3959. doi:10.1109/TSP.2005.855406

Rey, C., & Dugelay, J. L. (2002). A survey of watermarking algorithms for image authentication. *EURASIP Journal on Applied Signal Processing*, (6): 613–621. doi:10.1155/S1110865702204047

Swaminathan, A., Wu, M., & Liu, K. J. R. (2007). Non-intrusive component forensics of visual sensors using output images. *IEEE Transactions on Information Forensics and Security*, *2*(1), 91–106. doi:10.1109/TIFS.2006.890307

Wolfgang, R. B., & Delp, E. J. (1997). Overview of image security techniques with applications in multimedia systems. In *Proceedings of the SPIE International Conference on Multimedia Networks: Security, Displays, Terminals, and Gateways* (pp. 297-308).

This work was previously published in the International Journal of Digital Library Systems, Volume 2, Issue 3, edited by Chia-Hung Wei, pp. 49-66, copyright 2011 by IGI Publishing (an imprint of IGI Global).

Chapter 8
Digital Image Authentication:
A Review

Yue Li
Nankai University, Tianjin, China

Chia-Hung Wei
Ching Yun University, Taiwan

ABSTRACT

Digital image authentication refers to all the techniques performing anti-falsification, digital image copyright protection, or access control. A large number of DIA techniques have been developed to authenticate digital images, including cryptography-based digital image authentication (CBDIA) techniques and data-hiding-based digital image authentication (DHBDIA) techniques. This paper not only provides some practical applications on image authentication, but also describes general frameworks of image watermarking and the general techniques, including robust watermarking, fragile watermarking, and semi-fragile watermarking. This paper also addresses the potential issues on future research directions, including managing the PRNU database, development of advanced PRNU-based blind authentication techniques, and search for digital fingerprints.

1. DIGITAL IMAGE AUTHENTICATION

Due to the fast growth of digital technology, daily activities can be easily captured and saved in digital images, and then transmitted via the Internet. Despite the convenience, digital images suffer from problems, which can be summarised by the following questions: which person/device produces the image, who are authorised to access this image when it is stored and distributed, and whether the image is modified (Rey & Dugelay, 2002). As a result, digital image authentication (DIA) techniques have been developed in order to solve those security problems (Liu & Qiu, 2002). In the research of image authentication, DIA is a generic term for all the techniques performing

DOI: 10.4018/978-1-4666-2928-8.ch008

anti-falsification, digital image copyright protection or access control (Lu & Liao, 2001).

1. **Anti-Falsification:** Anti-falsification is one of the primary functions of DIA techniques, which aims to prove the authenticity and integrity of digital images (Li & Hong, 2008). If an image is modified, the DIA techniques for anti-falsification should be able to detect the modification and localise the modified areas. Figure 1 demonstrates the anti-falsification function by authenticating the image of a traffic scene, which may be used as evidence in the court of law. Figure 1(a) is the original image, while Figure 1(b) is a tampered version with a pedestrian embedded and the traffic lights altered. The

authentication result is illustrated as Figure 1(c), with the tampered region shaded.

2. **Digital Image Copyright Protection:** Copyright protection is another important authentication function in DIA (Wolfgang & Delp, 1997). In the application of copyright protection, the DIA techniques need to either identify the ownership of images or identify the source of images. To protect the commercial value of images and to fight against piracy, DIA techniques are applied to identify the ownership of the digital images. On the other hand, the trustworthiness of the source of digital images is also an important issue when the images are used in the news and media industry (Bartolini, Tefas, Barni, & Pitas, 2001). Therefore, the

Figure 1. The anti-falsification function of DIA

(a) Original image

(b) Forged image

(c) Authenticated image

DIA techniques are also used to identify the source of digital media, including scanners, digital cameras and computer graphic software. Figure 2 illustrates the two applications in copyright protection.

Figure 2(a) illustrates a computer graphic artwork where the visual signature on the upper-right corner can be easily removed or changed. Thus DIA techniques are required to ascertain the ownership of the work in the case of copyright infringement. Figure 2(b), on the other hand, illustrates a photo captured by a traffic surveillance camera, showing a car illegally parking aside the road.

3. **Access Control:** Access control is also an important authentication function for DIA.

In many applications, the images involve sensitive data. When these images are stored in the database or transmitted via the Internet, they should only be accessed by the authorised users with the proper level of access rights. For example, in the system for protecting digital mammogram proposed by Li and Li (2009), the access right is divided into three levels according to the role of the users as demonstrated in Table 1. For instance, the doctor in charge of a case can access the patient's information, such as the patient's medical history and the mammograms; therefore, he/she should be classified as Level 2 user. An intern or a trainee, on the other hand, can only access the mammograms for field work and training pur-

Figure 2. The copyright protection functions of DIA

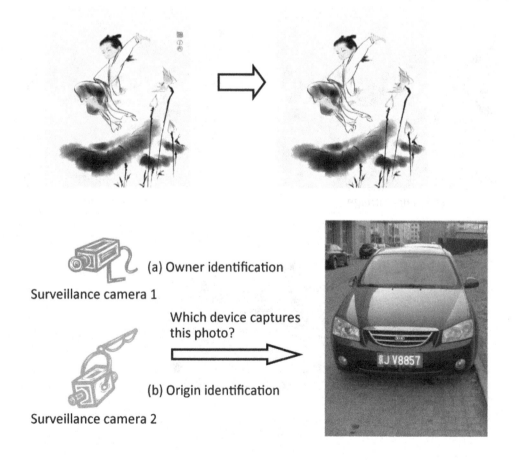

(a) Owner identification

Surveillance camera 1

Which device captures this photo?

(b) Origin identification

Surveillance camera 2

Table 1. Classification of the access rights

Roles / users	Access rights	Access keys issued
Level 0 user	No right given. (The contents of the mammograms are masked and unavailable to the users)	No key
Level 1 user	Only images (i.e., the mammograms with hidden patient information which cannot be extracted)	Half-authorised key
Level 2 user	Images and patient information	Full-authorised key

poses but cannot access the patient's medical history, so he/she is at Level 1. A system technician with only maintenance duties should not be allowed to access the patient's information and the contents of the mammograms so he/she is to be classified as Level 0. In the above example of access control, the DIA techniques generate different keys corresponding to different access levels and distribute these key to the users based on user access rights. Thus, only the authorised user with the correct key can access the images (Low & Christianson, 1994).

2. RELATED WORK TO DIA

Over the last couple of decades, a large number of DIA techniques have been developed to protect image systems (Fridrich, 2009; Liu, 2004; Potdar, Han, & Chang, 2003; Rey et al., 2002; Simmons, 1988), and generally speaking, these DIA techniques can be categorised into cryptography-based digital image authentication (CBDIA) techniques (Lin & Chang, 2003; Lu & Liao, 2009), and data-hiding-based digital image authentication (DHBDIA) techniques (Liu et al., 2002; Rey et al., 2002).

2.1. Cryptography-Based Digital Image Authentication (CBDIA)

CBDIA, a cryptographic scheme with an encryption function and a corresponding decryption function, is applied to encrypt/decrypt the image for authentication (Lin et al., 2003; Lu et al., 2009). The encryption function creates confusion and diffuses the data (Shannon, 1949), where confusion makes the relationship between the key and the encrypted data as complex as possible and the diffusion creates a complex dependence between the input bits of plaintext and the output bits of ciphertext. In cryptography, plaintext refers to the unencrypted data while ciphertext represents the encrypted data. The aim of confusion is to make it attacker hard for the attacker to find the key even if he/she has a large number of plaintext-ciphertext pairs produced by the same key. Due to the confusion, every bit of the ciphertext is dependent on the entire secret key. The aim of data diffusion is to spread the statistical redundancy of the plaintext over the whole ciphertext. Hence, if one bit of the plaintext is changed, then the ciphertext will be completely changed in an unpredictable or pseudorandom manner. In CBDIA techniques (Feng & Liu, 2008; Wu, 2002), an image is encrypted into ciphertext by the confusion and diffusion operations, and then transmitted via the Internet or stored in the database. When the ciphertext is received or accessed, the corresponding decryption function inversely translates it back to the image so that the authorised user can view the content of the image. The encryption algorithms for the CBDIA techniques include the Data Encryption Standard algorithm (Smid & Branstad, 1988), the Advanced Encryption Standard algorithm (Burr, 2003), the RSA encryption algorithm (Sun, Wu, Ting, & Hinek, 2007), etc. By using these encryption algorithms, CBDIA techniques can successfully protect images and authenticate them during transmission and storage (Feng et al., 2008; Lin et al., 2003; Lu et al., 2009; Wu, 2002). Despite the effectiveness, CBDIA techniques still have a major limitation, known as an "analogy hole" (Cox, Doerr, & Furon, 2006). The "analogy hole" refers to the lack of ability of the CBDIA techniques to provide continuing protection for the digital images. In other words, the image must be decrypted before it can be viewed and the CBDIA techniques cannot provide any further protection once the image is decrypted for viewing. Due to this deficiency, the applicability of CBDIA techniques are limited and data-hiding-based digital image authentication techniques are therefore developed to provide continuous protection to the digital images (Dittmann, Wohlmacher, & Nahrstedt, 2001).

2.2. Data-Hiding-Based Digital Image Authentication (DHBDIA)

In the DHBDIA techniques, a data-hiding method, called watermarking, imperceptibly embeds the authentication message into digital images for authentication (Kundur & Hatzinakos, 1999b). Since the human visual system is not sensitive to minor changes in images, images can be slightly modified to embed authentication messages without being perceived. Associated with the authentication messages, a watermarking scheme can either modify the intensity values of images in the spatial domain (Brisbane, Safavi-Nani, & Ogunbona, 2005; Hu, Ma, Dou, & Gao, 2008; Li & Yuan, 2006) or the coefficients in the transform domain (Fridrich, 1998a; Li & Si, 2007; Cox, Kilian, Leighton, & Shamoon, 1997). This modification is insignificant that it can only be detected by the authorised user who applies the corresponding extraction algorithm. By extracting and verifying the authentication messages, which are called watermarks, the user can identify the ownership of the image and verify the integrity of the image content. As long as the watermark exists in the image, the image is protected by the DHBDIA techniques. Therefore, compared to CBDIA, DHBDIA techniques can provide continuous protection of the images because the watermark

is always carried by the image for authentication. As a result, in the past decade, there has been a significant shift of research interest from CBDIA to DHBDIA. Due to this shift, improving current DHBDIA techniques and developing innovative DHBDIA techniques are the major research objectives in our studies.

However, despite their effectiveness, DHBDIA techniques are unable to authenticate images which do not carry watermarks due to both economic and technical reasons. Employing the watermarking schemes in the digital device increases the complexity of the digital imaging device and hence increases the cost of the digital imaging devices (Nakamura, 2006). As a result, non-data-hiding-based digital image authentication techniques have been developed as a complement to DHBDIA techniques in recent years in order to authenticate unwatermarked digital images (Bayram, Sencar, Memon, & Avcibas, 2005; Fridrich, 2002, 2009).

3. APPLICATION OF DIA TECHNIQUES

DIA techniques are normally applied to authenticate sensitive digital images, such as medical images, military images, entertainment images, etc. These images must be protected due to privacy and sensitive data, such as name of the device, data of the capturing, etc.

3.1. Medical Applications

Currently, medical image databases are primarily maintained on Picture Archiving and Communication Systems (PACS), which manages the storage and distribution of images to radiologists, physicians, medical specialists, clinics, and imaging centres (Huang, 1998). In PACS, medical images are strongly related to patients' privacy, including health care history and current health conditions. Therefore, DIA techniques need to prevent illegal access to and distribution of these types of information (Coatrieux, Lecornu, Sankur, & Roux, 2006; Giakoumaki, Pavlopoulos, & Koutsouris, 2006). Furthermore, the reliability and the authenticity of medical images are the precondition of a correct diagnosis. However, hackers can easily destroy this reliability and authenticity by modifying the contents of the images. For example, Figure 3 illustrates an attack on a mammogram stored in a PACS. In Figure 3(a), a mass, as circled, exists in the breast area, which is a clear indication of malignant cancer. However, in Figure 3(b) the mass is removed, deliberately to mislead diagnosis. Therefore, DIA techniques should be applied on PACS to detect such malicious manipulations of medical images (Coatrieux, Le Guillou, Cauvin, & Roux, 2009).

3.2. Military Applications

Due to the digital revolution, the importance of digital images in military applications has been greatly increased (Simmons, 1988). In such an application, to ensure that appropriate decisions are made based on correct intelligence (the images in this case), DIA techniques can be used to identify the origin of the military images in order to verify whether the image is captured by a trustworthy device or faked by the enemy (Steinder, Iren, & Amer, 1999). DIA techniques can also be used to verify content integrity of images. If the images are maliciously modified by the enemy, DIA techniques should be able to localise the modified area and consequently indicate the misleading information in the modified areas (Hammouri, Ozturk, & Sunar, 2008).

3.3. Entertainment Applications

In the digital entertainment business, one of the most serious problems is piracy, which has caused huge losses for the multimedia industry (Chellappa & Shivendu, 2003). Because digital multimedia products can be easily copied, the user can make profits from illegally distribution of the pirated copies of multimedia products without paying any copyright royalties. For example, in 2005 movie piracy were responsible for a loss of 18.2 billion dollars for the global movie industry and such a loss increased to 20.1 billion in 2006 (Jaisingh, 2009).

In the light of losses due to copyright piracy, DIA techniques, especially DHBDIA techniques,

Figure 3. The original and modified mammogram on PACS

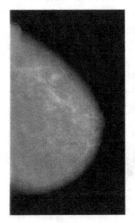

(a) The original mammogram with a mass

(b) The modified mammogram with the mass removed

are in urgently needed for copyright protection in the digital entertainment business. These techniques can restrict the operations on multimedia products so that the products can be viewed but are not able to be copied (Barni & Bartolini, 2004). Some DHBDIA techniques have also been developed to trace all users involved in piracy (Trappe, Wu, Wang, & Liu, 2003; Nakashima, Tachibana, & Babaguchi, 2009).

3.4. Forensics Applications

The widespread installing surveillance cameras have proved to be quite useful in capturing crime scenes and record them as digital images, which can be submitted to the court of law as evidence. However, the authenticity of the evidence must be firstly proved before the court of law can accept them, and such a requirement is described as the chain of evidence. In legal terminology, the chain of evidence (or chain of custody) refers to *"the ability to guarantee the identity and integrity of the specimen from collection through to reporting of the test results"* (Casey, 1999). For example, Figure 4(a) illustrates a photo from a traffic surveillance camera, recording a car parked on the road side. In Figure 4(b), the registration plate of this car is

modified, which should be rejected by the court of law if presented as evidence.

In order to determine whether a digital image satisfies the requirement of the chain of evidence, DIA techniques can be used to identify the source camera (Ho, Zhu, Vrusias, & Armstrong, 2006) and prove the authenticity of the images (Chen & Leung, 2008).

4. TECHNIQUES OF DIGITAL IMAGE AUTHENTICATION

4.1. General Framework of DHBDIA

DHBDIA techniques insert an authentication message into digital media before it is distributed, shared or transmitted. Such an authentication message, which is uniquely generated by the user, is later extracted to serve the purposes of anti-falsification, copyright protection and access control. In DHBDIA techniques, the methods of inserting the authentication message are called *watermarking*, whose working processes are illustrated in Figure 5. Watermarking schemes can be separated into two phases, the *embedding* phase and the *extraction* phase. In the embedding phase,

Figure 4. A photo from the traffic surveillance camera and a faked version

(a) The photo from surveillance camera

(b) The photo with faked registration plate

the authentication message (also called the watermark) W is embedded into the digital media I by the embedding algorithm. A secret key K is used as an important parameter for watermark generation and watermark embedding. Without this key, the unauthorised party cannot extract the watermark W from the watermarked images. In the extraction phase, the user extracts the watermark pattern W' carried by the image, using the shared secret key K. Then the extracted watermark pattern W' is compared to the original watermark W, which is either regenerated based on the invariant features of the image (such as the points of the edges in the contents (Huang & Zhang, 2006) and the secret key (Choi, Lee, & Kim, 2004; Chen & Yeh, 2006) or shared between the embedder and the recipient (Cox et al., 1997; Mukherjee, Maitra, & Acton, 2004). If the two watermarks are identical, then the digital image is deemed authentic; otherwise, the authentication system reports an authentication failure.

Under the framework demonstrated in Figure 5, a number of watermarking schemes have been developed for DIA, which can be divided into three categories: robust watermarking, fragile watermarking and semi-fragile watermarking (Lee & Jung, 2001; Liu et al., 2002; Macq, Dittmann, & Delp, 2004).

4.2. Robust Watermarking

Robust watermarking schemes can extract the watermark correctly from the images under common signal processing, manipulation and attack such as geometric distortion, collusion and forgery (Macq et al., 2004). Figure 6 demonstrates a robust watermarking scheme in the spatial domain, where the readable watermark "Mandrill" is embedded into the points of the edges of the image (Huang et al., 2006). Figure 6(a) is the original image and Figure 6(b) is the watermark. Figure 6(c) is the modified image, in which Gaussian noise has been added, while Figure 6(d) is the extracted watermark from Figure 6(c). In Figure 6(d), the word "Mandrill" is still clearly readable in the watermark despite the noise. Figure 6(e) is the cropped and re-scaled version of Figure 6(a) and the extracted watermark is illustrated in Figure 6(f), where the watermark has been seriously distorted; however, the word "Mandrill" remains

Figure 5. A general framework of DHBDIA techniques

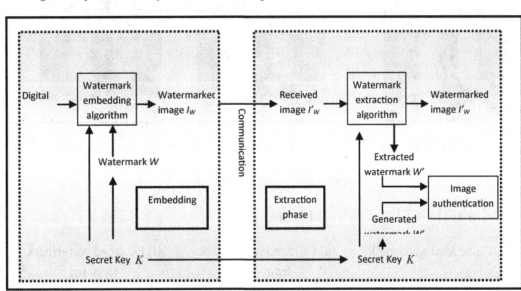

identifiable. Figure 7 demonstrates another robust watermarking scheme in the DCT domain, which is designed to be robust to the JPEG compression (Wu & Tsai, 1999). Figure 7(a) is the watermarked Lena after JPEG compressing with 50% quality, and the smaller logo on the right of Lena is the extracted watermark from the compressed Lena. In Figure 7(a), the extracted watermark is quite clear. Figure 7(b) illustrates the extraction result from the image with Gaussian noise and Figure 7(c) shows the extraction result from the cropped image. Although a quarter of the image has been cropped, the outline of the watermark is still clearly identifiable in Figure 7(c).

The spread spectrum-based method is one of the most widely applied techniques for robust watermarking (Cox et al., 1997). In these methods, the original image is first transformed to the frequency domain, then the watermark is either inserted into every coefficient for high robustness (Cox et al., 1997; Malvar & Florencio, 2003) or only inserted into the high-frequency coefficients for low distortion (Malik, Ansari, & Khokhar, 2008). After the inverse transform, the watermark is spread over the full range of frequencies, thus resulting in high robustness. Cox et al. (1997) proposed pioneering work for the spread spectrum-based watermarking in the DCT domain (Cox et al., 1997), where a watermark is inserted into coefficients of all frequencies by either directly adding the watermark to the coefficients or using an amplitude modulated factor to linearly transformed the coefficients. The watermark can be extracted by examining the correlations between the coefficients of the received images and watermark in the watermark database. The watermark, which leads to the highest correlation, is identified as the embedded watermark. Based on Cox's method, Altun et al. (2009) combined several methods to construct the optimal spread spectrum-based watermark techniques, including a method of maximising embedding strength, a method of minimising frequency-weighted perceptual distortion and a method of minimising watermark texture visibility. Gkizeli et al. (2007) proposed a method to maximise the embedding strength which is determined by the maximum signal-to-interference-plus-noise ratio. A linear

Figure 6. Demonstration of robust watermarking in the spatial domain

(a) Original image

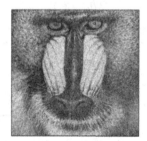

(c) Image with

additional Gaussian noise

(e) Image cropped

and rescaled

Mandrill

(b) Embedded watermark

Mandrill

(d) Extraced watermark
from (c)

Mandrill

(f) Extraced watermark
from (d)

Figure 7. Demonstration of robust watermarking in the DCT domain

| (a) JPEG compression with 50 % quality | (b) Gaussian noise has been added-in | (c) 1/4 of the image has been cropped |

transform is used to modulate the watermark to reach the maximum signal-to-interference-plus-noise ratio. As a result, Gkizeli's method reaches a very low error rate in the detection, implying higher robustness. Another spread spectrum technique (Liu, Dong, & Zeng, 2007) was proposed to minimise the watermark texture visibility by the aid of the just noticeable difference (JND). The JND, which is measures from the experiments in the human visual system, is a content-dependent feature indicating the maximum amount of data that can be embedded into the image without being noticed by humans. In Liu et al. (2007), a nonlinear function is designed based on the just noticeable difference, and this function modulates the watermark to achieve the minimal watermark texture visibility for lower distortion and higher robustness. Besides optimising the embedding algorithm discussed as above, Maity and Maity (2009)) optimised the watermarking extraction algorithm for spread spectrum-based methods in order to achieve low error rate in detection and thus higher robustness. In the extraction phase of their method, a minimum mean square error (MMSE) algorithm was applied to estimate the strength of the noise corrupted watermarked image, and then a fuzzy logic function, which is a machine learning function, was used to calculate the decision variable for the watermarks. The values of the decision variable are ranked as very strong, strong, weak and very weak. Then the

watermark, which corresponds to the decision variable with value "very strong", is identified as the embedded watermark. As a result, Maity's extraction method achieves lower detection error rate, implying higher robustness. Besides methods in the DCT domain, the spread spectrum-based methods can be applied in other transform domains in order to achieve better performance (Ghouti, Bouridane, Ibrahim, & Boussakta, 2006; Kumsawat, Attakitmongcol, & Srikaew, 2005). For example, Ghouti et al. (2006) proposed an adaptive spread spectrum-based method in the balanced wavelet transform domain. The watermark is adapted by a perceptual model therefore strikes a good balance between the distortion and robustness. Meanwhile, Kumsawat et al. (2005) used a genetic algorithm training the watermark with the image, in order to determine the optimal embedding strength parameter, and then embedding the watermark in a discrete multiwavelet transform domain for optimal performance.

While spread spectrum-based techniques have been widely used to embed a small number of watermark bits robustly in multimedia signals, quantisation-based embedding is more common for high capacity watermarking schemes for authentication (Wu, 2003). A popular technique, often known as Quantisation Index Modulation (QIM), was proposed by Chen and Wornell (2001a, 2001b). Their technique is considered to be the pioneering work of the quantisation-based watermarking schemes. QIM chooses a quantisation step size and uses it to round a feature, which can be an intensity value of the pixel or a coefficient in the transform domain, to the closest even multiples of the quantisation steps to embed a watermark bit "0" and to odd multiples of the quantisation steps to embed a watermark bit "1". To extract the QIM embedded watermark from the distorted images with noise, the original QIM method applies a nearest neighbour rule (Cover & Hart, 1967), which identifies the nearest quantised value to the received values. If this quantised value is an even multiple of the quantisation steps, then it represents watermark bit '0', and vice verse.

Besides this nearest neighbour rule, other extraction methods are developed for QIM in order to enhance the robustness and decrease the error rate in the extraction. Assuming the noise follows Cauchy and Gaussian distribution, the Cauchy (Hecht, 1987) detector, which is a probabilistic model for signal detection, is applied to detect the QIM embedded watermark (Alexia & Michael, 2004). In another method (Kang, Huang, & Zeng, 2008), a training sequence adaptively estimates irregular noise using a Fourier analysis and then the noise is subtracted from the received data. This method significantly enhances the robustness by decreasing the error rate in watermark extraction.

In quantisation-based watermarking (Wu, 2003), distortion control and robustness are conflicting factors. Generally speaking, larger quantisation steps ensure higher robustness; however, they also lead to higher embedding distortion. To decrease the embedding distortion at the cost of robustness, distortion compensation quantisation index modulation (DCQIM) (Boyer, Duhamel, & Blanc-Talon, 2007) was developed, which slightly modifies the quantised values towards original intensity values as a compensation. The compensation distance is determined by the Euclidean distance between the quantised values and the original values. Longer distances lead to a larger compensation and vice versa. Another distortion compensation method is proposed by

Pei and Chen (2006), in which the quantised value can be adaptively determined by associating the embedding distortion and the probability density function (PDF) of the intensities. If the intensity to be quantised has a higher probability density, implying a higher frequency of appearance in the image, then this value will be compensated more significantly. Conversely, a smaller compensation distortion is assigned to less frequent intensities in the images. Pei's method has greatly reduced the distortion of the quantisation-based watermarking schemes. Alternatively, quantisation-based methods can be applied in the transform domain in order to enhance the robustness. Wang and Lin (2004) grouped the wavelet coefficients of the image into so-called super trees, by associating the bit plane of the coefficients, and then embedded the watermark by quantising the super trees. The quantised tree exhibits a large enough statistical difference, so that even though the noise has been added into the images, the quantised result can still be correctly identified by statistically during the watermark extraction process. Since watermark bits are embedded in perceptually important frequency bands in the super trees, Wang and Lin's methods are more resistant to frequency-based attacks, such as low-pass filtering (Quendo, Rius, Person, & Ney, 2001). Also, the watermark is spread throughout spatial regions, yielding greater robustness against spatial domain geometric attacks.

There are other robust watermarking schemes in addition to the spread spectrum-based watermarking methods and the quantisation-based watermarking methods (Zhang, Cheng, Qiu, & Cheng, 2008; Kim & Lee, 2003; Simitopoulos, Koutsonanos, & Strintzis, 2003; Huang, Chiang, Chang, & Tu, 2005). For example, in Zhang et al. (2008), the watermark is embedded into feature points, which are calculated in the multiscale curvelet transform domain. Such feature points record the edges of the objects in the image content, therefore, if the content of the image is not changed, the feature points can be correctly identified and the watermark in the feature points can be extracted. In Kim et al. (2003), a similar technique was proposed to embed the watermark into the Zernike moments, which is also a feature representing the shape of objects in the content of the images. Feature points in the Radon transform, which is resistant to the majority of rotation and scaling manipulations, were also used to embed watermarks in (Simitopoulos et al., 2003).

4.3. Fragile Watermarking

A fragile watermarking scheme can be used for image authentication, in which the embedded watermark can be destroyed easily by any modification. This destruction may be either global, i.e. no part of the watermark can be recovered, or local, i.e. only part of the watermark is damaged. Figure 8 demonstrates an example of a fragile watermarking scheme, in which the watermark will be locally destroyed due to manipulation (Barni & Bartoloni, 2004). Figure 8(a) is a watermarked image of a F16 aircraft and in Figure 8(b), the characters on the aircraft have been removed. The authentication result is demonstrated in Figure 8(c), where the modified area is detected and highlighted in white in the authentication map.

In fragile watermarking, one of the key issues is to setup a block-wise/pixel-wise dependence

so that watermark embedding involves not only the block/pixel itself but also other blocks/pixels within a neighbourhood (Li et al., 2006, 2007). With the involvement of contextual information, the fragile watermarking scheme can successively raise the alarm of the modification and localise the modified area against common attacks, such as cover-up/cut-and-paste (Barreto, Kim, & Rijmen, 2002) and Holliman-Memon counterfeiting attack (Holliman & Memon, 2000) (also known as the birthday attack (Barreto et al., 2002), vector quantisation attack (Wong & Memon, 2000), or collage attack (Fridrich, 2002; Fridrich, Goljan, & Memon, 2002). A cover-up attack is the operation of cutting one region/block of the image and pasting it somewhere in the same or another image. The Holliman-Memon counterfeiting attack / birthday attack is devised on the basis of the so-called birthday paradox (Stallings, 1998). According to the birthday paradox, if the fragile watermarking system uses a hash function producing a bit string of length l, then the user can successfully modify the image without raising any alarm if only he/she can obtain $2^{l/2}$ copies of the watermarked images. In order to counter these attacks, Li (Li et al., 2006) proposed setting up a non-deterministic contextual dependence approach in the creation of the watermark. This dependence could either be block-wise, which

Figure 8. Demonstration of fragile watermarking (Li et al., 2006)

(a) Watermarked image   (b) Modified image   (c) Locally destroyed watermark

involves the information of neighbouring blocks to create a watermark (Li, 2004; Li et al., 2007), or pixel-wise, which involves all the surrounding pixels for watermark creation (Li & Wang, 2003). Meanwhile, this non-deterministic contextual dependence should be controlled by a secret key for higher security.

Besides watermark creation, there are many embedding methods proposed for fragile watermarking schemes, and one of the simplest and most common schemes is the least significant bit (LSB) method (Chang, Hsiao, & Chan, 2003). The luminance component of an image can be decomposed into bit planes through the binary representation, which is unique to every integer. Considering a gray-scale image (8 bits per pixel), each pixel can be represented by a non-negative integer D in the interval $[0, 255]$. The binary representation of this value D is

$$D = \sum_{i=0}^{7} b_i \cdot 2^i, \text{ where } b_i \in \{0, 1\} \tag{1}$$

where b_i is the binary value on the ith bit. The modification on b_0 leads to minimal distortion, therefore, b_0 is defined as the LSB of the pixels. In the LSB-based scheme, the watermark is inserted into the least-significant bit plane of the cover image either by directly replacing the LSBs (Chan & Cheng, 2004) or by modifying the LSBs according to a reversible function (van Schyndel, Tirkel, & Osborne, 1996). In Chan et al. (2004), the watermark is transformed into bit planes and replaces the LSB of the pixels directly. The watermark, which is embedded by the replacement, can be simply read out from the LSB of the watermarked images, which opens a security gap for potential attacks. Therefore, in Lu, Shen, and Chung (2003) the bit planes of the watermark are randomly permuted according to a secret key and then added to the LSB of the pixels by an XOR manipulation. This method introduces an extra key control security into the LSB-based water-

marking schemes. A more secure Fibonacci LSB-based watermarking scheme was proposed by Battisti et al. (2006). They decompose the bit planes of the pixels by the Fibonacci p-sequence, which is a method to transform the decimal integer into binary representation by using p-polynomials. Then the LSB of the intensities of the pixels, which fulfils the Zeckendorf condition, are replaced by the watermark bit. The Zeckendorf condition defines the unique Fibonacci representation for every positive integer.

Clustering algorithms can also be used to construct fragile watermarking schemes in the spatial domain in order to achieve high capacity and low distortion (Seppannen, Makela, & Keskinarkaus, 2000; Brisbane et al., 2005). The main idea of clustering-based watermarking schemes is to cluster similar intensity values into groups, and to use the index of the intensity values to represent the watermark bit (Seppannen et al., 2000; Brisbane et al., 2005). Seppannen et al. (2000) proposed a k-means clustering-based watermarking scheme for colour images. In their scheme, the RGB colour space is partitioned into many clusters and all the intensity values in the clusters are indexed. To embed watermark bits into a pixel, the cluster, to which the intensity of the pixel belongs, is identified and then the intensity whose index equals the watermark bits is used to substitute the original intensity. Although high embedding capacity for this scheme has been reported, high distortion makes this scheme unacceptable. Based on Seppannen et al.'s (2000) work, Brisbane et al. (2005) proposed another scheme aiming at trading capacity for lower distortion. In their method, instead of using every pixel for embedding, only the pixels nearer to the centre of the clusters are selected for embedding. This results in a lower distortion because the upper limit of distortion, which is determined by the distance from the substituted intensity to the centre of the clusters, is reduced. Meanwhile, the selection operation is controlled by a key, thus increasing the security of the scheme.

Clustering algorithms can also be applied in conjunction with a vector quantisation (VQ) algorithm, which is a popular image compression algorithm that uses a predefined vector to represent the block of pixels in the images (Cosman, Oehler, Riskin, & Gray, 1993). The predefined vector is called a codeword in VQ compression and the collection of the codewords is called a codebook. Lee et al. (2008) clustered the codewords for watermarking. In Lee's scheme, the codewords are grouped into pairs with the nearest distance in a minimum spanning tree, and then indexed to represent the watermark bit. Xing et al. (2003) utilised the k-means clustering algorithm for grouping the codewords into bigger clusters with more than two components, thus leading to higher capacity. Chang and Wu (2006) proposed another improved clustering-based watermarking scheme by applying codeword permutation and adaptive clustering. While embedding a certain amount of a watermark, the codeword is regrouped adaptively after a permutation. Despite the high computation load, Chang and Wu's scheme is capable of providing better image quality and embedding capacity.

Both the LSB-based watermarking and clustering-based watermarking are applicable in the spatial domain. However, they are not always applicable to where transformation is necessary for compressing the images because each small level of a quantised coefficient value corresponds to a big quantisation step in the spatial domain. This makes exhaustive embedding a visually intrusive operation (Li et al., 2006). To overcome this problem as well as to maintain low embedding distortion, watermarking schemes in the transform domain (Winne, Knowles, ll, & Nagarajah, 2002; Yuan & Zhang, 2003) tend to watermark some selected coefficients in the mid-frequencies of the host image. In the approach proposed by Winne

et al. (2002), to minimise the embedding distortion, only the coefficients of the high-frequency sub-bands at the finest scale of the luminance component are watermarked. All the other coefficients and components are neither watermarked nor involved during the watermarking process. Therefore, the major limitation of their algorithm is that it does not protect all the coefficients so that it is vulnerable to cut-and-paste, vector quantisation and transplantation attacks (Barreto et al., 2002). In Yuan and Zhang's (2003), work a Gaussian mixture model is used to obtain the distribution parameters of wavelet coefficients. Some coefficients of large value are modified to embed the watermark. However, since the neighbourhood is large, when the image is tampered with, the scheme cannot localise the tampering accurately. Li (2007) proposed a fragile watermarking scheme in the DWT domain in order to accurately localise all the modified area and protect all the coefficients in the images. The coefficients in the low frequency components, which are defined as non-watermarkable, are recursively projected to the watermarkable coefficients in the high frequency component. A secret key is used to determine the projection between the low-frequency components and the high-frequency component and consequently a key-controlled non-deterministic dependence is set up in Li's method. Although not every coefficient are watermarked, all of the coefficients are protected by the non-deterministic block-wise dependence. By examining the missing links in the dependence, the scheme can accurately localise the modified area. Beside the DCT and the DWT domains, Ho et al. (2008) embedded the watermark in the z-transform domain by exploiting the positions of zeros. The z-transform establishes a global dependence on the pixels in the images. This dependence is sensitive to the value change of even a single pixel so that the z-transform domain can effectively identify any minor modifications.

4.4. Semi-Fragile Watermarking

Semi-fragile watermarking is a watermarking technique where the watermark is expected to be destroyed by any modifications except a very limited number of incidental modifications (Barni et al., 2004). In contrast with the fragile watermarking, which is sensitive to any modification, semi-fragile watermarking is tolerant to some legal manipulations, such as lossy compression and quality enhancement. Hence, semi-fragile watermarking is capable of coping with complicated situations where illegal modifications must be identified and localised but legal manipulation should not raise an alarm during the authentication process (Chamlawi, Li, Usman, & Khan, 2009; Zhu, Ho, & Marziliano, 2006; Ho, 2007). Generally speaking, semi-fragile watermarking schemes need to be robust against incidental manipulations and non-deterministically dependent on the content of the image. The robustness is necessary because semi-fragile watermarking schemes must achieve a certain degree of robustness against legal manipulations, while, the non-deterministic dependence is necessary because the semi-fragile watermarking scheme needs to localise the modified area according to the watermark destroyed (Celik, Saber, Sharma, & Tekalp, 2001).

Semi-fragile watermarking in the spatial domain is generally developed based on statistical models. The features of the statistical models are preserved by incidental manipulations but destroyed by the modifications of the contents of images (Queluz, 2001; Queluz, 1999; Marvel, Hartwig, & Boncelet, 2000; Marvel, Boncelet, & Retter, 1999; Queluz & Lany, 2000). Meanwhile, the statistical models also set up dependence among pixels so that all pixels will be protected and manipulations on the content can be accurately localised. For example, Marvel et al. (1999, 2000) utilised the Gaussian model to develop semi-fragile watermarking scheme. In their work, the watermark as well as some bits of the error-correction code is firstly embedded into pixels in a polar coordinate system. The error-correction code increases the scheme's robustness to incidental modifications because it can be used to correct the watermark in the extraction phase. The watermarked area is modulated by a Gaussian signal to introduce globe dependence. In the extraction phase, the watermark is extracted from the demodulated area and then corrected by the error-correction code for authentication. Quelez et al. (1999, 2000, 2001) used a statistical model based on random basis functions for semi-fragile watermarking. The image is divided into blocks of the non-overlapping 3×3-pixels. Every block is treated as a matrix and then projected onto a random vector space by using the random basis functions. The projection result is then ordered by rank and the median value in the vector is quantised based on the watermark message. Incidental modifications should not change the rank of the values in the block, thus the quantisation process is robust to incidental modifications.

Semi-fragile watermarking schemes in the transform domain are mainly developed in the DCT domain and the Discrete Wavelet Transform (DWT) domain (Fridrich, 1998b, 1998a, 1999; Lin & Chang, 2000, 2001; Kundur et al., 1999a, 1999b). Since JPEG compression is a DCT-domain operation and JPEG 2000 is a DWT-domain operation (Grgic, Mrak, Grgic, & Zovko-Cihlar, 2003), semi-fragile watermarking schemes in these domains are capable of differentiating compression operations from illegal modifications such as cover-up/cut-and-paste (Barreto et al., 2002) and the low-pass filtering attacks (Quendo et al., 2001). Lin and Chang (2000, 2001) proposed semi-fragile watermarking in the DCT domain based on the invariant relationship of DCT coefficients after JPEG compression. The coefficients are randomly selected and forced to either odd or even multiples of the quantisation step, based on the watermark bit. The quantisation step is determined according to the quantisation table in the JPEG compression algorithm. Lin and Chang's schemes did not involved non-deterministic dependence so that their schemes are not sensitive enough to a Holliman-Memon counterfeiting attack (Holliman et al., 2000). Meanwhile, their methods are not robust against the salt-and-pepper noise (Ekici, Coskun, Umut, & Sankur, 2001). To overcome these problems, Fridrich et al. (1998b, 1998a, 1999) applied an indexing function on the DCT coefficients in the middle and low frequencies. The indexing function embeds the watermark into the coefficients by modifying the coefficients according to the watermark and the previous coefficient indexed based on zigzag searching. After the modification, the watermarked coefficients satisfy a predetermined geometric sequence, which is an increasing sequence controlled by a threshold α. The geometric sequence introduces the non-deterministic dependence among the coefficients. Therefore, these schemes can effectively localise tampered areas in the images. Fridich's schemes have shown to be more robust to the incidental manipulation and salt-and-pepper noise than Lin and Cheng's scheme (Ekici et al., 2001). In the DWT domain, Kundur and Hatzinakos (1999b, 1999a) quantised the DWT coefficients into even/odd multiples of the quantisation step based on the watermark. Their approach was particularly robust to JPEG 2000 compression (Ekici, Sankur, Coskun, Umut, & Akcay, 2004). Apart from the DCT and DWT domains, there are also other transforms used in semi-fragile watermarking schemes. Zhao et al. (2007) embedded the watermark into the LSB of the coefficients of the Slant transform, which is a linear transform for the images. The Slant transform establishes global dependence among pixels, therefore, this scheme can accurately localise the tampered area. On the other hand, the Slant transform is compatible with JPEG compression so that Zhao's method can differentiate JPEG compression from malicious manipulations, such as cut-and-paste attacks. Moreover, as a linear transform, the Slant transform leads to a faster processing speed than the DCT and DWT methods.

5. FUTURE RESEARCH DIRECTIONS

5.1. Future Research Directions on DHBDIA Techniques

DHBDIA and watermarking techniques have been developed over 10 years. However, several issues remain open in this research area.

5.1.1. Content-Based Image Authentication and Error Correction Watermarking

The objective of content-based image authentication is to develop multimedia authentication methods based on content analysis techniques (Liu & Tan, 2000). Most of the current watermark schemes globally embed the watermark for authentication. The content-based image authentication should allow the user to only modify the background area for embedding and authentication (Parameswaran & Anbumani, 2008; Kankanhalli & Ramakrishnan, 1998; Liu et al., 2000). The current schemes can find the background area using statistical techniques (Parameswaran et al., 2008; Kankanhalli et al., 1998; Liu et al., 2000), such as independent component analysis (Parameswaran et al., 2008), Neyman-Pearson criterion (Kankanhalli et al., 1998) and pseudo-noise sequence (Liu et al., 2000). Furthermore, determination of background areas should consider semantic interpretation so that the background area can be correctly and automatically detected in the image (Dyer, 1982).

With the content-based image authentication watermarking scheme, the user can treat the background area as a *redundant* area in the embedding. The redundancy can be utilised to embed the authentication message and the information about the region of interests. In this manner, the watermarking scheme will be able to reconstruct the region of interests even if the image is partially destroyed during transmission. In this way, this type of watermarking scheme can correct image errors caused by the transmission. This technique needs the support of the content-based watermarking; therefore this area has not been investigated in depth. Since error correction watermarking is important, future research into this area would be worthwhile.

5.1.2. Public-Key Watermarking and Digital Image Resource Management

Public-key watermarking is a newly developed branch of watermarking schemes (Xie, Wu, Du, & Li, 2007), where multiple security keys can be distributed to multiple users for extracting the watermark. The distribution of the key greatly extends the implementation range of the DHBDIA. Traditional DHBDIA is a one-to-one system where only one legal user can hold the key for authentication. Thus, the user of the DHBDIA is limited to single authorised users, such as the official third-party. In contrast, the public-key watermarking allows the DHBDIA system to be shared by multiple users (Xie et al., 2007). Currently, the public-key cryptographic schemes are widely applied in the Digital Resource Management (DRM) systems (Cui, Cui, & Meng, 2008). The study of public-key watermarking scheme has just started and been not sufficient yet (Chang & Chou, 2008; Fu, 2007). Developing more public-key watermarking scheme will be a new research direction in DHBDIA techniques.

5.2. Future Research Directions on NDBDIA Techniques

Intensive research effort in the last decade has led to the maturity of digital watermarking and data hiding. The last few years have seen an increasing number of researchers switching their interest toward the new area of digital forensics. It is expected that in the near future, the following research agendas will receive more attention.

5.2.1. Managing the PRNU Database

In the applications of the NDHBDIA techniques, a huge database is necessary to hold all of the reference PRNU pattern noises and hence the management of the database is an important issue. One of the challenges in the database management is to reduce the physical storage requirement of the PRNU database. To authenticate images taken by the same camera at different resolutions, current DIA techniques need to extract the individual reference PRNU pattern noises at different resolutions (Lukas, Fridrich, & Goljan, 2006; Chen, Fridrich, Goljan, & Lukas, 2007, 2008), and all of these reference PRNUs representing the same camera must be stored in the database, which incurs significant storage overhead. One potential solution to this problem is to study the relationship between the references PRNU pattern noises of different resolutions so that only one PRNU of a particular resolution is needed in the database. When images of different resolutions are under investigation, the reference PRNU in the database is re-sampled in some way to serve the authentication purpose. Therefore, re-sampling of PRNU is expected to be of interest in the near future.

5.2.2. Development of Advanced PRNU-Based Blind Authentication Techniques

Blind authentication techniques are to identify the source cameras and verify the content integrity based on the PRNU extracted from the images under investigation without the availability of the reference PRNU pattern noise. The applicability of current PRNU-based authentication techniques is seriously limited due to the availability requirement of the reference PRNU. In most situations, such reference pattern noises are not available. For example, in authenticating the trustworthiness of a military image released by an enemy, the source camera and the reference PRNU are unavailable. In civil cases, a criminal may destroy the camera so that the investigator cannot obtain any PRNU from the source camera. As a result, blind authentication techniques are more desirable in these applications. Li (2009a, 2009b) has done some work on blind source camera identification. In his method, without the reference PRNUs, a learning algorithm links/classifies the images into groups based only on the PRNU extracted from the images. The images within the same groups are deemed as the images captured by the same camera. In contrast with blind source camera identification, there is a research gap in blind content integrity verification. In content integrity verification, the reference PRNU pattern noise is necessary for the PRNU comparison (Farid, 2009; Chen et al., 2008). One of the potential methods to close this gap is to investigate the consistency of the PRNU. During the image acquisition process, the image may undergo the processes such as gamma correction, white balancing, enhancement and JPEG compression. These processes manipulate the whole image and introduce noise with a certain "pattern" into the image (Holst, 1998). Denoising and averaging the PRNU cannot perfectly remove the aforementioned noise and therefore by investigating the residual of this noise and looking for signs of inconsistency, the investigator can verify the integrity of the image content. In this way, the investigator should be able to blindly verify content integrity without the reference PRNU patter noise.

5.2.3. Search for New Digital Fingerprints

Current NDHBDIA techniques are developed based on PRNU and CFA (and the interpolation matrix). However these two fingerprints are not always feasible in the application listed below.

- Most mobile phones are equipped with a camera. However, authenticating images captured by mobile phone cameras is a difficult task due to the low quality of the im-

ages, which contains strong noise produced by the cheap electronic components in the mobile phone cameras (Gorokhovskiy, Flint, Atta, & Glushnev, 2007). This noise outweighs the sensor pattern noise in the camera noise and, on the other hand, some of the noise is random which is not usable for image authentication. Besides the infeasibility of the PRNU, the CFA may also be infeasible in authenticating the image taken by mobile phone cameras. Because the manufacturers tend to apply the most common CFA and interpolation algorithm, such as Bayer CFA and bilinear interpolation algorithm, in their products for economic reasons (Bradbeer, 1995). Therefore, looking for more effective fingerprints for the mobile phone camera is a challenge for NDHBDIA techniques.

- Computer graphic (CG) images are another important type of digital images. CG images are produced in large quantity by standard imaging software, such as Adobe Photoshop, Macromedia Firework, etc (Russ, 2001). Because these images are not captured by cameras, the fingerprints of the cameras, like PRNU and CFA, are not feasible for CG image authentication. Currently, the technique can only identify the software that has create the image under investigation by looking of the quantisation table used in the JPEG compression (Sorell, 2009a, 2009b). However, the same software may be installed on millions of computers and current techniques cannot serve the purposes of identifying individual computers that are responsible for producing an image. As a result, feasible fingerprints should be developed in order to identify the source computer of CG images.

There have been some preliminary research on using different types of digital fingerprints, such as camera response functions (Hsu & Chang, 2007), re-sampling artefacts (Popescu & Farid, 2005), JPEG compression (Sorell, 2009b, 2009c), lens aberration (Choi, Lam, & Wong, 2006; Lanh, Emmanuel, & Kankanhalli, 2007), as well as device attributes such as binary similarity measures, image quality measures and higher order wavelet statistics (Sankur, Celiktutan, & Avcibas, 2007; Xu, Gao, Shi, Su, & Hu, 2009; Sutthiwan, Ye, & Shi, 2009). Although their performance is not acceptable at present for various reasons for example, some require that specific assumptions be satisfied (Popescu et al., 2005; Hsu et al., 2007), they do point to the direction of future research.

REFERENCES

Alexia, B., & Michael, S. (2004). Optimal watermark detection under quantization the transform domain. *IEEE Transactions on Circuits and Systems for Video Technology, 14*, 1308–1319. doi:10.1109/TCSVT.2004.836753

Altun, H. O., Orsdemir, A., Sharma, G., & Bocko, M. F. (2009). Optimal spread spectrum watermark embedding via a multistep feasibility formulation. *IEEE Transactions on Image Processing, 18*, 371–387. doi:10.1109/TIP.2008.2008222

Barni, M., & Bartolini, F. (2004). Data hiding for fighting piracy. *Signal Processing Magazine, 21*, 28–39. doi:10.1109/MSP.2004.1276109

Barni, M., & Bartoloni, F. (2004). *Watermarking systems engineering*. Boca Raton, FL: CRC Press.

Barreto, P. S. L. M., Kim, H. Y., & Rijmen, V. (2002). Toward secure public-key blockwise fragile authentication watermarking. *Vision. Image and Signal Processing, 149*, 57–62. doi:10.1049/ip-vis:20020168

Bartolini, F., Tefas, A., Barni, M., & Pitas, I. (2001). Image authentication techniques for surveillance applications. *Proceedings of the IEEE, 89*, 1403–1418. doi:10.1109/5.959338

Battisti, F., Carli, M., Neri, A., & Egiaziarian, K. (2006). A generalized Fibonacci LSB data hiding technique. In *Proceedings of the Third International Conference on Computers and Devices for Communication*.

Bayram, S., Sencar, H. T., Memon, N., & Avcibas, I. (2005). Source camera identification based on CFA interpolation. In *Proceedings of the IEEE International Conference on Image Processing* (pp. 69-72).

Boyer, J.-P., Duhamel, P., & Blanc-Talon, J. (2007). Performance analysis of scalar DC-QIM for zero-bit watermarking. *IEEE Transactions on Information Forensics and Security, 2*, 283–289. doi:10.1109/TIFS.2007.897279

Bradbeer, R. (1995). A medium resolution intelligent video camera. *IEEE Transactions on Consumer Electronics, 41*, 573–578. doi:10.1109/30.468092

Brisbane, G., Safavi-Nani, R., & Ogunbona, P. (2005). High-capacity steganography using a shared colour palette. *IEEE Proceedings on Vision, Image, and Signal Processing, 152*, 787–792. doi:10.1049/ip-vis:20045047

Burr, W. E. (2003). Selecting the advanced encryption standard. *Security & Privacy, 1*, 43–52. doi:10.1109/MSECP.2003.1193210

Casey, E. (1999). *Digital evidence and computer crime: Forensic science, computers and the Internet*. New York, NY: Academic Publishing.

Celik, M. U., Saber, E., Sharma, G., & Tekalp, A. M. (2001). Analysis of feature-based geometry invariant watermarking. *Proceedings of the SPIE: Security and Watermarking of Multimedia Contents III, 4314*, 261–268.

Chamlawi, R., Li, C.-T., Usman, I., & Khan, A. (2009). Authentication and recovery of digital images: potential application in video surveillance and remote sensing. In *Proceedings of the Digest of Technical Papers in the International Conference on Consumer Electronics* (pp. 1-2).

Chan, C. K., & Cheng, L. M. (2004). Hiding data in images by simple LSB substitution export. *Pattern Recognition, 37*, 469–474. doi:10.1016/j.patcog.2003.08.007

Chang, C., & Chou, H. (2008). A new public-key oblivious fragile watermarking for image authentication using Discrete Cosine Transform. In *Proceedings of the Second International Conference on Future Generation Communication and Networking Symposium.*

Chang, C.-C., Hsiao, J.-Y., & Chan, C.-S. (2003). Finding optimal least-significant-bit substitution in image hiding by dynamic programming strategy. *Pattern Recognition, 36*, 1583–1595. doi:10.1016/S0031-3203(02)00289-3

Chang, C. C., & Wu, W. C. (2006). Hiding secret data adaptively in vector quantisation index tables. *IEEE Proceedings on Vision, Image, and Signal Processing, 153*, 589–597. doi:10.1049/ip-vis:20050153

Chellappa, R. K., & Shivendu, S. (2003). Economics of technology standards: Implications for offline movie piracy in a global context. In *Proceedings of the 36th Annual Hawaii International Conference on System Sciences* (p. 10).

Chen, B., & Wornell, G. W. (2001a). Quantization index modulation methods for digital watermarking and information embedding of multimedia. *Journal of Very Large Signal Processing Systems, 27*, 7–33. doi:10.1023/A:1008107127819

Chen, B., & Wornell, G. W. (2001b). Quantization index modulation methods: A class of provable good methods for digital watermarking and information embedding. *IEEE Transactions on Information Theory, 49*, 563–593.

Chen, I.-T., & Yeh, Y.-S. (2006). Security analysis of transformed-key asymmetric watermarking system. *Signal Processing Letters, 13*, 213–215. doi:10.1109/LSP.2005.863677

Chen, M., Fridrich, J., Goljan, M., & Lukas, J. (2007). Source digital camcorder identification using sensor photo response non-uniformity. *Proceedings of the SPIE, 6505.*

Chen, M., Fridrich, J., Goljan, M., & Lukas, J. (2008). Determining image origin and integrity using sensor noise. *IEEE Transactions on Information Security and Forensics, 3*, 74–90. doi:10.1109/TIFS.2007.916285

Chen, S. Y., & Leung, H. (2008). Chaotic watermarking for video authentication in surveillance applications. *IEEE Transactions on Circuits and Systems for Video Technology, 18*, 704–709. doi:10.1109/TCSVT.2008.918801

Choi, H., Lee, K., & Kim, T. (2004). Transformed-key asymmetric watermarking system. *Signal Processing Letters, 11*, 251–254. doi:10.1109/LSP.2003.819873

Choi, S., Lam, E. Y., & Wong, K. K. Y. (2006). Source camera identification using footprints from lens aberration. *Proceedings of the Society for Photo-Instrumentation Engineers, 6069*, 172–179.

Coatrieux, G., Le Guillou, C., Cauvin, J.-M., & Roux, C. (2009). Reversible watermarking for knowledge digest embedding and reliability control in medical images. *IEEE Transactions on Information Technology in Biomedicine, 13*, 158–165. doi:10.1109/TITB.2008.2007199

Coatrieux, G., Lecornu, L., Sankur, B., & Roux, C. (2006). A review of image watermarking applications in healthcare. In *Proceedings of the 28th Annual International Conference Engineering in Medicine and Biology Society* (pp. 4691-4694).

Cosman, P. C., Oehler, K. L., Riskin, E. A., & Gray, R. M. (1993). Using vector quantization for image processing. *Proceedings of the IEEE, 81*, 1326–1341. doi:10.1109/5.237540

Cover, T. M., & Hart, P. E. (1967). Nearest neighbor pattern classification. *IEEE Transactions on Information Theory, 13*, 21–27. doi:10.1109/TIT.1967.1053964

Cox, I. J., Doerr, G., & Furon, T. (2006). Watermarking is not cryptography. In *Proceedings of the 5th International Workshop on Digital Watermarking* (pp. 1-15).

Cox, I. J., Kilian, J., Leighton, T., & Shamoon, T. (1997). Secure spread spectrum watermarking for multimedia. *IEEE Transactions on Image Processing, 6*, 1673–1687. doi:10.1109/83.650120

Cui, H., Cui, X., & Meng, M. (2008). A public key cryptography based algorithm for watermarking relational databases. In *Proceedings of the International Conference on Intelligent Information Hiding and Multimedia Signal Processing* (pp. 1344-1347).

Dittmann, J., Wohlmacher, P., & Nahrstedt, K. (2001). Using cryptographic and watermarking algorithms. *Multimedia, 8*, 54–65. doi:10.1109/93.959103

Dyer, M. G. (1982). *A computer model of integrated process for narrative comprehension.* Cambridge, MA: MIT Press.

Ekici, Q., Coskun, B., Umut, N., & Sankur, B. (2001). Comparative assessment of semi-fragile watermarking techniques. *Proceedings of the SPIE: Multimedia Systems and Applications, IV*, 177–188.

Ekici, Q., Sankur, B., Coskun, B., Umut, N., & Akcay, M. (2004). Comparative evaluation of semifragile watermarking algorithms. *Journal of Electronic Imaging, 13*, 206–216. doi:10.1117/1.1633285

Farid, H. (2009). Image forgery detection. *Signal Processing Magazine, 26*, 16–25. doi:10.1109/MSP.2008.931079

Feng, W., & Liu, Z. Q. (2008). Region-level image authentication using Bayesian structural content abstraction. *IEEE Transactions on Image Processing, 17*, 2413–2424. doi:10.1109/TIP.2008.2006435

Fridrich, J. (1998a). Combining low frequency and spread spectrum watermarking. In *Proceedings of the SPIE International Symposium on Optical Science, Engineering, and Instrumentation* (pp. 19-24).

Fridrich, J. (1998b). Robust digital watermarking based on key-dependent basis functions. In *Proceedings of the Second Information Hiding Workshop* (pp. 143-157).

Fridrich, J. (1999). Methods for tamper detection in digital images. In *Proceedings of the ACM Workshop on Multimedia and Security* (pp. 19-23).

Fridrich, J. (2002). Security of fragile authentication watermarks with localization. *Proceedings of the SPIE: Security and Watermarking of Multimedia Contents, VI*, 691.

Fridrich, J. (2009). Digital image forensics using sensor noise. *IEEE Signal Processing Magazine, 26*, 26–37. doi:10.1109/MSP.2008.931078

Fridrich, J., Goljan, M., & Memon, N. (2002). Cryptanalysis of the Yeung-Mintzer fragile watermarking technique. *Journal of Electronic Imaging, 11*, 262–274. doi:10.1117/1.1459449

Fu, Y. (2007). A novel public key watermarking scheme based on shuffling. In *Proceedings of the International Conference on Convergence Information Technology* (pp. 312-317).

Ghouti, L., Bouridane, A., Ibrahim, M. K., & Boussakta, S. (2006). Digital image watermarking using balanced multiwavelets. *IEEE Transactions on Signal Processing, 54*, 1519–1536. doi:10.1109/TSP.2006.870624

Giakoumaki, A., Pavlopoulos, S., & Koutsouris, D. (2006). Multiple image watermarking applied to health information management. *IEEE Transactions on Information Technology in Biomedicine, 10*, 722–732. doi:10.1109/TITB.2006.875655

Gkizeli, M., Pados, D. A., & Medley, M. J. (2007). Optimal signature design for spread-spectrum steganography. *IEEE Transactions on Image Processing, 16*, 391–405. doi:10.1109/TIP.2006.888345

Gorokhovskiy, K., Flint, J. A., Atta, S., & Glushnev, N. (2007). Cost effective multiframe demosaicking for noise reduction. In *Proceedings of the 15th International Conference on Digital Signal Processing* (pp. 407-410).

Grgic, S., Mrak, M., Grgic, M., & Zovko-Cihlar, B. (2003). Comparative study of JPEG and JPEG2000 image coders. In *Proceedings of the 17th International Conference on Applied Electromagnetics and Communications* (pp. 109-112).

Hammouri, G., Ozturk, E., & Sunar, B. (2008). A tamper-proof and lightweight authentication scheme. *Pervasive and Mobile Computing, 4*, 807–818. doi:10.1016/j.pmcj.2008.07.001

Hecht, E. (1987). *Optics*. Reading, MA: Addison-Wesley.

Ho, A. T. S. (2007). Semi-fragile watermarking and authentication for law enforcement applications. In *Proceedings of the Second International Conference on Innovative Computing, Information and Control* (pp. 286-289).

Ho, A. T. S., Zhu, X., Shen, J., & Marziliano, P. (2008). Fragile watermarking based on encoding of the zeros of the z-transform. *IEEE Transactions on Information Forensics and Security, 3*, 567–579. doi:10.1109/TIFS.2008.926994

Ho, A. T. S., Zhu, X., Vrusias, B., & Armstrong, J. (2006). Digital watermarking and authentication for crime scene analysis. In *Proceedings of the Institution of Engineering and Technology Conference on Crime and Security* (pp. 479-485).

Holliman, M., & Memon, N. (2000). Counterfeiting attacks on oblivious block-wise independent invisible watermarking schemes. *IEEE Transactions on Image Processing, 9*, 432–441. doi:10.1109/83.826780

Holst, G. C. (1998). *CCD arrays, cameras, and displays* (2nd ed.). Bellingham, WA: SPIE Press.

Hsu, Y. F., & Chang, S. F. (2007). Image splicing detection using camera response function consistency and automatic segmentation. In *Proceedings of the IEEE International Conference on Multimedia and Expo* (pp. 28-31).

Hu, Y.-J., Ma, X.-P., Dou, L.-M., & Gao, L. (2008). A computation model for capacity and robustness of robust image watermarking scheme in spatial domain. In *Proceedings of the International Conference on Intelligent Information Hiding and Multimedia Signal Processing* (pp. 1154-1157).

Huang, H. K. (1998). *PACS: Basic principles and application* (1st ed.). New York, NY: John Wiley & Sons.

Huang, P. S., Chiang, C.-S., Chang, C.-P., & Tu, T.-M. (2005). Robust spatial watermarking technique for colour images via direct saturation adjustment. *Vision. Image and Signal Processing, 152*, 561–574. doi:10.1049/ip-vis:20041081

Huang, X., & Zhang, B. (2006). Robust detection of additive watermarks in transform domains. *Information Security, 153*, 97–106.

Jaisingh, J. A. (2009). Impact of piracy on innovation at software firms and implications for piracy policy. *Decision Support Systems, 46*, 763–773. doi:10.1016/j.dss.2008.11.018

Kang, X. G., Huang, J. W., & Zeng, W. J. (2008). Improving robustness of quantization-based image watermarking via adaptive receiver. *IEEE Transactions on Multimedia*, *10*, 953–959. doi:10.1109/TMM.2008.2001361

Kankanhalli, M. S., & Ramakrishnan, K. R. (1998). Content based watermarking of images. In *Proceedings of the Sixth ACM International Conference on Multimedia* (pp. 61-70).

Kim, H.-S., & Lee, H.-K. (2003). Invariant image watermark using Zernike moments. *IEEE Transactions on Circuits and Systems for Video Technology*, *13*, 766–775. doi:10.1109/TCSVT.2003.815955

Kumsawat, P., Attakitmongcol, K., & Srikaew, A. (2005). A new approach for optimization in image watermarking by using genetic algorithms. *IEEE Transactions on Signal Processing*, *53*, 4707–4719. doi:10.1109/TSP.2005.859323

Kundur, D., & Hatzinakos, D. (1999a). Towards a telltale watermarking technique for tamper-proofing. *Proceedings of the IEEE*, *87*, 1167–1180. doi:10.1109/5.771070

Kundur, D., & Hatzinakos, D. (1999b). Digital watermarking for telltale tamper proofing and authentication. *Proceedings of the IEEE*, *87*, 1167–1180. doi:10.1109/5.771070

Lanh, V. T., Emmanuel, S., & Kankanhalli, M. S. (2007). Identifying source cell phone using chromatic aberration. In *Proceedings of the IEEE Conference on Multimedia and Expo*.

Lee, C.-F., Chang, C.-C., & Wang, K.-H. (2008). Hiding data in VQ-compressed images using pairwise nearest codewords based on minimum spanning tree. In *Proceedings of the International Conference on Intelligent Information Hiding and Multimedia Signal Processing* (pp. 1293-1296).

Lee, S.-J., & Jung, S.-H. (2001). A survey of watermarking techniques applied to multimedia. In *Proceedings of the IEEE International Symposium on Industrial Electronics* (pp. 12-16).

Li, C. M., & Hong, L. X. (2008). Adaptive fragile watermark for image authentication with tampering localization. In *Proceedings of the Second International Conference on Anti-counterfeiting, Security and Identification* (pp. 22-25).

Li, C. T. (2004). Digital fragile watermarking scheme for authentication of JPEG images. *Vision, Image, and Signal Processing*, *151*, 460–466. doi:10.1049/ip-vis:20040812

Li, C.-T. (2009a). Unsupervised classification of digital images of unknown cameras using filtered sensor pattern noise. In *Proceedings of the International Workshop on Digital Watermarking*.

Li, C.-T. (2009b). Source camera linking using enhanced sensor pattern noise extracted from images. In *Proceedings of the 3rd International Conference on Imaging for Crime Detection and Prevention*.

Li, C. T., & Li, Y. (2009). Protection of digital mammograms on PACS using data hiding techniques. *International Journal of Digital Crime and Forensics*, *1*, 75–88. doi:10.4018/jdcf.2009010105

Li, C. T., & Si, H. (2007). Wavelet-based fragile watermarking scheme for image authentication. *Journal of Electronic Imaging*, *16*, 1–9. doi:10.1117/1.2712445

Li, C. T., & Wang, F.-M. (2003). One-dimensional neighborhood forming strategy for fragile watermarking. *Journal of Electronic Imaging*, *12*, 284–291. doi:10.1117/1.1557156

Li, C. T., & Yuan, Y. (2006). Digital watermarking scheme exploiting non-deterministic dependence for image authentication. *Optical Engineering (Redondo Beach, Calif.)*, *45*, 1–6. doi:10.1117/1.2402932

Lin, C. Y., & Chang, S. F. (2000). Semi fragile watermarking for authentication JPEG visual content. *Proceedings of the SPIE: Security and Watermarking of Multimedia Contents*, 113-118.

Lin, C. Y., & Chang, S. F. (2001). A robust image authentication method distinguishing JPEG compression from malicious manipulation. *IEEE Transactions on Circuits and Systems for Video Technology*, *11*, 153–168. doi:10.1109/76.905982

Lin, C.-Y., & Chang, S.-F. (2003). Robust digital signature for multimedia authentication. *Circuits and Systems Magazine*, *3*, 23–26. doi:10.1109/MCAS.2003.1267067

Liu, C. Y. (2004). Issues on image authentication. In Lu, C. S. (Ed.), *Multimedia Security* (pp. 173–206). Hershey, PA: IGI Global.

Liu, R., & Tan, T. (2000). Content-based watermarking model. In *Proceeding of the Fifteenth International conference on Pattern Recognition* (pp. 238-241).

Liu, T., & Qiu, Z.-D. (2002). A survey of digital watermarking-based image authentication techniques. In *Proceedings of the 6th International Conference on Signal Processing* (pp. 26-30).

Liu, W., Dong, L., & Zeng, W. J. (2007). Optimum detection for spread-spectrum watermarking that employs self-masking. *IEEE Transactions on Information Forensics and Security*, *2*, 645–654. doi:10.1109/TIFS.2007.908226

Low, M. R., & Christianson, B. (1994). Technique for authentication, access control and resource management in open distributed systems. *Electronics Letters*, *30*, 124–125. doi:10.1049/el:19940079

Lu, C. S., & Liao, H. Y. M. (2001). Multipurpose watermarking for image authentication and protection. *IEEE Transactions on Image Processing*, *10*, 1579–1592. doi:10.1109/83.951542

Lu, C.-S., & Liao, H.-Y. M. (2009). Structural digital signature for image authentication: An incidental distortion resistant scheme. *IEEE Transactions on Multimedia*, *5*, 161–173.

Lu, H. T., Shen, R. M., & Chung, F.-L. (2003). Fragile watermarking scheme for image authentication. *Electronics Letters*, *39*, 898–900. doi:10.1049/el:20030589

Lukas, J., Fridrich, J., & Goljan, M. (2006). Detecting digital image forgeries using sensor pattern noise. *Proceedings of the SPIE: Electronic Imaging*, *6072*, 362–372.

Macq, B., Dittmann, J., & Delp, E. J. (2004). Benchmarking of image watermarking algorithms for digital rights management. *Proceedings of the IEEE*, *92*, 971–984. doi:10.1109/JPROC.2004.827361

Maity, S. P., & Maity, S. (2009). Multistage spread spectrum watermark detection technique using fuzzy logic. *Signal Processing Letters*, *16*, 245–248. doi:10.1109/LSP.2009.2014097

Malik, H., Ansari, R., & Khokhar, A. (2008). Robust audio watermarking using frequency-selective spread spectrum. *Information Security*, *2*, 129–150. doi:10.1049/iet-ifs:20070145

Malvar, H. S., & Florencio, D. A. F. (2003). Improved spread spectrum: A new modulation technique for robust watermarking. *IEEE Transactions on Signal Processing*, *51*, 898–905. doi:10.1109/TSP.2003.809385

Marvel, L. M., Boncelet, C., & Retter, C. T. (1999). Spread spectrum image steganography. *IEEE Transactions on Image Processing*, *8*, 1075–1083. doi:10.1109/83.777088

Marvel, L. M., Hartwig, G. W., & Boncelet, C. (2000). Compression compatible fragile and semi-fragile tamper detection. In *Proceedings of the SPIE: International Conference on Security and Watermarking of Multimedia Contents*, *II*, 131–139.

Mukherjee, D. P., Maitra, S., & Acton, S. T. (2004). Spatial domain digital watermarking of multimedia objects for buyer authentication. *IEEE Transactions on Multimedia*, *6*, 1–15. doi:10.1109/TMM.2003.819759

Nakamura, K. (2006). *Image sensors and signal processing for digital still cameras*. Boca Raton, FL: Taylor & Francis.

Nakashima, Y., Tachibana, R., & Babaguchi, N. (2009). Watermarked movie soundtrack finds the position of the camcorder in a theater. *IEEE Transactions on Multimedia*, *11*, 443–454. doi:10.1109/TMM.2009.2012938

Parameswaran, L., & Anbumani, K. (2008). Content-based watermarking for image authentication using independent component analysis. *Informatica*, *32*, 299–306.

Pei, S. C., & Chen, J. H. (2006). Robustness enhancement for noncentric quantization-based image watermarking. *IEEE Transactions on Circuits and Systems for Video Technology*, *16*, 1507–1518. doi:10.1109/TCSVT.2006.885174

Popescu, A. C., & Farid, H. (2005). Exposing digital forgeries in color filter array interpolated images. *IEEE Transactions on Signal Processing*, *53*, 3948–3959. doi:10.1109/TSP.2005.855406

Potdar, V. M., Han, S., & Chang, E. (2003). A survey of digital image watermarking techniques. In *Proceedings of the Third IEEE International Conference on Industrial Informatics* (pp. 709-719).

Queluz, M. P. (1999). Content-based integrity protection of digital images. *Proceedings of the SPIE: Security and Watermarking of Multimedia Contents*, *3657*, 85–93.

Queluz, M. P. (2001). Authentication of digital image and video: Generic models and a new contribution. *Signal Processing Image Communication*, 461–475. doi:10.1016/S0923-5965(00)00010-2

Queluz, M. P., & Lany, P. (2000). Spatial watermark for image verification. In *Proceedings of the SPIE: International Conference on Security and Watermarking of Multimedia Contents*, *II*, 120–130.

Quendo, C., Rius, E., Person, C., & Ney, M. (2001). Integration of optimized low-pass filters in a band-pass filter for out-of-band improvement. *IEEE Transactions on Microwave Theory and Techniques*, *49*, 2376–2383. doi:10.1109/22.971624

Rey, C., & Dugelay, J. L. (2002). A survey of watermarking algorithms for image authentication. *EURASIP Journal on Applied Signal Processing*, 613–621. doi:10.1155/S1110865702204047

Russ, J. C. (2001). *The image processing handbook*. Charlotte, NC: Baker & Taylor Books.

Sankur, B., Celiktutan, O., & Avcibas, I. (2007). Blind identification of cell phone cameras. *Proceedings of the SPIE: Electronic Imaging, Security, Steganography, and Watermarking of Multimedia Contents IX*, *6505*, 1.

Seppannen, T., Makela, K., & Keskinarkaus, A. (2000). Hiding information in color images using small color palettes. In *Proceedings of the Third International Workshop on Information Security* (pp. 69-81).

Shannon, C. E. (1949). Communication theory of secrecy systems. *The Bell System Technical Journal*, *28*, 656–715.

Simitopoulos, D., Koutsonanos, D. E., & Strintzis, M. G. (2003). Robust image watermarking based on generalized Radon transformations. *IEEE Transactions on Circuits and Systems for Video Technology*, *13*, 732–745. doi:10.1109/TCSVT.2003.815947

Simmons, G. J. (1988). A survey of information authentication. *Proceedings of the IEEE*, *76*, 603–620. doi:10.1109/5.4445

Smid, M. E., & Branstad, D. K. (1988). Data encryption standard: Past and future. *Proceedings of the IEEE*, *78*, 550–559. doi:10.1109/5.4441

Sorell, M. (2009a). Unexpected artifacts in a digital photograph. *International Journal of Digital Crime and Forensics*, *1*, 45–48. doi:10.4018/jdcf.2009010103

Sorell, M. (2009b). Digital camera source identification through JPEG quantisation. In Li, C. T. (Ed.), *Multimedia forensics and security* (pp. 291–313). Hershey, PA: IGI Global.

Sorell, M. (2009c). Conditions for effective detection and identification of primary quantization of re-quantized JPEG images. *International Journal of Digital Crime and Forensics*, *1*, 13–27. doi:10.4018/jdcf.2009040102

Stallings, W. (1998). *Cryptography and network security - principles and practice*. Upper Saddle River, NJ: Prentice Hall.

Steinder, M., Iren, S., & Amer, P. D. (1999). Progressively authenticated image transmission. In *Proceedings of the Military Communications Conference* (pp. 641-645).

Sun, H.-M., Wu, M.-E., Ting, W.-C., & Hinek, M. J. (2007). Dual RSA and its security analysis. *IEEE Transactions on Information Theory*, *53*, 2922–2933. doi:10.1109/TIT.2007.901248

Sutthiwan, P., Ye, J., & Shi, Y. Q. (2009). An enhanced statistical approach to identifying photorealistic images. In *Proceedings of International Workshop on Digital Watermarking* (pp. 323-335).

Trappe, W., Wu, M., Wang, Z. J., & Liu, K. J. R. (2003). Anti-collusion fingerprinting for multimedia. *IEEE Transactions on Signal Processing*, *51*, 1069–1087. doi:10.1109/TSP.2003.809378

van Schyndel, R. G., Tirkel, A. Z., & Osborne, C. F. (1996). A digital watermark. In *Proceedings of the International Conference Image Processing* (pp. 86-90).

Wang, S.-H., & Lin, Y.-P. (2004). Wavelet tree quantization for copyright protection watermarking. *IEEE Transactions on Image Processing*, *13*, 154–165. doi:10.1109/TIP.2004.823822

Winne, D. A., & Knowles, H. D. ll, D. R., & Nagarajah, C. N. (2002). Digital watermarking in wavelet domain with predistortion for authenticity verification and localization. *Proceedings of the SPIE: Security and Watermarking of Multimedia Contents IV*, 349-356.

Wolfgang, R. B., & Delp, E. J. (1997). Overview of image security techniques with applications in multimedia systems. In *Proceedings of the SPIE International Conference on Multimedia Networks: Security, Displays, Terminals, and Gateways* (pp. 297-308).

Wong, P. W., & Memon, N. (2000). Secret and public key authentication watermarking schemes that resist vector quantization attack. *Proceedings of the SPIE: Security and Watermarking of Multimedia Contents*, *II*, 40–47.

Wu, C. W. (2002). On the design of content-based multimedia authentication systems. *IEEE Transactions on Multimedia*, *4*, 385–393. doi:10.1109/TMM.2002.802018

Wu, D. C., & Tsai, W. H. (1999). Embedding of any type of data in images based on a human visual model and multiple-based number conversion. *Pattern Recognition Letters, 20*, 1511–1517. doi:10.1016/S0167-8655(99)00118-X

Wu, M. (2003). Joint security and robustness enhancement for quantization based data embedding. *IEEE Transactions on Circuits and Systems for Video Technology, 13*, 831–841. doi:10.1109/TCSVT.2003.815951

Xie, R., Wu, K., Du, J., & Li, C. (2007). Survey of public key digital watermarking systems. In *Proceedings of the Eighth ACIS International Conference on Software Engineering, Artificial Intelligence, Networking, and Parallel/Distributed Computing*.

Xing, W., Lu, Z.-M., & Wang, H.-X. (2003). A digital watermarking method based on classified labeled-bisecting-k-means clustering. In *Proceedings of the International Conference on Machine Learning and Cybernetics* (pp. 2891-2895).

Xu, G., Gao, S., Shi, Y. Q., Su, W., & Hu, R. (2009). Camera-model identification using markovian transition probability matrix. In *Proceedings of the International Workshop on Digital Watermarking* (pp. 294-307).

Yuan, H., & Zhang, X. P. (2003). Fragile watermark based on the Gaussian mixture model in the wavelet domain for image authentication. In *Proceedings of the International Conference of Image Processing* (pp. 505-508).

Zhang, C., Cheng, L. L., Qiu, Z. D., & Cheng, L. M. (2008). Multipurpose watermarking based on multiscale curvelet transform. *IEEE Transactions on Information Forensics and Security, 3*, 611–619. doi:10.1109/TIFS.2008.2004288

Zhao, X., Ho, A. T. S., Treharne, H., Pankajakshan, V., Culnane, C., & Jiang, W. (2007). A novel semi-fragile image watermarking, authentication and self-restoration technique using the Slant transform. In *Proceedings of the Third IEEE International Conference on Intelligent Information Hiding and Multimedia Signal Processing* (pp. 283-286).

Zhu, X., Ho, A. T. S., & Marziliano, P. (2006). Image authentication and restoration using irregular sampling for traffic enforcement applications. In *Proceedings of the First International Conference on Innovative Computing, Information and Control* (pp. 62-65).

This work was previously published in the International Journal of Digital Library Systems, Volume 2, Issue 2, edited by Chia-Hung Wei, pp. 55-78, copyright 2011 by IGI Publishing (an imprint of IGI Global).

Chapter 9
Decomposed PRNU Library for Forensics on Photos

Yue Li
Nankai University, China

ABSTRACT

Today, the digital forensic techniques for digital images are developed with the origin identification and integrity verification functions for security reasons. Methods based on photo-response-non-uniform (PRNU) are widely studied and proved to be effective to serve the forensic purposes. However, due to the interpolation noise, caused by the colour filtering and interpolation function the accuracy of the PRNU-based forensic method has been degraded. Meanwhile, the tremendous physical storage requirement and computation consumption limit the applications of PRNU-based method. Therefore, an innovative DPRNU-based forensic method has been proposed in order to solve the above problems. In the method, the artificial component and physical component are separated according to the colour filtering array (CFA) and the PRNU are only extracted from the physical component in order to remove the interference caused by the interpolation noise, which increases the accuracy of the camera identification and integrity verification. Meanwhile, due to the separation, the DPRNU are only 1/3 of the size of the traditional PRNU, which saves considerable physical storage in setting up the digital library and fasters the comparison speed between the fingerprints.

INTRODUCTION

Nowadays, the widely applied digital imaging devices bring great convince to the people in daily life. At any time, people can capture scenes around them by the portable cameras or the built-in camera in the mobile; the government can achieve 24-hour surveillance by the widely installed CCTV; the journalists can records the 1/24-second-motions by the professional camera. However, the security of the captured digital images remains unprotected and such problem needs urgently investigation by the research and the engineer. The security problem can be summarized as which person/device produces the image and whether the image is modified. As a result, the digital forensic techniques for digital images are developed with the origin identification and integrity verification functions in order to solve the aforementioned problems.

DOI: 10.4018/978-1-4666-2928-8.ch009

Generally speaking, the forensic techniques extract a fingerprint, which is a digital feature left by the digital imaging device, and compared it to the reference fingerprints representing a set of imaging devices in the database (Dirik, Sencar, & Memon, 2008; Fridrich, 2009; Caldelli, Amerini, Picchioni, De Rosa, & Uccheddu, 2009; Cao & Kot, 2010). Depending on the comparing result, the forensic techniques can identify the origin and verify the integrity of the digital images (Lukas, Fridrich, & Goljan, 2006a; Lukas, Fridrich, & Goljan, 2006b). The framework of forensic techniques is illustrated in Figure 1. The scheme first extracts the digital fingerprint S_I of image I, and then S_I is compared to fingerprint S_D in the fingerprint database. To identify the origin of the image, the fingerprint database contains the reference fingerprints of a variety of imaging devices. If a correlation between a reference fingerprint and S_I is maximal among all correlations and greater than a predefined threshold, then the corresponding device is identified as the source device of the image under investigation. To verify content integrity, the fingerprint database consists of fingerprints on different areas of the reference image. If a reference fingerprint on a special area results in a correlation lower than the threshold, then this area is identified as a forged area.

Due to the necessity of the reference fingerprint, setting up a digital library, which stores the majority reference fingerprints of the digital devices and connect to internet/intranet, is essential to serve the forensic purposes. With the aids of the digital fingerprint library, the user can identify the source cameras by comparing the fingerprints of the camera under investigation and the fingerprint stored in the library and representing sample cameras (Lukas, Fridrich, & Goljan, 2006a; Lukas, Fridrich, & Goljan, 2006b). Meanwhile, the user can investigate the integrity of the photo using the fingerprints. Compared to the sample fingerprint in the library, if the investigated fingerprint is partially broken or entirely destroyed, then the corresponding photo can be verified as tampered in the corresponding area or entirely faked due to the destroyed fingerprint (Chen, Fridrich, Lukas, & Goljan, 2008; Chen, Fridrich, Goljan, & Lukas, 2007a). As a result, the digital library of the fingerprint can greatly benefits the user in the forensic application. However, in setting up such digital library, the user may face the serious problem in the physical storage requirement and tremendous time consuming in the computation. In the next section, a most representative and widely applied forensic method based on PRNU (Chen, Fridrich, Lukas, & Goljan, 2008; Chen, Fridrich, Goljan, & Lukas, 2008; Chen, Fridrich, Goljan, & Lukas, 2007b; Li, 2009a; Li, 2009b) is reviewed and the corresponding limitations in setting up a library on this method is discussed.

Figure 1. A general framework of NDHBDIA techniques

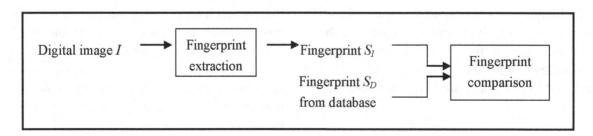

REVIEW OF THE FORENSIC TECHNIQUES

There are several kinds of forensic techniques for protecting the digital images. One kind of the widely studied techniques use the common feature shared by the same type or similar type of cameras as the fingerprint. Such features are irrelative to the image content but only determined by the presetting of the cameras in the manufacturing and therefore, these features are rather constant in the extraction. Colour filter array (CFA) is one of the most representative features in this kind of forensic techniques. In the digital camera, the CFA optically determined the lights been filtered during capturing the scene and the corresponding interpolation matrix (IM) creates the artificial electrical signal of the filtered lights (Lukas, Fridrich, & Goljan, 2006a). Therefore, by investigating the CFA and estimating the corresponding IM, the user can identify the originate camera of the images (Swaminathan, Wu, & Liu, 2007). However, forensic method cannot identify the camera in the same types or the camera in different types but employing same CFA

Another important kind of forensic techniques are developed based on the photo response non-uniformity (PRNU). PRNU is the content-dependent high-frequency noise, which is caused by the imperfections of the sensors during the manufacturing (Holst, 1998). Because the imperfections are unique to every single sensor and thus to every camera, forensic techniques based on the PRNU are accuracy enough to identify the unique camera. However, the techniques based on PRNU also cause higher computation load. The details of the forensic technique based on PRNU are reviewed in the next section.

FORENSIC TECHNIQUES BASED ON PRNU

In acquiring an image, the signals will inevitably be distorted when passing through each process and these distortions result in slight differences between the scene and the camera-captured image (Lukas, Fridrich, & Goljan, 2006a). Such distortions can be mathematically described as an additive noise to the signals, and hence the general expression of captured images is

$$I = Y + N \tag{1}$$

where I is the captured image, Y is the perfect representation of the scene and N is the additive noise representing the distortions (see Table 1).

With this additive noise, even if the camera takes pictures of the same scene, the resulting digital images will still exhibit slight differences (Lukas, Fridrich, & Goljan, 2006a). This is partly because of the *shot* noise (also known as photonic noise (Holst, 1998)), which is a random component uniquely produced in every acquisition process, and partly because of the *pattern noise*, which is a deterministic component that remains the same in pictures of the same scene taken by the same camera (Lukas, Fridrich, & Goljan,

Table 1. Noise type definition

Noise type	Definition	Dominant component
Shot noise	Random noise: It differs in every picture, even in the pictures of the same scene taken by the same camera.	Photonic noise (Holst, 1998)
PRNU	Content-dependent noise: It differs in the pictures of the different scenes, but remains the same in the pictures of the same scene taken by the same camera.	Sensor pattern noise (Lukas, Fridrich, & Goljan, 2006a)
FPN	Content-independent noise: It is fixed to the camera and is constant in every picture taken by the same camera.	Dark current (Qimage help, 2009)

2006a). Due to this property, the pattern noise can be utilised as a camera fingerprint for photo authentication. Figure 2 demonstrates the composition of the camera noise, in which the camera noise is separated into shot noise and pattern noise, and the pattern noise can be further classified into fixed pattern noise (FPN) and photo response pattern noise, known-as photo response non-uniformity (PRNU).

Figure 3 demonstrates two enhanced PRNU of different cameras. Figure 3 (a) shows the PRNU pattern from the Canon Power Shot A610 camera. In this figure, the PRNU has a circular distribution in the middle of the pattern. Figure 3 (b) is the PRNU pattern for the Fuji FinePix F50fd camera, in which the noise has a striped rather than a circular distribution.

DRAWBACKS OF THE METHOD BASED ON PRNU

While setting up a digital library for PRNU fingerprint, the users must face two challenges, as the degraded accuracy due to the interpolation noise and the heavy burden to the data storage and computation load.

THE DEGRADED ACCURACY DUE TO THE INTERPOLATION NOISE

According to the traditional definition, the sensor pattern noise is the dominant part of the PRNU, which is described in Figure 2 and Table 1.

However, by reviewing the image acquisition process demonstrated in Figure 4, we can see that the colour filtering and interpolation operation are both important processes but the effect of these operations are not considered in the PRNU definition in Figure 2 and Table 1. In the filtering, only one colour component of every pixel is captured by the sensor, while the other two colour components are generated by the interpolation functions for economical reasons. Figure 5 demonstrates the common Bayer CFA and the corresponding bilinear interpolation matrix (Gunturk, Glotzbach, Altunbasak, Schafer, & Mersereau, 2005). In this work, the colour components captured by the sensor are called *physical* components, while the colour components generated by the interpolation function are called *artificial* components (see Figure 5).

We use the term *artificial component* to represent the component generated by the interpolated function and the *interpolation noise* to present the difference between the filtered phys-

Figure 2. The composition of the camera noise

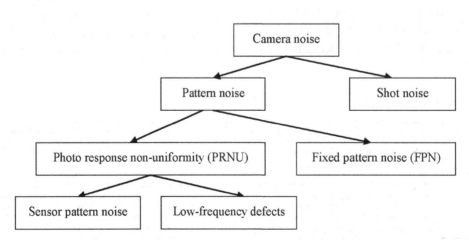

Figure 3. Illustration of the PRNU pattern noise of different cameras

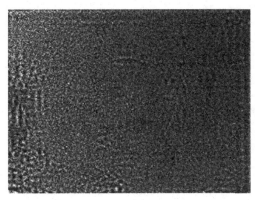 

(a) PRNU of camera Conon Power Shot A610   (b) PRNU of camera Fuji FinePix F50fd

ical colour components of the scene and the artificial components (Sorell, 2009). According to the CFA working process, only one third of the colour components of the pixels in the photo are physical components, which contain the sensor pattern noise, while the other two thirds of the colour components are artificial components and therefore, the majority of the noise extracted from these component are subsequently the interpolation noise (Gunturk, Glotzbach, Altunbasak, Schafer, & Mersereau, 2005). However, due to the exclusion of the definition of PRNU, the interpolation noise is extracted but not filtered in the PRNU fingerprint. As discussed in (Adams, 1995) such inclusion may lead to interference between the sensor pattern noise and the interpolation noise so that the accuracy of the forensic result will be consequently degraded. As a result, filtering the interpolation noise from the PRNU

is necessary to increase the accuracy of the forensic method.

HEAVY BURDEN TO THE DATA STORAGE AND COMPUTATION LOAD

In the digital library of PRNU, each PRNU represents a camera and therefore, the number of the fingerprint is determined the number of the camera need to be included in the database. Regarding to the huge amount of portable cameras, built-in cameras in the mobile, CCTV cameras and etc, the library of the PRNU will cost tremendous physical storage, which is a great challenge in setting up a fingerprint library (Rey & Dugelay, 2002). On the other hand, identifying PRNU fingerprints from the database need exhaustive comparisons,

Figure 4. The image acquisition process of a digital camera

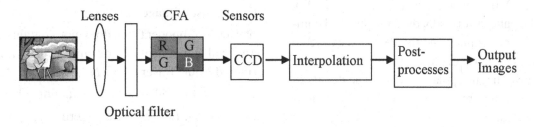

Figure 5. The Bayer CFA and the bilinear interpolation matrix

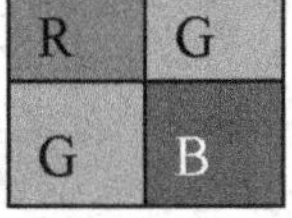

R G
G B

(a) A Bayer CFA

$$IM_{3\times 3} = \begin{bmatrix} 0 & 1 & 0 \\ 1 & 4 & 1 \\ 0 & 1 & 0 \end{bmatrix}$$

(b) Bilinear IM in the size of 3×3

$$IM_{7\times 7} = \begin{bmatrix} 0 & 0 & 0 & 1 & 0 & 0 & 0 \\ 0 & 0 & -9 & 0 & -9 & 0 & 0 \\ 0 & -9 & 0 & 81 & 0 & -9 & 0 \\ 1 & 0 & 81 & 256 & 81 & 0 & 1 \\ 0 & -9 & 0 & 81 & 0 & -9 & 0 \\ 0 & 0 & -9 & 0 & -9 & 0 & 0 \\ 0 & 0 & 0 & 1 & 0 & 0 & 0 \end{bmatrix}$$

(c) Bilinear IM in the size of 7×7

which consume considerable computation time and greatly increase the difficulties in forensics. As a result, a method can decrease the digital library size and increase the comparison speed is in need to improve the applicability of this kind of forensic method. In this paper, an innovative method removes the interpolation noise from PRNU is proposed to generate a smaller fingerprint database and correspondingly to faster the computing speed. Meanwhile, because the interference of the interpolation noise has been removed, the accuracy of the PRNU method will also be increased.

DECOMPOSED PRNU-BASED FORENSIC METHOD

In this section, an innovative method based on the Decomposed PRNU (DPRNU) has been proposed. In this method, first the CFA is determined by the method proposed by (Bayram, Sencar, Memon, & Avcibas, 2005; Swaminathan, Wu, & Liu, 2007), then the pattern corresponds to the physical components are obtained and the PRNU is extracted from these patterns of physical component in order to remove the interpolation noise. The details of this algorithm are presented in the following of this section.

To extract the DPRNU, we first separate the three colour channels I_c, $c \in \{R,G,B\}$ of a colour image I of $X \times Y$ pixels. Most CFAs are of 2×2 pixels as shown in Figure 5 and are repeatedly mapped to the sensors. We know that, for each pixel of I, only one of the three colour components is physical and the other two are artificial, so the second step is, for each channel I_c, we perform 2:1 down-sampling across both horizontal and vertical dimensions to get four sub-images, $I_{c,i,j}$, where i and $i,j \in \{0,1\}$, such that

$$I_{c,i,j}\left(x,y\right) = I_c\left(2x+i, 2y+j\right) \qquad (2)$$

where $x \in \left[0, \lfloor X/2 \rfloor - 1\right]$ and $y \in \left[0, \lfloor Y/2 \rfloor - 1\right]$.

Then applying the CFA estimation algorithm, developed in (Bayram, Sencar, Memon, & Avcibas, 2005; Swaminathan, Wu, & Liu, 2007), we can determine the employed CFA in the camera, and seek out the certain $\left(i,j\right)$ pairs which satisfies that the sub-image $I_{c,i,j}$ only consist of the physical component but does not contains any artificial components. For example, in an image filtered by the Bayer CFA, $I_{R,0,0}$, $I_{G,0,1}$, $I_{G,1,0}$ and $I_{B,1,1}$ are the sub-images containing physical components. PRNU noise pattern, $P_{R,0,0}$, $P_{G,0,1}$,

$P_{G,1,0}$ and $P_{B,1,1}$, extracted from these sub-images using the method in (Chen, Fridrich, Goljan, & Lukas, 2008), are the noise pattern contains majority sensor noise and no interpolation noise. By de-coupling the physical and virtual colour components in the fashion before extracting the PRNU noise pattern, we can prevent the interference error of the artificial components from contaminating the physical components during the DWT process. The wavelet-based denoising process, i.e., a DWT followed by a Wiener filtering operation (Lukas, Fridrich, & Goljan, 2006a) are used to obtain the PRNU noise patterns $P_{c,i,j}$. Meanwhile, the finally the DPRNU P is represented by the four noise pattern extracted from the sub-images of physical components

$$P = \{P_{c,i,j}\}, \text{where } P_{c,i,j} \text{ is extracted from } I_{c,i,j} \text{ of physical components} \tag{3}$$

According to the definition of CFA, only 1/3 of the components are captured by the sensor and recorded as physical components, and hence, the final DPRNU only contains 1/3 of the noise pattern of the original PRNU fingerprint. The framework of the DPRNU extraction algorithm is demonstrated in Figure 6, and the procedures are listed in Table 2.

EXPERIMENT RESULT

In this section, we carry out experiments in order to prove that 1) the DPRNU outperform the traditional PRNU in source camera identification and image content verification; 2) DPRNU save up the physical storage in setting up the digital library and increase the computing speed. In the experiments of source camera identification, we will trace the source cameras of digital photos by comparing the extracted DPRNU with the reference DPRNU of the cameras. In the experiments

of image content verification, we can detect forged area by investigating the integrity of the DPRNU.

CAMERA IDENTIFICATION

To demonstrate the performance of the proposed DPRNU, we have carried out identification tests on 300 2048×1536-pixel photos of natural scenes taken by six cameras, each responsible for 50. The six cameras are listed in Table 3. Each reference PRNU (i.e., r_d), that represents each camera, is generated according to Equation in Chen, Fridrich, Goljan, and Lukas (2008), which calculates the element-wise weighted average of the PRNUs extracted from 30 photos of blue sky taken by the digital camera.

Source camera identification requires similarity comparisons among PRNUs (DPRNUs) and therefore the feasibility of the chosen similarity metrics is important. Fridrich suggested the use of the Peak to Correlation Energy (PCE) measure in (Fridrich, 2009), which has been proved to be a more stable detection statistics than normalised cross-correlation when applied to the scenarios in which the images of interest may have undergone geometrical manipulations, such as rotation or scaling. The purpose of this experiment is to demonstrate the capability of the proposed DPRNU in dealing with the colour interpolation noise, so geometrical transformations will not be applied in order to prevent biased evaluation from happening. Therefore, in the following experiments, cross-correlation as formulated in Equation will be used to measure the similarity between PRNUs (DPRNUs).

In practice, the normalised cross-correlation has to be greater than a specified threshold for a camera to be identified as the source camera. However, in this experiment, the key point is about demonstrating the different performance of the traditional PRNU and the proposed DPRNU. Therefore, a camera is identified as the source

Figure 6. The DRPNU extraction algorithm

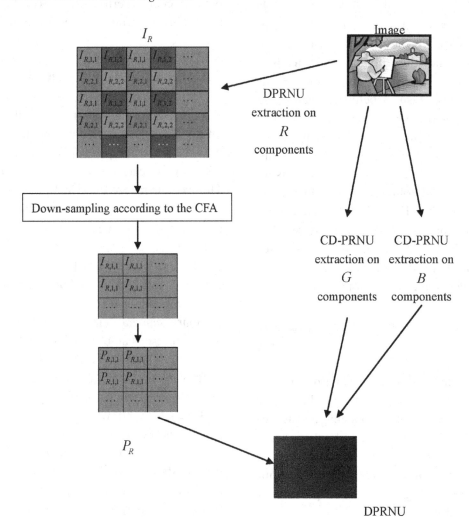

camera, if out of the six reference PRNU (or DPRNU), its reference PRNU (or DPRNU) is most similar to the PRNU (or DPRNU), n_I, of the image, I, under investigation. That is to say, camera C_i, $i \in [1, 6]$ is identified as the source camera if

$$d = \arg\max_i \left(\left\{ \rho(n_I, I \cdot r_i) \middle| i \in [1, 6] \right\} \right) \qquad (4)$$

Because PRNU is often used in content integrity verification, where smaller image blocks have to be analysed, e also compare the performance of the proposed DPRNU against that of the traditional PRNU when they are applied to blocks of 5 different sizes cropped from the centre of the full-sized PRNU (DPRNU). Table 4 lists the identification rates of the two methods, i.e. the traditional "PRNU" and the proposed "DPRNU". Individually speaking, C_1, C_3, C_4, C_5 and C_6 perform significantly better when DPRNU is used in all cases, except for a few cases when images are of full size (1536 × 2048 pixels) and the identification rates are close or equal to 100% (1.0000). Generally speaking, when the statistics of the six cameras are pooled together, as listed

Table 2. DPRNU extraction algorithm

Input: original image I

Output: DPRNU pattern noise P

DPRNU extraction algorithm

1) Decompose image I into R, G, and B components, I_R, I_G, and I_B, respectively.

2) $\forall c \in \{R, G, B\}$, decompose I_c into four sub-images, $I_{c,1,1}$, $I_{c,1,2}$, $I_{c,2,1}$ and $I_{c,2,2}$ by using Equation **Error!**.

3) $\forall c \in \{R, G, B\}$, $P_{c,1,1}$, $P_{c,1,2}$, $P_{c,2,1}$ and $P_{c,2,2}$ are obtained by denoising the sub-images $I_{c,1,1}$, $I_{c,1,2}$, $I_{c,2,1}$ and $I_{c,2,2}$ using the Wiener filtering in the DWT domain (Lukas, J., Fridrich, J., & Goljan, M., 2006a).

4) $\forall c \in \{R, G, B\}$, generate the DPRNU, P_c by combining $P_{c,1,1}$ to $P_{c,2,2}$ following Equation **Error!**

5) Combine the DPRNU noise pattern P_R, P_G, P_B to form the final DPRNU noise pattern P.

in the Total column of Table 4, we can see that DPRNU still outperforms PRNU significantly. This has been graphically presented in Figure 7.

CONTENT INTEGRITY VERIFICATION

To demonstrate the performance of the proposed DPRNU, we carry out integrity verification experiments on one 640×480-pixel images taken by Olympus C730 (C_6 in Table 3 of the camera list). In the experiments, we cut off an 80×100-pixel area from image in Figure 8(a), paste an area copied from a different location in the in Figure 8 (b) to create the forged (c). The PRNUs in the two areas are different due to the different locations, though both Figure 8 (a) and Figure 8 (b) are captured by the camera C_6.

To detect the manipulated areas, we create two 128×128-pixel sliding windows and one window is moved across the PRNU extracted form the image under investigation, whilst the other window

is moved across the reference PRNU of the cameras. The cross-correlation of the two PRNU pattern inside the two windows is calculated, and if the cross-correlation is lower than a predetermined threshold, the pixel in the centre of the window is deemed to be forged. In Chen's (Chen, Fridrich, Goljan, & Lukas, 2008) method, the windows are moved by a pixel at a time, which imposes a high computational load. On the other hand, this comparison method is not accurate to pixel level (Chen, Fridrich, Goljan, & Lukas, 2008). Therefore, we can increase the step by which the sliding windows are moved in order to reduce the computational load without sacrificing the accuracy. In our experiment, the sliding step/displacement is 5 pixels. Table 5 lists the number of manipulated and non-manipulated blocks of 5×5 pixels in the forged images.

We use the normalised cross-correlation as formulated in Equation to measure the similarity between PRNUs (DPRNUs). If the correlation is lower than a threshold, the centre pixel in the

Table 3. Camera list

Symbol	Camera	Symbol	Camera	Symbol	Camera
C_1	Canon IXUS 850IS	C_3	Canon IXY Digital 500	C_5	Olympus FE210
C_2	Canon PowerShot A400	C_4	FujiFilm A602	C_6	Olympus C730

Table 4. Source camera identification rates using traditional PRNU and proposed DPRNU

Block size	Methods	Identification rate of different cameras						
		C_1	C_2	C_3	C_4	C_5	C_6	*Total*
1536×2048	PRNU	0.9200	0.9600	0.9800	1.0000	0.9800	0.8000	**0.9400**
	DPRNU	0.9600	0.9600	0.9800	1.0000	1.0000	0.9600	**0.9767**
768×1024	PRNU	0.6800	0.8400	0.7200	1.0000	0.6200	0.7600	**0.7700**
	DPRNU	0.9400	0.9200	1.0000	1.0000	0.8200	0.9800	**0.9433**
384 × 512	PRNU	0.5000	0.7600	0.4600	0.9600	0.4200	0.6000	**0.6167**
	DPRNU	0.8400	0.8000	0.8400	0.9800	0.6800	0.8800	**0.8367**
192 × 256	PRNU	0.2200	0.6600	0.3200	0.7600	0.3000	0.3200	**0.4300**
	DPRNU	0.6000	0.6000	0.5800	0.8200	0.4600	0.5800	**0.6067**
96 ×128	PRNU	0.2600	0.4200	0.1600	0.5400	0.2200	0.3200	**0.3200**
	DPRNU	0.3000	0.4200	0.4800	0.6600	0.3200	0.5400	**0.4533**
48 × 64	PRNU	0.1400	0.4800	0.1600	0.3800	0.2000	0.1400	**0.2500**
	DPRNU	0.2400	0.4200	0.3000	0.6200	0.3600	0.2400	**0.3633**

window and the corresponding 5×5-pixel block centred at the pixel is deemed to be manipulated. As discussed in Chen (Chen, Fridrich, Goljan, & Lukas, 2008), the cross-correlation follows the Generalised Gaussian (GG) distribution, therefore, we use various thresholds defined as $\mu - c \cdot \sigma$ to analyse the performance of PRNU and DPRNU, where μ and σ are the mean and standard deviation of the correlations distribution, respectively, and c in the range from 0 to 3.

We use the four metrics, true positive (TP), false positive (FP), true negative (TN) and false negative (FN), to measure the performance of integrity verifications based on PRNU and DPRNU. The four metrics are defined in the following way. Let A be a 5×5-pixel block; and $M(A)$ and $F(A)$ be defined as

$$M(A) = \begin{cases} 0 & \text{if } A \text{ is not manipulated} \\ 1 & \text{if } A \text{ is manipulated} \end{cases}$$

(5)

$$F(A) = \begin{cases} 0 & \text{if } A \text{ is detected as not manipulated} \\ 1 & \text{if } A \text{ is detected as manipulated} \end{cases}$$

(6)

then, TP, FP, TN and FN are defined below.

$$\text{True Positive } (\text{TP}) = \left\| \left\{ A \,\middle|\, M(A) = 1 \text{ and } F(A) = 1 \right\} \right\|$$

(7)

$$\text{True Negative } (\text{TN}) = \left\| \left\{ A \,\middle|\, M(A) = 0 \text{ and } F(A) = 0 \right\} \right\|$$

(8)

$$\text{False Positive } (\text{FP}) = \left\| \left\{ A \,\middle|\, M(A) = 0 \text{ and } F(A) = 1 \right\} \right\|$$

(9)

$$\text{False Negative } (\text{FN}) = \left\| \left\{ A \,\middle|\, M(A) = 1 \text{ and } F(A) = 0 \right\} \right\|$$

(10)

Table 5. Number of manipulated and non-manipulated areas in each image (unit: block)

	Image $II.3$
Manipulated blocks	358
Non-manipulated blocks	7130

Figure 7. Overall identification rates when DPRNU and PRNU are used as fingerprint for identifying cameras

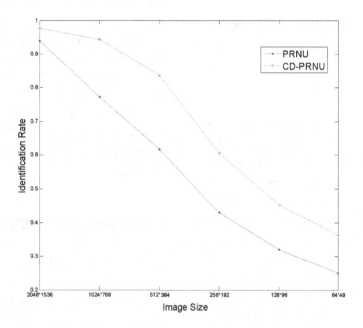

Higher TP and TN, and lower FP and FN indicate better performance. Because (TP, FP) and (TN, FN) are two pairs of conflicting factors. For example, we need to set a lower threshold in order to detect more manipulated blocks, bespeaking a higher TP. However, this low threshold also leads to the situation where more non-manipulated blocks are erroneously detected as manipulated, bespeaking a higher FP. Therefore, the ROC curve is used to evaluate the overall performance of the

PRNU and DPRNU and to determine the optimal balance point between TP and FP. Let P be the number of manipulated blocks and N be the number of non-manipulated blocks, i.e.,

$$\mathrm{P} = \| \{ A \mid \mathrm{M}(A) = 1 \} \| \qquad (11)$$

and

Figure 8. The original image, source image and forged images for the contents verification experiments

(a) Original Image   (b) Original Image   (b) Tampered Image

$$N = \| \{ A \mid M(A) = 0 \} \|. \tag{12}$$

Then the ROC is calculated as following

$$ROC = \frac{TP / P}{FP / N} \tag{13}$$

In the ROC curve, the x-axis is the false positive rate which is FP / N, and the y-axis is the true positive rate which is TP / P. At the same false positive rate, the scheme with better performance will results in a higher true positive rate. The ROC curve of the integrity verification experiment is illustrated as Figure 9.

Figure 9 demonstrates both schemes can effectively detect the manipulated blocks. But the ROC curve of DPRNU is slightly higher than the ROC curve of PRNU along y-axis, indicating a slightly better performance. Nevertheless, at the lower-left corner of Figure 9, the ROC curve of DPRNU is lower than the curve of random guess, when the false positive rate is low. This is because the high threshold leads to both low FP and TP (i.e., the lower-left corner of the figures) so that

only a few blocks are detected as manipulated. However, Chen's method (Chen, Fridrich, Goljan, & Lukas, 2008) is not accurate to small areas, which only contains a few blocks. Therefore, the experimental result is even worse than random guess. This error can be eliminated by using advanced similarity metrics (Fridrich, 2009). However, in this work we only concentrate on the evaluation of the PRNU and DPRNU and optimising integrity verification method is not studied in this chapter.

DATABASE OPTIMIZATION

In the proposed DPRNU method, the fingerprint has been decreased to 1/3 of the original size and thus DPRNU method can save a huge amount of the physical storage space of the fingerprint database. For example, one traditional PRNU fingerprint (Chen, Fridrich, Goljan, & Lukas, 2008) of a 2048×1536 RGB image will cost 68MB on the hard disk, while a DPRNU fingerprint only need 23MB for saving; one PRNU fingerprint of a 640×480 RGB image will cost 6MB on the

Figure 9. The ROC of the integrity verification experiments

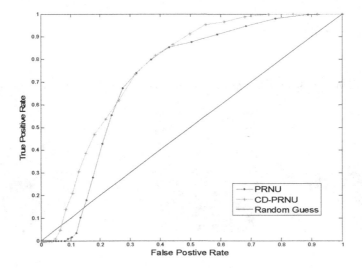

(b) ROC curve of integrity verification experiments on Image *II*

hard disk, while a DPRNU fingerprint only need 2MB for saving. Meanwhile, the DPRNU fingerprint also cost less time for computing. On a Pentium Core II 1.3G CPU and 3 GB Ram computer, computing the similarity between two PRNU fingerprint of two 2048×1536 images cost 0.66 second while time consuming of calculating the similarity between DPRNU is 0.23 second. As a result, when using the DPRNU for the fingerprint, the user can save 2/3 of both the physical storage and computing time in setting up and applying the digital library for forensic purposes.

CONCLUSION

In this paper, we have investigated the forensic method based on PRNU. Due to the interpolation noise, caused by the colour interpolation function and tied to the model of cameras, the accuracy of the PRNU-based forensic method has been degraded. Meanwhile, the tremendous physical storage requirement and computation consumption limit the applications of PRNU-based method. Therefore, an innovative DPRNU-based forensic method has been proposed in order to solve the above problems. In the method, the artificial component and physical component are separated according to the CFA and the PRNU are only extracted from the physical component in order to remove the interference caused by the interpolation noise, which increases the accuracy of the camera identification and integrity verification. Meanwhile, due to the separation, the DPRNU are only 1/3 of the size of the traditional PRNU, which saves considerable physical storage in setting up the digital library and fasters the comparison speed between the fingerprints.

REFERENCES

Adams, J. (1995). Interaction between color plane interpolation and other image processing functions in electronic photography. *Proceedings of the Society for Photo-Instrumentation Engineers, 2146,* 144–151.

Bayram, S., Sencar, H. T., Memon, N., & Avcibas, I. (2005). *Source camera identification based on CFA interpolation* (pp. 69–72).

Caldelli, R., Amerini, I., Picchioni, F., De Rosa, A., & Uccheddu, F. (2009). Multimedia Forensic Techniques for Acquisition Device Identification and Digital Image Authentication. In Li, C.-T. (Ed.), *Handbook of Research on Computational Forensics, Digital Crime and Investigation: Methods and Solutions.* Hershey, PA: IGI Global.

Cao, H., & Kot, A. C. (2010). Accurate Detection of Demosaicing Regularity for Digital Image Forensic. *IEEE Transactions on Information Forensics and Security, 4,* 889–910.

Chen, M., Fridrich, J., Goljan, M., & Lukas, J. (2007a). Digital imaging sensor identification. In *Proceedings of SPIE* (Vol. 6505).

Chen, M., Fridrich, J., Goljan, M., & Lukas, J. (2007b). Source digital camcorder identification using sensor photo response non-uniformity. In *Proceedings of SPIE* (Vol. 6505).

Chen, M., Fridrich, J., Goljan, M., & Lukas, J. (2008). Determining image origin and integrity using sensor noise. *IEEE Transactions on Information Security and Forensics, 3,* 74–90. doi:10.1109/TIFS.2007.916285

Chen, M., Fridrich, J., Lukas, J., & Goljan, M. (2008). *Imaging sensor noise as digital X-ray for revealing forgeries* (pp. 342–458).

Dirik, A. E., Sencar, H. T., & Memon, N. (2008). Digital single lens reflex camera identification from traces of sensor dust. *IEEE Transaction on Information Forensics Security*, *3*, 539–552. doi:10.1109/TIFS.2008.926987

Fridrich, J. (2009). Digital image forensics. *Signal Processing Magazine*, *26*, 26–37. doi:10.1109/MSP.2008.931078

Gunturk, B. K., Glotzbach, J., Altunbasak, Y., Schafer, R. W., & Mersereau, R. M. (2005). Demosaicking: color filter array interpolation. *Signal Processing Magazine*, *22*, 44–54. doi:10.1109/MSP.2005.1407714

Holst, G. C. (1998). *CCD Arrays, Cameras, and Displays* (2nd ed.). New York: JCD Publishing & SPIE Pres.

Li, C.-T. (2009a). *Source camera linking using enhanced sensor pattern noise extracted from images.*

Li, C.-T. (2009b). Unsupervised classification of digital images of unknown cameras using filtered sensor pattern noise.

Lukas, J., Fridrich, J., & Goljan, M. (2006a). Digital camera identification from sensor noise. *IEEE Transactions on Information Security and Forensics*, *1*, 205–214. doi:10.1109/TIFS.2006.873602

Lukas, J., Fridrich, J., & Goljan, M. (2006b). Detecting digital image forgeries using sensor pattern noise. In *Proceedings of the SPIE Electronic Imaging*, *6072*, 362–372.

Qimage help. (2009). *Dark Frame Subtraction* (Tech. Rep.). Retrieved from http://www.ddisoftware.com/qimage/qimagehlp/dark.htm

Rey, C., & Dugelay, J. L. (2002). A survey of watermarking algorithms for image authentication. *EURASIP Journal on Applied Signal Processing*, 613–621. doi:10.1155/S1110865702204047

Sorell, M. (2009). Unexpected artifacts in a digital photograph. *International Journal of Digital Crime and Forensics*, *1*, 45–48.

Swaminathan, A., Wu, M., & Liu, K. J. R. (2007). Non-intrusive component forensics of visual sensors using output images. *IEEE Transactions on Information Forensics and Security*, *2*, 91–106. doi:10.1109/TIFS.2006.890307

This work was previously published in the International Journal of Digital Library Systems, Volume 2, Issue 1, edited by Chia-Hung Wei, pp. 38-51, copyright 2011 by IGI Publishing (an imprint of IGI Global).

Chapter 10
Analysis the Typhoon Eyes of Megi from MTSAT Satellite Cloud Images with 3-D Profile Reconstruction

Yueh-Jyun Lee
Ching Yun University, Taiwan

Shih-Wen Liu
Ching Yun University, Taiwan

Ji-Chyun Liu
Ching Yun University, Taiwan

Yuh-Fong Lin
Ching Yun University, Taiwan

Lung-Chun Chang
Ching Yun University, Taiwan

ABSTRACT

In this paper, image reconstruction technique (IRT) is used to reconstruct a 3-D profile of typhoons from MTSAT satellite cloud image data and based on a 1691 MHz receiver and iDAP system. The satellite cloud image data gives a single line profile slicing from a surface cloud image which does match the typhoon distribution. The line profile is presented with the temperature of the cloud top. The 3-D profiles of typhoons are constructed with the surface cloud images and the temperatures. IRT is conducted using the data of the 2010 Megi event. The typhoon feature is studied and the various typhoon eyes in three time intervals are analyzed. An effective early-warning system may become feasible based on this work.

INTRODUCTION

The distribution of typhoon and its variation are very important for disaster prevention and worthy of study. The satellite data provides typhoon cloud image for analyzing the cloud structure and wind driven velocity of typhoon. The current geostationary satellites provided typhoon cloud image for weather broadcasting include US GOES-11 and GOES-12, Japan MTSTAT-1R, Dartcom, (http://www.dartcom.co.uk), Japan Meteorological Agency (http://www.jma.go.jp), Europe METEOSAT-6,7,8, China FY2, and METEOSAT-5 in Indian ocean. The typhoon cloud images are

DOI: 10.4018/978-1-4666-2928-8.ch010

not clear often, there are many kinds of noise in it, which may affect to accurately segment the helical cloud band or extract some information from the typhoon cloud images. Both noise reduction and contrast enhancement are usually applied in a typhoon cloud image for location, rotation, tracking, and forecast (Pun, Lin, Wu, Ko, & Liu, 2007; Pao, Yeh, Liu, & Hsu, 2006; Pao & Yang, 2008; Qian, Jiang, Zhang, & Wang, 2010; Qian & Jiang, 2011; Tsai, Hwang, Chen, & Lin, 2010; Wu, 2001; Wang, Guo, & Luo, 2006; Wang, Yang, Li Li, & Lu, 2005; Xu, Wang, & Xie, 2009; Wang, Xu, Shi, & Ye, 2008; Yeh, Pao, Lee, & Lai, 2007; Zhang, Lu, Lu, & Xu, 2008; Zhang & Wang, 2009; Zhang & Yang, 2011; Zhang, Lai, Wei, & Zong, 2006).

Recently, the typhoon eye is the interested behavior for research (Pun, Lin, Wu, Ko, & Liu, 2007; Pao, Yeh, Liu, & Hsu, 2006; Zhang & Wang, 2009; Zhang, Lai, Wei, & Zong, 2006). Since the portion surrounding the eye will do the most damage, the typhoon center recognition is important for weather forecast and typhoon analysis. When the typhoon reaches to certain strength, there will be an eye appeared at the center. As the strength of the typhoon getting stronger, the eye tends to a circle and also becomes clearer. When the typhoon arrive the land, its strength will decrease and the eye may be non-clear. However, the typhoon cloud images are planar pictures. Recently a 3-D profile reconstruction is an interesting research topic for recognizing the practical typhoon. The segmentation of the satellite cloud image was sliced in horizontal plane to obtain a series of 2D surfaces, and reconstruct the 3D cloud or storm (Somporn, Willi, Hans, Susanne, Wattana, & Suchada, 2008).

Based on the vertical segmentation, IRT is used to reconstruct a 3-D profile of typhoons from MTSAT satellite cloud image data in this paper. The objectives of this paper are three fold: first, to slice the line profile from that satellite cloud image data and present the height variations under the conversion of the temperature; second, to construct the mesh-amplitude model in

Figure 1. Three cloud images of Megi typhoon: (a) first interval, (b) second interval, (c) third interval

(a)

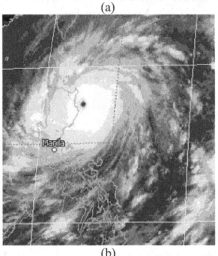

(b)

(c)

Figure 2. Line profile with cloud top temperature: (a) toggle profile mode with starting and stop points, (b) distance, bearing and profile window

(a)

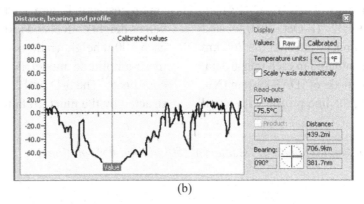

(b)

Figure 3. Mesh-amplitude model for 3-D profile of typhoon

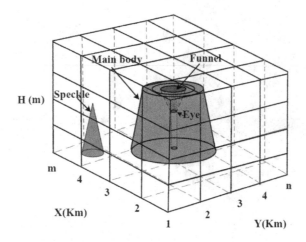

depicting the height distribution of the cloud top from a surface cloud image. The 3-D profiles of typhoons are constructed with the surface cloud images and the temperatures and third, to recognize the eye of the typhoon. IRT is conducted using the data of the 2010 Megi typhoon in three time interval. An effective early-warning system may become feasible based on this work. We present the numerical results with discussion and conclusions finally.

IMAGE RECONSTRUCTION TECHNIQUE AND METHODOLOGY

The three typhoon cloud images of Megi typhoon were occurred and shown in Figure 1 (a) to (c) respectively, typhoons in first interval, second interval and third interval when 01:32, 17 Oct. 01:32, 18 Oct. and 04:32, 18 Oct. 2010 located near Taiwan. The boundary covered the 760 km by 840 km area has contoured in each image data.

By toggle profile mode of iDAP system (Xu, Wang, & Xie, 2009), the line profile with cloud top temperature is sliced from that satellite cloud image data and presented in Figure 2. In Figure 2(a), when the toggle profile mode chose, we click a point on the image to set the starting point (P1) of a line and then determine the stop point (P2). The distance, bearing and profile window is obtained and display in Figure 2(b). The window is a floating display, means it can be moved anywhere on the screen, the distance (horizontal axis) and temperature (vertical axis) will be presented in the Display and Read-out screen.

The mesh-amplitude model in depicting the height distribution of the cloud top from a surface cloud image is constructed in Figure 3. For a rectangular coordinate (X, Y, H), the projective cloud image is located on the X-Y plane, and the height of typhoon is presented along the H-axis. The two-cut patterns with mxn points in X-Y plane are processed in Figure 3. Cloud top temperature versus height conversion is 0.650 C reduction per each 100m height (ratio is -0.650 C/100m). The mesh-amplitude model is with 25 × 25 mesh coordinate. The 3-D profile of typhoon is reconstructed by the nineteen latitudinal line profiles.

Figure 4. Rotation of Megi typhoon in 1st interval (50^0 tilt and 45^0 rotations)

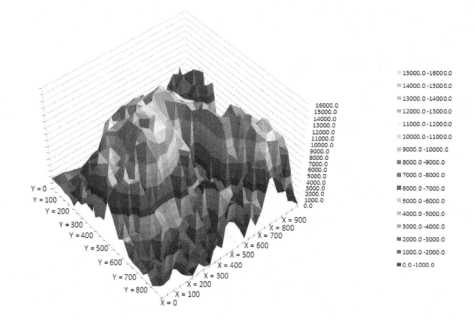

Figure 5. Eye of Megi typhoon in 1st interval

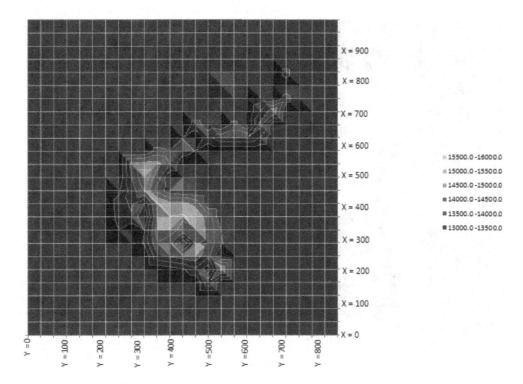

Figure 6. Rotation of Megi typhoon in 2nd interval (50⁰ tilt and 45⁰ rotations)

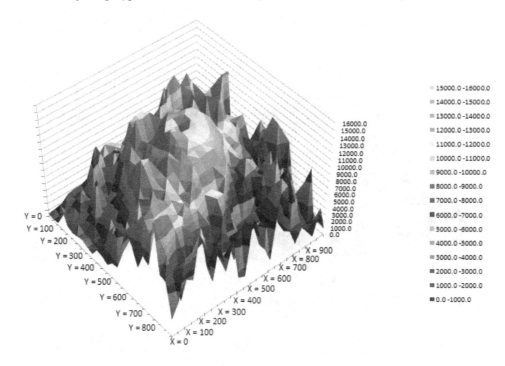

Figure 7. Eye of Megi typhoon in 2nd interval

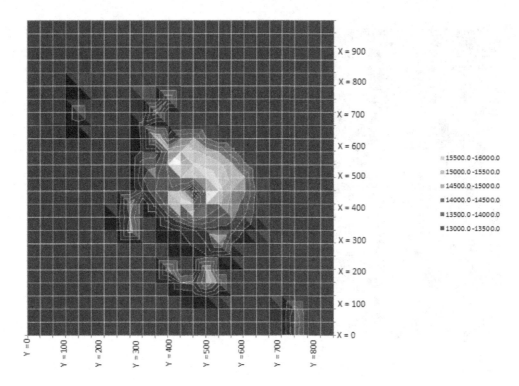

Figure 8. Rotation of Megi typhoon in 3rd interval (50⁰ tilt and 45⁰ rotations)

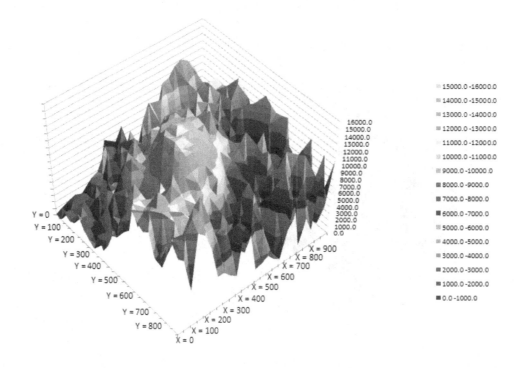

Figure 9. Funnel of Megi typhoon in 3rd interval

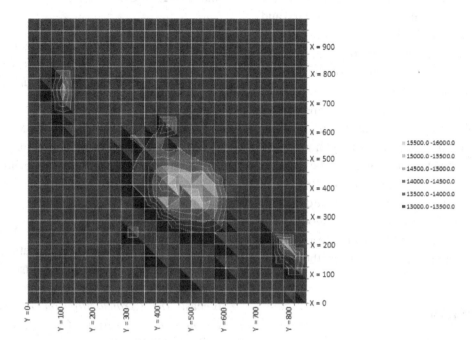

ANALYSIS AND RESULTS

By the mesh-amplitude model and the graphical CAD (Excel 3D plot), 3-D profile of typhoon Megi is reconstructed. The height (15.4 km), head distribution (750 km by 710 km, at 10 km height) and coverage (1200 km by 930 km) of typhoon Megi in first interval is observed. When

3-D profile of typhoon Megi is rotated with 500 tilt and 450 rotations, it is shown in Figure 4. In which the typhoon eye is observed and enlarged in Figure 5, the eye size is 83 km by 72 km and deep from top-down is about 2 km.

The 3-D profile of typhoon Megi in 2nd interval is reconstructed and the rotated 3-D profile is presented in Figure 6. Typhoon eye is pre-

Table 1. Features of various Megi typhoon

		1st interval	2nd interval	3rd interval
Main body	head (km², at 10 km height)	750×710	790×610	710×820
	coverage (km²)	1200 × 930	1400 ×1000	2040× 1860
	height (km)	15.4	15.9	15.5
Typhoon funnel	open-end size (km²)	120× 100	85×72	45×52
	deep (km)	2	2.5	0
	clarity of eye	clear	clear	non-clear
	eye size (km²)	83 × 72	42×36	0
Speckle	number	3	6	8
	height (km)	11	12	12

sented in Figure 7. As well as, 3-D profile of typhoon Megi in 3rd interval is reconstructed and the rotated 3-D profile is presented in Figure 8. The funnel is presented in Figure 9.

For comparison, the features of the various typhoons are listed in Table 1. In 1st interval and 2nd interval, the typhoon main bodies are smaller and the typhoon eyes are clear. When touching Taiwan island in 3rd interval, the typhoon main body becomes bigger and higher, and the typhoon eye are non-clear. The typhoon eye in 2nd interval is larger size and more deep. They are quite different. The more detailed features of three typhoons with 3-D profile are obtained by using the proposed image reconstruction technique and methodology.

CONCLUSION

Three applications of MTSAT satellite cloud image data are proposed to reconstruct 3-D profiles of typhoon distribution around Taiwan. In summary, using a 1691 MHz receiver and iDAP system in Ching Yun university campus and based on toggle profile mode and mesh-amplitude model with the cloud images, we can reconstruct a fair profile to exhibit the main features of typhoon Megi. With the additional graphical computations, the reconstructed profiles can be further improved.

Three various satellite cloud images of typhoon Megi existed around Taiwan are studied. The typhoon main body included head, coverage and height; the typhoon eye expressed with funnel open, funnel deep and eye size and the speckle are observed. As the typhoon main body is smaller and the typhoon eye is clear when it locates around Philippine island. And the typhoon main body is larger and the typhoon eye is non-clear when it touch Philippine island. The results can be used as a test bench for this proposed new technique, based on which a possible early-warning system can be implemented. The typhoon profile included main body, head, height, coverage, eye, funnel, and speckle can be observed for any perspective viewpoint.

REFERENCES

Pao, T. L., & Yang, P. L. (2008). Typhoon locating and reconstruction from the infrared satellite cloud image. *Journal of Multimedia*, *3*, 45–51. doi:10.4304/jmm.3.2.45-51

Pao, T. L., Yeh, J. H., Liu, M. Y., & Hsu, Y. C. (2006). Locating the typhoon center from the IR satellite cloud images. In *Proceedings of the IEEE International Conference on Systems* (pp. 484-488).

Pun, I. F., Lin, I. I., Wu, C. R., Ko, D. S., & Liu, W. T. (2007). Validation and application of altimetry-derived upper ocean thermal structure in the Western North Pacific Ocean for typhoon-intensity forecast. *IEEE Transactions on Geoscience and Remote Sensing*, *45*(6), 1616–1630. doi:10.1109/TGRS.2007.895950

Qian, H., & Jiang, B. (2011). Method base on multi-channel satellite cloud image for typhoon segmentation. [Journal of Beijing University of Aeronautics and Astronautics]. *Beijing Hangkong Hangtian Daxue Xuebao*, *37*, 466–471.

Qian, H., Jiang, B., Zhang, Z., & Wang, L. (2010). A level set-based framework for typhoon segmentation with application to multi-channel satellite cloud images. In *Proceedings of the 3rd International Congress on Image and Signal Processing* (pp. 1273-1275).

Somporn, C. A., Willi, J. A., Hans, G. B., Susanne, K. O., Wattana, K., & Suchada, S. (2008). 3D cloud and storm reconstruction from satellite image modeling. In *Proceedings of the International Conference on Simulation and Optimization of Complex Processes* (pp. 187-206).

Tsai, F., Hwang, J. H., Chen, L. C., & Lin, T. H. (2010). Post-disaster assessment of landslides in southern Taiwan after 2009 Typhoon Morakot using remote sensing and spatial analysis. *Natural Hazards and Earth System Sciences*, *10*, 2179–2190. doi:10.5194/nhess-10-2179-2010

Wang, J., Xu, S. Y., Shi, C., & Ye, M. W. (2008). Dynamic assessment of typhoon disaster condition based on multi-sources remote sensing imagery: Research progress. *Journal of Natural Disasters, 17,* 22–28.

Wang, P., Guo, C., & Luo, Y. (2006). Local spiral curves simulating based on Hough transformation and center auto-locating of developing typhoon. *Transactions of Tianjin University, 12,* 142–146.

Wang, P., Yang, P. L., Li Li, W., & Lu, H. Q. (2005). Extracting the rotation feature of the developing typhoon. In *Proceedings of the Fourth International Conference on Machine Learning and Cybernetics* (pp. 5229-5234).

Wu, C. C. (2001). Numerical simulation of Typhoon Gladys (1994) and its interaction with Taiwan terrain using the GFDL hurricane model. *Monthly Weather Review, 129,* 1533–1549. doi:10.1175/1520-0493(2001)129<1533:NSOTGA>2.0.CO;2

Xu, J. W., Wang, P., & Xie, Y. Y. (2009). Image segmentation of typhoon spiral cloud bands based on support vector machine. In *Proceedings of the Eighth International Conference on Machine Learning and Cybernetics* (pp. 1088-1093).

Yeh, J. H., Pao, T. L., Lee, C. L., & Lai, W. T. (2007). Reconstruction of typhoon path and cloud image from descriptors. In *Proceedings of the IEEE International Conference on Systems, Man and Cybernetics* (pp. 2097-2101).

Zhang, C. J., Lu, X. Q., Lu, J., & Xu, J. P. (2008). Segmentation for main body of typhoon from satellite cloud image by genetic algorithm in contourlet domain. In *Proceedings of the Third International Conference on Convergence and Hybrid Information Technology* (pp. 352-357).

Zhang, C. J., & Wang, X. D. (2009). Typhoon cloud image enhancement and reducing speckle with genetic algorithm in stationary wavelet domain. *IET Image Process, 3*(4), 200–216. doi:10.1049/iet-ipr.2008.0044

Zhang, C. J., & Yang, B. (2011). A novel nonlinear algorithm for typhoon cloud image enhancement. *International Journal of Automation and Computing, 8,* 161–169. doi:10.1007/s11633-011-0569-1

Zhang, Q. P., Lai, L. L., Wei, H., & Zong, X. F. (2006). Non-clear typhoon eye tracking y artificial ant colony. In *Proceedings of the Fifth International Conference on Machine Learning and Cybernetics* (pp. 4063-4068).

This work was previously published in the International Journal of Digital Library Systems, Volume 2, Issue 3, edited by Chia-Hung Wei, pp. 39-48, copyright 2011 by IGI Publishing (an imprint of IGI Global).

Chapter 11
Agent Negotiation in Water Policy Planning

Menq-Wen Lin
Ching Yun University, Taiwan

Chia-Hung Wei
Ching Yun University, Taiwan

Pei-Cheng Cheng
Ching Yun University, Taiwan

ABSTRACT

With the growing demand for water, and many challenges related to water availability, food security, pollution, and environmental degradation, it becomes imperative to establish good water policy planning for a sufficient supply of water consumption. This paper presents a general problem-solving framework for modeling multi-issue agent negotiation in water policy planning via fuzzy constraint processing. All participants involved in water policy planning are modeled as agents. Agent negotiation is formulated as a distributed fuzzy constraint satisfaction problem. Fuzzy constraints are used to define each participant's professional views and demands. The agent negotiation simulates the interactive process of all participants' water policy planning. This approach provides a systematic method to reach an agreement that benefits all participants' water policy planning with a high satisfaction degree of fuzzy constraints, and move towards the deal more quickly since their search focuses only on the feasible solution space. An example application to Negotiation for Water Policy Planning is considered to demonstrate the usefulness and effectiveness of the proposed approach.

1. INTRODUCTION

With the boosting demand for water, and many challenges related to water availability, food security, pollution, and environmental degradation, it becomes imperative and necessity to establish good water policy planning for sufficient supply of water consumption. Many studies have been presented to address such problems. Adams and Simon (1996) proposed game theory-based negotiation model for California water policy planning. Randall et al. (1997) proposed water supply planning simulation model using mixed-integer linear programming. Watkins et al. (1998) presented

DOI: 10.4018/978-1-4666-2928-8.ch011

decomposition methods for water resources optimization models with fixed costs. Blackstock and Richards (2007) proposed an approach to evaluate stakeholder involvement in river basin planning. Larson (2009) investigated the new water planning processes from the perspective of the design principles for the robust institutions.

An agent (Bradshaw, 1997; Huhns & Munindar, 1998) with autonomy, self-learning, and coordination can serve as an efficient approach for water policy planning in view of its following features. Firstly, an agent can stand for different institutes or groups related to water resource and fulfill autonomously its duty that is assigned to itself. Secondly, an agent can self-learn and anticipate the oncoming water demand and trend in water resource development, in a changeable and unpredictable environment of water resource. Thirdly, an agent can coordinate and solve a problem in water policy planning from perspectives of its self- and overall-interest. In Addition, agent negotiation (Pruitt, 1981) is an iterative process through which a joint decision is made by two or more agents in order to reach a mutually acceptable agreement. Many approaches to such negotiation have been proposed, including negotiation support systems (NSSs) (Kersten & Lo, 2001), a game theory-based model (Rosenschein & Zlotkin, 1994), a Bayesian model (Ren, Anumba, & Ugwu, 2002), evolutionary computation (Oliver, 1996), and distributed artificial intelligence (Eaton, Freuder, & Wallace, 1998).

NSSs emphasize support, rather than automation. In the game theory-based model, the agent's utility for each possible outcome of an interaction is used to construct into a pay-off matrix. The aim of the game theory-based model is to formalize agent negotiation in a context in which each agent tries to maximize its own utility with respect to other agents. However, the pay-off matrices are generally based on some unrealistic assumption that all agents have common knowledge of the pay-off matrix. Even if the pay-off matrix is known, it may quickly become intractable for large

games that involve multiple issues and agents. As a result, the use of negotiation strategies based on game theory should generally be treated with skepticism. In the Bayesian model, a Bayesian network is used to update an agent's knowledge and beliefs about other agents, and Bayesian probabilities are employed to generate offers. Based on this model, Zeng and Sycara (1998) modeled multi-issue negotiation as a sequential decision making model, but their system could not easily capture users' demands on attributes of a product. Evolutionary computation shows how a rational agent can learn to mimic human negotiation. Oliver (1996) and Choi et al. (2001) presented a genetic agent-based automated negotiation system for application in electronic business. However, evolutionary approach requires many trials to acquire good strategies. Another cluster of work on agent negotiation draws on the field of distributed artificial intelligence (DAI). Sycara (1989) presented a negotiation model based on the integration of case-based reasoning and multi-attribute utility theory (MAUT). Sathi and Fox (1989) argued that negotiations can be viewed as constraint-directed problems.

As declared in Luo et al. (2003), fuzzy constraints can serve as a natural means of modeling a buyer's requirements over products' single issues and the combination of the products' multiple issues. They are also appropriate for modeling trade-offs between different issues of a product, and capturing the process by which a buyer relaxes his constraints to reach a partially satisfactory deal. Hence, this paper presents a general problem-solving framework for modeling multi-issue agent negotiation in e-marketplace via fuzzy constraint processing. In this framework, all participants involved in water policy planning are modeled as agents. Agent negotiation is formulated as a distributed fuzzy constraint satisfaction problem (DFCSP). Fuzzy constraints are used to define each participant's professional views and demands. The agent negotiation can simulate the interactive process of all participants' water policy planning. A concession strategy, based on fuzzy constraint-based problem-solving, is proposed to relax demands and a trade-off strategy is presented to evaluate existing alternatives. This approach provides a systematic method to reach an agreement that benefits all participants' water policy planning with a high satisfaction degree of fuzzy constraints, and move towards the deal more quickly since their search focuses only on the feasible solution space. An example application for modeling water policy planning via agent negotiation is considered to demonstrate the usefulness and effectiveness of the proposed approach.

The remainder of this paper is organized as follows. Section 2 introduces the theoretical basis of formulating agent negotiation as a DFCSP. Section 3 presents the negotiation strategies and negotiation process. Section 4 demonstrates the effectiveness of the approach by an example application to Negotiation for Water Policy Planning. Finally, Section 5 draws some comparisons and conclusions.

2. AGENT NEGOTIATION AS DFCSP

Fuzzy constraint satisfaction problems (FCSPs) are defined by a collection of objects with the associated domains and a set of crisp or fuzzy constraints that relate the objects to the objective of determining whether a tuple exists that satisfies all the constraints to an extent that is greater than or equal to the threshold of acceptability (Lai, 1992; Zadeh, 1975, 1978). However, real-world environments are heterogeneous and inherently distributed. Thus, the FCSP is extended to a distributed FCSP (DFCSP), which can be represented as a set of fuzzy constraint networks (FCNs) that are connected by constraints. Thus, a distributed fuzzy constraint network (DFCN) is defined as below.

Definition 1 (Distributed fuzzy constraint network): A distributed fuzzy constraint network (U,X,C) can be defined as a set of fuzzy constraint networks $\left\{N^1, ..., N^L\right\}$, $N^k = (U^k, X^k, C^k)$ being an FCN k, where:

○ U^k is a universe of discourse for FCN k;

○ X^k is a tuple of n^k non-recurring objects $X_{1^k}^k, ..., X_{n^k}^k$;

○ C^k is a set of $m^k \geq n^k$ fuzzy constraints, which is the union of a set of internal fuzzy constraints C^{k_i} existing among objects in X^k and a set of external fuzzy constraints C^{k_e} referring to at least one object in X^k and another not in X^k;

○ N^k is connected to other FCNs by C^{k_e};

○ U is a universe of discourse;

○ $X = (\bigcup_{k=1}^{L} X^k)$ is a tuple of all non-recurring objects;

○ $C = (\bigcup_{k=1}^{L} C^k)$ is a set of all fuzzy constraints.

In Definition 1, the intent of an FCN k viewed as a set of solutions of FCN k can be defined as follows.

Definition 2 (The intent of a fuzzy constraint network): The intent of a fuzzy constraint network (U^k, X^k, C^k), written Π_{U^k, X^k, C^k}, is an n-ary possibility distribution for the objects involved in the FCN k. That is

$$\Pi_{U^k, X^k, C^k} = \bar{C}_1^k(T_1) \cap ... \cap \bar{C}_m^k(T_m), \qquad (1)$$

where, for each constraint $C_j^k(T_j) \in C^k$, $\bar{C}_j^k(T_j)$ is its cylindrical extension in the space $X^k = (X_1^k, ..., X_n^k)$.

Meanwhile, $_\alpha\Pi_{U^k, X^k, C^k}$, the α-level cut of Π_{U^k, X^k, C^k}, can be viewed as a set of solutions satisfying all the internal and external constraints in FCN k simultaneously to an extent that is greater than or equal to an acceptable threshold α.

Furthermore, the overall satisfaction degree of the constraints of FCN k reached by a solution u, denoted by $\mu_{\Pi_{U^k,X^k,C^k}}(u)$, is defined as the satisfaction degree of the least satisfied constraint. That is

$$\mu_{\Pi_{U^k,X^k,C^k}}(u) = \min_{j=1...n}(\mu_{C_j^k}(u)). \qquad (2)$$

For simplification, $\mu_{\Pi_{U^k,X^k,C^k}}(.)$ can be written as $\mu_{C^k}(.)$.

The intent of a distributed fuzzy constraint network (U,X,C), written $\Pi_{U,X,C}$, is an n-ary possibility distribution for the objects X, which must hold for every constraint in C. Thus, a distributed fuzzy constraint satisfaction problem (DFCSP) can be viewed as a decision problem for determining whether a solution exists that satisfies all the constraints to an extent that is greater than or equal to a threshold α.

Definition 3 (Distributed fuzzy constraint satisfaction): Given a distributed fuzzy constraint network (U,X,C), which is defined as a set of fuzzy constraint networks, and a threshold value α in the interval [0, 1] of the real number line, a distributed fuzzy constraint satisfaction problem is a decision problem which involves determining if

$$_\alpha\Pi_{U,X,C} \neq \{\}, \qquad (3)$$

where $\Pi_{U,X,C}$ can be viewed as a set of solutions satisfying all the constraints.

That is, the task is to discover a solution, a whole set of solutions, or an optimal solution to a DFCSP that satisfies all the constraints in a DFCN. However, the solution to a DFCSP is much more complicated than that to a FCSP, mainly because a DFCN needs a communication model to facilitate the information exchanges among FCNs. Hence, an order of information exchanges and a leadership token are defined to construct an interaction mechanism. Each FCN can be considered to be an agent that is used in the description of the interaction mechanism.

Agent negotiation is closely related to a distributed fuzzy constraint satisfaction problem in that coming up to an agreement that satisfies two or more agents is the same as uncovering a consistent solution that satisfies all the constraints in a distributed fuzzy constraint network in which the fuzzy relationships inside each agent and among agents are specified. Thus, agent negotiation can be formulated as a DFCSP to yield agents' potential agreements and reach a mutually satisfactory outcome. Each agent in the negotiation can be represented as a different fuzzy constraint network; issues negotiated among agents can correspond to constrained objects; agent's demands and preferences can be naturally represented by fuzzy constraints.

The consent of all agents is required for an agreement, so possible agreements among agents that satisfy all of their demands can be viewed as the intent, $\Pi_{U,X,C}$, of all fuzzy constraints in a distributed fuzzy constraint network. However, no agent knows about its opponents' feasible proposals and possible agreements a priori. Agents take turns to propose offers to explore potential agreements, thereby moving the negotiation toward a consensus.

The following aggregated satisfaction value of the solutions is defined to evaluate counteroffers and find more satisfactory outcomes.

Definition 4 (Aggregated satisfaction value): Given the value of an offer (or counteroffer) u involving a number of issues $(x_1,...,x_n)$, the aggregated satisfaction value of the offer u to agent k, denoted by $\Psi^k(u)$, can be defined as a function of the values of satisfaction with the issues as follows:

$$\Psi^k(\mathrm{u}) = \frac{1}{n} \sum_{j=1}^{n} \mu_{C_j^k}(x_j), \qquad (4)$$

where $\mu_{C_j^k}(.)$ is the satisfaction degree of the constraint C_j^k of agent k over issue j.

$\Psi^k(\mathrm{u})$ can be viewed as a constraint among the issues to represent the preference over the combination of issues. Thus, $\Psi^k(\mathrm{u})$ can be used to make tradeoffs among issues for offers.

The procedure of offer generation by agents will continue until the expected proposal u^* is generated or no more solution can be proposed. However, assuming that agent k proposes an offer u to k' and agent k' subsequently proposes a counteroffer u' to agent k, agent k will accept the offer u' proposed by its opponent k' as an agreement if

$$\left(\mu_{C^k}(\mathrm{u}') \geq \alpha_i^k\right) \wedge \left(\Psi^k(\mathrm{u}') \geq \Psi^k(\mathrm{u})\right). \qquad (5)$$

Notably, a rational agent will not propose a counter-offer that is worse than the offer proposed already by the opponent. Thus, assuming that the counter-offer u' is proposed by agent k' and the u^* is the next offer of agent k, a rational agent k would also accept the offer u' proposed by its opponent k' as an agreement if

$$\left(\mu_{C^k}(\mathrm{u}') \geq \alpha_i^k\right) \wedge \left(\Psi^k(\mathrm{u}') \geq \Psi^k(\mathrm{u}^*)\right). \qquad (6)$$

where α_i^k is the acceptable threshold of agent k.

3. AGENT NEGOTIATION STRATEGY

The development of the negotiation process is determined by the negotiation strategies of the involved agents. These strategies determine how agents evaluate and generate offers to reach an agreement that is most in their self-interest. Agents exchange offers throughout the negotiation according to their own negotiation strategies. Typically, each agent starts a negotiation by proposing the ideal offer which is most in its self-interest. Whenever an offer is not acceptable by other agents, they make counter-offers by making concessions or by finding new alternatives to move towards an agreement. Hence, a concession strategy is presented, and a trade-off strategy is proposed to find alternatives.

3.1. Concession Strategy

A concession is a revision of a previous position that has been held and justified publicly. An agent's concession strategy is employed to generate a new proposal by reducing the agent's demands, thereby moving the negotiation toward a consensus. In the proposed approach, an agent makes a concession by decreasing its previously aggregated satisfaction value to generate an offer from a certain solution space. In that space, the satisfaction degrees of the constraints associated on the solutions equal or exceed a certain threshold of acceptability. Even if no solution enables the preference within the proposal space to be met, an agent can use self-relaxation to lower gradually the threshold of acceptability and thus generate new, feasible proposals without giving up on any of the agent's demand. Therefore, the set of feasible concession proposals for agent k with a threshold α_i^k is defined as follows.

Definition 5 (Set of feasible concession proposals): Given the latest offer u and a threshold α_i^k of agent k, the set of feasible concession proposals at the threshold α_i^k for the next offer of agent k, given by $_{\alpha_i^k}C_{\mathrm{u}}^k$, can be defined as

$$_{\alpha_i^k}C_{\mathrm{u}}^k = \left\{ \mathrm{v} \mid \left(\mu_{C^k}(\mathrm{v}) \geq \alpha_i^k\right) \wedge \left(\Psi^k(\mathrm{v}) = \Psi^k(\mathrm{u}) - r\right) \right\},$$
$$(7)$$

where r is the concession value.

The agent's concession value r for its next offer may be determined from the agent's mental state and the opponent's responsive state. Hence, using $\mathrm{x}^p = (x_1^p, \ldots, x_m^p)$ to represent the negotiator's mental state, $\mathrm{x}^q = (x_1^q, \ldots, x_n^q)$ to represent the opponent's responsive state, and r to represent the negotiator's concession value, the *flexible concession strategy* is specified by a set of fuzzy constraints as follows:

$$C_\lambda(\mathrm{x}^p, \mathrm{x}^q, r) = \left\{ (\mathrm{x}^p, \mathrm{x}^q, r) @ \pi \mid \pi = \min(\tilde{\mathbf{A}}_i^p(\mathrm{x}^p), \tilde{\mathbf{A}}_i^q(\mathrm{x}^q), \tilde{R}_i(r)), \ r = \xi(\mathrm{x}^p, \mathrm{x}^q) \right\},$$
(8)

where $\xi(\mathrm{x}^p, \mathrm{x}^q)$ is a fuzzy predicate, and $\tilde{\mathbf{A}}_i^p = (\tilde{A}_{i1}^p, \ldots, \tilde{A}_{im}^p)$, $\tilde{\mathbf{A}}_i^q = (\tilde{A}_{i1}^q, \ldots, \tilde{A}_{im}^q)$ and $\tilde{R}_i$ are the fuzzy regions of x^p, x^q and r respectively. Then, given x^p and x^q, the fuzzified negotiator's concession value R^* can be computed as follows:

$$R^* = Max\left[Min\left[\tilde{\mathbf{A}}_i^p(\mathbf{x}^p), \tilde{\mathbf{A}}_i^q(\mathbf{x}^q) \right] \cdot \tilde{R}_i(r) \right],$$
(9)

where $\tilde{\mathbf{A}}_i^p(\mathbf{x}^p) = Min\left(\tilde{A}_{i1}^p(x_1^p), \ldots, \tilde{A}_{im}^p(x_m^p) \right)$ and $\tilde{\mathbf{A}}_i^q(\mathbf{x}^q) = Min\left(\tilde{A}_{i1}^q(x_1^q), \ldots, \tilde{A}_{im}^q(x_m^q) \right)$.

Then, in the discrete case, in which $R*$ is defined on a finite universal set $(r_1, r_2, \ldots, r_t)$, the negotiator's concession value r can be calculated from $R*$ by the center of gravity method as follows:

$$r = \frac{\sum_{j=1}^{t} r_j \cdot \tilde{R}_i(r_j)}{\sum_{j=1}^{t} \tilde{R}_i(r_j)}.$$
(10)

The proposed system also includes various concession strategies. The *fixed concession strategy* and the *response-based concession strategy* are special cases of the flexible concession strategy. In the fixed concession strategy, an agent will translate its urgency into its concession value.

Thus, a greater urgency corresponds to the making of more concessions. However, in response-based concession strategies, including *reactive*, *bluff*, and *collaborative* strategies, the concession behavior considers only the negotiator's response. The reactive strategy is an approach by which the negotiator concedes more when the opponent concedes more and concedes less when the opponent concedes less. The bluff strategy is an approach by which an agent concedes less when the opponent concedes more and concedes more when the opponent concedes less. In the collaborative strategy, an agent concedes more than its opponent does to reach a consensus quickly. These do not complete the set of possible concession strategies, but are those considered herein.

3.2. Tradeoff Strategy

A tradeoff strategy is one by which an agent generates an alternative without reducing its demands. Agents can consider options for reaching a mutual satisfactory outcome by reconciling their interests. In the proposed method, the agent generates and develops alternative in a specific solution space without reducing its aggregated satisfaction value. In that space, the degrees of satisfaction in the constraints associated with the solutions equal or exceed a particular threshold. Thus, this method can reach an agreement that acceptably benefits all agents.

The set of feasible tradeoff proposals is defined as follows.

Definition 6 (Set of feasible tradeoff proposals): Given the latest offer u and a threshold α_i^k of agent k, the set of feasible tradeoff proposals at threshold α_i^k in response to the alternatives of agent k, denoted by $_{\alpha_i^k}\Im_{\mathbf{u}}^k$, is defined as

$$_{\alpha_i^k}\Im_{\mathbf{u}}^k = \{\mathrm{v} \mid (\mu_{C^k}(\mathrm{v}) \geq \alpha_i^k) \wedge (\Psi^k(\mathrm{v}) = \Psi^k(\mathrm{u}))\}.$$
(11)

In a semi-competitive environment, the agents simply maximize their individual payoffs, and also maximize the outcome to benefit all negotiators. Thus, a normalized Euclidean distance can be applied in establishing a trade-off strategy to measure the similarity between alternatives, and thus generate the best possible offer. This function tends to distinguish options whose satisfaction values are relatively close. Hence, a similarity function and the expected trade-off proposal may be defined as follows.

Definition 7 (Similarity function): Assuming that $\mathbf{v}$ is a feasible trade-off proposal of agent k and U' is the set of counteroffers made by other agents, the similarity function between v and U' on the negotiated issues for agent k, denoted by $\Theta^k(v, U')$, is defined as

$$\Theta^k(v, U') = 1 - \frac{\sqrt{\sum_{j=1}^{m}(\mu_{C_j^k}(v) - \mu_{C_j^k}(u') + P_{C_j^k}(u'))^2}}{m},$$

(12)

where $u' = = \arg_{v'} \max_{v' \in U'}(\mu_{C_j^k}(v) - \mu_{C_j^k}(v'))$, $\mu_{C_j^k}(v)$ and $\mu_{C_j^k}(u')$ denote the satisfaction degree of the jth (weighted) fuzzy constraint associated with the v and the u' for agent k, $P_{C_j^k}(u')$ denotes the penalty from the jth dissatisfied (weighted) fuzzy constraint associated with the offer u' made by agent k, and m is the number of fuzzy constraints of agent k on issues.

Definition 8 (Expected trade-off proposal): Assuming that agent k proposes an offer u to its opponents, and that the opponents subsequently proposes a set of counter-offer U' to agent k, the expected trade-off proposal u^* for the next offer by agent k is defined as

$$u^* = \arg_{\mathbf{v}}(\max_{\mathbf{v} \in_{\alpha_i^k} \mathfrak{I}_{\mathbf{u}}^k} \Theta^k(v, U')),$$

(13)

where α_i^k is the highest possible threshold such that $_{\alpha_i^k}\mathfrak{I}_{\mathbf{u}}^k \neq \{\ \}$ and $\Theta^k(v, U') > \Theta^k(\mathbf{u}, U')$.

The constraint $\Theta^k(\mathbf{v}, \mathbf{U'}) > \Theta^k(u, U')$ is used to ensure that the next solution is better than the previous solution. Thus, based on the fuzzy similarity, an agent can use a trade-off strategy to generate a proposal that may benefit all parties without lowering the agent's demands.

Different combinations of strategies can be applied to particular situations. Hence, the trade-off strategy and/or concession strategy can be further meshed and ordered into a meta strategy M over the whole scenario of negotiation. The proposed model considers that agent k has a mental state that includes beliefs, desires, intentions, goals, and knowledge of the opponent's possible behavior; this mental state affects the strategy chosen by an agent. Hence, assuming that the mental state (psyche) of agent k at the state n is noted as P_n^k, the meta strategy from state n to the next state n + 1 for agent k, denoted by M_{n+1}^k, can be defined as

$$M_{n+1}^k = f(M_n^k, P_n^k),$$

(14)

where P_n^k is the mental state n of agent k. Agents apply meta strategies and take turns to propose offers to explore the agents' potential agreements and pursue a satisfactory outcome that meets their demands.

4. MULTILATERAL NEGOTIATIONS FOR WATER POLICY PLANNING

In an island nation, due to the development of industrial zones, golf courses, and real estate, mountain deforestation has severely damaged watersheds. Excluding the prohibition of deforestation, there seems to be no easy remedy for such upstream pollution beyond finding new water sources and spending money on downstream water cleanup. With this in mind, the government plans to add new reservoirs to the island's current. However, environmentalists worry about environmental degradation resulting from reservoir construction, and reservoir proposals almost always provoke public protest. After the lift of martial law, in the face of dramatically changed political situation and increased democratic awareness, government can no longer deal with conflicts and protests regarding water resources through coercive way as before, but rather needs negotiate a common acceptable solution. Moreover, because of the island's failure to develop its sewage system, many of island's rivers and coastal waters have been seriously polluted. To carry out reservoir pollution control programs, the cities of island thus urgently need to build adequate sewage systems and formulate water processing regulations in order to curb water pollution. Besides, for water conservation, the government plans a differentiated charging system on water consumption, which means those consuming more water than average should pay more, and those using water within certain quota can pay at a lower price. In order to focus attention on the major issues and interests, this application abstracts from the complicated negotiation process. Thus, three major issues, including the volume (one hundred million cube meter) of the new water resource exploitation, the degree of the environmental standard (waste water processing treatment, water recycle), and the degree of the raised price for consuming water more than average in differentiated charging system, have arisen in the negotiation.

Meanwhile, the island nation has the world's second largest IC design industry and world's No. 1 foundry industry. The industry sector contributes lots of GDP of the nation. Hence, in the bargain the representatives of industrial water users (or Industrial Development Bureau, hereafter the industrial agent I, residents (hereafter the resident agent R), and environmentalists (or Environmental Protection Administration, hereafter the environmentalist agent E) will negotiate the volume of new water resource, the degree of the environmental standard, and the degree of the differentiated charge. The multilateral negotiation on the three groups indicates economic, ethical (disparities), and environmental features of the debate.

Industrial water users views new resource exploitation (Infrastructure) as the best method of facilitating regular water availability, and they strongly support the new resource exploitation. The equipments for the waste water processing regulations (water recycle) will increases the financial burden, but the water from recycle also can be reused. Thus, industrial water users generally oppose the high environmental standard. Industrial water users almost consume more water than average. Thus, they hope smaller charging difference on the differentiated charging system.

Resident water users are primarily concerned with the availability of affordable water supplies to support continued growing population. Thus, resident users support the new infrastructure development. Although resident water users disagree with strong environmental regulations regarding water use, the high value of water in resident use tempers this opposition. Thus, they only weakly oppose the high environmental standard. In a differentiated charging system, residents using water within certain quota can pay at a lower price. Thus, they may support greater charging difference on the differentiated charging system.

Environmentalists are strongly opposed to the new resource exploitation (Infrastructure) because they are primarily concerned with controlling adverse environmental consequences. Strong environmental regulations are the primary negotiating objective of environmentalists. Thus, environmentalists strongly stand up for the high environmental standard. By paying more, people will become more aware of the value of water, and water conservation. Thus, environmentalists support the higher price for consuming more water.

Accordingly, industrial agent *I* specifies the requirements as fuzzy constraints, namely "*More* New_resource," "*Low* Environ_standard," "*Small* Differentiated_Charge," along with the relative importance of issues, urgency, and minimal satisfaction degree. The situation is the same for resident agent R, who represents the requirements as fuzzy constraints "*More* New_resource," "*Low* Environ_standard," "*Great* Differentiated_charge," and for environmentalist agent E, who represents the requirements as fuzzy constraints "*Less* New_resource," "*High* Environ_standard," "*Great* Differentiated_charge," and so on. Sup-

pose that agents *I*, *R*, and *E* all adopt the fixed concession strategies with urgency=0.1. Figure 1 shows the user interfaces of industrial agent I, resident agent R, and environmentalist agent E.

Industrial agent I, resident agent R, and environmentalist agent *E* take turns to propose offers to reach an agreement. As shown in Figure 1, at the threshold $a_1^I = 1$, agent I proposes its ideal feasible proposals $u_1^I = (120, 60\%, 6\%)$ related to New_resource, Environ_standard, and Different_charge to agents *R* and *E*. However, according to (5) agents *R* and *E* cannot accept u_1^I as an agreement. Subsequently, agent *R* proposes its

Figure 1. User interfaces of industrial agent, resident agent, and environmentalist agent

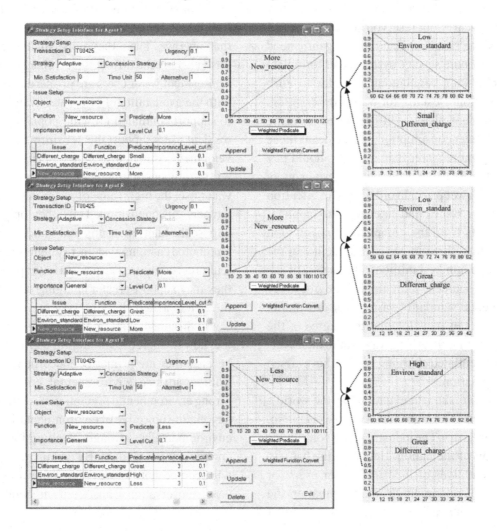

best counter-offer $u_1^R = (120, 58\%, 42\%)$ at the threshold $a_1^R = 1$ to agents I and E. However, according to (5), agents I and E cannot accept u_1^R as an agreement. Agent E also proposes its best counter-offer $u_1^E = (0, 84\%, 42\%)$ at the threshold $a_1^E = 1$ to agents I and R. However, according to (5), agents I and R also cannot accept u_1^E as an agreement.

Furthermore, since agent I adopts the fixed concession strategy and has no expected proposal at the threshold $a_1^I = 1$, by (7) in Definition 5, agent I lowers its threshold to the next threshold $a_1^I = 0.9$ and creates I new set of feasible proposals as follows:

$$\mathbf{v}_{2a}^I = (120, 62\%, 6\%), \mathbf{v}_{2b}^I = (110, 60\%, 6\%), \mathbf{v}_{2c}^I = (120, 60\%, 9\%),$$

Next, using (12) in Definition 7, the similarity among these feasible proposals is computed by agent I as follows.

$$\Theta(\mathbf{v}_{2a}^I) = 0.263, \quad \Theta(\mathbf{v}_{2b}^I) = 0.282, \quad \Theta(\mathbf{v}_{2c}^I) = 0.272.$$

Thus, agent I selects the most likely acceptable solution $\mathbf{v}_{2b}^I = (110, 60\%, 6\%)$ which $\Theta(\mathbf{v}_{2b}^I) = 0.282$ as the offer u_2^I for proposing to agents R and E. This procedure of offer evaluation and generation for agents I, R and E will continue until an agreement is reached or no more solution can be proposed. Figure 2 shows only the partial results in order to converse space.

Consequently, the negotiation reaches an agreement over (New_resource, Environ_standard, Different_charge) at (50, 72%, 24%), of

Figure 2. Negotiation results of agent I, (agent R, and agent E)

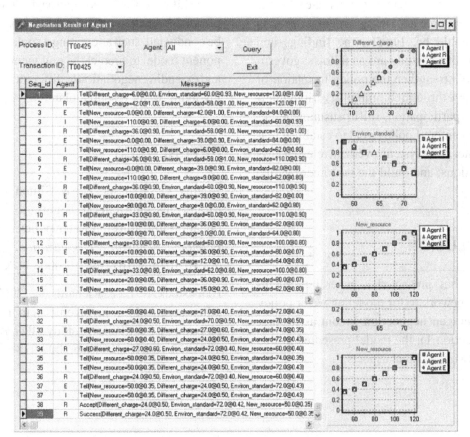

which the satisfaction degree for industrial agent I is (0.4, 0.5, 0.47), that of the resident agent R is (0.35, 0.42, 0.5), and that of the environmentalist agent E is (0.5, 0.4, 0.4). Thus Water Resources Agency will provide agents the plan at the 50 (hundred million cube meter) new water resource, 72% environmental standard, and 24% differentiated charge. The reached deal u=(50, 72%, 24%), of which Ψ^I =0.456, Ψ^R =0.423, Ψ^E =0.433, a^I =0.4, a^R =0.35, and a^E =0.4 shows that the proposed approach, involving fuzzy constraint relaxation and similarity, can apply on the multi-issue multilateral negotiation to reach a fair agreement that benefits all agents and maximize the overall satisfaction degree of requirements. The application also shows that our approach will avoid resulting in an agreement that benefits one's side on balance but fails to generate sufficient gain for special industrial groups that can block ratification.

This application attempts to illustrate what the new water resource policies and regulations government should be. Finally, the findings and suggestions of the study are as follows: government should strengthen the policy formation of water resource through community (various interest groups) participation, fulfill sustainable-development-centered policy goal to establish reasonable water price system, overhaul relevant laws and regulations, and build the customer-pay-fee system.

5. CONCLUSION

This paper has presented a general problem-solving framework to for modeling water policy planning via agent negotiation. In contrast to other models (Section 1), the model presented in this paper has two important aspects:

- Systematic problem solving: Fuzzy constraints enable an agent, in case of no solution, to relax its demands to generate a proposal without the necessity to delete any of its desires, and in case of too many solutions, to specify possibilities prescribing to what extent the solutions are suitable for its proposal to rank the solutions. With the capability of self-relaxation, our approach provides a systematic approach to explore proposals.

- Search offers only from a feasible region: the proposed approach enables an agent to systematically relax fuzzy constraints to generate a proposal, and employ fuzzy similarity to select the alternative that is subject to its acceptability by the opponents. Thus, our approach can yield an agreement more quickly.

While the proposed approach yielded some promising results, considerable works remain to be conducted, such as creating a sophisticated opponent model to predict the opponent's behavior, and extending negotiation to different applications involving water resource planning.

REFERENCES

Adams, G., Rausser, G., & Simon, L. (1996). Modelling multilateral negotiations: An application to California water policy. *Journal of Economic Behavior & Organization*, *30*, 97–111. doi:10.1016/S0167-2681(96)00844-X

Blackstock, K. L., & Richards, C. (2007). Evaluating stakeholder involvement in river basin planning: a Scottish case study. *Water Policy*, *9*, 493–512. doi:10.2166/wp.2007.018

Bradshaw, J. M. (1997). *Software agents*. Cambridge, MA: MIT Press.

Choi, S. P. M., Liu, J., & Chan, S. P. (2001). A genetic agent-based negotiation system. *Computer Networks*, *37*, 195–204. doi:10.1016/S1389-1286(01)00215-8

Eaton, P. S., Freuder, E. C., & Wallace, R. J. (1998). Constraints and agents: Confronting ignorance. *AI Magazine*, *19*, 51–65.

Huhns, M. N., & Munindar, P. S. (1998). *Readings in agents*. San Francisco, CA: Morgan Kaufmann.

Kersten, G. E., & Lo, G. (2001). Negotiation support systems and software agents in e-business negotiations. In *Proceedings of the First International Conference on Electronic Business* (pp. 19-21).

Lai, R. (1992). *Fuzzy constraint processing*. Raleigh, NC: NCSU Press.

Lai, R., & Lin, M. W. (2004). Modeling agent negotiation via fuzzy constraints in e-business. *Computational Intelligence*, *20*, 624–642. doi:10.1111/j.0824-7935.2004.00257.x

Larson, S. (2009). Designing robust water planning institutions in remote regions: A case of Georgina and Diamantina catchment in Australia. *Water Policy*, *12*, 357–368. doi:10.2166/wp.2009.266

Lin, M. W., Lai, R., & Yu, T. J. (2005). Fuzzy constraint-based agent negotiation. *Journal of Computer Science and Technology*, *20*, 319–330. doi:10.1007/s11390-005-0319-3

Luo, X., Jennings, N. R., & Shadbolt, N. (2003). A fuzzy constraint based model for bilateral, multi-issue negotiations in semi-competitive environments. *Artificial Intelligence*, *148*, 53–102. doi:10.1016/S0004-3702(03)00041-9

Oliver, J. R. (1996). On artificial agents for negotiation in electronic commerce. In *Proceedings of the 29th Annual Hawaii International Conference on System Sciences* (pp. 337-346).

Pruitt, D. G. (1981). *Negotiation behavior*. New York, NY: Academic Press.

Randall, D., Cleland, L., & Kuehne, C. S. (1997). Water supply planning simulation model using mixed-integer linear programming. *Journal of Water Resources Planning and Management*, *123*, 116–124. doi:10.1061/(ASCE)0733-9496(1997)123:2(116)

Ren, Z., Anumba, C. J., & Ugwu, O. O. (2002). Negotiation in a multi-agent system for construction claims negotiation. *Applied Artificial Intelligence*, *16*, 359–394. doi:10.1080/08839510290030273

Rosenschein, J. S., & Zlotkin, G. (1994). *Rules of encounter: Designing conventions for automated negotiation among computers*. Cambridge, MA: MIT Press.

Sathi, A., & Fox, M. (1989). Constraint-directed negotiation of resource reallocation. In Gasser, L., & Huhns, M. (Eds.), *Distributed artificial intelligence* (*Vol. 2*, pp. 163–195). San Francisco, CA: Morgan Kaufmann.

Sycara, K. (1989). Multi-agent compromise via negotiation. In Gasser, L., & Huhns, M. (Eds.), *Distributed artificial intelligence* (*Vol. 2*, pp. 119–139). San Francisco, CA: Morgan Kaufmann.

Watkins, D. W. Jr, & McKinney, D. C. (1998). Decomposition methods for water resources optimization models with fixed costs. *Water Resources*, *21*, 283–295. doi:10.1016/S0309-1708(96)00061-9

Zadeh, L. A. (1975). The concept of a linguistic variable and its application to approximate reasoning. *Information Sciences*, *8*, 199–249. doi:10.1016/0020-0255(75)90036-5

Zadeh, L. A. (1978). Fuzzy sets as a basis for a theory of possibility. *Fuzzy Sets and Systems*, *1*, 3–28. doi:10.1016/0165-0114(78)90029-5

Zeng, D., & Sycara, K. (1998). Bayesian learning in negotiation. *International Journal of Human-Computer Studies*, *48*, 125–141. doi:10.1006/ijhc.1997.0164

This work was previously published in the International Journal of Digital Library Systems, Volume 2, Issue 2, edited by Chia-Hung Wei, pp. 1-12, copyright 2011 by IGI Publishing (an imprint of IGI Global).

Chapter 12
An Affinity Based Complex Artificial Immune System

Wei Wang
Nankai University, China

Mei Chang
Neusoft Institute of Information, China

Xiaofei Wang
University of Toyama, Japan

Zheng Tang
Toyama University, Japan

ABSTRACT

This paper proposes an affinity based complex artificial immune system considering the fact that the different eptitopes located on the surface of antigen can be recognized by a set of different paratopes expressed on the surface of immune cells. A neighborhood set consisting of immune cells with different affinities to a certain input antigen is built to simulate the nature immune behavior. Furthermore, the complex numbers are adopted as the data representation, besides the weight between different layers. In the simulations, the recognition on transformation patterns is performed to illustrate that the proposed system is capable of recognizing the transformation patterns and it has obviously higher noise tolerance ability than the previous system models.

1. INTRODUCTION

Along with the interest in studying the immune system increasing over the last few years, a new field of research called artificial immune systems has arisen. The artificial immune systems, which is inspired by theoretical immunology and observed immune functions, principles and models, has been applied to the various fields of engineering science to solve many complex problems, such as pattern recognition (de Castro, & Timmis, 2002), robotics (Jakimovsk, & Maehle, 2008), anomaly detection Dasgupta & Forrest, 1996; Gonzalz, & Dasgupta, 2004), data mining (Knight, & Timmis, 2001) and optimization (Hajela, & Yoo, 1999).

DOI: 10.4018/978-1-4666-2928-8.ch012

In our previous works, some artificial immune system models motivated by nature immune system were proposed, such as binary model (Tang, Hebishima, Tashima, Ishizuka, & Tanno, 1997), real value system (Sun, Tang, Tamura, & Ishii, 2003), multi-valued system (Yamaguchi, Tang, Ishizuka, & Tanno, 2001; Tang, Yamaguchi, Tashima, Ishizuka, & Tanno, 1997; Tang Yamaguchi, Tashima, Ishizuka, & Tanno, 1999) clonal selection theory based network (Tang, Tashima, & Cao, 2001), and TI-TD-based model (Dai, Tang, Tamura, & Yang, 2006). Furthermore, a complex artificial immune system model, which adopts complex number data representation and affinity evaluations was also proposed to recognize transformation patterns (Wang, Gao, Li, & Tang, 2008; Wang, Gao, & Tang, 2009). These earlier papers treated the immune response as a competition process by using WTA (Winner-Take-All) rule (Hagan, Demuth, & Beale, 1995). In another word, there is only one immune cell (the winner immune cell) that is selected to respond to a certain input antigen. On the other hand, immune cells with different receptors respond to input antigen with different strength in natural immune system. This is quite different from the nature immune system model, based on which we proposed our artificial immune system previously.

In this paper, we propose an affinity based complex artificial immune system model to simulate the actual immune response. In this model, we build a neighborhood set consisting of several immune cells with higher affinities to a certain input antigen than the other immune cells based on the SOM principles. All the weights of cells located in the neighborhood set have their weights updated according to the affinities. The results of simulation on pattern recognition shows that the proposed system model can recognize the transformation patterns in high accuracy and it has obvious higher noise tolerance ability than the previous system models.

The rest of the paper is organized as follows. In section 2 we introduce some basic concepts of nature immune response mechanism. In section 3 we introduce the affinity based complex artificial immune system model based on the immune response mechanism briefly. Followed by this, we depict the algorithm in detail in section 4. In section 5, we represent the simulation on transformation pattern recognition. Finally, we give some general conclusions.

2. IMMUNE RESPONSE MECHANISM

Figure 1 depicts the immune response process in detail considering the affinity interactions. When an antigen invades the host, antigen present cells first internalize the invaded antigen to secrete antigenic peptides, either by phagocytosis or by endocytosis. These antigenic peptides join to major histocompatibility complex (MHC) and display on the surface of antigen presenting cell together. Th cells recognize the peptide-MHC molecules through T-cell receptors. Activated Th

Figure 1. Immune response process

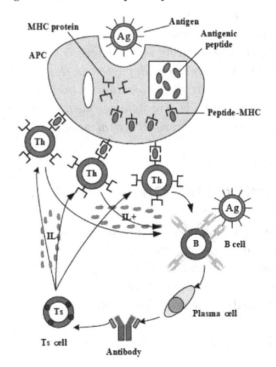

cells divide and secrete interleukin (IL+), or other chemical signals, which mobilize other components (B cells etc.) of the immune system. It is remarked that Th cells with different receptors recognize complex of peptide-MHC with different affinity. If Th cell receptors and antigens are not quite complementary, they may still bind, but with a low affinity. However, B cells can also be activated by antigens directly. Activated B cells can divide and differentiate into plasma cells and memory cells. Plasma cells secrete the antibodies to destroy the invaded antigen. When antigen is destroyed, Ts cells are activated and secrete suppressing signal interleukin (IL-) to Th cells to terminate immune response. As for the memory B cells, when they encounter the same antigens once again, they will divide into plasma cells rapidly, and generate abundant antibodies soon, which is called the second response.

3. AFFINITY BASED COMPLEX ARTIFICIAL IMMUNE SYSTEM MODEL

Based on the nature immune response mechanism, we propose the affinity based complex artificial immune system. As shown in Figure 2, this model consists of four layers: APC layer, MHC layer, Th cell layer and B cell layer. The antigen (AG) and antibody (AB) are considered as the input and the output of the model respectively. When an input antigen is presented to the system, first it is processed by ACP layer. The input antigen is transformed into the complex forms and outputted to the MHC layer. The key feature of the input antigen calculated in this layer is considered as the input of the competitive layer (Th cell layer). In this model, the obvious improvement is the introduction of the affinity based neighborhood instead of inappropriate previously adopted WTA rule. In B cell layer, B cells are activated by the stimuli form Th cells located in neighborhood set. Antibody is regarded as the difference

between the key feature of input antigen and the memory information memorized in B cells. Ts cells modulate the weights of the immune cells located in neighborhood set according to the state of antibody.

4. ALGORITHM

In this section, we will discuss the algorithm of the affinity based complex artificial immune system model.

4.1. Complex Antigen Transformation in APC Layer and Invariant Feature Extraction in MHC Layer

In the natural immune system, the antigens are cut into smaller pieces called peptides by antigen-presenting cells (APC). Mathematically the antigen can be expressed as a set of binary value as: $AG = (ag_1, ag_2, \cdots, ag_M)$ (Tang, Hebishima, Tashima, Ishizuka, & Tanno, 1997), each element

Figure 2. Affinity based complex artificial immune system model

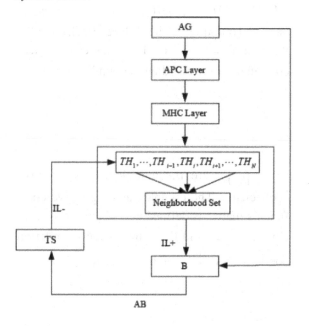

of which is binary numbers, i.e. 0 or 1. However, small disturbance easily causes binary representation loss of some feature information. In order to avoid this disadvantage and extract the invariant features of the antigens, the sequence of boundary points of the input antigen with the value of "1" are explored and represented as complex numbers. The number of input antigens is M. The number of the cells in the APC layer is M', which actually depends upon the number of the boundary points. As shown in Figure 3, the output of APC layer is expressed as $AG' = (ag'_1, ag'_2, \cdots, ag'_{M'})$, and each element in AG' has a complex expression as:

$$ag'_i = x_{ag_i} + y_{ag_i} i \tag{1}$$

where i is the imaginary number. x_{ag_i} and y_{ag_i} are the horizontal and vertical value of boundary point ag_i respectively when mapping the whole antigen to a two dimensional space and regarding the left-upper point as the origin.

Similarly, the MHC layer receives AG' from APC layer as: $MHC_i = ag'_i$. In this layer, the complex partial autocorrelation coefficients (Sekita, Kurita, & Otsu, 1992) of AG' namely $MHC' = (MHC'_1, MHC'_2, \ldots, MHC'_m)$ are calculated and outputted to the Th layer. Each complex input number MHC_i can be expressed by a linear combination of preceding m boundary points as:

$$MHC_i = \sum_{k=1}^{m} a_k \cdot MHC_{i-k} \tag{2}$$

where $\{a_k\}_{k=1}^{m}$ are the complex autoregressive coefficients. The complex autoregressive coefficients matrix is defined as $A = [a_1, a_2, \cdots, a_m]'$. On the other hand the complex autocorrelation coefficients $\{r_j\}_{j=0}^{m}$ can be calculated as:

$$r_j = \sum_{k=0}^{M'-1} MHC_k \cdot \overline{MHC}_{(k+j)\bmod(M')} \tag{3}$$

where the bar denotes a scalar complex conjugate and mod represents the modulo operation. $\overline{MHC}_{(k+j)\bmod(M')}$ is the complex conjugate of MHC_k, which has been transposed m. Thus, we can get the complex autocorrelation coefficients given by:

$$MHC'_1 = A_{11} = \frac{r_1}{r_0}$$

$$A_{jk} = A_{(j-1)k} - MHC'_j \cdot \overline{A}_{(j-1)(j-k)}, \qquad k < j$$

$$MHC'_j = A_{jj} = \frac{r_j - \sum_{k=1}^{j-1} r_{j-k} A_{(j-1)k}}{r_0 - \sum_{k=1}^{j-1} r_k \overline{A}_{(j-1)k}}, \quad j \geq 2$$

$$\tag{4}$$

where $\overline{A}$ is the complex conjugate matrix of A.

Hereby, according to Equation (2) to Equation (4), the MHC' can be calculated and each element can be expressed as:

Figure 3. Process in APC layer and MHC layer

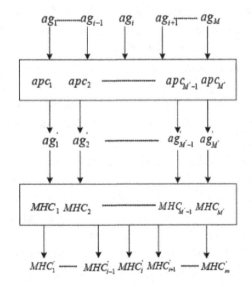

$$MHC_i^{'} = x_i + y_i i \qquad (5)$$

where x_i is the real part and y_i is the imaginary part of $MHC^{'}$.

4.2. Affinity Based Competition in Th Cell layer

As introduced above, Th cells in competitive layer received the input from MHC layer through different weight channels. As shown in Figure 4, the weight W between Th cell layer and MHC layer is given by:

$$w_{ij} = a_{ij} + b_{ij} i \qquad (6)$$

where a_{ij} is the real part and b_{ij} is the imaginary part. Thus, the state of each Th cell is given by:

$$TH_j = (MHC_i^{'}, w_{ij}) = \sum_{i=1}^{m} (x_i \cdot a_{ij} + y_i \cdot b_{ij}) \quad (j=1,2,...,N) \qquad (7)$$

In the previous complex artificial immune system model, winner-take-all rule (WTA) is used to determine the maximally stimulus Th cell using:

$$TH_{j\max} = \max\{TH_j\} \qquad (j=1,2,...,N) \qquad (8)$$

Thus, only one Th cell is activated by a certain stimulus, while other Th cells are inhibited. As a fact that Th cells with different receptors can recognize MHC molecules by different affinities, another method is necessary to simulate the nature immune response instead of the WTA rule.

Self-organizing maps (SOMs) have been received great interest recently and can be applied to many areas. For instance, image processing and speech recognition, process control, economical analysis, and diagnostics in industry and in medicine (Kohonen, Oja, Simula, Visa, & Kangas, 1996). As a new and useful tool for pattern recognition in chemical sensing (Lemos, Nakamura, Sugimoto, & Kuwano, 1993), SOMs show a particular ability for solving the problem of classification in pattern recognition.

Based on the SOM algorithm, the weight w can be updated according to the following equations:

$$a_{ij}(t+1) = a_{ij}(t) + \eta(t)h_j(t)[x_i - a_{ij}(t)]$$
$$b_{ij}(t+1) = b_{ij}(t) + \eta(t)h_j(t)[y_i - b_{ij}(t)]$$
$$(9)$$

$$h_j(t) = \exp(-\frac{\rho^2(j)}{2\sigma^2}) \qquad (10)$$

$$\rho(j) = | P(j) - P(j\max) | \qquad (11)$$

where

- $\eta(t)$ is the learning rate at time t.
- $h_j(t)$ is the Gaussian neighborhood function kernel centered on the $TH_{j\max}$ cell, and σ is called the neighborhood radius.
- $\rho(j)$ is the distance between the jth Th cell and $TH_{j\max}$ cell.
- $P(j)$ is the position of the jth Th cell on the SOM grid.

As shown in Figure 4, the Th cells receive stimulus from the output of MHC layer, unlike the previous model, in which only one Th cell with highest affinity is outputted, reorganization is performed according to the affinity between input MHC stimulus and Th cells. As a result, an affinity based neighborhood set (the marked part) composed of the $TH_{j\max}$ cell and other Th cells with higher affinity than other Th cells is generated. In this condition, the reorganized Th cells are arranged by affinity sequence given by:

$$A(r1) > A(r2) > \cdots > A(rd) > \cdots > A(rN) \qquad (12)$$

Figure 4. Process in Th cell layer

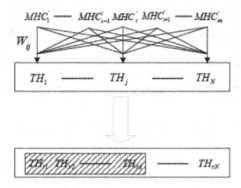

where

$rj (j = 1, 2, ..., N)$ is the index of the rj th Th cell.

d is the neighborhood distance, which indicates the response depth in Th cell layer.

$A(rj)$ is the affinity between the rj th Th cell and input stimulus expressed as:

$$A(rj) = (MHC_i', w_{srj}) = \sum_{i=1}^{m} (x_i \cdot a_{srj} + y_i \cdot b_{srj}) \quad (j = 1, 2, ..., N)$$

$$(13)$$

As shown above, the neighborhood set consists of $TH_{rj} (j = 1, 2, ..., d)$. The Th cells located in the neighborhood set are activated while others are inhibited given by:

$$O(TH_{rj}) = 1 \quad when \quad j = 1, 2, ..., d$$
$$O(TH_{rj}) = 0 \quad when \quad otherwise$$

$$(14)$$

where $O(*)$ is the activation function of Th cell.

4.3. B Cells Activation

As shown in Figure 5, B cells are stimulated by interleukin (IL+) secreted by activated Th cells located in the neighborhood set (masked part) through different weight channels V namely:

$$v_{rji} = a_{rji}' + b_{rji}' i \quad (15)$$

where a_{rji}' is the real part and b_{rji}' is the imaginary part. Referring to the Equation (10) and Equation (11), the weight v_{rji} is given by:

$$a_{rji}'(t + 1) = a_{rji}'(t) + \eta(t)h_j(t)[x_i - a_{rji}'(t)]$$
$$b_{rji}'(t + 1) = b_{rji}'(t) + \eta(t)h_j(t)[y_i - b_{rji}'(t)]$$

$$(16)$$

The memory patterns can be defined as:

$$B_{rji} = O(TH_{rj})v_{rji} \quad (j = 1, 2, ..., m) \quad (17)$$

4.4. System Update

In the proposed complex artificial immune system, the antibody AB is defined as the difference between the antigen key feature and memory pattern. An affinity evaluation parameter E is defined in advance in order to calculate antibody given by:

$$E_{rj} = (MHC_i', B_{rji}) = \sum_{i=1}^{m} (x_i \cdot a_{rji}' + y_i \cdot b_{rji}')$$

$$(18)$$

For all the Th cells located in the neighborhood set, the corresponding antibody can be expressed as:

$$AB_{rj} = 1 - \frac{\| E_{rj}(t) - E_{rj}(t-1) \|}{\| \sum_{i=1}^{N} E_i(t-1) \|} \quad (19)$$

where $E_{rj}(t)$ is the present affinity between the rj th Th cell in the neighborhood set and the memory pattern at time t, while $E_{rj}(t-1)$ is the preceding affinities called memory affinity.

If the similarity is less than the system tolerance namely,

Figure 5. B cells' response to Th cells located in neighborhood set

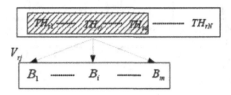

$$AB_{rj} < \rho \quad (0 < \rho < 1) \qquad (20)$$

The result is reserved and another evaluation using a lower affinity Th cell located in the neighborhood set is performed according to Equation (18) and Equation (19). If all $TH_{j\max}$ the similarities of Th cells in the neighborhood set are less than the system tolerance, it will be considered as the recognition failed, and system is updated using TH_{r1} cell.

If the similarity is equal to or more than the system tolerance namely,

$$AB_{rj} \geq \rho \quad (0 < \rho < 1) \qquad (21)$$

This means that, this TH_{rj} th cell is accepted and it represents the category of this kind of antigen, and the antigen is recognized successfully. The TH_{rj} cell becomes to the winner Th cell, marked as $TH_{j\max}$

In nature immune system, Ts cells have the function of regulating cells' activation. During the period of immune response T, the Ts cells adjust the weight of by:

$$
\begin{aligned}
a_{ij}(t+1) &= a_{ij}(t) + Ts(t)\eta[x_i - a_{ij}(t)] \\
b_{ij}(t+1) &= b_{ij}(t) + Ts(t)\eta[y_i - b_{ij}(t)]
\end{aligned} \qquad (22)
$$

where η is the learning rate, $Ts(t) = 1 - \dfrac{t}{T}$ is the state of the Ts cell at time t.

As mentioned above, the neighborhood set in SOM consists of the winner cell $TH_{j\max}$ and some

other Th cells with higher affinities. That is to say, the Th cells in the neighborhood set are bound by the affinity of the input antigen and memory pattern. Hereby, based on the affinity relation, the update of weights v associated with the Th cells located in the neighborhood set is given by:

$$
\begin{aligned}
a'_{rji}(t+1) &= a'_{rji}(t) + Ts(t)\eta f(rj, j\max)[x_i - a'_{rji}(t)] \\
b'_{rji}(t+1) &= b'_{rji}(t) + Ts(t)\eta f(rj, j\max)[y_i - b'_{rji}(t)]
\end{aligned}
$$
$$(23)$$

where indicates the similarity between the TH_{rj} and $TH_{j\max}$.

5. SIMULATION

In our previous work (Wang, Gao, Li, & Tang, 2008; Wang, Gao, & Tang, 2009), we have illustrated that the complex artificial immune system maintains the immunity of the traditional artificial immune system and has the ability of recognizing transformation patterns along with the better noise tolerance through the simulation on numbers' recognition. In view of the improvement of the neighborhood set output of Th cell layer, the proposed affinity based artificial immune system should have improved recognition ability theoretically. In this section, a simulation on pattern recognition is performed to illustrate the enhanced recognition ability of the affinity based artificial immune system. Furthermore, a comparison with the previous model is also done to expound the anti-noisy ability of the proposed system model. In the simulation on the pattern recognition, the system operations are divided into two steps: Learning and recognition, corresponding to the primary response and second response of the nature immune system respectively. In learning process, in order to adjust the system weights to make the correct output can be obtained for a certain input, the standard patterns are inputted into the system and learned repeatedly.

Figure 6. Patterns for simulation

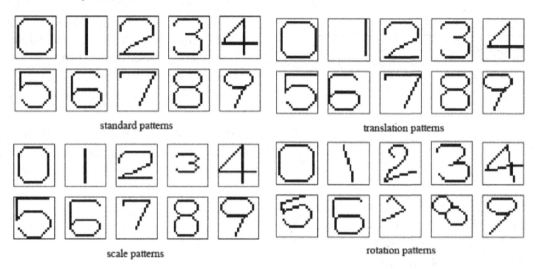

standard patterns   translation patterns

scale patterns   rotation patterns

Figure 7. Recognition with different system tolerance

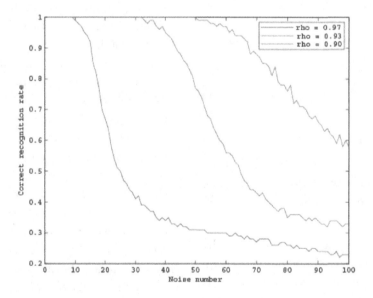

The patterns for simulations are shown in Figure 6. Each pattern is composed of 19x19 pixels. The learning process of the system is performed according to following steps:

Step 1: Initialize the real part and imaginary part of weights w_{ij} and v_{ji}.

Step 2: In APC layer, seek the boundary points of input pattern, and calculate the complex coordinates of boundary points. The input of this layer AG's number M is calculated to be 361, and the cells number of this layer M' depends on the number of boundary points.

Figure 8. Classification process of number "5"

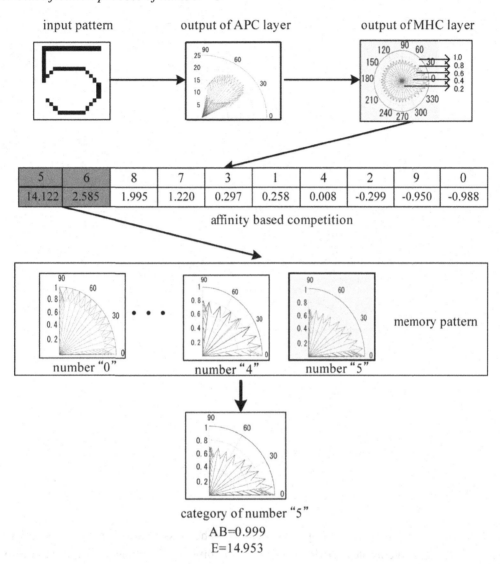

category of number "5"
AB=0.999
E=14.953

Step 3: In MHC layer, calculate the value of MHC' using Equation (2)-(4). In addition, the number of MHC' m is set to be 50.

Step 4: In Th cell layer, output the affinity based neighborhood set. The response depth d is set to be 2 and cell number N is set to be 10.

Step 5: Compute the antibody AB using Equation (18) and (19), and decide whether to perform a better match in neighborhood set or not by Equation (20) and (21). If the similarity is less than the system tolerance, use the Th cell with lower affinity in the neighborhood set until the similarity satisfy the system tolerance. Otherwise, go to next step. If all of the Th cells do not satisfy the system tolerance, the recognition is considered to be failed. Then update the system using the Th_{r1} cell and go to step 7.

Step 6: Update the weights using Equation (22) and (23).

Step 7: Go to step 2 for next input pattern.

Figure 9. Transformation noisy pattern recognition

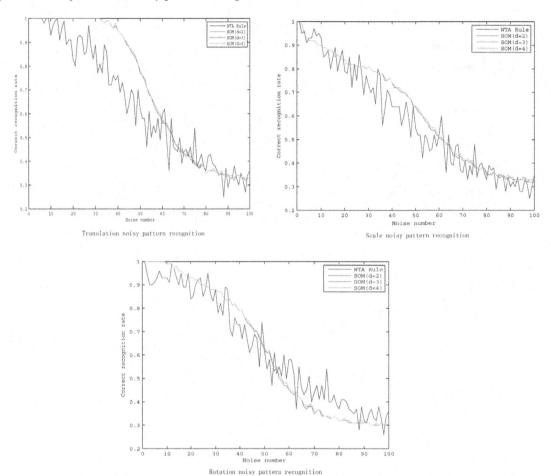

Translation noisy pattern recognition

Scale noisy pattern recognition

Rotation noisy pattern recognition

The system tolerance ρ is the most important parameter in the proposed complex artificial immune system, by which the recognition accuracy of transformation patterns can be controlled. Figure 7 depicts the noise recognition result with different system tolerance with the response depth is set to be $d = 2$.

If the system tolerance is set as $\rho = 0.97$, although the accuracy of the recognition can be maintained, the anti-noise ability will be lost. On the contrary, if ρ is set to be too low (0.90), the system will lose the ability of recognizing similar input pattern. Therefore, in the following simulation, we set ρ as the experimental value 0.93.

The classification process of standard pattern of number "5" is shown in Figure 8 as an example. The complex coordinates of the boundary points are calculated and shown in the middle. The key feature is shown on the right of the first row. The second row is the result of the affinity based competition, which is organized by affinity descending order. As the response depth d is set to be 2, the neighborhood set marked as grey part is outputted to the B cell layer. Thus, the AB is calculated using the memory pattern of first category in the neighborhood set and the value (0.999) satisfy the system tolerance, which means that the input pattern can be classified to the category of number "5". It should be emphasized that in

Figure 10. Increased noisy pattern recognition

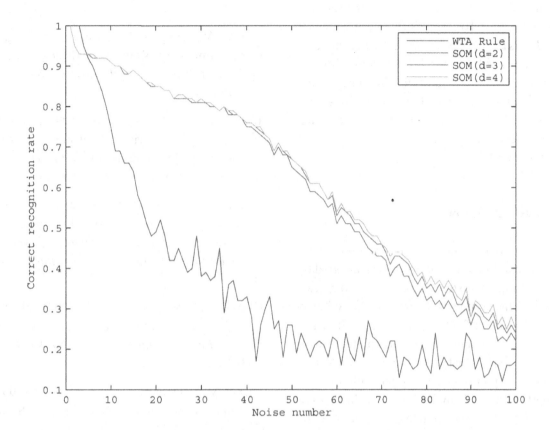

some cases, the first category does not satisfy the system tolerance. Then system will try another category with lower affinity in the neighborhood set.

A comparison of noisy pattern recognition is performed using the proposed affinity based complex artificial immune system and the previous complex artificial immune system. We generate noisy patterns by adding noise to the transformation patterns. The noise is defined as the antigen presentation values we changed randomly. In addition, one parameter called CRR is defined to evaluate recognition ability. We define the correct recognition rate CRR as CR/N, where, CR is the number of presented patterns correctly recognized, and N is the number of patterns presented to the system.

The results of translation, scale and rotation recognition are shown in Figure 9. The horizontal axis is noise number and vertical axis is the correct recognition rate. From the results, we can see that the affinity based the complex artificial immune system has obvious higher noise tolerance than the complex artificial immune system using WTA rule. In addition, the recognition results using different response depths do not show evident discrepancies. The following consideration is given: the recognition rate is controlled by the system tolerance, not the response depth, and the noises are not sufficient to obtain the obvious recognition results of different response depths.

In the noisy pattern recognition above, the noises are added to the antigen presentation randomly. Therefore, it is probably that the noises are added to one antigen presentation repeatedly.

To avoid this, increased noisy pattern recognition of translation patterns is done, and the result is shown in Figure 10. The position, where noise is added to, is memorized to insure that the duplicate noise does not be generated. Obviously, the affinity based complex artificial immune system has higher noise tolerance than the previous complex artificial immune system using WTA rule, and the deeper response depth shows the better anti-noise ability.

5. CONCLUSION

In our previous works, we have proposed different artificial immune system models inspired by nature immune system (binary and complex). However, these models adopted WTA (Winner-Take-All) rule in the competitive layer. It means that only one winner Th cell is outputted, which disregards the fact that immune cells with different receptors respond to input antigen with different strength in natural immune system. In this paper, an affinity based complex artificial immune system is proposed based on SOM principles. An affinity based neighborhood set of Th cells is introduced. When updating the system, all the cells located in the neighborhood set have their weights modified according to the input antigen and the similarity to the winner Th cell. In the simulation, we emphasize that the proposed system has not only the ability of recognizing the transformation patterns, but also the enhanced noise tolerance, especially to the increased noise recognition, the proposed affinity based artificial immune system shows obvious strong anti-noise tolerance capacity. Hereby, this proposed model possesses better pattern recognition ability than that of earlier models.

REFERENCES

Dai, H. W., Tang, Z., Tamura, H., & Yang, Y. (2006). Immune system inspired model and its applications. *International Journal of Soft Computing*, 22-29.

Dasgupta, D., & Forrest, S. (1996). Novelty detection in time series data using ideas from immunology. In *Proceedings of the ISCA 5th International Conference on Intelligent Systems*.

de Castro, L. N., & Timmis, J. (2002). Artificial immune systems: A novel paradigm to pattern recognition. In *Proceedings of the Conference on Artificial Neural Networks in Pattern Recognition* (pp. 67-84).

Gonzalz, F., & Dasgupta, D. (2004). Nomaly detection using real-valued negative selection. *Genetic Programming and Evolvable Machines*, 383–403.

Hagan, M. T., Demuth, H. B., & Beale, M. (1995). *Neural network design*. Boston, MA: PWS Publishing.

Hajela, P., & Yoo, J. S. (1999). Immune network modelling in design optimization. *New Ideas in Optimization*, 203-215.

Jakimovsk, B., & Maehle, E. (2008). Artificial immune system based robot anomaly detection engine for fault tolerant robots. In *Proceedings of the 5th International Conference on Autonomic and Trusted Computing* (pp. 177-190).

Knight, T., & Timmis, J. (2001). AINE: An immunological approach to data mining. In *Proceedings of the IEEE International Conference on Data Mining* (pp. 297-304).

Kohonen, T., Oja, E., Simula, O., Visa, A., & Kangas, J. (1996). Engineering applications of the self-organizing map. *Proceedings of the IEEE*, *84*(10), 1358–1384. doi:10.1109/5.537105

Lemos, R. A., Nakamura, M., Sugimoto, I., & Kuwano, H. (1993). A self-organizing map for chemical vapor classification. In *Proceedings of the 7th International Conference on Solid State Sensors and Actuators.*

Sekita, I., Kurita, T., & Otsu, N. (1992). Complex autoregressive model for shape recognition. *IEEE Transactions on Pattern Analysis and Machine Intelligence*, *14*(4), 489–496. doi:10.1109/34.126809

Sun, W. D., Tang, Z., Tamura, H., & Ishii, M. (2003). An artificial immune system architecture and its applications. *IEICE Transactions on Fundamentals*, *86*, 1858–1868.

Tang, Z., Hebishima, H., Tashima, K., Ishizuka, O., & Tanno, K. (1997). An immune network based on biological immune response network and its immunity. *IEICE Transactions on Fundamentals*, *80*(11), 1940–1950.

Tang, Z., Tashima, K., & Cao, Q. P. (2001). A pattern recognition system using clonal selection-based immune network. *Systems and Computers in Japan*, *34*(12), 56–63. doi:10.1002/scj.10243

Tang, Z., Yamaguchi, T., Tashima, K., Ishizuka, O., & Tanno, K. (1997). Multiple-valued immune network model and its simulations. In *Proceedings of the 27th International Symposium on Multiple-Valued Logic* (pp. 233-238).

Tang, Z., Yamaguchi, T., Tashima, K., Ishizuka, O., & Tanno, K. (1999). Multiple-value immune network and its applications. *IEICE Transactions on Fundamentals*, *82*, 1102–1108.

Wang, W., Gao, S., Li, F., & Tang, Z. (2008). A complex artificial immune system and its immunity. *International Journal of Computer Science and Network Security*, *8*, 287–295.

Wang, W., Gao, S., & Tang, Z. (2009). Improved pattern recognition with complex artificial immune system. *Soft Computing - A Fusion of Foundations. Methodologies and Applications*, *13*, 1209–1217.

Yamaguchi, T., Tang, Z., Ishizuka, O., & Tanno, K. (2001). Adaptive multiple-valued immune system. *IEEE Transactions on Electronics. Information Systems*, *121*(11), 1747–1754.

This work was previously published in the International Journal of Digital Library Systems, Volume 2, Issue 2, edited by Chia-Hung Wei, pp. 13-26, copyright 2011 by IGI Publishing (an imprint of IGI Global).

Section 3
User Studies

Chapter 13
Attitudes of Librarians in Selected Nigerian Universities towards Digital Libraries in E-Learning

Edwin I. Achugbue
Delta State University, Nigeria

Sylvester O. Anie
Delta State Polytechnic, Nigeria

ABSTRACT

The attitude of librarians in Nigerian university libraries has the potential to encourage or discourage digital libraries in e-learning. This paper addresses and discusses the attitudes of librarians towards digital library in e-learning, the imperativeness of training and knowledge for effective functionality of digital libraries in Nigerian universities. The paper uses the descriptive survey method to explore the attitudes of librarians towards digital libraries, advantages of digital libraries, and the types of e-learning that can be supported by digital libraries. It was discovered that training and knowledge are sine qua non of a positive attitude towards digital libraries in e-learning. And there was a high interest in the use of online information by researchers and learners but lack of awareness and how best to integrate e-learning resources into digital libraries pose a great challenge to the librarians in Nigerian universities.

INTRODUCTION

Integrating e-learning resources into digital libraries in Nigerian universities depends largely on librarians' attitudes towards it. The application of ICT to library services has caused significant changes in Nigerian university libraries. Cooper

DOI: 10.4018/978-1-4666-2928-8.ch013

(1998) opined that the advent of the internet, digitisation, e-learning resources and the ability to access library and research materials from remote locations created dramatic changes in the functionality of university libraries.

The term "digital library" according to Lynch is simply "an electronic information access system that offers users coherent view of an organised, selected and managed body of information".

Sharifabadi (2006) suggested the following working definition of the digital library:

Digital libraries are organisations that provide the resources, including the specialised staff, to select, structure, offer intellectual access to, interpret, distribute, preserve the integrity of, and ensure the persistence over time of collections of digital works so that they are readily and economically available for use by a defined community or set of communities.

Based on this working definition, Sharifabadi (2006) asserted that a digital library is not merely equivalent to a digitised collection with information management tools. It is also a series of activities that brings together collections, services, and people in support of the full life circle of creation, dissemination, use, and preservation of data, information and knowledge.

The booming of new learning methods built on an underlying foundation of computer and Information Technology (IT) over the past decades has offered various "solutions" to educational and training activities. Most of the early "solutions" were adaptations of text-based training delivered electronically. Today, the 'solutions" are more than duplicating non-electronic learning materials and transmitting them online – they are mainly embodied in the internet environment, containing variant elements, such as virtual learning environments, online mutual interaction, and managed learning environments. Among the numerous present applications of e-learning are online training, distance learning, learning with threaded discussions or interactive bulletin boards, website-based curriculum, courses that post assignments online, correspondence course-style read-and-test programmes, etc (McLester, 2001).

It is important to note here that not all professional librarians concur to these changes in educational methods and environment due to the concern of the possible dehumanisation of the learning process (Self, 1996) and the volatility of computers (Oppenheimer, 1997). However, many proponents argued that e-learning is able to offer more choices that suit learners' flexibility, provide stimulus, reinforcement and instant feedbacks, foster interactions, and stimulate understanding and the recall of information. These claimed advantages have made e-learning very appealing. This technological change is posing a particular challenge to librarians in developing countries. Librarians in developed countries moved quickly to learn and adopt new information technologies (Ramzan, 2004). Digital library was introduced to perform library functions and provide innovative user services. Librarians gained knowledge of new technologies through continuing education programmes, professional training, and revisions to university curricula. University libraries in Nigeria, though not all, became equipped with appropriate hardware and software to enhance digitisation.

Ramzan (2004) has described the situation in Pakistan and other developing countries such as Nigeria. He declared that the librarians in developing countries are not readily prepared to embrace the changes introduced with the advent of Information Technology (IT). Most librarians are uncertain about digitisation of university libraries and the benefits for their organisations, especially when huge amount of money is involved and they are having little knowledge about digital librarian in e-learning. The problems associated with this lack of knowledge are also discussed by Khan (1995), and Mahmood (1999). This study will explore attitudes of librarians in Nigeria towards digitisation of university libraries. It is useful to have empirical evidence from a population of Nigerian librarians in this topical issue, which is important to the development of libraries at this knowledge era.

Literature Review

Attitudes represent the conceptual value of these technologies in the minds of the librarians, not the values of the technologies themselves. According to Spacey et al. (2003), Fine (1986) and Evald (1996), positive attitudes are fundamental in implementing new technologies. Jones et al. (1999) carried out a research that reinforced the importance of a positive attitude on the implementation of digital library in e-learning.

Introduction of digital libraries in e-learning is growing in Nigerian university libraries. Popoola (2002) asserts that microcomputers will create remarkable changes in the nature of the professional work. He further argued that there is widespread fear and negative attitudes that have slowed the progress of digital library in Nigeria. Johnson (1991) observes that a major reason for failure of digitalisation of libraries or ICT implementation projects in developing countries is that librarians plan without sufficient knowledge of the purchase of hardware, software, and power supply requirements. Johnson sought to establish a connection between current knowledge and personality types in measuring librarians' attitudes toward digital library. The researchers hypothesised that those with more knowledge and more innovative personalities were likely to have more positive attitude toward innovation. The hypotheses about knowledge were supported. Jones (2002) found that reference librarians with digital reference experience had more positive attitudes than those who have no experience.

The introduction of digital libraries into the education process was made easier by distance education, which has developed over the years. Digital libraries have the potential to significantly change fundamental aspects of the classroom in ways that could have an enormous impact on teaching and learning. New pedagogical methods should accompany digital libraries as an emerging technology for education (Sharifadi, 2006). Raitt (2000) reports some of the digital library projects in Europe that are forming the next generation of libraries.

Peacock (2005) notes also that librarians as educators, must demonstrate the hypothesis that

the design and delivery of information literacy rich curriculum rooted in rigorous pedagogical principles and blended with the astute use of ICT will result in profound learning. In order to lead a shift in practice, we must prove that such an approach is not only viable but vital. Lippincott (2002) advocates librarian involvement in learning communities" "The librarian can shift the focus from explaining library resources to meeting the ongoing information needs of the students in the broad information environment".

The concept of "e-learning" is becoming more prevalent in this information age. Kaplan-Leiserson (2001) declares that e-learning "covers a wide set of applications and processes such as web-based learning, computer-based learning, virtual classrooms, and electronic collaboration. Waller and Wilson (2001): e-learning "is the effective learning process created by combining electronically delivered content with (learning) support and services. E-learners learn in a multi-faceted learning programme that utilises distance learning, interactive cable TV, and internet to connect learning environment to homes, places of work, and the community at large (Mason, 1999; Baker College System, 2002).

METHODOLOGY

The design for this study is descriptive survey and utilises questionnaire to collect data from respondents.

Table 1. Sample selection

Name of Library	Number of Librarians Surveyed
Benson Idahosa University Library	8
Igbinedion University Library	10
University of Benin Library	15
Total	33

Table 2. Attitude statement

S/N.	Attitude Statement	No.	Mean	Agree	Disagree
1.	Digital library enables most effective way of resource sharing	33	5.42	32(96.97%)	1(3.03%)
2.	Digital library makes e-learning resources easy to discover and retrieve.	33	5.33	32(96.97%)	1(3.03%)
3.	Digital library in e-learning increases the quantity, quality and comprehensiveness of internet-based educational resources.	33	5.25	32(96.97%)	1(3.03%)
4.	Digital library services are essential components of a quality e-learning system.	33	5.22	31(93.94%)	2(6.04%)
5.	Digital library in e-learning is able to offer choices that suit learners.	33	5.19	31(93.94%)	2(6.04%)
6.	Automated acquisition is feasible for Nigerian libraries.	33	4.62	21(63.64%)	12(36.36%)
7.	Implementation of digital library in the e-learning has created job fears among librarians.	33	3.31	14(42.42%)	19(57.58%)
8.	Data retrieved through print resources is not authentic.	33	3.24	6(18.18%)	27(81.82%)
9.	Digitalisation of university libraries in Nigeria will not appreciably reduce the number of library staff.	33	3.08	4(12.12%)	29(87.88%)
10.	Data storage on computers is highly risky in the library.	33	3.05	3(9.09%)	30(90.91%)

POPULATION AND SAMPLE

The study targeted librarians in university libraries in Edo State of Nigeria that have automated systems. These are Benson Idahosa University Library, Benin City; Igbinedion University Library, Okada Land; and University of Benin Library, Benin City. All librarians in the population were included in the survey (see Table 1).

Of the total population, 21 were male and 12 female. The 33 respondents have their M.Sc. or MLS degree certificates.

Part 1: Demographic Variables of the Respondents

Part one of the instrument used for the collection of data on this study was focused on the respondents' gender, age, highest educational qualification, department/ division, and length of service.

Part 2: Attitude Towards ICT

Part two of the survey focused on measuring librarians' attitudes toward digital library in e-learning. Respondents were asked to rate their belief about digitalisation of library in e-learning applications to library practices on a 2-point scale: 2=Agree and 1=Disagree.

Part 3: ICT Experience and Training

Table 3. Librarian training / knowledge and attitudes toward digital library in e-learning

Variables	No.	Mean	SD	Df	r.obs	p	Remarks
Librarian training / knowledge	33	35.7	6.8	31	4.37	0.05	S**
Librarians' attitude to ICT/digital library	33	33.9	6.3				

This part focuses on assessing librarians' ICT experience and training relating to query language, library software packages, operating systems, knowledge of programming, participation in design and implementation of digital library in e-learning, and method of acquiring ICT experience.

FINDINGS

The results of the analyses on the study are presented as follows: A Friedman Test with percentage and frequency count was used to analyse the responses. The result is contained in Table 2.

Table 2 shows that the result of the Friedman test mean, and percentage, which indicates that the librarians in the study have a positive attitude toward digital library in e-learning with large majorities agreeing about its usefulness. These results generally show that respondents have a positive response to all attitude items.

Table 3 shows a significant difference between training / knowledge of ICT and attitude towards digital library in e-learning. This is shown with the Pearson correlation matrix where df=3.

DISCUSSION

The results reveal generally that librarians in the study have a positive attitude towards the use and implementation of digital library in e-learning. The reasons may include the provision of electronic resources and information that are readily and economically available for use by a defined community or set of communities. The results reveal further that librarians' training and knowledge of ICT influence their attitudes toward digital library in e-learning. This is in consonant with the findings of earlier studies of Finlay and Finlay (1990), which established a connection between current knowledge and personality types in measuring librarians' attitudes toward the internet. These findings lend credence to this study. Furthermore,

Jones (2002) reveals that reference librarians with digital reference experience tended to have more positive attitudes than those who have no experience. Adequate training and knowledge of ICT are crucial in encouraging librarians to show a positive attitude toward digital library in e-learning.

CONCLUSION

Libraries are essentially educational in purpose, but seeking momentous and meaningful manifestation in e-learning environments is not an easy process. Mere provision and connection to e-learning resources and services does not automatically provide a better learning environment for learners. Skilful guidance and tactical presentation from insightful involvement is required for designing the digital library in e-learning. Training and knowledge are the sine qua non of a positive attitude towards digital library in e-learning. The fear of some librarians in developing countries toward ICT is widening the digital divide. Africans should awake and take their stand to bridge the digital gap through training and acknowledgement of the benefits of digital library in e-learning.

REFERENCES

Baker College System. (2002). *Blended/Hybrid Delivery*. Retrieved from www.baker.edu/ departments/instructech/blended.html

Cooper, R., & Dempsey, D. R. (1998). Remote Library Users; needs and expectations. *Library Trends, 47*(1), 42–64.

Evald, P. (1996). Information Technology in Public Libraries. In Adesola, P. A., Omoba, R. O., & Adeyinka, T. (Eds.), *Attitudes of Librarians toward Selected Nigerian Universities toward the use of ICT*. Library Philosophy and Practice.

Fine, S. (1986). Technological Innovation Diffusion and Resistance: an Historical Perspective. *Journal of Library Administration, 7*(1).

Graghill, D., Neale, C., & Wilson, T. D. (1989). *The Impact of IT on Staff Deployment in UK Public Libraries*. London: British Library.

Jones, B. (1999). *Staff in the New Library: Skill Needs and Learning Choices, Findings from Training the Future, a Public Library Research Project*. London: British Library.

Jones, D. (2002). Ten Year later: support staff perceptions and opinions on technology in the workplace. *Library Trends, 47*, 4.

Kaplan-Leiserson, E. (2001). *E-learning Glossary in Learning Circuits*. Retrieved from www.learningcircuits.org/glossary.html

Khan, N. A. (1995). Information technology in the University Libraries of Pakistan: Stresses and Strains. *Pakistan Library Bulletin, 26*, 1.

Lipincott, J. K. (2003). Developing Collaborative Relationships: Librarians, Students and Faculty creating Learning Communities. *College & Research Libraries News, 3*(3).

Mahmood, K. (1999). The Development of Computerised Library Services in Pakistan: a Review if the Literature. *Asian Libraries, 8*(9). doi:10.1108/10176749910293803

Mason, R. (1999). The Impact of Telecommunications. In Harry, K. (Ed.), *Higher Education through Open and Distance Learning*. London: Routledge.

Mclester, S. (2001). The e-learning phenomenon. *Technology and Learning, 22*(1).

Oppenheimer, T. (1997). The Computer Delusion. *Atlantic Monthly, 28*(1).

Peacock, J. (2000). Information Literacy Education in Practice. In Levy, P., & Roberts, S. (Eds.), *Changing Roles of the Academic Librarian*. London: Facet Publishing.

Popoola, S. O. (2002). 'Users' Attitude towards Microcomputer use in Agricultural Research Libraries in Nigeria. *Journal of Librarianship and Information Science in Africa, 2*(1).

Ramzan, M. (2004). Does level of Knowledge impact Librarians' Attitudes toward Information Technology (IT) Applications? In *Proceedings of the 2nd International CALIBER-2004*, New Delhi, India.

Self, J. (1996). *The Development of the Computer Based Learning Unit: a Discussion Document*. Retrieved from http://eblslca.leeds.ac.uk/jas/discussion.html

Sharifabadi, S. R. (2006). How digital libraries can support e-learning. *The Electronic Library, 24*(3). Retrieved from www.emeraldinsight.com/0264-0473.htm. doi:10.1108/02640470610671231

Spacey, R., Goulding, A., & Murray, I. (2003). ICT and Change in UK Public Libraries:does Training matter? *Library Management, 24*(1/2). doi:10.1108/01435120310454520

Walter, C. (2001). *A definition for e-learning*. The OPL Newsletter.

This work was previously published in the International Journal of Digital Library Systems, Volume 2, Issue 1, edited by Chia-Hung Wei, pp. 52-57, copyright 2011 by IGI Publishing (an imprint of IGI Global).

Chapter 14
Role of Public Libraries in Bridging the Digital Divide

Owajeme Justice Ofua
Delta State University, Nigeria

Ogochukwu Thaddaeus Emiri
Delta State University, Nigeria

ABSTRACT

This paper reviews the role of public libraries in bridging the digital divide in Delta State. It calls for the adoption of appropriate infrastructure and other innovative measures like introduction of appropriate computer related programmes in schools, encouraging citizenry to pick up carrier in the area of science and technology, embanking on enlightenment and awareness programmes and setting up regional/local information resource centers by government especially through the use of the internet also, the challenges of digital divide was revealed. The work concludes that unless appropriate measures are taken in Delta State and Nigeria generally they will be relegated to the background in this knowledge age.

INTRODUCTION

The United National Education, Scientific and Cultural Organization (UNESCO, 2000) defined the digital divide as a phenomenon that results from the unequal application of, and access to, information and communication technologies leading to a global knowledge gap between information 'haves' and have-nots' This dichotomy threatens to create an underclass of inform poor who risk further marginalization in societies where computer skills open the doors to economic success and personal advancement, entry to good careers and education opportunities, full access to social

DOI: 10.4018/978-1-4666-2928-8.ch014

networks and opportunities for civic engagement (Norris, 2000). Public libraries offer three essential ingredients needed to ensure benefits in the digital era. Infrastructure, content and access (Newman, 2004). In the digital information age people who don't have access to the internet and World Wide Web through the application of information and communication technologies (ICTs) are increasingly disadvantaged in their access to information (Culler, 2003).

Digital divide can be seen as the growing gap between those parts of the world which have easy access to knowledge, information, ideas and works of information through technology and those who do not (Deschamps, 2001). In the same vein, Salina (2003) sees digital divide as that disparity between individual and or communities who can use electronic information and communication tools, such as the internet, to better the quality of their lives and those who cannot.

Initially the 'divide' referred to the gap that was forming between the richer and the poorer sections of society. However, some people were talking about the digital divide as a complex and dynamic phenomenon' while some denied the existence of a digital divide, others claimed that it would disappear on its own (Djik & Harken, 2003). According to World Bank (2002) quoted in Ani, Uchendu, and Astseye (2007) in its report contend that, in the rapidly evolving electronic environment, developing countries face opportunity cost if they delay greater access to and use of information technology (IT), which together make up ICT. According to the report, ICT is the key for economic development and growth; it offers opportunities for global integration while retaining the identity of traditional societies. ICTs can also increase the economic and social being of poor people, empower individuals and communities, and enhance the effectiveness and efficiency of the public sector. However, in Nigeria, there is disparity in the level of accessibility to ICT, between the private and public sectors of the economy (Ani, Uchendu, & Astseye, 2007). This present study is

therefore and attempt to investigate and examine the role of public libraries in bridging the digital divide in Delta State.

Research Questions

This study sought answers to the following questions:

1. What is the level of awareness of the concept of digital divide in public libraries?
2. What are the causes of digital divide?
3. What is the role of public libraries in bridging the digital divide?
4. What are the infrastructures for bridging the digital divide?
5. What are the challenges faces by public libraries in bridging the digital divide?

Background

Causes of Digital Divide

Mutala (2002), Singh (2004), Cullen (2001), Kenny (2004), and Salina (2003) identified the following factors that contribute to digital divide:

- **Gender:** It was found that fewer males have limited access to the internet than females. This disparity is partly attributed to perception that it is a technical subject for men, with many females consequently shying away from it.
- **Physical disability:** The internet is inaccessible to the blind and visually impaired used, because the screen reader is unable to read the graphically based web page.
- **Physical access:** The main barriers under this point are lack of telecommunication infrastructure with insufficient reliable bandwidth for internet connections and costs.
- **Lack of ICT skills and support:** People in many disadvantaged groups are often

excluded from making use of ICT'S because of low levels of computer and technology skills and also very importantly literacy skills. This is a significant factor in preventing certain people from using the internet technology.

- **Attitudinal factors:** This is derived from cultural and behavioral attitudes towards technology e.g., that computers are for "brainy" people for males for young people, and difficult to user or belong to a middle class "white" culture. Attitudinal factors can also be culturally-based.

- **Relevant content:** One of the reasons why some people do not use internet technologies is because the content is not relevant and interesting to them. This may apply to specific group such as elderly or ethnic gap.

- **Age:** It is clear that a digital divide exist between age group because the youths are more exposed to technology and are willing to use it, whereas older people are resistant to change and avoid those technology.

- **Racial Segregation:** The legacy of some countries policy such as apartheid as the case in South Africa has contributed a lot to the digital divides whereby white people have more access to technology than blacks.

- **Illiteracy rate:** The general population of Africa is predominantly rural and the continent is the lowest urbanized in the world. In addition a large number of people do not have access to education facilities and sometimes where these are available, they are of very poor quality number of people who cannot read or write in Africa is still relatively high.

Roles of Public Libraries in Bridging the Digital Divide

Public libraries can make a huge impact in bridging the digital divide by providing access to computer and the internet to those who do not have such facilities. The perception that libraries are for the elite in universities should be eradicated. Libraries are for everyone, educated and uneducated, rich and poor. They are equalizers and democrat force in access to computer, the internet information learning and training (Learning and Libraries, 2004). Public libraries need to establish effec-

Table 1. Distribution of staff in public libraries Delta Central Senatorial District (Asaba, 2009)

Name of Public Libraries	No of Staff
Orerokpe	4
Sapele	8
Mosogar	3
Oghara	4
Ughelli	10
Effurun	3
Iyarra	12
Total	44

Table 2. Gender and digital divide

Sex	Frequency	Percentage
Male	28	70
Female	12	30
Total	40	100

Table 3. Digital divide and age of respondents

Age	Frequency	Percentage
16-25	26	65
26-35	8	20
36-40	4	10
45 and above	2	5
Total	40	100

Table 4. Perception of librarians on digital divide

Perception						
It is the gap between those who have computer and internet, and those who do not have.	38	95	1	2.5	1	2.5
It is the disparity between the information rich and the information poor.	38	95	2	5	0	0
It is the disparity between those who use electronic and communication tools to better their lives and those who cannot	26	65	10	25	4	10
It is the gap between those people with effective access to digital and information technology.	36	90	2	5	2	5

tive resources sharing schemes. As a result of present proliferation of information, high cost of information resources and dwindling library budget, it is difficult for any library to provide all the information need of it client. Sharing this available resource will assist in meeting user's information needs hence, the digital divide. The availability of full internet access and facsimile machine in public libraries would facilitate online access to the world of information and also the sharing of information resources as suggested by Adeogun (2003)

Secondly, he argues that the new knowledge economy emphasizes that knowledge from wherever it is produced can be transferred to where it's needed.

Infrastructure for Bridging the Digital Divide

The following facilities and services can be adopted by public libraries in an effort to ensure equal access to global knowledge in Africa:

1. Public internet access facilities.
2. Telecenters.
3. Wireless and satellite technologies.
4. Mobile phone technologies.
5. Information and computer literacy training.
6. Use of solar energy.

Challenges Faced by Public Libraries in Bridging the Digital Divide

Current challenges for libraries are to sustain their ability to provide public access. This requires ongoing investment and support in five key areas which includes:

- Hardware and software upgrades.
- Internet connectivity.
- Keeping systems running.
- Staff training.
- Keeping libraries open.

Remedies for the Problem Facing Public Libraries in Bridging the Digital Divide

Deschamps (2003), suggested ways of bridging digital divide by calling on the UN summit on information society 2003 to:

- Commit member states to connect all their public libraries to the internet by 2006.
- Support skill development by librarians.
- Ensure that intellectual property laws for electronic publications do not prevent public access.
- Recommend public investment in information and telecommunication technologies.
- Ensure that libraries providing public access are eligible for affordable connection charges.
- The skill, energy and commitment of the world's librarians will not fail you in the struggle to bridge the digital divide-provided you give them the resources required, was the challenge made by the IFLA president to the world summit.

Methodology

The sample for this study is drawn from the public libraries in Delta State. Researcher used the balloting method to select from three senatorial district of Delta State (Central, North and Delta South). The Delta Central Senatorial district was selected. This means the staff of the public libraries in Delta Central was used for the study. The 40 library staff whose questionnaires were retrieved in the public libraries in Delta central were used for the study. Table 1 shows the staff of public libraries in Delta central senatorial district.

Sample

The questionnaire is the instrument used for the study which was distributed to all public library staff concerned and forty (40) questionnaires were retrieved. The sample size for the study is 40.

RESULT OF THE STUDY AND DISCUSSIONS

Analysis of data was done following the research questions.

Table 2 shows that male respondents were 28 (70%) while female respondents were 12 (30%). This means male are more inclined to digital divide. This finding is in line with LU, DU, Zhang, Ma, and Le (2002) that the ration of male to female internet users in main land China is greater than 2 to 1. And that the males seem to be more inclined to access the internet than the females. Also a survey by Effa and Parvyn Wamahid (2003) is in agreement with the finding of this study since fewer females than males use telecenter sources of the internet in Africa.

Table 3 shows that respondents with the age bracket 16- 25(65%) use the internet more than the other groups. This shows that younger people (singles) are more inclined to use of internet.

Table 5. How did you get to know about the digital divide

Response	Frequency	Percentage
Friend/colleagues	6	15
Lecturers	2	5
Computer Programme	8	20
Personal Research	20	50
Textbooks	4	10
Total	40	100

Table 6. Causes of digital divide

Causes	Agree		Disagree		Undecided	
Gender	5	12.5	30	75.0	5	12.5
Physical disability	5	12.5	30	75	5	12.5
Lack of ICT Skills and support	30	75	8	20	2	5

Table 7. Roles of public libraries in bridging the digital divide

Roles	A	%	D	%	U	%
Providing access to computer and internet	32	80	5	12.5	3	7.5
Educate library patrons in modern information technology usage	28	70	12	30	0	0
Establish effective resource centers	38	95	0	0	2	5
Equip themselves with good online information databases	38	95	2	5	0	0
Provide free public access computing	27	67.5	1.0	25	3	7.5

Table 8. Infrastructures for bridging digital divide

Infrastructures	Agreed		Disagreed		Undecided	
1. Public internet access facilities	35	87.5	5	12.5	0	0
2. Telecentres	10	25	27	67.5	3	7.5
3. Wireless and satellite technologies.	30	75	10	25	0	0
4. Mobile phone technology	40	100	0	0	0	0
5. ICT literary training	25	62.5	10	25	5	12.5
6. Use of solar energy	0	0	30	75	10	25

Table 9. Challenges to digital divide

Factors	Agreed		Disagreed		Undivided	
	F	%	F	%	F	%
Lack of access to internet	25	62.5	10	25	5	12.4
Inadequate skills to browse the internet	20	50	20	50	0	0
Lack of financial capacity to pay the bill by internet users	10	25	25	62.5	5	12.5
Poor internet service	39	97.5	1	2.5	0	0
Frequency interruption of power	39	97.5	1	2.5	0	0
Lack of awareness of the potentials of internet by potential user	15	37.5	25	62.5	0	0
Poor maintenance culture of available facilities.	10	25	28	70	2	5

Table 4 reveals that majority of respondents are not familiar with the concept of digital divide. A good percentage of the respondents had positive response to the above points which are correct about digital divide.

This finding is in line with the American Library Association (ALA, 2000) definition of digital divide as disparities/differences based on economic status, gender, and race.

Table 5 shows that majority of respondents got to know about digital divide through personal research 20(50%) while lecturers 2(5%) ranked lowest.

Table 6 shows that illiteracy rate 40 (100%) ranked highest while gender 5 (12.5%) and physical disability 5 (12.5) ranked lowest.

Table 7 indicates that the roles of public libraries to bridging digital divide are numerous. This ranges from, equipping themselves with good online information database 38 (95%), establish effective resource centers 38 (95%) providing access to computer and internet 32 (80%) and providing free public access computing 27 (67.5%). This finding is in line with the assertion by Deschamps (2003) that the 70th coming United Nations World summit on information society to recognize that libraries have the key in talking the growing digital divide.

Table 8 shows that various infrastructure needed for bridging digital divide. Mobile phone technology 40 (100%) ranked highest while use of solar energy 0 (0%) ranked Lowest.

From Table 9 is revealed that poor internet access 39(97.5%) and frequency interruption of power 39(97.5%) ranked highest while lack of finance 10(25%) and poor maintenance culture ran ked lowest as challenges of digital divide.

SUMMARY OF FINDINGS

Arising from the study, the following findings were made:

1. Males are more inclined to the use of internet than females.
2. Age bracket 16-25 use the internet more. This shows that 80% of internet users are single.
3. Majority of respondents got to know about digital divide through personal research.
4. Illiteracy rate ranked highest as major cause of the digital divide while gender and physical disability ranked lowest.
5. The role in bridging digital divide is enormous. This includes equipping themselves with good online information database among others.

CONCLUSION AND RECOMMENDATIONS

The consequence of digital divide in Delta state is expected to be severe if not handled on time. The study revealed that digital divide exists in the area of gender and age. Gender disparity which was evident in this work is not unconnected with the fact that males are more scientifically and technologically oriented than females which has affected their pattern of use of internet and other related infrastructures. Also the study revealed that a good percentage of the respondents are not familiar with the concept of digital divide which they got to know through personal research. The following recommendations were suggested:

1. Government and relevant non-governmental organizations should introduce appropriate programmes that will enhance the citizenry especially females to be interested in the use of internet and other technologies.
2. Also, females and other citizenry should be encouraged to pick up career in the areas of science and technologies.
3. Government and other relevant international and non- government organization should embark on enlightenment and awareness programmes regarding ICT's. This will encourage both educated and uneducated citizens to make use of available internet infrastructure.
4. Government should set up regional/local information resource centers to enable the citizenry use the internet and at subsidized rate.

REFERENCES

Adeogun, M. (2003). The digital divide and university educations systems in Sub-Saharan Africa. *Journal of Library. Archives and Information Science, 13*(2), 11–20.

Bill & Melinda Gates Foundation. (2004). *Toward equality of access: The role of public libraries in addressing the digital divide.* Retrieved from http://www.worldcat.org/title/toward-equality-of-access-the-role-of-public-libraries-in-addressing-the-digital-divide/oclc/54706779

Borgman, C. (2000). *From Gutenberg to the global infrastructure: Access to information in the networked world.* Cambridge, MA: MIT Press.

Chowdhury, G. C. (2003). *Introduction to digital libraries.* London, UK: Facet Publishing.

Cleveland, G. (1998). *Digital libraries: Definitions, issues and challenges.* Retrieved from http://www.ifla.org/VI/5/op/udtop8/udtop8.htm

Cool, C., & Spink, A. (1999). Education for digital libraries. *D-Lib Magazine, 5*(5).

Cullen, R. (2001). Addressing the digital divide. *Online Information Review, 25*(5), 311–320. doi:10.1108/14684520110410517

Deschamp, C. (2001). *Can libraries help bridges the digital divide?* Retrieved from http://www.nordinfo.helsink.fi/publications/nordnytt/nnytt4-01/deschamps

Dijk, J. V., & Hacker, K. (2001). The digital divide as a complex and dynamic phenomenon. *The Information Society, 19*, 315–326. doi:10.1080/01972240309487

Dutta, S. (2003). Impact of information communication technology on society. *Yojna, 47*(7), 24.

Etta, F. E., & Pargn Wamahu, S. (2003). *Information and communication technologies for development in Africa: Volume 2: The experience with community telecentres.* Ottawa, ON, Canada: International Development research Center (IDRC).

Gosh, S. (2004). Indian telecom scenario. *Yojna, 48*(1), 20.

International Telecommunication Union. (2003). *World summit on the information society.* Retrieved from http://www.itu.int/wsis

Kenny, C. (2004). *Should we try to bridge the global digital divide?* Retrieved from http://charleskenny.blogs.com/weblog/files/infopiece.pdf

Learning and Libraries. (2004). *The sophist.* Retrieved from http://www/sophinstitute.com/soplist-no8-editor.aspx

Lu, W., Du, J., Zhang, J., Ma, F., & Le, T. (2002). Internet development in China. *Journal of Information Science, 28*(3), 207–223. doi:10.1177/016555150202800303

Mahajan, S. (2003). Impact of digital divide on developing countries with special reference to India. *SERALS Journal of Information Management, 40*(4), 328–329.

Mutala, S. M. (2002, April 15-19). The digital divide in Sub-Saharan Africa: Implications of RHT revitalization and preservation of indigenous knowledge systems. In *Proceedings of the 15th Standing Conference of Eastern, Central and Southern African Library and Information Association on Africa to the World: The Globalization of Indigenous Knowledge Systems* (pp. 119-141).

Newman, W. (2004). *Public libraries in the priorities of Canada: Acting on the assets and opportunities.* Retrieved from http://www.collectionscanada.gc.ca/6/7/s7-3000-e.html

Norris, P. (2001). *Digital divide: Civil engagement, information poverty and the Internet in democratic societies*. Cambridge, UK: Cambridge University Press.

Rao, R. K. (2003). E-governance gaining in popularity. *Kurukhetra*, *9*(12), 1.

Satyanarayana, M. N., & Sathyamurthy. (2005). Telemedicine: Specialty health care for all. *Employment News*, *30*(4), 1–2.

Singh, A. M. (2004). Bridging the digital divide the role of universities in getting South Africa closer to the global information society. *South African Journal of Information Management, 6*(2).

UNESCO. (2000). *World education reports*. Retrieved from http://www.unesco.org/education/information/wer/

World Bank. (2002). *Information and communication technologies: A World Bank ground strategy*. Washington, DC: World Bank.

This work was previously published in the International Journal of Digital Library Systems, Volume 2, Issue 3, edited by Chia-Hung Wei, pp. 14-22, copyright 2011 by IGI Publishing (an imprint of IGI Global).

Chapter 15
Perceptions and Attitude of Students in Relation to Vandalism in University Libraries in South–South Zone of Nigeria

Owajeme Justice Ofua
Delta State University, Nigeria

Ogochukwu Thaddaeus Emiri
Delta State University, Nigeria

ABSTRACT

This study was conducted in December 2010 to find out students perception and attitude toward vandalism in the library. To gather the required information, a questionnaire was distributed to 1400 randomly selected students of university libraries in the South-South zone of Nigeria out of which 718 responded. Results of their responses revealed that vandalism of library materials in the form of theft, mutilation and hiding of books and journals, is largely regarded as a form of academic survival, this makes student to put up "I Don't care" attitude to library materials. The major causes of vandalism of library materials include limited library collections; restrictions in the use of some materials; number and duration of loans; insufficient number of copies of recommended textbooks; unaffordable cost of personal textbooks; high cost of photocopying as well as peer-influence. Amongst others, researchers recommend the following: training and retraining programme for users, extension of loan period; adequate funding; robust security measures and punishment of offenders.

DOI: 10.4018/978-1-4666-2928-8.ch015

INTRODUCTION

Vandalism is a problem that affects libraries of all types. As custodian of library collections, it is part of librarians' responsibility to ensure they are adequately informed in order to prevent vandalism as much as possible and to be prepared in the inevitable event that vandalism occurs in their libraries (Heat, 2003). The threat of intellectual properly through theft vandalism, mutilation and other forms of abuse has posed tremendous challenge to the library profession worldwide. Incidents of theft, non-return of materials and mutilation of library stock are on the increase (Jackson, 1991). According to Salaam and Onitade (2010), Vandalism of library materials has been an age- long problem of libraries. This takes the form of ripping off pages of books and documents, deliberate defacement of materials and sabotage of library equipments and outright theft of books and other library materials and equipment. Unlike professional thieves who steal for economic reasons, some library patrons vandalize library materials for selfish motive. Others rip of pages of books because they cannot afford the cost of the book or they cannot fine particular books anywhere else. Vandalism of books and non-books materials are a common phenomenon in Nigerian University libraries and if not checked will increase a serious threat to Nigerian Libraries collection and preservations. This study, therefore sought to find out student perception and attitude to vandalism in the south-south university libraries of Nigeria.

REVIEW OF THE LITERATURE

Various writers have expressed their view on what contributes to the cause of different forms of abuse in the library. However, many researchers bases their argument on economic depress and security as the main cause of abuse of library materials. These include Ajegbomogun (2004), Agboola (2001), Afolabi (1993), Akinfolarin (1992), and Bello (1997) among others. Others authors reveal that theft is motivated by societal problems. Verner (1983) listed a series of factors that contribute to library malpractices which include in adequate services staff at night and during the weekends, lack of multiple copies of library materials in high demand and inadequate photocopying facilities. Any shift from this, may cause a negative impact on users' disposition to library materials. According to Goldstein (1996) identified three central concepts of vandalism: Intentionality, destructiveness and property ownership. Therefore, Vandalism is intentional act of destruction or defacement of property not one's own.

Goldstein (1996), Cohen (1989), Lincolin (1996), and Cornog and Perper (1996) recognized six categories of Vandalism, many of which are common in libraries which include:

- Acquisitive Vandalism, this involves acts done to obtain property or money. Example of acquisitive vandalism that may occur in libraries include damages to parking meters, public telephones, vending machines and photocopiers.
- Tactical vandalism: it includes act done to accomplish goals other than monetary gain, such as defacement of material by a student to prevent the use of that material by fellow student
- Ideological Vandalism: which is an act done in promotion of a social, political or other cause such as the placement of KKK stickers within materials in a library.
- Vindictive Vandalism: involves acts to gain revenge.
- Play vandalism, it include acts of destruction or disfigurement in the course of play, such as a group of students who decide to play target practice with library windows
- Malicious vandalism, these acts express rage or frustration such as library might encounter includes the clogging of toilets or sinks, setting off five alarms or sprinkler systems or urinating in public areas.

The issues of Vandalism in library has been well flogged in the professional literature, but very little has been done on perception and attitude of students to vandalism in university libraries in south-south zone of Nigeria.

Goldstein (1996) suggested that the most successful approach and prevention strategies for vandalism in libraries will be comprehensive, prescriptive, and appreciative. He also recommended that the strategies must be implemented with adequate attention to the integrity, intensity and coordination of the intervention. In other words, librarian's approach to vandalism should take into account to the individual needs of their library. Their effect should be planned and carried out in an intentional manner. Onatola (1998) quoted in Salaam and Onitade (2010), expressed that human beings as agents of destruction in libraries have been the most difficult to control. He recommended that library security personnel as well as reader's services staff and indeed all library staff should be exposed to short training course in library security at least once in very four years. Abareh (2001) also quoted in Salaam and Onifade (2010) the results of a study designed to gather information on how best to reduce the theft, loss and mutilation in a university library in Nigeria. He concluded with a number of useful suggestions on more effective library security measures.

OBJECTIVES OF THE STUDY

- To find out the students perception of vandalism of library materials,
- To know about the student attitude to vandalism of library materials, and
- To examine factors responsible for vandalism of library materials.

METHODOLOGY

The survey method was used for the study. A questionnaire was designed to obtain students perception and attitudes to vandalism in the library. The student population for the actual library users of the selected university libraries in South-South Zone of Nigeria. Six university libraries were selected through balloting from the nine (9) university libraries in the South-South zone of

Table 1. Distribution of respondents according to actual university library users

Selected University Libraries	Actual Library Users.	Retrieved questionnaires
University of Benin	1745	162
University of Calabar	2156	184
University of Port-Harcourt	1340	155
Ambrose Alli University Ekpoma	870	107
Delta state university, abraka	660	58
Rivers state University of Science and Technology	580	52
TOTAL	**7325**	**718**

Source: University Library Records, as of December, 2010

Table 2. Distribution of respondents by level of study

Level of study	Respondents	Percentages
500 level	35	4.9
400 level	103	14.3
300 level	315	43.9
200 level	185	25.1
100 level	85	11.8
Total	**718**	**100**

Nigeria. The actual library users are gotten from average library users from peak and low periods.

The university porters were instructed to distribute the questionnaires to every twentieth student entering the library during December, 2010. In all 1400 copies (200 each) of the questionnaires were distributed, out of which 718 were returned; representing 51.3% responses

The questionnaire was designed following the objectives raised for the study which is on students' perception and attitude to library vandalism. Using likert scale of rating, students were asked to respond to the various questions showing their level of agreement/disagreement i.e., Agree, strongly Disagreement, strongly disagree (see Table 1).

FINDINGS AND DISCUSSION

The data collected showed that, out of 718 respondents, 407 (56.7%) were male while 311 (43.3%) were female. The gender difference tends to suggest that male students are more in number.

The River State University of Science and Technology 52 (7.3%) and Delta State University (58 (8.1%) have low respondents because they are newly created universities and their population is very low when compared to other universities.

Analysis of data shows that majority of the respondents are 300 level students in most universities in Table 2. This implies that the respondents have in the system for at least three (3) years and would have been familiar with use of the library facilities.

Data analysis in Table 3 shows that the majority of the respondents representing 315 (43.9%) of the total respondents strongly agreed that vandalism is inevitable in libraries while only 90 (12.5)% respondents strongly disagreed with this. This indicated that the perception of students on vandalism of library materials is negative. Students possess "I don't care" attitude towards library materials. Salaam and Onitade (2010) posited that among the reasons for inevitability of vandalism

in the library include limited collections, insufficient number of copies of recommended textbooks, exorbitant cost of text books, high cost of photocopying and less number of books allowed to be borrowed and duration of loans respectively.

Table 4 shows that the majority of the respondents perceive library materials as being public property which also belong to them and therefore can be removed and used for their private use. Hence, vandalism of library materials was not seen as a real crime. This makes respondents see library materials as public property and can be misused by all the way they like.

Salaam and Onitade (2010) opined that student is selfish in the issues of vandalism because in their opinion since they are paying for use of library resources, they have the right to use library resources the way they like it. This has resulted in mutilation, defacing and the sort, while some hide the materials so that others would not have access to them. This corroborated Mansfield (2009) view that students want unlimited access to information by any means because they are

Table 3. Vandalism is inevitable

Perception	Responses	%
Strongly agreed	315	43.9
Agreed	185	25.8
Strong disagreed	90	12.5
Disagreed	128	17.8
Total	**718**	**100**

Table 4. Library materials are public property

RESPONSES	NO	%
Strongly agreed	365	50.8
Agreed	128	17.8
Strong disagreed	115	16.1
Disagreed	110	15.3
Total	**718**	**100**

paying increased fees for it. In a study by Mansfield (2009) 116 respondents (30%) felt that it is foolish not to participate in vandalism since others are doing, while the majority, 270 representing 70% of the respondents argued that vandalism could be avoided if users can be considerate and patient. This also emphasized that fact that frequent users education programmes needed to be organized to change negative perception of the students. In addition to this, efforts should be made to increase funding for the libraries so that they will be able to satisfy a considerate number of users which might eventually reduce or minimize vandalism (Salaam & Onitade, 2009).

RECOMMENDATIONS

Arising from the adverse effect of vandalism to the library the following recommendations are made:

1. There is need for libraries to do intensive training and retraining education programme for students and the punitive measures for vandalism should be emphasized.
2. Loan period for library materials which used to be two weeks can be extended to make students use borrowed materials effectively before return.
3. Adequate funding is necessary for libraries to provide multiple copies of library materials.
4. Sophisticated security measures should be put in place by libraries to check vandalism.
5. Students who indulge in vandalism should be punished and this should be made public. This would help assuage vandalism in libraries.

CONCLUSION

This study has revealed that students in university libraries in the south-south zone of Nigeria do not see anything wrong with vandalizing library materials. They see it as one of the way to survive in their academic pursuit

Factors which encourage vandalism include limited library collection, restrictions in the use of some materials, inadequate number of books to be borrowed short duration of loans, high cost of books, and photocopying. However, with stringent measures taken vandalism can be reduced to its barest minimum, if not wipe away completely.

REFERENCES

Abarach, H. M. (2001). An exploratory survey of book loss, theft and damage in Abubakar Tafawa Balewa University (ATBU), Bauchi. *Nigeria. Library & Archival Security, 17*(1), 31–42.

Afolabi, M. (1993). Factors influencing theft and mutilation among library users and staff in Nigeria. *Journal of Leading Libraries and Information Centres, 1*(3-4), 2–8.

Agboola, A. T. (2001). Penetration of stock security in a Nigerian university library. *Lagos Librarian, 22*(1-2), 45–50.

Ajegbomogun, F. O. (2004). Users' assessment of library security: A Nigerian university case study. *Library Management, 25*(8-9), 386390.

Akinfolarin, W. A. (1992). Towards improving security measures in Nigerian libraries. *African Journal of Library. Archives and Information Sciences, 2*(1), 51–56.

Alokun, N. A. T. (1993). The impact of pilfering and mutilation on library collection. *Library Scientists, 17*, 70–79.

Bezuidenhout, M. (1996). How does one deal with vandalism? *Cape Librarian, 40*(3), 37.

Cohen, S. (1973). Property destruction: Motives and meanings. In Ward, C. (Ed.), *Vandalism* (pp. 23–53). London, UK: H.E Warne.

Constantinou, C. (1995). Destruction of knowledge: A study of journal mutilation at a large university library. *College & Research Libraries*, *56*, 497–507.

Cornog, M., & Perper, T. (1996). From access to vandalism. In Greenwood Press (Ed.), *For sex education, see librarian: A guide to issues and resources* (pp. 115-136). Westport, CT: Greenwood Press.

Curry, A., Flodin, S., & Matheson, K. (2000). Theft and mutilation of library materials: Coping with biblio-bandits. *Library & Archival Security*, *15*(2), 9–26. doi:10.1300/J114v15n02_03

Goldstein, A. P. (1996). *The psychology of vandalism*. New York, NY: Plenum Press.

Gouke, M. N., & Murfin, M. (1980). Periodical mutilation: The insidious disease. *Library Journal*, *105*(16), 95–97.

Hart, S. (2009). *Vandalism in libraries: Causes, common occurrences and prevention strategies.* Retrieved from http://capping.slis.ualberta.ca/cap05/sandy/capping.htm

Huntsberry, J. S. (1992). Student library security patrols: A viable alternative. *Conservation Administration News*, *49*, 1–2.

Lincoln, A. J. (1989). Vandalism: Causes, consequences and prevention. *Library & Archival Security*, *9*(3-4), 37–61.

Mansfield, D. (2009). Reducing book theft at university libraries. *Library and Information Research*, *33*(103).

Oche, A. N. (2000). Book theft and mutilation and their effect on the services of the Benue State Polytechnic Library, Ogbokolo. *Frontiers of Information and Library Sciences: Journals of the World Information Community*, *1*(1), 57–64.

Onatola, A. (1998). Staff assessment of security lapses and stock losses in two selected Nigerian University Libraries. *Gateway Library Journal*, *1*(1), 40–45.

Pedersen, T. L. (1990). Theft and mutilation of library materials. *College & Research Libraries*, *51*, 120–128.

Prasad, B. (1986). *Problems of misplacement, mutilation and theft of books in libraries*. Raigarh, India: BP Goswami.

Rogers, M. (2003). Serial slasher stalks in stacks. *Library Journal*, *122*(10), 14–15.

Salaam, M. O., & Onifade, F. N. (2010). Perception and attitude of students in relation to vandalism in a university library. *Annals of Library and Information Studies*, *57*(5), 146–149.

Schumm, R. W. (1994). Periodicals mutilation revisited: A two-year follow up study. *The Serials Librarian*, *25*, 201–205. doi:10.1300/J123v25n01_16

Smith, E. H., & Olszak, L. (1997). Treatment of mutilated art books: A survey of academic ARL institutions. *Library Resources & Technical Services*, *41*, 7–16.

University of Alberta. (2003). Gay books defaced at university. *American Libraries*, *27*, 32.

This work was previously published in the International Journal of Digital Library Systems, Volume 2, Issue 3, edited by Chia-Hung Wei, pp. 23-28, copyright 2011 by IGI Publishing (an imprint of IGI Global).

Chapter 16
ICT Readiness of Higher Institution Libraries in Nigeria

Pereware A. Tiemo
Niger Delta University, Nigeria

Nelson Edewor
Delta State Polytechnic, Nigeria

ABSTRACT

This article surveys the Information Communication Technology (ICT) readiness of higher institution libraries in Delta State, Nigeria. By means of questionnaires and observation techniques, data were collected from the higher institution libraries. Frequency counts and percentages were used to analyze the data generated. Findings revealed the higher institution libraries ICT demographics, available ICT facilities and equipment, critical service areas automated in these libraries, as well as constraints to ICT use to include poor funding, inadequate skilled manpower, non reliability of electricity supply, inadequate technical support, and poor implementation of policies and lack of maintenance. The study concludes that higher institution libraries in Delta State, Nigeria, are yet to fully embrace ICT in library and information service delivery. Some recommendations that can facilitate the use of ICT in these libraries were also set forth.

INTRODUCTION

Information Communication Technology has been greatly described in several ways. According to Dewatteville and Gilbert (2000) ICT is the acquisition, analysis, manipulation, storage and distribution of information and the design and provision of equipment and software for these purposes. ICT encompasses array of networks, hardware and applications of communication and information creation, management, processing, storage and dissemination. The ICT sector is a gamut of industries and services – internet service provision, telecommunications equipment and services, information technology (IT) equipments

DOI: 10.4018/978-1-4666-2928-8.ch016

and services, media and broadcasting, libraries and documentation centers, commercial information providers, network-based information services and other related information and communication activities (Ajayi, 2003).

ICT is central to the development of contemporary society in all ramifications. That every facet of human life is affected by ICT is no longer in doubt – of which the library is not an exception. The use of ICT for library and information service delivery has undergone various level of development. Today the library mission of providing information service and access to information resources is greatly enhanced by the use of ICT. With ICT, these services are taking on new meanings and constructs. Al-Qallaf (2006) summed this up, when he stated that "librarians provide access to eclectic e-collections, create and maintain digital content, support e-learning, provide real time e-reference, negotiate contracts and licensing agreements and struggle with the economies of electronic information". With Internet protocols as platforms, libraries are now virtual – available anytime, anywhere, without brick and mortar physical structure, but are able to inform educate, create, store, and process data/information.

Akintunde (2004) succinctly captured this, 'libraries worldwide since the last two decades have undergone significant metamorphosis from a purely traditional modeled manual service delivery system to a more dynamic technologically driven system …. Like a cyclone the technology environment has enveloped the library and is taking it to unprecedented heights in knowledge acquisition, management and communication'.

From the foregoing, the relevance and benefits of ICT in higher institution's libraries cannot be over-emphasized. As new technologies emerge all over the globe; the question that easily comes to mind is; what are some of the technologies available in Nigerian higher institutions' libraries? To what extent are libraries ICT driven? What is the state of existing ICT facilities? What are the factors enhancing ICT usage or imped-

ing ICT utilization? Research on these and other related questions will help academic, policy makers, librarians, professionals and researchers in planning and developing effective strategies for implementation and utilization of ICT in library and information services.

LITERATURE REVIEW

A search of the literature dealing with state of ICT facilities in higher institutions libraries revealed several studies. Jones (1989) surveyed three university libraries in the United States. The result showed that participating libraries have On-line Public Access Catalogue (OPAC) with state of the Art ICT facilities. A similar study involving academic Libraries in Wisconsin by Palmine (1994) showed that only cataloguing, acquisition, reference and circulation functions of the participating libraries were automated.

On the African scene, Magara (2002) provided a detailed report on the state of ICT in Ugandan libraries. By means of a questionnaire, he sought to find out the number of computers, level of automation and types of software in use. The results showed that although most participants had computers and software packages for library and information service delivery; responses indicated a low level of ICT utilization. Isaac (2002) examined the level of ICT implementation and use in South Africa. He found that insufficient funds, lack of infrastructure, high telephone and internet cost are amongst the factors affecting effective ICT implementation in Tertiary Institutions. The Scenario in Botswana academic libraries was greatly captured in Ojedokun and Owolabi (2003). They reported the low level of Internet access competence (18%) among teaching and research staff of universities in Botswana. Their study was aimed at determining the level of use of Internet for teaching and research activities by university of Botswana academics. Kavulya (2004) also studied ICT use in selected university libraries in Kenya. A particular area addressed was the use of ICT in the provision of library services for distance education. The finding showed that some libraries in Kenya are already promoting distance learning through the provision of online access to relevant collection centers for the students.

In Nigeria, a wealth of data has been collected on determining the state of ICT in higher institution libraries. A perusal of the literature revealed a low number of computers in libraries, minimal level of automation of the critical service areas, with a corresponding inadequate number of staff and expertise (Gambari & Chike, 2007; Ogunleye, 1997; Igben & Akobo, 2007; Akintudnde, 2006; Obasuyi, 2005, Faboyinde 2006; Oketunji, 2002). Babafime and Adedibu (2007) conducted a study on the application of computer technology to circulation subsystem in Federal University of Agriculture, Abeokuta. The purpose of the study was to examine the extent of automation in the circulation section of the library. Simple survey method was adopted. The result showed that there were only 2 desktops and 2 laptops were available. This indicated that there were inadequate computers in the library. Odion and Adetona (2009) conducted a research on Information and Communication Technology (ICT) as a tool for effective performance by in academic libraries in Edo state, Nigeria. The result showed that 77.3% of respondents use their personal computer to perform official activities. It was also revealed that with the use of ICT facilities such as computers, internet, CD ROMs, cable satellite, telephone, television, and fax machine if provided will greatly improve the job performance of librarians. Adebisi (2009) conducted a study on ICT availability, accessibility and resource sharing in the Federal Polytechnic libraries in South-West, Nigeria. The objective was the find out the numbers and conduction of ICT in the libraries. The instrument used for data collection was the questionnaire. It was discovered that all the libraries had Local Area Network (LAN). It was also discovered that only 47 computers were available in the libraries of

the four Federal Polytechnics used for the study. Internet connectivity was available in only three Polytechnics and there were no fax machine in any of the polytechnics libraries. Disiru (2009) conducted a study on the availability of ICT in Colleges of Education (COE) in Minna, Nigeria. The objective of the study was to investigate the availability and utilization of the various ICT components in COE in Minna. Majority of the respondents (82%) accepted that there is availability of ICT in the various departments such as the internet, computers, photocopying machine and CD ROMs. Majority of the staff use these facilities in teaching and learning. Harunna and Oyelekan (2010) conducted a research on provision utilization of Information Resources and Services in Nigeria Defence Academic (NDA) Library, Kaduna, Nigeria. The finding shows that 89% (55.6%) of respondents accepted to inadequate ICT facilities in the library. Ilorah, Nwafor, and Onwudinjo (2007) conducted a research on E- learning in Universities in Anambra State, Nigeria. Among the purpose of the study was to find out the availability of ICT in university libraries in the state. The instrument used in collecting data was the questionnaire was the questionnaire with a response rate of 85%. The finding shows that the university libraries in the state had computers, printers, DC ROMs and photocopying machines. Regrettably, other ICT facilities such as fax machines, computer work stations, emails and Online Public Access Catalogue (OPAC), internet and multimedia were lacking. Anaehobi (2007) conducted a research work on availability of ICT facilities in academic libraries in Anambra State. The objective of the study was meant to provide data on the facilities and high light the status of ICT in academic libraries in the state. Observation and questionnaire methods were used in collecting data institution librarians. The finding revealed that only 2 libraries had scanners, e libraries had email facilities and only 2 libraries render internet facilities to users. These were out of the eight libraries used for the study. Nkanu

Table 1. Demographic profile of higher institution

Name of institution	Institution type	Year established	Library e-mail ID	Library website
FUPRE	Government owned	2007	None	None
PTI	--------	1987	-------	--------
DELSU	--------	1991	-------	-------
NU	Privately owned	2000	--------	-------
DSPG	Govt. owned	2002	--------	--------
DSPT	Govt. Owned	2002	------	-------
DSPQ	Govt. Owned	2002	-------	--------
COEWA	Govt. Owned	1982	---------	------
COEA	Govt. Owned	1983	--------	-------
FCET	Govt. owned	1979	------	----
COPEM	Govt. owned	2002	------	--------

(2008) findings on utilization of ICT facilities in Nigeria university libraries shows that with the advent of the telecommunication facilities in Nigeria, some libraries has given ways to the traditional methods of providing information resources to users. With high agreed percentage it has being accepted that photocopying machines, CD-ROM database, printers, video tape, and audio tape are in use in libraries in Nigeria. Adullahi and Haruna (2008) conducted a study on utilization of Information and Communication Technology for information services delivery in university libraries in Adamawa State, Nigeria. The survey method was used for the study from the study, three university libraries namely: the Federal University Library, Yola, American University of Nigeria library, Yola and Adamawa State University Library, Muba were sampled. A sampled size of 578 was drawn from the entire population of 2,890. The findings shows that 517 respondents indicated that there are high level of ICT usage in information delivery services in the three (3) selected university libraries used for the study.

Following the general awareness of ICT as a relevant tool in the "Information Business" the need for continued re-appraisal of the current state of ICT facilities in Higher Institutions libraries

becomes imperative. Thus, the study responds to the need to continually investigate the current state of ICT deployment and use in higher institutions libraries in Nigeria, with particular reference to Delta State, an oil rich state in the Niger Delta region of the Country. This study has become necessary because no such study had been carried out to determine the current ICT level of higher institutions libraries in Delta State. It is also believed that this study will have significance for other Niger Delta region states taking into consideration their social, cultural and educational similarities.

Research Objectives

The purpose of this research is to determine the current state of ICT facilities in higher institutions libraries in Delta State, Nigeria. Specific questions addressed are:

- What is the ICT demographic profile of libraries in Delta State, Nigeria?
- What are the various ICT facilities available?
- What is the extent of automation and the areas/services automated?

- Are there constrains affecting the deployment and use of ICT in libraries of higher institutions in Delta State, Nigeria?

Methodology

The survey research design was adopted for this study. The instrument for the collection of data was the questionnaire and observation methods. The questionnaire consisted of 20 questions in four parts. The first part of the questionnaire asked demographic information aimed at determining year of establishment, e-mail ID and website address. Part two asked respondents on ICT facilities available; part three sought to know the services automated in the libraries while part four was designed to know the factors affecting the use of ICT.

The questionnaire was validated through the expert judgment of a systems librarian and a computer scientist whom are of the rank of senior lecturers and above in Delta State University, Abraka and Delta State Polytechnic, Ozoro respectively; after which it was pre-tested on three libraries of higher institutions to determine its reliability. The population consisted of heads of libraries of higher institutions in Delta State, Nigeria. Eleven higher institutions were sampled for this study. The sampled institution libraries include; Federal University of Petroleum Resources, Effurun (FUPRE); Delta State University (Delsu), Abraka; Novena University, Ogume (NU), Delta State Polytechnic, Ogwashi-uku (DSPG), Delta State Polytechnic, Otefe-Oghara (DSPT); Delta State Polytechnic, Ozoro (DSPZ)' College of Education, Warri (COEWA); College of Education, Agbor (COEA); Federal College of Education Technical, Asaba (FCET); College of Physical and Sport Education; Mosogar (COPEM); and Petroleum Training Institution (PTI). However, the Asaba and Oleh campuses of Delsu were eliminated, because Abraka is the mother campus. The researchers personally visited the participating libraries to administer the questionnaire. Collected data were analyzed using frequency counts and percentages.

Data Analysis and Presentation of Result

The eleven participating libraries completed the questionnaires. Most heads of libraries delegated other staff members (librarians) deemed fit such as systems librarians; heads of audio-visual units etc to respond to the questionnaire.

ICT DEMOGRAPHIC PROFILE

From the collated data, none of the institution libraries had an e-mail ID neither a website for library and information service delivery. This is summarized in Table 1. Ugboma and Edewor (2007) had earlier revealed this in the libraries they investigated. From the table; majority (10) were government funded institutions and one private institutions. Most of the libraries have been in existence for over 10 years and above without a website dedicated to the provision of library and information services. However, librarians and information practitioners in these libraries have e-mail ID for personal/private purposes as revealed in the study

AVALIABLE ICT FACILITIES/ EQUIPMENT

There are various types of ICT facilities and equipments available in higher institution libraries in Delta State. The questionnaire listed twenty-six perceived ICT facilities and respondents reacted to them. The data in Tables 2a, 2b, and 2c shows in numbers the available ICT facilities.

The eleven higher institution libraries had a total of one hundred and twenty-two desktop computers. The number of computer per library ranged from 2-10, with an average of 4 computers

Table 2a. ICT facilities/equipment available

INSTITUTION LIBRARY	DESKTOPS	LAPTOPS	LAN	WAN	SOFTWARE IN USE	INTERNET	ELECTRONIC DATABASE	CD DUPLICATORS	TV SATELLITE DISH
FUPRE	2	-	-	-	-	-	-	-	-
PTI	72	-	Yes	-	X-LIB	Yes	-	2	Yes
DELSU	9	-	-	-	-	-	-	-	Yes
NU	2	-	-	-	-	-	-	-	Yes
DSPG	5	15	Yes	-	-	Yes	-	1	Yes
DSPT	2	-	-	-	-	-	-	-	Yes
DSPZ	13	-	Yes	-	-	Yes	-	1	Yes
COEWA	4	-	-	-	-	-	-	-	Yes
COEA	4	-	-	-	-	-	-	-	Yes
FCET	4	-	-	-	-	-	-	-	Yes
COPEM	5	-	Yes	-	-	Yes	-	-	Yes

Table 2b. ICT facilities/equipment available

INSTITUTION LIBRARY	CCTV	WEBCAM	TELEVISIONS	PRINTERS	PROJECTOR SCREEN	PHOTOCOPY MACHINE	OVERHEAD PROJECTOR	DIGITAL VIDEO CAMERA	MULTIMEDIA PROJECTOR
FUPRE	-	-	-	1	-	-	-	-	-
PTI	-	-	6	4	-	2	-	2	1
DELSU	-	-	2	4	1	1	-	-	-
NU	-	-	1	1	-	-	-	-	-
DSPG	-	-	2	3	1	2	1	2	2
DSPT	-	-	1	1	1	1	1	-	-
DSPZ	-	-	6	2	1	1	1	2	-
COEWA	-	-	1	1	-	1	-	-	-
COEA	-	-	1	1	-	1	-	-	-
FCET	-	-	1	1	-	-	-	-	-
COPEM	-	-	-	1	-	-	-	-	-

per library, except the PTI library. This corroborates the finding of Igben and Akobo (2007) that the available number and distribution of computer in libraries is clearly inadequate. More so the existing computers have no webcam, with a total of 20 units of printers for the entire libraries. In all the libraries, there was clear absence of electronic database; OPAC system; Intranet system and fax machine. The implication is that online resource sharing and other information service would be impossible. Only 4 libraries have internet facility for general browsing purpose. In the face of the wide array of information resources available through the internet and WWW, it is therefore imperative for all libraries to provide internet access to users across the state.

Service Automated in Libraries

The study was interested in critical service areas automated in higher institution libraries. None of the eleven libraries had automated any of their services (see Table 3). While DELSU is currently automating its circulation services, though still

Table 2c. ICT facilities/equipment available

INSTITUTION LIBRARY	VIDEO TAPE PLAYER	AUDIO TAPE PLAYER	SCANNERS	FAX	BARCODE READER	OPAC	SYSTEM INTRANET	ANTENNA MAST
FUPRE	-	-	-	-	-	-	-	-
PTI	4	3	3	-	1	-	-1	-
DELSU	-	-	1	-	-	-	-	-
NU	-	-	-	-	-	-	-	-
DSPG	2	-	-	-	-	-	-	1
DSPT	1	-	-	-	-	-	-	-
DSPZ	2	2	2	-	-	-	-	-
COEWA	-	-	-	-	-	-	-	-
COEA	-	-	-	-	-	-	-	-
FCET	-	-	-	-	-	-	-	-
COPEM	-	-	1	-	-	-	-	-

in its infancy stage, the PTI library automated its Cataloguing section. This does not portend well for the library and information service delivery of higher institution libraries in Delta State.

CONSTRAINTS TO ICT USE

There could be a number of reasons for non use of ICT in libraries. The questionnaire listed seven perceived reasons and respondent reacted to them. The result were analyzed using the statistical method of summation of weighted values (SWV) as shown in Table 4. Five ratings namely; strongly Agree; Agree; Disagree; Strongly Disagree and None; corresponding to scale of preference of 5,4,3,2,1 respectively were adopted. The preference index is obtained by dividing the SWV for each attribute by the total number of respondents. The result in the Table 4 shows that poor funding tops the chart with an index of 4.7. Lack of maintenance had an index of 4.2, while irregular breakdown

Table 3. Services automated in higher institution libraries

Institution library	Inter library	Selection/acquisition	Circulation	Cataloging	Reference
FUPRE	Nil	Nil	Nil	Nil	Nil
PTI	-	-	-	Yes	-
DELSU	-	-	In progress	Nil	-
NU	-	-	Nil	-	-
DSPG	-	-	-	-	-
DSPT	-	-	-	-	-
DSPZ	-	-	-	-	-
COEWA	-	-	-	-	-
COEA	-	-	-	-	-
FCET	-	-	-	-	-
COPEM	-	-	-	-	-

Table 4. Constraints to ICT use

Constraints	SA	A	D	SD	NONE	TOTAL	INDEX
Poor funding	45	8	-	-	-	53	4.8
Inadequate skilled manpower	30	12	-	-	-	42	3.8
Non reliability of electricity supply	45	4	3	-	-	52	4.7
Irregular breakdown of ICT equipment	15	12	15	2	-	44	4
Inadequate technical support	30	12	-	-	2	44	4
Poor implementation of policies	25	12	6	2	-	45	4.1
Lack of maintenance	20	20	6	-	-	46	4.2

of ICT facilities and inadequate technical support had the lowest index of 4 respectively. This corroborates the finding of Akintunde (2004) that most libraries now have maintenance agreement with ICT equipment suppliers.

CONCLUSION AND RECOMMENDATION

This study has shown that higher institution libraries in Delta state, Nigeria, had not yet embraced ICT. This has implication for information service delivery. The study reveals non automation of critical service in the libraries. Further revelation showed that the number of computers in libraries was low, averaging 4 computers per library. This few computers are mainly used for administrative purposes. None of the participating libraries had a websites

The study also identified reasons for the non use of ICT in the libraries. These include poor funding, inadequate skilled manpower, non-reliability of electricity supply; inadequate technical support and poor implementation of poor policies, among others.

Results from the study also indicate several areas where future research will have positive implications on higher institution libraries in Nigeria; one area for further research might be to conduct

the study using a larger sample and a broader geographical base. Another possibility is to replicate the study to include available ICT skilled librarians. More attention needs to be directed towards how library personnel in this part of the world are complaint with ICT. Finally researchers could adapt a comparative study of ICT use in libraries from different cultural backgrounds.

Considering the ramifications of ICT in an information environment such as libraries in higher institution; Nigeria libraries needs to focus on strategies and plans that will enhance the use of ICT in libraries. They must take practical measures to provide a stable ICT infrastructure that facilitates the provision of fundamental library information Community. As presented in the discussions, reasons for non use of ICT by higher institution libraries in Nigeria exist; recommendations for improvement in these areas are as follows:

- Regular training on ICT hardware and software for library personnel.
- Increased funding to take care of automation; ICT infrastructure(hardware, software, connectivity, bandwidth etc.) and Subscription to e-resources.
- Uninterrupted power supply.
- Adequate technical support.
- Design and faithful implementation of ICT policy in higher institution libraries.

REFERENCES

Abdullahi, Z. M., & Haruna, I. (2008). Utilization of information and communication technology (ICT) for information services delivery in university libraries in Adamawa State. *Information Technologist: An International Journal of Information and Communication Technology*, *5*(2), 24–30.

Adebisi, O. L. (2002). Information and communication technology availability, accessibility and resource sharing in the federal polytechnic libraries in South West Nigeria. *Information Technologist: An International Journal of Information and Communication Technology*, *6*(2), 169–176.

Ajayi, G. O. (2005). *E-Government in Nigeria's e-strategy*. Paper presented at the 5th Annual African Computing and Telecommunication Summit, Abuja, Nigeria.

Akintunde, S. A. (2004). *Libraries as tools for ICT development*. Paper presented at the 42nd Annual Nations Conference and AGM of the Nigerian Library Association, Akure, Nigeria.

Akintunde, S. A. (2006, June 18-23). State of ICT's tertiary institutions in Nigeria: Windows on the universities. In *Proceedings of the 44th Annual National Conference and Annual General Meeting of the Nigerian Library Association*, Abuja, Nigeria (pp. 123-127).

Al-Qallaf, C. L. (2006). Librarians and technology in academic and research libraries in Kuwait: Perceptions and effects. *Libri*, *56*, 168–179. doi:10.1515/LIBR.2006.168

Anaehobi, E. S. (2007). Availability of ICT facilities in academic libraries in Anambra State. *Journal of the Nigeria Library Association. Anambra State Chapter*, *1*(1), 57–64.

Babafemi, G. O., & Adedibu, L. O. (2007). Application of computer technology to circulation subsystem of the Federal University of Agriculture, Abeokuta. *Nigerbiblios*, *18*(1-2), 23–30.

De Watterille, A., & Gilbert, L. (2000). *Advanced information and communication technology*. Oxford, UK: Heinemann Educational Publishers.

Dirisu, B. M. (2009). The availability and unitization of information and communication technologies (ICTs) in college of education (COE) Minna, a survey. *Information Technologist: An International Journal of Information and Communication Technology*, *6*(2), 149–153.

Faboyubde, E. O. (2006). The state of information and communication technology (ICT) in selected libraries in Lagos and Ibadan Metropolis in libraries: Dynamic engines for the knowledge and information society proceedings of the NLA. In *Proceedings of the 44th Annual National Conference and AGM*, Abuja, Nigeria (pp. 61-68).

Gambari, A. I., & Chike, O. A. (2007). Availability and utilization of ICT facilities higher institution in Nigeria State, Nigeria. *Information Technologist*, *4*(1), 35–46.

Haruna, I., & Oyelakan, G. O. (2010). Provision and utilization of information resources in Nigerian Defense Academy (NDA) Library, Kaduna. *Information Technologist*, *7*(1), 11–18.

Igben, M. J., & Akobo, D. I. (2007). State of information and communication technology (ICT) in libraries in Rivers State, Nigeria. *African Journal of Library . Archives and Information Science*, *17*(2), 135–143.

Ilorah, H. C., Nwofor, F. A., & Onwudinjo, O. T. (2007). The place of university libraries in e-learning in Universities in Anambra State: A case study of Nnamdi Azikiwe University, Awka, Anambra State University, Uli and Madonna University Okija. *Journal of the Nigeria Library Association . Anambra State Chapter, 1*(1), 51–56.

Jones, E. E. (1989). Library support staff and technology: Perceptions and opinions. *Library Trends, 37*(4), 432–456.

Kavulya, J. M. (2004). Challenges in the provision of library services for distance education: A case of selected universities in Kenya. *African Journal of Library . Archives and Information Science, 13*(1), 43–53.

Magara, E. (2002). Application of digital libraries and electronic technology in Uganda. *African Journal of Library . Archives and Information Science, 13*(1), 43–53.

Nkanu, W. O. (2008). Utilization of information and communication technology facilities in Nigeria university libraries. *Information Technologist: An International Journal of Information and Communication Technology, 5*(2), 1–6.

Obasuyi, L. (2005). Impact of computer and internet applications on library and information services delivery in NARIS libraries in Nigeria. In *Proceedings of the 43rd Annual National Conference and AGM of Nigeria Library Association* (pp. 76-86).

Odion, F., & Adetona, C. (2009). Information and communication technology (ICT) as a tool for effective performance by academic librarians in Edo State of Nigeria. *Communicate: Journal of Library and Information Science, 11*(1), 27–37.

Ogunleye, G. O. (1977). Automating the Federal University in Nigeria: A state of art. *African Journal of Library . Archives and Information Science, 7*(1), 71–79.

Ojedoknen, A. A., & Owolabi, E. O. (2003). Internet access competence and the use of internet for teaching and research activities by University of Botswana academic staff. *African Journal of Library . Archives and Information Science, 13*(1), 43–53.

Oketunji, J. (2002). *40 years of information and communication technology (ICT) library services to the National Paper.* Paper presented at the 40th Annual National Conference and AGM of the Nigeria Library Association, Badagry, Nigeria.

Palmini, C. C. (1994). The impact of computerization on library support staff: A study of support staff in academic libraries in Wisconsin. *College & Research Libraries, 55*(1), 119–127.

Ugboma, M. U., & Edewor, N. (2008). Use of e-mail in library and information service provision in higher institutions of delta State, Nigeria. *Information Technologist, 5*(1), 42–51.

This work was previously published in the International Journal of Digital Library Systems, Volume 2, Issue 3, edited by Chia-Hung Wei, pp. 29-38, copyright 2011 by IGI Publishing (an imprint of IGI Global).

Chapter 17

A Presentation-Preserved Compositional Approach for Integrating Heterogeneous Systems:
Using E-Learning as an Example

Fang-Chuan Ou Yang
Ching Yun University, Taiwan

ABSTRACT

In traditional SCW environments, related web services are integrated into business processes. Web service still brings less than expected benefits to small corporations and end-users for two reasons: 1) the web service only focuses on data level and is difficult to implement the presentation-centric business contexts. 2) The small corporations and end-users usually do not have enough IT competences to write a client or user interface to interact with web service(s). In order to solve these problems, the author proposes a presentation-preserved compositional approach for service-oriented architecture (PCSOA), which extends the existing data-oriented compositional approaches for web services to provide a more flexible methodology to orchestrate both data level and presentation level services during the workflow integration. A prototype is also built to validate the feasibility of the approach.

1. INTRODUCTION

Software developments of online business have adopted component-based distributed services and web services (W3C, 2002) as better system integration solutions (Stanford University, 2002; Blake & Gomaa, 2005; Medjahed & Bouguettaya,

DOI: 10.4018/978-1-4666-2928-8.ch017

2005; Tsalgatidou et al., 2006; Zhao, 2006; Wang, 2006). To realize complete commercial processes, particular services often need to be further incorporated and composed with other processes to achieve complete end-to-end business activities. Flexible and solid frameworks for the services-based cross-organizational workflow (SCW) (Blake & Gomaa, 2005) are becoming critical and indispensable.

The term so called virtual enterprise (Camarinha-Matos & Afsarmanesh, 1999; Gijsen et al., 2002) describes a business task consisting of multiple services from different third-party organizations. The workflow coordination in the virtual enterprise is responsible for controlling the execution sequence of each service, mediating messages passed throughout the services, and ultimately returning the aggregated data to the upper presentation layer to perform the result for end-users. Each service is only responsible for sending and receiving the data, hence the service consumer (the service-integrated organization) must implement GUIs (graphic user interfaces) such as web pages, in order to present the result and interact with end-users. In this typical service-oriented architecture, we use the term, data-oriented compositional approaches, to describe the workflow compositional approaches which employ standard web service technologies adhere to the W3C specifications (W3C, 2002).

Without considering the interaction with end users, data-oriented web services have been successful. In fact, this is also the original intension of SOA to separate GUI out of the service. However, without any mechanism to reuse the required presentation and interaction with users within the data-oriented workflow composition, the data-oriented compositional approaches usually demand additional implementation cost on the presentation and interaction management. In these data-oriented approaches, service consumers often need to program and implement the presentation level interfaces to display the retrieved data. In the real world, not all business organizations can finish these missions by themselves, especially for the companies with no IT departments and technicians. Due to the nature of data-based service, separate presentation-layer interfaces are remained to be implemented by each service consumer respectively without proper reuse. In some business environments where the providers and consumers have asymmetrical IT competences, these problems will make the service-

based cross-organizational workflow integration to be infeasible and unrealistic. Therefore, the web service's original intension to completely separate GUI from data should be amended with certain mechanism that promotes the reuse of GUI works to make SOA a more efficient distributed architecture.

Moreover, the presentation level integration has been more and more important to the next generation software as developed in the concept of Web 2.0 (O'Reilly, 2005). One of the key points in Web 2.0 is to generate the synergy of small sites to make up the bulk of the web's content. For example, the video files hosted on Youtube (www.youtube.com, a web platform which provides web users to upload and perform their own movies) can easily be reused and plugged into any web site with only simple codes and configurations. This web site can then reuse Youtube's video clip to produce related multimedia content and programs on a new web page without worrying the source video. Combining this observation of Web 2.0 and our aforementioned shortcomings of data-centric SOA, we believe SOA should be further extended to treat diverse web resources (esp., presentation-based services) as reusable components to makes these services and resources manageable and assembled in an easy and efficient way.

In this article, we propose a presentation-preserved compositional approach for service-oriented architecture (called PCSOA) to show that, in many cases, the reuse and integration of presentation-based resources is also necessary in addition to the data level integration within the enterprise service compositional environments. For example, in applying SCW technologies to coordinate various product catalogue and material resources in the product design processes (Hou & Su, 2006; Richardson & Midwinter, 2006). Other frequently occurred examples are to compose diverse learning services into e-learning environments (Fuji & Tanigawa, 2002; Gaeta et al., 2002; Liao & Ou Yang, 2004; Liao et al., 2005). In the traditional SCW approaches, the functionality of each process/service is delivered by the data-based web service while the presentation interfaces are left to be implemented separately by each involving consumers. By careful analysis of the daily operation, the presentation-centric and data-centric processes usually coexist in the corporate workflow activity as shown in Table 1. However, the discussions of the workflow composition incorporating both data-based and presentation-based services are lack in the previous researches.

The first and foremost difference of our approach is that both the data-based services and presentation-based services can be composed into the workflow activities in the PCSOA. The general concept of the service composition in the PCSOA is depicted in Figure 1. Figure 1 shows that the service#1 and service#3 include only pure data-oriented web services, briefly the data-based services. Service#2 includes presentational markups and a data-oriented web service, and service#4 includes the presentational markups, both in the PCSOA are defined as presentation-based services. The presentation-based services also have metadata and can be discovered the same way as the data-based services. Second, the presentation-based services have standard and open service-oriented protocols to deliver presentational markups, perform page flows, handle message state, and have ways of doing URL-mapping following WSRP standards (Kropp, Leue, & Thompson, 2003). Third, to compose and drive the

presentation-based services for workflow orchestration, we stick on existing standards (e.g., Web Services, Web Service for Remote Portlet, BPEL4WS) in the PCSOA expecting its ease of adaptation. The proposed PCSOA can be executed on any service-based platforms as long as they support web standards. A further contribution of this work is to align the developmental processes of PCSOA with industry-standard software engineering processes, which make our approach easy to be implemented on various programming languages and platforms based on the service-oriented architectures.

The remainder of this paper is organized as follows: related works are discussed in Section 2 Section 3 presents the PCSOA architecture and elaborate each functional component. Section 4 presents and evaluates the prototype of our proposed PCSOA and Section 5 presents our conclusion and future works.

2. RELATED WORK

2.1. Data-Oriented Web Services and Presentation-Oriented Web Services

The service-oriented architecture (SOA) provides the core technology of integrating heterogeneous applications (The TimesTen Team, 2000; Friesen & Mazloumi, 2004; Puustjärvi, 2004; Medjahed

Table 1. Two examples of presentation-intensive workflow composition

	Presentation-Intensive Workflow examples	
	E-learning resource integration	**Product design**
Service1	Getting learning content (**p**)	Getting customer needs (**d**)
Service2	Getting testing questions (**d**)	Moving design information into specs. (**p**)
Service3	Retrieving learning status and scores (**d**)	Transforming the specs. into engineering requirements. (**p**)
Service4	Obtaining personalized configurations (**d**)	Defining the family of solutions (**p**)
Service5	Organizing and performing learning contents on the web GUIs (**p**)	Completing the description of the artifacts (**p**)
Note: (**d**) represents the data-based service. (**p**) represents the presentation-centric service.		

Figure 1. The general concept of the service composition in the PCSOA

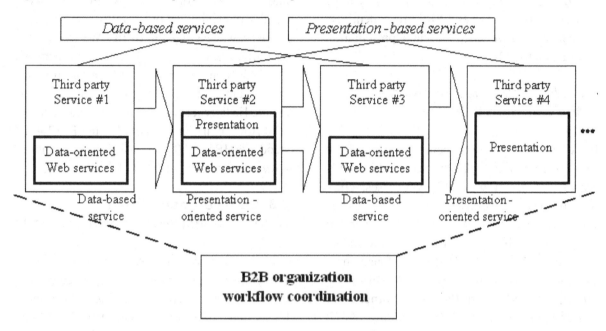

& Bouguettaya, 2005; Liao et al., 2005; Zhao, 2006). The SOA consists of three standards: Web Service Description Language (WSDL) (Christensen, Curbera, Meredith, & Weerawarana, 2002), Simple Object Access Protocol (SOAP) (Ericsson & Lafon, 2002), and Universal Description, Discovery, and Integration (UDDI) (Universal Description, Discovery, and Integration (UDDI) specification, http://www.uddi.org/), and SOA solves the problems of "naming" for the distributed environments and makes heterogeneous systems capable of communication and interaction.

However, the SOA only provides integration in the functional level, but lacks the definition of presentation level reuse and integration across heterogeneous environments due to the nature of data communicational mechanisms. Currently, even though the SOA can invoke diverse external web services and get results from them, front-end web interfaces must be handled with additional implementations. In order to solve the shortcomings of the data-based web services, many organizations employ portals to support presentation level integration for their web sites (Puschmann &

Alt, 2004). In applying portal technologies, portlet (JCP, 2003) is one of the most important elements. A portlet is a web component for handling HTTP requests and generating dynamic web contents through the portlet container, which makes portal technology excellent in implementing various web contents aggregation. Portlets can be designed as sharable presentation-oriented web services, such as WSRP(Web Service for Remote Portlets) (Kropp, Leue, & Thompson, 2003) services. Different from the data-oriented web services, presentation-oriented WSRP services provide the definition in the presentation level to make portlets capable of being invoked from remote endpoints, as well as pluggable into local portal without handling front-end web interfaces during the integration. The major difference is that the data-oriented web services only response a set of name value pairs with simple datatypes to the consumer sides while the presentation-oriented web services return the presentational markups such as HTML, XHTML, and JavaScripts. WSRP services use exactly the same standard as the data-oriented web services, such as WSDL, SOAP and

UDDI for publishing and subscribing in the SOA environments. This makes WSRP an excellent base for extension if we want to include presentation materials into SOA.

2.2. Workflow Specifications in the Software Industry

In a collaborative environment constructed from web services, and workflow control standard is crucial for describing public processes, composition, private workflow, and other common workflow artifacts. There are various popular workflow specifications in the software industry, such as Wf-XML (Workflow Management Coalition, http://www.wfmc.org/), WSFL (IBM, 2002), XLANG (http://www.gotdotnet.com/team/xml_wsspecs/xlang-c/default.htm), WSCI (Arkin et al., 2000), WSCL (Banerji et al., 2000), BPEL4WS (IBM, 2002), PIPs (RosettaNet, 2000), and JDF (CIP4, 2000).

Out of several workflow specifications, BPEL4WS has been frequently used and discussed in several researches and projects (Hsu & Ou Yang, 2005; Blake & Gomaa, 2005; Medjahed & Bouguettaya, 2005; ActiveBPEL, http://www.activebpel.org/; Wang, 2006) because: 1) A workflow in the BPEL4WS is a composite web service as a component which can enhance application usability and flexibility for enterprise application integration. 2) BPEL4WS can fit into SOA to control the flow of a set of web services that make up an application. 3) BPEL4WS merges the advantages of WSFL (IBM, 2002) and XLANG and specifies a collection of primitive activities such as invoke, receive, and reply, as well as structures for combining them such as sequence and while.

BPEL4WS is designed to promote the service-based workflow where the services it integrates are mainly data-oriented. To make our proposed PCSOA a practical and easy-to-use extension to SOA, we propose to add extra components to BPEL4WS to allow BPEL4WS to invoke and integrate presentation-oriented web services

into PCSOA. In order to make the BPEL4WS capable of driving the presentation-oriented web services, we leverage the BPEL4WS standard to design an agent to mediate the interaction between BPEL4WS engine and the invocation proxy for the presentation-based services. The agent (as detailed in later section) can be easily added to any workflow engine products following BPEL4WS standards (IBM, 2002; Microsoft BizTalk, http://www.microsoft.com/biztalk/default.mspx).

2.3. Service-Based Cross-Organizational Workflow Integration

With the popularity of SOA, the SCW integration is becoming indispensable. Many researches in this domain discuss the underlying infrastructure for services composition (Chen et al., 2000; Shen & Norrie, 2001; Shen et al., 2001; Zeng et al., 2001; Korhonen et al., 2003) via the use of agent technologies. Other researches place emphasis on how to make the SCW environments more flexible and smart to reconfigure and update dynamically in order to overcome the stateless nature of web services (Blake, 2003; Sycara et al., 2004; Vieira et al., 2004; Blake & Gomaa, 2005; Kumar & Wainer, 2005). However, considering the practical issues of applying SCW to business environments, the SOA requires more enhancements such as security, resource management, and implementation flexibility to meet the real business needs. In this paper, we discuss two critical issues in the SCW environments:

1. **Presentation-centric workflow integration:** In the traditional SCW environments, web services are delivered, shared, composed, and managed at data level. However, this approach sometimes causes workflow orchestration more difficult and cost-expensive especially in the presentation-centric business contexts.

2. **Implementation cost:** Although SOA provides an interoperable infrastructure for the

SCW environments, it usually only stays at verbal discussion within the technical community but rarely brings the benefits to the end-users. The major problem is the end-users do not have enough IT competences to communicate with a web service nor write a user interface to interact with it. SCW also faces similar problem in the business environment.

In this study, we propose the PCSOA which focuses on discussing the approach of reusing the presentation-oriented web service and its composition into the SCW environments for solving the aforementioned practical problems. To our best knowledge, the concept of PSCOA is novel and has not been discussed in the previous SCW researches.

3. SYSTEM DEVELOPMENT OF PCSOA

3.1. The PCSOA Architecture

To meet the aforementioned requirements on PC-SOA, there are several architectural characteristics for the PCSOA:

1. Different from the data-based service, the presentation-based services are provided based on the portlet technologies (JCP, 2003) to address the flexible configuration and management of web interfaces, which at least consist of presentational tags and script such as HTML, XHTML, and JavaScript.
2. A portal server is required as the integration endpoint for presenting the UI contents via portlets to the end-users. With the high popularity of portal servers, we see this as a reasonable architectural decision.
3. The works done on each participating service points may include both data-based and presentation-based services.

4. The workflow management system should be capable of driving presentation-based services, data-based web services, and incorporating other legacy service resources based on popular web and workflow standards.
5. The design of PCSOA has to follow the software engineering principals; each element should be loosely coupled, autonomous, and easily integrated into enterprise applications.

We can divide the working principles of PC-SOA into two phases: the preparation phase and execution phase, as shown in Figure 2. We also separate the different components for service provider and consumer while describing these two phases:

1. **Preparation phase:** in the service provider, the to-be-published services may come from distributed components, web service, or other resource types. If a presentation component is ready to be reused by others, it can be wrapped and published as a presentation-based service to be reused globally and coordinated into workflow processes under PCSOA. The Service Resource Wrapping Agent (SRWA) is responsible for converting resources to presentation-based services. The wrapped presentation-based services can be published into the public UDDI registries. This completes the service providing side of the preparation phase. On the service consuming side, a PCSOA process, which may invoke presentation-based services, should first be defined in a workflow management system, which supports PCSOA. The process definitions for PCSOA can be generated by either the process definition tools or made in manual since the process definition of PCSOA are similar to the regular process definition as it is in BPEL4WS environments.
2. **Execution phase:** at the execution time, the presentation-based services in the service

Figure 2. Core components of the preparation and execution phase for PCSOA

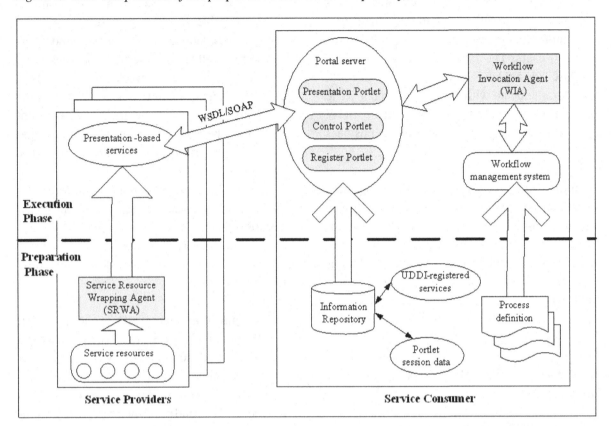

provider are deployed and waiting for the SOAP invocation from the service consumer. In the service consumer, its portal server is responsible for obtaining the registered information of desired presentation services, calling the external presentation-based services for presentation in the portal UIs, and talking with the workflow management system. Thus, a portal server supporting PCSOA consists of additional three portlets: Register Portlet, Control Portlet, and Presentation Portlet. An appropriate communication mechanism is necessary for the portal server to communicate with the back-end workflow management system. The Workflow Invocation Agent (WIA) is designed to support specific actions for connecting the portal server and workflow management system.

For readers who are familiar with SOA, we illustrate the differences between SOA and PC-SOA from several perspectives in Table 2. Note that the additional components that we designed for PCSOA (i.e., WIA, three functional portlets, and SRWA) all follow existing web standards. This guarantees that our proposed PCSOA can be realized at any workflow engines and portal servers supporting BPEL4WS, Web Service, WSRP, and Portlet 168 standards (e.g., WebSphere and WebLogic platforms).

Key features of the PCSOA architecture are service resources wrapping, presentation level integration, and workflow orchestration of services. These three features can be mapped to their corresponding components in the PCSOA, namely SRWA, the extended portal server, and WIA. In Section 3.2, we discuss SRWA on how to wrap into presentation-based services from

Table 2. Comparisons of SOA and PCSOA

Service providing				
Preparing phase	Functions	Required components	Required actions	Used standards
	Construct the service	Manual programming if presentation is required	Implement a web service	WS
		SRWA	Wrapping web content with SWRA into a WSRP service	WS+WSRP
	Publish the service	N/A	Send to UDDI or service consumer	WS
		N/A	Send to UDDI or service consumer	WS
	Published format	WSDL	N/A	WS
		WSDL	N/A	WS
Execution phase	Providing service	Running WSRP service	Send back messages via SOAP	WS
		Running WSRP service	Send back messages via SOAP	WS+WSRP
Service consuming via BPEL4WS				
Preparing phase	Functions	Required components	Required actions	Used standards
	Workflow arrangement	Tool for BPEL4WS workflow definition	Define process using workflow tool (where all presentation content should be programmed outside the workflow definition)	BPEL4WS
		Tool for BPEL4WS workflow definition (with WIA available as a standard web service)	Define process using workflow tool (where presentation-based service can also be included declaratively)	BPEL4WS
Execution phase	Workflow execution	BPEL4WS engine	BPEL4WS engine execute the defined workflow process	BPEL4WS+WS
		Portal server (with 3 additional portlets)+WIA +BPEL4WS engine	BPEL4WS engine execute the defined workflow process whose steps with WSRP are dispatched to portal user via WIA	BPEL4WS+WSRP+WS
Note: *Dark areas represent the characteristics of SOA and the light areas represent the characteristics of PCSOA.*				

diverse service resources and contents. In Section 3.3, we discuss how standard portal server can be extended with three proposed functional portlets to freely invoke presentation-based services for better content resue. The workflow modeling of data-based and presentation-based services via WIA is detailed in Section 3.4.

3.2. Service Resource Wrapping Agent (SRWA)

Different from the data-based service, the design of presentation-based service in PCSOA should consider the flexible configuration and management of web interfaces (e.g., presentational tags and script such as HTML, XHTML, and JavaScript). The portlet standard (JCP, 2003) and its extended standard WSRP are chosen in PCSOA to fit this need. If a presentation component is ready to be reuse by many others, a wrapping process is needed to publish it as a presentation-based service to be invoked globally and coordinated into workflow processes under PCSOA.

Figure 3 depicts the resource wrapping concept of the presentation-based services. Two kinds of resources can be wrapped to the presentation-based services: 1) web contents: it can be the texts, pictures, videos, or other types of multimedia files. 2) Web services and distributed components: it's the traditional data-oriented web services following the SOA architecture or distributed components such as EJB, Java bean and COM+. The Service Resource Wrapping Agent (SRWA) is responsible for wrapping those resources to standard presentation-based services. There are two steps involved in the wrapping procedure: linking and feeding. In the linking step, the SRWA will initially get the resource address of web contents or the service description of web services and distributed components. The SRWA then assigns those resources to related URIs (Uniform Resource Identifiers) via the Resource Identifier which provides simple and extensible means to identify those resources on the web. In the feeding step, the SRWA will pass those URIs to the related presentation-based services via the Resource Matchmaker. Finally, the presentation-based services can directly link/invoke those resources and response presentational markups of those web contents to consumers.

3.3. Three Functional Portlets in the Portal Server

The portal server of the PCSOA includes three functional portlets: Register Portlet, Control Portlet, and Presentation Portlet. Those portlets are designed as web components which can be plugged into a web page and have UIs for the end-users to interact with. The Register Portlet is a local portlet for the web administrators to register remote services and stored required information used at the runtime workflow control. The required information for the Register Portlet can be captured from the public/private UDDI registries or specific endpoint addresses. The Control portlet is responsible for communicating with the WIA for the workflow control and notifying the Presentation Portlet to initialize related actions associated with the service invocation. The Presentation Portlet is a service proxy in charge of sending request and obtaining response messages where the messages are passed in the SOAP payloads. For clearly elaborating the interaction pattern among the Control Portlet, Presentation

Figure 3. The resource wrapping of the presentation-based services

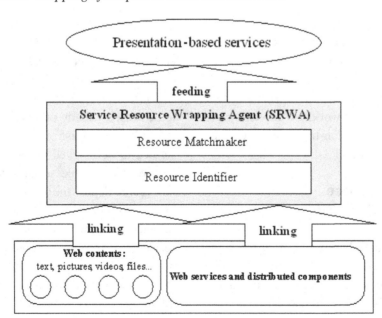

Portlet, and related roles in the PCSOA, the UML swimlane diagram is used to depict several critical actions, as shown in the Figure 4. We highlight those actions:

1. An end user chooses a workflow from the list of the Control Portlet.
2. The Control Portlet sends a request to the WIA for obtaining the service ID used in the following service invocation actions.
3. The WIA is a mediator for connecting the portal server and the back-end workflow management system in charge of obtaining the decided service ID for the Control Portlet and storing the portlet preferences. The portlet preferences have several required information such as the end-user ID, process ID, service ID, and session data for the runtime execution of Presentation Portlet. The further detail of the WIA and workflow modeling is discussed in Section 3.4.
4. After getting the service ID, the Control Portlet calls the Presentation Portlet to initialize relative actions for the service invocation.

Figure 4. The interaction of the key roles in PCSOA

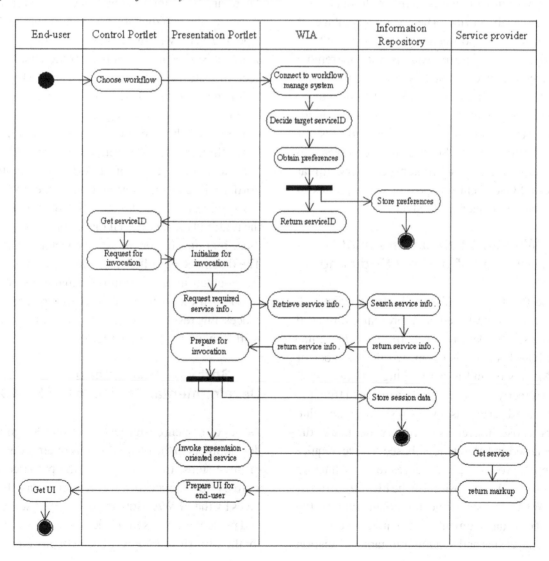

5. The Presentation Portlet invokes remote presentation-based service of the service provider and gets the markups through the standardized SOAP messages. The markups essentially comprise of the HTML codes which can be directly plugged into a fragment of web page. Finally, the Presentation Portlet returns those markups to the portal server and shows UIs for the end-user.

These three functional portlets in the PCSOA architecture are designed to mediate between service provider and service consumer. In other words, those portlets play the same role of service invocation clients as in the traditional data-oriented web service. The major advantage of those functional portlet designs in the PCSOA is that the service consumer can easily invoke remote services via several simple settings in the portal server without additional efforts of implementation and deployment. This extension to standard portal server allows its invocation and reuse of presentation material/services to be completed in a declarative manner for content designers, similar to how SOA client composing web services in declarative manner via WSDL.

3.4. Workflow Invocation Agent (WIA) and the Workflow Modelling

In the PCSOA, the WIA is the key mediator to weave the data-based and presentation-based services. The data returned from the presentation-based service is composed of a number of HTML codes and it can be plugged into a web page directly; however, the data returned from the data-based service is always a set of name value pairs. Those different output data generated by the data-based and presentation-based services require adaptive processing procedures for coordinating the workflow composition in the PCSOA. Briefly, the WIA is responsible for connecting to the workflow management system, judging different types of service and assigning suitable invocation

proxy, and send commands to the Control Portlet to initialize related invoking actions.

Figure 5 depicts the working mechanism of WIA. For the service binding, the WIA will perform different actions according to the service types. Initially, the WIA receives the input parameters of process definition PD, service descriptions SD, and service type lists STlist from the workflow management systems. The validateProcessDefinition() function checks if the required information defined in the PD is valid and sufficient. After the PD validation check has been conducted, each service invocation request will be recursively assigned according to the service type. There are two judged conditions defined in the PCSOA: 1) when the target service is data-based type, the WIA will bind the service through the standard SOAP proxy, get the returned data, and keep the returned data which will be used in the following data-based services or presentation-based services. The assignDataServiceProxy() function will be executed in this condition. 2) When the target service is presentation-based, the WIA will notify the Control Portlet, the Control Portlet will call the Presentation Portlet to bind the service through standard SOAP proxy, get the returned presentational markups, and capture those markups to perform on the web interfaces. The delegateControlPortletProxy() function will be executed in this condition. Finally, the WIA will return the state number that represents the processing result of workflow modeling to the workflow management system.

3.5. Software Design and Developmental Processes of PCSOA

At the component design level, software design and development in the PCSOA environment consists of three steps. In the first step, the prepared resources are wrapped to the presentation-based services by the SRWA. Both the data-based services and presentation-based services that are required for the workflow composition are deployed in the

Figure 5. The workflow modeling plan of WIA

```
Algorithm The workflow modeling plan of WIA
Input:
1) PD: it is a document-based process definition to represent the process logic
elements of a workflow and their partner relationships .
2) SD[]: it is a set of service descriptions for each service in the process
definition .
3) STlist[]: it is a set of service type lists for each service in the process
definition .
Output: SN: it is a state number representing the processing result .
validateProcessDefinition (): the function is used for validating the process
definition .
validateService (): the function is used for validating the required information
of service descriptions and service type .
assignDataServiceProxy (): the function is used for assigning the target data -
based service to the SOAP proxy to remote invocation .
delegateContorlPortletInvocation (): the function is used for delegating the job
of  presentation -based service invocation to the Control Portlet which has
permission to drive the Presentation Portlet  (a presentation -based SOAP
proxy).
begin
  SN=Null;
   if validateProcessDefinition (PD)==true then
    for each service Si where validateService (SD[Si], STlist[Si])==true do
       if judgeType(Si) ==Data_Based_Service then
         SN=assignDataServiceProxy (SD[Si]);
        else if judgeType(Si) ==Presentation_Based_Service then
         SN=delegateContorlPortletInvocation (SD[Si]);
     end for
    return SN;
end
```

local or remote endpoints. For discovering these services, the service descriptions can be published in the private or public UDDI registry where the workflow authors can search for to compose the workflow in the second step. In the second step, domain experts define the workflow activities and the system developers convert those documents to standardized workflow specification via the visual or text-based workflow authoring tools. Those specifications are then necessary to be deployed on the workflow management system of the consumer's portal as the reference of runtime execution. In the third step, all required portlets are developed and deployed on the consumer's portal server. The WIA is also set to connect to the portal server and workflow management system for the workflow modeling. Several configurations can be also done for the arrangement of web layouts for the end-users. In the Section 4, there is a discussion of the implementation result and operational evaluation of the PCSOA prototype.

4. IMPLEMENTATION AND OPERATIONAL EVALUATION

4.1. The PCSOA Prototype

There are many service-based application areas where presentations are important. Making presentations available as presentation-based services will greatly enhance the presentation reuse. Making these presentation-based services compositional for the service compositional environment further extend their ease of use into SCW domains.

For example, during the different phases of commercial product design, many digital engineering sketches and materials from various processes/services will be reused and reviewed by related engineers and supervisors. Integrating those resources into presentation-based services and use PCSOA to orchestrate the workflow activities with legacy enterprise applications and components can efficiently reduce the implementation cost and complexity of process integration for the product design.

Another frequently occurred example is from the e-learning domain. At an e-learning environment where many lessons from different hosts/service points should be integrated into a complete workflow and the same lesson from a host can be integrated into many different workflows if it is a commonly reusable unit. Making each lesson a presentation-based service and use PCSOA to integrate these presentation-based services, an organic workflow consisting of lesson presentation and retrieving learner-related information using regular data-based web services can be tied together easily under our proposed PCSOA.

Figure 6 depicts the implementation mappings of primary elements in the PCSOA. The WSRP technology is applied to develop the presentation-based services. Java APIs are used to implement the SRWA to wrap the e-learning resources to presentation-based services. To simulate cross-organizational interactions, all services hosted on providers are distributed across multiple Windows 2000 server endpoints. In the consumer side, we use the Liferay4.1.1 (http://www.liferay.com) as the portal server for hosting and managing several necessary portlets in the PCSOA. Register Portlet, Control Portlet, and Presentation Portlet are implemented adhere to the JSR 168 standard (JCP, 2003). The activeBPEL2.0 (AtiveBPEL, http://www.activebpel.org/) is used as the workflow management system which employs the BPEL4WS as the workflow specification. The WIA connected to the workflow management system is implemented as a standard web service which will be instantiated with individual workflow instance. Finally, to simplify the UDDI calls in the PCSOA, all service endpoint addresses are directly assigned to the invocation proxy instead of being published in the public registry.

Regardless of the application domain, there are two crucial implementation issues which we have successfully validated in this PCSOA prototype: first, how the workflow engine (BPEL4WS engine) drives the various services following predefined sequence, and secondly how the portal server (WSRP consumer) dynamically renders markups from different presentation-based service on the specific web layout (of portlet)? The solution for the first question is WIA. The programming logic and algorithm has already been detailed in the Section 3.4. It deserves to be mentioned, considering the compatibility with BPEL4WS, the WIA is implemented in the type of standard web service (in the BPEL4WS, each process is defined to a standard web service) and instantiated initially before the workflow activity. Notice that the markups rendered from the designate WSRP service are originally performed in a specific local portlet layout. The solution of the second question on dynamic invocation of various WSRP services (i.e., perform diverse WSRP services in the same portlet layout) is done via the presentation portlet proposed in Section 3.

Figure 6. The implementation mappings of the PCSOA prototype

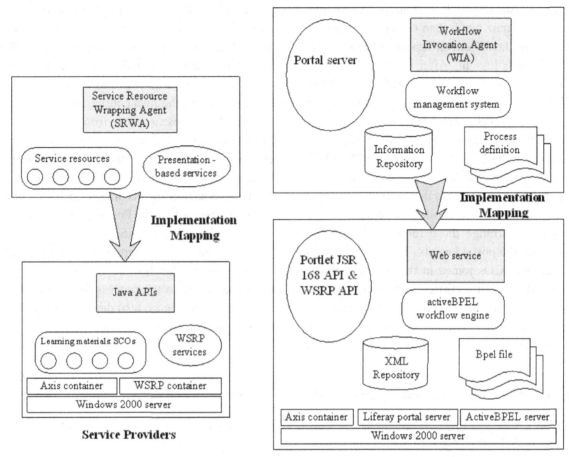

4.2. Testing and Evaluation of the PCSOA Architecture

In this section, we illustrate a real Java e-learning course to justify the feasibility of the presentation-based composition in PCSOA. Here, Java APIs and SCROM RTE (ADL, 2003) are used to implement the SRWA to wrap the e-learning resources to presentation-based services. In this testing case, three tentative lesson resources are used and wrapped to separate SCORM-compatible zip files (SCOs): "Java Syntax and quiz", "Java General", and "Java Methods" (The "Java Gengral" and "Java Methods" lessons contain only common web contents, such as web pages and

power points; the "Java Syntax and quiz" lesson contains common web contents and a web service to obtain the testing score form the database of service provider.). All SCOs are wrapped to presentation-based services via the SRWA and deployed across multiple service providers' endpoints. Those lessons are composed initially with a visual process definition which follows the activity-based workflow modeling notations proposed by Bi and Zhao (2003), as shown in the top of Figure 7. The visual process definition is easy to be understood and convenient to revise during the workflow design phase for the domain experts and course designers. A simple course activity defined in this case is: "The learners start to learn with the Java Syntax lesson, and then take the quiz of this lesson. If the learners get testing score of the quiz better than 60 will continue to enter to the Java General lesson, otherwise the Java Methods lesson." After the visual process definition is confirmed, the workflow engineer will transform it to BPEL4WS specification via the activeBPEL workflow authoring tools, as shown in the bottom of Figure 7. Finally, the BPEL4WS specification will be uploaded to the BPEL4WS workflow engine for the runtime execution.

For the portal server of the PCSOA, two configurations are required to set the registry information and arrange those rendered lesson resources on the portal layouts. The first one is to register the SCOs joined in the course activity through the Register Portlet. The other one is to place the Control Portlet and Presentation Portlet on the appropriate layouts. In Figure 8(a), for example, there are five portlets placed on the E-

learning page, namely the "Dictionary", "Search", "Analog Clock", "Subscribe (Control Portlet)", and "WSRP Proxy (Presentation Portlet)". The web administrator can flexibly adjust the layout position of each functional block in order to meet the learners' requirements and preferences. For starting to learn the Java course, learners will be prompted to choose a course from the course list in the "Subscribe" block. After the course being chosen by learners, the course ID is sent to the back-end workflow engine and the workflow will be instantiated (during this time, serial interactions occur among the Control Portlet, WIA, workflow engine, as described in the Section 3.3 and Section 3.4). Consequently, the rendered markups of lesson resource will be shown in the "WSRP Proxy" block according to the process definition of the course activity. Figure 8(b) depicts the whole e-learning workflow in this case.

Figure 7. An e-learning process definition in PCSOA prototype

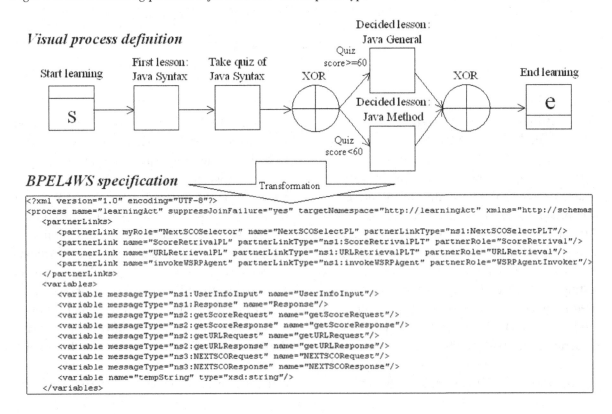

Figure 8. Two screenshots on the demonstrated e-learning workflow

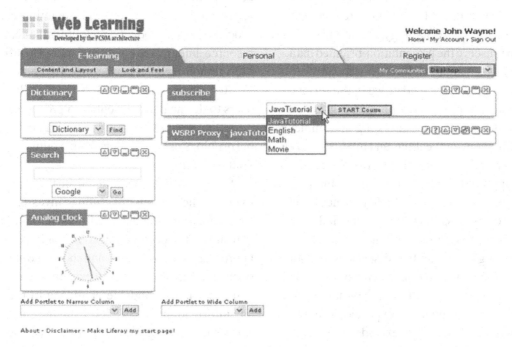

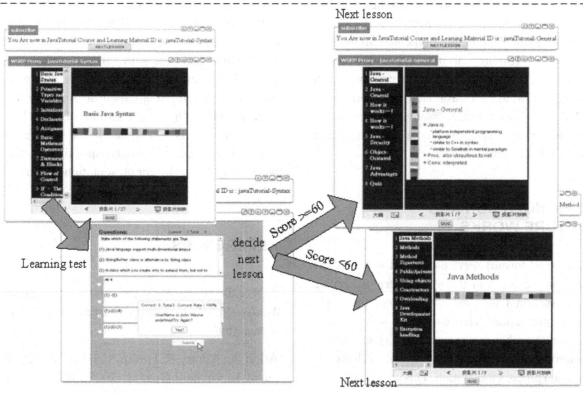

In this demonstration, the experimental result proves the feasibility of the PCSOA architecture. By using the portlet technology, the service providers can preserve the presentation-oriented data (markups) and share them through standard web service protocols. On the other hand, the service consumers can rapidly add a presentation-based service in the portal without coding and implementing for client applications and interfaces. By using the WIA, the back-end workflow engine will be supported to connect and drive the presentation-based services, which enhances the flexibility of process integration; especially the process is presentation-required and presentation-centric. Though the data-based services are not used to experiment in the prototype system, the feasibility of the combination of data-based and presentation-based should be expected. The major reason is the PCSOA only extends the existing web service architectures and open standards but destroys and modifies them. Moreover, the SRWA is implemented in the prototype system to wrap the service resources to presentation-based services. In this experiment, two common web content resources ("Java Gengral" and "Java Methods" lessons) and a web service included resource ("Java Syntax and quiz") are tested and justified successfully.

5. CONCLUSION AND FUTURE WORKS

The trend toward service-oriented web ecosystem has resulted in the use of various service compositional approaches to enhance the workflow integration. The data-based services and presentation-based services are both required in a heterogeneous business environment for flow control and process integration. This paper presented a presentation-preserved compositional approach for the workflow integration to allow existing standardized workflow framework to orchestrate both data-based and presentation-based services. This approach integrates diverse presentation-centric processes (e.g., product development, e-learning resource integration) to bring more benefits of SOA to non-technical end-users. In the vision of PCSOA, the service providers should allow end users to define their presentation process as supported in PCSOA, such as web users can easily define blogs using contents from Youtube (www.youtube.com).

Several issues encountered in this approach may be the source for future investigations. First, since the standardized presentation-based consumer (the portal of PCSOA) only performs appropriate URL rewriting and shows the markups on the web layout during the execution phase, the consumer has formidable challenge to preserve any information and data left from the end-users. It is a shortcoming of presentation-based service especially for an integrated and collaborative environment where the sharable presentation content needs to be coordinated and customized for different end-uses with various preferences. A standard interaction pattern may be needed to solve this problem. At last, there are many discussions regarding the error-handling of workflow, they mainly focus on the data-based services or non service-based workflow composition. Further works may be needed for presentation-based services in this area.

REFERENCES

ADL. (2003). *Sharable Content Object Reference Model (SCORM)*. Retrieved from. http://www.adlnet.gov/

Arkin, A., Askary, S., Fordin, S., Jekeli, W., Kawaguchi, K., Orchard, D., et al. (2000). *Web Services Choreography Interface (WSCI)*. Retrieved from http://www.w3.org/TR/wsci/

Banerji, A., Bartolini, C., Beringer, D., Chopella, V., Govindarajan, K., Karp, A., et al. (Eds.). (2000). *Web Services Conversation Language (WSCL).* Retrieved from http://www.w3.org/TR/wscl10/

Bi, H. H., & Zhao, J. L. (2003). Mending the lag between commercial needs and research prototypes: a logic-based workflow verification approach. In *Proceedings of the 8th INFORMS Computing Society Conference.*

Blake, M. B. (2003). Coordinating multiple agents for workflow-oriented process orchestration. *Information System and e-Business Management, 1*(2), 387-405.

Blake, M. B., & Gomaa, H. (2005). Agent-oriented compositional approaches to services-based cross-organizational workflow. *Decision Support Systems, 40*, 31–50. doi:10.1016/j.dss.2004.04.003

Camarinha-Matos, L. M., & Afsarmanesh, H. (1999). The virtual enterprise concept. In Camarinha-Matos, L. M., & Afsarmanesh, H. (Eds.), *Infrastructures for virtual enterprises: Networking industrial enterprises* (pp. 3–14). Boston, MA: Kluwer Academic.

Chen, Q., Dayal, U., Hsu, M., & Griss, M. L. (2000). Dynamic-agents, workflow and XML for e-commerce automation. In *Proceedings of the First International Conference on Electronic Commerce and Web Technologies*, London, UK (pp. 314-323).

Christensen, E., Curbera, F., Meredith, G., & Weerawarana, S. (2002). *Web Service Description Language (WSDL) specification.* Retrieved from http://www.w3.org/TR/wsdl

CIP4. (2000). *Job definition format (JDF).* Retrieved from http://www.cip4.org/

Ericsson, N. M., & Lafon, Y. (2002). *Simple Object Access Protocol (SOAP) specification.* Retrieved from http://www.w3.org/TR/soap12-part0/

Friesen, K., & Mazloumi, N. (2004). Integration of learning management systems and web applications using web services. *Advanced Technology for Learning, 1*(1).

Fuji, T., & Tanigawa, T. (2002). The methodology for reuse of e-learning resources. In *Proceedings of the E-Learn World Conference on E-Learning in Corporate, Government, Healthcare, & Higher Education*, Montreal, QC, Canada (Vol. 1, pp. 305-310).

Gaeta, M., Ritrovato, P., & Salerno, S. (2002, September). Implementing new advanced learning scenarios through GRID technologies. In *Proceedings of the First LeGE-WG International Workshop on Educational Models for GRID Based Services*, Lausanne, Switzerland.

Gijsen, J. W. J., Szirbik, N. B., & Wagner, G. (2002). Agent technologies for virtual enterprises in the one-of-a-kind-production industry. *International Journal of Electronic Commerce, 7*(1), 9–34.

Hou, J., & Su, D. (2006). Integration of web services technology with business models within the total product design process for supplier selection. *Computers in Industry, 57*(8-9), 797. doi:10.1016/j.compind.2006.04.008

Hsu, K. C., & Ou Yang, F. C. (2005, July 5-8). OEPortal: an open, unified, and interoperable presentation-preserving e-learning portal. In *Proceedings of the 5th IEEE International Conference on Advanced Learning Technologies*, Kaohsiung, Taiwan (pp. 628-632)

IBM. (2002). *Business Process Execution Language for Web Services (BPEL4WS).* Retrieved from http://www-128.ibm.com/developerworks/library/specification/ws-bpel/

IBM. (2002). *Web Services Flow Language Specification (WSFL)*. Retrieved from http://www-3.ibm.com/software/solutions/webservices/pdf/WSFL.pdf

JCP. (2003). *Portlets Specification final release, JSR168*. Retrieved September 20, 2004, from http://jcp.org/en/jsr/detail?id=168

Korhonen, J., Pajunen, J., & Puustjarvi, J. (2003). Automatic composition of web services workflows using a semantic agent. In *Proceedings of the IEEE/WIC International Conference on Web Intelligence*, Beijing, China (pp. 566-569).

Kropp, A., Leue, C., & Thompson, R. (Eds.). (2003). *Web Services for Remote Portles (WSRP) specification of OASIS version 1.0*. Retrieved October 2, 2004, from http://www.oasis-open.org/committees/download.php/3343/oasis-200304-wsrp-specification-1.0.pdf

Kumar, A., & Wainer, J. (2005). Meta workflows as a control and coordination mechanism for exception handling in workflow systems. *Decision Support Systems, 40*, 89–105. doi:10.1016/j.dss.2004.04.006

Liao, C. J., & Ou Yang, F. C. (2004, July 21-25). A workflow framework for mobile learning objects integration by employing grid services flow language. In *Proceedings of the International Conference on Education and Information Systems, Technologies and Applications*, Orlando, FL (Vol. 1, pp. 155-160).

Liao, C. J., Ou Yang, F. C., & Hsu, K. C. (2005). A service-oriented approach for the pervasive learning grid. *Journal of Information Science and Engineering, 1*(5), 959–971.

Medjahed, B., & Bouguettaya, A. (2005). Customized delivery of e-government web services. *IEEE Intelligent Systems, 20*, 77–84. doi:10.1109/MIS.2005.103

O'Reilly, T. (2005). *What is Web 2.0*. Retrieved from http://www.oreillynet.com/pub/a/oreilly/tim/news/ 2005/09/30/ what-is-web-20.html

Puschmann, T., & Alt, R. (2004, January 5-8). Process portals - Architecture and integration. In *Proceedings of the 37th Hawaii International Conference on System Sciences*, Big Island, HI.

Puustjärvi, J. (2004). Using one-stop portal in integrating e-learning systems. *Advanced Technology for Learning, 1*(2).

Richardson, M., & Midwinter, T. (2006). Product catalogue management with semantic web services. *BT Technology Journal, 24*(4), 21. doi:10.1007/s10550-006-0094-x

RosettaNet. (2000). *Partner Interface Process (PIPs)*. Retrieved from http://www.rosettanet.org/

Shen, W., & Norrie, D. H. (2001). Dynamic manufacturing scheduling using both functional and resource related agents. *Integrated Computer-Aided Engineering, 8*(1), 17–30.

Shen, W., Norrie, H., & Barthes, J. P. (2001). *Multi-agent systems for concurrent intelligent design and manufacturing*. London, UK: Taylor & Francis.

Stanford University. (2002). *The CHAIMS project*. Retrieved from http://www-db.stanford.edu/CHAIMS/

Sycara, K., Paolucci, M., Soudry, J., & Srinivasan, N. (2004). Dynamic discovery and coordination of agent-based semantic web services. *IEEE Internet Computing, 8*(3), 66–73. doi:10.1109/MIC.2004.1297276

The TimesTen Team. (2000). High performance and scalability through application-tier, in-memory data management. In *Proceedings of the 26th International Conference on Very Large Databases*, Cairo, Egypt (pp. 677-680).

Tsalgatidou, A., Athanasopoulos, G., Pantazoglou, M., Pautasso, C., Heinis, T., & Grønmo, R. (2006). Developing scientific workflows from heterogeneous services. *SIGMOD Record, 35.*

Vieira, T. A. S. C., Casanova, M. A., & Ferrao, L. G. (2004). An ontology-driven architecture for flexible workflow execution. In *Proceedings of the WebMedia & LA-Web Joint Conference and 10th Brazilian Symposium on Multimedia and the Web and the 2nd Latin American Web Congress*, São Carlos, Brazil (pp.70-77).

W3C. (2002) *Web services.* Retrieved from http://www.w3.org/2002/ws/desc/

Wang, S. (2006). An agent-based Web service workflow model for inter-enterprise collaboration. *Expert Systems with Applications, 31,* 787–799. doi:10.1016/j.eswa.2006.01.011

Zeng, L., Ngu, A., Bentallah, B., & O'Dell, M. (2001). An agent-based approach for supporting cross-enterprise workflows. In *Proceedings of the 12th Australasian Database Conference*, Gold Coast, Queensland, Australia (pp. 123-130).

Zhao, J. L. (2006). Process-driven collaboration support for intra-agency crime analysis. *Decision Support Systems, 41,* 616–633. doi:10.1016/j.dss.2004.06.014

This work was previously published in the International Journal of Digital Library Systems, Volume 2, Issue 3, edited by Chia-Hung Wei, pp. 67-85, copyright 2011 by IGI Publishing (an imprint of IGI Global).

Chapter 18
Technostress:
Effects and Measures Among Librarians in University Libraries in Nigeria

Owajeme Justice Ofua
Delta State University, Nigeria

Tiemo Aghwotu Pereware
Niger Delta University Library, Nigeria

ABSTRACT

This study examines technostress, its effects, and measures taken to avoid it among librarians at university libraries in Nigeria. The descriptive survey design was adopted and 5 (five) university libraries in Edo and Delta States were used for the study. The sample size for the study was 79, using the purposive sampling technique, a questionnaire was the main instrument used for data collection, and simple percentage and Chi square were used to analyze the data collected. The authors found that technostress could be avoided by librarians, by taking the following measures: purchasing user friendly interface software, regular staff training on ICTs, and developing positive attitude toward technology, and so forth.

INTRODUCTION

Information and communication technology (ICT) has undoubtedly brought along many changes in libraries environment today, technological revolution in organization has not only improved efficiency but also helps reduces the problems or boredom in the workplace (Vieitez, Carcia, &

Rodriquez, 2001). The application of ICTs has immensely improved the effectiveness of library activities such as acquisition, circulation, Cataloging, references and serial services (Bichteler, 1986; Murthy & Cholin). The ability of libraries to offer access to digital information regardless of location and time has given birth to the term "Virtual Library", "Electronic Library" or "Digital library" (Saunders, 1999; Gorman, 2001,).

DOI: 10.4018/978-1-4666-2928-8.ch018

ICTs is the sine-qua-non for effective modern library management and services (Wombo & Abba, 2008). According to Aina (2004) Information and communication technology (ICT) has radically transformed most of the services provided by library. ICT is heavily utilized in the storage, processing and dissemination of information. It has made the organization of information very efficient, the delivery of basic information services more effective and the dissemination of information to users easier. It has eliminated a lot of routine and repetitive tasks in a library. ICT is now a core component of any library and information science curriculum at all levels. Any modern library and information professional must be knowledgeable in library automation, networking, internet surfing, database management processing software, statistical software, etc.

Although, technology has allowed work to be carried out faster and more efficient, many employees are not comfortable with the implementation of this technology and it involves changes and uncertainty. As a result, they experience additional stress known as techno-stress which may have negative consequence in the library activities.

Technostress is the general feeling of anxiety and the negative impact on thoughts, behavior, attitudes and body when a person is expected to deal with technology (Kupersmith, 2007, Weil & Rosen, 2000). The usage of computer integrated system, CD-ROMS and multiples database, the internet and World Wide Web (WWW) and the rapid changes of information technology has also caused enormous amounts of strain on librarians (Davis-Milles, 1998; Kupersmith, 2007).

Although, Brod (1984) looked at technostress as a disease, other researchers considered it more as an inability to adopt to change brought by technology. Davis-Milles (1998) identified technostress as a condition whereby a person has to adapt to new technology especially when there is inadequacy of the equipment, support, or the technology itself.

In the same vein, Clark and Kalin (1996), sees technostress as a resistance to change".

TECHNOSTRESS IN LIBRARIES

While technostress is well documented in libraries the world seems unaware of library work as computer related (Clute, 1998). Interestingly, Poole and Emmett (2001) explain that the 1994 job rated almanac ranked librarianship among the 25 least stressful occupations, thereby reinforcing a publicly held image that library work is not a technological field. However, in the process of adapting to the increasingly complex technologies, more users and staff have been experiencing physical and emotional stress (Saunders, 1999).

This resulted in higher level of absenteeism and turnover, higher cost for retaining new staff and increase in litigation costs related to workplace stress (Harper, 2000). Bichteler (1986) discovered that as a result of library automation some librarians feel that their personalities has changed, in which they became more computer oriented. They were easily irritated and impatient when dealing with unorganized or illogical people and found it hard to communicate with non programmers. The pressure to use the equipment efficiently and to stay on schedule has reduced their opportunities for conversation and let them to isolate themselves from other people. Moreover, the librarian also felt frustrated when there is incapability between micros and mainframe, inaccessible and unhelpful sales representative, lacking of training and inadequate time provided to practice what they have learned (Ahmad, Amin, & Ismail, 2009).

Research Questions

The research work will be guided with the following research questions:

1. What are the effects of techno-stress among librarians in the universities libraries in Delta and Edo State?
2. What measures are taken by librarians to avoid techno-stress in the universities libraries Delta and Edo State?

RESEARCH HYPOTHESES

The following null hypotheses were tested in this research work:

1. There is no significant differences in the effects of techno-stress experienced by librarians in the universities libraries in Delta and Edo State.
2. There is no significant difference in the measures taken to avoid techno-stress by librarians in the universities libraries in Delta and Edo State.

OBJECTIVES OF THE STUDY

The aim of the present study is to investigate and examine the effect of techno-stress and measure taken to avoid it among librarians in the university libraries in Nigeria. While the specific objectives are as follows:

1. The effect of techno-stress among librarians in the university in Delta and Edo State.
2. The measures taken to avoid techno-stress by librarians in the universities in Delta and Edo State.

LITERATURE REVIEW

Effect of Technostress

Inadequate staff and insufficient number of printers, terminals and work stations which caused the librarians to share equipments were more likely to lead to frustration and avoidance (Kupersmith, 1992). More so, librarians who work in an unsupportive climate perceived that their ideas were being ignored, their effort going unnoticed, there were no reward for professional development or when the organization priorities were unclear, such factors would contribute to librarian's beings much less able to deal with technology and its demands (Kupersmith, 1992).

Kupersmith (2007) confirmed that technostress existed in the library setting, in fact, more than half of the librarians surveyed (59%) felt that stress has increased in the past five years and almost two thirds of the respondents believed that the problem was somewhat serious. The study also revealed that the major causes of technostress in the library were information overload, networking problem, security issues and computer hardware, and economics. The development of internet and electronic networked resources encouraged the development of new services such as digital libraries. However, this might pose a greater challenge since the internet was also seen as a threat as it created a lot of uncertainty (Melchionda, 2007). He further explained that, the transition from automation to digitization meant that librarian had to acquire new skills and competencies be educated in new technologies which in turn added a further burden and stress to them.

Research has also shown that librarian experiences high levels of Adrenaline and Mordrenaline during work periods with computers (Arntez & Berg, 1993). Adrenaline and Noradrenaline are caterchomines secreted by the adrenal gland. Increased secretion notes of adrenaline and noradrenaline are associated with both under load and overload (stress) stimulation and emotional arousal. An aspect of technostress experienced by many librarians has been the worry that continual use of computer can change ones through pattern, value system, view of reality and ability to solve problems (Ganga, 1985). This is a stress that hit many librarians during the automation process.

Many librarians feared that their image was suffering as a result of automation. Users, they felt were viewing librarians more and more to be merely "equipment technicians and search experts" (Stewart et al., 1990). As automation unfolded, many librarians also began to experience longer working hours, as the tools needed to complete office duties become more mobile (Bichteler, 1986).

Another worry of many librarians was the possible loss of interpersonal communication in their libraries (Daskshinamuriti, 1985). Many feared that the libraries would become less human as patron turned to computers instead of professionals for information required by the terminal itself can indeed produce (Daskshinamuriti, 1985). Library workers today find that electronic mail systems, automated workstations, and the intense concentration required by the terminal itself can indeed produce an altered state, a "lonely state" (Fine, 1986). With the advent of technology in the library environment, many librarians experienced a change in their work place culture. According to Joseph (1980), in his work entitled" technocrats and mandarins; the two cultures of librarianship which identified a schism developing between two types of librarians… those who admire innovation and those are suspicious of change and respectful of tradition."

Measures Taken to Avoid Technostress

Champion (1988) suggested that in order to succeed in avoiding technostress, manager must "recognize that technology will, by its nature, result in changes in (1) the environment, (2) relationship; (3) self-imposed role of the librarians". She offers the following recommendations for managers:

- Meet the challenges of technology head on-think about change and what is data mean and how it can be use.
- Rewrite job descriptions as often as needed.

- Be aware of techno stressor, discuss them and plans for them.
- Get support from computer enthusiasts in your community.
- Design a special area that let staff works on computer in a quiet, adult only area.
- Regard technology as a tool, not a force for maintaining power.
- Encourage inquiry and problem solving.
- Convince workers to participate in planning.
- Reassure staff that mistakes will be made and tolerated.
- Reinforce the belief that people are more important than machine.
- Delegates details that people are more important than machines.
- Delegates details that can be handled efficiently by someone else.
- Build teams of co-workers to learn the technology.

The following recommendations were reported to help avoid technostress, training of staffing, communication with staff, better technical support, sufficient, staffing, user friendly interfaces, positive attitudes, goal setting, standardization, co-evolve with technology ergonomics. Other include, accept diversity, contingency plan, counseling, training for users and user friendly jargon (Clute, 1989).

RESEARCH METHODOLOGY

The research design was a descriptive study. The sample size for the study was 79. The purposive technique was used. The instrument used was the questionnaire. Seventy-nine questionnaires were administered to academic and non academic librarians in 5 (five) university libraries in Edo and Delta States, out of which 69 questionnaires were retrieved and found usable for data analysis. The data obtained from the retrieved copies of the questionnaire were analyzed using simple percentage in order to answer the research questions, and t-test statistical technique to test the formulated hypotheses.

Table 1 indicates the number of university libraries for the study. Copies of the questionnaires were sent to 79 academic and non academic librarians of which 69 response were returned from the 5 university libraries in Edo and Delta States as at the time of this study (2007/2008 session). It is observed that high responses came from the government owned universities. The reason for this is that those universities have the highest number of librarians and they are old generation university libraries. 39(57%) of the 69 respondents were males and 30 (43%) were females.

As can be seen from Table 2, avoidance of some technologies ranked highest with 7 (10%) male on strongly agree and 20 (29%) on agree respectively. while female 9 (13%) on strong agree and 11(16%) on agree as a major effect of technostress among (males /female) librarians in universities libraries under study. This is followed by continued use of manual techniques to perform some operation with 6 (8%) on strongly agree and 22 (23%) on agree by male, while female had 7 (10%) on strongly agree and 12 (17%) on agree respectively.

One of the purposes of this study was to find out the effect of technostress among librarians. The respondents agreed on range of issues as major effects of technostress among librarians, some of the effects indentified include; avoidance of some technologies, use of manual techniques to perform some operation, poor job performance, job burnout, longer working hour, loss of interpersonal communication in working place, fear that technologies will alter/ taken over one's job/ loss of status and others. Some of the finding of this study agreed with those of Ganga (1985) that an aspect of technostress experienced by many librarians has been the worry that continual use of computer can change one's thought patterns, value system view of reality and ability to solve problems. It is also in agreement with Convey (1982) quoted in Dakshinamuritit (1985) that a significant aspect of technostress is the fear technology brings to workplace, that one's position might one day be not just changed but even eliminated, and that the very culture of profession can be changing.

As can be seen in Table 3, positive attitudes toward technology ranked highest as the major measures taken by librarians to avoid technostress with male 26 (38%) and female 22 (32%) on strong agreed respectively. This is followed by buying/using users friendly interface software in the libraries with male 22 (32%) and female 12 (17%) who agreed on this, includes adequate staff training, counseling, user friendly language/jargon co-evolve/live with technology among others.

The second purpose of this study was to determined measures taken by librarians to avoid technostress. From these findings over 80% of respondents supported staff training on information and communication technologies, positive

Table 1. University libraries and number of respondents (Field work 2007/2008)

Name of library	No administered	No retrieved	Male	Female
Delta State University Library	41	34	21	13
University of Benin Library	18	16	10	6
Novena University Library, Amai	3	3	2	1
Benson Idahosa University Library, Benin-city	8	7	2	5
Iginedon University Libraries, Okada	9	9	4	5
Total	79	69	39	30

Table 2. Effect of technostress

Effect	Sex	Strongly agree		Agree		Disagree		Strongly disagree		Undecided	
		N	%	N	%	N	%	N	%	N	%
Avoidance of some technologies	Male	7	10	20	29	2	3	7	10	3	4
	Female	9	13	11	16	2	3	8	2	-	-
Continued use of manual techniques to perform some operation	Male	6	9	22	32	5	7	2	3	4	6
	Female	7	10	12	17	6	9	4	6	1	1
Poor job performance	Male	6	9	14	20	13	19	4	6	2	3
	Female	3	4	13	19	11	16	2	3	1	1
Error in judgment	Male	3	4	8	12	22	32	4	6	2	3
	Female	-	-	9	13	13	9	5	7	3	4
Cardiac problem	Male	-	-	9	13	13	19	5	7	3	4
	Female	2	3	3	12	11	16	5	7	4	6
Hypertension	Male	4	6	5	7	22	32	6	9	2	3
	Female	2	3	6	9	12	17	5	7	5	7
Magrine/headaches	Male	2	3	9	13	14	20	9	13	5	7
	Female	3	4	7	10	13	19	7	10	-	-
Job burnout	Male	5	7	13	19	12	17	4	6	5	7
	Female	5	7	13	19	8	12	4	6	-	-
Fear that technologies will alter/take one job/loss of job status	Male	4	6	7	10	14	20	6	9	8	12
	Female	3	4	7	10	15	22	5	7	-	-
Longer working hours	Male	6	9	15	22	11	16	5	7	2	3
	Female	3	4	13	19	10	14	2	3	2	3
Loss of interpersonal communication workplace	Male	2	3	12	17	21	30	4	6	-	-
	Female	2	3	8	12	11	36	4	6	5	7

attitude towards technology, setting realistic goals, and purchasing user friendly interface to avoid technostress. These findings collaborates with Clute (1989) who reported measures taken to avoid technostress for staff to include, communication with staff, better technical support, sufficient user friendly interface, positive attitude toward technologies, goal setting, standardization, co-evolve with technology, training for users, buying friendly jargon software, etc.

Hypotheses Testing

Hypothesis I

There is no significance mean difference in the effect of technostress experienced by both males and female librarians. The data in Table 4 were use to test this hypothesis.

It is observed that the t-calculated of 0.74 is less than the t-critical of 1.67. This means that null hypothesis which states that there is no significant mean difference in the effect of technostress experienced by both male and female librarians is accepted. Therefore both male and females librarians in the university libraries ex-

Table 3. Measures taken to avoid technostress

Measures	Sex	Strongly agree		Agree		Disagree		Strongly disagree		Undecided	
		N	%	N	%	N	%	N	%	N	%
Staff training	Male	22	23	13	19	3	4	-	-	1	1
	Female	15	22	15	22	-	-	-	-	-	-
Communication with staff	Male	13	19	20	29	3	4	1	1	2	3
	Female	14	20	12	17	2	3	2	3	-	-
Good technological support	Male	15	22	17	25	5	7	-	-	2	3
	Female	14	20	16	23	-	-	-	-	-	-
Adequate staffing	Male	11	16	22	32	6	9	-	-	-	-
	Female	11	16	13	19	5	7	-	-	-	-
User friendly	Male	13	19	22	32	4	6	-	-	-	-
	Female	14	20	12	17	4	6	-	-	-	-
Positive attitudes toward technology	Male	26	38	13	19	-	-	-	-	-	-
	Female	22	32	11	16	2	3	2	3	2	3
Setting realistic goals	Male	22	32	11	16	2	3	2	3	2	3
	Female	15	2	11	16	2	3	1	1	1	1
Standardizations	Male	13	19	20	29	4	6	2	3	-	-
	Female	13	19	10	14	2	3	1	1	4	6
Co evolve/low with technology	Male	11	16	23	33	4	6	1	1	-	-
	Female	8	12	13	19	4	6	-	-	5	7
Ergonomic	Male	7	10	15	22	8	12	-	-	9	13
	Female	7	10	14	20	5	7	-	-	4	6
Developing contingency plans	Male	9	13	20	35	2	6	-	-	2	3
	Female	7	10	15	22	-	-	-	-	8	12
Accept diversity	Male	9	13	20	29	6	9	1	1	3	4
	Female	8	12	11	16	3	4	-	-	8	12
Counseling	Male	9	10	24	35	5	7	-	-	1	1
	Female	7	13	14	20	8	12	-	-	1	1
Providing I T training to user	Male	17	25	15	22	6	9	-	-	1	1
	Female	16	23	13	19	-	-	-	-	1	1
User friendly language Jargon	Male	9	13	22	32	4	6	-	-	4	6
	Female	9	13	15	22	4	6	-	-	2	2

Table 4. t-test summary table for effects of technostress

SEX	N	X	SD	DF	T-CAL	T-CRITICAL	DECISION
Male	39	3.35	0.29	67	0.74	1.67	Accepted
Female	30	3.27	0.54				

Table 5. t-test summary table for measures taken to avoid technostress

SEX	N	X	SD	DF	T-CAL	T-CRITICAL	DECISION
Male	39	4.00	0.30	67	-1.25	1.67	Accepted
Female	30	4.00	0.35				

perienced almost the same effect of technological stress, as also reported by Ganga (1985) an aspect of technostress experience by many librarian has been the worry that continual use of computers can change ones thought, value, system, views of reality and ability to solve problems.

Hypothesis II

There is no significant mean difference in the measure taken to avoid technostress by both male and female librarians. The data in Table 5 are use to test this hypothesis.

The t-test analysis indicates that the t-calculated of -1.25 is less than the t-critical of 1.67. This means that the null hypothesis which states that there is no significant mean difference in the measure taken to avoid techno stress by both male and female librarians is accepted.

SUMMARY OF FINDINGS

The following are the summary of findings of this study,

1. Avoidance of some technologies and continued used of manual technique to perform some operation in the libraries had been discovered to be the major effects of technostress among librarians in university libraries.
2. Technostress can be avoided by librarians, by taking the following measure:
   a. Purchasing user friendly interface software,
   b. Regular Staff training on ICTs, and
   c. Develop positive attitude towards technology
3. There is no significance mean difference in the effect of technostress experienced by both male and female librarians in university libraries.
4. There is no significance mean difference in the measure taken to avoid technostress by both males and females librarians in university libraries.

CONCLUSION AND RECOMMENDATION

Based on the finding of this study it could be concluded that among those who have been heavily affected by technostress are librarians. Thus, this paper proposed a study on the effect and measures taken by librarians working in the academic libraries in Nigerian's higher institutions of learning with particular references to academic libraries in Edo and Delta State. The results of these findings will generate new knowledge and provide fresh insights that will improve libraries and librarians in dealing with the problem of technostress. Knowing the effect of technostress, and measures taken to avoid it by librarians and libraries will enable public and private higher learning institution libraries and librarians to plans appropriate mechanisms in managing stress due to technology and maintain a high level of modern libraries in this information age.

REFERENCES

Ahmed, U. N. U., Amin, W. K. W., & Ismali, W. K. (2009). The impact of technostress on organization commitment among Malaysian academic librarians. *Singapore Journal of Library & Information Management*, *38*, 103–123.

Aina, L. O. (2004). Coping with the challenges of library and information delivery services: The need for institutional professional development. In *Proceedings of the Nigerian Library Association Conference*.

Arnetz, B. B., & Berg, M. (1993). Tehnolosress psychological consequences of poor man-machine interface. In Smith, M. J., & Salvend, G. (Eds.), *Human computer interaction: applications and case studies* (pp. 891–896). Amsterdam, The Netherlands: Elsevier.

Barlette, V. (1995). Avoiding computer avoidance. *Library Administration and Management*, *9*(4), 225–230.

Bichteler, J. (1986). Human aspect of high tech in special Libraries. *Special Libraries*, *9*(3), 121–128.

Brod, C. (1984). *Technostress: The human cost of the computer revolution*. Reading, MA: Addison-Wesley.

Brosnan, M., & Thorpe, S. (2001, July 12-14). Does technophobia conform to DSM-1V criteria for a specific phobia (300.29)? In *Proceedings of the 22nd International Conference of STAR, the International Society for Stress and Anxiety Research*, Palma de Mallorca, Spain.

Champion, S. (1988). Technostress: Technology toll. *School Library Journal*, *3*(3), 48–51.

Chua, S. L., Chen, D., & Wong, A. F. L. (1999). Computer anxiety and its correlates: a meta-analysis. *Computers in Human Behavior*, *15*, 609–623. doi:10.1016/S0747-5632(99)00039-4

Clark, K., & Kalin, S. (1996). Technostress out? *Library Journal*, *121*(13), 30–32.

Clute, R. (1998). *Technostress: A content analysis* (Unpublished master's thesis). Kent State University, East Liverpool, OH.

Dakshinamurti, C. (1985). Automations effect on library personnel. *Canadian Library Journal*, 343-351.

David-mills, N. (1998). *Technostress and the organization*. Retrieved September 9, 2008, from http://webmt.edu/ninadm/mia.htm

Fine, S. F. (1986, April 14-16). Terminal paralysis or showdown at the interface. In D. Shaw (Ed.), *Human aspects of library automation: Helping staff and patrons cope (clinic on library applications of data processing)* (pp. 3-15). Urbana-Champaign, IL: Graduate School of Library and Information Sciences, University of Illinois.

Gorman, M. (2001). Technostress and library value. *Library Journal*, *26*(7), 48–50.

Harper, S. (2000). *Managing technostress in UK libraries. A realistic guide*. Retrieved September 12, 2007 from http://www.ariadne.ac.uk/issue25/technostress

Kupersmith, J. (2007). *Technostress in libraries*. Retrieved September 9, 2007, from http://www.net/stres.html

Marcoulides, G. A. (1988). The relationship between computer anxiety and computer achievement. *Journal of Educational Computing Research*, *4*(2), 151–158. doi:10.2190/J5N4-24HK-567V-AT6E

Melchionda, M. G. (2007). Librarians in the age of the Internet: Their attitudes and roles. *New Library World*, *108*(3-4), 123–140. doi:10.1108/03074800710735339

Murthy, T. A. V., & Cholin, V. S. (2003). *Library automation*. Retrieved December 19, 2008, from http://dspace.inflibnet.ac.in/bitstream/1994/170/3/03cali_1.pdf

Poole, C. E., & Emment, D. (2001). *Technological change in the work place: A Starwide survey of community college library and learning resources personnel*. Retrieved March 16, 2006, from http://www.ct.org

Saunders, L. M. (1999). The human element in the virtual library. *Library Trends*, *47*(4), 771–789.

Stewart, L., Chiang, K. S., & Coons, B. (2006). *Public access CD-ROMS in libraries: case studies (supplement to computers in libraries)*. Westport, CT: Mecklermedia.

Thorpe, S., & Brosnan, M. (2001, July 12-14). A single treatment for technopbobia. In *Proceedings of the 22nd International Conference of STAR, the International Society for Stress and Anxiety Research*, Palma de Mallorca, Spain.

Vieitez, J. C., Carcia, A. D. L. T., & Rodriguez, M. T. V. (2001). Perception of job security in a process of technological change: Its influence on psychological well-being. *Behaviour & Information Technology*, *20*(3), 213–223.

Weil, M. M., & Rosen, L. D. (2000). *Four years study shows more Technology @ work and @ home but more hesitancy about trying new technology*. Retrieved March 19, 2006, from http://www.Human-warecom/businessstudy.htm

Womboh, B. S. H., & Tukur, A. (2008). The state of Information and Communication Technology (ICT) in Nigeria University libraries: The experience of Ibrahim Babangida Libraries, Federal University of Technology, Yola. *Library Philosophy and Practice, 2008*.

Chapter 19
Predicting Users' Acceptance of E–Library from the Perspective of Technology Acceptance Model

Adeyinka Tella
University of Ilorin, Nigeria

ABSTRACT

Universities are investing heavily in electronic resources. As a way of embracing new developments, the University of Ilorin, Nigeria, has spent millions of dollars building a usable e-library. However, research indicates that potential users may still not use e-libraries. This study examines user acceptance of e-library from the perspective of technology acceptance mode (TAM). E-library system characteristics, organisational context, and individual characteristics are identified as variables that determine acceptance. Data was collected through self-designed questionnaire from 1,500 undergraduate users of the e-library. The findings revealed that the acceptance constructs, ease of use, perceived usefulness, actual use, satisfaction, relevance, awareness, computer/internet self-efficacy, and social influence, significantly correlate with e-library acceptance. The study suggests that all eight factors jointly pulled 69% prediction of the users' acceptance of e-library. The study recommends that e-library users at the university increase their computer and internet self-efficacy, which significantly enhances their use of the e-library system. The university can assist in this matter by organising computer training for the students.

DOI: 10.4018/978-1-4666-2928-8.ch019

INTRODUCTION

Electronic library is understood to be digital collection of real or virtual resources, which may also be available elsewhere. These resources must be whole works, with which humans can have a complete cognitive or affective engagement. E-libraries are collections of information that have associated services delivered to user communities using a variety of technologies (Arms, 2000). The collections of information can be scientific, business or personal data and can be represented as a digital text, image, audio, video or other media (Frias-Martinez & Chen, 2005). Electronic libraries provide opportunities for widespread dissemination of information in a timely fashion. With this development, access to information in a networked world is now the concerned of many people. Electronic libraries are one of the most common web services for information seeking. Their main advantage is also their main disadvantages. Digital libraries are designed with a global approach for everyone. This implies that all users are presented with the same interface. Previous studies have proved to help users search information by matching the interface to their preferences.

Due to the amount and great variety of information stored by e-libraries, they have become, with search engines in general, one of the major web services (Liaw & Huang, 2003), which are faced by a diverse population of users who have heterogeneous background, skills, and preferences. Considering how the interfaces of e-libraries can support different users to accomplish their tasks is important. As suggested by previous studies in information seeking (Marchionini et al., 1998; Blandford et al., 2001), matching the interface with users' preferences can help them to achieve their tasks in a satisfactory way. Nevertheless, in general, e-libraries have a global approach in which the entire users are presented with the same interface, regardless of the diversity of users' preferences.

Increased use of ICT in University libraries results in hybrid systems. It is now the common practice in Africa and other developing countries to find donors providing funding to support ICT infrastructure in university libraries as also the case in Nigeria. The availability of ICT is now making it possible for libraries to provide electronic services to users. With this these development, it is now the thought of many people that introduction of new technology will results into its use (Tibenderana & Ogao, 2008). However, technology acceptance model makes it clear that there are other factors. At the University of Ilorin, Nigeria; resources have been heavily invested on the electronic library to support the services provided by the manual library. In this context, it is essential to study the degree of users' acceptance of the library with the interface and functionalities provided by it.

Extant literature has revealed lack of evaluation models for library ICT use at the university of Ilorin and universities in Africa as a whole (Tibenderana & Ogao, 2008). Similarly, study has revealed absence of tested and validated technology acceptance models under the e-library prevalent in developing countries (Baba & Broady, 1998). It is against this backdrop that this study examined the predictors of users' acceptance of e-library at the University of Ilorin, Nigeria. Specifically, the study will achieve the following objectives:

1. Determine the predictors of e-library acceptance.
2. Develop a framework for measuring e-library acceptance from the perspective of technology acceptance model.
3. To examine the predictive capability of each of the TAM variables and other variables not included in TAM on acceptance of e—library.

LITERATURE REVIEW

Background of the University of Ilorin

The University of Ilorin was established by a decree of the Federal Military Government of Nigeria in August, 1975 with mandate to implement one of the educational directives of the country's national development plans which aimed at providing more opportunities for Nigerians aspiring to acquire university education and to generate high level of man-power. In line with this goal, the University of Ilorin Library was established in May 1976 to support teaching and learning of the parent institution. In order to meet information needs of the University community, the library acquired numerous print and electronic materials that cut across all disciplines of studies in the University. The University library, through the support of the National University Commission (NUC), subscribed to a number of electronic information resources (Databases) that are expected to also enhance teaching, learning and research activities of the University community. These electronic resources can be accessed either from the Electronic library centre or from any computer connected to the internet with the aid of User name and password already provided to members of the University community.

E-Library at the University of Ilorin

The e-library at the University of Ilorin was established as a result of positive working relationship between the university and the United Bank for Africa Plc. Based on this, the bank donated a building on a land provided by the university. On completion, the building was equipped with 60 desktop computers connected to the internet and two printers. The e-library was commissioned on 23rd October, 2008, headed by a deputy librarian digitization. Users of the library have the opportunity of access to online materials such as books,

journals, etc., and databases that the university subscribed. Since inception in 2008, students and staff at the university have been enjoying the facility for research and teaching.

E-Library

An electronic library is a managed collection of information, with associated services, where the information is stored in digital formats and accessible over a network. What could be noted from this definition is that the information is managed. Therefore, a stream of data sent to earth from a satellite is not a library. The same data, when organized systematically, becomes a digital library collection (Arms, 2000).

In terms of characteristics, electronic libraries contain diverse collections of information for use by many different users. Electronic libraries range in size from tiny to huge. They can use any type of computing equipment and any suitable software. The unifying theme is that information is organized on computers and available over a network, with procedures to select the material in the collections, to organize it, to make it available to users, and to archive it. As electronic libraries are different from the traditional libraries, so also there are some similarities between them. The shift from traditional libraries to the electronic or digital is not merely a technological evolution, but requires a change in the paradigm by which people access and interact with information.

Going by Reddy et al. (1999) position, a traditional library is characterized by "its emphasis on storage and preservation of physical items, particularly books and periodicals, cataloguing at a high level rather than one of detail, e.g., author and subject indexes as opposed to full text, browsing based on physical proximity of related materials". By contrast, an electronic library differs from the above in the following ways: emphasis on access to digitized materials wherever they may be located, with digitization eliminating the need to own or store a physical item, cataloguing down to individual words, browsing based on hyperlinks, keyword, or any defined measure of relatedness; materials on the same subject do not need to be near one another in any physical sense, broadcast technology; users need not visit a digital library except electronically (Reddy et al., 1999). According to Reddy et al. (1999), e-library exists at any place they can access it, e.g., home, school, office, or in a car.

Acceptance and Use of E-Library

Extant literature has revealed factors which promote or hinder the adoption and usage of ICT especially in digital libraries including: *benefits/ usefulness*: (Bar-Ilan, Peritz, & Wolman, 2003; Baruchson-Arbib & Shor, 2002; Entlich et al., 1996; Harless & Allen, 1999; Marchonini, 2000; Theng et al., 2007; Thong, Hong, & Tam, 2002, 2004), *awareness* (Bar-Ilan, Peritz, & Wolman, 2003; Bishop, 2002; Harless & Allen, 1999; Nicholson, 2004), *relevance* (Kwak et al., 2002; Nicholson, 2004; Vaidyanathan et al., 2005; Nov & Ye, 2008), among others, and *ease of use* (Buttenfield, 1999; Lagier, 2002; Nov & Ye, 2008) and many others.

In an effort to design an evaluation model for libraries, Nicholson (2004) developed a matrix conceptual framework for holistic measurement and cumulative evaluation of library services. He analyzed the relevance of information and introduced the concept of aboutness, which is based on a content match between the query and the documents being sought. In Nicholson's view, *aboutness* refers to the location of the information within the system (e-library in this case). *Usability* refers to how well the system can be used without one having problems. *Knowledge status* refers to how well one is aware of what is available, and is linked to the introduced concept of awareness. *Value of* works refers to the value/ benefits that the material has to the user, which is largely influenced by the relevance of the work, and is linked to the introduced independent vari-

able of relevancy where an information seeker puts in a query, the system searches through to answer the query. If e-library services are relevant or valuable to the information seeker, the query will be answered accordingly. Nicholson (2004) therefore views users' use of library services as being affected by their awareness and by the relevance to them of the library's offerings. The two factors are further stressed by Vaidyanathan et al. (2005), who studied digital library system components' acceptability.

Technology Acceptance Model

To put very simply, electronic libraries offer the potential to greatly improve how individuals search and retrieve information (Borgman, Smat, Milwood, & Finley, 2005). However, as with other information systems, user acceptance is a key factor in the success and full utilization of electronic libraries (Nov & Ye, 2008).

The technology acceptance model is one of the pioneer and most powerful models for determining acceptance and adoption of information system. It is one of the early IS model developed from the Theory of Reason Action (TRA) by Fishbein and Ajzen (1975). The technology acceptance model (TAM) (Davis, 1989) is the most widely used conceptual model in the technology-acceptance literature. Following the introduction of TAM, numerous studies have replicated and extended Davis' work (e.g., Lee, Kozar, & Larsen, 2003), including some in the realm of electronic libraries (e.g., Hong et al., 2002; Kim, 2006; Thong et al., 2002). According to TAM, perceived usefulness (PU) and perceived ease of use (PEOU) are the two key user beliefs affecting intention to adopt a technology. Given the importance of PU and PEOU in determining user acceptance, researchers have taken great interest in identifying the antecedents of these user beliefs. For PEOU, researchers have identified two main categories of antecedents (Hong et al., 2002), namely, system characteristics and individual differences. System characteristics such as compatibility (Karahanna et al., 2006) and objective usability (Venkatesh & Davis, 1996), as well as individual differences in computer self-efficacy and computer anxiety (e.g., Venkatesh, 2000) were found to influence PEOU.

Though research is advancing the understanding of PEOU antecedents stemming from individual differences, this area of research still requires more work (Nov & Ye, 2008). As pointed out by Lee et al. (2003) "a deeper understanding of factors contributing to ease of use and usefulness is needed" and "more efforts to examine the broader environmental factors are necessary." (pp. 766–767). This study is a response to this suggestion.

Modification of TAM

Technology acceptance model TAM was modified in to arrive at a variables or factors for predicting e-libraries acceptance. By the way of modification, some variables were added. These are:

- **Social Influence:** The degree to which important others believed s/he should use the digital libraries and services provided. This variable was added because it is assumed that significant others like peers can influence acceptance of digital libraries.
- **Relevance:** The degree to which something is closely connected with the subject of concern or the situation one is thinking about (Thong et al., 2004). Relevance was added because it is assumed that a service must be appropriate before it can attract usage.
- **Usage:** The degree to which one plans to use a technology after he/she has found out its usefulness.
- **Awareness:** The degree an individual knows the existence of something, and its availability for his/her uses (Nicholson, 2004).

- **Computer/Internet self-efficacy:** This is the degree to which an individual is able to use the computer and the internet. It is assumed that this will influence the use of the services provided by digital libraries. The effective use is expected to lead to acceptance.

Statement of Hypotheses

1. Ease of use will predict users' acceptance of e- libraries.
2. Perceived usefulness will leads to users' acceptance of e libraries.
3. Usage will leads to users' acceptance of e-libraries.
4. User satisfaction will lead to acceptance of e-libraries.
5. Relevance will lead to users' acceptance of e-libraries.
6. Awareness will lead to users' acceptance of e-libraries.
7. Computer/Internet self-efficacy will lead to users' acceptance of e-libraries.
8. Social influence will lead to users' acceptance of e-libraries.
9. All the eight constructs/factors will significantly lead to uses' acceptance of e-library.

METHODOLOGY

A pure quantitative method using survey approach was adopted for the study. This approach was chosen to allow the researcher drawn on large sample which is representative of the total population (Babie, 2004). Moreover, survey approach was chosen because it is the most prominent approach used in previous related studies (e.g., Amroso & Hunsinger, 2009).

Population and Sample

The target population for this study comprised the undergraduate students at the University of Ilorin, Nigeria. Currently, the total population of undergraduate students in this university is 16,800. Israel (2003) model was used to select the sample for the study. The model states that: Sample size for ±3%, ±5%, ±7% and ±10% precision levels where confidence level is 95% and P=.5. In the light of this, ±3% was taken for precision, while the population is 16,800 at 95% confidence. Therefore, the sample should be 1,034. The target of this study was to include only the users of e-libraries at the university in the study. At the first stage of the sample, 2,500 undergraduate students were included, out of which 1,500 were identified as users of the university e-library. This 1500 constituted the sample for the study.

Instrument

A self-designed questionnaire with items adapted from various scale used in previous related studies was used. The various constructs in the question-naire were measured to examine the predicting factors of users' acceptance of digital libraries. Previous TAM related studies were used to derive the constructs for the study. Five-point Likert format ranging from strongly agree to strongly disagree was adopted for the instrument. The instrument (the questionnaire) consisted of eight sections to measure the constructs for predicting acceptance and to capture demographic data.

Reliability and Validity

To determine the validity of the instrument (questionnaire), it was given to two experts in IS research in order to assist in ensuring its face and content validity. Strong support for construct validity was found by examining the factor analysis data. The results assisted in the modification of the items in the instrument. To establish the reli-ability of the questionnaire, it was administered on 20 students who did not eventually participated in the study. Data collected were subjected to Cronbach Alpha. By examining the Cronbach Alpha reliability coefficients, strong support was reported for construct reliability. All the sub-section of the instrument showed relatively high Cronbach Alpha co-efficients at $\alpha > 0.80$. Principal component analysis was conducted with a nine-factor solution, with eigen values greater than 1.0, explaining 82.5% of the variance in the data set. Tables for Cronbach Alpha coefficients, factor analysis, and eigen values are not included but are available upon request.

Procedure for Data Collection

The questionnaire was administered personally by the researcher to the respondents. All the respondents were administered the questionnaire in their respective faculty during a core course (core courses are course which the entire students of the faculty must offer and pass before graduation). The administration exercise took ten days. A total of 2500 copies of questionnaire were administered out of which 1500 were identified as users of e-libraries. This eventually constituted the sample for the study.

Data Analysis and Results

Pearson Correlations Method was used to examine the relationships between the dependent variable (users' acceptance) with the independent variables (i.e., predictive constructs) while regression analysis was used to find out the predictors of users' acceptance among the constructs. The results of analyses are presented as follows.

BIO-DATA INFORMATION

Table 1 reveals that the highest number of respondents was from the faculty of Communication and

Table 1. Respondents distribution by faculties (1500)

Faculties	Frequency	Percentage
Art	131	8.7
Agric. Science	125	8.3
Business and Soc. Sciences	227	15.1
Comm. & Info. Sciences	280	18.6
Education	242	16.1
Engineering	164	10.9
Science	213	14.2
Law	118	7.8
Total	1500	100.0

Information Sciences with 18.6%. This is followed by the faculty of Education 16.1% respectively. The faculty of Business and Social sciences is the next with 15.1%. Other faculties followed in this order: Science, 14.2%; faculty of Engineering, 10.9% and faculty of Art 8.7%, faculty of Agricultural Science 8.3% while faculty of Law had the least with 7.8%. Summarily, eight (8) faculties out of the 11 faculties that made up the university participated in the studies. The higher number of respondents from the faculty of Communication and Information Sciences indicates that they have the highest number of students using the e-library in the university. This may be attributed to the nature of the courses in the faculty majority of which are computer and ICT oriented.

The results in Table 2 reveal that respondents in 100 levels (year one) were the majority with 462 (30.8This is followed by respondents in 200 level (year two) with 369 (24.6%). Respondents in 300 level (year three) followed with 305 (20.3%), respondents in 400 level (year four) were 297 (19.8%) while respondents in 500 level were the lowest with 67 (4.5%). The lower rate of participation of the respondents in 500 level (year five) may be attributed to the fact that very limited

number of faculties and departments has course duration of five years.

RESULTS OF HYPOTHESES 1 THROUGH 8

The results in Table 3 suggest all the constructs significantly correlate with users' acceptance of e-library. This confirms hypotheses 1 through 8. To establish the joint prediction of the construct and contribution of each to the prediction of e-library acceptance, a multiple regression analysis was conducted. The result is presented as follows.

Table 4 suggests that the R square = 0.853, R value adjusted =0.544, and the overall correlation of all the e-payment predictors yielded an R = 69, while the standard error of the estimate yielded 15.91. In the second step, the analysis of variance performed on multiple regressions yielded an F-ratio value of 10.61. This was found to be significant at 0.05 levels. These results suggest that all the nine e-library acceptance constructs together made 69% of users' acceptance of e-library. This suggests that all eight factors jointly predict the users' acceptance of e-library.

Table 5 suggests that each of the independent variables (factors) made a significant prediction of e-library acceptance. In terms of the magnitude of the prediction, perceived ease of use made the most significant with (Beta, .084, t = 5.27), followed by user satisfaction with (Beta = 0. 144, t = 4.79). The next predicting value was exerted by computer/internet self-efficacy (Beta = 0.224, t = 4.61. This is followed by perceived usefulness (Beta = 0144, t = 4.44). The other factors made a significant prediction in the following order: actual use (Beta 0.95, t = 3.10); relevance (Beta = 0.3.014; t = 3.01); awareness (Beta = 0.75; t = 1.88); while social influence made the least prediction with (Beta = 0.158; t = 1.40). These suggest that all the constructs, are good predictors of e-library acceptance. This confirms hypothesis 9.

Table 2. Respondents distribution by levels of studies (1500)

Levels Faculties	100	200	300	400	500	Total
Art	21	31	37	42	-	131
Agric. Science	23	25	30	30	17	125
BBS	74	60	48	45	-	227
Comm. & Info. Sciences	120	60	50	50	-	280
Education	74	68	50	50	-	242
Engineering	40	33	31	30	30	164
Science	78	66	39	30	-	213
Law	32	26	20	20	20	118
Total	462	369	305	297	67	1500

Discussion of Findings

This study has examined the predictors of e-library acceptance by the undergraduate students at the University of Ilorin, Nigeria. The findings of the study have revealed among others that all the e-library acceptance constructs significantly correlate with users' acceptance of e-library. Similarly, the results suggest that all eight factors jointly predict the users' acceptance of e-library. At the same time, all the constructs are good predictors of e-library acceptance.

The correlation of the factors, ease of use, perceived usefulness, actual use, satisfaction, relevance, awareness, computer/internet self-efficacy and social influence with e-library acceptance corroborate the earlier findings in the literature, e.g., *usefulness* (Bar-Ilan, Peritz, & Wolman, 2003; Baruchson-Arbib & Shor, 2002), *awareness* (Bar-Ilan, Peritz, & Wolman, 2003; Bishop, 2002), *relevance* (Kwak et al., 2002; Nicholson, 2004), and *ease of use* (Lagier, 2002; Nov & Ye, 2008). Similarly, it also confirms Nicholson (2004) who viewed users' use of library services as being affected by their awareness and by the relevance of

Table 3. Pearson correlation between the constructs and the dependent variable (e-library acceptance (1500)

Constructs	Number	Mean	Standard Deviation	Correlation Co-Efficient
Perceived ease of use	1500	5.12	.670	.66**
Perceived usefulness	1500	5.09	.610	.45**
Actual use	1500	4.28	.540	.48**
Satisfaction	1500	5.46	.640	.67**
Relevance	1500	5.24	.570	.53**
Awareness	1500	4.63	.510	.40**
Computer/internet self-efficacy	1500	5.74	.520	.60**
Social Influence	1500	4.32	.490	.38**
Acceptance (constant)	1500	4.19	.770	.77**

** Significant correlation

Table 4. Summary of multiple regression analysis on the combine prediction of e-library (dependent variable) by the nine predictive factors (Independent variables) (N = 1500)

Model Summary				
Model	R	R. Square	Adjusted Square	Standard Error of the Estimate
1	.694	0.853	.544	15.91284
ANOVA				
Model		Sums of Squares	Df	Mean Square	F.ratio	Sig.
1	Regression	255154.766	9	2,296.392	10.61	.05
	Residual	145243.131	1491	216.557		
	Total	400397.897	1500			

the library's offerings. Vaidyanathan et al. (2005), also stressed the importance of relevance and awareness in his study on digital library system components' acceptability. Furthermore, researchers such as Lee, Kozar, and Larsen (2003), Hong et al. (2002), Kim (2006), and Thong et al. (2002) have all reported most of the constructs in this study as good determinant of e-library adoption/acceptance. Therefore, it can be emphatically stated that this results is not a co-incidence but rather revealing the constructs used in this study as important and good determinant of acceptance of e-library.

SUMMARY AND CONCLUSION

So far, predictors and accompanying tool to measure users' acceptance of e-library at the University of Ilorin, Nigeria has been identified and developed. The preliminary results of the factors in this study predict 69% of users' acceptance of e-library. This is considered a further improvement on TAM model by Davies et al. (1989). Similarly, the findings of the study have revealed among others that the entire e-library acceptance constructs: ease of use, perceived usefulness, actual use, satisfaction, relevance, awareness, computer/internet self-efficacy and social influence significantly correlate with users'

Table 5. Contribution of the factors to the prediction of acceptance of e-library acceptance (N = 1500)

Model		Unstandardised Coefficients		Standardised Coefficients	T	Sig.
		B	Std Error	Beta		
1	(Constant)	11.231	4.145		7.209	.000
	Perceived ease of use	.689	.352	.084	5.270	.000
	Perceived usefulness	1.225	.427	.144	4.441	.000
	Actual use	.518	.322	.095	3.100	.000
	Satisfaction	1.069	.466	.108	4.788	.000
	Relevance	1.211	.328	.150	3.014	.000
	Awareness	.776	360	.075	1.881	.000
	Comp/Internet SE	1.330	.294	.224	4.612	.000
	Social influence	.962	.275	.158	1.402	.000

acceptance. Moreover, the study suggests that all eight factors jointly predict the users' acceptance of e-library; and that, all the constructs are good predictors of e-library acceptance.

Limitation of the Study and Future Direction

A large as the population of the university is, very few respondents are users of e-library services. Respondents were selected only from the University of Ilorin, Nigeria. It would be important for future researchers to consider extending the study to cover a wider scope so that generalisation to the entire population of e-library users in Nigeria as a country and Africa in general could be possible. The study is also limited based on the use of self reporting instrument. There are some available standardised instruments that future researcher may consider using in a similar studies. The fact that respondents were drawn mainly from the University of Ilorin, Nigeria, the results of the study may not be representative of Nigeria, Africa and developing countries as a whole.

Recommendations

The results on this study have demonstrated that users are aware about the existence of e-library in the university and this awareness couple with other factors contributed to the acceptance and actual use. In the light of this, the university needs to continue investing more funds on the e-library at the university so that it can attract more users.

The results particularly table two revealed that respondents at the lower levels (year one and two) were aware and use the e-library more than other levels. The reason for this may the results of the orientation given to them as fresher to the university. However, students at the higher levels (years 3, 4 and 5) are called upon to increase their use of the e-library.

Moreover, the results have suggested that computer and internet self-efficacy contributed to the acceptance of e-library. This implies that this factor is very important when talking about e-library use. However, the less computer/internet self-efficacy may limit the users from using the e-library. In the light of this, users of e-library in the university are called upon to increase their computer and internet self-efficacy as this is expected to significantly enhance their use of the e-library system. The university can as well assist in this matter by organising computer training for the students. If this is done, it assumed that it will assist the students to develop internet browsing skills.

REFERENCES

Amoroso, D. L., & Hunsinger, D. S. (2009). Measuring the acceptance of internet technology by consumers. *Journal of E-Adoption*, *1*(3).

Arms, J. (2000). *Digital libraries*. Delhi, India: MIT Press.

Baba, Z., & Broady, J. (1998). Organizational effectiveness assessment: case studies of the National Library of Wales and Perpustakaan Negara Malaysia. In *Proceedings of the 2nd Northumbria International Conference on Performance Measurement in Libraries and Information Services*, Newcastle upon Tyne, UK (pp. 319-339).

Babbie, E. (2004). *The practice of social research* (10th ed.). Belmont, CA: Thomson/Wadsworth.

Bar-Ilan, J., Peritz, B. C., & Wolman, Y. (2003). A survey on the use of electronic databases and electronic journals accessed through the web by the academic staff of Israeli universities. *Journal of Academic Librarianship*, *29*(6), 346–361. doi:10.1016/j.jal.2003.08.002

Baruchson-Arbib, S., & Shor, F. (2002). The use of electronic information sources by Israeli college students. *Journal of Academic Librarianship, 28*(4), 255–257. doi:10.1016/S0099-1333(02)00289-6

Bishop, A. P. (2002). Measuring access, use and success in digital libraries. *Journal of Electronic Publishing*. Retrieved February 10, 2007, from http://www.press.umich.edu/jep/04-02/bishop.html

Blandford, A., Stelmaszewska, H., & Bryan-Kinns, N. (2001). Use of multiple digital libraries: a case study. In *Proceedings of the 1st ACM/IEEE-CS Joint Conference on Digital Libraries*.

Borgman, C., Smat, L., Milwood, K., & Finley, J. (2005). Comparing faculty information seeking in teaching and research: Implications for the design of digital libraries. *Journal of the American Society for Information Science and Technology, 56*(6), 636–657. doi:10.1002/asi.20154

Buttenfield, B. (1999). Usability evaluation of digital libraries. In Stern, D. (Ed.), *Philosophies, technical design considerations, and example scenarios*. New York, NY: Haworth Press.

Callan, J., Smeaton, A., Beaulieu, M., Borlund, P., Brusilovsky, P., & Chalmers, C. (2000). Personalization and recommender systems in digital libraries. *International Journal on Digital Libraries, 57*(4), 299–308. Retrieved from http://doras.dcu.ie/205/

Davis, F. D. (1989). Perceived usefulness, perceived ease of use and user acceptance of information technology. *Management Information Systems Quarterly, 13*(3), 319–340. doi:10.2307/249008

Entlich, R., Garson, L., Lesk, M., Normore, L., Olsen, J., & Weibel, S. (1996). Testing a digital library: User response to the CORE project. *Library Hi Tech, 14*(4), 99–118. doi:10.1108/eb048044

Fishbein, M., & Ajzen, I. (1975). *Belief, attitude, intention and behavior. An introduction to theory and research*. Reading, MA: Addison-Wesley.

Frias-Martinez, E., & Chen, S. Y. (2005, August 17-19). Evaluation of user satisfaction with digital library interfaces. In *Proceedings of the 5th WSEAS International Conference on Simulation, Modeling and Optimization*, Corfu, Greece (pp. 172-177).

Harless, D. W., & Allen, F. R. (1999). Using the contingent valuation method to measure patron benefits of reference desk services in an academic library. *College & Research Libraries, 60*(1), 59–69.

Hong, W., Wong, W., Thong, J., & Tam, K. (2002). Determinants of user acceptance of digital libraries: An empirical examination of individual differences and system characteristics. *Journal of Management Information Systems, 18*(3), 97–124.

Israel, G. D. (2003). *Determining sample size*. Retrieved February 10, 2007, from http://edis.ifas.edu

Karahanna, E., Straub, D. W., & Chervany, N. L. (1999). Information technology adoption across time: a cross-sectional comparison of pre-adoption and post-adoption beliefs. *Management Information Systems Quarterly, 23*(2), 183–213. doi:10.2307/249751

Kim, J.-A. (2006). Toward an understanding of Web-based subscription database acceptance. *Journal of the American Society for Information Science and Technology, 57*(13), 1715–1728. doi:10.1002/asi.20355

Kwak, B. H., Jun, W., Gruenwold, L., & Hong, S.-K. (2002). A study on the evaluation model for university libraries in digital environments. In M. Agosti & C. Thanos (Eds.), *Proceedings of 6th European Conference on Research and Advanced Technology for Digital Libraries*, Rome, Italy (LNCS 2458, pp. 204-217).

Lagier, J. (2002). *Measuring usage and usability of online databases at Haltnell College: An evaluation of selected electronic resources* (Unpublished doctoral dissertation). Nova Southeaster University, Davie, FL.

Lee, Y., Kozar, K. A., & Larsen, K. R. T. (2003). The technology acceptance model: Past, present, and future. *Communications of the Association for Information Systems, 12*, 752–780.

Liaw, S., & Huang, H. (2003). An investigation of user attitude toward search engines as an information retrieval tool. *Computers in Human Behavior, 19*(6), 751–765. doi:10.1016/S0747-5632(03)00009-8

Marchionini, G., Plaisant, C., & Komlodi, A. (1998). Interfaces and tools for the Library of Congress National Digital Library Program. *Information Processing & Management, 34*(5), 535–555. doi:10.1016/S0306-4573(98)00020-X

Marchonini, G. (2000). Evaluating digital libraries: A longitudinal and multifaceted view. *Library Trends, 49*(2), 303–333.

Nicholson, S. (2004). A conceptual framework for the holistic measurement and cumulative evaluation of library services. *The Journal of Documentation, 60*, 164–182. doi:10.1108/00220410410522043

Nov, O., & Ye, C. (2008). User's personality and perceived ease of use of digital libraries: The case for resistance to change. *Journal of the American Society for Information Science and Technology, 59*(5), 845–851. doi:10.1002/asi.20800

Reddy, S., Lowry, D., Reddy, S., Henderson, R., Bavis, J., & Babich, A. (1999). *Searching for citations to document sorted by number of citations*. Retrieved March 12, 2011, from http//www.webdav.org/dasl/protocol/draft-dasl-protocol-00.html

Theng, Y., Tan, K., Lim, E., Zhang, J., Goh, D. H., & Ghatterjea, K. …Vo, M. C. (2007, June 18-23). Mobile G-Portal supporting collaborative sharing and learning in geography fieldwork: An empirical study. In *Proceedings of the ACM/IEEE-CS Joint Conference on Digital Libraries*, Vancouver, BC, Canada.

Thong, J. Y. L., Hong, W., & Tam, K. (2002). Understanding user acceptance of digital libraries: what are the roles of interface characteristics, organizational context, and individual? *International Journal of Human-Computer Studies, 57*(3), 215–242. doi:10.1016/S1071-5819(02)91024-4

Thong, J. Y. L., Hong, W., & Tam, K. (2004). What leads to user acceptance of digital libraries? *Communications of the ACM, 47*(11), 79–83. doi:10.1145/1029496.1029498

Tibenderana, P., & Ogao, P. J. (2008, June 19). Acceptance and use of e-library services in Ugandan Universities. In *Proceedings of the 8th ACM/IEEE-CS Joint Conference on Digital Libraries*, Pittsburgh, PA.

Vaidyanathan, G., Sabbaghi, A., & Bargellini, M. (2005). User acceptance of digital library: An empirical exploration of individual and system components. *Issues in Information Systems, 6*(2), 279–285.

Venkatesh, V. (2000). Determinants of perceived ease of use: Integrating control, intrinsic motivation, and emotion into the technology acceptance model. *Information Systems Research, 11*(4), 342–365. doi:10.1287/isre.11.4.342.11872

Venkatesh, V., & Davis, F. D. (1996). A model of the antecedents of perceived ease of use: Development and test. *Decision Sciences, 27*(3), 451–481. doi:10.1111/j.1540-5915.1996.tb01822.x

This work was previously published in the International Journal of Digital Library Systems, Volume 2, Issue 4, edited by Chia-Hung Wei, pp. 34-44, copyright 2011 by IGI Publishing (an imprint of IGI Global).

Chapter 20
Analysis of Success Factors of Introducing SAP System for ERP Implementation in Small and Midsize Enterprises in Taiwan

Hsin-Ju Wei
Information Technology Total Services Corp., Taiwan

Chia-Liang Wei
Allis Electric Co. Ltd., Taiwan

ABSTRACT

Enterprise Resource Planning (ERP) has become the core of successful information management and is also the foundation of corporate information systems for treating with everything related to corporate processes. The ERP implementation has been considered a complicated process because introducing process is involved with different potential conditions and factors so that they may affect the ultimate performance of ERP systems. The aim of this study is to analyze success factors of introducing SAP system for ERP implementation in small and midsized firms. The authors first found out past critical factors affecting the ERP implementation by means of literature review in order to understand results of past studies. Next, the authors widely collected the critical success factors from previous studies and sifted out representative factors to make up a questionnaire. Through the pilot study and questionnaire revision, the authors identified the content of the questionnaire and started interviewing job. When interviewing activities were finished, they began to study and analyze the data. Survey results indicate that three of the most important factors affecting ERP implementation are "top management support and commitment", "project manager's competence" and "communication and coordination effectiveness".

DOI: 10.4018/978-1-4666-2928-8.ch020

INTRODUCTION

In the early era, information systems were simply used to manage production planning and raw material in the factory. With diversity of products in enterprises, they needed powerful information systems to manage them and compete in the complex market in order to survive. An integrated information system, Enterprise Resource Planning (ERP), was gradually developed and extended many functions, such as supply chain management, customer relationship management and warehouse function. With the competition of globalization, both e-business and Internet function were also increased to ERP systems. This make ERP become a function-oriented and modular information system.

The ERP implementation has been considered a complicated process because introducing process is involved with different potential conditions and factors so that they may affects the ultimate performance of ERP systems (Soja, 2006). Besides, ERP systems own the characteristics of real time and integration. By integrating the work process of different department, organizations can establish standardization of processes so that different database can be mutually used in the same information system in time. In the past decade, ERP was usually introduced by large-scale enterprises due to the business requirement and implementation costs. In recent years, more and more small and midsize enterprises express the need for introducing ERP systems in order to keep competitiveness in their industry. Moreover, they also expect to realize any potential crucial factors in the ERP implementation. However, success factors usually involve local culture, business environment and organizational itself. Therefore, in the report, we will study the success factors affecting ERP implementation in small and medsized enterprises (SMEs) and the result will help enterprises to create positive conditions and avoid negative effects.

Aim and Objectives

The aim of this study is to analyze success factors of introducing SAP system for ERP implementation in small and midsize firms. To achieve this aim, it is necessary to fulfil the following objectives:

- To understand what factors are considered determinants for the success of implementation before ERP systems are introduced into SMEs.
- To understand how those determinant factors impact on an ERP implementation When ERP systems have introduced into SMEs.
- To understand what factors are valued by enterprises and consultants in the implementing period when ERP systems are introduced into SMEs.

Contributions

The contributions of this report include: (1) This report investigates the success factors of ERP implementation and the result can provide companies intending to introduce ERP and consults with implementing reference. (2) The result can help organizations to understand the importance of implementing factors in different period and to advance the successful implementation.

LITERATURE REVIEW

Introduction to ERP

Enterprise Resource Planning (ERP) system has become the core of successful information management and is also the foundation of corporate information systems for treating with everything related to corporate processes (Bylinsky, 1999). An original concept of ERP was introduced by Garner Group, an IT research and advising company, in 1990 and the company stated that the next generation of manufacturing business systems and manufacturing resource planning software (Stoilov & Stoilova, 2008). They will be a set of integrated information system of operations and function management in an enterprise for dealing with corporate daily routine and the system will satisfy all commercial requirements of all the departments in a company. Through the system, enterprises can promptly respond to client's needs and make whole enterprise reach the optimum. American Production and Inventory Control Society (APICS) in 1995 defined ERP system as "*An accounting oriented information system for identifying and planning the enterprise wide resources needed to take, make, ship and account for customer orders. An ERP system differs from the typical MRPII system in technical requirements such as graphical user interface, relational database, and computer aided software engineering tools in development, client/server architecture, and open-system portability.*"(Geng, 2004, p. 556)

ERP is introduced to enterprises to resolve different corporate problems, especially in a large enterprise and offer an integrated infrastructure. ERP system can integrate all information flows and make a company share general data, corporate processes and practices all over whole enterprise and let access of information keep within a real-time environment (Davenport, 1998).

ERP Development History

The root of ERP was originally developed for manufacturing industry along with the development of business oriented software in 1960s. The first integrated information system was called Material Requirements planning (MRP), which can make factory's managers to coordinate the production plan and raw material requirements (Todor & Krasimira, 2008; Brady, Monk, & Wagner, 2001). In 1970s, plant managers began to realize the significance of combining the material requirements planning (MRP) with distribution resource planning (DRP). The goal was to promote

overall production scheduling and production planning automatically.

From 1980, the notion of the MRP grew to the second generation of MRP systems (MRPII), which increased many functions along with order processing, manufacture and distribution. The target of MRPII was to let various departments in a company implement the same information system. In 1990, company's managers began to combine other corporate functions together, including finance, human resources and project management. Finally the MRPII evolved into the ERP systems.

Since 2000, ERP system have extended much more functions, such as supply chain management, knowledge management, forecasting, purchasing, customer relationship management, material management, sale operation planning, warehouse management, plant maintenance, sales and marketing, e-business and the Internet function (Todor & Krasimira, 2008; Shehab et al., 2004; Boykin, 2001; Helo, 2008). As a result, ERP become a central business management system which integrates all corporate management functions and makes use of database technology and control information for enterprise businesses. It will provide an enterprise with available information, correct data, communication and services to all related clients, and emphasizes the global real-time information system.

ERP System: SAP

SAP (System, Applications and Products in Data processing) was founded in Germany in 1972 and began to develop the first set of ERP system about accounting packages along with other modules, including, purchasing and inventory management (Todor & Krasimira, 2008; Shehab et al., 2004). In 1978, SAP released the R/2 system which possessed more integrated modules and could make different modules interactive. In 1992, SAP addressed R/3 system. The system had been mature integrated business software which included finance, manufacture, distribution, logistics and human resource (Shehab et al., 2004; Al-Mashari & Zairi, 2000; Bancroft, Seip, & Sprengel, 1999). At the same time, the software was also be broadly used as a means to facilitate the change of business process and IT systems.

With the development of the ERP systems during 1990s, the whole ERP market dramatically increased many competitors, including Oracle, JD Edwards, PeopleSoft and Baan. The five main ERP software companies occupied the most of EPR market share (Shehab et al., 2004; Mabert, Soni, & Venkataramanan, 2001). According to the report addressed by Gartner, the world's renowned independent research company, SAP was the largest ERP software company in the world and its total worldwide market share attained 27 percent in 2006 (Janet, 2008; SAP, 2007). One of its main advantages possesses the extensive capability of the software functionality than other ERP providers (Vidyaranya & Cydnee, 2005).

Implementation Methodology

Wildemann (1990) ever mentioned that enterprises can make use of the method of deploying strategic information system to implement integrated software packages. He also suggested processes of implementation through five stages, including analysis of current circumstance, analysis of difference, evaluation of structure, occasion of implementation and speed of implementation. On the other hand, enterprises themselves also have to begin to process the organizational changes, training of employees and establishment of database.

Heinrich (1994) mentioned implementation of standardized software packages by means of tactics/operation and suggested companies carrying out five stags. Firstly, preliminary study means to decide the goal of the implementation, to define conceptual target and to design main concept and project planning in an enterprise. Secondly, detailed study means to analyze advantages and disadvantage of systems. Thirdly, rough project planning means to perform analysis, design and integration of systems. Fourthly, detailed project plan means systemic design and integration of sub-assignment procedure. Fifthly, the installation of systems means to prepare installation and implementation.

In addition, SAP, an ERP provider, developed the methodology of the AcceleratedSAP (ASAP) for implementing (SAP, 2009). The ASAP can help enterprises implement their EPR systems easier and efficiently. It consists of the five phases, including project preparation, business blueprint, realization, final preparation and go live & support (Lukman, 2003; SAP, 2009; SAP, 1999) (see Figure 1).

Firstly, project preparation means to plan the ERP project. In the stage, enterprises have to set up their project goals, project schedule, budget plan and implementing sequence, and they also need to clarify the implementing scope and establish the project team. Secondly, business blueprint means to assist enterprises to establish future business processes and organizational structure. Thus, project team has to document enterprises' all needs. Thirdly, realization means to start to build the prototypal ERP systems in the enterprise. Key users begin overall tests in the system and make operating manual. Fourthly, final preparation means to finish all preparations, including testing, training of key users and system management. Fifthly, go live & support means that enterprises begin to transform legacy systems to live production operation. Enterprises will continuously improve work processes to meet future requirements of business.

Although each ERP package vendor has different methodologies of implementation in the market, they, accordingly, have the similar processes of implementation. In general, these steps usually include project planning, analyzing, designing, implementing, going live preparation and going live support. Thus, when organizations intend to introduce ERP systems and examine the different methods of the implementation

Figure 1. The ASAP roadmap consists of five phases

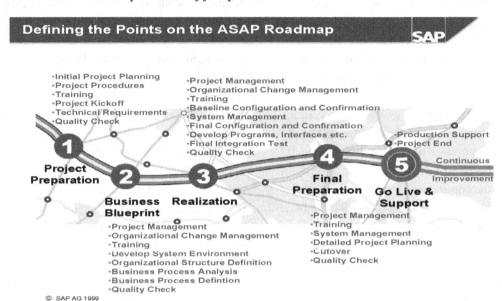

from each provider, they should focus on implementing methods which are simple and easy to understand, with sound design. These key points will help enterprises shorten processes and time of implementing ERP. However, each methodology of the implementation is applied in each unique ERP system based on different corporate characteristics. Thus, the customized ERP systems from different providers have to use different implementation methodologies.

ERP Implementation Impact

The implementation of system projects often bring organizations many impacts in order to correspond to new information systems. Accordingly, the organization itself and its business processes have to be rebuilt and redesigned. Thus, in the following part, we will discuss the several impacts that the ERP implementation brings.

Total Cost of Ownership (TCO)

TCO usually means all direct and indirect costs which are involved in the whole life-cycle stages of an ERP system, including costs of building and running the system (West & Daigle, 2004; Wilderman, 2003). From the beginning of an ERP system, TCO is set to carry out the successful project and also has to manage whole related costs during its life cycle. Thus, when enterprises estimate the purchasing cost of ERP systems, other related costs, such as installation, software deployment, professional services, maintenance, internal staff costs, have to be taken into consideration. Thus, TCO is an important component for implementing a successful EPR system.

However, TCO is a huge expenditure of ERP projects and common companies cannot afford it. Moreover, it is also different for enterprises to forecast the return on investment (ROI) (Mabert et al., 2001; Buonanno et al., 2005). Meta Group, a well-known research company, ever investigated 63 companies deploying different ERP systems and found that the result was a negative net return of 1.5 million in average after implementing ERP within five years (Stamford, 1999). Some studies pointed out that deploying ERP systems is a complicated and costly task (Buonanno et al., 2005; Al-Mudimigh et al., 2001). Although the effective use of large-scale administrative systems is a strategic target for enterprises in any size, current ERP systems in the market are still so expensive that small businesses do not have the financial capabilities to deploy it (Chau, 1995; Buonanno et al., 2005; Gartner Group and Dataquest, 1999). Thus, high TCO can affect SMEs to deploy ERP systems.

Business Process Changes

To survive in current business environments, an organization needs to continuously change their business processes (Vuksic & Spremic, 2005). ERP systems are regarded as a tool of improving organization and they can bring about business process changes. The key systems replace legacy systems, obtain greater control and manage globalization throughout whole organization (Marnewick & Labuschagne, 2005). The new systems can promote organizations to begin a succession of reengineering of business process. Thus, business process changes are related to business process reengineering (BPR) and information technology (IT).

Business Process Reengineering (BPR)

Business process reengineering (BPR) is an organizational method which is concerned with finding out how to operate business processes, redesign business processes, decrease the waste, advance efficiency and carry out process changes in order to achieve several improvement of current performance and gain competitiveness (Vuksic & Spremic, 2005; Rock, 2003; Al-Mashair, 2001; Siriginidi, 2000). The BPR is the re-thinking of business processes and it is to design new ways to reorganize tasks, reorganize internal employees and redeploy IT systems so that the new business processes can support the organizational goals (Rock, 2003; Vuksic & Spremic, 2005; Siriginidi, 2000). The focus of BPR is to integrate redesign-

ing of business processes and deployment of information technology (IT) in order to support organizational reengineering work (Rock, 2003). Siriginidi (2000) mentioned that BPR revolves around information technology, continuous change and changing requirements of organizations. BPR promotes organizations to become more customer-focused and responsive by changes in the competitive environment.

Davenport (1992) set up a five-step guideline to business process reengineering model.

- Developing the business vision and process objectives;
- Identifying the business processes to be redesigned;
- Understanding and measuring the existing processes;
- Identifying IT levers;
- Designing and building a prototype of the new processes.

BPR and Information Technology (IT)

Information technology (IT) plays an important role which improves coordination and information access throughout whole organizations and enables organizations to perform effective management (Siriginidi, 2000; Vuksic & Spremic, 2005). The IT capabilities in an organization provide the following functions (Siriginidi, 2000):

- **Transactional:** Changing loosen processes into structured transactions;
- **Geographical:** Delivering information quickly and easily across long distances;
- **Automatic:** Decreasing manpower in processes;
- **Analytical:** Introducing complicated analytical ways to extend the field;
- **Informational:** Bringing a great quantity of complete information into the processes;
- **Sequential:** Promoting changes in a series of tasks processes;

- **Knowledge management:** Making collection and extension of knowledge and expertise to manage the processes;
- **Tracking:** Tracing the work condition;
- **Disintermediation:** Combining two sides or internal and external within a process.

BPR is the radical redesign of organizational processes in order to improve current performance in quality, cost, services and customers' satisfaction. IT and BPR have a close relationship based on the ERP implementation. IT capabilities will influence performance of BPR, and reengineering of business processes can be carried out based on the capabilities that IT can offer.

Organizational Changes

The ERP implementation can often promote organizations to begin a large-scale organizational change (Davenport, 1998). When an organization decides to introduce the ERP systems, the organization needs to carefully manage and control each process of the implementation. Thus, change management in an ERP project plays a very key role which is directly involved with the adoption, adaptation and acceptance phases of a system (Kemp & Low, 2008).

Change management is seen as a tool which is used to manage such a change that the ERP implementation brings and change management is also related to various issues, mainly including culture, IT, organizational structure, management systems and performance measures (Al-Mashari et al., 2001; Bancroft et al., 1999; Kemp & Low, 2008). During the implementation of ERP systems, change management should concentrate on creating an environment where the change can be introduced (Kemp & Low, 2008). Thus, some activities are suggested as follows (Schneider, 1999; Al-Mashari, 2001; Kemp & Low, 2008; Debrabander & Thiers, 1984; Grover et al., 1995; Allen & Kilmann, 2001; Igbaria et al., 1997),

- Encouraging and training internal employees to change their job roles through incentives and rewards;
- Setting up some anticipations and goals and valuing the internal gaps and conflicts in the present working environment;
- Making effort to eliminate the organizational resistance by explaining the reasons of change and communicating features and benefits of system;
- Preventing projects from delay by technical and daily problems and choosing strong and experienced teams;
- Observing the implementation of ERP systems from a business aspect rather than an IT aspect, and educating proper manager;
- Communicating new business processes and organizational structures at all level of internal employees.

Cultural Change

The implementation of ERP systems refers to the organizational cultural changes (Al-Mashari, 2001). The important issue is that organizations need to understand the cultural differences and preferences in accordance with organizational and geographical perspectives (Finney & Corbett, 2007; Davison, 2002). To manage cultural change, an organization needs to understand the business features and the requirements for a culture which is related to change (Finney & Corbett, 2007; Tarafdar & Roy, 2003). On the other hand, organizational cultural change will be new way of work and communication because these affect how internal employees work together (Remus, 2007; Collins, 2001). This means that employees have to change the way they think about their work and their organization. Several important areas have to be identified (Finney & Corbett, 2007):

- Recognizing the organizational cultural to organizational affects;

- Needing to understand organizational cultural strengths;
- Appling the cultural advantages to organizational change;
- Understand the organizational cultural weakness that may interfere with the cultural change.

Organizational Structure

When ERP systems are introduced, they can often cut down the traditional route. They need an extensive change from a functional system to a process-oriented structure (Al-Mashari, 2001; Schneider, 1999). The structure stresses positive value which possesses an effect on the promotion or limit of creativity and innovation in organizations (Martins & Terblanche, 2003; Armstrong, 1995). The organizational structure under the ERP implementation can bring the competitiveness.

IT Change Management

When legacy systems of an organization are complicated and possesses different IT platforms to administrate ordinary business processes, the amount of technical and organizational changes required is usually higher (Holland & Light, 1999). An organization faces the transformation of different information systems, several procedures should be carried out, as follows (Al-Mashari, 2001):

- Administering a great quantity of modifications to the new information systems through the use of version control;
- Developing an auditing systems to record all data of modifications ;
- Defining and controlling each stage of a project by using processes and workflow to control procedures;
- Establishing tracking systems to inform all project members about changes and problems which develop project over life cycle.

Risk Management

Organizational change may concern with risks which is usually from the change itself or the organizational previous experiences of change (Talwar, 1993). Many ERP project managers are thoughtful about how to control the risks when they are responsible for ERP projects. This is because managers' control in the processes of the implementation will affect the outcome of ERP systems. Thus, risk management is an important issue. In general, in the implementation of large integrated information systems, organizations can usually encounter some risks, including financial risk, technical risk, project risk, functionality risk and political risk (Clemons, 1995).

Financial Risk

Financial risk can make the ERP project unable to finish on schedule and on budget (Clemons, 1995). Since ERP systems are widely realized to be expensive and costly, common small-scale companies have to seriously control the risk. In the solution of financial risk management, increasing funds or omitting certain functions may reduce this risk and cost (Al-Mashari, 2001). In addition, through setting up the reserved expense, the risk may be also lowered.

Technical Risk

When new information systems are exploited, there is usually quite large gap between new and old systems (Al-Mashari, 2001; Clemons, 1995). In general, the possible technical risks are described below (Peng & Nunes, 2008).

Firstly, ERP systems cannot seamlessly integrate other information systems. Secondly, legacy systems cannot accommodate in the new ERP systems. Thirdly, when users boot the systems, invalid data cannot be automatically detected. Fourthly, hardware or software may generate crash.

Project Risk

When the ERP projects are phased and the activities are not normally preceded, the implementing processes can generate the project risks (Al-Mashari, 2001; Clemons, 1995). The risks can lead to the delay of the project and increase the cost of implementation. The most causes of project risks concentrate on inadequate technology knowledge, insufficient re-skilling, insufficient training of end-users, ineffective information communication, poor consultancy service and insufficient definition of project scope (Al-Mashari, 2001; Sumner, 2000).

Functionality Risk

When business requirements cannot be satisfied in the information systems, the systems can generate functionality risks (Al-Mashari, 2001). Although most ERP systems possess complicated functions, this does not mean that they possess the same characteristics as other systems. Thus, each system owns its advantages and disadvantages. It is difficult for an organization to understand the functionalities of systems.

Political Risk

Political risk is involved with the organizational resistance and the lack of commitment (Clemons, 1995; Al-Mashari, 2001). They are an obstacle which affects whole implementing effort. The implementation of ERP systems are a quite complicated processes which concern with adoption of a new information technology and the technology combines with business process re-engineering and change management of organizations (Al-Mashari, 2001; Bancroft et al., 1999). When a company encounters the difficult combination, it is likely to bring a company with inadequate control over the managerial abilities (Al-Mashari, 2001). This condition could make end-users refuse the new information systems and raise internal conflicts.

Performance Measures

The degree of organizational change is decided by the level of company transformation (Buonanno et al., 2005). This means that organizational change can bring more potential benefits. This measure is based on the assessment of the organization of economic impacts, such as the ability of internal employees or anticipated resistance. Thus, many factors will affect the organizational performance. Venkatraman (1994) pointed out that the levels of organizational transformation can be classified into five main levels (see Figure 2).

Local Automation

This level only displays for automation of local and independent procedures. Organizations can simply make use of technology to deal with current job more efficiently and effectively, and cannot acquire competitive advantages through simple automation of existing procedures (Buonanno et al., 2005; Bertin, 2004). However, organizations in the stage need to express their anticipated results. Thus, they need to set the objectives and plans, and make efforts to achieve them.

Internal Integration

This level focuses on integrating the existing business processes and corporal information systems (IS) in order to strengthen organizational competitiveness (Buonanno et al., 2005). At the same time, it makes use of advantages of information technology (IT) to establish seamless organizational processes (Buonanno et al., 2005; Bertin, 2004). The degree of integration has to establish on technical interconnectivity and organizational interdependence.

Business Process Redesign

Business process redesign refers to the partial or entire redesign of key processes and can affect organizational procedures and organizational structures (Buonanno et al., 2005; Bertin, 2004).

Business Network Redesign

With regard to the redesign of information exchange among all participants, business network redesign could enhance the organizational abilities of coordination, control, services and provision of products (Buonanno et al., 2005; Bertin, 2004). Due to the redesign of information exchange, each participant can explore the abilities of the business network.

Business Scope Redefinition

Information communication technologies (ICT) redefines the company scope by inter-organizational relationships (Buonanno et al., 2005; Bertin, 2004). In addition to company scopes, it would adjust internal activities, new partnerships, alignment and the value chain (Bertin, 2004).

From the above classifications, we understand that the degree of organizational transformation is directly related to the use of information systems. In other words, as the degree of the organizational transformation is the greater, the extent of use of ERP systems is the higher (Buonanno et al., 2005) (see Figure 2).

Technology Support

The competitive pressure has promoted many companies to consider the adoption of the new information technology (Crage & King, 1993; Iacovou et al., 1995). However, most small-scale companies usually own little experience in computer use and lack enough professional knowledge in managing IT and internal information systems (Gable, 1991; Thong, 1999). They usually do not

have the proficient experts and it is difficult to hire the experts for a long time mainly because of the lack of financial resource (Gable, 1991; Hung et al., 2004).

In general, small-scale companies have to depend on external support, such as consultants or system vendors when they need to maintain the ERP systems. The technical support of consultants and support vendors can provide the comprehensive performance of information systems (Thong et al., 1996). Through the external experts, small-scale enterprises can focus on strengthening their core competencies and they do not need to waste their resources for non-essential activities. At the same time, they can eliminate difficulty for recruiting and retaining resource of the information technology.

Challenges of ERP Implementation in SMEs

The organizational structures of small and midsize enterprises (SMEs) are different from larger companies. Current operating tendency of SMEs are generally showing a critical requirement for coordination and control of business activities which is related to the complex information systems (Buonanno et al., 2005; MacGregor & Kartiwi, 2007; Bunker & MacGregor, 2000). Since current SMEs face more and more complex business processes, including complex business activities and business environments, they need ERP to manage their information flows more effectively. In the following parts, we will proceed with the research of SMEs.

ERP for Small and Midsized Enterprises

Although the implementation of ERP systems normally can assist small and midsize enterprises in reinforcing their strategic and competitive capabilities, several reasons indicate why firms are unwilling to install the ERP systems (Smith,

Figure 2. Level of organizational transformation

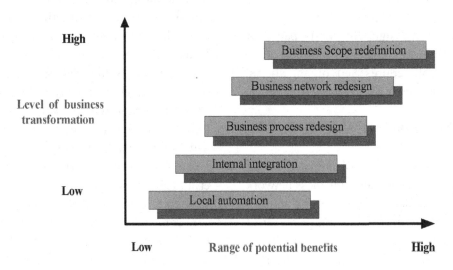

Source: (Venkatraman, 1994)

1999; Jenson & Johnson, 1999). Firstly, only 40 percent of those ERP installed firms successfully adopt ERP systems while 60 percent of those are considered partial success or total failures (Trunick, 1999). Secondly, SMEs are usually subject to their financial limits so that they cannot afford expensive and costly ERP systems (Ferman, 1999). Unlike large-scale enterprises, SMEs are usually unable to support enough IT staff and adequate training for ERP installation (Hill, 1997). These reasons imply the difficulty in implementing ERP systems for SMEs. Currently, there is not much of research done on identifying the factors of ERP implementation success based on the small and midsize enterprises.

In past several years ago, ERP systems had been implemented on large organizations. Most of previous studies indicated that they mainly analyzed successful factors for large enterprises and little studies focused on the SMEs. However, each company has its own organizational culture, business markets, business processes, business requirements and business challenges. In particular, the ERP implementation of SMEs is also affected

by the organization itself and business environments. Hence, the factors of the organization and environment would affect the introduction of ERP systems in SMEs.

SMEs are foundation stone for economic development and performance of any country and its features are flexibility and innovation. In Taiwan, SMEs are defined as the number of employee inside 200 employees and amount of capital invested less than 80,000,000 NT dollars. About 1,200,000 enterprises are SMEs in Taiwan. According to Taiwan government statistics, 98% of enterprises in Taiwan are small and midsize enterprises (SMEA, 2008).

In the past, ERP systems are designed to apply in large-scale enterprises and some studies pointed out that ERP system can bring great efficiency and beneficiary. However, the ERP markets in large-scale enterprises have gradually appeared saturation. Many ERP vendors have begun to turn their marketing sights on SMEs. Since the resource of SMEs is limited, now more and more ERP vendors provide best practices or templates for SMEs.

Characteristics of SMEs

Small and midsize enterprises should not be regarded as miniaturized version of large-scale enterprises because the organizational structures of SMEs differ from large-scale companies. Moreover, SMEs are usually more risky than its larger counterpart mainly because it tends to be higher failure rates (MacGregor et al., 2002; Klatt, 1973). SMEs usually possess the following characteristics (MacGregor et al., 2002; Poba-Nzaou et al., 2008; Raymond & Uwizeyemungu, 2007; Sledgianowski et al., 2007).

- Lack of large management team, specialist staff and promotable staff;
- Strong proprietor's influence and desire for independence with centralized power and control;
- Multi-functional management;
- Lack of sufficient planning and control systems;
- Limited business environment and heavy dependence on few customers;
- Lack of handling through the business environment;
- Limited business processes and product technology;
- Labor intensive work and low manpower turnover;
- Full of Management of proprietor's personal idiosyncrasies;
- Narrow educational background, work experience and skills;
- Intuitive reaction rather than reasonable judgment;
- Limited competence to acquire funds;
- Reactive responses rather than innovative responses to change;
- Intrusion of family interests.

Through above mentioned characteristics, we know that the use of the information systems in the SMEs business environment cannot simply be seen as miniature version of the large-scale organization. When information systems are introduced in SMEs, a variety of characteristics of SMEs operations should be considered.

Prior Studies and their Methodologies

Several prior studies have indicated the importance of investigating critical success factors (CSF) in the process of the ERP implementation. Loh and Koh (2004) mentioned the most frequent critical factors for successful implementation in SMEs as follows (Juell-Skielse, 2006):

- **Project champion:** The project leader's ability to address the system project based on business perspective and eliminate the organizational conflicts;
- **Project management:** The project leaders' ability to control and plan the system project based on time, cost and schedule;
- **Top management support:** Corporate top managers have the willingness to support the project;
- **Effective communication:** The organizational ability to convey expectations, requirements and goal at each level;
- **Project teamwork and composition:** The organizational ability to appoint best employees to make up project tem;
- **Minimum package adjustments:** The project's ability to decrease adjustments of the software package.
- **BPR and organizational adjustments:** The organizational ability to redesign business processes and organizational structures to meet the processes of the software package;
- **Change management program and culture:** The project's ability to promote organizations to change culture, IT, structure and processes and provide the accurate training;

- **Software development, testing and troubleshooting:** The ability to install, test and revise the errors in the IS structure;
- **Monitoring and evaluation of project performance:** The ability to examine and assess the performance of the project based on organizational goal;
- **Monitoring and evaluation of business benefits:** The ability to review and assess the finished business benefits.

In addition, Thong (2001) presented a model of IS introduction for small businesses in accordance with Welsh and White's (1981) framework of resource constraints as well as Attewell's (1992) knowledge barrier theory. This model showed that a small business with successful IS should possess the following factors, including effective external experts, enough IS investment, high user's IS knowledge, high user participation and high CEO support (Thong, 2001).

Leavitt's Diamond Organization Model

The Leavitt's Diamond Model (see Figure 3) develops a balance concept and is broadly used and cited to analyze management change and organizational change (Okunoye & Bertaux, 2006; Keen, 1981). The model consists of four organizational variables, including technology (tools), people (actors), task and structure (Leavitt, 1965).

Technology in the model means all software and hardware to support organizational tasks and include some assignment technology. People means to carry out the organizational mission and the people have to possess the knowledge, ability and concept of executing tasks. Besides, they can coordinate and cooperate with each other. Task means to include all corporate project plan and assignment process. Structure means to offer an environment to support tasks and manpower, including management system, organizational structure and culture. These four variables are highly interdependent relationship as showed by the arrowheads.

When one variable is changed, others will be impacted. In Figure 3, technologies can be seen as tools which help organizations finish work for converting inputs to outputs. According to the above points of view, we can realize that the ERP implementation not only affects information processes or people who perform these processes, but also impacts organizational structures and technologies. This model equally considers the four variables so that projects can reach maximal success.

METHODOLOGY

Research Structure

The aim of the research is to find out the successful key of ERP implementation in small and midsize enterprises. The outcome of research is to provide SMEs intending to implement the ERP systems with preparation of implementation and to advance the successful organizational changes. The structure of the research is designed in Figure 4.

With regard to the method of the research, we firstly found out past critical factors affecting the ERP implementation by means of literature review in order to understand the results of past studies. Next, we widely collected the critical success factors from previous studies and sifted out representative factors to make up the questionnaire in according with the purpose of the research. Through the pilot study and questionnaire revision, we identified the content of the questionnaire and started interviewing job. When interviewing activities were finished, we began to study and analyze these data. Finally, we generated results.

In the following sections, we will explain the researching procedures, including the design of the questionnaire, source of data, choice of interviewee, data analysis and research tools.

Figure 3. Leavitt's Diamond Organization Model

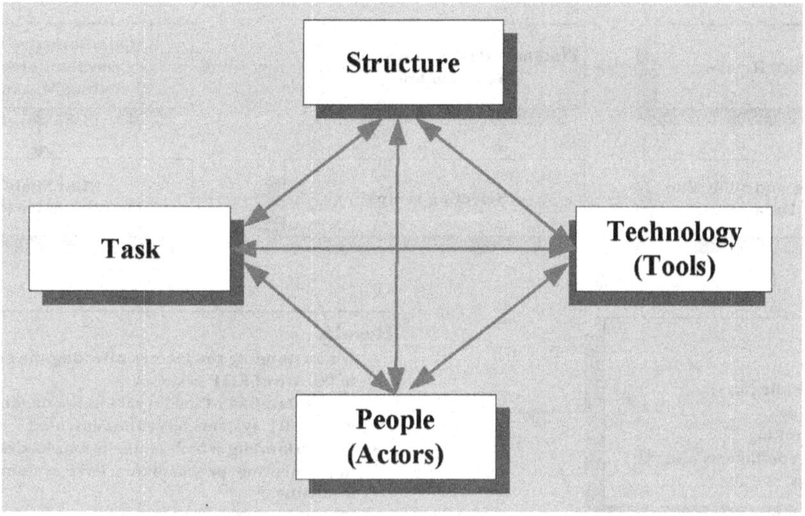

Source: (Leavitt, 1965)

Questionnaire Design

The content of the questionnaire was designed in two parts, including background information and testing questions. In the part of background information, we adopted the way of nominal scale to differentiate the status of the interviewee in order to classify them into different category for analysis. In the part of the testing question, we mainly collected them from past literatures. After we were engaged in literature review, we found out the critical success factors and adopted a wide range of collection. At the same time, we selected those suited critical factors. We expected to make up the completed content of the questionnaire in this research.

The designing way of the questionnaire adopted the structured questionnaire of the closed way because data could be quantified for statistical analysis. Regarding questionnaire formulation and measure scale, we made use of the way of Likert Scale developed by Likert (1932). In general, the way is used for psychological test. Respondents can directly answer their feeling degree in accordance with statements of the questionnaire. The feeling degree is classified into five stages from unimportant to very important.

- Very important
- Important
- Moderately important
- Of little important
- Unimportant

Finally, we finished the investigation and statistics of the questionnaire (see Appendix A, Appendix B and Appendix C).

Selecting Sample

This research mainly explores the critical success factors which small and midsize enterprise implementing ERP systems. At the same time, we analyzed the impacts generated from organizational interior during and after implementing ERP systems. Thus, the interviewees of our study included SAP consultants, corporate key users, corporate officers, divisional managers, project leaders and various project team members during and after the implementation of the ERP projects.

Figure 4. Flow chart of research

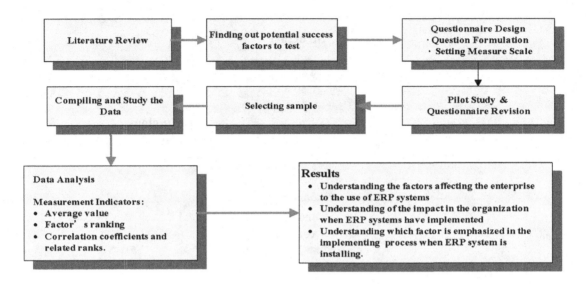

Since each participant ever owned directly deep experience in each stage of SAP implementation and building of new IT/IS, we thought that they could provide more objective answers to the content of the questionnaire.

Since the ERP implementation is generally seen as a core task in enterprises, ERP systems have been built in different industries. Thus, in order to pick up the suitable interviewees, we reviewed some reports from related financial magazines and we collected the corporate roll of implementing SAP. Besides, we referred to "*All information on 5000 trading companies in Taiwan*" provided from Importers and Exporters Association of Taipei and "*2009 Taiwan area industrial name list*" provided from China Credit Information Service, Ltd (CCIS), Taiwan's largest and leading credit information agency.

According to the SMEs' definition mentioned in the previous section, we adopted the way of artificial selection to generate the interviewing companies possessing the SAP implementing experience in order to avoid generating deviation. This could help us focus on our study interviewees. We made totally 100 copies of the questionnaires and collected them. We intended to establish two

groups of the questionnaires, including the enterprise group and the consultant group. 50 copies of the questionnaires were distributed among corporate key users, corporate officers and divisional managers. Other 50 copies of the questionnaires were answered by SAP consultants. The questionnaires were sent out in the early April, 2009 and we collected them by the end of April, 2009. After the questionnaire was collected, we conducted a pilot survey in order to revise the potential errors and mistakes in the questionnaires.

The collecting number of the questionnaire reached 44 copies (Whole Collection Rate: 44%) (see Table 1). After deducting from the invalidity of 3 questionnaires, we totally obtain 41 copies of effective questionnaires (Whole Effective Collection Rate: 41%). In other words, the enterprise group obtained 17 copies of effective samples and the consultant group obtained 24 copies of effective samples.

The profile from the respondent companies is listed in Table 2. In the effective questionnaire of the enterprise group, all respondent enterprises belonged to manufacturing industries. About 76.5% of companies were established over 16 years. The number of employee (100 ~ 200

Table 1. The statistics of questionnaires in enterprise group and consultant group

Item	Enterprise Group	Consultant Group	Total
Number of Questionnaire	50	50	100
Collection of Questionnaire	18	26	44
Effective Questionnaire	17	24	41
Invalid Questionnaire	1	2	3
Collection Rate	36%	52%	44%
Effective Collection Rate	34%	48%	41%

Table 2. The profile of sample from enterprise group enterprise information

	Item	Number of sample	Percentage (%)
Industry category	Manufacturing	17	100
Year of establishment	10 years	1	5.9
	11 years ~ 15 years	3	17.6
	16 years ~ 20 years	10	58.8
	20 years and more	3	17.7
Number of Employee	0 ~ 20 people	0	0
	21~ 100 people	3	17.6
	100 ~ 200 people	14	82.4
	200 people and more	0	0
Number of MIS staff	None	0	0
	1 ~ 3 people	1	5.9
	3 ~ 5 people	10	58.8
	5 ~ 10 people	5	29.4
	10 people and more	1	5.9

people) reached about 82.4 percent in all respondent companies and the number of MIS staff (3 ~5 people) was around 58.8 percent. This showed that most respondent enterprises only employed MIS staff inside 3 ~ 5 people.

On the other hand, with regard to the profile of the consultant group (see Table 3), working experience of respondent consults was mainly between 4 and 9 years and reached about 83.4 percent. The professional specialty of respondent consultants was dispersed in different ERP modules on overage and their ages were mainly between 26 and 45 years old and were about 91.7 percent.

Compiling and Studying the Data

After conducting interview, we had to compile the data and study the data we collected. This facilitated us to conduct data analysis at the following stage.

Analysis Structure

In the research, we adopted three ways of studying models to analyzing organizational impacts of different period and these models could provide different purposes (see Table 4).

Table 3. The profile of sample from consultant group

Consultant information	Item	Number of sample	Percentage (%)
Work Module of ERP	Sales and distribution	7	29.1
	Materials management	6	25
	Production planning	4	16.7
	Financial accounting	4	16.7
	Controlling	3	12.5
Work Experience	1 ~ 3 years	2	8.3
	4 years ~ 6 years	11	45.9
	7 years ~ 9 years	9	37.5
	10 years and more	2	8.3
Age	18 ~ 25 years old	0	0
	26 ~ 35 years old	14	58.4
	36 ~ 45 years old	8	33.3
	46 ~ 55 years old	2	8.3
	56 and more	0	0

In the analyzing model I, we divided the questionnaire into the enterprise group and the consultant group. By statistics of the questionnaire from enterprises and ERP consultants, we could understand which factor may affect a company to build the ERP systems.

In the analyzing model II, we made use of the Leavitt's diamond model as our researching basis (see Figure 5). Since its four variables, including task, people, structure and technology, can analyze the organizational changes, we put critical factors separately into the four variables in accordance to its definition of the diamond model. We tried to analyze their mutual relationship. Through this model, we could understand that these factors in each variable may impact other relevant factors, when an organization used ERP systems.

In the analyzing model III, we combined the mentioned ASAP roadmap and Leavitt's diamond model to develop an analyzing model in order to understand which factor is emphasized in whole implementing process (see Figure 6). We realize that when an organization implements ERP systems, whole organization may generate huge changes of the organizational structure. From beginning of implementation to end of implementation, an organization itself could have to plan and carry out many tasks, such as project planning, staff training, business process re-definition and system management. Such a complex rebuilding engineering has to obtain support and participa-

Table 4. The purpose of three analysis structures

Item	Purpose
Model I	Understanding of the factors affecting the enterprise to the use of ERP systems
Model II	Understanding of the impact in the organization when organizations have implemented ERP systems
Model III	Understanding which factor is emphasized in the implementing process when organizations is implementing ERP systems

Figure 5. Critical factors are put into four variables in the diamond model

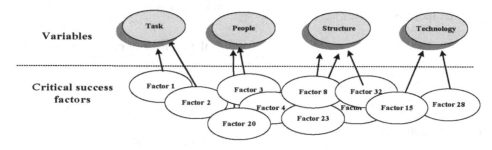

tion from whole organizational members. Thus, we can understand this change through the analysis of the model.

Indicators of Data Analysis

By means of the questionnaire, we received a large number of data and analyzed our data by the following statistic indicators:

Background Information

In order to explore the points of view of different position, we classified questionnaires into

the enterprise group and the consultant group in order to understand their background information.

Descriptive Statistics

According to the frequency and percentage of the sample, we could obtain the distribution and construction of the sample. In order to examine the respondent's opinions about the important factors, a mean (average) was calculated for each factor. The calculations are made from different groups.

The mean is the average of all the observations. It means that the total of the measurements is divided by the number of the observations. The

Figure 6. An analyzing model combined from ASAP roadmap and Leavitt's diamond model

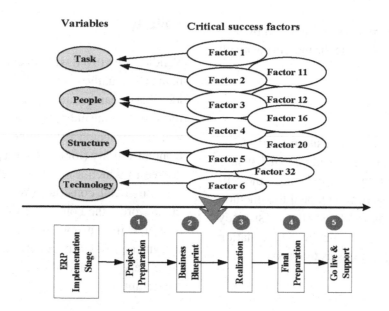

mean is usually denoted by $\overline{X}$. Thus, the equation for calculating the mean is as follows:

$$\overline{X} = \frac{X_1 + X_2 + X_3 + \ldots\ldots + X_n}{n} = \frac{\sum_{i=1}^{n} X_n}{n}$$

$\sum_{i=1}^{n} X_n$ = the total of all observations of size n in one sample

X_i = the value of each observation. $i = 1, 2, 3\ldots.n$

n = the number of observations

Factor's Ranking

The factors' ranking was calculated on the basis of decreasing average importance evaluated with a given group in order to easily focus on important factors. According to the factor's ranking, we can understand which factor is valued by the enterprise group and the consultant group and we can also compare their mutual relationship by different analysis methods.

Examination of Reliability and Validity

A rigid questionnaire needs to be tested by reliability and validity. We state the measuring result as follows.

Reliability

Reliability refers to the consistent and stable degree in any measuring procedure which generates the same result. In order to identify the reliability in this research, we adopted this method of Cronbach's Alpha (α) to test the consistency and stability of the questionnaire. The equation for Cronbach's Alpha (a) is as follows:

$$\text{Cronbach's } \alpha = \frac{N}{N-1} \left(1 - \frac{\sum_{i=1}^{N} \sigma_{Y_i}^2}{\sigma_X^2}\right)$$

N = the number of components (items)

σ_x^2 = the variance for the total of all items

$\sigma_{Y_i}^2$ = the variance of component i

When the Cronbach's Alpha coefficient is between 0.35 and 0.7, the value is seen as acceptable reliability. When the Alpha coefficient is under 0.35, it is seen as low reliability and when the Alpha coefficient is more than 0.7, it indicates high reliability. In the research, this questionnaire is classified into two groups, including enterprise group and consultant group.

Through the test of Cronbach's Alpha, we obtained relative coefficients. The Alpha coefficient in enterprise group was 0.891 and the value in consultant group was 0.907. The Alpha coefficient is all group was 0.893. We find that above mentioned Alpha coefficients all were over 0.7. This showed that the questionnaire possesses high consistency and stability in individual group and entire group.

Validity

Validity is involved with an extent which a study plan can actually assesses or reflects the definite idea that researcher undertakes to measure. Validity is an accurate indication and means a degree to which the research result coincides with actuality. Content validity (logical validity) means that the degree to which a measure includes all way of a given social construct (Wikipedia, 2009). In other words, the content of the measure is able to aim at the purpose of the questionnaire and it owns representative content. Content validity quite depends on community identification to the definition.

The development of the questionnaire in this research was based on past literatures as a basis. According to current researching context, we revised them to reach a reasonable questionnaire. Besides, before we began to make questionnaire, all questionnaires were tested and discussed by an experienced expert Professor Chia-hung Wei, Department of Information Management, Ching Yun University, Taiwan. Through the expert's guidance, we revised the unsuitable content to the questionnaire and eventually obtained a better version. Thus, the questionnaire on content validity can obtain well examination.

DATA ANALYSIS AND DISCUSSION

In this section, we analyze a sequence of questionnaires surveyed from enterprises and ERP consultants. Through the statistics of data, we can understand which critical success factor may affect SAP implementation in small and midsize enterprises in Taiwan. In order to analyze the results of the questionnaire, we make use of three analysis models to understand the impact of critical factors in different period.

Data Analysis I

According to the responding questionnaires from different interviewee, we classify these responding data into three groups, including the enterprise group, consultant group and all respondents' group. Through the classifications and rank, we can analyze and understand which factor is concerned by respondents before ERP implementation.

Enterprise Group

The data obtained from the enterprise group is tabulated in Table 5. In the table, we find out that 76.47 percent of respondents think that "top management support and commitment" was the most important factor in the enterprise group. In general, top management usually has crucial affection in the SMEs and only a few top managers possess authorities to decide policies in an organization. When a company intends to install EPR systems and needs to face such a huge organizational change, the commitment of top management becomes an important support. Thus, the above responding result seems to show out that respondents also support the point of view.

Table 5. Statistical data of the critical success factors from enterprise group

Critical Success Factors (CSFs)	Percent (%)
Top management support and commitment	76.47
Project manager's competence	70.59
System reliability	70.59
Consultant's experience	64.71
Domain knowledge of suppliers	64.71
Appropriate training	64.71
Knowledge transfer from consultant to the company	64.71
Product functionality and quality of ERP	64.71
Supplier support and training	58.82
Fast effects	58.82

Notes: The table 1 only shows the most previous 10 critical success factors (CSFs). Each percentage in the each item is counted based on total respondents from the enterprise group. The whole percentages of all CSFs can refer to appendix A.

The second important factor, project manager's competence, is 70.59 percent. During introducing the ERP systems, the project managers' abilities are enough to affect the progress of ERP introduction. This is because their experiences, integration and controlling abilities directly respond to the implementing plans. Excellent project managers can successfully lead a company to transform into another company. This is also why project managers play an important role during ERP implementation. The third factor is "system reliability" in the rate of 70.59 percent. The enterprise group sees system reliability as one of the previous three important factors. This situation shows that these interviewed enterprises may quite respect the quality of ERP systems and also value the results of ERP implementation. After all, the implementation of ERP systems has to spend quite great costs. They would carefully choose the well-known ERP product.

In addition, other factors, including consultant's experience, domain knowledge of suppliers, appropriate training, knowledge transfer from consultant to the company, and product functionality and quality of ERP, are the same percentage of 64.71. The last two factors are supplier support and training and fast effects with 58.82 percent.

Consultant Group

Table 6 shows the survey results from the consultant group. Likewise, the factor of "top management support and commitment" is thought of as the most important factor by professional consultants and listed in the first rank in the table. It reaches the highest rate of 91.67 percent. Since the ERP implementation often involves with huge changes of organizational structures and business processes, responding consultants might think that top managers' support and commitment can affect the introducing results. The second factor is also "project manager's competence" in the rate of 83.33 percent. The aforementioned two factors

are regarded as two main affecting factors as the point of view of enterprise group.

The two factors "clear implementation goals" and "communication and coordination effectiveness" are ranked in the third place with the same rate of 75 percent. However, not all ERP systems can be successfully deployed in any organization. Some failing cases are resulted from the above mentioned two factors. The two factors could affect the progress and outcome of introduction. Besides, other factors, including team involvement (66.67%), cross-function coordination (62.5%) and, system testing and maintain capabilities (50%), were identified by more than a half of respondents.

Comparison Between Enterprises and Consultants

Table 5 and Table 6 indicate the statistical results of the enterprise group and the consultant group. In order to compare the mutual relationship between two groups, we respectively divide the 10 critical success factors of each group into internal factors (relating to organizational perspective factors) and external factors (relating to external expertise). By mutually comparing them, we find out some interesting phenomenon as follows.

In Figure 7, we find out that the enterprise group almost emphasizes external factors. The ratio of external factors to internal factors is 80%:20%. This result displays that these small and midsize firms might quite need the assistance of external expertise when they introduced ERP systems or deploy IT infrastructures. The possible cause is that SMEs did not have a great quality of resources to employ IT experts for a long term. As soon as ERP systems were introduced to an organization, corporate staffs were usually concerned with how to obtain and learn external IT knowledge, and gain training. In the organizational perspective factor, in addition to the factor of top manager's support and commitment, another emphasized factor was "fast effects". A possible reason is that

Table 6. Statistical data of the critical success factors from consultants group

Critical Success Factors (CSFs)	Percent (%)
Top management support and commitment	91.67
Project manager's competence	83.33
Clear implementation goals	75
Communication and coordination effectiveness	75
Team involvement	66.67
Cross-functional coordination	62.5
System testing and maintenance capabilities	50
Work time schedule	45.83
Data conversion and integrity	45.83
Project timeframe and implementation strategy	41.67

Notes: The table 2 only shows the most previous 10 critical success factors (CSFs). Each percentage in the each item is counted based on total respondents from the consultant group. The whole percentages of all CSFs can refer to appendix B.

since SMEs usually owns the ability to fast adapt new technologies/environments for survival, they might need to obtain fast effects in the system integration. When SMEs intend to introduce the ERP systems, they often have to consider many factors more than large companies. Those factors might affect their willingness to adopt ERP systems.

Figure 8 shows that the consultant group mainly stressed organizational perspective factors. 90% of the internal factors is compared with 10% of external factors. The possible cause displays that when consultants help enterprises implement ERP systems, respondents might often encounter many resistances from their organizational factors. For example, organizational top managers lack awareness or organizations do not have clear goals for ERP implementation. Thus, Figure 8 shows that the successful key of implementing ERP depends on organization itself.

All Respondents Group

Table 7 shows the results of whole respondents which include enterprise group and consultant group. The result indicates that "top management support and commitment", "project manager's competence" and "communication and coordination effectiveness" are three most important factors affecting ERP implementation. We find out that "top management support and commitment" reaches around 85.37 percent on average. This result is similar to previous studies and top management support and commitment are also the most broadly discussed factor (Finney & Corbett, 2007; Remus, 2007; Siriginidi, 2000).

Another important factor, "project manager's competence", reaches approximately 78.05 percent. The two factors are commonly thought of as the key factors by whole respondents. The third factor is "communication and coordination effectiveness", which reaches about 65.85 percent. From the overall statistics of Table 7, we find that although the ERP is an expensive information system, the factor of building cost does not seem to be seen as one of the most important factors by all respondents. On the contrary, technology, system function, maintenance abilities, relative training, IT knowledge transfer, expert support and top management support are concern of all respondents.

Data Analysis II

The Leavitt's diamond model can be used to explain changes of organizational processes when an organization introduces new systems. In the section, we make use of the model to analyze critical success factors to organizational affections when ERP systems have been installed in a company. In order to clearly appear organizational changes, we only used statistical data from the enterprise group to analyze their results. We sorted all criti-

cal success factors into four variables of the diamond model, including task, people, technology and structure, based on their definitions. These variables, which mutually affect each other, are further discussed as follows.

Task Perspective

In the task variable, the factor of "knowledge transfer from consultant to the company" is mainly stressed and it reaches 64.71 percent or

Figure 7. Critical success factors in enterprise group are classified into internal and external factor

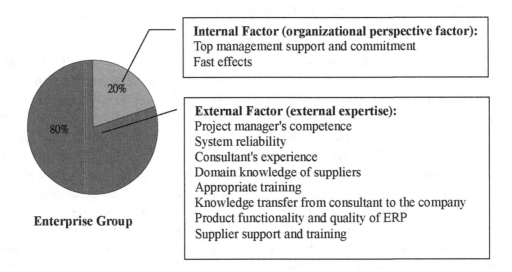

Figure 8. Critical success factors in consultant group are classified into internal and external factor

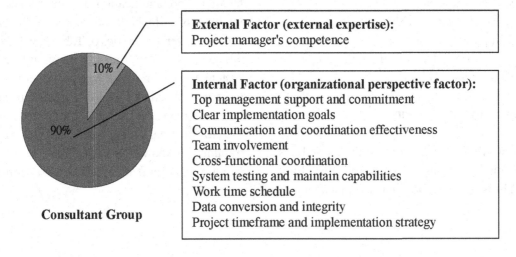

Table 7. Statistical data of the critical success factors from all respondents

Critical Success Factors (CSFs)	Percent (%)
Top management support and commitment	85.37
Project manager's competence	78.05
Communication and coordination effectiveness	65.85
Team involvement	60.98
Cross-functional coordination	58.54
Clear implementation goals	56.10
System testing and maintenance capabilities	53.66
Knowledge transfer from consultant to the company	51.22
System reliability	51.22
Product functionality and quality of ERP	51.22
Notes: The table 3 only shows the most previous 10 critical success factors (CSFs). Each percentage in the each item is counted based on total respondents from enterprises and ERP consultants. The whole percentages of all CSFs can refer to appendix C.	

so (see Table 8). The factor might affect other factors in people and technology variables, such as "appropriate training (64.71%)", "system testing and maintain capabilities (58.82%)" and "system troubleshooting capabilities (58.82%)". We find that the factor of "knowledge transfer from consultant to the company" owns higher percentage. When we view other affected factors, they likewise have higher percentage. This condition is mentioned in the diamond model because each factor in organization might mutually draw other relative factors.

Another factor is fast effects with about 58.82% and it might also affect factors in other variables, such as "project manager's competence (70.59%)", "consultant's experience (64.71%) and "top management support and commitment (76.47)". Other factors, including "fit with business process" and "project cost planning and management" also reaches 58.82%. They can similarly affect other factors.

Structure Perspective

Table 9 shows percentages of factors in the structure variable. As the definition of the structure variable mentioned in previous chapter, it can offer an organizational environment to support all organizational tasks and manpower. The factor of "top management support and commitment" reaches 76.47%. Obviously, the percentage displays the importance of the factor in the organization. Thus, the factor of "top management support and commitment" might bring both task variable and people variable a wide affection. Moreover, the factor is also a key role of business process reengineering (BPR) of an organization.

Others factors, such as "cross-functional coordination (52.94%)" and "communication and coordination effectiveness (52.94%)" could also bring affection to other factors, such as integration of legacy system and ERP (52.94%),

People Perspective

The people variable usually involves with external experts and internal key users who need mutual coordination and cooperation. At the same time, the variable is also the most complicated part in ERP implementation because it is involved with whether the whole project plan can be finished on schedule and whether the system can be implemented successfully. Since it involved a

Table 8. The task variable in the diamond model

Task	Percent (%)
Knowledge transfer from consultant to the company	64.71
Fast effects	58.82
Fit with business process	58.82
Project cost planning and management	58.82
Organization change management	41.18
Feedback and monitoring	41.18
Project timeframe and implementation strategy	35.29
Work time schedule	35.29
Notes: The above factors are classified into the task variable based on the definition of the diamond model.	

broad layer, it could bring overall affections in different variable.

Table 10 shows that "project managers' competence (70.59)" is the key factor in the variable. Likewise, its importance is similar to the aforementioned factor, top management support and commitment, because it involves with the implementing results of whole project plan. The possible affected factors include project cost planning and management (58.82%), integration of legacy system and ERP (52.94%), minimal customization to meet organizational process (29.41%) and IT infrastructure (23.53%). In fact, "the project managers' abilities" is a quite important factor because project managers are responsible for the success of ERP implementation.

The second ranking factor in the variable is domain knowledge of suppliers (64.71%). Since core knowledge and characteristics of each industry have quite great differences, suppliers' abundant knowledge and experiences can help to understand organizational related knowledge and provide organization with actual requirements. The factor of "domain knowledge of suppliers" might affect other factors, such as system reliability (70.59%), integration of legacy system and ERP (52.94%) and fit with business process (58.82%).

Another factor consultant's experience (64.71%) can affect the progress of project plan. Professional consultants can offer similar cases

and experiences to organizations for references and can make right analysis to help organization make right decisions. The factor could draw other factors, such as integration of legacy system and ERP (52.94%) and knowledge transfer from consultant to the company (64.71%). Other factors, such as "appropriate training (64.71%)" and "training staff (end-users) support (64.71%), may affect many perspectives, such as "knowledge transfer from consultant to the company (64.71%)", "system testing and maintain capabilities (58.82)" and "system troubleshooting capabilities (58.82)".

Technology Perspective

Table 11 shows that "system reliability (70.59%)" and "product functionality and quality of ERP (64.71%)" are stressed by respondents. Since the organizational structure of SMEs usually owns the characteristics of fast change, they might especially value the reliability, functionality and quality of ERP system. This factor might affect the other factors, such as "fast effects (58.82%)" and "minimal customization to meet organizational process (29.41%)".

Other factors in the table, "system testing and maintenance capabilities (58.82%)", "system troubleshooting capabilities (58.82%), might involve other factors, such as "appropriate training

Table 9. The structure variable in the diamond model

Structure	Percent (%)
Top management support and commitment	76.47
Cross-functional coordination	52.94
Communication and coordination effectiveness	52.94
Motivation/ Incentives program	41.18
Clear implementation goals	29.41
Risk management and allocation	29.41
Human resource commitment	23.53
Notes: The above factors are classified into the structure variable based on the definition of the diamond model.	

(64.71%)" and "training staff (end-users) support (64.71%)".

Through the above analyzing way of Leavitt's diamond model, we find that each factor is mutually affected and can reach the state of a balance. In fact, all critical factors in organizations possess a relationship of interdependence. In other words, when information technology (IT) of an organization is changed, it can affect the original way of executing tasks. When organizational structures or strategies generate changes, they can also affect the adoption of IT. When tasks are changed, staff's concepts and behaviors need to match such a change. Thus, when an organization introduces ERP systems and begin business process reengineering (BPR), four variables, including task, structure, people and technology, can mutually be affected. The important concept of this model states that IT's change has to match new task, people and structure so that the old structure can reach another new balance point. In the above tables, the percentage stands for the degree of interviewee's response. The higher the percentage is, the more the conflict is. Thus, whole organizations might be involved. On the contrary, as the percentage is lower, it presented that the success is easier to reach.

Data Analysis III

In this section, we build a methodology which consists of the Leavitt's diamond model and the

Table 10. The people variable in the diamond model

People	Percent (%)
Project manager's competence	70.59
Domain knowledge of suppliers	64.71
Consultant's experience	64.71
Appropriate training	64.71
Training staff (end-users) support	64.71
Supplier support and training	58.82
Team involvement	52.94
Local support	47.06
External expertise support	35.29
Notes: The above factors are classified into the people variable based on the definition of the diamond model.	

Table 11. The technology variable in the diamond model

Technology	Percent (%)
System reliability	70.59
Product functionality and quality of ERP	64.71
System testing and maintenance capabilities	58.82
System troubleshooting capabilities	58.82
Data conversion and integrity	58.82
Integration of legacy system and ERP	52.94
Minimal customization to meet organizational process	29.41
IT infrastructure	23.53
Notes: The above factors are classified into the technology variable based on the definition of the diamond model.	

Table 12. An analysis model built from the diamond model and ASAP roadmap

ERP Implementation Roadmap				
Organization variables	Phase 1	Phase 2	Phase 3	Phase 4	Phase 5
	Project Preparation	Business Blueprint	Realization	Final Preparation	Go Live & Support
Task	oFit with business process (58.82%) oProject cost planning and management (58.82%) oProject timeframe and implementation strategy (35.29%)	oOrganization change management (41.18%) oWork time schedule (35.29%)	oKnowledge transfer from consultant to the company (64.71%)	oFeedback and monitoring (41.18%)	oFast effects (58.82%)
People	oProject manager's competence (70.59%) oConsultant's experience (64.71%)		oTraining staff (ending-users) support (64.71%) oTeam involvement (52.94%) oExternal expertise support (35.29%) oLocal support (47.06%)	oAppropriate training (64.71%) oSupplier support and training (58.82%)	
Structure	oTop management support and commitment (76.47%) oHuman resource commitment (23.53%) oDomain knowledge of suppliers (64.71%)	oCross-functional coordination (52.94%) oCommunication and coordination effectiveness (52.94%) oClear implementa-tion goals (29.41%)	oMotivation/ Incentives program (41.18%) oRisk management and allocation (29.41%)		
Technology	oProduct functionality and quality of ERP (64.71%) oIT infrastructure (23.53%)	oMinimal customization to meet organizational process (29.41%) oSystem reliability (70.59%)	oIntegration of legacy system and ERP (52.94%) oData conversion and integrity (58.82%)		oSystem testing and maintenance capabilities (58.82%) oSystem troubleshooting capability (58.82%)

ASAP Roadmap. At the same time, we put the critical factors of enterprise group into the built methodology and analyze them (see Table 12). Through the methodology, we can understand which factor is emphasized during ERP implementation.

Firstly, we find that, in the phase of the project preparation, most respondents mainly focus on help of external knowledge and experiences because the percentage related to external experts is higher than others. These factors include project manager's competence, consultant's experience and domain knowledge of suppliers. On the contrary, IT infrastructure in the phase is not especially considered. The possible cause shows that this phase expressed the requirements of professional scope. Secondly, 70.50 percent of respondents think that system reliability is the most important factor in the phase of business blueprint. This phase displays that system quality and function are taken into account. At the same time, stability and history of the ERP suppliers could affect firms to choose them. Thirdly, two factors, knowledge transfer from consultant to the company and training staff (ending-users) support, are regarded as important factors in the phase of realization. Fourthly, relative training is valued in the phase of final preparation. Fifthly, system testing and maintenance abilities are stressed in the phase of go live & support. Through the built methodology, we find out that most concerned factors mainly concentrate on the phase of project preparation and are mainly from people and structure variable.

Discussion

In this study, we focus on the analysis of success factors of implementing SAP system for ERP implementation in small and midsize firms in Taiwan. Since the related researches involved with SMEs are not found in Taiwan yet, we propose methodologies to analyze the questionnaire obtained from different interviewees. In the study,

we obtain some important results. Main critical success factors are emphasized by interviewees, as follows:

- Top management support and commitment;
- Project manager's competence;
- Communication and coordination effectiveness;
- Team involvement;
- Cross-functional coordination;
- Clear implementation goals;
- System testing and maintain capabilities;
- Knowledge transfer from consultant to the company;
- System reliability;
- Product functionality and quality of ERP.

In addition, we compare previous literatures and there are some interesting findings. There are some same points of view listed as follows:

- Top management support and commitment (Finney & Corbett, 2007; Nah et al., 2001; Siriginidi, 2000; Remus, 2007);
- Project manager's competence (Finney & Corbett, 2007);
- Communication and coordination effectiveness (Nah et al., 2001; Woo, 2006; Remus, 2007);
- Clear implementation goals (Remus, 2007);
- Team involvement (Finney & Corbett, 2007; Woo, 2006; Remus, 2007);
- Product functionality and quality of ERP (Finney & Corbett, 2007; Siriginidi, 2000).

There are some different points of view listed as follows:

- Project cost planning and management (Ferman, 1999; Finney & Corbett, 2007);
- IT infrastructure (Siriginidi, 2000; Finney & Corbett, 2007);

- Risk management and allocation (Talwar, 1993; Clemons, 1995).

Regarding the above three factors, they are not seen as the critical factors by Taiwan's interviewees. This result is different from previous literatures.

CONCLUSION

With diversification and complexity of product in an enterprise, an integrated information system, ERP, is developed to manage an organization. In general, the ERP systems are deployed in the large-scale enterprises. Since they usually possess more complicated organizational structures and business processes, they need the ERP information systems to treat with a large number of daily activities. By implementing ERP systems, an enterprise can streamline their organizational structure and business processes and advance their competitiveness. Thus, the system can bring an organization obvious benefit and the ERP is a quite expensive information system. Only large-scale enterprises can possess enough resources to afford such a costly system. However, currently, more and more SMEs are considering implementing ERP in order to advance their competitiveness.

In the study, we explored the critical factors affecting SMEs to adopt ERP and surveyed the Taiwan's companies using SAP systems. The result displays that the factor of implementing costs was not regarded as key factor in the SMEs. On the contrary, interviewees were mainly concerned about acquirement of IT knowledge and support and commitment of top management. We think that most companies belong to SMEs and possess well competitiveness. However, SMEs are usually subject to insufficient resources so that they cannot have their own IT knowledge and technology, including software and hardware. On the other hand, top management support and commitment is considered the most important factor to introduce successful ERP systems because top management has the decisive affection in an organization. This result is also similar to past studies. Therefore, through the study, we can understand the key factors to the ERP implementation of current SMEs in Taiwan.

REFERENCES

Al-Mashari, M. (2001). Process orientation through enterprise resource planning (ERP): A review of critical issues. *Knowledge and Process Management*, 8(3), 175–185. doi:10.1002/kpm.114

Al-Mashari, M., & Zairi, M. (2000). The effective application of SAP R/3: A proposed model of best practice. *Losidtics Information Management*, 13(3), 156–166. doi:10.1108/09576050010326556

Al-Mudimigh, A., Zairi, M., & Al-Mashari, M. (2001). ERP implementation: An integrative framework. *European Journal of Information Systems*, 10, 216–226. doi:10.1057/palgrave.ejis.3000406

Allen, R. S., & Kilmann, R. H. (2001). The role of the reward system for a total quality management based strategy. *Journal of Organizational Change*, 14(2), 110–131. doi:10.1108/09534810110388036

Armstrong, M. (1995). *A handbook of personnel management practice* (5th ed.). London: Kogan Page.

Attewell, P. (1992). Technology diffusion and organizational learning: The case of business computing. *Organization Science*, 3(1), 1–19. doi:10.1287/orsc.3.1.1

Bancroft, N. H., Seip, H., & Sprengel, A. (1999). *Implementing SAP R/3: How to introduce a large system into a large organization* (2nd ed.). Upper Saddle River, NJ: Prentice-Hall.

Bertin, C. K. (2004). *Government business process transformation: From automation to paradigm shift; from localize exploitation to business scope redefinition*. Retrieved from http://www.comnet-it.org/news/stlucia/Tue- 10th-CletusBert-Govt-Business-Process-Transformation1.ppt#2

Boykin, R. F. (2001). Enterprise resource-planning software: A solution to the return material authorization problem. *Computers in Industry, 45*, 99–109. doi:10.1016/S0166-3615(01)00083-5

Brady, J., Monk, E., & Wagner, B. (2001). *Concepts in enterprise resource planning*. Course Technology Thomson Learning.

Bunker, D. J., & MacGregor, R. C. (2000). Successful generation of information technology (IT) requirements for small/medium enterprises (SMEs)-cases from regional Australia. In *Proceedings of the SMEs in a Global Economy*, Wollongong (pp. 72-84).

Buonanno, G., Pigni, F., Ravarini, A., Sciuto, D., & Tagliavini, M. (2005). Factors affecting ERP system adoption: A comparative analysis between SMEs and large companies. *Journal of Enterprise Information Management, 18*(4), 384–426. doi:10.1108/17410390510609572

Bylinsky, G. (1999). The challengers move in on ERP. *Fortune*, 306.

Chau, P. Y. K. (1995). Factors used in the selection of packaged software in small business: Views of owners and manager. *Information & Management, 29*(2), 71–78. doi:10.1016/0378-7206(95)00016-P

Clemons, E. (1995). Using scenario analysis to manage the strategic risks of reengineering. *Sloan Management Review*, 61–71.

Collins, H. (2001). *Corporate portals revolutionizing information access to increase productivity and drive the bottom line*. New York: American Management Association.

Crage, P. B., & King, M. (1993). Small-firm computing: Motivators and inhibitors. *Management Information Systems Quarterly, 17*(1), 47–60. doi:10.2307/249509

Davenport, T. H. (1992). *Process innovation: Reengineering work through information technology*. Boston: Harvard Business School Press.

Davenport, T. H. (1998). Putting the enterprise into the enterprise system. *Harvard Business Review*, 121–131.

Davison, R. (2002). Cultural complications of ERP. *Association for Computing Machinery Communications of the AC, 45*, 109.

Debrabander, B., & Thiers, G. (1984). Successful information system development in relation to situational factors which affect effective communication between MIS users and EDP specialists. *Management Science, 30*(2), 137–155. doi:10.1287/mnsc.30.2.137

Ferman, J. E. (1999). Strategies for successful ERP connections. *Manufacturing Engineering, 123*, 48–60.

Finney, S., & Corbett, M. (2007). ERP implementation: A compilation and analysis of critical success factors. *Business Process Management Journal, 13*(3), 329–347. doi:10.1108/14637150710752272

Gable, G. G. (1991). Consultant engagement for first time computerization: A pro-action role in small business. *Information & Management, 20*(2), 83–93. doi:10.1016/0378-7206(91)90046-5

Gartner Group and Dataquest. (1999). *ERP Software Publishers: Service Strategies and Capabilities*. New York: Gartner Group and Dataquest.

Geng, H. (2004). *Manufacturing Engineering Handbook*. New York: McGraw Hill.

Grover, V., Jeong, S. R., Kettinger, W., & Teng, J. (1995). The implementation of business process reengineering. *Journal of Management Information Systems, 12*(1), 109–144.

Heinrich, J. (1994). *System planning I: Planning and realizing of information project*. Munchen, Germany: Wien.

Helo, P. (2008). Expectation and reality in ERP implementation: Consultant and solution provider perspective. *Industrial Management & Data Systems, 108*(8), 1045–1059. doi:10.1108/02635570810904604

Hill, S. (1997). The wait is over. *Manufacturing Systems, 15*, II–X.

Holland, C., & Light, B. (1999). A critical success factors model for ERP implementation. *IEEE Software*, 30–35. doi:10.1109/52.765784

Hung, S.-T., Chang, S.-J., & Lee, P.-J. (2004). *Critical factors of ERP adoption for small- and medium-sized enterprise: An empirical study*. Retrieved http://74.125.153.132/search?q=cache:3B8wrg1IB84J:www.pacis-net.org/file/2004/S15-002.PDF+critical+factors+of+erp+adoption+for+samll+and+medium&cd=1&hl=zh-TW&ct=clnk&gl=tw

Iacovou, C. L., Benbasat, I., & Dexter, A. S. (1995). Electronic data interchange and small organizations: Adoption and impact of technology. *Management Information Systems Quarterly, 19*(4), 465–485. doi:10.2307/249629

Igbaria, M., Zinatelli, N., Cragg, P., & Cavaye, A. M. (1997). Personal computing acceptance factors in small firms: A structural equation model. *Management Information Systems Quarterly, 21*(3), 279–305. doi:10.2307/249498

Janet, P. (2008, August 1). *The ERP software market share leader. ERPsoftware360*. Retrieved http://www.erpsoftware360.com/erp.htm

Jenson, R. L., & Johnson, I. R. (1999). The enterprise resource planning system as a strategic solution. *Information Strategy. The Executive's Journal, 15*, 28–33.

Juell-Skielse. (2006). *ERP adoption in small and medium sized companies*. Retrieved from http://kth.diva-portal.org/smash/get/diva2:10252/FULLTEXT01

Keen, P. G. W. (1981). Information systems and organizational change. *Communications of the ACM, 24*(1), 24–33. doi:10.1145/358527.358543

Kemp, M. J., & Low, G. C. (2008). ERP innovation implementation model incorporating change management. *Business Process Management, 14*(2), 228–242. doi:10.1108/14637150810864952

Klatt, L. A. (1973). *Small business management: Essential in entrepreneurship*. CA: Wadsworth.

Leavitt, H. J. (1965). Applied organizational change in industry: Structural, technological, and humanistic approaches. In March, J. (Ed.), *Handbook of organizations* (pp. 1144–1170). Chicago: Rand McNally & Co.

Likert, R. (1932). *A Technique for the Measurement of Attitudes*. New York: Archives of Psychology.

Loh, T. C., & Koh, S. C. L. (2004). Critical elements for a successful enterprise resource planning implementation in small-and medium-sized enterprises. *International Journal of Production Research, 42*(17), 3433–3455. doi:10.1080/00207540410001671679

Lukman, S. (2003). *Business process reengineering and ASAP: Side-by-side*. Retrieved from http://www.susanto.id.au/papers/BPEASAP.asp

Mabert, V. A., Soni, A., & Venkataramanan, M. A. (2001). Enterprise resource Planning: Common myths versus evolving reality. *Business Horizons*, 69–76. doi:10.1016/S0007-6813(01)80037-9

MacGregor, R. C., & Kartiwi, M. (2007). Electronic commerce adoption barriers in small to medium-sized enterprises (SMEs) in developed and developing countries: A cross-country comparison. *Journal of Electronic Commerce in Organizations, 5*(3), 35–51.

MacGregor, R. C., Vrazalic, L., Carlsson, S., Bunker, D., & Magnusson, M. (2002). The impact of business size and business type on small business investment in electronic commerce: A study of Swedish small business. *Australasian Journal of Information Systems, 9*(2), 31–39.

Marnewick, C., & Labuschagne, L. (2005). A conceptual model for enterprise resource planning (ERP). *Information Management & Computer Security, 13*(2), 144–155. doi:10.1108/09685220510589325

Martins, E. C., & Terblanche, F. (2003). Building or organisational culture that stimulates creativity and innovation. *European Journal of Innovation Management, 6*(1), 64–74. doi:10.1108/14601060310456337

Nah, F. F.-h., Lau, J. L.-s., & Kuang, J. (2001). Critical factors for successful implementation of enterprise systems. *Business Process Management Journal, 7*(3), 285–296. doi:10.1108/14637150110392782

Okunoye, A., & Bertaux, A. (2006). KAFRA: A context-aware framework of knowledge management in global diversity. *International Journal of Knowledge Management, 2*(2), 26–45.

Peng, G. C., & Nunes, M. B. (2008). Identification and assessment of risks to successful exploitation of ERP systems in China. In *Proceedings of the European and Mediterranean Conference on Information Systems* (pp. 1-13).

Poba-Nzaou, P., Raymond, L., & Fabi, B. (2008). Adoption and risk of ERP systems in manufacturing SMEs: A positivist case study. *Business Process Management Journal, 14*(4), 530–550. doi:10.1108/14637150810888064

Raymond, L., & Uwizeyemungu, S. (2007). A profile of ERP adoption in manufacturing SMEs. *Journal of Enterprise Information Management, 20*(4), 487–502. doi:10.1108/17410390710772731

Remus, U. (2007). Critical success factors for implementing enterprise portals. A comparison with ERP implementations. *Business Process Management Journal, 13*(4), 538–552. doi:10.1108/14637150710763568

Rock, N. L. (2003). *Examining the relationship between business process reengineering and information technology.* Retrieved from http://faculty.ed.umuc.edu /~meinkej/inss690/larock.pdf

SAP. (1999). *Accelerated SAP.* Retrieved from http://help.sap.com/printdocu/core/print46b /en/data/en/pdf/SVASAP.pdf

SAP. (2000). *SAP implementation* (PowerPoint slides). Retrieved from http://www.mi s.cmich.edu/bis697c/asap91_ph/46asap9105.pdf

SAP. (2007). *Independent research firm states SAP as worldwide market share leader for CRM, ERP and SCM.* Retrieved from http://www.sap.com/solutions/business-suite/scm/newsevents/press.epx?pressid=8309

SAP. (2009). *ASAP Roadmap.* Retrieved from http://help.sap.com/saphelp_47x200/helpdata/en/48/623972d55a11d2bbf700105a5e5b3c/content.htm

Schneider, P. (1999). Wanted: ERPeople skills. *CIO Magazine, 12*(10), 30–37.

Shehab, E. M., Sharp, M. W., Supramaniam, L., & Spedding, T. A. (2004). Enterprise resource planning an integrative review. *Business Process Management Journal, 10*(4), 359–386. doi:10.1108/14637150410548056

Singla, A. R., & Goyal, D. P. (2004). *Managing risk factors in design and implementation of ERP systems: An empirical investigation of the Indian industry*. International Association for Management of Technology.

Siriginidi, S. R. (2000). Enterprise resource planning in reengineering business. *Business Process Management Journal, 6*(5), 376–391. doi:10.1108/14637150010352390

Sledgianowski, D., Tafti, M. H. A., & Kierstead, J. (2007). SME ERP system sourcing strategies: A case study. *Industrial Management & Data Systems, 108*(4), 421–436. doi:10.1108/02635570810868317

SMEA. (2008). *Annual blue print in small, medium-sized enterprises*. Retrieved from http://book.moeasmea.gov.tw/book/doc_detail.jsp?pub_SerialNo=2008A00937&click=2008A00937

Smith, D. (1999). Better data collection for greater efficiency. *Manufacturing Engineering, 123*, 62–68.

Soja, P. (2006). Success factors in ERP systems implementations: Lessons from practice. *Journal of Enterprise Information Management, 19*, 646–661. doi:10.1108/17410390610708517

Somers, T. M., & Nelson, K. (2001). The impact of critical success factors across the stages of enterprise resource planning implementations. In *Proceedings of the 34th Hawaii International Conference on System Sciences (HICSS)*.

Stamford, C. (1999). *Meta group study dispels common myths about ERP/ERM implementation costs and overall value comprehensive study assesses ERP/ERM issues and compares top vendors*. Retrieved from http://findarticles.com/p/articles/mi_m0EIN/is_1999_April_1/ai_54277417/

Stoilov, T., & Stoilova, K. (2008). Functional analysis of enterprise resource planning systems. In *Proceedings of the International Conference on Computer Systems and Technologies* (pp. 1-6).

Sumner, M. (2000). Risk factors in enterprise-wide/ERP projects. *Journal of Information Technology, 15*, 317–327. doi:10.1080/02683960010009079

Talwar, R. (1993). Business re-engineering – A strategy-driven approach. *Long Range Planning, 26*(6), 22–40. doi:10.1016/0024-6301(93)90204-S

Tarafdar, M., & Roy, R. K. (2003). Analyzing the adoption of enterprise resource planning systems in Indian organizations: A process framework. *Journal of Global Information Technology Management, 6*, 31–38.

Thong, J. Y. L. (1999). An integrated model of information systems adoption in small business. *Journal of Management Information Systems, 15*(4), 187–214.

Thong, J. Y. L. (2001). Resource constrains and information systems implementation is Singaporean small business. *Omega, 29*, 143–156. doi:10.1016/S0305-0483(00)00035-9

Thong, J. Y. L., Yap, C. S., & Raman, K. S. (1996). Top management support, external expertise and information systems implementation in small business. *Information Systems Research, 7*(2), 248–267. doi:10.1287/isre.7.2.248

Todor, S., & Krasimira, S. (2008). Functional analysis of enterprise resource planning Systems. In *Proceedings of the International Conference on Computer Systems and Technologies* (pp. 1-6).

Trunick, P. A. (1999). ERP: Promise or pipe dream? *Transportation & Distribution*, *40*, 23–26.

Venkatraman, N. (1994). IT-enabled business transformation: From automation to business scope redefinition. *Sloan Management Review*, 429–442.

Vidyaranya, B. G., & Cydnee, B. (2005). Success and failure factors of adopting SAP in ERP system implementation. *Business Process Management Journal*, *11*(4), 501–516.

Vuksic, V. B., & Spremic, M. (2005). ERP system implementation and business process change: Case study of p pharmaceutical company. *Journal of Computing and Information Technology- Cit*, *13*(1), 11-24.

Welsh, J. A., & White, J. F. (1981). A small business is not a little big business. *Harvard Business Review*, *59*(4), 81–32.

West, R., & Daigle, S. L. (2004). Total cost of ownership: A strategic tool for ERP planning and implementation. *Educause Center for Applied Research*, *1*, 1–14.

Wikipedia. (2009). *Content validity*. Retrieved from http://en.wikipedia.org/wiki/Co ntent_va lidity

Wildemann, H. (1990). *The implementation of computer integrated manufacturing system*. Munchen.

Wilderman, B. (2003). Taking the measure of ERP implementations. *Meta Delta*, *2240*, 1–5.

Woo, H. S. (2006). Critical success factors for implementing ERP: The case of a Chinese electronics manufacturer. *Journal of Manufacturing Technology Management*, *18*(4), 431–442. doi:10.1108/17410380710743798

APPENDIX A

Statistical table of questionnaire from enterprise group

Enterprise Group Critical Success Factor	Unimportant (%)	Little importance (%)	Moderately important (%)	Important (%)	Very Important (%)
Top management support and commitment				23.53	76.47
Project manager's competence			5.88	23.53	70.59
Team involvement			5.88	41.18	52.94
External expertise support		11.77	29.41	23.53	35.29
Consultant's experience			5.88	29.41	64.71
Supplier support and training			11.77	29.41	58.82
Domain knowledge of suppliers				35.29	64.71
Local support			17.65	35.29	47.06
Human resource commitment			35.29	41.18	23.53
Clear implementation goals			23.53	47.06	29.41
Organization change management			11.76	41.18	41.18
Cross-functional coordination		11.77		35.29	52.94
Fast effects			11.77	29.41	58.82
Fit with business process		5.885	5.885	29.41	58.82
Project cost planning and management		5.885	5.885	29.41	58.82
Feedback and monitoring		5.88	5.88	47.06	41.18
Risk management and allocation		11.76	5.89	52.94	29.41
Communication and coordination effectiveness				47.06	52.94
Project timeframe and implementation strategy			11.77	52.94	35.29
Work time schedule			11.77	52.94	35.29
Appropriate training		5.88	5.88	23.53	64.71
Motivation/Incentives program		11.76	23.53	23.53	41.18
IT infrastructure			23.53	52.94	23.53
Knowledge transfer from consultant to the company				35.29	64.71
Minimal customization to meet organizational process		5.88		64.71	29.41
System reliability			5.88	23.53	70.59
Product functionality and quality of ERP				35.29	64.71
Integration of Legacy system and ERP			17.65	29.41	52.94
System testing and maintenance capabilities			5.89	35.29	58.82
System troubleshooting capabilities				41.18	58.82
Training staff (end-users) support				47.06	52.94
Data conversion and integrity			5.89	35.29	58.82
Note: "Unimportant" to "very important"					

APPENDIX B

Statistical table of questionnaire from consultant group

Consultant Group Critical Success Factor	Unimportant (%)	Little importance (%)	Moderately important (%)	Important (%)	Very Important (%)
Top management support and commitment				8.33	91.67
Project manager's competence				16.67	83.33
Team involvement				33.33	66.67
External expertise support		12.5	25	62.5	0
Consultant's experience			12.5	66.67	20.83
Supplier support and training			12.5	70.83	16.67
Domain knowledge of suppliers				83.33	16.67
Local support			20.83	62.5	16.67
Human resource commitment		8.33	12.5	41.67	37.5
Clear implementation goals				25	75
Organization change management			33.34	33.33	33.33
Cross-functional coordination			8.33	29.17	62.5
Fast effects			41.67	33.33	25
Fit with business process			25	54.17	20.83
Project cost planning and management				66.67	33.33
Feedback and monitoring				70.83	29.17
Risk management and allocation			8.33	54.17	37.5
Communication and coordination effectiveness				25	75
Project timeframe and implementation strategy			4.16	54.17	41.67
Work time schedule			12.5	41.67	45.83
Appropriate training			16.67	45.83	37.5
Motivation/Incentives program		12.5	20.83	54.17	12.5
IT infrastructure			41.67	45.83	12.5
Knowledge transfer from consultant to the company			12.5	45.83	41.67
Minimal customization to meet organizational process		4.16	29.17	50	16.67
System reliability		4.17	20.83	37.5	37.5
Product functionality and quality of ERP		4.16	16.67	37.5	41.67
Integration of Legacy system and ERP		4.17	33.33	45.83	16.67
System testing and maintenance capabilities			8.33	41.67	50
System troubleshooting capabilities			8.33	54.17	37.5
Training staff (end-users) support			16.67	58.33	25
Data conversion and integrity			16.67	37.5	45.83
Note: "Unimportant" to "very important"					

APPENDIX C

Statistical table of questionnaire from all interviewees

All Respondents Critical Success Factors	Unimportant (%)	Little importance (%)	Moderately important (%)	Important (%)	Very Important (%)
Top management support and commitment				14.63	85.37
Project manager's competence			2.44	19.51	78.05
Team involvement			2.44	36.58	60.98
External expertise support		12.2	26.83	46.34	14.63
Consultant's experience			9.76	51.22	39.02
Supplier support and training			12.2	53.66	34.15
Domain knowledge of suppliers				63.41	36.59
Local support			19.51	51.22	29.27
Human resource commitment		4.88	21.95	41.47	31.71
Implementation goals clear			9.76	34.15	56.10
Organization change management			24.39	36.58	36.59
Cross-functional coordination		4.88	4.88	31.71	58.54
Fast effects			29.27	31.71	39.02
Fit with business process		2.44	17.07	43.9	36.59
Project cost planning and management		2.44	2.44	51.22	43.90
Feedback and monitoring		2.44	2.44	60.97	34.15
Risk management and allocation		4.88	7.32	53.66	34.15
Communication and coordination effectiveness				34.15	65.85
Project timeframe and implementation strategy			7.32	53.66	39.02
Work time schedule			12.2	46.34	41.46
Appropriate training		2.44	12.2	36.58	48.78
Motivation/Incentives program		12.19	21.95	41.47	24.39
IT infrastructure			34.15	48.78	17.07
Knowledge transfer from consultant to the company			7.32	41.46	51.22
Minimal customization to meet organizational process		4.87	17.08	56.1	21.95
System reliability		2.44	14.63	31.71	51.22
Product functionality and quality of ERP		2.44	9.76	36.58	51.22
Integration of Legacy system and ERP		2.44	26.83	39.02	31.71
System testing and maintain capabilities			7.32	39.02	53.66
System troubleshooting capabilities			4.88	48.78	46.34
Training staff (end-users) support			9.76	53.66	36.59
Data conversion and integrity			12.2	36.58	51.22
Note: "Unimportant" to "very important"					

APPENDIX D

Questionnaire

Part 1: Background Information

☐ Enterprise (Key user or Top management)

Enterprise category: ☐ Trading company ☐ Manufacturing industry ☐ Other _____

Year of establishment: ☐ 1-10 years ☐ 11-15 years ☐ 16-20 years ☐ 20 years and more Employee number: ☐ below 20 people ☐ 21-100 people ☐ 100-200 people ☐ 200 people and more MIS staff number: ☐ None ☐ 1-3 people ☐ 3-5 people ☐ 5-10 people ☐ 10 people and more

☐ Consultant

Work module: ☐ Sales and distribution ☐ Materials management ☐ Production planning ☐ Financial accounting ☐ Controlling

Year of work: ☐ 1-3 years ☐ 4-6 years ☐ 7-9 years ☐ 10 years and more

Age: ☐ 18-25 years old ☐ 26-35 years old ☐ 36-45 years old ☐ 46-55 years old ☐ 55 years old and more

Part 2: Please identify the degree of importance for ERP implementation. (Score 1-5: ☐ 1-Unimportant ☐ 2-Of Little Importance ☐ 3-Moderately Important ☐ 4-Important ☐ 5-Very Important)

1. Top management support and commitment 1☐ 2☐ 3☐ 4☐ 5☐
2. Project manager's competence 1☐ 2☐ 3☐ 4☐ 5☐
3. Team involvement 1☐ 2☐ 3☐ 4☐ 5☐
4. External expertise support 1☐ 2☐ 3☐ 4☐ 5☐
5. Consultant's experience 1☐ 2☐ 3☐ 4☐ 5☐
6. Supplier support and training 1☐ 2☐ 3☐ 4☐ 5☐
7. Domain knowledge of suppliers 1☐ 2☐ 3☐ 4☐ 5☐
8. Local support 1☐ 2☐ 3☐ 4☐ 5☐
9. Human resource commitment 1☐ 2☐ 3☐ 4☐ 5☐
10. Clear implementation goals 1☐ 2☐ 3☐ 4☐ 5☐
11. Organization change management 1☐ 2☐ 3☐ 4☐ 5☐
12. Cross-functional coordination 1☐ 2☐ 3☐ 4☐ 5☐
13. Fast effects 1☐ 2☐ 3☐ 4☐ 5☐
14. Fit with business process 1☐ 2☐ 3☐ 4☐ 5☐
15. Project cost planning and management 1☐ 2☐ 3☐ 4☐ 5☐
16. Feedback and monitoring 1☐ 2☐ 3☐ 4☐ 5☐
17. Risk management and allocation 1☐ 2☐ 3☐ 4☐ 5☐
18. Communication and coordination effectiveness 1☐ 2☐ 3☐ 4☐ 5☐
19. Project timeframe and implementation strategy 1☐ 2☐ 3☐ 4☐ 5☐
20. Work time schedule 1☐ 2☐ 3☐ 4☐ 5☐
21. Appropriate training 1☐ 2☐ 3☐ 4☐ 5☐
22. Motivation/ Incentives program 1☐ 2☐ 3☐ 4☐ 5☐
23. IT infrastructure 1☐ 2☐ 3☐ 4☐ 5☐
24. Knowledge transfer from consultant to the company 1☐ 2☐ 3☐ 4☐ 5☐
25. Minimal customization to meet organizational process 1☐ 2☐ 3☐ 4☐ 5☐

26. System reliability 1☐ 2☐ 3☐ 4☐ 5☐
27. Product functionality and quality of ERP 1☐ 2☐ 3☐ 4☐ 5☐
28. Integration of legacy system and ERP 1☐ 2☐ 3☐ 4☐ 5☐
29. System testing and maintenance capabilities 1☐ 2☐ 3☐ 4☐ 5☐
30. System troubleshooting capabilities 1☐ 2☐ 3☐ 4☐ 5☐
31. Training staff (end-users) support 1☐ 2☐ 3☐ 4☐ 5☐
32. Data conversion and integrity 1☐ 2☐ 3☐ 4☐ 5☐

End of Questionnaire

This work was previously published in the International Journal of Digital Library Systems, Volume 2, Issue 1, edited by Chia-Hung Wei, pp. 1-37, copyright 2011 by IGI Publishing (an imprint of IGI Global).

Compilation of References

Abarach, H. M. (2001). An exploratory survey of book loss, theft and damage in Abubakar Tafawa Balewa University (ATBU), Bauchi. *Nigeria* . *Library & Archival Security, 17*(1), 31–42.

Abdullahi, Z. M., & Haruna, I. (2008). Utilization of information and communication technology (ICT) for information services delivery in university libraries in Adamawa State. *Information Technologist: An International Journal of Information and Communication Technology, 5*(2), 24–30.

Adams, G., Rausser, G., & Simon, L. (1996). Modelling multilateral negotiations: An application to California water policy. *Journal of Economic Behavior & Organization, 30,* 97–111. doi:10.1016/S0167-2681(96)00844-X

Adams, J. (1995). Interaction between color plane interpolation and other image processing functions in electronic photography. *Proceedings of the Society for Photo-Instrumentation Engineers, 2146,* 144–151.

Adebisi, O. L. (2002). Information and communication technology availability, accessibility and resource sharing in the federal polytechnic libraries in South West Nigeria. *Information Technologist: An International Journal of Information and Communication Technology, 6*(2), 169–176.

Adeogun, M. (2003). The digital divide and university educations systems in Sub-Saharan Africa. *Journal of Library* . *Archives and Information Science, 13*(2), 11–20.

ADL. (2003). *Sharable Content Object Reference Model (SCORM)*. Retrieved from. http://www.adlnet.gov/

Afolabi, M. (1993). Factors influencing theft and mutilation among library users and staff in Nigeria. *Journal of Leading Libraries and Information Centres, 1*(3-4), 2–8.

Agboola, A. T. (2001). Penetration of stock security in a Nigerian university library. *Lagos Librarian, 22*(1-2), 45–50.

Ahmed, U. N. U., Amin, W. K. W., & Ismali, W. K. (2009). The impact of technostress on organization commitment among Malaysian academic librarians. *Singapore Journal of Library & Information Management, 38,* 103–123.

Aida-zade, K. R., & Hasanov, J. Z. (2009). Word base line detection in handwritten text recognition system. *International Journal of Electrical and Computer Engineering, 4*(5), 310–314.

Aina, L. O. (2004). Coping with the challenges of library and information delivery services: The need for institutional professional development. In *Proceedings of the Nigerian Library Association Conference*.

Ajayi, G. O. (2005). *E-Government in Nigeria's e-strategy*. Paper presented at the 5th Annual African Computing and Telecommunication Summit, Abuja, Nigeria.

Ajegbomogun, F. O. (2004). Users' assessment of library security: A Nigerian university case study. *Library Management, 25*(8-9), 386390.

Akinfolarin, W. A. (1992). Towards improving security measures in Nigerian libraries. *African Journal of Library* . *Archives and Information Sciences, 2*(1), 51–56.

Akintunde, S. A. (2004). *Libraries as tools for ICT development*. Paper presented at the 42nd Annual Nations Conference and AGM of the Nigerian Library Association, Akure, Nigeria.

Akintunde, S. A. (2006, June 18-23). State of ICT's tertiary institutions in Nigeria: Windows on the universities. In *Proceedings of the 44th Annual National Conference and Annual General Meeting of the Nigerian Library Association*, Abuja, Nigeria (pp. 123-127).

Alexia, B., & Michael, S. (2004). Optimal watermark detection under quantization the transform domain. *IEEE Transactions on Circuits and Systems for Video Technology, 14*, 1308–1319. doi:10.1109/TCSVT.2004.836753

Algazi, V. R., Ford, G. E., & Potharlanka, R. (1991). Directional interpolation of images based on visual properties and rank order filtering. In *Proceedings of the IEEE Int. Conf. Acoustics, Speech . Signal Processing, 4*, 3005–3008.

Allen, R. S., & Kilmann, R. H. (2001). The role of the reward system for a total quality management based strategy. *Journal of Organizational Change, 14*(2), 110–131. doi:10.1108/09534810110388036

Al-Mashari, M. (2001). Process orientation through enterprise resource planning (ERP): A review of critical issues. *Knowledge and Process Management, 8*(3), 175–185. doi:10.1002/kpm.114

Al-Mashari, M., & Zairi, M. (2000). The effective application of SAP R/3: A proposed model of best practice. *Losidtics Information Management, 13*(3), 156–166. doi:10.1108/09576050010326556

Al-Mudimigh, A., Zairi, M., & Al-Mashari, M. (2001). ERP implementation: An integrative framework. *European Journal of Information Systems, 10*, 216–226. doi:10.1057/palgrave.ejis.3000406

Alokun, N. A. T. (1993). The impact of pilfering and mutilation on library collection. *Library Scientists, 17*, 70–79.

Al-Qallaf, C. L. (2006). Librarians and technology in academic and research libraries in Kuwait: Perceptions and effects. *Libri, 56*, 168–179. doi:10.1515/LIBR.2006.168

Altun, H. O., Orsdemir, A., Sharma, G., & Bocko, M. F. (2009). Optimal spread spectrum watermark embedding via a multistep feasibility formulation. *IEEE Transactions on Image Processing, 18*, 371–387. doi:10.1109/TIP.2008.2008222

Amerini, I., Ballan, L., Caldelli, R., Del Bimbo, A., & Serra, G. (2011). A SIFT-based forensic method for copy–move attack detection and transformation recovery. *IEEE Transactions on Information Forensics and Security, 3*(6).

Amoroso, D. L., & Hunsinger, D. S. (2009). Measuring the acceptance of internet technology by consumers. *Journal of E-Adoption, 1*(3).

Anaehobi, E. S. (2007). Availability of ICT facilities in academic libraries in Anambra State. *Journal of the Nigeria Library Association . Anambra State Chapter, 1*(1), 57–64.

Anderson, R. H. (1977). Two-dimensional mathematical notation. In *Proceedings of the Syntactic Pattern Recognition Applications* (pp. 147-177).

Aoyagi, Y., & Asakura, T. (1996). A study on traffic sign recognition in scene image using genetic algorithms and neural networks. In *Proceedings of the 22nd International Conference on Industrial Electronics, Control, and Instrumentation*.

Arkin, A., Askary, S., Fordin, S., Jekeli, W., Kawaguchi, K., Orchard, D., et al. (2000). *Web Services Choreography Interface (WSCI)*. Retrieved from http://www.w3.org/TR/wsci/

Arms, J. (2000). *Digital libraries*. Delhi, India: MIT Press.

Armstrong, M. (1995). *A handbook of personnel management practice* (5th ed.). London: Kogan Page.

Arnetz, B. B., & Berg, M. (1993). Tehnolosress psychological consequences of poor man- machine interface . In Smith, M. J., & Salvend, G. (Eds.), *Human computer interaction: applications and case studies* (pp. 891–896). Amsterdam, The Netherlands: Elsevier.

Attewell, P. (1992). Technology diffusion and organizational learning: The case of business computing. *Organization Science, 3*(1), 1–19. doi:10.1287/orsc.3.1.1

Baba, Z., & Broady, J. (1998). Organizational effectiveness assessment: case studies of the National Library of Wales and Perpustakaan Negara Malaysia. In *Proceedings of the 2nd Northumbria International Conference on Performance Measurement in Libraries and Information Services*, Newcastle upon Tyne, UK (pp. 319-339).

Babafemi, G. O., & Adedibu, L. O. (2007). Application of computer technology to circulation subsystem of the Federal University of Agriculture, Abeokuta. *Nigerbiblios*, *18*(1-2), 23–30.

Babbie, E. (2004). *The practice of social research* (10th ed.). Belmont, CA: Thomson/Wadsworth.

Bahlmann, C., Zhu, Y., Ramesh, V., Pellkofer, M., & Koehler, T. (2005). A system for traffic sign detection, tracking, and recognition using color, shape, and motion information. In *Proceedings of the Intelligent Vehicles Symposium* (pp. 255-260).

Baker College System. (2002). *Blended/Hybrid Delivery*. Retrieved from www.baker.edu/ departments/instructech/blended.html

Bancroft, N. H., Seip, H., & Sprengel, A. (1999). *Implementing SAP R/3: How to introduce a large system into a large organization* (2nd ed.). Upper Saddle River, NJ: Prentice-Hall.

Banerji, A., Bartolini, C., Beringer, D., Chopella, V., Govindarajan, K., Karp, A., et al. (Eds.). (2000). *Web Services Conversation Language (WSCL)*. Retrieved from http://www.w3.org/TR/wscl10/

Bar-Ilan, J., Peritz, B. C., & Wolman, Y. (2003). A survey on the use of electronic databases and electronic journals accessed through the web by the academic staff of Israeli universities. *Journal of Academic Librarianship*, *29*(6), 346–361. doi:10.1016/j.jal.2003.08.002

Barlette, V. (1995). Avoiding computer avoidance. *Library Administration and Management*, *9*(4), 225–230.

Barni, M., & Bartolini, F. (2004). Data hiding for fighting piracy. *Signal Processing Magazine*, *21*, 28–39. doi:10.1109/MSP.2004.1276109

Barni, M., & Bartoloni, F. (2004). *Watermarking systems engineering*. Boca Raton, FL: CRC Press.

Barreto, P. S. L. M., Kim, H. Y., & Rijmen, V. (2002). Toward secure public-key blockwise fragile authentication watermarking. *Vision . Image and Signal Processing*, *149*, 57–62. doi:10.1049/ip-vis:20020168

Bartolini, F., Tefas, A., Barni, M., & Pitas, I. (2001). Image authentication techniques for surveillance applications. *Proceedings of the IEEE*, *89*, 1403–1418. doi:10.1109/5.959338

Baruchson-Arbib, S., & Shor, F. (2002). The use of electronic information sources by Israeli college students. *Journal of Academic Librarianship*, *28*(4), 255–257. doi:10.1016/S0099-1333(02)00289-6

Battisti, F., Carli, M., Neri, A., & Egiaziarian, K. (2006). A generalized Fibonacci LSB data hiding technique. In *Proceedings of the Third International Conference on Computers and Devices for Communication*.

Bayram, S., Sencar, H. T., Memon, N., & Avcibas, I. (2005). Source camera identification based on CFA interpolation. In *Proceedings of the IEEE International Conference on Image Processing* (pp. 69-72).

Belaid, A., Pierron, L., & Valverde, N. (2000). Part-of-speech tagging for table of contents recognition. In *Proceedings of the 15th International Conference on Pattern Recognition*, Barcelona, Spain (Vol. 4, pp. 451-454).

Belaid, Y., Panchevre, J. L., & Belaid, A. (1998). Form analysis by neural classification of cells. In *Proceedings of the 3rd Workshop on Document Analysis Systems*, Nagano, Japan (pp. 69-78).

Belaid, A. (2001). Recognition of table of contents for electronic library consulting. *International Journal on Document Analysis and Recognition*, *4*(1), 35–45. doi:10.1007/PL00013572

Belaid, A., & Haton, J. P. (1984). A syntactic approach for handwritten mathematical formula recognition. *IEEE Transactions on Pattern Analysis and Machine Intelligence*, *6*(1), 105–111. doi:10.1109/TPAMI.1984.4767483

Berman, B. P., & Fateman, R. J. (1994). Optical character recognition for typset mathematics. In *Proceedings of the International Symposium on Symbolic and Algebraic Computation*, Oxford, UK (pp. 348-353).

Bertin, C. K. (2004). *Government business process transformation: From automation to paradigm shift; from localize exploitation to business scope redefinition*. Retrieved from http://www.comnet-it.org/news/stlucia/Tue- 10th-CletusBert-Govt-Business-Process-Transformation1.ppt#2

Bezdek, J. C., Ehrlich, R., & Full, W. (1984). FCM: The fuzzy c-means clustering algorithm. *Computers & Geosciences*, *10*(2-3), 191–203. doi:10.1016/0098-3004(84)90020-7

Bezuidenhout, M. (1996). How does one deal with vandalism? *Cape Librarian*, *40*(3), 37.

Bhattacharya, U., & Chaudhuri, B. B. (2009). Handwritten numeral databases of Indian scripts and multistage recognition of mixed numerals. *IEEE Transactions on Pattern Analysis and Machine Intelligence*, *31*(3), 444–457. doi:10.1109/TPAMI.2008.88

Bi, H. H., & Zhao, J. L. (2003). Mending the lag between commercial needs and research prototypes: a logic-based workflow verification approach. In *Proceedings of the 8th INFORMS Computing Society Conference*.

Bichteler, J. (1986). Human aspect of high tech in special Libraries. *Special Libraries*, *9*(3), 121–128.

Bill & Melinda Gates Foundation. (2004). *Toward equality of access: The role of public libraries in addressing the digital divide*. Retrieved from http://www.worldcat.org/title/toward-equality-of-access-the-role-of-public-libraries-in-addressing-the-digital-divide/oclc/54706779

Bishop, A. P. (2002). Measuring access, use and success in digital libraries. *Journal of Electronic Publishing*. Retrieved February 10, 2007, from http://www.press.umich.edu/jep/04-02/bishop.html

Biswas, A., Bhowmick, P., & Bhattacharya, B. B. (2010). Construction of isothetic covers of a digital object: A combinatorial approach. *Journal of Visual Communication and Image Representation*, *21*(4), 295–310. doi:10.1016/j.jvcir.2010.02.001

Blackstock, K. L., & Richards, C. (2007). Evaluating stakeholder involvement in river basin planning: a Scottish case study. *Water Policy*, *9*, 493–512. doi:10.2166/wp.2007.018

Blake, M. B. (2003). Coordinating multiple agents for workflow-oriented process orchestration. *Information System and e-Business Management*, *1*(2), 387-405.

Blake, M. B., & Gomaa, H. (2005). Agent-oriented compositional approaches to services-based cross-organizational workflow. *Decision Support Systems*, *40*, 31–50. doi:10.1016/j.dss.2004.04.003

Blancard, M. (1992). Road sign recognition: A study of vision-based decision making for road environment recognition . In Masaki, I. (Ed.), *Vision based vehicle guidance* (pp. 162–175). Berlin, Germany: Springer-Verlag. doi:10.1007/978-1-4612-2778-6_7

Blandford, A., Stelmaszewska, H., & Bryan-Kinns, N. (2001). Use of multiple digital libraries: a case study. In *Proceedings of the 1st ACM/IEEE-CS Joint Conference on Digital Libraries*.

Borgman, C. (2000). *From Gutenberg to the global infrastructure: Access to information in the networked world*. Cambridge, MA: MIT Press.

Borgman, C., Smat, L., Milwood, K., & Finley, J. (2005). Comparing faculty information seeking in teaching and research: Implications for the design of digital libraries. *Journal of the American Society for Information Science and Technology*, *56*(6), 636–657. doi:10.1002/asi.20154

Boubaker, H., Kherallah, M., & Alimi, A. M. (2009). New algorithm of straight or curved baseline detection for short Arabic handwritten writing. In *Proceedings of the 10th International Conference on Document Analysis and Recognition* (pp. 778-782).

Boyer, J.-P., Duhamel, P., & Blanc-Talon, J. (2007). Performance analysis of scalar DC-QIM for zero-bit watermarking. *IEEE Transactions on Information Forensics and Security*, *2*, 283–289. doi:10.1109/TIFS.2007.897279

Boykin, R. F. (2001). Enterprise resource-planning software: A solution to the return material authorization problem. *Computers in Industry*, *45*, 99–109. doi:10.1016/S0166-3615(01)00083-5

Bradbeer, R. (1995). A medium resolution intelligent video camera. *IEEE Transactions on Consumer Electronics*, *41*, 573–578. doi:10.1109/30.468092

Bradshaw, J. M. (1997). *Software agents*. Cambridge, MA: MIT Press.

Brady, J., Monk, E., & Wagner, B. (2001). *Concepts in enterprise resource planning*. Course Technology Thomson Learning.

Brisbane, G., Safavi-Nani, R., & Ogunbona, P. (2005). High-capacity steganography using a shared colour palette. *IEEE Proceedings on Vision, Image, and Signal Processing*, *152*, 787–792. doi:10.1049/ip-vis:20045047

Brod, C. (1984). *Technostress: The human cost of the computer revolution*. Reading, MA: Addison-Wesley.

Brosnan, M., & Thorpe, S. (2001, July 12-14). Does technophobia conform to DSM-1V criteria for a specific phobia (300.29)? In *Proceedings of the 22ⁿᵈ International Conference of STAR, the International Society for Stress and Anxiety Research*, Palma de Mallorca, Spain.

Brun, L., & Kropatsch, W. (2006). Contains and inside relationships within combinatorial pyramids. *Pattern Recognition, 39*(4), 515–526. doi:10.1016/j.patcog.2005.10.015

Buciu, I., & Gacsadi, A. (2011). Directional features for automatic tumor classification of mammogram images. *Biomedical Signal Processing and Control, 6*(4), 370–378. doi:10.1016/j.bspc.2010.10.003

Bunker, D. J., & MacGregor, R. C. (2000). Successful generation of information technology (IT) requirements for small/medium enterprises (SMEs)-cases from regional Australia. In *Proceedings of the SMEs in a Global Economy*, Wollongong (pp. 72-84).

Buonanno, G., Pigni, F., Ravarini, A., Sciuto, D., & Tagliavini, M. (2005). Factors affecting ERP system adoption: A comparative analysis between SMEs and large companies. *Journal of Enterprise Information Management, 18*(4), 384–426. doi:10.1108/17410390510609572

Burr, W. E. (2003). Selecting the advanced encryption standard. *Security & Privacy, 1*, 43–52. doi:10.1109/MSECP.2003.1193210

Buttenfield, B. (1999). Usability evaluation of digital libraries . In Stern, D. (Ed.), *Philosophies, technical design considerations, and example scenarios*. New York, NY: Haworth Press.

Bylinsky, G. (1999). The challengers move in on ERP. *Fortune*, 306.

Caldelli, R., Amerini, I., Picchioni, F., De Rosa, A., & Uccheddu, F. (2009). Multimedia forensic techniques for acquisition device identification and digital image authentication . In Li, C.-T. (Ed.), *Handbook of research on computational forensics, digital crime and investigation: Methods and solutions*. Hershey, PA: Information Science Reference. doi:10.4018/978-1-60566-836-9.ch006

Callan, J., Smeaton, A., Beaulieu, M., Borlund, P., Brusilovsky, P., & Chalmers, C. (2000). Personalization and recommender systems in digital libraries. *International Journal on Digital Libraries, 57*(4), 299–308. Retrieved from http://doras.dcu.ie/205/

Camarinha-Matos, L. M., & Afsarmanesh, H. (1999). The virtual enterprise concept . In Camarinha-Matos, L. M., & Afsarmanesh, H. (Eds.), *Infrastructures for virtual enterprises: Networking industrial enterprises* (pp. 3–14). Boston, MA: Kluwer Academic.

Cao, H., & Kot, A. C. (2010). Accurate Detection of Demosaicing Regularity for Digital Image Forensic. *IEEE Transactions on Information Forensics and Security, 4*, 889–910.

Carrato, S., Ramponi, G., & Marsi, S. (1996). A simple edge--sensitive image interpolation filter. In *Proceedings of the IEEE Int. Conf. Image Processing* (Vol. 3, pp. 711-714).

Casey, E. (1999). *Digital evidence and computer crime: Forensic science, computers and the Internet*. New York, NY: Academic Publishing.

Celik, M. U., Saber, E., Sharma, G., & Tekalp, A. M. (2001). Analysis of feature-based geometry invariant watermarking. *Proceedings of the SPIE: Security and Watermarking of Multimedia Contents III, 4314*, 261–268.

Chamlawi, R., Li, C.-T., Usman, I., & Khan, A. (2009). Authentication and recovery of digital images: potential application in video surveillance and remote sensing. In *Proceedings of the Digest of Technical Papers in the International Conference on Consumer Electronics* (pp. 1-2).

Champion, S. (1988). Technostress: Technology toll. *School Library Journal, 3*(3), 48–51.

Chan, C. K., & Cheng, L. M. (2004). Hiding data in images by simple LSB substitution export. *Pattern Recognition, 37*, 469–474. doi:10.1016/j.patcog.2003.08.007

Chandran, S., Balasubramanian, S., Gandhi, T., Prasad, A., Kasturi, R., & Chhabra, A. (1996). Structure recognition and information extraction from tabular documents. *International Journal of Imaging Systems and Technology, 7*(4), 289–303. doi:10.1002/(SICI)1098-1098(199624)7:4<289::AID-IMA4>3.0.CO;2-4

Chang, C., & Chou, H. (2008). A new public-key oblivious fragile watermarking for image authentication using Discrete Cosine Transform. In *Proceedings of the Second International Conference on Future Generation Communication and Networking Symposium*.

Chang, C. C., & Wu, W. C. (2006). Hiding secret data adaptively in vector quantisation index tables. *IEEE Proceedings on Vision, Image, and Signal Processing, 153*, 589–597. doi:10.1049/ip-vis:20050153

Chang, C.-C., Hsiao, J.-Y., & Chan, C.-S. (2003). Finding optimal least-significant-bit substitution in image hiding by dynamic programming strategy. *Pattern Recognition, 36*, 1583–1595. doi:10.1016/S0031-3203(02)00289-3

Chang, S. K. (1970). A method for the structural analysis of 2-d mathematical expression. *Information Sciences, 2*(3), 253–272. doi:10.1016/S0020-0255(70)80052-4

Chan, K. F., & Yeung, D. Y. (1999, July). Recognizing on-line handwritten alphanumeric characters through flexible structural matching. *Pattern Recognition, 32*(7), 1099–1114. doi:10.1016/S0031-3203(98)00155-1

Chan, K. F., & Yeung, D. Y. (2000). Mathematical expression recognition: A survey. *International Journal on Document Analysis and Recognition, 3*(1), 3–15. doi:10.1007/PL00013549

Chaudhuri, B. B., & Bera, S. (2009). Handwritten text line identification in Indian scripts. In *Proceedings of the 10th International Conference on Document Analysis and Recognition* (pp. 636-640).

Chau, P. Y. K. (1995). Factors used in the selection of packaged software in small business: Views of owners and manager. *Information & Management, 29*(2), 71–78. doi:10.1016/0378-7206(95)00016-P

Chellappa, R. K., & Shivendu, S. (2003). Economics of technology standards: Implications for offline movie piracy in a global context. In *Proceedings of the 36th Annual Hawaii International Conference on System Sciences* (p. 10).

Chen, M., Fridrich, J., Goljan, M., & Lukas, J. (2007). Source digital camcorder identification using sensor photo response non-uniformity. *Proceedings of the SPIE, 6505*.

Chen, M., Fridrich, J., Goljan, M., & Lukas, J. (2007a). Digital imaging sensor identification. In *Proceedings of SPIE* (Vol. 6505).

Chen, M., Fridrich, J., Lukas, J., & Goljan, M. (2008). Imaging sensor noise as digital x-ray for revealing forgeries. In *Proceedings of the 9th Information Hiding Workshop* (pp. 342-458).

Chen, Q., Dayal, U., Hsu, M., & Griss, M. L. (2000). Dynamic-agents, workflow and XML for e-commerce automation. In *Proceedings of the First International Conference on Electronic Commerce and Web Technologies*, London, UK (pp. 314-323).

Chen, B., & Wornell, G. W. (2001a). Quantization index modulation methods for digital watermarking and information embedding of multimedia. *Journal of Very Large Signal Processing Systems, 27*, 7–33. doi:10.1023/A:1008107127819

Chen, B., & Wornell, G. W. (2001b). Quantization index modulation methods: A class of provable good methods for digital watermarking and information embedding. *IEEE Transactions on Information Theory, 49*, 563–593.

Chen, I.-T., & Yeh, Y.-S. (2006). Security analysis of transformed-key asymmetric watermarking system. *Signal Processing Letters, 13*, 213–215. doi:10.1109/LSP.2005.863677

Chen, L. H., & Yin, P. Y. (1992). A system for on-line recognition of handwritten mathematical expressions. *Computer Processing of Chinese and Oriental Languages, 6*(1), 19–39.

Chen, M., Fridrich, J., Goljan, M., & Lukas, J. (2007). Source digital camcorder identification using sensor photo response non-uniformity. *Proceedings of the Society for Photo-Instrumentation Engineers, 6505*.

Chen, M., Fridrich, J., Goljan, M., & Lukas, J. (2008). Determining image origin and integrity using sensor noise. *IEEE Transactions on Information Security and Forensics, 3*, 74–90. doi:10.1109/TIFS.2007.916285

Chen, M., Fridrich, J., Lukas, J., & Goljan, M. (2008). *Imaging sensor noise as digital X-ray for revealing forgeries* (pp. 342–458).

Chen, S. Y., & Leung, H. (2008). Chaotic watermarking for video authentication in surveillance applications. *IEEE Transactions on Circuits and Systems for Video Technology, 18*, 704–709. doi:10.1109/TCSVT.2008.918801

Choi, H., Lee, K., & Kim, T. (2004). Transformed-key asymmetric watermarking system. *Signal Processing Letters, 11*, 251–254. doi:10.1109/LSP.2003.819873

Choi, S. P. M., Liu, J., & Chan, S. P. (2001). A genetic agent-based negotiation system. *Computer Networks, 37*, 195–204. doi:10.1016/S1389-1286(01)00215-8

Choi, S., Lam, E. Y., & Wong, K. K. Y. (2006). Source camera identification using footprints from lens aberration. *Proceedings of the Society for Photo-Instrumentation Engineers, 6069*, 172–179.

Chou, P. (1989). Recognition of equations using a two-dimensional stochastic context-free grammar. *Visual Communications and Image Processing*, 852-863.

Chowdhury, G. C. (2003). *Introduction to digital libraries.* London, UK: Facet Publishing.

Christensen, E., Curbera, F., Meredith, G., & Weerawarana, S. (2002). *Web Service Description Language (WSDL) specification.* Retrieved from http://www.w3.org/TR/wsdl

Chua, S. L., Chen, D., & Wong, A. F. L. (1999). Computer anxiety and its correlates: a meta-analysis. *Computers in Human Behavior, 15*, 609–623. doi:10.1016/S0747-5632(99)00039-4

CIP4. (2000). *Job definition format (JDF).* Retrieved from http://www.cip4.org/

Clark, K., & Kalin, S. (1996). Technostress out? *Library Journal, 121*(13), 30–32.

Clemons, E. (1995). Using scenario analysis to manage the strategic risks of reengineering. *Sloan Management Review*, 61–71.

Cleveland, G. (1998). *Digital libraries: Definitions, issues and challenges.* Retrieved from http://www.ifla.org/VI/5/op/udtop8/udtop8.htm

Clute, R. (1998). *Technostress: A content analysis* (Unpublished master's thesis). Kent State University, East Liverpool, OH.

Coatrieux, G., Lecornu, L., Sankur, B., & Roux, C. (2006). A review of image watermarking applications in healthcare. In *Proceedings of the 28th Annual International Conference Engineering in Medicine and Biology Society* (pp. 4691-4694).

Coatrieux, G., Le Guillou, C., Cauvin, J.-M., & Roux, C. (2009). Reversible watermarking for knowledge digest embedding and reliability control in medical images. *IEEE Transactions on Information Technology in Biomedicine, 13*, 158–165. doi:10.1109/TITB.2008.2007199

Cohen, S. (1973). Property destruction: Motives and meanings . In Ward, C. (Ed.), *Vandalism* (pp. 23–53). London, UK: H.E Warne.

Collins, H. (2001). *Corporate portals revolutionizing information access to increase productivity and drive the bottom line.* New York: American Management Association.

Constantinou, C. (1995). Destruction of knowledge: A study of journal mutilation at a large university library. *College & Research Libraries, 56*, 497–507.

Cool, C., & Spink, A. (1999). Education for digital libraries. *D-Lib Magazine, 5*(5).

Cooper, R., & Dempsey, D. R. (1998). Remote Library Users; needs and expectations. *Library Trends, 47*(1), 42–64.

Cornog, M., & Perper, T. (1996). From access to vandalism. In Greenwood Press (Ed.), *For sex education, see librarian: A guide to issues and resources* (pp. 115-136). Westport, CT: Greenwood Press.

Cosman, P. C., Oehler, K. L., Riskin, E. A., & Gray, R. M. (1993). Using vector quantization for image processing. *Proceedings of the IEEE, 81*, 1326–1341. doi:10.1109/5.237540

Cover, T. M., & Hart, P. E. (1967). Nearest neighbor pattern classification. *IEEE Transactions on Information Theory, 13*, 21–27. doi:10.1109/TIT.1967.1053964

Cox, I. J., Doerr, G., & Furon, T. (2006). Watermarking is not cryptography. In *Proceedings of the 5th International Workshop on Digital Watermarking* (pp. 1-15).

Cox, I. J., Kilian, J., Leighton, T., & Shamoon, T. (1997). Secure spread spectrum watermarking for multimedia. *IEEE Transactions on Image Processing, 6,* 1673–1687. doi:10.1109/83.650120

Cox, I. J., Miller, M., Bloom, J., Fridrich, J., & Kalker, T. (2007). *Digital watermarking and steganography* (2nd ed.). San Francisco, CA: Morgan Kaufmann.

Cox, I. J., Miller, M., Minka, T. P., Papathomas, T., & Yianilos, P. (2000). The Bayesian image retrieval system, PicHunter: Theory, implementation, and psychophysical experiments. *IEEE Transactions on Image Processing, 9*(1), 20–37. doi:10.1109/83.817596

Crage, P. B., & King, M. (1993). Small-firm computing: Motivators and inhibitors. *Management Information Systems Quarterly, 17*(1), 47–60. doi:10.2307/249509

Cui, H., Cui, X., & Meng, M. (2008). A public key cryptography based algorithm for watermarking relational databases. In *Proceedings of the International Conference on Intelligent Information Hiding and Multimedia Signal Processing* (pp. 1344-1347).

Cullen, R. (2001). Addressing the digital divide. *Online Information Review, 25*(5), 311–320. doi:10.1108/14684520110410517

Curry, A., Flodin, S., & Matheson, K. (2000). Theft and mutilation of library materials: Coping with biblio-bandits. *Library & Archival Security, 15*(2), 9–26. doi:10.1300/J114v15n02_03

Dai, H. W., Tang, Z., Tamura, H., & Yang, Y. (2006). Immune system inspired model and its applications. *International Journal of Soft Computing,* 22-29.

Dakshinamurti, C. (1985). Automations effect on library personnel. *Canadian Library Journal,* 343-351.

Das, A. K., & Chanda, B. (1998a, February 18-20). Detection of tables and headings from document image: A morphological approach. In *Proceedings of the International Conference on Computational Linguistics, Speech and Document Processing,* Calcutta, India (pp. 57-64).

Das, A. K., & Chanda, B. (1998b, April 6-8). Extraction of half-tones from document images: A morphological approach. In *Proceedings of the International Conference on Advances in Computing,* Calcutta, India (pp. 15-19).

Das, A. K., & Chanda, B. (2001). A fast algorithm for skew detection of document images using morphology. *International Journal of Document Analysis and Recognition, 4,* 109–114. doi:10.1007/PL00010902

Dasgupta, D., & Forrest, S. (1996). Novelty detection in time series data using ideas from immunology. In *Proceedings of the ISCA 5th International Conference on Intelligent Systems.*

Davenport, T. H. (1992). *Process innovation: Reengineering work through information technology.* Boston: Harvard Business School Press.

Davenport, T. H. (1998). Putting the enterprise into the enterprise system. *Harvard Business Review,* 121–131.

David-mills, N. (1998). *Technostress and the organization.* Retrieved September 9, 2008, from http://webmt.edu/ninadm/mia.htm

Davis, F. D. (1989). Perceived usefulness, perceived ease of use and user acceptance of information technology. *Management Information Systems Quarterly, 13*(3), 319–340. doi:10.2307/249008

Davison, R. (2002). Cultural complications of ERP. *Association for Computing Machinery Communications of the AC, 45,* 109.

de Castro, L. N., & Timmis, J. (2002). Artificial immune systems: A novel paradigm to pattern recognition. In *Proceedings of the Conference on Artificial Neural Networks in Pattern Recognition* (pp. 67-84).

de la Escalera, A., & Salichs, A. M. (1997). Road traffic sign detection and classification. *IEEE Transactions on Industrial Electronics, 44*(6). doi:10.1109/41.649946

de la Escalera, A., & Salichs, A. M. (2003). Traffic sign recognition and analysis for intelligent vehicles. *Image and Vision Computing, 21,* 247–258. doi:10.1016/S0262-8856(02)00156-7

De Watterille, A., & Gilbert, L. (2000). *Advanced information and communication technology.* Oxford, UK: Heinemann Educational Publishers.

DeAngelis, C. D., & Fontanarosa, P. B. (2010). US preventive services task force and breast cancer screening. *Journal of the American Medical Association, 303*(2), 172–173. doi:10.1001/jama.2009.1990

Debrabander, B., & Thiers, G. (1984). Successful information system development in relation to situational factors which affect effective communication between MIS users and EDP specialists. *Management Science*, *30*(2), 137–155. doi:10.1287/mnsc.30.2.137

Deschamp, C. (2001). *Can libraries help bridges the digital divide?* Retrieved from http://www.nordinfo.helsink.fi/publications/nordnytt/nnytt4-01/deschamps

Dietrich, C. F. (1991). *Uncertainty, calibration, and probability: the statistics of scientific and industrial measurement*. Bristol, UK: Institute of Physics.

Dijk, J. V., & Hacker, K. (2001). The digital divide as a complex and dynamic phenomenon. *The Information Society*, *19*, 315–326. doi:10.1080/01972240309487

Dimitriadis, Y. A., & Coronado, J. L. (1995). Towards an art based mathematical editor that uses on-line handwritten symbol recognition. *Pattern Recognition*, *28*(6), 807–822. doi:10.1016/0031-3203(94)00160-N

Dirik, A. E., Sencar, H. T., & Memon, N. (2008). Digital single lens reflex camera identification from traces of sensor dust. *IEEE Transaction on Information Forensics Security*, *3*, 539–552. doi:10.1109/TIFS.2008.926987

Dirisu, B. M. (2009). The availability and unitization of information and communication technologies (ICTs) in college of education (COE) Minna, a survey. *Information Technologist: An International Journal of Information and Communication Technology*, *6*(2), 149–153.

Dittmann, J., Wohlmacher, P., & Nahrstedt, K. (2001). Using cryptographic and watermarking algorithms. *Multimedia*, *8*, 54–65. doi:10.1109/93.959103

Dong, H., & Kim, H.-J. (2001). A fast content-based indexing and retrieval technique by the shape information in large image database. *Journal of Systems and Software*, *56*(2), 165–182. doi:10.1016/S0164-1212(00)00095-9

Drake, D., & Baird, H. (2005). Distinguishing mathematics notation from English text using computational geometry. In *Proceedings of the 8th International Conference on Document Analysis and Recognition*, Seoul, South Korea (pp. 1270-1274).

Dunn, P. F. (2005). *Measurement and data analysis for engineering and science*. New York, NY: McGraw-Hill.

Dutta, S. (2003). Impact of information communication technology on society. *Yojna*, *47*(7), 24.

Dyer, M. G. (1982). *A computer model of integrated process for narrative comprehension*. Cambridge, MA: MIT Press.

Early, D. S., & Long, D. G. (2001). Image reconstruction and enhanced resolution imaging from irregular samples. *IEEE Transactions on Geoscience and Remote Sensing*, *39*, 291–302. doi:10.1109/36.905237

Eaton, P. S., Freuder, E. C., & Wallace, R. J. (1998). Constraints and agents: Confronting ignorance. *AI Magazine*, *19*, 51–65.

Eberl, M. M., Fox, C. H., Edge, S. B., Carter, C. A., & Mahoney, M. C. (2006). BI-RADS classification for management of abnormal mammograms. *Journal of the American Board of Family Medicine*, *19*(2), 161–164. doi:10.3122/jabfm.19.2.161

Ekici, Q., Coskun, B., Umut, N., & Sankur, B. (2001). Comparative assessment of semi-fragile watermarking techniques. *Proceedings of the SPIE: Multimedia Systems and Applications*, *IV*, 177–188.

Ekici, Q., Sankur, B., Coskun, B., Umut, N., & Akcay, M. (2004). Comparative evaluation of semifragile watermarking algorithms. *Journal of Electronic Imaging*, *13*, 206–216. doi:10.1117/1.1633285

El Aroussi, M., El Hassouni, M., Ghouzali, S., Rziza, M., & Aboutajdine, D. (2011). Local appearance based face recognition method using block based steerable pyramid transform. *Signal Processing*, *91*(1), 38–50. doi:10.1016/j.sigpro.2010.06.005

Elfiky, N. M., Shahbaz Khan, F., van de Weijer, J., & Gonzàlez, J. (2012). Discriminative compact pyramids for object and scene recognition. *Pattern Recognition*, *45*(4), 1627–1636. doi:10.1016/j.patcog.2011.09.020

El-Naqa, I., Yang, Y., Galatsanos, N. P., Nishikawa, R. M., & Wernick, M. N. (2004). A similarity learning approach to content-based image retrieval: Application to digital mammography. *IEEE Transactions on Medical Imaging*, *23*(10), 1233–1244. doi:10.1109/TMI.2004.834601

Eltoukhy, M. M., Faye, I., & Samir, B. B. (2010). Breast cancer diagnosis in digital mammogram using multiscale curvelet transform. *Computerized Medical Imaging and Graphics*, *34*(4), 269–276. doi:10.1016/j.compmedimag.2009.11.002

Embley, D. W., Hurst, M., Lopresti, D., & Nagy, G. (2006). Table processing paradigms: A research survey. *International Journal on Document Analysis and Recognition*, *8*, 66–86. doi:10.1007/s10032-006-0017-x

Entlich, R., Garson, L., Lesk, M., Normore, L., Olsen, J., & Weibel, S. (1996). Testing a digital library: User response to the CORE project. *Library Hi Tech*, *14*(4), 99–118. doi:10.1108/eb048044

Ericsson, N. M., & Lafon, Y. (2002). *Simple Object Access Protocol (SOAP) specification*. Retrieved from http://www.w3.org/TR/soap12-part0/

Etta, F. E., & Pargn Wamahu, S. (2003). *Information and communication technologies for development in Africa: Volume 2: The experience with community telecentres*. Ottawa, ON, Canada: International Development research Center (IDRC).

Evald, P. (1996). Information Technology in Public Libraries . In Adesola, P. A., Omoba, R. O., & Adeyinka, T. (Eds.), *Attitudes of Librarians toward Selected Nigerian Universities toward the use of ICT*. Library Philosophy and Practice.

Faboyubde, E. O. (2006). The state of information and communication technology (ICT) in selected libraries in Lagos and Ibadan Metropolis in libraries: Dynamic engines for the knowledge and information society proceedings of the NLA. In *Proceedings of the 44ᵗʰ Annual National Conference and AGM*, Abuja, Nigeria (pp. 61-68).

Fang, C.-Y., Chen, S.-W., & Fuh, C.-S. (2003). Road-sign detection and tracking. *IEEE Transactions on Vehicular Technology*, *52*(5), 1329–1341. doi:10.1109/TVT.2003.810999

Farid, H. (2009). Image forgery detection. *Signal Processing Magazine*, *26*, 16–25. doi:10.1109/MSP.2008.931079

Fateman, R. J., Tokuyasu, T., Berman, B., & Mitchell, N. (1996). Optical character recognition and parsing of typeset mathematics. *Visual Communication and Image Representation*, *7*(1).

Fateman, R. J., & Tokuyasu, T. (1996). Progress in recognizing typeset mathematics. *Proceedings of the Society for Photo-Instrumentation Engineers*, *2660*, 37–50.

Feng, W., & Liu, Z. Q. (2008). Region-level image authentication using Bayesian structural content abstraction. *IEEE Transactions on Image Processing*, *17*, 2413–2424. doi:10.1109/TIP.2008.2006435

Ferman, J. E. (1999). Strategies for successful ERP connections. *Manufacturing Engineering*, *123*, 48–60.

Fine, S. F. (1986, April 14-16). Terminal paralysis or showdown at the interface. In D. Shaw (Ed.), *Human aspects of library automation: Helping staff and patrons cope (clinic on library applications of data processing)* (pp. 3-15). Urbana-Champaign, IL: Graduate School of Library and Information Sciences, University of Illinois.

Fine, S. (1986). Technological Innovation Diffusion and Resistance: an Historical Perspective. *Journal of Library Administration*, *7*(1).

Finney, S., & Corbett, M. (2007). ERP implementation: A compilation and analysis of critical success factors. *Business Process Management Journal*, *13*(3), 329–347. doi:10.1108/14637150710752272

Fishbein, M., & Ajzen, I. (1975). *Belief, attitude, intention and behavior. An introduction to theory and research*. Reading, MA: Addison-Wesley.

Forsyth, D. A., & Ponce, J. (2003). *Computer vision: A modern approach*. Upper Saddle River, NJ: Prentice Hall.

Frias-Martinez, E., & Chen, S. Y. (2005, August 17-19). Evaluation of user satisfaction with digital library interfaces. In *Proceedings of the 5th WSEAS International Conference on Simulation, Modeling and Optimization*, Corfu, Greece (pp. 172-177).

Fridich, J., Lukas, J., & Soukal, D. (2003). Detection of copy-move forgery in digital images. In *Proceedings of the Digital Forensics Research Conference*.

Fridrich, J. (1998a). Combining low frequency and spread spectrum watermarking. In *Proceedings of the SPIE International Symposium on Optical Science, Engineering, and Instrumentation* (pp. 19-24).

Fridrich, J. (1998b). Robust digital watermarking based on key-dependent basis functions. In *Proceedings of the Second Information Hiding Workshop* (pp. 143-157).

Fridrich, J. (1999). Methods for tamper detection in digital images. In *Proceedings of the ACM Workshop on Multimedia and Security* (pp. 19-23).

Fridrich, J. (2002). Security of fragile authentication watermarks with localization. *Proceedings of the SPIE: Security and Watermarking of Multimedia Contents, VI*, 691.

Fridrich, J. (2009). Digital image forensics. *IEEE Signal Processing Magazine, 26*(2), 26–37. doi:10.1109/MSP.2008.931078

Fridrich, J., Goljan, M., & Memon, N. (2002). Cryptanalysis of the Yeung-Mintzer fragile watermarking technique. *Journal of Electronic Imaging, 11*, 262–274. doi:10.1117/1.1459449

Friesen, K., & Mazloumi, N. (2004). Integration of learning management systems and web applications using web services. *Advanced Technology for Learning, 1*(1).

Fu, Y. (2007). A novel public key watermarking scheme based on shuffling. In *Proceedings of the International Conference on Convergence Information Technology* (pp. 312-317).

Fuji, T., & Tanigawa, T. (2002). The methodology for reuse of e-learning resources. In *Proceedings of the E-Learn World Conference on E-Learning in Corporate, Government, Healthcare, & Higher Education*, Montreal, QC, Canada (Vol. 1, pp. 305-310).

Gable, G. G. (1991). Consultant engagement for first time computerization: A pro-action role in small business. *Information & Management, 20*(2), 83–93. doi:10.1016/0378-7206(91)90046-5

Gaeta, M., Ritrovato, P., & Salerno, S. (2002, September). Implementing new advanced learning scenarios through GRID technologies. In *Proceedings of the First LeGE-WG International Workshop on Educational Models for GRID Based Services*, Lausanne, Switzerland.

Gambari, A. I., & Chike, O. A. (2007). Availability and utilization of ICT facilities higher institution in Nigeria State, Nigeria. *Information Technologist, 4*(1), 35–46.

Gangolli, A. R., & Tanimoto, S. L. (1983). Two pyramid machine algorithms for edge detection in noisy binary images. *Information Processing Letters, 17*(4), 197–202. doi:10.1016/0020-0190(83)90040-6

Gartner Group and Dataquest. (1999). *ERP Software Publishers: Service Strategies and Capabilities*. New York: Gartner Group and Dataquest.

Geng, H. (2004). *Manufacturing Engineering Handbook*. New York: McGraw Hill.

Ghouti, L., Bouridane, A., Ibrahim, M. K., & Boussakta, S. (2006). Digital image watermarking using balanced multiwavelets. *IEEE Transactions on Signal Processing, 54*, 1519–1536. doi:10.1109/TSP.2006.870624

Giakoumaki, A., Pavlopoulos, S., & Koutsouris, D. (2006). Multiple image watermarking applied to health information management. *IEEE Transactions on Information Technology in Biomedicine, 10*, 722–732. doi:10.1109/TITB.2006.875655

Gijsen, J. W. J., Szirbik, N. B., & Wagner, G. (2002). Agent technologies for virtual enterprises in the one-of-a-kind-production industry. *International Journal of Electronic Commerce, 7*(1), 9–34.

Gkizeli, M., Pados, D. A., & Medley, M. J. (2007). Optimal signature design for spread-spectrum steganography. *IEEE Transactions on Image Processing, 16*, 391–405. doi:10.1109/TIP.2006.888345

Goedemé, T. (2008). Traffic sign recognition with constellations of visual words. In *Proceedings of the International Conference on Informatics in Control, Automation and Robotics* (pp. 222-227).

Goesele, M., Heidrich, W., & Seidel, H.-P. (2001). Entropy based dark frame subtraction. In *Proceedings of the Image Processing, Image Quality, Image Capture Systems Conference* (pp. 293-298).

Goldstein, A. P. (1996). *The psychology of vandalism*. New York, NY: Plenum Press.

Gomes, J., Darsa, L., Costa, B., & Velho, L. (1999). *Warping and morphing of graphical objects*. San Francisco: Morgan Kaufmann.

Gonzalez, R. C., & Wood, R. (1992). *Digital image processing*. Reading, MA: Addison-Wesley.

Gonzalez, R. C., & Woods, R. E. (2002). *Digital image processing*. Upper Saddle River, NJ: Prentice Hall.

Gonzalz, F., & Dasgupta, D. (2004). Nomaly detection using real-valued negative selection. *Genetic Programming and Evolvable Machines*, 383–403.

Gopisetty, S., Lorie, R., Mao, J., Mohiuddin, M., Sorin, A., & Yair, E. (1996). Automated forms processing software and services. *IBM Journal of Research and Development*, *40*(2), 211–230. doi:10.1147/rd.402.0211

Gorman, M. (2001). Technostress and library value. *Library Journal*, *26*(7), 48–50.

Gorokhovskiy, K., Flint, J. A., Atta, S., & Glushnev, N. (2007). Cost effective multiframe demosaicking for noise reduction. In *Proceedings of the 15th International Conference on Digital Signal Processing* (pp. 407-410).

Gorski, N., Anisimov, V., Augustin, E., Baret, O., Price, D., & Simon, J. C. (1999). A2iA check reader: A family of bank check recognition systems. In *Proceedings of the 5th International Conference on Document Analysis and Recognition* (pp. 523-526).

Gosh, S. (2004). Indian telecom scenario. *Yojna*, *48*(1), 20.

Gouke, M. N., & Murfin, M. (1980). Periodical mutilation: The insidious disease. *Library Journal*, *105*(16), 95–97.

Graghill, D., Neale, C., & Wilson, T. D. (1989). *The Impact of IT on Staff Deployment in UK Public Libraries*. London: British Library.

Grauman, K., & Darrell, T. (2007). The pyramid match kernel: Efficient learning with sets of features. *Journal of Machine Learning Research*, *8*, 725–760.

Grbavec, A., & Blostein, D. (1995). Mathematical expression recognition using graph rewriting. In *Proceedings of the International Conference on Document Analysis and Recognition* (pp. 417-421).

Grgic, S., Mrak, M., Grgic, M., & Zovko-Cihlar, B. (2003). Comparative study of JPEG and JPEG2000 image coders. In *Proceedings of the 17th International Conference on Applied Electromagnetics and Communications* (pp. 109-112).

Grover, V., Jeong, S. R., Kettinger, W., & Teng, J. (1995). The implementation of business process reengineering. *Journal of Management Information Systems*, *12*(1), 109–144.

Guillevic, D., & Suen, C. Y. (1998). Recognition of legal amounts on bank cheques. *Pattern Analysis & Applications*, *1*(1), 28–41. doi:10.1007/BF01238024

Gunturk, B. K., Glotzbach, J., Altunbasak, Y., Schafer, R. W., & Mersereau, R. M. (2005). Demosaicking: color filter array interpolation. *Signal Processing Magazine*, *22*, 44–54. doi:10.1109/MSP.2005.1407714

Ha, J., Haralick, R. M., & Philips, I. T. (1995). Understanding mathematical expressions from document images. In *Proceedings of the International Conference on Document Analysis and Recognition* (pp. 956-959).

Hagan, M. T., Demuth, H. B., & Beale, M. (1995). *Neural network design*. Boston, MA: PWS Publishing.

Haizhou, L., & Baosheng, Y. (1998). Chinese word segmentation. In *Proceedings of the 12th Pacific Asia Conference on Language, Information, and Computation* (pp. 212-217).

Hajela, P., & Yoo, J. S. (1999). Immune network modelling in design optimization. *New Ideas in Optimization*, 203-215.

Hammouri, G., Ozturk, E., & Sunar, B. (2008). A tamper-proof and lightweight authentication scheme. *Pervasive and Mobile Computing*, *4*, 807–818. doi:10.1016/j.pmcj.2008.07.001

Harless, D. W., & Allen, F. R. (1999). Using the contingent valuation method to measure patron benefits of reference desk services in an academic library. *College & Research Libraries*, *60*(1), 59–69.

Harper, S. (2000). *Managing technostress in UK libraries. A realistic guide*. Retrieved September 12, 2007 from http://www.ariadne.ac.uk/issue25/technostress

Hart, S. (2009). *Vandalism in libraries: Causes, common occurrences and prevention strategies*. Retrieved from http://capping.slis.ualberta.ca/cap05/sandy/capping.htm

Haruna, I., & Oyelakan, G. O. (2010). Provision and utilization of information resources in Nigerian Defense Academy (NDA) Library, Kaduna. *Information Technologist, 7*(1), 11–18.

Hecht, E. (1987). *Optics*. Reading, MA: Addison-Wesley.

He, F., Ding, X., & Peng, L. (2004). Hierarchical logical structure extraction of book documents by analyzing table of contents. *Proceedings of the Society for Photo-Instrumentation Engineers, 5296*, 6–13.

Heinrich, J. (1994). *System planning I: Planning and realizing of information project*. Munchen, Germany: Wien.

Helo, P. (2008). Expectation and reality in ERP implementation: Consultant and solution provider perspective. *Industrial Management & Data Systems, 108*(8), 1045–1059. doi:10.1108/02635570810904604

Hill, S. (1997). The wait is over. *Manufacturing Systems, 15*, II–X.

Ho, A. T. S. (2007). Semi-fragile watermarking and authentication for law enforcement applications. In *Proceedings of the Second International Conference on Innovative Computing, Information and Control* (pp. 286-289).

Ho, A. T. S., Zhu, X., Vrusias, B., & Armstrong, J. (2006). Digital watermarking and authentication for crime scene analysis. In *Proceedings of the Institution of Engineering and Technology Conference on Crime and Security* (pp. 479-485).

Ho, A. T. S., Zhu, X., Shen, J., & Marziliano, P. (2008). Fragile watermarking based on encoding of the zeros of the z-transform. *IEEE Transactions on Information Forensics and Security, 3*, 567–579. doi:10.1109/TIFS.2008.926994

Holland, C., & Light, B. (1999). A critical success factors model for ERP implementation. *IEEE Software*, 30–35. doi:10.1109/52.765784

Holliman, M., & Memon, N. (2000). Counterfeiting attacks on oblivious block-wise independent invisible watermarking schemes. *IEEE Transactions on Image Processing, 9*, 432–441. doi:10.1109/83.826780

Holst, G. C. (1998). *CCD Arrays, Cameras, and Displays* (2nd ed.). New York: JCD Publishing & SPIE Pres.

Hong, W., Wong, W., Thong, J., & Tam, K. (2002). Determinants of user acceptance of digital libraries: An empirical examination of individual differences and system characteristics. *Journal of Management Information Systems, 18*(3), 97–124.

Hou, J., & Su, D. (2006). Integration of web services technology with business models within the total product design process for supplier selection. *Computers in Industry, 57*(8-9), 797. doi:10.1016/j.compind.2006.04.008

Hsu, C. C., Hung, T. Y., Lin, C. W., & Hsu, C. T. (2008). Video forgery detection using correlation of noise residue. In *Proceedings of the IEEE 10th Workshop on Multimedia Signal Processing*.

Hsu, K. C., & Ou Yang, F. C. (2005, July 5-8). OEPortal: an open, unified, and interoperable presentation-preserving e-learning portal. In *Proceedings of the 5th IEEE International Conference on Advanced Learning Technologies*, Kaohsiung, Taiwan (pp. 628-632)

Hsu, Y. F., & Chang, S. F. (2007). Image splicing detection using camera response function consistency and automatic segmentation. In *Proceedings of the IEEE International Conference on Multimedia and Expo* (pp. 28-31).

Hu, Y.-J., Ma, X.-P., Dou, L.-M., & Gao, L. (2008). A computation model for capacity and robustness of robust image watermarking scheme in spatial domain. In *Proceedings of the International Conference on Intelligent Information Hiding and Multimedia Signal Processing* (pp. 1154-1157).

Huang, C., & Srihari, S. (2008). Word segmentation of off-line handwritten documents. In *Proceedings of the IST/SPIE Annual Symposium on Document Recognition and Retrieval*.

Huang, H. K. (1998). *PACS: Basic principles and application* (1st ed.). New York, NY: John Wiley & Sons.

Huang, H. K. (2003). *PACS, image management, and imaging informatics*. New York, NY: Springer.

Huang, P. S., Chiang, C.-S., Chang, C.-P., & Tu, T.-M. (2005). Robust spatial watermarking technique for colour images via direct saturation adjustment. *Vision . Image and Signal Processing, 152*, 561–574. doi:10.1049/ip-vis:20041081

Huang, X., & Zhang, B. (2006). Robust detection of additive watermarks in transform domains. *Information Security, 153*, 97–106.

Huhns, M. N., & Munindar, P. S. (1998). *Readings in agents.* San Francisco, CA: Morgan Kaufmann.

Hu, J., Kashi, R., Lopresti, D., & Wilfong, G. (2000). Medium-independent table detection. *Proceedings of the Society for Photo-Instrumentation Engineers, 3967*, 291–302.

Hung, S.-T., Chang, S.-J., & Lee, P.-J. (2004). *Critical factors of ERP adoption for small-and medium-sized enterprise: An empirical study.* Retrieved http://74.125.153.132/search?q=cache:3B8wrg1IB84J:www.pacis-net.org/file/2004/S15-002.PDF+critical+factors+of+erp+adoption+for+samll+and+medium&cd=1&hl=zh-TW&ct=clnk&gl=tw

Huntsberry, J. S. (1992). Student library security patrols: A viable alternative. *Conservation Administration News, 49*, 1–2.

Iacovou, C. L., Benbasat, I., & Dexter, A. S. (1995). Electronic data interchange and small organizations: Adoption and impact of technology. *Management Information Systems Quarterly, 19*(4), 465–485. doi:10.2307/249629

IBM. (2002). *Business Process Execution Language for Web Services (BPEL4WS).* Retrieved from http://www-128.ibm.com/developerworks/library/specification/ws-bpel/

IBM. (2002). *Web Services Flow Language Specification (WSFL).* Retrieved from http://www-3.ibm.com/software/solutions/webservices/pdf/WSFL.pdf

Igbaria, M., Zinatelli, N., Cragg, P., & Cavaye, A. M. (1997). Personal computing acceptance factors in small firms: A structural equation model. *Management Information Systems Quarterly, 21*(3), 279–305. doi:10.2307/249498

Igben, M. J., & Akobo, D. I. (2007). State of information and communication technology (ICT) in libraries in Rivers State, Nigeria. *African Journal of Library . Archives and Information Science, 17*(2), 135–143.

Ilorah, H. C., Nwofor, F. A., & Onwudinjo, O. T. (2007). The place of university libraries in e-learning in Universities in Anambra State: A case study of Nnamdi Azikiwe University, Awka, Anambra State University, Uli and Madonna University Okija. *Journal of the Nigeria Library Association . Anambra State Chapter, 1*(1), 51–56.

International Telecommunication Union. (2003). *World summit on the information society.* Retrieved from http://www.itu.int/wsis

Ishikawa, Y., Subramanya, R., & Faloutsos, C. (1998). MindReader: Querying databases through multiple examples. In *Proceedings of the 24th International Conference on Very Large Data Bases.*

Israel, G. D. (2003). *Determining sample size.* Retrieved February 10, 2007, from http://edis.ifas.edu

Itonori, K. (1993). Table structure recognition based on textblock arrangement and ruled line position. In *Proceedings of the International Conference on Document Analysis and Recognition* (pp. 765-768).

Jaisingh, J. A. (2009). Impact of piracy on innovation at software firms and implications for piracy policy. *Decision Support Systems, 46*, 763–773. doi:10.1016/j.dss.2008.11.018

Jakimovsk, B., & Maehle, E. (2008). Artificial immune system based robot anomaly detection engine for fault tolerant robots. In *Proceedings of the 5th International Conference on Autonomic and Trusted Computing* (pp. 177-190).

Janet, P. (2008, August 1). *The ERP software market share leader. ERPsoftware360.* Retrieved http://www.erpsoftware360.com/erp.htm

JCP. (2003). *Portlets Specification final release, JSR168.* Retrieved September 20, 2004, from http://jcp.org/en/jsr/detail?id=168

Jenkins, F. A., & White, H. E. (1976). *Fundamentals of Optics.* New York: McGraw-Hill.

Jenson, R. L., & Johnson, I. R. (1999). The enterprise resource planning system as a strategic solution. *Information Strategy. The Executive's Journal, 15*, 28–33.

Jones, B. (1999). *Staff in the New Library: Skill Needs and Learning Choices, Findings from Training the Future, a Public Library Research Project*. London: British Library.

Jones, D. (2002). Ten Year later: support staff perceptions and opinions on technology in the workplace. *Library Trends, 47*, 4.

Jones, E. E. (1989). Library support staff and technology: Perceptions and opinions. *Library Trends, 37*(4), 432–456.

Juell-Skielse. (2006). *ERP adoption in small and medium sized companies*. Retrieved from http://kth.diva-portal.org/smash/get/diva2:10252/FULLTEXT01

Kacem, A., Belaid, A., & Ahmed, M. B. (2001). Automatic extraction of printed mathematical formulas using fuzzy logic and propagation of context. *International Journal of Document Analysis and Recognition, 4*(2), 97–108. doi:10.1007/s100320100064

Kang, D. (1994). *Invariant pattern recognition system based on sequential processing and geometrical transformation* (Unpublished doctoral dissertation). Texas A&M University, College Station, TX.

Kang, D., Griswold, N., & Kehtarnavaz, N. (1994). An invariant traffic sign recognition system based on sequential color processing and geometrical transformation. In *Proceedings of the IEEE Southwest Symposium on Image Analysis* (pp. 88-93).

Kang, X. G., Huang, J. W., & Zeng, W. J. (2008). Improving robustness of quantization-based image watermarking via adaptive receiver. *IEEE Transactions on Multimedia, 10*, 953–959. doi:10.1109/TMM.2008.2001361

Kankanhalli, M. S., & Ramakrishnan, K. R. (1998). Content based watermarking of images. In *Proceedings of the Sixth ACM International Conference on Multimedia* (pp. 61-70).

Kaplan-Leiserson, E. (2001). *E-learning Glossary in Learning Circuits*. Retrieved from www.learningcircuits.org/glossary.html

Karahanna, E., Straub, D. W., & Chervany, N. L. (1999). Information technology adoption across time: a cross-sectional comparison of pre-adoption and post-adoption beliefs. *Management Information Systems Quarterly, 23*(2), 183–213. doi:10.2307/249751

Kavulya, J. M. (2004). Challenges in the provision of library services for distance education: A case of selected universities in Kenya. *African Journal of Library. Archives and Information Science, 13*(1), 43–53.

Keen, P. G. W. (1981). Information systems and organizational change. *Communications of the ACM, 24*(1), 24–33. doi:10.1145/358527.358543

Kehtarnavaz, N., & Ahmad, A. (1995). Traffic sign recognition in noisy outdoor scenes. In *Proceedings of the Intelligent Vehicles Symposium*.

Kehtarnavaz, N., Griswold, N., & Kang, D. (1993). Stop-sign recognition based on color and shape processing. *Machine Vision and Applications, 6*, 206–208. doi:10.1007/BF01212298

Kemp, M. J., & Low, G. C. (2008). ERP innovation implementation model incorporating change management. *Business Process Management, 14*(2), 228–242. doi:10.1108/14637150810864952

Kenny, C. (2004). *Should we try to bridge the global digital divide?* Retrieved from http://charleskenny.blogs.com/weblog/files/infopiece.pdf

Kersten, G. E., & Lo, G. (2001). Negotiation support systems and software agents in e-business negotiations. In *Proceedings of the First International Conference on Electronic Business* (pp. 19-21).

Khan, N. A. (1995). Information technology in the University Libraries of Pakistan: Stresses and Strains. *Pakistan Library Bulletin, 26*, 1.

Kieninger, T. G. (1998). Table structure recognition based on robust block segmentation. *Proceedings of the Society for Photo-Instrumentation Engineers, 3305*, 22–32.

Kim, G., & Govindaraju, V. (1997). A lexicon driven approach to handwritten word recognition for real-time applications. *IEEE Transactions on Pattern Analysis and Machine Intelligence, 19*(4), 366–379. doi:10.1109/34.588017

Kim, H.-S., & Lee, H.-K. (2003). Invariant image watermark using Zernike moments. *IEEE Transactions on Circuits and Systems for Video Technology, 13*, 766–775. doi:10.1109/TCSVT.2003.815955

Kim, J.-A. (2006). Toward an understanding of Web-based subscription database acceptance. *Journal of the American Society for Information Science and Technology, 57*(13), 1715–1728. doi:10.1002/asi.20355

Kirchner, M., & Boehme, R. (2008). Hiding traces of resampling in digital images. *IEEE Transactions on Information Forensics and Security, 3*, 582–592. doi:10.1109/TIFS.2008.2008214

Klatt, L. A. (1973). *Small business management: Essential in entrepreneurship.* CA: Wadsworth.

Knight, T., & Timmis, J. (2001). AINE: An immunological approach to data mining. In *Proceedings of the IEEE International Conference on Data Mining* (pp. 297-304).

Kohonen, T., Oja, E., Simula, O., Visa, A., & Kangas, J. (1996). Engineering applications of the self-organizing map. *Proceedings of the IEEE, 84*(10), 1358–1384. doi:10.1109/5.537105

Korhonen, J., Pajunen, J., & Puustjarvi, J. (2003). Automatic composition of web services workflows using a semantic agent. In *Proceedings of the IEEE/WIC International Conference on Web Intelligence*, Beijing, China (pp. 566-569).

Kountchev, R., Rubin, S., Milanova, M., & Todorov, V. (2007, 13-15 Aug. 2007). Image multi-layer search based on spectrum pyramid. In *Proceedings of the IEEE International Conference on Information Reuse and Integration.*

Kropp, A., Leue, C., & Thompson, R. (Eds.). (2003). *Web Services for Remote Portles (WSRP) specification of OASIS version 1.0.* Retrieved October 2, 2004, from http://www.oasis-open.org/committees/download.php/3343/oasis-200304-wsrp-specification-1.0.pdf

Kumar, A., & Wainer, J. (2005). Meta workflows as a control and coordination mechanism for exception handling in workflow systems. *Decision Support Systems, 40*, 89–105. doi:10.1016/j.dss.2004.04.006

Kumsawat, P., Attakitmongcol, K., & Srikaew, A. (2005). A new approach for optimization in image watermarking by using genetic algorithms. *IEEE Transactions on Signal Processing, 53*, 4707–4719. doi:10.1109/TSP.2005.859323

Kundur, D., & Hatzinakos, D. (1999a). Towards a telltale watermarking technique for tamper-proofing. *Proceedings of the IEEE, 87*, 1167–1180. doi:10.1109/5.771070

Kundur, D., & Hatzinakos, D. (1999b). Digital watermarking for telltale tamper proofing and authentication. *Proceedings of the IEEE, 87*, 1167–1180. doi:10.1109/5.771070

Kupersmith, J. (2007). *Technostress in libraries.* Retrieved September 9, 2007, from http://www.net/stres.html

Kushki, A., Androutsos, P., Plataniotis, K. N., & Venetsanopoulos, A. N. (2004). Query feedback for interactive image retrieval. *IEEE Transactions on Circuits and Systems for Video Technology, 14*(5), 644–655. doi:10.1109/TCSVT.2004.826759

Kutter, M., Voloshynovskiy, V., & Herrigel, A. (2000). Watermark copy attack. *Proceedings of SPIE Security and Watermarking of Multimedia Contents, II*, 3971.

Kwak, B. H., Jun, W., Gruenwold, L., & Hong, S.-K. (2002). A study on the evaluation model for university libraries in digital environments. In M. Agosti & C. Thanos (Eds.), *Proceedings of 6th European Conference on Research and Advanced Technology for Digital Libraries*, Rome, Italy (LNCS 2458, pp. 204-217).

Kwon, J. B., & Yeom, H. Y. (2004). Generalized data retrieval for pyramid-based periodic broadcasting of videos. *Future Generation Computer Systems, 20*(1), 157–170. doi:10.1016/S0167-739X(03)00151-1

Lagier, J. (2002). *Measuring usage and usability of online databases at Haltnell College: An evaluation of selected electronic resources* (Unpublished doctoral dissertation). Nova Southeaster University, Davie, FL.

Lai, R. (1992). *Fuzzy constraint processing.* Raleigh, NC: NCSU Press.

Lai, R., & Lin, M. W. (2004). Modeling agent negotiation via fuzzy constraints in e-business. *Computational Intelligence, 20*, 624–642. doi:10.1111/j.0824-7935.2004.00257.x

Lanh, V. T., Emmanuel, S., & Kankanhalli, M. S. (2007). Identifying source cell phone using chromatic aberration. In *Proceedings of the IEEE Conference on Multimedia and Expo.*

Larson, S. (2009). Designing robust water planning institutions in remote regions: A case of Georgina and Diamantina catchment in Australia. *Water Policy, 12,* 357–368. doi:10.2166/wp.2009.266

Le Bourgeois, H. E., & Bensafi, S. S. (2001). Document understanding using probabilistic relaxation: Application on tables of contents of periodicals. In *Proceedings of the 6th International Conference on Document Analysis and Recognition*, Seattle, WA (p. 508-512).

Learning and Libraries. (2004). *The sophist.* Retrieved from http://www/sophinstitute.com/soplist-no8-editor.aspx

Leavitt, H. J. (1965). Applied organizational change in industry: Structural, technological, and humanistic approaches . In March, J. (Ed.), *Handbook of organizations* (pp. 1144–1170). Chicago: Rand McNally & Co.

Lee, C.-F., Chang, C.-C., & Wang, K.-H. (2008). Hiding data in VQ-compressed images using pairwise nearest codewords based on minimum spanning tree. In *Proceedings of the International Conference on Intelligent Information Hiding and Multimedia Signal Processing* (pp. 1293-1296).

Lee, H. J., & Lee, M. C. (1993). Understanding mathematical expression in a printed document. In *Proceedings of the International Conference on Document Analysis and Recognition* (pp. 502-505).

Lee, H. J., & Wang, J. S. (1995). Design of mathematical expression recognition system. In *Proceedings of the International Conference on Document Analysis and Recognition* (pp. 1084-1087).

Lee, S.-J., & Jung, S.-H. (2001). A survey of watermarking techniques applied to multimedia. In *Proceedings of the IEEE International Symposium on Industrial Electronics* (pp. 12-16).

Lee, H. J., & Lee, M. C. (1994). Understanding mathematical expressions using procedure-oriented transformation. *Pattern Recognition, 27*(3), 447–457. doi:10.1016/0031-3203(94)90121-X

Lee, H. J., & Wang, J. S. (1997). Design of a mathematical expression understanding system. *Pattern Recognition Letters, 18,* 289–298. doi:10.1016/S0167-8655(97)87048-1

Lee, S. W., & Paik, J. K. (1993). Image interpolation using adaptive fast B--spline filtering. In *Proceedings of the IEEE Int. Conf. Acoustics, Speech . Signal Processing, 5,* 177–180.

Lee, W., Lee, D. J., & Park, H. S. (1996). A new methodology for gray scale character segmentation and recognition. *IEEE Transactions on Pattern Analysis and Machine Intelligence, 18*(10), 1045–1050. doi:10.1109/34.541415

Lee, Y., Kozar, K. A., & Larsen, K. R. T. (2003). The technology acceptance model: Past, present, and future. *Communications of the Association for Information Systems, 12,* 752–780.

Lehmann, T. M., Guld, M. O., Thies, C., Plodowski, B., Keysers, D., Ott, B., et al. (2004). IRMA - content-based image retrieval in medical applications. In *Proceedings of the 14th World Congress on Medical Informatics*

Lemos, R. A., Nakamura, M., Sugimoto, I., & Kuwano, H. (1993). A self-organizing map for chemical vapor classification. In *Proceedings of the 7th International Conference on Solid State Sensors and Actuators.*

Lew, M. S., Sebe, N., & Eakins, J. P. (2002). Challenges of image and video retrieval. In *Proceedings of the International Conference on Image and Video Retrieval.*

Li, C. M., & Hong, L. X. (2008). Adaptive fragile watermark for image authentication with tampering localization. In *Proceedings of the Second International Conference on Anti-counterfeiting, Security and Identification* (pp. 22-25).

Li, C.-T. (2009). Source camera linking using enhanced sensor pattern noise extracted from images. In *Proceedings of the 3rd International Conference on Imaging for Crime Detection and Prevention.*

Li, C.-T. (2009). Unsupervised classification of digital images of unknown cameras using filtered sensor pattern noise. In *Proceedings of the International Workshop on Digital Watermarking.*

Li, Y. (2011). A robust forensic method based on scale-invariance feature transform. In *Proceeding of the 2nd International Conference on Multimedia Technology.*

Li, Y., & Li, C. T. (2011). Optimized digital library for digital forensic based on decomposed PRNU. In *Proceeding of the 2nd International Conference on Multimedia Technology*.

Liao, C. J., & Ou Yang, F. C. (2004, July 21-25). A workflow framework for mobile learning objects integration by employing grid services flow language. In *Proceedings of the International Conference on Education and Information Systems, Technologies and Applications*, Orlando, FL (Vol. 1, pp. 155-160).

Liao, C. J., Ou Yang, F. C., & Hsu, K. C. (2005). A service-oriented approach for the pervasive learning grid. *Journal of Information Science and Engineering*, *1*(5), 959–971.

Liaw, S., & Huang, H. (2003). An investigation of user attitude toward search engines as an information retrieval tool. *Computers in Human Behavior*, *19*(6), 751–765. doi:10.1016/S0747-5632(03)00009-8

Li, C. T. (2004). Digital fragile watermarking scheme for authentication of JPEG images. *Vision, Image, and Signal Processing*, *151*, 460–466. doi:10.1049/ip-vis:20040812

Li, C. T., & Li, Y. (2009). Protection of digital mammograms on PACS using data hiding techniques. *International Journal of Digital Crime and Forensics*, *1*, 75–88. doi:10.4018/jdcf.2009010105

Li, C. T., & Si, H. (2007). Wavelet-based fragile watermarking scheme for image authentication. *Journal of Electronic Imaging*, *16*, 1–9. doi:10.1117/1.2712445

Li, C. T., & Wang, F.-M. (2003). One-dimensional neighborhood forming strategy for fragile watermarking. *Journal of Electronic Imaging*, *12*, 284–291. doi:10.1117/1.1557156

Li, C. T., & Yuan, Y. (2006). Digital watermarking scheme exploiting non-deterministic dependence for image authentication. *Optical Engineering (Redondo Beach, Calif.)*, *45*, 1–6. doi:10.1117/1.2402932

Li, C.-T. (2010). Medical image protection through steganography and digital watermarking . In Li, C.-T. (Ed.), *Handbook of research on computational forensics, digital crime and investigation: Methods and solutions*. Hershey, PA: IGI Global.

Likert, R. (1932). *A Technique for the Measurement of Attitudes*. New York: Archives of Psychology.

Lin, C. Y., & Chang, S. F. (2000). Semi fragile watermarking for authentication JPEG visual content. *Proceedings of the SPIE: Security and Watermarking of Multimedia Contents*, 113-118.

Lin, C., Niwa, Y., & Narita, S. (1997). Logical structure analysis of book document images using contents information. In *Proceedings of the International Conference on Document Analysis and Recognition* (pp. 1048-1054).

Lin, C. Y., & Chang, S. F. (2001). A robust image authentication method distinguishing JPEG compression from malicious manipulation. *IEEE Transactions on Circuits and Systems for Video Technology*, *11*, 153–168. doi:10.1109/76.905982

Lin, C.-Y., & Chang, S.-F. (2003). Robust digital signature for multimedia authentication. *Circuits and Systems Magazine*, *3*, 23–26. doi:10.1109/MCAS.2003.1267067

Lincoln, A. J. (1989). Vandalism: Causes, consequences and prevention. *Library & Archival Security*, *9*(3-4), 37–61.

Lin, M. W., Lai, R., & Yu, T. J. (2005). Fuzzy constraint-based agent negotiation. *Journal of Computer Science and Technology*, *20*, 319–330. doi:10.1007/s11390-005-0319-3

Lin, X., & Xiong, Y. (2006). Detection and analysis of table of contents based on content association. *International Journal of Document Analysis and Recognition*, *8*(2-3), 132–143. doi:10.1007/s10032-005-0149-4

Lipincott, J. K. (2003). Developing Collaborative Relationships: Librarians, Students and Faculty creating Learning Communities. *College & Research Libraries News*, *3*(3).

Liu, R., & Tan, T. (2000). Content-based watermarking model. In *Proceeding of the Fifteenth International conference on Pattern Recognition* (pp. 238-241).

Liu, T., & Qiu, Z.-D. (2002). A survey of digital watermarking-based image authentication techniques. In *Proceedings of the 6th International Conference on Signal Processing* (pp. 26-30).

Liu, X. (2003). Text mining based journal splitting. In *Proceedings of the International Conference on Document Analysis and Recognition*, Edinburgh, UK.

Liu, C. Y. (2004). Issues on image authentication . In Lu, C. S. (Ed.), *Multimedia Security* (pp. 173–206). Hershey, PA: IGI Global.

Liu, W., Dong, L., & Zeng, W. J. (2007). Optimum detection for spread-spectrum watermarking that employs self-masking. *IEEE Transactions on Information Forensics and Security, 2*, 645–654. doi:10.1109/TIFS.2007.908226

Liu, Y.-Y., Chen, M., Ishikawa, H., Wollstein, G., Schuman, J. S., & Rehg, J. M. (2011). Automated macular pathology diagnosis in retinal OCT images using multi-scale spatial pyramid and local binary patterns in texture and shape encoding. *Medical Image Analysis, 15*(5), 748–759. doi:10.1016/j.media.2011.06.005

Li, X., & Orchard, M. T. (2001). New edge--directed interpolation. *IEEE Transactions on Image Processing, 10*, 1521–1527. doi:10.1109/83.951537

Loh, T. C., & Koh, S. C. L. (2004). Critical elements for a successful enterprise resource planning implementation in small-and medium-sized enterprises. *International Journal of Production Research, 42*(17), 3433–3455. doi:10.1080/00207540410001671679

Lopresti, D., & Nagy, G. (1999). Automated table processing: An opinionated survey. In *Proceedings of the 3rd International Workshop on Graphics Recognition*, Jaipur, India (pp. 109-134).

Louloudis, G., Gatos, B., Pratikakis, I., & Halatsis, C. (2009). Text line and word segmentation of handwritten documents. *Journal of Pattern Recognition, 42*(12), 3169–3183. doi:10.1016/j.patcog.2008.12.016

Lowe, D. G. (1999). Object recognition from local scale-invariant features. In *Proceedings of the International Conference on Computer Vision.*

Low, M. R., & Christianson, B. (1994). Technique for authentication, access control and resource management in open distributed systems. *Electronics Letters, 30*, 124–125. doi:10.1049/el:19940079

Lu, C. S., & Liao, H. Y. M. (2001). Multipurpose watermarking for image authentication and protection. *IEEE Transactions on Image Processing, 10*, 1579–1592. doi:10.1109/83.951542

Lu, C.-S., & Liao, H.-Y. M. (2009). Structural digital signature for image authentication: An incidental distortion resistant scheme. *IEEE Transactions on Multimedia, 5*, 161–173.

Lu, H. T., Shen, R. M., & Chung, F.-L. (2003). Fragile watermarking scheme for image authentication. *Electronics Letters, 39*, 898–900. doi:10.1049/el:20030589

Lukas, J., Fridrich, J., & Goljan, M. (2006). Detecting digital image forgeries using sensor pattern noise. *Proceedings of the SPIE: Electronic Imaging, 6072*, 362–372.

Lukas, J., Fridrich, J., & Goljan, M. (2006). Digital camera identification from sensor noise. *IEEE Transactions on Information Security and Forensics, 1*(2), 205–214. doi:10.1109/TIFS.2006.873602

Lukman, S. (2003). *Business process reengineering and ASAP: Side-by-side.* Retrieved from http://www.susanto.id.au/papers/BPEASAP.asp

Luo, Q., Watanabe, T., & Nakayama, T. (1996). Identifying contents page of documents. In *Proceedings of the International Conference on Document Analysis and Recognition* (pp. 696-700).

Luo, X., Jennings, N. R., & Shadbolt, N. (2003). A fuzzy constraint based model for bilateral, multi-issue negotiations in semi-competitive environments. *Artificial Intelligence, 148*, 53–102. doi:10.1016/S0004-3702(03)00041-9

Lu, W., Du, J., Zhang, J., Ma, F., & Le, T. (2002). Internet development in China. *Journal of Information Science, 28*(3), 207–223. doi:10.1177/016555150202800303

Mabert, V. A., Soni, A., & Venkataramanan, M. A. (2001). Enterprise resource Planning: Common myths versus evolving reality. *Business Horizons*, 69–76. doi:10.1016/S0007-6813(01)80037-9

MacGregor, R. C., & Kartiwi, M. (2007). Electronic commerce adoption barriers in small to medium-sized enterprises (SMEs) in developed and developing countries: A cross-country comparison. *Journal of Electronic Commerce in Organizations, 5*(3), 35–51.

MacGregor, R. C., Vrazalic, L., Carlsson, S., Bunker, D., & Magnusson, M. (2002). The impact of business size and business type on small business investment in electronic commerce: A study of Swedish small business. *Australasian Journal of Information Systems, 9*(2), 31–39.

Macq, B., Dittmann, J., & Delp, E. J. (2004). Benchmarking of image watermarking algorithms for digital rights management. *Proceedings of the IEEE, 92*, 971–984. doi:10.1109/JPROC.2004.827361

Magara, E. (2002). Application of digital libraries and electronic technology in Uganda. *African Journal of Library . Archives and Information Science, 13*(1), 43–53.

Mahajan, S. (2003). Impact of digital divide on developing countries with special reference to India. *SERALS Journal of Information Management, 40*(4), 328–329.

Mahmood, K. (1999). The Development of Computerised Library Services in Pakistan: a Review if the Literature. *Asian Libraries, 8*(9). doi:10.1108/10176749910293803

Maity, S. P., & Maity, S. (2009). Multistage spread spectrum watermark detection technique using fuzzy logic. *Signal Processing Letters, 16*, 245–248. doi:10.1109/LSP.2009.2014097

Majumdar, A., & Chaudhuri, B. B. (2007). Curvelet-based multi-SVM recognizer for offline handwritten Bangla: A major Indian script. In *Proceedings of the 9th International Conference on Document Analysis and Recognition* (pp. 491-495).

Malik, H., Ansari, R., & Khokhar, A. (2008). Robust audio watermarking using frequency-selective spread spectrum. *Information Security, 2*, 129–150. doi:10.1049/iet-ifs:20070145

Malvar, H. S., & Florencio, D. A. F. (2003). Improved spread spectrum: A new modulation technique for robust watermarking. *IEEE Transactions on Signal Processing, 51*, 898–905. doi:10.1109/TSP.2003.809385

Mandal, S., Chowdhury, S. P., Das, A. K., & Chanda, B. (2003b). Automated detection and segmentation of table of contents page from document images. In *Proceedings of the International Conference on Document Analysis and Recognition* (pp. 398-402).

Mandal, S., Chowdhury, S. P., Das, A. K., & Chanda, B. (2003c). Automated segmentation of math-zones from document images. In *Proceedings of the International Conference on Document Analysis and Recognition* (pp. 755-759).

Mandal, S., Chowdhury, S. P., Das, A. K., & Chanda, B. (2004). A complete system detection and identification of tabular structures from document images. In *Proceedings of the International Conference on Document Analysis and Recognition* (pp. 217-225).

Mandal, S., Chowdhury, S. P., Das, A. K., & Chanda, B. (2006a, April 27-28). Detection and segmentation of table of contents and index pages from document images. In *Proceedings of the 2nd IEEE International Conference on Document Analysis for Libraries*, Lyon, France (pp. 70-81).

Mandal, S., Chowdhury, S. P., Das, A. K., & Chanda, B. (2006b). A simple and effective table detection system from document images. *International Journal on Document Analysis and Recognition, 8*(2-3), 172–182. doi:10.1007/s10032-005-0006-5

Mansfield, D. (2009). Reducing book theft at university libraries. *Library and Information Research, 33*(103).

Mao, J., Sinha, P., & Mohiuddin, K. (1998). A system for cursive handwritten address recognition. In *Proceedings of the 14th International Conference on Pattern Recognition* (pp. 1285-1287).

Marchionini, G., Plaisant, C., & Komlodi, A. (1998). Interfaces and tools for the Library of Congress National Digital Library Program. *Information Processing & Management, 34*(5), 535–555. doi:10.1016/S0306-4573(98)00020-X

Marchonini, G. (2000). Evaluating digital libraries: A longitudinal and multifaceted view. *Library Trends, 49*(2), 303–333.

Marcoulides, G. A. (1988). The relationship between computer anxiety and computer achievement. *Journal of Educational Computing Research, 4*(2), 151–158. doi:10.2190/J5N4-24HK-567V-AT6E

Marnewick, C., & Labuschagne, L. (2005). A conceptual model for enterprise resource planning (ERP). *Information Management & Computer Security, 13*(2), 144–155. doi:10.1108/09685220510589325

Martins, E. C., & Terblanche, F. (2003). Building or organisational culture that stimulates creativity and innovation. *European Journal of Innovation Management, 6*(1), 64–74. doi:10.1108/14601060310456337

Marvel, L. M., Boncelet, C., & Retter, C. T. (1999). Spread spectrum image steganography. *IEEE Transactions on Image Processing, 8*, 1075–1083. doi:10.1109/83.777088

Marvel, L. M., Hartwig, G. W., & Boncelet, C. (2000). Compression compatible fragile and semi-fragile tamper detection. In . *Proceedings of the SPIE: International Conference on Security and Watermarking of Multimedia Contents, II*, 131–139.

Mason, R. (1999). The Impact of Telecommunications . In Harry, K. (Ed.), *Higher Education through Open and Distance Learning*. London: Routledge.

Mclester, S. (2001). The e-learning phenomenon. *Technology and Learning, 22*(1).

Medjahed, B., & Bouguettaya, A. (2005). Customized delivery of e-government web services. *IEEE Intelligent Systems, 20*, 77–84. doi:10.1109/MIS.2005.103

Melchionda, M. G. (2007). Librarians in the age of the Internet: Their attitudes and roles. *New Library World, 108*(3-4), 123–140. doi:10.1108/03074800710735339

Meselhy Eltoukhy, M., Faye, I., & Belhaouari Samir, B. (2012). A statistical based feature extraction method for breast cancer diagnosis in digital mammogram using multiresolution representation. *Computers in Biology and Medicine, 42*(1), 123–128. doi:10.1016/j.compbiomed.2011.10.016

Meyer-Arendt, J. R. (1989). *Introduction to Classical and Modern Optics*. Upper Saddle River, NJ: Prentice-Hall.

Milanova, M., Kountchev, R., Rubin, S., Todorov, V., & Kountcheva, R. (2009). Content based image retrieval using adaptive inverse pyramid representation. In G. Salvendy & M. Smith (Eds.), *Proceedings of the International Symposium on Human Interface and the Management of Information: Information and Interaction* (LNCS 5618, pp. 304-314).

Miller, E. G., & Viola, P. A. (1998). Ambiguity and constraint in mathematical expression recognition. In *Proceedings of the 15th National Conference on Artificial Intelligence*, Madison, WI (pp. 784-791).

Mohamed, M., & Gader, P. (1996). Handwritten word recognition using segmentation free hidden markov modeling and segmentation based dynamic programming techniques. *IEEE Transactions on Pattern Analysis and Machine Intelligence, 18*(5), 548–554. doi:10.1109/34.494644

Mukherjee, D. P., Maitra, S., & Acton, S. T. (2004). Spatial domain digital watermarking of multimedia objects for buyer authentication. *IEEE Transactions on Multimedia, 6*, 1–15. doi:10.1109/TMM.2003.819759

Müller, H., Müller, W., Squire, D. M., Marchand-Maillet, S., & Pun, T. (2001). Performance evaluation in content-based image retrieval: overview and proposals. *Pattern Recognition Letters, 22*(5), 593–601. doi:10.1016/S0167-8655(00)00118-5

Murthy, T. A. V., & Cholin, V. S. (2003). *Library automation*. Retrieved December 19, 2008, from http://dspace.inflibnet.ac.in/bitstream/1994/170/3/03cali_1.pdf

Mutala, S. M. (2002, April 15-19). The digital divide in Sub-Saharan Africa: Implications of RHT revitalization and preservation of indigenous knowledge systems. In *Proceedings of the 15th Standing Conference of Eastern, Central and Southern African Library and Information Association on Africa to the World: The Globalization of Indigenous Knowledge Systems* (pp. 119-141).

Nah, F. F.-h., Lau, J. L.-s., & Kuang, J. (2001). Critical factors for successful implementation of enterprise systems. *Business Process Management Journal, 7*(3), 285–296. doi:10.1108/14637150110392782

Nakamura, K. (2006). *Image sensors and signal processing for digital still cameras*. Boca Raton, FL: Taylor & Francis.

Nakashima, Y., Tachibana, R., & Babaguchi, N. (2009). Watermarked movie soundtrack finds the position of the camcorder in a theater. *IEEE Transactions on Multimedia, 11*, 443–454. doi:10.1109/TMM.2009.2012938

Nakayama, Y. (1993). A prototype pen-input mathematical formula editor. In *Proceedings of the Ed-Media World Conference on Educational Multimedia and Hypermedia*, Orlando, FL (pp. 400-407).

Newman, W. (2004). *Public libraries in the priorities of Canada: Acting on the assets and opportunities.* Retrieved from http://www.collectionscanada.gc.ca/6/7/s7-3000-e.html

Nguyen, N., Milanfar, P., & Golub, G. (2001). Efficient generalized cross--validation with applications to parametric image restoration and resolution enhancement. *IEEE Transactions on Image Processing, 10,* 1299–1308. doi:10.1109/83.941854

Nicholson, S. (2004). A conceptual framework for the holistic measurement and cumulative evaluation of library services. *The Journal of Documentation, 60,* 164–182. doi:10.1108/00220410410522043

Nkanu, W. O. (2008). Utilization of information and communication technology facilities in Nigeria university libraries. *Information Technologist: An International Journal of Information and Communication Technology, 5*(2), 1–6.

Norris, P. (2001). *Digital divide: Civil engagement, information poverty and the Internet in democratic societies.* Cambridge, UK: Cambridge University Press.

Nov, O., & Ye, C. (2008). User's personality and perceived ease of use of digital libraries: The case for resistance to change. *Journal of the American Society for Information Science and Technology, 59*(5), 845–851. doi:10.1002/asi.20800

O'Gorman, L. (1992). Image and document processing techniques for the right pages electronic library system. In *Proceedings of the 11th International Conference on Pattern Recognition* (pp. 260-263).

O'Reilly, T. (2005). *What is Web 2.0.* Retrieved from http://www.oreillynet.com/pub/a/oreilly/tim/news/2005/09/30/what-is-web-20.html

Obasuyi, L. (2005). Impact of computer and internet applications on library and information services delivery in NARIS libraries in Nigeria. In *Proceedings of the 43rd Annual National Conference and AGM of Nigeria Library Association* (pp. 76-86).

Oche, A. N. (2000). Book theft and mutilation and their effect on the services of the Benue State Polytechnic Library, Ogbokolo. *Frontiers of Information and Library Sciences: Journals of the World Information Community, 1*(1), 57–64.

Odion, F., & Adetona, C. (2009). Information and communication technology (ICT) as a tool for effective performance by academic librarians in Edo State of Nigeria. *Communicate: Journal of Library and Information Science, 11*(1), 27–37.

Ogunleye, G. O. (1977). Automating the Federal University in Nigeria: A state of art. *African Journal of Library . Archives and Information Science, 7*(1), 71–79.

Ojedoknen, A. A., & Owolabi, E. O. (2003). Internet access competence and the use of internet for teaching and research activities by University of Botswana academic staff. *African Journal of Library . Archives and Information Science, 13*(1), 43–53.

Okamoto, M., & Miao, B. (1991). Recognition of mathematics by using the layout structures of symbols. In *Proceedings of the International Conference on Document Analysis and Recognition* (pp. 242-250).

Okamoto, M., & Miyazawa, H. (1992). An experimental implementation of a document recognition system for papers containing mathematical expression. *Structured Document Image Analysis,* 36-53.

Oketunji, J. (2002). *40 years of information and communication technology (ICT) library services to the National Paper.* Paper presented at the 40th Annual National Conference and AGM of the Nigeria Library Association, Badagry, Nigeria.

Okunoye, A., & Bertaux, A. (2006). KAFRA: A context-aware framework of knowledge management in global diversity. *International Journal of Knowledge Management, 2*(2), 26–45.

Oliver, J. R. (1996). On artificial agents for negotiation in electronic commerce. In *Proceedings of the 29th Annual Hawaii International Conference on System Sciences* (pp. 337-346).

Onatola, A. (1998). Staff assessment of security lapses and stock losses in two selected Nigerian University Libraries. *Gateway Library Journal, 1*(1), 40–45.

Oppenheimer, T. (1997). The Computer Delusion. *Atlantic Monthly, 28*(1).

Osborne, D., Abbott, D., Sorell, M., & Rogers, D. (2004). Multiple embedding using robust watermarks for wireless medical images. In *Proceedings of the Third International Conference on Mobile and Ubiquitous Multimedia* (pp. 245-250).

Otsu, N. (1979). A threshold selection method from graylevel histogram. *IEEE Transactions on Systems, Man, and Cybernetics, 9*(1), 62–66. doi:10.1109/TSMC.1979.4310076

Palmini, C. C. (1994). The impact of computerization on library support staff: A study of support staff in academic libraries in Wisconsin. *College & Research Libraries, 55*(1), 119–127.

Pao, T. L., Yeh, J. H., Liu, M. Y., & Hsu, Y. C. (2006). Locating the typhoon center from the IR satellite cloud images. In *Proceedings of the IEEE International Conference on Systems* (pp. 484-488).

Pao, T. L., & Yang, P. L. (2008). Typhoon locating and reconstruction from the infrared satellite cloud image. *Journal of Multimedia, 3*, 45–51. doi:10.4304/jmm.3.2.45-51

Papakostas, G. A., Boutalis, Y. S., Karras, D. A., & Mertzios, B. G. (2007). A new class of Zernike moments for computer vision applications. *Information Sciences, 177*(13), 2802–2819. doi:10.1016/j.ins.2007.01.010

Parameswaran, L., & Anbumani, K. (2008). Content-based watermarking for image authentication using independent component analysis. *Informatica, 32*, 299–306.

Parui, S. K., Guin, K., Bhattacharya, U., & Chaudhuri, B. B. (2008). Online handwritten Bangla character recognition using HMM. In *Proceedings of the 19th International Conference on Pattern Recognition* (pp. 1-4).

Peacock, J. (2000). Information Literacy Education in Practice. In Levy, P., & Roberts, S. (Eds.), *Changing Roles of the Academic Librarian*. London: Facet Publishing.

Pedersen, T. L. (1990). Theft and mutilation of library materials. *College & Research Libraries, 51*, 120–128.

Pedrotti, F. L., & Pedrotti, L. S. (1987). *Introduction to Optics*. Upper Saddle River, NJ: Prentice Hall.

Pei, S. C., & Chen, J. H. (2006). Robustness enhancement for noncentric quantization-based image watermarking. *IEEE Transactions on Circuits and Systems for Video Technology, 16*, 1507–1518. doi:10.1109/TCSVT.2006.885174

Peng, G. C., & Nunes, M. B. (2008). Identification and assessment of risks to successful exploitation of ERP systems in China. In *Proceedings of the European and Mediterranean Conference on Information Systems* (pp. 1-13).

Plamondon, R. (Ed.). (1993). Handwriting processing and recognition. *Pattern Recognition, 26*(3), 379. doi:10.1016/0031-3203(93)90165-S

Plamondon, R., & Leedham, C. G. (Eds.). (1990). *Computer processing of handwriting*. Singapore: World Scientific.

Poba-Nzaou, P., Raymond, L., & Fabi, B. (2008). Adoption and risk of ERP systems in manufacturing SMEs: A positivist case study. *Business Process Management Journal, 14*(4), 530–550. doi:10.1108/14637150810888064

Poilpre, M. C., Perrot, P., & Talbot, H. (2008). Image tampering detection using Bayer interpolation and JPEG compression. In *Proceedings of the First International Conference on Forensic Applications and Techniques in Telecommunications, Information and Multimedia*.

Poole, C. E., & Emment, D. (2001). *Technological change in the work place: A Starwide survey of community college library and learning resources personnel*. Retrieved March 16, 2006, from http://www.ct.org

Popescu, A. C., & Farid, H. (2005). Exposing digital forgeries in color filter array interpolated images. *IEEE Transactions on Signal Processing, 53*(10), 3948–3959. doi:10.1109/TSP.2005.855406

Popoola, S. O. (2002). 'Users' Attitude towards Microcomputer use in Agricultural Research Libraries in Nigeria. *Journal of Librarianship and Information Science in Africa, 2*(1).

Potdar, V. M., Han, S., & Chang, E. (2003). A survey of digital image watermarking techniques. In *Proceedings of the Third IEEE International Conference on Industrial Informatics* (pp. 709-719).

Prasad, B. (1986). *Problems of misplacement, mutilation and theft of books in libraries*. Raigarh, India: BP Goswami.

Pruitt, D. G. (1981). *Negotiation behavior*. New York, NY: Academic Press.

Pun, I. F., Lin, I. I., Wu, C. R., Ko, D. S., & Liu, W. T. (2007). Validation and application of altimetry-derived upper ocean thermal structure in the Western North Pacific Ocean for typhoon-intensity forecast. *IEEE Transactions on Geoscience and Remote Sensing, 45*(6), 1616–1630. doi:10.1109/TGRS.2007.895950

Puschmann, T., & Alt, R. (2004, January 5-8). Process portals - Architecture and integration. In *Proceedings of the 37th Hawaii International Conference on System Sciences*, Big Island, HI.

Puustjärvi, J. (2004). Using one-stop portal in integrating e-learning systems. *Advanced Technology for Learning, 1*(2).

Qian, H., Jiang, B., Zhang, Z., & Wang, L. (2010). A level set-based framework for typhoon segmentation with application to multi-channel satellite cloud images. In *Proceedings of the 3rd International Congress on Image and Signal Processing* (pp. 1273-1275).

Qian, H., & Jiang, B. (2011). Method base on multi-channel satellite cloud image for typhoon segmentation. [Journal of Beijing University of Aeronautics and Astronautics]. *Beijing Hangkong Hangtian Daxue Xuebao, 37*, 466–471.

Qiao, Y.-L., Lu, Z.-M., Pan, J.-S., & Sun, S.-H. (2010). Fast k-nearest neighbor search algorithm based on pyramid structure of wavelet transform and its application to texture classification. *Digital Signal Processing, 20*(3), 837–845. doi:10.1016/j.dsp.2009.10.011

Qimage help. (2009). *Dark Frame Subtraction* (Tech. Rep.). Retrieved from http://www.ddisoftware.com/qimage/qimagehlp/dark.htm

Queluz, M. P. (1999). Content-based integrity protection of digital images. *Proceedings of the SPIE: Security and Watermarking of Multimedia Contents, 3657*, 85–93.

Queluz, M. P. (2001). Authentication of digital image and video: Generic models and a new contribution. *Signal Processing Image Communication*, 461–475. doi:10.1016/S0923-5965(00)00010-2

Queluz, M. P., & Lany, P. (2000). Spatial watermark for image verification. In . *Proceedings of the SPIE: International Conference on Security and Watermarking of Multimedia Contents, II*, 120–130.

Quendo, C., Rius, E., Person, C., & Ney, M. (2001). Integration of optimized low-pass filters in a bandpass filter for out-of-band improvement. *IEEE Transactions on Microwave Theory and Techniques, 49*, 2376–2383. doi:10.1109/22.971624

Ramel, J. Y., Crucianu, M., Vincent, N., & Faure, C. (2003). Detection, extraction and representation of tables. In *Proceedings of the International Conference on Document Analysis and Recognition*, Edinburgh, UK (pp. 374-378).

Ramzan, M. (2004). Does level of Knowledge impact Librarians' Attitudes toward Information Technology (IT) Applications? In *Proceedings of the 2nd International CALIBER-2004*, New Delhi, India.

Randall, D., Cleland, L., & Kuehne, C. S. (1997). Water supply planning simulation model using mixed-integer linear programming. *Journal of Water Resources Planning and Management, 123*, 116–124. doi:10.1061/(ASCE)0733-9496(1997)123:2(116)

Rao, R. K. (2003). E-governance gaining in popularity. *Kurukhetra, 9*(12), 1.

Raymond, L., & Uwizeyemungu, S. (2007). A profile of ERP adoption in manufacturing SMEs. *Journal of Enterprise Information Management, 20*(4), 487–502. doi:10.1108/17410390710772731

Reddy, S., Lowry, D., Reddy, S., Henderson, R., Bavis, J., & Babich, A. (1999). *Searching for citations to document sorted by number of citations*. Retrieved March 12, 2011, from http//www.webdav.org/dasl/protocol/draft-dasl-protocol-00.html

Remus, U. (2007). Critical success factors for implementing enterprise portals. A comparison with ERP implementations. *Business Process Management Journal, 13*(4), 538–552. doi:10.1108/14637150710763568

Ren, Z., Anumba, C. J., & Ugwu, O. O. (2002). Negotiation in a multi-agent system for construction claims negotiation. *Applied Artificial Intelligence, 16*, 359–394. doi:10.1080/08839510290030273

Rey, C., & Dugelay, J. L. (2002). A survey of watermarking algorithms for image authentication. *EURASIP Journal on Applied Signal Processing*, 613–621. doi:10.1155/S1110865702204047

Richardson, M., & Midwinter, T. (2006). Product catalogue management with semantic web services. *BT Technology Journal*, 24(4), 21. doi:10.1007/s10550-006-0094-x

Rocchio, J. J. (1971). Relevance feedback in information retrieval . In Salton, G. (Ed.), *The SMART retrieval system - Experiments in automatic document processing* (pp. 313–323). Upper Saddle River, NJ: Prentice Hall.

Rock, N. L. (2003). *Examining the relationship between business process reengineering and information technology*. Retrieved from http://faculty.ed.umuc.edu/~meinkej/inss690/larock.pdf

Rogers, M. (2003). Serial slasher stalks in stacks. *Library Journal*, 122(10), 14–15.

Rosenschein, J. S., & Zlotkin, G. (1994). *Rules of encounter: Designing conventions for automated negotiation among computers*. Cambridge, MA: MIT Press.

RosettaNet. (2000). *Partner Interface Process (PIPs)*. Retrieved from http://www.rosettanet.org/

Rui, Y., Huang, T. S., & Mehrotra, S. (1998). Human perception subjectivity and relevance feedback in multimedia information retrieval. In *Proceedings of the IS&T/SPIE Storage and Retrieval of Image and Video Database*.

Russ, J. C. (2001). *The image processing handbook*. Charlotte, NC: Baker & Taylor Books.

Salaam, M. O., & Onifade, F. N. (2010). Perception and attitude of students in relation to vandalism in a university library. *Annals of Library and Information Studies*, 57(5), 146–149.

Sankur, B., Celiktutan, O., & Avcibas, I. (2007). Blind identification of cell phone cameras. *Proceedings of the SPIE: Electronic Imaging, Security, Steganography, and Watermarking of Multimedia Contents IX*, 6505, 1.

SAP. (1999). *Accelerated SAP*. Retrieved from http://help.sap.com/printdocu/core/print46b /en/data/en/pdf/SVASAP.pdf

SAP. (2000). *SAP implementation* (PowerPoint slides). Retrieved from http://www.mi s.cmich.edu/bis697c/asap91_ph/46asap9105.pdf

SAP. (2007). *Independent research firm states SAP as worldwide market share leader for CRM, ERP and SCM*. Retrieved from http://www.sap.com/solutions/business-suite/scm/newsevents/press.epx?pressid=8309

SAP. (2009). *ASAP Roadmap*. Retrieved from http://help.sap.com/saphelp_47x200/helpdata/en/48/623972d55a11d2bbf700105a5e5b3c/content.htm

Sarkar, A., Biswas, A., Bhowmick, P., & Bhattacharya, B. B. (2010). Word segmentation and baseline detection in handwritten documents using isothetic covers. In *Proceedings of the 12th International Conference on Frontiers in Handwriting Recognition* (pp. 445-450).

Sathi, A., & Fox, M. (1989). Constraint-directed negotiation of resource reallocation . In Gasser, L., & Huhns, M. (Eds.), *Distributed artificial intelligence* (Vol. 2, pp. 163–195). San Francisco, CA: Morgan Kaufmann.

Satoh, S., Takasu, A., & Katsura, E. (1995). An automated generation of electronic library based on document image understanding. In *Proceedings of the International Conference on Document Analysis and Recognition* (pp. 163-166).

Satyanarayana, M. N., & Sathyamurthy. (2005). Telemedicine: Specialty health care for all. *Employment News*, 30(4), 1–2.

Saunders, L. M. (1999). The human element in the virtual library. *Library Trends*, 47(4), 771–789.

Schneider, P. (1999). Wanted: ERPeople skills. *CIO Magazine*, 12(10), 30–37.

Schumm, R. W. (1994). Periodicals mutilation revisited: A two-year follow up study. *The Serials Librarian*, 25, 201–205. doi:10.1300/J123v25n01_16

Sekita, I., Kurita, T., & Otsu, N. (1992). Complex autoregressive model for shape recognition. *IEEE Transactions on Pattern Analysis and Machine Intelligence*, 14(4), 489–496. doi:10.1109/34.126809

Self, J. (1996). *The Development of the Computer Based Learning Unit: a Discussion Document*. Retrieved from http://eblslca.leeds.ac.uk/jas/discussion.html

Senior, A. W., & Robinson, A. J. (1998). An off-line cursive handwriting recognition system. *IEEE Transactions on Pattern Recognition and Machine Intelligence, 20*(3), 309–322. doi:10.1109/34.667887

Seppannen, T., Makela, K., & Keskinarkaus, A. (2000). Hiding information in color images using small color palettes. In *Proceedings of the Third International Workshop on Information Security* (pp. 69-81).

Shannon, C. E. (1949). Communication theory of secrecy systems. *The Bell System Technical Journal, 28*, 656–715.

Sharifabadi, S. R. (2006). How digital libraries can support e-learning. *The Electronic Library, 24*(3). Retrieved from www.emeraldinsight.com/0264-0473.htm. doi:10.1108/02640470610671231

Shehab, E. M., Sharp, M. W., Supramaniam, L., & Spedding, T. A. (2004). Enterprise resource planning an integrative review. *Business Process Management Journal, 10*(4), 359–386. doi:10.1108/14637150410548056

Shen, W., & Norrie, D. H. (2001). Dynamic manufacturing scheduling using both functional and resource related agents. *Integrated Computer-Aided Engineering, 8*(1), 17–30.

Shen, W., Norrie, H., & Barthes, J. P. (2001). *Multi-agent systems for concurrent intelligent design and manufacturing.* London, UK: Taylor & Francis.

Simitopoulos, D., Koutsonanos, D. E., & Strintzis, M. G. (2003). Robust image watermarking based on generalized Radon transformations. *IEEE Transactions on Circuits and Systems for Video Technology, 13*, 732–745. doi:10.1109/TCSVT.2003.815947

Simmons, G. J. (1988). A survey of information authentication. *Proceedings of the IEEE, 76*, 603–620. doi:10.1109/5.4445

Simner, M. L., Leedham, C. G., & Thomassen, A. J. W. M. (Eds.). (1996). *Handwriting and drawing research: Basic and applied issues.* Amsterdam, The Netherlands: IOS Press.

Simner, M., Hulstijn, W., & Giouard, P. (Eds.). (1994). *Forensic, developmental and neuropsychological aspects of handwriting.* Journal of Forensic Document Examination.

Singh, A. M. (2004). Bridging the digital divide the role of universities in getting South Africa closer to the global information society. *South African Journal of Information Management, 6*(2).

Singla, A. R., & Goyal, D. P. (2004). *Managing risk factors in design and implementation of ERP systems: An empirical investigation of the Indian industry.* International Association for Management of Technology.

Siriginidi, S. R. (2000). Enterprise resource planning in reengineering business. *Business Process Management Journal, 6*(5), 376–391. doi:10.1108/14637150010352390

Sledgianowski, D., Tafti, M. H. A., & Kierstead, J. (2007). SME ERP system sourcing strategies: A case study. *Industrial Management & Data Systems, 108*(4), 421–436. doi:10.1108/02635570810868317

SMEA. (2008). *Annual blue print in small, medium-sized enterprises.* Retrieved from http://book.moeasmea.gov.tw/book/doc_detail.jsp?pub_SerialNo=2008A00937&click=2008A00937

Smid, M. E., & Branstad, D. K. (1988). Data encryption standard: Past and future. *Proceedings of the IEEE, 78*, 550–559. doi:10.1109/5.4441

Smith, D. (1999). Better data collection for greater efficiency. *Manufacturing Engineering, 123*, 62–68.

Smith, E. H., & Olszak, L. (1997). Treatment of mutilated art books: A survey of academic ARL institutions. *Library Resources & Technical Services, 41*, 7–16.

Soja, P. (2006). Success factors in ERP systems implementations: Lessons from practice. *Journal of Enterprise Information Management, 19*, 646–661. doi:10.1108/17410390610708517

Somers, T. M., & Nelson, K. (2001). The impact of critical success factors across the stages of enterprise resource planning implementations. In *Proceedings of the 34th Hawaii International Conference on System Sciences (HICSS).*

Somporn, C. A., Willi, J. A., Hans, G. B., Susanne, K. O., Wattana, K., & Suchada, S. (2008). 3D cloud and storm reconstruction from satellite image modeling. In *Proceedings of the International Conference on Simulation and Optimization of Complex Processes* (pp. 187-206).

Sorell, M. (2009a). Unexpected artifacts in a digital photograph. *International Journal of Digital Crime and Forensics*, *1*, 45–48. doi:10.4018/jdcf.2009010103

Sorell, M. (2009b). Digital camera source identification through JPEG quantisation . In Li, C. T. (Ed.), *Multimedia forensics and security* (pp. 291–313). Hershey, PA: IGI Global.

Sorell, M. (2009c). Conditions for effective detection and identification of primary quantization of re-quantized JPEG images. *International Journal of Digital Crime and Forensics*, *1*, 13–27. doi:10.4018/jdcf.2009040102

Spacey, R., Goulding, A., & Murray, I. (2003). ICT and Change in UK Public Libraries:does Training matter? *Library Management*, *24*(1/2). doi:10.1108/01435120310454520

Srihari, S. N., & Keubert, E. J. (1997). Integration of handwritten address interpretation technology into the United States postal service remote computer reader system. In *Proceedings of the 4ᵗʰ International Conference on Document Analysis and Recognition* (pp. 892-896).

Srihari, S. N., Shin, Y. C., Ramanaprasad, V., & Lee, D. S. (1996). A system to read names and addresses on Tax Forms. *Proceedings of the IEEE*, *84*(7), 1038–1049. doi:10.1109/5.503302

Stallings, W. (1998). *Cryptography and network security - principles and practice*. Upper Saddle River, NJ: Prentice Hall.

Stamford, C. (1999). *Meta group study dispels common myths about ERP/ERM implementation costs and overall value comprehensive study assesses ERP/ERM issues and compares top vendors*. Retrieved from http://findarticles.com/p/articles/mi_m0EIN/is_1999_April_1/ai_54277417/

Stanford University. (2002). *The CHAIMS project*. Retrieved from http://www-db.stanford.edu/CHAIMS/

Steinder, M., Iren, S., & Amer, P. D. (1999). Progressively authenticated image transmission. In *Proceedings of the Military Communications Conference* (pp. 641-645).

Stewart, L., Chiang, K. S., & Coons, B. (2006). *Public access CD-ROMS in libraries: case studies (supplement to computers in libraries)*. Westport, CT: Mecklermedia.

Stoilov, T., & Stoilova, K. (2008). Functional analysis of enterprise resource planning systems. In *Proceedings of the International Conference on Computer Systems and Technologies* (pp. 1-6).

Story, G. A., O'Gorman, L., Fox, D., Schaper, L. L., & Jagadish, H. V. (1992). The right pages image-based electronic library for alerting and browsing. *Computer*, *25*(9), 17–26. doi:10.1109/2.156379

Su, C., Zhuang, Y., Huang, L., & Wu, F. (2005). Steerable pyramid-based face hallucination. *Pattern Recognition*, *38*(6), 813–824. doi:10.1016/j.patcog.2004.11.007

Suckling, J., Parker, J., Dance, D., Astley, S., Hutt, I., Boggis, C., et al. (1994). The mammographic images analysis society digital mammogram database. *Experta Medica International Congress Series, 1069*, 375-378.

Sumner, M. (2000). Risk factors in enterprise-wide/ERP projects. *Journal of Information Technology*, *15*, 317–327. doi:10.1080/02683960010009079

Sun, H.-M., Wu, M.-E., Ting, W.-C., & Hinek, M. J. (2007). Dual RSA and its security analysis. *IEEE Transactions on Information Theory*, *53*, 2922–2933. doi:10.1109/TIT.2007.901248

Sun, W. D., Tang, Z., Tamura, H., & Ishii, M. (2003). An artificial immune system architecture and its applications. *IEICE Transactions on Fundamentals*, *86*, 1858–1868.

Sutthiwan, P., Ye, J., & Shi, Y. Q. (2009). An enhanced statistical approach to identifying photorealistic images. In *Proceedings of International Workshop on Digital Watermarking* (pp. 323-335).

Swaminathan, A., Wu, M., & Liu, K. J. R. (2007). Non-intrusive component forensics of visual sensors using output images. *IEEE Transactions on Information Forensics and Security*, *2*, 91–106. doi:10.1109/TIFS.2006.890307

Sycara, K. (1989). Multi-agent compromise via negotiation . In Gasser, L., & Huhns, M. (Eds.), *Distributed artificial intelligence* (Vol. 2, pp. 119–139). San Francisco, CA: Morgan Kaufmann.

Sycara, K., Paolucci, M., Soudry, J., & Srinivasan, N. (2004). Dynamic discovery and coordination of agent-based semantic web services. *IEEE Internet Computing*, *8*(3), 66–73. doi:10.1109/MIC.2004.1297276

Talwar, R. (1993). Business re-engineering – A strategy-driven approach. *Long Range Planning*, *26*(6), 22–40. doi:10.1016/0024-6301(93)90204-S

Tanaka, T., & Tsuruoka, S. (1998). Table form document understanding using node classification method and HTML document generation. In *Proceedings of the 3rd IAPR Workshop on Document Analysis Systems*, Nagano, Japan. (pp. 157-158).

Tang, Z., Yamaguchi, T., Tashima, K., Ishizuka, O., & Tanno, K. (1997). Multiple-valued immune network model and its simulations. In *Proceedings of the 27th International Symposium on Multiple-Valued Logic* (pp. 233-238).

Tang, Z., Hebishima, H., Tashima, K., Ishizuka, O., & Tanno, K. (1997). An immune network based on biological immune response network and its immunity. *IEICE Transactions on Fundamentals*, *80*(11), 1940–1950.

Tang, Z., Tashima, K., & Cao, Q. P. (2001). A pattern recognition system using clonal selection-based immune network. *Systems and Computers in Japan*, *34*(12), 56–63. doi:10.1002/scj.10243

Tang, Z., Yamaguchi, T., Tashima, K., Ishizuka, O., & Tanno, K. (1999). Multiple-value immune network and its applications. *IEICE Transactions on Fundamentals*, *82*, 1102–1108.

Tarafdar, M., & Roy, R. K. (2003). Analyzing the adoption of enterprise resource planning systems in Indian organizations: A process framework. *Journal of Global Information Technology Management*, *6*, 31–38.

Tersteegen, W. T., & Wenzel, C. (1998). Scantab: Table recognition by reference tables. In *Proceedings of the 3rd IAPR Workshop on Document Analysis Systems*, Nagano, Japan (pp. 356-365).

The TimesTen Team. (2000). High performance and scalability through application-tier, in-memory data management. In *Proceedings of the 26th International Conference on Very Large Databases*, Cairo, Egypt (pp. 677-680).

Theng, Y., Tan, K., Lim, E., Zhang, J., Goh, D. H., & Ghatterjea, K. …Vo, M. C. (2007, June 18-23). Mobile G-Portal supporting collaborative sharing and learning in geography fieldwork: An empirical study. In *Proceedings of the ACM/IEEE-CS Joint Conference on Digital Libraries*, Vancouver, BC, Canada.

Thong, J. Y. L. (1999). An integrated model of information systems adoption in small business. *Journal of Management Information Systems*, *15*(4), 187–214.

Thong, J. Y. L. (2001). Resource constrains and information systems implementation is Singaporean small business. *Omega*, *29*, 143–156. doi:10.1016/S0305-0483(00)00035-9

Thong, J. Y. L., Hong, W., & Tam, K. (2002). Understanding user acceptance of digital libraries: what are the roles of interface characteristics, organizational context, and individual? *International Journal of Human-Computer Studies*, *57*(3), 215–242. doi:10.1016/S1071-5819(02)91024-4

Thong, J. Y. L., Hong, W., & Tam, K. (2004). What leads to user acceptance of digital libraries? *Communications of the ACM*, *47*(11), 79–83. doi:10.1145/1029496.1029498

Thong, J. Y. L., Yap, C. S., & Raman, K. S. (1996). Top management support, external expertise and information systems implementation in small business. *Information Systems Research*, *7*(2), 248–267. doi:10.1287/isre.7.2.248

Thorpe, S., & Brosnan, M. (2001, July 12-14). A single treatment for technopbobia. In *Proceedings of the 22nd International Conference of STAR, the International Society for Stress and Anxiety Research*, Palma de Mallorca, Spain.

Tibenderana, P., & Ogao, P. J. (2008, June 19). Acceptance and use of e-library services in Ugandan Universities. In *Proceedings of the 8th ACM/IEEE-CS Joint Conference on Digital Libraries*, Pittsburgh, PA.

Todor, S., & Krasimira, S. (2008). Functional analysis of enterprise resource planning Systems. In *Proceedings of the International Conference on Computer Systems and Technologies* (pp. 1-6).

Tong, S., & Chang, E. (2001). Support vector machine active learning for image retrieval. In *Proceedings of the Ninth ACM International Conference on Multimedia*.

Toumit, J. Y., Garcia-Salicetti, S., & Emptoz, H. (1999). A hierarchical and recursive model of mathematical expressions for automatic reading of mathematical documents. In *Proceedings of the International Conference on Document Analysis and Recognition* (pp. 116-122).

Trappe, W., Wu, M., Wang, Z. J., & Liu, K. J. R. (2003). Anti-collusion fingerprinting for multimedia. *IEEE Transactions on Signal Processing*, *51*, 1069–1087. doi:10.1109/TSP.2003.809378

Trunick, P. A. (1999). ERP: Promise or pipe dream? *Transportation & Distribution*, *40*, 23–26.

Tsai, F., Hwang, J. H., Chen, L. C., & Lin, T. H. (2010). Post-disaster assessment of landslides in southern Taiwan after 2009 Typhoon Morakot using remote sensing and spatial analysis. *Natural Hazards and Earth System Sciences*, *10*, 2179–2190. doi:10.5194/nhess-10-2179-2010

Tsalgatidou, A., Athanasopoulos, G., Pantazoglou, M., Pautasso, C., Heinis, T., & Grønmo, R. (2006). Developing scientific workflows from heterogeneous services. *SIGMOD Record*, 35.

Tsuruoka, S., Hirano, C., Yoshikawa, T., & Shinogi, T. (2001). Image-based structure analysis for a table of contents and conversion to a XML documents. In *Proceedings of the Workshop on Document Layout Interpretation and its Application*

Tsuruoka, S., Takao, K., Tanaka, T., Yoshikawa, T., & Shinogi, T. (2001). Region segmentation for table image with unknown complex structure. In *Proceedings of the International Conference on Document Analysis and Recognition* (pp. 709-713).

Ugboma, M. U., & Edewor, N. (2008). Use of e-mail in library and information service provision in higher institutions of delta State, Nigeria. *Information Technologist*, *5*(1), 42–51.

UNESCO. (2000). *World education reports*. Retrieved from http://www.unesco.org/education/information/wer/

University of Alberta. (2003). Gay books defaced at university. *American Libraries*, *27*, 32.

Urdiales, C., Dominguez, M., de Trazegnies, C., & Sandoval, F. (2010). A new pyramid-based color image representation for visual localization. *Image and Vision Computing*, *28*(1), 78–91. doi:10.1016/j.imavis.2009.04.014

Vaidyanathan, G., Sabbaghi, A., & Bargellini, M. (2005). User acceptance of digital library: An empirical exploration of individual and system components. *Issues in Information Systems*, *6*(2), 279–285.

Vajda, S., Roy, K., Pal, U., Chaudhuri, B. B., & Belaïd, A. (2009). Automation of Indian postal documents written in Bangla and English. *International Journal of Pattern Recognition and Artificial Intelligence*, *23*(8), 1599–1632. doi:10.1142/S0218001409007776

Van Galen, G. P., & Morasso, P. (Eds.). (1998). Neuromotor control in handwriting and drawing. *Acta Psychologica*, *100*(1-2), 236.

Van Galen, G. P., & Stelmach, G. E. (Eds.). (1993). Handwriting: Issues of psychomotor control and cognitive models. *Acta Psychologica*, *82*(1-3).

van Schyndel, R. G., Tirkel, A. Z., & Osborne, C. F. (1996). A digital watermark. In *Proceedings of the International Conference Image Processing* (pp. 86-90).

Venkatesh, V. (2000). Determinants of perceived ease of use: Integrating control, intrinsic motivation, and emotion into the technology acceptance model. *Information Systems Research*, *11*(4), 342–365. doi:10.1287/isre.11.4.342.11872

Venkatesh, V., & Davis, F. D. (1996). A model of the antecedents of perceived ease of use: Development and test. *Decision Sciences*, *27*(3), 451–481. doi:10.1111/j.1540-5915.1996.tb01822.x

Venkatraman, N. (1994). IT-enabled business transformation: From automation to business scope redefinition. *Sloan Management Review*, 429–442.

Vidyaranya, B. G., & Cydnee, B. (2005). Success and failure factors of adopting SAP in ERP system implementation. *Business Process Management Journal*, *11*(4), 501–516.

Vieira, T. A. S. C., Casanova, M. A., & Ferrao, L. G. (2004). An ontology-driven architecture for flexible workflow execution. In *Proceedings of the WebMedia & LA-Web Joint Conference and 10th Brazilian Symposium on Multimedia and the Web and the 2nd Latin American Web Congress*, São Carlos, Brazil (pp.70-77).

Vieitez, J. C., Carcia, A. D. L. T., & Rodriguez, M. T. V. (2001). Perception of job security in a process of technological change: Its influence on psychological well-being. *Behaviour & Information Technology*, *20*(3), 213–223.

Viola, P., & Jones, M. (2001). *Robust real-time object detection (Tech. Rep. No. CRL 2001/01)*. Cambridge, MA: Cambridge Research Laboratory.

Vuksic, V. B., & Spremic, M. (2005). ERP system implementation and business process change: Case study of p pharmaceutical company. *Journal of Computing and Information Technology- Cit, 13*(1), 11-24.

W3C. (2002) *Web services*. Retrieved from http://www.w3.org/2002/ws/desc/

Walter, C. (2001). *A definition for e-learning*. The OPL Newsletter.

Wang, P., Yang, P. L., Li Li, W., & Lu, H. Q. (2005). Extracting the rotation feature of the developing typhoon. In *Proceedings of the Fourth International Conference on Machine Learning and Cybernetics* (pp. 5229-5234).

Wang, F.-Y. (2006). Driving into the future with ITS. *IEEE Intelligent Systems, 21*(3), 94–95. doi:10.1109/MIS.2006.45

Wang, F.-Y., Zeng, D., & Yang, L. (2006). Smart cars on smart roads: An IEEE intelligent transportation systems society. *IEEE Pervasive Computing / IEEE Computer Society [and] IEEE Communications Society, 5*(4), 68–69. doi:10.1109/MPRV.2006.84

Wang, J., & Jean, J. (1994). Segmentation of merged characters by neural networks and shortest path. *Pattern Recognition, 27*(5), 649–658. doi:10.1016/0031-3203(94)90044-2

Wang, J., Xu, S. Y., Shi, C., & Ye, M. W. (2008). Dynamic assessment of typhoon disaster condition based on multi-sources remote sensing imagery: Research progress. *Journal of Natural Disasters, 17*, 22–28.

Wang, P., Guo, C., & Luo, Y. (2006). Local spiral curves simulating based on Hough transformation and center auto-locating of developing typhoon. *Transactions of Tianjin University, 12*, 142–146.

Wang, S. (2006). An agent-based Web service workflow model for inter-enterprise collaboration. *Expert Systems with Applications, 31*, 787–799. doi:10.1016/j.eswa.2006.01.011

Wang, S.-H., & Lin, Y.-P. (2004). Wavelet tree quantization for copyright protection watermarking. *IEEE Transactions on Image Processing, 13*, 154–165. doi:10.1109/TIP.2004.823822

Wang, W., Gao, S., Li, F., & Tang, Z. (2008). A complex artificial immune system and its immunity. *International Journal of Computer Science and Network Security, 8*, 287–295.

Wang, W., Gao, S., & Tang, Z. (2009). Improved pattern recognition with complex artificial immune system. *Soft Computing - A Fusion of Foundations . Methodologies and Applications, 13*, 1209–1217.

Wan, J., Wing, A. M., & Sovik, N. (Eds.). (1991). *Development of graphic skills: Research, perspectives and educational implications*. London, UK: Academic Press.

Watanabe, T., Luo, Q. L., & Sugie, N. (1995). Layout recognition of multi-kinds of table-form documents. *IEEE Transactions on Pattern Analysis and Machine Intelligence, 17*(4), 432–446. doi:10.1109/34.385976

Watkins, D. W. Jr, & McKinney, D. C. (1998). Decomposition methods for water resources optimization models with fixed costs. *Water Resources, 21*, 283–295. doi:10.1016/S0309-1708(96)00061-9

Wei, C.-H. (2008). *Content-based mammogram retrieval* (Unpublished doctoral dissertation). University of Warwick, Coventry, UK.

Wei, C.-H., & Li, C.-T. (2006). Calcification descriptor and relevance feedback learning algorithms for content-based mammogram retrieval. In *Proceedings of the 8th International Workshop on Digital Mammography*.

Wei, C.-H., Li, C.-T., & Wilson, R. (2005). A general framework for content-based medical image retrieval with its application to mammogram retrieval. In *Proceedings of the SPIE International Symposium on Medical Imaging*.

Wei, C.-H., & Li, C.-T. (2008). *Content analysis from user's relevance feedback for content-based image retrieval*. Hershey, PA: Idea Group.

Wei, C.-H., Li, C.-T., & Wilson, R. (2006). *A content-based approach to medical image database retrieval*. Hershey, PA: Idea Group.

Wei, C.-H., Li, Y., Chau, W. Y., & Li, C.-T. (2009). Trademark image retrieval: Using synthetic features for describing global shape and interior structure of trademark. *Pattern Recognition*, *42*(3), 386–394. doi:10.1016/j.patcog.2008.08.019

Weil, M. M., & Rosen, L. D. (2000). *Four years study shows more Technology @ work and @ home but more hesitancy about trying new technology.* Retrieved March 19, 2006, from http://www.Human-warecom/businessstudy.htm

Welsh, J. A., & White, J. F. (1981). A small business is not a little big business. *Harvard Business Review*, *59*(4), 81–32.

West, R., & Daigle, S. L. (2004). Total cost of ownership: A strategic tool for ERP planning and implementation. *Educause Center for Applied Research*, *1*, 1–14.

Wikipedia. (2009). *Content validity.* Retrieved from http://en.wikipedia.org/wiki/Co ntent_va lidity

Wildemann, H. (1990). *The implementation of computer integrated manufacturing system.* Munchen.

Wilderman, B. (2003). Taking the measure of ERP implementations. *Meta Delta*, *2240*, 1–5.

Winne, D. A., & Knowles, H. D. ll, D. R., & Nagarajah, C. N. (2002). Digital watermarking in wavelet domain with predistortion for authenticity verification and localization. *Proceedings of the SPIE: Security and Watermarking of Multimedia Contents IV*, 349-356.

Wolfgang, R. B., & Delp, E. J. (1997). Overview of image security techniques with applications in multimedia systems. In *Proceedings of the SPIE International Conference on Multimedia Networks: Security, Displays, Terminals, and Gateways* (pp. 297-308).

Womboh, B. S. H., & Tukur, A. (2008). The state of Information and Communication Technology (ICT) in Nigeria University libraries: The experience of Ibrahim Babangida Libraries, Federal University of Technology, Yola. *Library Philosophy and Practice, 2008.*

Wong, P. W., & Memon, N. (2000). Secret and public key authentication watermarking schemes that resist vector quantization attack. *Proceedings of the SPIE: Security and Watermarking of Multimedia Contents, II*, 40–47.

Woo, H. S. (2006). Critical success factors for implementing ERP: The case of a Chinese electronics manufacturer. *Journal of Manufacturing Technology Management*, *18*(4), 431–442. doi:10.1108/17410380710743798

World Bank. (2002). *Information and communication technologies: A World Bank ground strategy.* Washington, DC: World Bank.

Wu, C. C. (2001). Numerical simulation of Typhoon Gladys (1994) and its interaction with Taiwan terrain using the GFDL hurricane model. *Monthly Weather Review*, *129*, 1533–1549. doi:10.1175/1520-0493(2001)129<1533:NSOTGA>2.0.CO;2

Wu, C. W. (2002). On the design of content-based multimedia authentication systems. *IEEE Transactions on Multimedia*, *4*, 385–393. doi:10.1109/TMM.2002.802018

Wu, D. C., & Tsai, W. H. (1999). Embedding of any type of data in images based on a human visual model and multiple-based number conversion. *Pattern Recognition Letters*, *20*, 1511–1517. doi:10.1016/S0167-8655(99)00118-X

Wu, M. (2003). Joint security and robustness enhancement for quantization based data embedding. *IEEE Transactions on Circuits and Systems for Video Technology*, *13*, 831–841. doi:10.1109/TCSVT.2003.815951

Xie, R., Wu, K., Du, J., & Li, C. (2007). Survey of public key digital watermarking systems. In *Proceedings of the Eighth ACIS International Conference on Software Engineering, Artificial Intelligence, Networking, and Parallel/ Distributed Computing.*

Xing, W., Lu, Z.-M., & Wang, H.-X. (2003). A digital watermarking method based on classified labeled-bisecting-k-means clustering. In *Proceedings of the International Conference on Machine Learning and Cybernetics* (pp. 2891-2895).

Xu, G., Gao, S., Shi, Y. Q., Su, W., & Hu, R. (2009). Camera-model identification using markovian transition probability matrix. In *Proceedings of the International Workshop on Digital Watermarking* (pp. 294-307).

Xu, J. W., Wang, P., & Xie, Y. Y. (2009). Image segmentation of typhoon spiral cloud bands based on support vector machine. In *Proceedings of the Eighth International Conference on Machine Learning and Cybernetics* (pp. 1088-1093).

Yamaguchi, T., Tang, Z., Ishizuka, O., & Tanno, K. (2001). Adaptive multiple-valued immune system. *IEEE Transactions on Electronics . Information Systems*, *121*(11), 1747–1754.

Yeh, J. H., Pao, T. L., Lee, C. L., & Lai, W. T. (2007). Reconstruction of typhoon path and cloud image from descriptors. In *Proceedings of the IEEE International Conference on Systems, Man and Cybernetics* (pp. 2097-2101).

Yuan, H., & Zhang, X. P. (2003). Fragile watermark based on the Gaussian mixture model in the wavelet domain for image authentication. In *Proceedings of the International Conference of Image Processing* (pp. 505-508).

Zadeh, L. A. (1975). The concept of a linguistic variable and its application to approximate reasoning. *Information Sciences*, *8*, 199–249. doi:10.1016/0020-0255(75)90036-5

Zadeh, L. A. (1978). Fuzzy sets as a basis for a theory of possibility. *Fuzzy Sets and Systems*, *1*, 3–28. doi:10.1016/0165-0114(78)90029-5

Zanibbi, R., Blostein, D., & Cordy, J. R. (2004). A survey of table recognition: Models, observations, transformations, and inferences. *International Journal on Document Analysis and Recognition*, *7*, 1–16.

Zeng, L., Ngu, A., Bentallah, B., & O'Dell, M. (2001). An agent-based approach for supporting cross-enterprise workflows. In *Proceedings of the 12th Australasian Database Conference*, Gold Coast, Queensland, Australia (pp. 123-130).

Zeng, D., & Sycara, K. (1998). Bayesian learning in negotiation. *International Journal of Human-Computer Studies*, *48*, 125–141. doi:10.1006/ijhc.1997.0164

Zhang, C. J., Lu, X. Q., Lu, J., & Xu, J. P. (2008). Segmentation for main body of typhoon from satellite cloud image by genetic algorithm in contourlet domain. In *Proceedings of the Third International Conference on Convergence and Hybrid Information Technology* (pp. 352-357).

Zhang, Q. P., Lai, L. L., Wei, H., & Zong, X. F. (2006). Non-clear typhoon eye tracking y artificial ant colony. In *Proceedings of the Fifth International Conference on Machine Learning and Cybernetics* (pp. 4063-4068).

Zhang, C. J., & Wang, X. D. (2009). Typhoon cloud image enhancement and reducing speckle with genetic algorithm in stationary wavelet domain. *IET Image Process*, *3*(4), 200–216. doi:10.1049/iet-ipr.2008.0044

Zhang, C. J., & Yang, B. (2011). A novel nonlinear algorithm for typhoon cloud image enhancement. *International Journal of Automation and Computing*, *8*, 161–169. doi:10.1007/s11633-011-0569-1

Zhang, C., Cheng, L. L., Qiu, Z. D., & Cheng, L. M. (2008). Multipurpose watermarking based on multiscale curvelet transform. *IEEE Transactions on Information Forensics and Security*, *3*, 611–619. doi:10.1109/TIFS.2008.2004288

Zhang, D., & Lu, G. (2002). A comparative study of curvature scale space and fourier descriptors for shape-based image retrieval. *Journal of Visual Communication and Image Representation*, *14*(1), 39–57. doi:10.1016/S1047-3203(03)00003-8

Zhao, X., Ho, A. T. S., Treharne, H., Pankajakshan, V., Culnane, C., & Jiang, W. (2007). A novel semi-fragile image watermarking, authentication and self-restoration technique using the Slant transform. In *Proceedings of the Third IEEE International Conference on Intelligent Information Hiding and Multimedia Signal Processing* (pp. 283-286).

Zhao, J. L. (2006). Process-driven collaboration support for intra-agency crime analysis. *Decision Support Systems*, *41*, 616–633. doi:10.1016/j.dss.2004.06.014

Zhong, S., Hongjiang, Z., Li, S., & Shaoping, M. (2003). Relevance feedback in content-based image retrieval: Bayesian framework, feature subspaces, and progressive learning. *IEEE Transactions on Image Processing*, *12*(8), 924–937. doi:10.1109/TIP.2003.815254

Zhu, X., Ho, A. T. S., & Marziliano, P. (2006). Image authentication and restoration using irregular sampling for traffic enforcement applications. In *Proceedings of the First International Conference on Innovative Computing, Information and Control* (pp. 62-65).

Zuyev, K. (1997). Table image segmentation. In *Proceedings of the International Conference on Document Analysis and Recognition* (pp. 705-707).

About the Contributors

Chia-Hung Wei is currently an Assistant Professor of the Department of Information Management at Chien Hsin University of Science and Technology, Taiwan. He obtained his PhD degree in Computer Science from the University of Warwick, UK, and Master's degree from the University of Sheffield, UK, and Bachelor's degree from the Tunghai University, Taiwan. His research interests include content-based image retrieval, digital image processing, medical image processing and analysis, machine learning for multimedia applications, and information retrieval. He has published over 10 research papers in those research areas.

Chih-Ying Gwo received his Bachelor's degree from the National Tsing Hua University, Taiwan, MS degree in Computer Engineering from Syracuse University, New York, USA, and PhD in Electrical Engineering from University of Southern California, USA. He is currently an Assistant Professor of Department of Information Management at Chien Hsin University of Science and Technology, Taiwan. His current research interests include online character recognition and pattern recognition.

* * *

Partha Bhowmick graduated from the Indian Institute of Technology, Kharagpur, India, and received his Masters and PhD from the Indian Statistical Institute, Kolkata, India. He is currently an Assistant Professor in Computer Science and Engineering Department, Indian Institute of Technology, Kharagpur, India. His primary research area is digital geometry, with applications to low-level image processing, approximate pattern matching, document image processing and analysis, shape analysis, and biometrics. He has published more than 60 research papers in international journals, edited volumes, and refereed conference proceedings, and holds 4 US patents.

Arindam Biswas graduated from Jadavpur University, Kolkata, India, and received his master's and doctorate degree both from the Indian Statistical Institute, Kolkata, India, where he has submitted his doctoral thesis also. He is currently an Assistant Professor in the Department of Information Technology, Bengal Engineering and Science University, Shibpur, India. His research interests include digital geometry, image processing, approximate shape matching and analysis, medical image analysis, and biometrics. He has published over 40 research papers in international journals, edited volumes, and refereed conference proceedings, and holds one US patent.

Bhabatosh Chanda received B.E. in Electronics and Telecommunication Engineering and PhD in Electrical Engineering from University of Calcutta in 1979 and 1988 respectively. His research interest includes Image and Video Processing, Pattern Recognition, Computer Vision and Mathematical Morphology. He has published more than 100 technical articles in refereed journals and conferences, authored one book and edited five books. He has received `Young Scientist Medal' of Indian National Science Academy in 1989, `Computer Engineering Division Medal' of the Institution of Engineers (India) in 1998, 'Vikram Sarabhai Research Award in 2002, and IETE-Ram Lal Wadhwa Gold medal in 2007. He is also recipient of UN fellowship, UNESCO-INRIA fellowship and Diamond Jubilee fellowship of National Academy of Science, India. He is fellow of Institute of Electronics and Telecommunication Engineers (FIETE), of National Academy of Science, India (FNASc.), of Indian National Academy of Engineering (FNAE) and of International Association of Pattern Recognition (FIAPR). He is a Professor in Indian Statistical Institute, Kolkata, India.

Jinn-Ming Chang received his Bachelor of Medicine from Graduate of National Defense Medial Center Faculty of Medicine, in 1975. He currently serves as department head of Health-Care Management Center and department staff of Diagnostic Radiology, Chi Mei Foundation Hospital, Tainan, Taiwan. He is also a Lecturer, Department of Child Care Education, Southern Taiwan University of Technology, Taiwan. His research interests include magnetic resonance imaging, computed tomography, ultrasound, breast medical imaging and interventional radiology.

Lung-Chun Chang received the B.S. degree in mathematics from Tunghai University, Taichung, Taiwan, in 1995, the M.S. degree from the Graduate School of Engineering Technology, National Taiwan Institute of Technology, Taipei, Taiwan, in 1997, and the Ph.D. degree in the Department of Information Management of the National Taiwan University of Science and Technology, Taipei, Taiwan, in 2002. He is now an Assistant Professor with the Department of Information Management at Ching Yun University. His research interests include image processing and human-computer interaction.

Mei Chang is a lecturer of Department of Computer Science and Technology, Neusoft Institute of Information. She received the B.S. degree from Shandong Normal, Shandong, China in 2004 and M.S. degree from Dalian Maritime University, Liaoning, China in 2007. Her main research interests are computer networks technology and application.

Chee-Chiang Chen received his medical degree from the Cebu Institute of Medicine, Philippine. He currently serves in the Department of Diagnostic Radiology, Tungs' Taichung MetroHarbor Hospital, Taiwan. He specializes in general radiology and ultrasound examinations.

Pei Cheng Cheng received the Ph.D. degree in Computer Science and Engineering from National Chiao Tung University (NCTU), HsinChu, Taiwan in 2006. Now he is an associate professor of the Department of Information Management, Ching Yun University, Taoyuan, Taiwan. His current research interests include content-based image retrieval, machine learning, knowledge management, and artificial intelligence.

Amit Kumar Das was born in Calcutta and completed his Masters and PhD at Calcutta University and Bengal Engineering College (DU), India, respectively. He is presently a Professor in the Computer Science and Technology Department, Bengal Engineering and Science University, Shibpur, Howrah, India. His field of interest includes embedded system design and document image processing.

Mousumi Dutt graduated from St. Thomas' College of Engineering and Technology, Kolkata, and received M.E. degree in Information Technology from Bengal Engineering and Science University, Shibpur. She is now pursuing Ph.D. from the Department of Information Technology from Bengal Engineering and Science University, Shibpur. Her primary research interest is digital geometry and its application in image processing.

Neslon Edewor is a practicing librarian with Delta State Polytechnic,Ozoro. He holds a BLS and MSc in Library and Information Science. His research areas are Library and information, Knowledge Management, Database management and Information policy. He has published in various local and international journals.

Ogochukwu T. Emiri is an Assistant Librarian with Delta State University Library, Delta State University, Abraka. He holds a B.LS and M.Sc. in Library and Information Science both from Delta State University, Abraka. His research interests are in information science, knowledge management, information and communication Technology and Internet/Internet Security. He has a number of research publications in reputable international journals and chapters in books.

Yu-Ching Hsu was born in Changhua, Taiwan, 1988. She is now a student with the Department of Information Management at Ching Yun University. Her research interests include project planning and database design.

Hui-Yun Hu was born in Hsinchu, Taiwan, 1988. She is now a student with the Department of Information Management at Ching Yun University. Her research interests include web design and human-computer interaction.

Pai-Jung Huang is the Chief and Medical Director of Comprehensive Breast Health Center. He earned his medical degree and master's degree in medical informatics at Taipei Medical University. Dr. Huang then received his professional training at Columbia University Medical Center, New York and started his international career. After six years of intensive training, Dr. Huang extended his career back to his home country, Taiwan. Not only was he one of the attending surgeons at Mackay Memorial Hospital, but also he took challenging roles in the medical informatics field at several renowned institutions. In 2001, Dr. Huang ignited his international career again. At Faulkner Breast Center, Massachusetts, Dr. Huang dedicated himself to becoming an expert in mini-invasive surgery of breast. Since 2007 when Dr. Huang came back to Taiwan again, he has been involved in the expansion of comprehensive breast healthcare, and to establish three breast centers in Taiwan, the first one in China, and one in Ho Chi Ming City, Vietnam. In addition, he is actively involved in R&D, cooperating with top academic and research institutions both domestically and internationally.

Yueh-Jyun Lee was born in Taichung, Taiwan, R.O.C. in 1960. He received the B.S., M.S. and Ph.D. degree in Electrical Engineering from Chung Cheng Institute of Technology, Taiwan, R.O.C. in 1982, 1988 and 1997, respectively. Since 2001 he has been an Assistant Professor in the Department of Information Management at Ching Yun University. His research interests include neural network and digital signal processing.

Yue Li received his PhD degree in computer science from University of Warwick, UK, in 2009, M.S. in Information Technology from Department of Computer Science, University of Nottingham, UK, in 2005, and BSc in Mathematics from Nankai University, China, in 2003. He is currently an assistant professor of Collage of Software, University of Nankai, China. He serves as a member of editorial review board of International Journal of Digital Crime and Forensics. His research interests include digital forensics, multimedia security, digital watermarking, pattern recognition, machine learning and content-based image retrieval.

Menq-Wen Lin received his M.S. degree in computer science from New Jersey Institute of Technology, New Jersey, USA, and Ph.D. in computer science and engineering from Yuan Ze University, Taiwan in 2004. In 1990, he joined Ching Yun University, Taiwan, where he is now an associate professor. His current research interests include data mining and agent technologies.

Yuh-Fong Lin was born in Hualien, Taiwan, R.O.C. in 1957. He received the B.S. degree in surveying and mapping from Chung Cheng Institute of Technology, Taiwan, R.O.C. in 1978, the M.S. degree from the Graduate School of Photogrammetry, National Cheng Kung University, Tainan, Taiwan, in 1982, and the PhD degree in the Department of geography of the National Taiwan Normal University, Taipei, Taiwan, in 1996. He is now an Associate Professor with the Department of Information Management at Ching Yun University. His research interests include digital mapping and quantitative research.

Ji-Chyun Liu was born at Taiwan in 1951. He obtained the B.S., M.S. and PhD degrees from Chung-Cheng Institute of Technology in 1974, 1981 and 1993 respectively. From 1981 to 2003, he was instructor, associate professor and professor of Chung Cheng Institute of Technology. Now, he has been the professor of Ching Yun University since 2003. His research has included microwave integrated circuit design, wide-band filter, wide-band amplifier, chaotic oscillator, broadband antenna, fractal antenna, active integration antenna, broadband absorber, ceramic metamaterials as well as EMI/EMC and microwave instrumentation and measurement.

Shih-Wen Liu was born in Taoyuan, Taiwan, 1987. He is now a student with the Institute of Information Management at Ching Yun University. His research interests include satellite cloud image and 3-D profile reconstruction.

Sekhar Mandal received his BTech and MTech degrees in Radiophysics and Electronics from University of Calcutta. He did his PhD from Bengal Engineering and Science University, Shibpur, Howrah, India, where is presently an Assistant Professor in the Computer Science and Technology Department. His primary research area is document image processing.

Owajeme J. Ofua is an Assistant Librarian in Delta State University Library, Delta State University, Abraka. He holds a B.Sc. and M.Sc. in Library and Information Science from Delta State University, Abraka, Nigeria and is currently a doctoral student in the same department. His research interest lie in Information and Communication Technology in Libraries, African Indigenous knowledge system and bibliometric analysis.

Tiemo Aghwotu Pereware is currently a senior librarian with Niger Delta University library, Wilberforce Island. He has previous worked with the British Council Library Nigeria and in Delta state University Library, Abraka, where he was also an associate lecturer in the Department of Library and Information Science. He has published chapters in books and article in leading international and local journals.

Aisharjya Sarkar graduated from Narula Institute of Technology, Kolkata, and and received M.E. degree in Information Technology from Bengal Engineering and Science University, Shibpur. Her specific areas of research include digital geometry and image analysis.

Zheng Tang is a professor of Toyama University, Toyama, Japan, he received the B.S. degree from Zhejiang University, Zhejiang, China in 1982 and an M.S. degree and a D.E. degree from Tshinghua University, Beijing, China in 1984 and 1988, respectively. From 1988 to 1989, he was an Instructor in the Institute of Microelectronics at Tshinhua University. From 1990 to 1999, he was an associate professor in the Department of Electrical and Electronic Engineering, Miyazaki University, Miyazaki, Japan. In 2000, he joined Toyama University, Toyama, Japan, where he is currently a professor in the Department of Intellectual Information Systems. His current research interests include intellectual information technology, neural networks, and optimizations.

Pereware A. Tiemo is a Senior Librarian in Niger Delta University Bayelsa State Nigeria. He holds a BLS and MSc in Library and Information Science. He has prevoiusly worked with the British Council library, Lagos office and also in Delta State University library, Abraka as a librarian and an associate lecturer in the Dept of library and information Science. He has published articles in local and international journals. His areas of interest are Internet, Information magement, e-library and librarianship in general.

Wei Wang is a lecturer of College of Software, Nankai University,China. He received the B.S. degree from Dalian Maritime University, Liaoning, China in 2003 and a MS degree and a DE degree from University of Toyama, Toyama, Japan in 2007 and 2010, respectively. In 2010, he joined Nankai University, China. His main research interests are artificial neural networks, artificial immune networks and pattern recognition.

Xiaofei Wang received the B.S. degree from University of Toyama, Toyama, Japan in 2005 and a M.S. degree and a D.E. degree from University of Toyama, Toyama, Japan in 2007 and 2010, respectively. His main research interests are artificial neural networks and optimizations.

Chia-Liang Wei is currently a section chief of purchasing division in Allis Electric Co., Ltd. He obtained his Master degree in Logistics and Business Management from University of Bedfordshire, UK in 2006. His research interests include operation management, logistics, international trade and business process. During work, he assisted his organization to develop its own import and export trading system in 1996. By 2002, he participated in the introduction of ERP systems in his company.

Hsin-Ju Wei is currently a senior SAP FI/CO module consultant of ERP. She obtained her Master degree in MBA from University of Leicester UK in 2009. Her research interests include coordination and analysis of business process, and planning, integration and implementation of information system. She has worked over 20 years in those research areas. At present, she assists Taiwan's small and midsize enterprises in introducing ERP systems.

Yi-Syuan Wu was born in Taoyuan, Taiwan, 1988. She is now a student with the Department of Information Management at Ching Yun University. Her research interests include system analysis and database design.

Fang-Chuan Ou Yang is an Assistant Professor in Department of Information Management at Ching Yun University in Taiwan. He received his PhD of Information Management from Nation Central University (2009) in Taiwan. He teaches professional computer courses in several software training centers before joining Ching Yun University. He has extensive experience on software design, distributed technologies, and e-learning systems. His current research interests include digital content, multimedia/hypermedia, e-learning, distributed computing, web 2.0, mobile learning, and cloud computing. He is also sponsored by National Science Council for preceding several research projects regarding L2 English vocabulary learning, mobile learning, and constructivist learning.

Index